Fodor's

# NEW ZEALAND



**FODOR'S TRAVEL PUBLICATIONS**

NEW YORK • TORONTO
LONDON • SYDNEY • AUCKLAND

WWW.FODORS.COM

# CONTENTS

**KEY TO SYMBOLS**

- Map reference
- Address
- Telephone number
- Opening times
- Admission prices
- Underground station
- Bus number
- Train station
- Ferry/boat
- Driving directions
- Tourist office
- Tours
- Guidebook
- Restaurant
- Café
- Bar
- Shop
- Number of rooms
- Air conditioning
- Swimming pool
- Gym
- Other useful information
- ▷ Cross reference
- ★ Walk/drive start point

175
115
243
194

# UNDERSTANDING NEW ZEALAND

Understanding New Zealand is an introduction to the country, its geography, economy, history and its people, giving a real insight into the nation. Living New Zealand gets under the skin of New Zealand today, while The Story of New Zealand takes you through the country's past.

New Zealand took its place on the tourist map in 1880, when modish travellers included it on their route around the world. Although facilities were distinctly basic, visitors managed to fill several letters with enthusiastic reports of the countryside and its varied populations. These days, tourists can opt out of 'tent hotels' for world-class luxury, but New Zealand's beauty remains sublime. There are dozens of ways to experience it, too, from the high-adrenalin of jet-boats and bungy jumps to the serenity of walks, drives or alfresco dining. It is an easy country to enjoy—attractions, transport and Kiwi attitudes welcome more than 2.5 million visitors a year.

## THE LANDSCAPE

New Zealand consists of three main islands—the North Island, the South Island and Stewart Island—with a handful of small, far-flung islands completing the family. The total land area is approximately 270,500sq km (104,795 square miles).

Although compact in size, New Zealand's landscape is rich and varied, with glaciers, braided rivers, lakes, fiords, sounds (flooded riverbeds, found predominantly in the South Island), lowlands, alluvial plains, wetlands, large natural coastal harbours and a rash of offshore islands.

Because New Zealand is located at the meeting point of the Pacific and Indo-Australian tectonic plates, it also experiences frequent earthquakes. A string of volcanoes stretches from the currently active Whakaari/White Island in the Bay of Plenty to Mount Ruapehu in the heart of the North Island. The area also has numerous thermal features, including geysers, mineral springs, blowholes and mud pools, most of which can be found around Rotorua and Taupo.

The South Island is far more mountainous than the North and boasts the country's highest peak, Mount Cook/Aoraki (▷ 203). The country's longest river is the Waikato, which stretches 425km (264 miles) from Tongariro National Park to the Tasman Sea.

Great stretches of these wonderful landscapes are unmarked by humans—no roads, no houses, no telegraph poles. Within an hour's drive from most main towns you can find the edge of habitation. Another hour or two in a chosen mode of transport—such as walking, horse-riding or kayaking—and you can be totally remote. While some outdoor areas are deservedly popular, like the tramping tracks of Fiordland, in plenty of other spots you can explore for miles without seeing another soul. Where else in the world can you do that without threat of a poisonous snake or spider?

## PEOPLE AND POPULATION

The population of New Zealand currently stands at about 4.3 million, with more than 3 million in the North Island

and more than 1 million in the South Island. Greater Auckland is home to more than 1 million people.

New Zealand is essentially a bicultural society made up of Maori and Europeans, with many other nationalities also present. Maori make up about 14 per cent of New Zealand's total population, with the vast majority living in the North Island. There are around 266,000 Pacific Islanders, with many living in greater Auckland. Asians make up nine per cent of New Zealand's total population and are the fastest-growing minority group, again settled mainly in the greater Auckland area.

New Zealanders are famous for being the world's greatest travellers, and at any one time a large proportion of citizens are absent or living abroad. More than 450,000 live and work in Australia alone. Through their close trans-Tasman ties, Australian and New Zealand citizens are free to live and work in both countries.

## MAORI CULTURE

A big draw for visitors is the vibrant culture of New Zealand's first inhabitants, the Maori. After their culture was suppressed throughout the 19th century, Maori society enjoyed a renaissance towards the end of the 1970s. Language, art and *kapa haka* (performance arts) are thriving. The most popular place for visitors to experience these is Rotorua.

## POLITICS

Things change quickly in New Zealand. With its small population and triennial elections, it's sometimes seen as a social laboratory. Currently under the microscope is Mixed Member Proportional representation (MMP), an electoral system that has helped a wider range of MPs into parliament since it was introduced in 1996. As well as the two long-established parties, Labour and National, significant political stakes are held by the environmentally friendly Green Party, family-values oriented United Future and migrant-watching New Zealand First. A number of distinctive personalities have made it big in national and local politics—Georgina Beyer, the world's first transsexual MP; Nandor Tanczos, the Rastafarian Green with waist-length dreadlocks; Tim Shadbolt, the flower-power activist turned mayor of Invercargill; and Dick Hubbard, breakfast cereal magnate and mayor of Auckland.

## RELIGION

The dominant religion is Christianity, with Anglican, Presbyterian and Roman Catholic denominations being the most prominent. Minority religions include Hinduism, Islam, Judaism and Buddhism. The Maori developed two of their own minority Christian-based faiths, Ratana and Ringatu, both of which were formed in the late 19th to early 20th centuries. At least a quarter of the total population are atheists or have no religion, and this number is growing.

**Opposite** *The towering snow-capped peak of Mount Cook*
**Above** *Natural steam clouds rise from mud pools at Wai-O-Tapu*

## VISITING NEW ZEALAND

Many visitors from Asia experience New Zealand in three days flat—Auckland, Rotorua and Queenstown. These are great spots, but to get a feel for the country, its people and culture, you really need two weeks minimum. If your flight takes more than 12 hours, three weeks is a preferable time to allow, simply because jet lag can spoil the first few days.

The easiest way to travel is by road. Coaches are inexpensive, reliable and connect most visitor areas, while campervans have become incredibly popular, providing flexible access to remote quarters with no worry of finding a bed for the night. Rail is limited, with some notable exceptions—the TranzAlpine trip from Christchurch to Greymouth is an attraction in its own right. If time is limited, a good way to see the highlights of both islands is to fly. If you have a contact, it's less expensive to book from within the country, and the earlier the better.

There are ample opportunities to try outdoor activities such as hiking, fishing, hunting and mountain biking. Just be aware that if you bring your own equipment, it must be scrupulously cleaned before you try to get it through customs. Most gear can be easily hired anyway, and the results are all but guaranteed if you use the services of an experienced guide.

## LANGUAGE

▷ 293–294.

# NEW ZEALAND'S REGIONS

## AUCKLAND, NORTHLAND AND COROMANDEL

**Auckland:** New Zealand's commercial hub and largest city, with 1.25 million residents. Ferries give access to prettier areas such as Devonport and Waiheke Island, while the Sky Tower gives a 360-degree view of the city and its harbours.
**Northland:** Warm, humid and sparsely populated, with impressive coastal landscapes. North of Ninety Mile Beach is sacred Cape Reinga. The Waipoua Forest Sanctuary is home to New Zealand's largest kauri tree. The Bay of Islands, known for big-game fishing, has historic sites, including Waitangi National Reserve.
**Coromandel:** Conservationists and artisans now fiercely defend the sunny peninsula, once exploited for gold, coal and kauri.

## CENTRAL NORTH ISLAND

**Rotorua:** Spectacular geothermal activity includes bubbling mud pools, geysers, steaming lakes and a spa complex. The tourist capital of Maori culture.
**Lake Taupo:** New Zealand's biggest lake. Its crystal waters are famed for trout fishing.
**The Volcanic Plateau:** Three volcanoes rise from an austere plain, including Mount Ruapehu, whose crater still simmers.
**New Plymouth:** Wedged between Mount Taranaki (Mount Egmont) and the Tasman Sea, the city gains an artistic edge from its cosmopolitan oil industry.
**Napier:** Destroyed by an earthquake in 1931, the city was rebuilt as an art deco delight.

## SOUTHERN NORTH ISLAND

**Wellington:** The capital city looks a gem from the Botanic Garden's lookout, accessed by cable car. Home to national museum Te Papa, the Beehive parliament building and hundreds of excellent cafés.
**The Wairarapa:** Wine-making has brought boutique shopping and dining to villages like Martinborough and Greytown.
**Kapiti Coast:** Long white-sand beaches and a pleasant climate. Kapiti Island, 6km (4 miles) off the coast, is one of New Zealand's most important nature reserves.
**Wanganui:** The serene Whanganui River is rich in Maori history and legend. The river is popular for jet-boating and kayaking.

## NELSON AND MARLBOROUGH

**Nelson:** Warm, sandy beaches rival the best of the North Island's, while craggy mountains and rough rivers are distinctly South Island. Its many attractions include the vast stretch of Golden Bay and the easy-to-stroll Abel Tasman National Park.
**Nelson City:** The quality of local clay has attracted successful potters and other established artists. The town's creativity pulses through The World of Wearable Art and Classic Cars museum.
**Marlborough:** The first Marlborough wineries were instrumental in putting New Zealand on the world wine map. Now there are around 100 wineries, most of them also offering world-class cuisine.

**Below** *Auckland's Sky Tower rises above the city*

**CANTERBURY AND THE WEST COAST**

**Christchurch:** Called the Garden City, the South Island's largest city has vast areas of parkland. Visitors can punt on the Avon, visit the landmark Anglican cathedral on Cathedral Square and explore the lively Arts Centre. The Port Hills and beaches make a delightful change to the city's flatness.

**Canterbury:** From the farms of the Canterbury Plains, the region suddenly rears up into the Southern Alps. Star of these great mountains is Aoraki (Mount Cook). Azure Lake Tekapo has a memorial to sheepdogs of the harsh McKenzie Country.

**The West Coast:** This area consists of a thin strip of land between the Southern Alps and the ocean. Narrow State Highway 6 winds through dense rainforest, near Fox and Franz Josef Glaciers, and past Punakaiki Pancake Rocks. Evocative scenery is guaranteed, unlike the weather.

**OTAGO AND THE FAR SOUTH**

**Dunedin:** Victorian and Edwardian architecture beckon in Larnach Castle, Olveston and the railway station. The Otago Peninsula is home to the distinguished Royal Albatross Centre, plus many penguins and seals.

**Otago:** Queenstown is New Zealand's adventure capital, with world-renowned bungy jumping and jet-boating. Quieter but equally scenic towns include Wanaka and Arrowtown, with incredible mountains, lakes and rivers.

**Fiordland:** The wettest, wildest corner of New Zealand, consisting of mountains and water. Milford Sound is the most accessible of the fiords. Its photographic gems are Mitre Peak and the immense Bowen Falls.

# THE BEST OF NEW ZEALAND

## AUCKLAND, NORTHLAND AND COROMANDEL

**Auckland Art Gallery** (▷ 61) has what is probably the biggest and best collections of New Zealand art, including famous paintings by Goldie and Lindauer.

**Auckland Museum Tamaki Paenga Hira** (▷ 61), set in the Auckland Domain (park), contains some of the finest collections of Maori and Pacific Island objects in the country.

**The Bay of Islands** (▷ 72) offers some of the most outstanding coastal scenery in the North Island, and doubles as a popular watersports venue.

**Bungy jump** from Auckland's Sky Tower (▷ 66, 89)—even watching it from the viewing platform makes your stomach lurch!

**The Matakohe Kauri Museum** (▷ 75) celebrates a native New Zealand tree with creative displays about its value to early settlers, from ships' masts to the uses of its valuable gum resin.

**Ninety Mile Beach** is an unequalled stretch of soft white sands on the Aupouri Peninsula (▷ 59), near the northern tip of the country, but don't be tempted to drive on it yourself.

**Pukematu Lodge, Russell** (▷ 97), is a modern B&B with great hospitality and fabulous views.

**Tiritiri Matangi Island** (▷ 74) is an accessible haven in the Hauraki Gulf, just 35 minutes from Auckland, where endangered native birds such as takahe and little spotted kiwi thrive.

**Waiheke Island** has a number of excellent vineyards—try Stonyridge for its Cabernet Sauvignon (▷ 92), or join in the annual winefest (▷ 93).

**White, Auckland** (▷ 94): Try this for high-class dining in the City of Sails.

## CENTRAL NORTH ISLAND

**Blackwater rafting** in the Waitomo cave system is great (▷ 116–117, 131), if you're fearless.

**Hawke's Bay** is famous in international wine circles, and you can compare some of the best at its annual wine festival (▷ 131).

**Huka Lodge, Taupo** (▷ 135) is the luxury lodge where the stars go to be pampered.

**Luge** down a steep hill on little more than a tray, with Skyline Skyrides near Rotorua (▷ 111)—take the gondola up and the luge down.

**The Museum of Caves at Waitomo** (▷ 117) is a world-class introduction to the formation of limestone caves and the creatures and people who have used them.

**Napier** is surrounded by extensive vineyards, including the venerable Church Road winery (▷ 128), where you can also explore the country's only wine museum.

**Rotorua's extensive geothermal landscape** (▷ 108–111) is unrivalled, with steaming sulphur mud pools, spouting geysers of boiling water, and multi-hued lakes.

**Zorb at Rotorua** (▷ 130)—but when you've finished rolling downhill in an inflated ball you may not recall which part of Down Under is down under!

## SOUTHERN NORTH ISLAND

**Boulcott Street Bistro and Wine Bar** (▷ 159) is one of Wellington's top restaurants.

**The Lighthouse, Wellington** (▷ 169) is good for unusual accommodation in the capital.

**Martinborough's** chief advantage (▷ 139, 153) is that there are around 20 vineyards within strolling distance of its Wine Centre—so no danger of drinking and driving as you sample your way around.

**The Museum of Wellington City and Sea** (▷ 148) marks the maritime heritage of the 'windy city', with excellent displays of local exhibits.

**Pukaha Mount Bruce Wildlife Centre** (▷ 140) is the Department of Conservation's flagship breeding centre, where you can see many species, including stitchbirds, wild eels and kaka parrots.

**Te Papa Tongarewa-Museum of New Zealand** (▷ 142–143), the national museum, set in an architecturally intriguing building on Wellington's harbourfront, opened in 1998 with highlights of a vast collection.

## NELSON AND MARLBOROUGH

**Abel Tasman National Park** (▷ 166–167), with its sandy bays and azure sea, lush coastal vegetation and famous tramping trail, is a popular holiday destination for Kiwis.

**Blenheim** (▷ 165) is an otherwise unremarkable town at the heart of the Marlborough/Wairau Valley wineries (▷ 175); for some of the best wine in the South Island, head to Cloudy Bay (▷ 182).

**Kaikoura** (▷ 169, 182–183) is known around the world for the success of its whale- and dolphin-watching tours, and you can also get up close (within smelling distance) to fur seals along this coast.

**Kaiteriteri**, on the Abel Tasman coast of the South Island (▷ 167), offers golden sands on a stunningly lovely bay.

**The Old Convent, Kaikoura** (▷ 189) combines monastic architecture with comfort and fine food.

**Rabbit Island**, by Nelson (▷ 172), offers seemingly endless miles of volcanic grey sands backed by splendid pine forest.

**Smokehouse Café, Mapua** (▷ 187) is the place for top-notch fish, close by Nelson.

**Wharariki**, on Farewell Spit (▷ 165), is a patch of golden sands on a curving spit that harbours wading birds and fur seals.

**Whitewater raft** on the Buller Gorge from Murchison (▷ 171) or Westport (▷ 220)

**The World of Wearable Art and Classic Cars** (▷ 173) put Nelson firmly on the fashion map, with its wacky and outrageous costume designs and its light-hearted presentation—and the cars are pretty special, too.

## CANTERBURY AND THE WEST COAST

**Coaltown Museum at Westport** (▷ 205) gives an insight into the heyday of mining on the west coast—both for coal and gold—with evocative items including the massive brake drum from the Denniston Incline.

**Harbour 71, Akaroa** (▷ 222) has great views from its waterfront building, serving Pacific Rim cuisine.

**The International Antarctic Centre** in Christchurch (▷ 200) is the public face of a lively, working campus, giving a great introduction to the science and history of south polar exploration.

**Westland Tai Poutini National Park** (▷ 206–207) boasts two of the great sights of New Zealand—the Franz Josef and Fox glaciers.

## OTAGO AND THE FAR SOUTH

**Corstorphine House, Dunedin** (▷ 256) is a private hotel in a historic, stylish setting.

**Fiordland National Park** (▷ 233) takes in a spectacular landscape of steep forested peaks and drowned glaciated valleys, seen to advantage from the Milford Track (▷ 234).

**Jet-boat** on the Shotover River through Skippers Canyon (▷ 239), with tours from Queenstown (▷ 240–241)—after all, New Zealanders developed the craft specially.

**Moeraki beach** (▷ 236) comes with the bonus of a bizarre clutch of rounded boulders, a natural phenomenon well worth seeing.

**Oamaru** (▷ 238) is the chosen home of little blue and yellow-eyed penguins, with opportunities to see both rare species.

**The Otago Peninsula** (▷ 239) stretches northeastwards from Dunedin and is home to the only mainland-based royal albatross colony in the world.

**Saffron, Arrowtown** (▷ 254) offers wild local ingredients perfectly combined, in a historic setting.

**Opposite** *A cruise boat on Milford Sound in Fiordland National Park*
**Below** *Dolphin-spotting in the Bay of Islands*

## TOP EXPERIENCES

**Go for a walk.** The Kiwis call it tramping, and there's a huge choice of longer trails (▷ 284–285) and short strolls to get you closer to nature.

**Eat a top-class meal** of local delicacies (▷ 288–290). New Zealand lamb is hard to beat for taste and tenderness, the seafood is superb and the modern Pacific-influenced style of cooking is refreshing.

**Learn about Maori culture.** There are lots of opportunities in major towns to enjoy a Maori cultural event, partake of a *hangi* (▷ 290) or visit a *marae*—Rotorua offers some of the best (▷ 108–111).

**Take to the water,** even if it's only the Interislander ferry (▷ 52–53), and look for dolphins and seabirds. Sailing, kayaking and wildlife watching are just some of the options (▷ 280–285).

**Ride on the TranzAlpine,** the fabulous scenic rail route through the Southern Alps that links Christchurch and Greymouth (▷ 51).

**Shop 'til you drop.** There's much more to modern New Zealand fashion than the hard-working Swanndri (▷ 217), and the lively markets are a great way to source original souvenirs—try Aotea Square in Auckland (▷ 88), or Nelson (▷ 183), or Dunedin (▷ 249).

**Watch sport** and talk about it. It's probably the best way to blend in with the locals, whether you pick Ellerslie for racing (▷ 88), the Basin Reserve for cricket (▷ 154), Addington for trotting (▷ 215), or just about anywhere for rugby.

**Sit in an outdoor thermal pool** and experience natural reinvigoration. Rotorua (▷ 108–111) or Hanmer Springs (▷ 195) are the most obvious venues, but smaller places include Maruia Springs (▷ 202).

**Fly over a glacier** to experience a bird's-eye view of a moving snow-field—or better still, land on one and see it close up (▷ 218, 220)

**Do something that sets your heart racing.** New Zealand is becoming the world capital of adventure and adrenaline sports, and Queenstown (▷ 240–241) and Rotorua (▷ 108–111) are the main places, but you'll find opportunities everywhere. Go on—have a try!

**Below** *A close-up look at the Tasman Glacier from Terminal Lake in Mount Cook National Park*

# LIVING NEW ZEALAND

# NEW ZEALAND'S PEOPLE

It's barely been 200 years since European settlers moved into Aotearoa, the land they called New Zealand. In this short time, each city has developed an identity as distinctive as its new residents. Auckland's cosmopolitan citizens are known for their laptops, mobile phones and boating obsessions. Wellington is home to politicians, civil servants and cultured café society. Christchurch people, with their good manners and manicured gardens, are more English than the English. Dunedinites celebrate their Scottish heritage and the untamed freedoms of their wildlife and students. Beyond the cities, the farming folk are characterized by their bush-shirts, gumboots and staunched emotion. The Maori maintain their cultural stronghold in places such as Rotorua and Gisborne, but their influence touches all parts of the country. Against all odds, Maori culture survived colonization and continues to gain strength and standing. It is a highly regarded element of the national identity, for despite minor regional differences, the overriding belief is that New Zealanders—Kiwis—are one. They value a practical, down-to-earth approach, with nothing too frilly. They are great travellers who are unencumbered by tradition, and relish new ideas. They see themselves as 'laid back' but stand firm on issues they hold dear.

**Above** *New Zealanders express their national identity strongly at sporting events, especially at All Blacks rugby test matches*

**KIWI INGENUITY**

New Zealanders reckon they can make just about anything with a good whack of No. 8 fencing wire. Their flair for lateral thinking has led to a disproportionate number of successful inventions—for example, the three-wheeled Mountain Buggy, developed by Allan Croad in his family garage from an old golf trundler bought for NZ$5 at a school gala in 1992. The company now exports to 16 countries and makes blokes proud to push the pram.

Classic Kiwi inventions include the tranquillizer dart gun, now exported from Timaru to zoologists, farmers and gamekeepers worldwide, and the electric fence, brainchild of a Waikato farmer. Then there's the Hamilton jet-boat—which thrills visitors by speeding through mere centimetres of water—eartags for livestock, the electronic petrol pump, childproof bottle tops, spring-free trampolines and spreadable butter...

**SCRUFFY ICON**

New Zealand's devotion to Oscar-winning film-maker Peter Jackson is absolute.

Jackson has ticked every box on the Kiwi Hero scorecard. He was a DIY self-starter who made war films on his parents' back lawn, aged eight. His breakthrough movie, cult gorefest *Bad Taste*, was created with home-made equipment and a bunch of mates. He stuck by New Zealand when Hollywood offers flowed in, and insisted the *Lord of the Rings* trilogy should be made in his own backyard. New Zealanders love him just as he is...although there was a murmur of approval when, for a *King Kong* press launch, he was rumoured to have trimmed his hair.

**THE NEW IMMIGRANTS**

The New Zealand government has worked hard to attract migrants with investment capital or much-needed job skills—such as trades people and medical specialists. The impact showed clearly in the 2006 census. During the previous five years the Asian population increased by more than 100,000 to 354,000, 9 per cent of New Zealand's total. Those of European ethnic origin declined by 13 per cent, to two-thirds of the total population. Just over 14 per cent were Maori. The melting-pot effect is particularly noticeable in Auckland, which is home to two-thirds of Asian and Pacific peoples.

The total population tipped 4 million for the first time in 2003. This figure is always slightly skewed as at any one time more than half a million Kiwis are overseas. The majority live in Australia, thanks to the absence of work restrictions.

**Above** *This brightly painted rainbow kiwi is part of the Kiwiana displays in Otorohanga*
**Below** *Oscar-winning film-maker Peter Jackson*

**WOMEN'S WORLD**

Despite New Zealand's macho history of farming and rugby, women have played a significant role in the nation's development. New Zealand was the first country in the world to give women the vote, in 1893; the first country where two women leaders fought in a general election, in 1999; and the first country to elect a transsexual MP.

In the early 21st century women occupied all the top roles in the government—Head of State (Queen Elizabeth II), the Governor-General (Dame Silvia Cartwright, whose term finished in 2006), the Prime Minister (Helen Clark), the Chief Justice (Dame Sian Elias) and the Speaker of the House of Representatives (Margaret Wilson). In Parliament, 39 of the 121 MPs are women, including another party leader—Jeanette Fitzsimons, co-leader of the Green Party.

**LOCAL LINGO**

*The Dictionary of New Zealand English* (OUP, 1997) contains 6,000 main entries and 9,300 sub-entries, proving that although the country's official language is English, a visitor should not expect to understand it all. Phrases like 'rattle your dags' (hurry up) reflect a farming background, while 'half pie' (not great) stems from the Maori word *pai* (good). *Jandals* (flip flops), *jaffas* (chocolate balls with an orange coating) and *pikelets* (hotcakes) have become part of everyday life and language.

A strong New Zealand accent can be difficult to penetrate—it is similar to Australian, but the 'i' sound gives it away. Kiwis tend to turn it into a 'u' sound, as in 'fush and chups', while Australians say 'feesh and cheeps'. The accent is more-or-less consistent across the country except for Southland, where a rolled 'r' is common.

# THE GREAT OUTDOORS

When Canadian country-pop star Shania Twain visited Central Otago, New Zealand was thrilled. When she decided to buy a slice of it in 2004, the reception was rather cooler. New Zealanders are strongly connected with their land and love to share it with visitors. But they became wary around 1998, when the world's super-rich started snapping up beauty spots at bargain prices. Land values shot up. Young farmers now struggle to get started and traditional baches (holiday cottages) are vanishing. The most sensitive issue is public access to the land on the coast, under threat from developers, and the foreshore, where Maori customary rights and recently enacted Crown ownership don't always sit comfortably. In Twain's case, her company, Soho Properties, took out pastoral leases for Motatapu and Mount Soho Stations near Wanaka that were approved with stringent conservation and access conditions, some being suggested by Soho. Part of the agreement was the establishment of a walking track through both properties and the building of two new huts, funded by Soho Properties. Her land also hosts a walk/bicycle event, The Motatapu Icebreaker. So it's positive outcomes for all, as New Zealanders love being able to use and enjoy their countryside.

**Above** *Sailing is an extremely popular outdoor activity—this yacht race is on Lake Wakatipu*
**Opposite left** *Thrills and spills on a jet-boat ride near Hanmer Springs*
**Opposite right** *Bungy jumping is not a sport for the faint-hearted*

## A BEAUTIFUL GAME

Rugby is New Zealand's national addiction, but despite the awesome spectacle of their *haka* (traditional dance), New Zealand's All Blacks national rugby team has not lived up to expectations in recent years. New Zealand has not won the Rugby World Cup since 1987, considered a national disgrace.

By contrast, New Zealand has defeated Australia in 38 out of 50 events to win the Bledisloe Cup, the annual rugby series between the two nations—and Australia is currently one of the giants of world rugby.

The next Rugby World Cup will be contested in New Zealand in 2011, and hopes are high that home turf will make a difference. On the other hand, since 1990 the Black Ferns, New Zealand's women's rugby team, have lost only two of the international rugby events they have contested.

## SAILING HOPES

New Zealand is a nation of yachties—it's not for nothing that Auckland is known as the City of Sails, and at the Anniversary Day Regatta at the end of January the whole population seems to be out on the water.

The whole country was swept up in the enthusiasm in 2000, when Team New Zealand became the first non-US syndicate to retain the America's Cup. This all fell to pieces in the next defence, in 2003, after star skipper Russell Coutts was lured to the Swiss Alinghi team, and the Kiwi team suffered a series of major equipment failures—the boat was swamped by waves in one race, and the mast snapped in half in another.

In the 2007 America's Cup competition, the Kiwis lost to Alinghi once again—with Brad Butterworth, yet another New Zealander, in command of the victorious Swiss boat.

## CRAZY, BUT SMART

When A.J. Hackett jumped off the Eiffel Tower in a dinner suit in 1987, attached only to his prototype bungy cord, the world declared Kiwis crazy. Perhaps—but Hackett and co-founder Henry van Asch were on to something. Some 450,000 tourist jumps later, in 2004 a multi-million dollar Bungy Centre was opened at Kawarau Bridge in Queenstown by Prime Minister Helen Clark.

New buzzes are invented every year to enhance New Zealand's reputation as the adventure capital of the world, but bungy is queen bee. New Zealand now has four A.J. Hackett bungy sites (and many non-Hacketts), offering something for everyone, including the original Kawarau site (43m/141ft) for history buffs, Auckland Harbour Bridge (40m/131ft) for those who like smart technology, or Nevis Highwire, near Queenstown (134m/440ft), for the truly brave.

## MOUNTAIN MADNESS

Normal people take three hours to drive west-to-east across the South Island. But once a year, hardy souls do it the hard way, in the Speight's Coast to Coast multisport race from Kumara Beach, near Greymouth, to Sumner Beach, near Christchurch. The 243km (151-mile) course consists of 140km (87 miles) cycling, 67km (42 miles) kayaking and 36km (22 miles) running, including a 33km (20-mile) mountain stage across the Southern Alps. Competitors take anything from 10 hours 45 minutes (the course record) to 24 hours. The race's hero is Christchurch man Steve Gurney, who has competed 19 times and won 9 times since it began in 1983. More than 800 competitors vied for a place in the 2008 event, attracted by the promise of personal achievement and a free beer at the finishing line.

## DON'T GET MAD, GET CROSS

It's not for purists, but anyone looking for a unique—yet sedate—outdoor experience in New Zealand couldn't do better than GolfCross. The game is much like golf but uses an oval ball and a large rubber tee. Players use regular clubs but the putter isn't required—instead of holes and greens, the ball is pitched into a triangular goal with a two-sided net.

Surprisingly, the oval ball is easier to control than a round one. How the ball is set on the tee determines whether it will fly straight, hook or slice. The game's creator, Wellington inventor and writer Burton Silver, says this encourages players to take greater risks. The four GolfCross courses are in beautiful farmland (complete with sheep) near Rotorua, Wanaka, Martinborough and Mount Cook/Aoraki.

After suffering years of 'cultural cringe', New Zealanders are finding their own confident voice. Through the 1970s and 80s there was a perception that homegrown meant awful. Only accolades from abroad could guarantee artistic acceptance locally. High expectations perhaps had benefits—per head of population, New Zealand has a remarkable success rate. Literature had a good start with Katherine Mansfield (▷ 35) and the murder mysteries of Dame Ngaio Marsh (▷ 275). These days, children's fiction stands out, with Margaret Mahy, Joy Cowley and Lynley Dodd's *Hairy Maclary* selling millions of books worldwide. Split Enz and Kiri Te Kanawa led the way into the international music scene in the 1980s; performers like Hayley Westenra and opera star Jonathan Lemalu now follow on. In the 1990s, a strong film industry emerged with *An Angel at my Table, Once Were Warriors, The Piano* and *Heavenly Creatures*. They laid the foundations for the proudest moment in the history of Kiwi arts: Peter Jackson, director of *The Lord of the Rings* trilogy, and Keisha Castle-Hughes, star of *Whale Rider*, together on the red carpet at the 2003 Academy Awards. Fabulous locations and tax breaks should keep the film-makers coming, but the greatest benefit is New Zealand's new pride in its cultural identity.

**Above** *A Maori carving on the waterfront at Auckland*

**THE NEXT PRECIOUS...**

After starring as Middle Earth, New Zealand's next major film role was as Narnia, under Kiwi director Andrew *(Shrek)* Adamson. Work on *The Lion, the Witch and the Wardrobe* began in Auckland in early 2004, the production's budget of more than NZ$150 million nicely helping to fill the economic void left by the America's Cup (▷ 17). Later that year, filming moved on to locations down in the South Island, including high country, coast, alpine plateau, forests and mock English countryside.

The only major hiccup was the Ministry for Agriculture and Forestry (MAF)'s refusal to let 14 American reindeer into the country in case they carried potentially deadly Q fever. It took six months to create a replacement team—of animatronic reindeer—out of fibreglass and motors.

**Above** *Singer Hayley Westenra on stage*
**Below** *A sculpture carved from driftwood on Stewart Island*

## SINGING BELLES

New Zealand's latest music export is Hayley Westenra (b.1987), young, gorgeous and acclaimed the world over. In 2004, 17-year-old Hayley's album *Pure* stormed into the UK pop chart at No. 8 and the classical chart at No. 1. In New Zealand, the album's 18-week stay at No. 1 made her the country's biggest-selling artist ever. Soon after, she was dovetailing exams at her Christchurch high school with international appearances alongside Pavarotti, José Carreras and Bryn Terfel. She has performed for the Queen and other world leaders, past and present.

For those who like something a little more Norah Jones, New Zealand offers Brooke Fraser. She was just 20 when she won 'Tuis' at the 2004 Vodafone New Zealand Music Awards for best female and breakthrough artist of the year.

## WOW-WEE!

The Montana World of Wearable Art (WOW) awards show is big and getting bigger. Sculptor Suzie Moncrieff started it in 1987 to promote her Nelson art gallery, and it quickly boomed into a two-hour theatrical extravaganza. The televised awards are held each September before an audience of thousands. Entrants, from overseas designers to first-time locals, submit fantastical costume creations in any materials: Stained glass, wood panelling, flax, car parts and dried sausage skins have featured.

In 2004 the awards' last night was in Nelson; the show then moved to Wellington as part of an expansion plan. The ultimate vision is to stage events in different parts of the world and bring the winners to a grand final in New Zealand. The World of Wearable Art museum remains in Nelson (▷ 172–173).

## EEYORE MEETS MICHELANGELO

What do you get when you cross a Portaloo with sounds of a braying donkey and a volcano? Some say ground-breaking art, others a shocking waste of taxpayers' money. For sure, it's an animated fracas when the work's creator is to represent New Zealand at the most important contemporary arts event in the world.

The 'Donkey Toilet' (real title *Rapture 2004)*, created by a collective known as et al, caused a stink when it was exhibited at Wellington's City Gallery. But the stuff really hit the fan when CreativeNZ revealed that it provided NZ$500,000 to send et al's work to the 2005 Venice Biennale. It transpired that the 'collective' was established artist Merilyn Tweedie, and her Venice installation would feature computer hardware rather than a noisy toilet—but Joe Kiwi remained staunchly unimpressed.

## FRAME AND MIRROR

One of New Zealand's literary giants was Janet Frame, and since her death in 2004 her life has been commemorated in a Heritage Trail in Oamaru (▷ 238). Born in 1924 in Dunedin, Frame grew up shy, poor and marked by a head of frizzy orange hair. A misdiagnosed schizophrenic, she passed most of her 20s in psychiatric institutions. Despite the fact she was intensely reclusive, readers knew her through her novels (especially *Owls Do Cry)* and her three-part autobiography: *To the Is-land, An Angel at My Table* and *The Envoy from Mirror City*. She became widely recognized in New Zealand after 1983, when her autobiographies brought international acclaim, and she was tipped for the Nobel Prize in 2003. The Janet Frame Heritage Trail in Oamaru includes the railway worker's house where she grew up, and places featured in her books.

New Zealand is riding a wave of economic stability. Gross domestic product has been growing since 1999, outperforming growth is the US and British economies for most of that period. The unemployment rate has stood at under five per cent almost continuously since the beginning of the decade. The national sheep flock is in decline, from a high of 70 million in the 1980s to 43 million today. Dairy products earn more export income for New Zealand than meat or wool these days, and in many parts of South Island in particular, former sheep pastures have become dairy farms. Other industries such as forestry, fishing and deer farming have grown, each nurturing their niche products—such as mussels for the US and ice cream for Japan. New Zealand's 'clean, green' image is ruthlessly exploited to market agriculture and the other big earner—tourism. The tourism industry brings in more foreign exchange than any other sector of the economy, providing about one job in ten. More than 2.4 million international visitors spend an estimated NZ$8.3 billion a year on unique Kiwi experiences. As prosperity has increased, so has the share price of Kiwi retail icon The Warehouse. The red sheds are 'where everyone gets a bargain', bulk discounting everything from sofas to face cream.

**Above** *Sheep outnumber citizens by ten to one, although the national flock is in decline*

**SPREADING THE WEB**

The *Rings* trilogy shone the spotlight on New Zealand's IT industry, highlighting Kiwis' ability to combine creativity with computer genius. Gollum's parents at Weta Workshop continue to lead the way; aside from *King Kong*, their digital experts have been developing cost-effective animation for children's TV since 2003. Kiwis' other successful projects tend to be niche, such as web and email security, e-health systems, farming software, and the technology behind new-wave mobile phone services. It's hard going, though. Despite proven potential, the industry suffers from remoteness and lack of local investment capital. The story is all too common: Small development company is nurtured to world-class standing, then sold to US heavyweight who regrettably shuts the New Zealand office and makes the original staff redundant.

## DEER ME!

France has Champagne; New Zealand has Cervena. This is top grade, trademarked venison—mild, tender, low in fat, and heavy on the clean, green imagery.

With a national herd of 1.4 million, the industry is small fry compared with sheep and dairy. Nevertheless, it holds international significance as the world's number one source of farmed venison, exporting particularly to the US, Europe, Australia and Japan. Some 85 per cent of venison served in American restaurants comes from New Zealand.

Deer velvet, known for its medicinal properties, is also in demand and earns around NZ$38 million a year. The deer population has grown 12 per cent since 1994, and the South Island herd by 45 per cent. The name Cervena comes from *cervidae*—Latin for deer—and venison.

**Below** *Dairy products and sophisticated wines are top export earners for New Zealand*

## MUSSELING IN

What's so special about New Zealand mussels that makes them worth counterfeiting? The green-lipped mussel *(Perna canaliculus)* is native and unique to New Zealand. Its green-and-gold shell contains plump meat that is creamy white when male or apricot when female. Their size and taste give them a top reputation among mussel-buffs the world over, especially in the US, where inferior Chinese mussels *(Perna viridis)* have been sold in fake New Zealand packaging. The big concern—other than economic, as the industry is worth NZ$209 million a year—is that Chinese imposters are a potential health hazard. Mussels farmed under the New Zealand Greenshell trademark are grown under such stringent conditions they are safe to eat raw, but Chinese mussels are not. New Zealand's biggest mussel farms are in the Marlborough Sounds.

## A POWERFUL WIND

New Zealand's geographical quirks aren't just for looks—they keep the country running. Mighty rivers like the Clutha and Waikato are dammed for hydro-electricity, which is the main source of power (61.4 per cent). Geothermal activity provides another 6.9 per cent, while gas, sourced particularly from the Taranaki offshore field, Maui, provides 24.4 per cent. But crisis looms. Drought in 2003 lowered lake levels so severely that the country was threatened with blackouts; and Maui reserves are expected to run out around 2015. The government aims to develop renewable energy to take up the slack. In 2004, Te Apiti wind farm was opened in the Manawatu. The country's fifth wind farm, it is expected to become the biggest in the southern hemisphere, with 55 turbines, each able to power 700 homes.

## TOP TIPPLE

Accessible and elegant, wine is perhaps the Kiwis' best-loved export. The industry burgeoned from a historical fondness for beer and sherry, surprising the world in 1988 when it was highly featured at the London Wine Trade Fair. Export earnings have rocketed from NZ$18 million in 1990 to NZ$700 million in 2007: more New Zealand wine is drunk overseas than domestically. New Zealand Sauvignon blanc is a reliable award-winner and has become the world's benchmark. Chardonnay, Pinot noir and Cabernet/ Merlot blends are also gaining recognition.

New Zealand has 10 main wine-growing areas from Northland to Central Otago, the most established being Gisborne, Hawke's Bay and Marlborough. Many vineyards rate highly on the tourist trail, offering exceptional cuisine to complement tastings.

# NATURE AND WILDLIFE

Even as they step off the plane, visitors discover how serious New Zealand is about protecting its environment. No foreign plant or animal matter slips easily across the border; and a forgotten apple earns a NZ$250 spot fine. Vigilance has been learned the hard way. Before man's arrival the country's only land mammals were bats. The bush was thick with birds, many of which safely evolved as ground-dwellers—including the moa, kakapo and kiwi. The meaty moa was hunted to extinction by the Maori, and with the arrival of Europeans, many more species vanished as their habitats were destroyed. Introduced animals compounded the disaster. With no natural predators, possums, cats, dogs, stoats, ferrets and rats ran rampant and are still a severe menace to native birds. What's truly remarkable is that in spite of all the losses, wildlife remains one of New Zealand's greatest marvels. Native flora and fauna flourish in wilderness pockets all over the country, as well as a few inner-city areas such as Karori Wildlife Sanctuary in Wellington, where populations of rare kiwis, saddlebacks and kereru thrive. Much can be attributed to the expertise of local conservationists, who are in hot demand as far away as Indonesia and Madagascar.

**Above** *The flightless weka, endemic to New Zealand, has been classified as a vulnerable species*

## SUPER BUGS

The giant weta is a heavyweight of the insect world. It can grow 9cm (3.5 inches) long, excluding antennae, and weigh up to 80g (3oz)—the same as four average mice. Even so, it is the sweetest-looking of New Zealand's five types of weta and by far the rarest. These nocturnal super-bugs evolved good defences against their natural enemies—birds—but are poor jumpers and no match for hungry stoats, rats or weasels. However, weta breed well in captivity and their track record for survival is good—in evolutionary terms they are older than dinosaurs. The mountain rock weta of the Southern Alps is the largest insect known to tolerate being frozen solid in winter. Most weta eat foliage or animal remains, but will try a human finger if threatened.

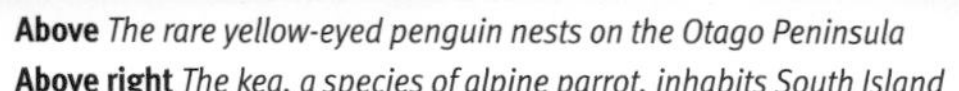
**Above** *The rare yellow-eyed penguin nests on the Otago Peninsula*
**Above right** *The kea, a species of alpine parrot, inhabits South Island*

## KEEPING THE BALANCE

When Penguin Place on the Otago Peninsula opened to visitors in 1984, there were eight pairs of rare yellow-eyed penguins on the reserve. By 2004 that number had tripled. The attraction now runs programmes for scientific research, native reforestation, predator control and an ornithological hospital. It's cost thousands, but every project was funded with tourist dollars.

Eco-tourism creates a win–win situation—if the operators create the best environment possible, wildlife thrives, creating an even more attractive tourist destination. In exchange for their dollars, tourists access a unique, hands-on experience. Top eco-friendly activities include spotting endangered Hector's dolphins near Christchurch, the Waimangu valley near Taupo, and guided nature walks around Queenstown in the south of South Island.

## THREATENED IDENTITY

Human Kiwis were shocked in the 1980s to realise their feathered namesake was in serious trouble. Despite urgent action, the numbers continued to decline by up to five per cent a year. The current total population across six varieties is estimated at between 50,000 and 60,000.

However, the Bank of New Zealand Kiwi Recovery Trust is striking back. Operation Nest Egg (ONE) increases chicks' chances of reaching adulthood from five per cent to forty, at which point they can defend themselves. The enormous egg is taken from the sitting adult, and the chick is hatched and reared in captivity. Kiwi chicks fend for themselves once hatched, so in some situations the parents can be left undisturbed and the newly hatched chick removed to a predator proof 'kiwi crèche' within the birds' wild habitat.

## THE PROBLEM WITH POSSUMS

One feature of every New Zealand highway is the squashed possum. Never mind, there's plenty more. An estimated 70 million Australian brushtail possums (introduced in 1837) are stripping native forests in 98 per cent of the country, often decimating prized trees such as rata for miles around. Their main food is young tree foliage, but they tuck into flowers, fruit, berries and insects if available. It was originally thought their impact on native birdlife was indirect, but time-lapse video has caught them eating eggs, chicks and adult birds. The NZ$60 million spent each year on possum control is not working. Current hopes lie in a contraceptive vaccine. A fur trade makes a tiny dint in the population, with luxury products like Merinomink (possum/fine wool) clothing, bedspreads, gloves and… nipple warmers.

## TREASURE OR TRAITOR?

A unique conservation debate was highlighted in June 2004, when the Department of Conservation (DoC) dropped 55 tonnes of rat poison on Little Barrier Island in the Hauraki Gulf. It was the first stage of a NZ$700,000 operation to wipe out the kiore, or Polynesian rat, from what is New Zealand's oldest nature reserve.

The issue was sensitive because some Maori tribes consider the kiore a *taonga*, or treasure. It has probably been in New Zealand as long as the Maori, having arrived with the early canoes, and was once important for food and cloak-making. However, it's a predatory rodent and considered a threat to native weta, frogs, skinks, birds and other wildlife. Although kiore are common in the southwestern Pacific and on some of New Zealand's offshore islands, they are rare on the mainland.

Far from dying out, as predicted by colonists, Maori culture is an integrated component of everyday New Zealand. Te Reo (Maori language) is taught in schools and culturally specific words like *iwi* (tribe), *taonga* (treasure), *whanau* (family) and *tapu* (sacred) are commonly used without elaboration. A Maori television channel was launched in 2003, the same year as the Maori Party in politics. Understanding and value of New Zealand's Maori heritage continues to grow; it's part of what makes the country unique. Indeed, when cyclist Sarah Ulmer won gold at the 2004 Athens Olympics, it was her supporters' spontaneous *haka*, not the medal ceremony, that touched her most.

**THE BIG ISSUE**

Does the Crown own New Zealand's foreshore and seabed? In 1997 the Ngati Apa tribe of Marlborough asked the court. In 2003 the Court of Appeal ruled it was Maori customary land. As no laws had been made to change this, the foreshore and seabed did not belong to the Crown absolutely. Kiwis prize nothing more than a day at the beach, so the Government leaped to legislate in 2004, giving ownership of the foreshore and seabed to the state. Their principles were that these areas should be public domain, with open access for all New Zealanders, but the customary interests of Maori would be protected. Maori—and the Waitangi Tribunal—called the ruling discriminatory because it abolished Maori property rights while apparently protecting everyone else's.

**KA MATE, KA MATE!**

*Haka* were around long before the All Blacks, but the rugby team certainly helped to cement the dance in Kiwi culture. Traditionally *haka* could refer to all Maori dance, but now it implies a vigorous posture dance. Men and women both perform *haka* but the men have the more spirited role, slapping thighs and chests, enlarging their eyes and sticking out their tongues. *Haka* can intimidate first-time spectators but they are not necessarily war dances—they are also performed at times of welcome, success or strong emotion.

**UNFURLING ECONOMY**

The emerging phrase 'Maori economy' describes enterprises run in line with Maori cultural values, such as *whanaugatanga* (kinship), *kotahitanga* (unity), *kaitiakitanga* (guardianship) and *mana whenua* (control of land). The end product doesn't need a particularly Maori flavour to qualify—Maori exports largely consist of fisheries, beef cattle, sheep meat, wool and forest products. But in some cases the Maori-ness is the product's selling point. Entrepreneurial chef Charles Royal has developed a demand for *pikopiko* (delicately unfurling fern fronds), a traditional Maori food that can be poached, grilled, barbecued or stir-fried. Under the label Kinaki Wild Herbs, he also produces medicinal body rubs containing *horopito* (bush pepper), a traditional aid to skin repair, and *kawakawa*, considered a blood purifier.

**Above** *The All Blacks perform the Haka Kapa o Pango Maori dance before their matches*

# THE STORY OF NEW ZEALAND

New Zealand was 680 million years in the making. Humans arrived on its shores perhaps a thousand years ago—hardly a tick on the geological clock—but their effect was profound and irreversible. The first settlers from East Polynesia probably numbered between one and two hundred, but within a century several species of bird were extinct, seals and other seabirds were all but eradicated from the main islands and large tracts of land were destroyed by fire. The easy pickings from New Zealand's great natural store cupboard had gone and the settlers were forced into more considered methods of survival. This marked the transition from the 'archaic' era of Maori settlement to the 'classic'. Groups became more settled as they developed sustainable food production such as gardening. The tubers of their *kumara* (sweet potato) became more valuable and had to be protected, giving rise to *pa* (fortified villages). By the 16th century a tribal system had developed. Now fully adjusted to the challenges of their environment, settlers could keep warm, build appropriate shelters and grow food. The focus moved to building social and cultural systems based on the old ways, but suited to their new country. They were no longer immigrants from Polynesia, but Maori.

**Above** Te Mata O Hoturua, *a carved Maori war canoe in the Wanganui Regional Museum*

**IN THE BEGINNING**

There are two quite different Maori myths about New Zealand's origins. One concerns Maui, the heroic trickster, who hauled up the North Island while he was out fishing.

The other is of Papatuanuku (the Earth Mother) and Ranginui (the Sky Father), who embraced each other so tightly their 70 sons were squashed between them. After much discussion, all the sons except one agreed their parents should be prized apart. Tanemahuta stood on his shoulders and pushed up the sky with his feet. He then clothed Papa with the green of the forest and adorned Rangi with the sun and stars, but still they wept for each other, creating rain and mist. Tawhiri-matea, the son who objected to his parents' separation, angrily followed Rangi into the sky and created the wind and storms.

### MAN BECOMES MYTH

Until recently, Maori arrival in New Zealand was neatly tied up: in AD950, a Polynesian navigator, Kupe, left Hawaiki (Tahiti) with his family and crew. Eventually, he sighted a white cloud *(aotea)*, which revealed a bush-covered land. He called it Aotearoa—Land of the Long White Cloud. In 1350, a 'Great Fleet' of seven canoes followed in his wake.

However, 1970s research found these 'truths' were not authenticated by Maori sources but had been cobbled together by a European scholar.

What we do know for sure is the Maori came from East Polynesia, a race of seafarers with the sophisticated navigation needed to complete the 3,000km (1,860-mile) journey and return home. It seems likely that after voyages of discovery, men and women came in several canoes, equipped for settlement, during the 13th century.

### HUNTED DOWN

Maori settlers walked into a teeming store cupboard in New Zealand. The moa was not the only ground-dwelling bird with little fear of predators in the country, but it remains by far the most distinctive.

The moa looked like a chunky ostrich, or an enormous kiwi with a long neck. At around 3m (10ft), the giant moa was the world's tallest bird, with drumsticks equivalent to a leg of beef. Even the smaller bush moa were as large as turkeys.

They were zealously rounded up and killed in their thousands by settlers until, in little more than 100 years, they were gone. Archaeologists have found traces of massive fires that destroyed forests, especially in Hawke's Bay and on the east coast of the South Island—these may have been started as a last-ditch effort to flush out the last of the species.

### CODES OF CONDUCT

As Maori culture developed into the tribally organized 'classic' phase, common values emerged. Links between tribes were strong enough for these values to be shared by all, just like the language.

For example, it was accepted that people were either *rangatira* (aristocrats) or *tutua* (commoners). *Rangatira* had more *mana* (honour), but anyone could gain or lose *mana* according to their skills and achievements.

Another common concept was *utu*. This idea of reciprocation could be positive or destructive, in response to a favour or an insult. It could sweeten relationships between tribes or families—one could gift basalt while the other returned with fish, raising the *mana* of both parties. Or it could mean war, as one tribe rectified another tribe's misdeed, which could have occurred days or possibly decades before.

### A RACE WRONGED

The Moriori came from East Polynesia and settled in the Chatham Islands (Rekohu). They shared the same genes as the Maori and travelled at around the same time, but away from the mainland they developed cultural differences: a society without hierarchy, their own dialect and a covenant to settle disputes by one-on-one combat, rather than warfare. During the 20th century historians portrayed Moriori as an inferior race exterminated by the Maori—a useful justification for European colonization. Moriori numbers were indeed decimated by the 1835 invasion of two Maori tribes, but descendants survived. However, most kept their heritage quiet until these presumptions were challenged in the late 20th century. In 2004, three Moriori groups signed terms with the Government under the Treaty of Waitangi, and three more were expected to follow suit.

**Left** *The first settlers soon hunted the flightless moa to extinction*
**Below** *Throwing a spear was a sign of welcome at a feast*

New Zealand's appearance on the world map did not suddenly change life for the Maori. English navigator Captain James Cook came and went in 1769, and the next 70 years brought an odd assortment of Europeans who settled around the edges of Maoridom. Many coastal tribes happily adopted individual missionaries or traders—it was a boost to *mana*, having one's own white man. Similarly, they adopted the goods that suited them best and discarded the rest. Maori bred pigs and grew flax, fruit and vegetables—especially the new white potatoes—specifically to barter with the Europeans. Europeans depended on this trade for survival; Maori came to depend on it for muskets. By the 1830s the entire country was consumed by a bloody carnage known as the Musket Wars. Traditional power balances were abolished as tribes such as Ngapuhi and Ngati Toa swept across the country, annihilating rival tribes. During 3,000 or so battles that took place from 1818 to 1840, an estimated 30,000 of the total 100,000 Maori population was killed by warfare, disease, starvation, slavery or in the cannibal feasts of victory.

**Above** *Maori chiefs recognized British sovereignty by signing the Treaty of Waitangi*
**Opposite top** *Portrait of Te Pehi Kupe in western dress, c1826*

**A FLOATING LABORATORY**

The first map of New Zealand represented disappointment. Captain James Cook's 1769 circumnavigation proved the country was not the hoped-for corner of a Southern Continent, as suggested by Dutch explorer Abel Tasman in 1642. But Cook's scientific expedition had many successes. He observed the transit of Venus across the sun from Tahiti as directed by London's Royal Society, providing vital data to map the solar system. He proved that regular doses of sauerkraut (rich in vitamin C) prevented sailors from dying of scurvy. And with naturalists headed by Joseph Banks, hundreds of plant and animal specimens were collected.

## PAKEHA MAORI

New Zealand's early Europeans were a diverse group. Among the sealers, whalers and missionaries was a small group known as Pakeha Maori—people like Barnet Burns, a trader who came in 1830 and went native. He lived in Mahia, south of Gisborne, under the protectorate of a chief he called 'Awhawee'. He married the chief's daughter, Amotawa, with whom he had three children. Over three intensive years he was abducted by rival tribesmen, escaped, led two major battles and claimed to have been made chief of a tribe of 600. He sailed to England on business in 1835 and gave a series of lectures—resplendent in full Maori dress and *moko* (facial and body tattoos). He never returned to New Zealand, but numerous descendants still live on the East Coast.

**Right** *British naval commander William Hobson was appointed first governor of New Zealand*

## GOD AND GRAMMAR

Christianity came to the Maori in 1814. Anglican chaplain Samuel Marsden planted three lay workers at Rangihoua, in the Bay of Islands. One, Thomas Kendall, approached his task by immersing himself in Maori culture and language. To his dismay, he nearly converted himself to heathen ways long before any Maori turned Christian.

Marsden dismissed him for misdemeanours including adultery, but not before Kendall could accompany his friend chief Hongi Hika and a younger chief, Waikato, to England in 1820. There, Hongi Hika (a fearsome figure of the Musket Wars) had an audience with George IV. The threesome worked with a Cambridge linguist to produce the foundations of written Maori. The conversion rate stayed on zero until the late 1820s, when Christian peace gave an alternative to the bloodshed of the Musket Wars.

## THE TREATY OF WAITANGI

In 1839, naval officer William Hobson was sent from London to formally establish New Zealand as a British colony. He invited chiefs from the North Island to sign a treaty at Waitangi on 5 February 1840. The government provided no draft document, so, with no legal training, Hobson and his officials hurriedly prepared the treaty in the four days preceding. Most inter-racial communication occurred in Maori, so it was also translated the night before. Forty-five chiefs signed after extended deliberations on 6 February; by September more than 500 had signed. The question was—and still is—what did they agree to? Discrepancies between British and Maori understandings were quickly realized but not easily rectified. Despite good intentions, the Treaty of Waitangi became the most contentious issue in New Zealand's history.

## NAMES FOR FACES

The word Maori means ordinary. It was widely used by Maori to describe themselves by the 1830s, although to most Europeans they were simply 'New Zealanders'. The Maori version of the Treaty of Waitangi uses the phrase *tangata maori*—ordinary people. As for Europeans, Maori had used the word *Pakeha* since at least 1814, when missionary William Hall recorded he had been referred to as a 'rungateeda pakehaa' *(rangatira pakeha)*, meaning a European gentleman. By the 1830s the word's usage among Maori was widespread. Europeans still described themselves according to their home countries, such as British. Pakeha probably originates from *pakepakeha*, an imaginary light-skinned being. The word's use was purely descriptive rather than derogatory, although it was also used for turnip (because of its white flesh) and flea.

The year 1840 marked the start of mass migration to New Zealand. The imminent tide of settlers was one reason Hobson needed to push through the Treaty of Waitangi—the Crown's right to purchase land had to be secured before private enterprise companies (notably the New Zealand Company) could steal the march. The next 20 years passed in relative peace, as Maori and Pakeha traded goods and land, but shady deals sowed seeds for future discontent. Maori land was communally owned, and wide consultation was required for a valid sale. New Zealand Company agents in Wellington, Nelson and Wanganui often found it easier to skip difficult owners and close a quick deal, while some Maori found their land had been 'sold' from under them by rivals. In 1840 there were just over 2,000 Pakeha settlers. By 1858 there were 59,000—3,000 more than there were Maori. As the numbers changed, so did the countryside; settlers made it more homely. Hundreds of plants, birds and animals were introduced, including 1.5 million sheep. The land was surveyed and mapped. Mountains, lakes and rivers known by the Maori for generations were 'discovered' and given European names. New Zealand was becoming 'the Britain of the South'.

**Above** *Land was cleared of spear grass and matagouri to make way for sheep*
**Opposite bottom** *Maori chief Hone Heke defied authorities, sparking the Northern War, in 1845*

## END OF AN EMPIRE

The most powerful man in 1840 was Te Rauparaha—warrior chief, strategist and entrepreneur. Kicked out of his Kawhia homeland by Waikato relatives, Te Rauparaha and his Ngati Toa tribe conquered Horowhenua with guns in 1823. From his stronghold on Kapiti Island he led murderous raids as far south as Banks Peninsula, and soon dominated the lower North Island and upper South Island. Wellington and Nelson were established only with his permission in the 1840s, but disputes later arose over which areas he actually sold. In 1843 a confrontation over land on the Wairau Plains, north of Blenheim, ended violently and settlers became nervous. Governor George Grey decided Te Rauparaha could not be trusted and arrested him in 1846. During 10 months in prison his *mana* waned. Te Rauparaha died in 1849.

## MAORI MONARCHY

As Maori felt their land and culture slipping away, they looked for strength in unity. Tribes around Waikato, Taranaki and the central North Island acted by selecting the first Maori king: the Waikato chief Te Wherowhero.

In 1858, he took his seat at Ngaruawahia, north of Hamilton, in the district now known as the King Country. Maori intended their monarchy to complement the British Crown—the Maori king and Queen Victoria would be joined in accord. They hoped this unity would give Maori a chance against the confident and cohesive settlers. Instead, it aggravated the colonists, who thought it showed disloyalty to the Queen. It was also seen as a stumbling block to further land sales, and fuelled the popular idea that Maori were getting too big for their boots.

## DREAMS FOR SALE

For the equivalent of NZ$101, the New Zealand Company sold investors one town acre (0.4ha) and 100 country acres (40ha). Not that the company had any land to sell—the ships containing buyers and surveyors scooted into Port Nicholson (Wellington) just 18 days before 1,000 unsuspecting migrants. They found no sign of the undulating plains promised in company propaganda, described as perfect for grapevines, wheat, olives and bananas—only swamp, forest, steep hills and sand hummocks. The plan of 1,100 one-acre sections simply wouldn't fit into the proposed Hutt Valley site. Migrants camped on the Petone foreshore, with possessions from beds to pianos heaped around them. At least they wouldn't starve: From the moment they stepped off the boat, they started shooting birds.

## GREAT SHAKES

As if the Wellington settlers hadn't enough to contend with, their fledgling town was struck by the country's biggest recorded earthquake in January 1855. It measured 8 on the Richter scale—the 1999 Taiwan quake that claimed 2,330 lives was 7.6. In this case, one person died in Wellington and three in Wairarapa. But it wasn't all bad. The shoreline rose 1m (3ft) on average, leaving Lambton Quay high and dry—it is now a main shopping street. Plans for a new dock had to be shelved (the area is now Basin Reserve cricket ground, ▷ 148, 154), but there was suddenly space for a road to link Wellington with the Hutt Valley, reclaimable land around the harbour and another 100m (110 yards) of beach at Petone. Wooden buildings were proved to be safer than brick, and carpenters rejoiced.

## HEAVEN OR HELL?

The primitive conditions of New Zealand shocked new arrival Georgiana Bowen. She wrote to her sister in 1851: 'It is only Colonists who can have any idea of what roughing it is, and it is ill suited for any but the young, strong and active… We are now in wooden shanties or tents of which perhaps you can form no idea.' Maria Richmond, on the other hand, was smitten after just six months. In 1853 she wrote: 'I have never felt so wide awake as I have done since I landed in New Zealand…the feeling of coming home, as it were, to a country wanting you, asking for people to enjoy and use it, with a climate to suit you, a beauty to satisfy and delight, and with such possibilities for the future.'

**Above** *A view of Auckland's Queen Street, around 1853, from the wharf*

# THE COLONY GAINS CONFIDENCE

The colony entered an unsettled time of change. Rapid growth put pressure on towns like Auckland and New Plymouth, which in turn put pressure on Maori to sell more land. Discontent on both sides sparked a series of land wars, which ripped through the North Island from 1860 to 1872. Colonial forces fought Maori and Maori fought each other. By the turn of the century, Maori were considered a dying race. Many tribes had lost their livelihoods and their morale with the confiscation of millions of hectares of land. They were also ravaged by influenza, measles, whooping cough and dysentery. Meanwhile, the European population boomed. Premier Julius Vogel borrowed a staggering amount of money on the London capital market during the 1870s to put in thousands of kilometres of roads, railways and telegraph lines, and to assist another 100,000 settlers into the country. It was not enough to protect New Zealand from worldwide recession, which lasted into the 1890s, but the advent of refrigeration brought new hope. The first successful shipment of frozen lamb and mutton to England in 1882 granted the country a major new export earner.

**Above** *The Cardrona Hotel, just outside Wanaka, dates from the gold rush era and is one of the oldest surviving hotels in New Zealand*

**THE BACHELOR LIFE**

In 1871, men outnumbered women two to one. With no prospect of marrying, many vanished into a men's world of shearing, farm work, timber milling, mining or public works. Once in the back blocks, they would live in shanty camps for years. It was the start of New Zealand's 'bloke' culture, where hard work, honesty, camaraderie, sense of humour and mateship were highly valued. The government aimed to boost the population by offering free passage to single British women. Many obliged; domestic servants could earn more than in England. Even so, mistresses had to bargain hard to keep their staff, and domestics with an apparent impediment to matrimony—such as Gaelic speakers—were preferred. Twenty years later, the sex ratios were nearly balanced.

## CHINATOWN

Gold in Otago and Westland brought a new wave of immigrants—the Chinese. They made up 6 per cent of the Otago population in 1871, virtually all men who lived on the breadline to send money back to their wives and families. Isolated by appearance and culture, they stuck together and were treated with suspicion by Europeans. Their greatest success story was Choie Sew Hoy, whose pioneer gold dredge enabled miners to winkle sand out of river flats as well as the river bed. Hoy established a store in Dunedin importing Chinese goods and became a mentor for other Chinese in the area. Unlike his compatriots, he opted to stay in New Zealand and married. By 1880 he was the best-known Chinese figure in Dunedin. Sew Hoy's store still trades on Stafford Street.

## A GREAT EXPLOSION

On 10 June 1886, the ground south of Rotorua shook violently as Mount Tarawera split open, sending a column of fire into the night sky. Tourists staying at the Rotomahana Hotel fled to the *whare* of Sophia, a Maori guide. Her small house sheltered 60 people through the night and was one of only two buildings in Wairoa village to survive the eruption. The rest were buried under tonnes of mud, rock and ash.

An estimated 153 people were killed, including the school teacher and five of his children. His wife was later pulled from the mud alive. Lake Rotomahana is now 30m (98ft) higher than before the eruption. The blasted face of Mount Tarawera still tells a tale, and destroyed the famous Pink-and-White Terraces (⊳ 111).

## TAKING THE LEAD

Two remarkable world firsts passed into law under Richard ('King Dick') Seddon's Liberal government: old-age pensions (1898) and universal suffrage. Winning the world's first national votes for women took a good deal of hard graft by Kate Sheppard, temperance supporter, writer, speaker and early feminist. She liked women to be 'hearty and hale', and rode a bike around Christchurch when women were considered too fragile for such activity. But she also had the tact, intellect and determination to win allies and advance her battle. Her first petition in 1891 contained 9,000 signatures. Her second, a year later, had 19,000. Her final petition was signed by nearly 32,000 women—around a third of the female population. The Women's Suffrage Bill passed by two votes in 1893.

## BLOWING THE WHISTLE

New Zealand stamped its first mark on rugby in 1884, when referee W.H. Atack of Canterbury got sick of shouting himself hoarse at two marauding teams. According to the official historian of the NZ Rugby Football Union, Atack was mulling over the problem when his fingers strayed to a waistcoat pocket. There, they encountered a dog whistle. With a flash of inspiration, he realized it would be a perfect way to stop the game. The next time he refereed, he called the teams together and they agreed to play to the whistle. It was a great success and was adopted all over the country.

New Zealand's first national rugby team was invited to tour the UK in 1888–89. The team called itself the New Zealand Native Team. The current name, the All Blacks, was not adopted until 1905.

**Left** *Gold miners take a break at Monteith's Brewery, Greymouth*

**Below** *Gottfried Lindauer's portrait of Ana Rupene and child, c1880*

There was no doubt that New Zealand would fight alongside Mother England when World War I broke out in 1914. After a period of relative peace and prosperity, many of the country's young men jumped at the chance to take part—both Pakeha and Maori. It was exciting, patriotic, a chance for blokes to get together and see the world. They would fight alongside Australians as the Australia and New Zealand Army Corps—ANZACs. But the euphoria rapidly vanished when 3,000 New Zealanders landed at Gallipoli on the Turkish Coast on 25 April 1915. The campaign was a disaster from the outset—troops were landed 3km (2 miles) from the intended beach and faced a wall of cliffs. One soldier in five was mown down on the first day. For eight months, the men existed in trenches metres away from the Turkish troops, prey to disease, snipers, heat, blizzards and the stench of irretrievable bodies. Despite valiant attempts to claim the peninsula, the attack was an utter failure. When the troops were finally pulled out in mid-December, the casualty rate stood at an appalling 88 per cent. New Zealanders went on to fight at the Western Front and in the Middle East but Gallipoli is still the campaign most remembered. April 25 is ANZAC Day, a national day of commemoration.

**WELFARE FOR ALL**

Few prime ministers have their photos hung over the mantelpiece, but Michael Joseph Savage was different. He was the benign face of the Labour government that stormed to victory in 1935, just as the Great Depression was tailing off. Their mission to look after New Zealanders 'from the cradle to the grave' had a positive effect—a free hospital system, universal superannuation at 65, a 40-hour working week and a basic wage considered enough to keep a man, wife and three children comfortably. In three years, 3,500 state houses were built with modern kitchens and an indoor toilet.

**Above** *An expression of architectural confidence in Dunedin's railway station, 1907, featuring a Royal Doulton mosaic floor and decorative wrought iron railings*

## TAKING OFF

When does 'powered flight' become 'controlled'? If you can land in a river and still be 'controlled', then Richard Pearse was a world-class achiever. And even if you can't, his 1902 aircraft still flew nine months before the Wright brothers'. The South Canterbury farmer created a plane with a two-cylinder engine, vertical rudder, tricycle undercarriage and propeller. Eyewitnesses say that on 31 March 1902 this craft took off from a farm paddock, climbed slowly, turned right and flew 1,200m (3,963ft) before landing in a river. A modified version flew 50m (164ft) one year later before colliding with a gorse bush.

Pearse patented ailerons—flaps that give planes vertical control—in 1906, but he let the patent lapse in 1910 because he saw little prospect of selling planes in New Zealand.

## DEADLY VIRUS

On 11 October 1918, the passenger liner *Niagara* was permitted to dock in Auckland harbour, despite radioed warnings that Spanish influenza was on board. Why wasn't the ship quarantined?

Among the passengers were New Zealand Prime Minister William Massey and his Minister of Finance, anxious to return to work after meetings in Britain and Europe. It's not known if they influenced the decision to let passengers disembark, but by 3 November, 120 cases of influenza were admitted to Auckland Public Hospital.

There was no cure. The disease quickly spread south through the country, forcing the shutting of schools, shops and pubs, and disrupting industry. More than 6,700 New Zealanders died of the disease, including an estimated 2,160 Maori.

## LITERARY TALENT

Katherine Mansfield is New Zealand's best-known writer. Even though she was 'ashamed' of her young country's stifling lack of creativity, her childhood memories gave richness to her masterful short stories.

She was born in 1888 to a socialite Wellington family. At the age of 14 she went to England for three years of schooling, and on returning home found she couldn't wait to get back to London. 'It is Life,' she wrote.

Her avid pursuit of 'Life' took her back to London in 1908, where she mingled with D. H. Lawrence and the intellectual Bloomsbury group of writers. After passionate affairs with both men and women, an inexplicable marriage and a last-ditch hunt for inner peace, she died of tuberculosis near Paris in 1923, aged 34.

Katherine Mansfield was the first New Zealand-born writer to earn international recognition for her work.

## MAORIS ENTER POLITICS

By the start of the 20th century, a group of well-educated leaders emerged to fight the Maori cause through politics: Maui Pomare, James Carroll and Apirana Ngata.

Less conventional was Tahupotiki Wiremu Ratana. The ploughman's journey began in 1918, when he heard the voice of God telling him that Maori were God's chosen people, and that he should unite Maori and turn them towards God. Ratana began faith healing and was so successful that a settlement grew around his house, south of Wanganui (it is now called Ratana). Ratana MPs held all four Maori parliamentary seats by 1943 and provided Labour with a vital alliance during 1946 to 1949. Attention to Maori land development, schooling, housing and unemployment brought a marked improvement to Maori conditions. The Ratana church now has more than 49,000 members.

**Above** *Memorials to the troops who fell in New Zealand's service*
**Top** *Writer Katherine Mansfield (1888–1923)*

Mother England gently loosened the apron strings in 1931 by proclaiming her Dominions autonomous. New Zealand remained in denial, even as she backed out of their stifling economic relationship in preference for Europe. In 1984, a new Labour government showed the first signs of the rebellious teenager. It was led by quick-witted barrister David Lange, who soon had to grasp the prickly end of Labour's anti-nuclear stance. When the US ship *Buchanan* refused to confirm or deny its nuclear capabilities, Lange denied it entry. This signalled the effective end of ANZUS, a key defence treaty with Australia and America. The US's subsequent bullying did not impress the public, but on 10 July 1985 the Kiwis' nuke-free stance turned absolute. That night, the Greenpeace ship *Rainbow Warrior* was blown up in Auckland harbour, killing one crew member. The ship was about to sail to Mururoa atoll in the Pacific to protest against French nuclear tests. In a matter of days the New Zealand police caught those responsible—two French agents. The leaders of the US, Britain and Australia barely said a word against it. New Zealanders were outraged, and determined to stand by their principles. The agents were later decorated by the French government.

**Above** *The Greenpeace ship* Rainbow Warrior *which was sunk in Auckland harbour by French agents*

**LAND RIGHTS TO THE FORE**

The government continued to take Maori land in the 1970s but there was a difference—Maori numbers, awareness and anger had grown. In 1975, a march from Northland ended in Wellington with 50,000 supporters asking the government to guarantee that not one more hectare of Maori land would be lost. The government did not commit. Rather, in 1976, it decided to sell land at Bastion Point, which originally belonged to Ngati Whatua. The tribe had reserved it nearly 100 years before, after selling thousands of hectares for Auckland development. Over time, pockets were lost—much of it to compulsory Crown acquisition. Maori patience ran out when the government tried to sell the land for housing—protesters occupied the site for 17 months before being arrested in May 1978.

### THE OPEN MARKET

The Labour government created the welfare state in 1935; in 1984 they took most of it away. With the over-protected economy verging on bankruptcy, finance minister Roger Douglas opened New Zealand to the ravages of the free market.

The resulting changes were abrupt, unexpected and painful. Agriculture subsidies were phased out; farmers walked off the land. The dollar was devalued and later floated on the international market.

In addition, government enterprises such as the Post Office and New Zealand Steel became State Owned Enterprises and were expected to turn a profit. The government actions resulted in thousands of public servants being made redundant and unions reeled as their power base was chipped away. 'Rogernomics' changed New Zealand's fundamental economic values forever.

### DIVIDED FANS

Could any other country be so divided by rugby? In 1981, the New Zealand Rugby Union invited the South African Springboks to play three test matches against the All Blacks. Prime Minister Rob Muldoon refused to intervene even though he had signed the Gleneagles Agreement, discouraging sporting contact with apartheid South Africa. It sparked an unofficial civil war—barbed-wire fences, street blockades and riot police became as common as street marches.

The first match in Hamilton was abandoned when 300 protestors sat on the pitch, tempting the wrath of 27,000 fans. The violence peaked at the final match in Auckland. Protesters made 362 complaints against the police; 75 were eventually upheld. In all, around 2,000 arrests were made and tour defence cost the country NZ$7.2 million.

### RUNNING THE RACE

Ever been for a jog? Thank Aucklander Arthur Lydiard, who formed the world's first jogging group.

In 1944, at the age of 27, he struggled to run 10km (6 miles) with a friend. The training method of the day—speeding round a track to point of collapse—didn't work for him. Instead, he devised a programme of gradual build-up. By his early 30s he was New Zealand's top marathon runner, and his times over shorter distances had also improved.

A group of younger runners started training under Lydiard's guidance. Two members of the group became stars of the 1960 Rome Olympics—Murray Halberg, who won the 5,000m gold, and Peter Snell, who won the 800m and smashed the Olympic record by 1.4 seconds. Lydiard later applied his training principles to fitness for the general public and invented 'jogging'.

### HOMEGROWN SUPERMODEL

When everyone was talking about the supermodels of Britain, the US and Europe, New Zealand was surprised to realize it had one too. Rachel Hunter (born in Auckland in 1969) started modelling at the age of 17. After starring as 'the Trumpet girl' in an ice cream advertisement on TV, she leapt to the pages of *Sports Illustrated*—the magazine famed for making models famous. She appeared on thousands of covers worldwide, including *Cosmopolitan* and *Vogue*. Not only that, but by 1990 Hunter had married Rockin' Rod Stewart—the British crooner 24 years her senior. For a while she was the ultimate home girl made good—she even brought Rod and her two children home for holidays. In 1999 the pair split but Rachel continued to dominate magazine headlines. She now lives in the US.

**Right** *Many marathon runners follow Lydiard's training programme*
**Below** *Former Prime Minister David Lange*

# INTO THE NEW MILLENNIUM

New Zealand's taste for independence has grown to a hearty appetite and the country has bravely adopted its new position as a Pacific nation, closer to Asia than Europe. In trade, the country gradually recovered to establish healthy relationships with countries other than Britain, particularly Australia, the US, Europe, Japan and China. Agricultural products like meat and dairy remained substantial export earners, but tourism, forestry and fisheries widened the economic base. The surprise boon of the new century was film-making. New Zealand has stormed into the world of big-budget film production with a string of successes including the *Lord of the Rings* series.

**COMPETITIVE SPIRIT**
Kiwis were devastated to lose the America's Cup in 2003, and appalled to see England crowned rugby world champions in the same year. The 2008 Beijing Olympics was New Zealand's most successful since 1988, with a total of nine medals, including three golds. New Zealand's athletes performed particularly well in the rowing where they won two bronze medals and one gold.

**RACE RELATIONS**
The Waitangi Tribunal was created in 1975 to inquire into Maori grievances against the Crown but grew teeth only in 1985, when it was able to consider claims dating back to 1840. In October 2000, 870 claims had been registered with the Tribunal. Claims could be historical, such as compensation for confiscated land, or contemporary, if current government actions were thought to breach treaty principles. Apart from tribal land, claims have been made about sharing resources as diverse as the airwaves, oil, fisheries, airspace and, in 2004–05, the foreshore and seabed. Successful claimants, such as Ngai Tahu in the South Island, who settled on a NZ$170 million compensation package, have generated business success and morale. The Tribunal expects to report on all claims by 2012.

**WAR AGAINST TERROR**
After September 11, New Zealand joined the United Nations in disagreeing with the need to invade Iraq. Prime Minister Helen Clark clearly believed the US was wrong to proceed without UN backing. After the invasion, nearly 70 per cent of New Zealanders approved of her Labour government's opposition to the war. The stand was principled but it wasn't easy, especially as New Zealand had high hopes of jumping on Australia's free trade deal with the US. Clark's widely reported comment that the war would never have happened if Al Gore was president was considered by some a major gaffe. New Zealand soldiers have helped to ensure security in Afghanistan's Banyan province since 2003.

**Above** *Queen Elizabeth II with New Zealand's Prime Minister John Key at a New Zealand tourism exhibition in London*

# ON THE MOVE

On the Move gives you detailed advice and information about the various options for travelling to New Zealand before explaining the best ways to get around the country once you are there. Handy tips help you with everything from buying tickets to renting a car.

**Above** *Air New Zealand, the national airline, serves many international and domestic destinations*

## ARRIVING BY AIR

The vast majority of visitors to New Zealand arrive by air. The three main international airports are Auckland, Christchurch and Wellington, with Auckland being the principal entry point. Palmerston North and Hamilton in North Island and Christchurch, Dunedin and Queenstown in South Island all offer regular air services to airports in eastern Australia.

### Auckland International Airport

Auckland airport, a relatively small, modern gateway to the nation, is 21km (13 miles) south of the city's central business district. The airport has two terminals—international and domestic. A free transit shuttle operates between them every 20 minutes from 6am to 10.30pm, and there is a connecting walkway.

» At the i-SITE visitor information office on the ground floor of the Arrivals hall you can book hotels, check transport details and store luggage. Hospitality ambassadors, dressed in bright blue jackets, or customer service officers, dressed in red jackets, are available for assistance.

» Shops, food outlets, mail boxes, internet access, nursery, free showers (towels are rented out from the florist on the ground floor for a small fee plus deposit) and phones are all available at the airport.

» Additional services include dayrooms containing a bed, desk, TV, coffee, tea and shower, which can be rented from NZ$30 for four hours. There are banks with currency exchange facilities throughout Departures and Arrivals in the International Terminal. ATMs can be found in various locations in the International Terminal. A medical facility operates just outside the International Terminal.

» All the well-known rental car operators (▷ 42) are represented at both terminals on the ground floor.

| AIRPORT CONTACTS | | |
|---|---|---|
| **NORTH ISLAND** | | |
| Auckland | tel 09-276 8899 | www.auckland-airport.co.nz |
| Wellington | tel 04-388 9900 | www.wellington-airport.co.nz |
| Palmerston North | tel 06-351 4415 | www.pnairport.co.nz |
| Hamilton | tel 07-848 9027 | www.hamiltonairport.co.nz |
| **SOUTH ISLAND** | | |
| Christchurch | tel 03-358 5029 | www.christchurch-airport.co.nz |
| Dunedin | tel 03-486 2879 | www.dnairport.co.nz |
| Queenstown | tel 03-442 3505 | www.queenstownairport.co.nz |

### Wellington International Airport

Wellington airport, in the suburb of Rongotai, 6km (3 miles) south of the heart of the city, handles both international and domestic flights from one terminal. Take-offs and landings along its short runway are particularly memorable.

» Although there are dozens of Trans-Tasman and Pacific Island flights per week, Wellington primarily operates a busy domestic schedule, with regular daily flights to most principal cities. Air New Zealand and Qantas are the main carriers, but a number of smaller operators fly to upper South Island destinations. These include Sounds Air, who offer flights to Picton, Nelson and Blenheim for relatively low fares.

» The terminal has all the usual facilities, including food outlets, shops, luggage deposit and an information office.

» All the major car rental companies (⊳ 42) are represented at the airport. Both shuttles and taxis depart from directly outside baggage reclaim.

| NEW ZEALAND INTERNATIONAL AIRLINES |
|---|
| **Air New Zealand** tel 0800-028 4149 (UK) www.airnz.co.nz |
| **Freedom Air International** tel 0800-600 500 www.freedomair.com |
| |
| **FOREIGN AIRLINES OPERATING TO NEW ZEALAND** |
| **Aerolineas Argentinas** tel 0800 0969 747 (UK), 800-333 0276 (US) www.aerolineas.com.ar |
| **Air Pacific** tel 01206 264283 (UK), 800-227 4446 (US) www.airpacific.com |
| **British Airways** tel 0870-850 9850 (UK), 800-AIRWAYS (US) www.british-airways.com |
| **Cathay Pacific** tel 020-8834 8888 (UK), 800-233 2742 (US) www.cathaypacific.com |
| **Emirates** tel 0870 243 2222 (UK), 800-777 3999 (US) www.emirates.com |
| **Garuda Indonesia** tel 020-7467 8600 (UK), 800-3 GARUDA (US) www.garuda-indonesia.com |
| **Japan Airlines** tel 0845 774 7700 (UK), 800-525 3663 (US) www.jal.com |
| **Jetstar** tel 866-397 8170 (US) www.jetstar.com |
| **Korean Air** tel 0800 413 000 (UK), 800-438 5000 (US) www.koreanair.com |
| **Malaysia Airlines** tel 0870 607 9090 (UK), 800-552 9264 (US) www.malaysiaairlines.com |
| **Pacific Blue** tel +61 7 3295 2284 www.flypacificblue.com |
| **Qantas Airways** tel 0845 774 7767 (UK), 800-227 4500 (US) www.qantas.com.au |
| **Singapore Airlines** tel 0844 800 2380 (UK), 800-742 3333 (US) www.singaporeair.com |
| **Thai Airways International** tel 0870 606 0911 (UK), 800-426 5204 (US) www.thaiair.com |
| **Virgin Blue** tel +61 7 3295 2296 www.virginblue.com.au |

### Christchurch International Airport

Christchurch airport is 12km (7 miles) northwest of the city. The international and domestic terminals are housed in one building; domestic transfer check-in counters are in the international arrivals hall. The terminal is open for all flight arrivals and departures, while the domestic terminal is open from 7.30am to 8pm.

» The international terminal has direct links with Australia, Singapore and Japan.

» There are bars and restaurants in both terminals. The International Atrium has duty-free shopping and other shops, including clothes stores in the departures hall. A smaller variety of shops is available in the domestic terminal. ATMs are found in both terminals.

» Information desks in both the domestic terminal and international arrivals hall can make reservations for local hotels and tours, provide full travel agency services and arrange any further international or domestic travel plans.

**Below** *Air pockets and strong winds enliven flights into Wellington*

**Above** *Many visitors use minivans to get to top locations*

## VEHICLE RENTAL

### CAR

As well as the major car rental firms, there are many local operators. Shop around, and always read the small print before you sign. Some of the less expensive companies have an insurance excess of NZ$700.

» Always ask for a list of any dents or scratches that you see on the vehicle.

» If you do not have a credit card you may have to leave a cash deposit of NZ$500–NZ$1,000.

» You must be over 21 and have a valid driver's licence. Insurance premiums for under-25s can be high.

» You can rent a vehicle in one city and drop it off at another. This will almost certainly involve a drop-off fee of around NZ$120–NZ$150.

» Insurance is not compulsory but highly recommended. You will not be covered if you venture onto any of the 'sand highways' on the coast, such as Ninety Mile Beach (▷ 69), and many companies do not provide cover in the Catlins (▷ 229).

### MOTORCYCLE

Motorcycle rental can be a superb way to see the country.

» Depending on the model and package, renting a motorcycle for a week can cost anything between NZ$80 and NZ$1,000.

### CAMPERVAN (RV)

Campsites are readily available. Powered sites cost around NZ$10–NZ$15 per night. Note that lay-by (turnout) overnight parking is illegal.

» Rates vary and are seasonal. The average daily charge for a basic two-berth/six-berth for rent over 28 days, including insurance, is around NZ$195/ NZ$350 in high season and NZ$70/NZ$140 in low season.

| RENTAL CONTACTS |
|---|
| **CAR RENTAL CONTACTS** |
| **About New Zealand** tel 0800-455 565 www.rentalcar.co.nz |
| **Ace Rental Cars** tel 0808-234 8561 www.acerentals.co.nz |
| **Avis** tel 0800-655 111 www.avis.com |
| **Budget** tel 0800-283 438 www.budget.co.nz |
| **Ezy Rentals** tel 0800-559 3292 www.ezy.co.nz |
| **Hertz** tel 0800-654 321 www.hertz.com |
| |
| **MOTORCYCLE RENTAL CONTACTS** |
| **Adventure Motorcycles** tel 0508 RIDE BMW www.adventuremotorcycles.co.nz |
| **Adventure Trailrides** tel 0274 510 584 www.adventureride.co.nz |
| **New Zealand Motorcycle Rentals & Tours** tel 0800-917 3941 (UK), 866-490 7940 (US) www.nzbike.com |
| **South Pacific Motorcycle Tours** tel 03 312 0444 www.motorcycletours.co.nz |
| **Te Waipounamu Motorcycle Hire and Tours** tel 03-372 3537 www.motorcycle-hire.co.nz |
| |
| **BICYCLE RENTAL CONTACTS** |
| **Bicycle Rentals** tel 0800 444 144 www.bicyclerentals.co.nz (throughout New Zealand) |
| **City Cycle Hire (Christchurch)** tel 03-339 4020 www.cyclehire-tours.co.nz |
| **Hedgehog Bikes (Auckland)** tel 09 486 6559 www.hedgehog.co.nz |
| |
| **CAMPERVAN RENTAL CONTACTS** |
| **Britz** tel 0800-831 900 www.britz.co.nz |
| **Kea Campers** tel 09-441 7833 www.kea.co.nz |
| **Kiwi Campers** tel 0800 549 44, www.nzcampers.com |
| **Maui** tel 09-275 3013/0800 651 080 www.maui.co.nz |

## GETTING AROUND IN AUCKLAND

**Auckland's public transportation system has been overhauled to provide a more consistent service between buses, ferries and trains. Information on all types of transport is available from MAXX (see Useful Contacts, below).**

The handiest way to travel in the city is by bus. Several travel pass schemes are available: the Auckland Discovery Day Pass gives unlimited travel on the five major bus companies, suburban trains and inner port ferries between 5am on the day of purchase and 4.59am the following morning. Auckland Pass gives one day's unlimited travel on North Star and Stagecoach Auckland buses (including the Link; see below) and includes travel on ferry services to the North Shore. A similar deal is offered by the Three-Day Rover, but for three consecutive days.

### BUS

» Most central and suburban buses stop at the Britomart Transport Centre, between Customs and Quay streets, near the waterfront.

» An Auckland Busabout Guide is available from the bus terminal and all major tourist information offices, showing routes and departure points for the main attractions. Fares are on a staged system, 1–8 (NZ$1.60–NZ$9.70).

» City Circuit is a red bus providing a free service around the city's heart every 10 minutes, daily 8–6.

» The Link bus has a flat fare of $1.60 and runs every 10 minutes 6am–7pm weekdays, 7am–6pm Saturdays, every 15 minutes evenings and Sundays. The route is Britomart–Quay Park–Parnell– Museum–Domain–Newmarket– Hospital–University–AUT– Library–Karangahape Road– Ponsonby–Victoria Park–SKYCITY–Queen Street–Britomart.

» The double-decker Auckland Explorer bus has all-day sightseeing with commentary (NZ$30 day pass).

### TRAIN

» Local and intercity trains arrive and depart from the Britomart Transport Centre, near the waterfront.

» Two main commuter lines run west to Waitakere and south to Papakura. Contact MAXX.

### FERRY AND WATER TAXI

» Almost all ferries depart from around the Ferry Buildings on the waterfront, at Quay Street. Commuter service is expanding.

» The main ferry company is Fullers, with an information office on the ground floor of the Ferry Building, tel 09-367 9111, www.fullers.co.nz.

» Water taxis sail from the North Shore, tel 0800 111 616, www.reubens.co.nz.

### TAXI

» Taxis are generally widely available and can be flagged down, ordered by phone or picked up at ranks.

» Fares are based on time as well as distance, and they vary from one taxi company to another.

### GREEN TRAVEL

Walking is a good way of getting to know the cities. Wellington and Christchurch are compact enough to walk to most central attractions, while Auckland's Link and City Circuit buses connect the main areas. Wellington's electric trolleybuses, Auckland's free hybrid electric City Circuit and Christchurch's City Shuttle buses all help minimize effects on the environment.

### USEFUL CONTACTS

**AUCKLAND**

**Auckland Explorer** tel 0800 4 EXPLORER www.explorerbus.co.nz

**Britomart Transport Centre** tel 09-374 3873 www.britomart.co.nz

**MAXX** tel 09-366 6400 www.maxx.co.nx

**CHRISTCHURCH**

**Metro** tel 03-366 8855 www.metroinfo.org.nz

**Trams** tel 03-366 7830 www.tram.co.nz

**Tram dining tour** tel 03-366 7511 www.tram.co.nz

**WELLINGTON**

**Metlink** tel 04-801 7000 www.metlink.org.nz

**Right** *The Britomart Transport Centre is a hub for bus routes and a useful source of travel information*

## GETTING AROUND IN CHRISTCHURCH

**Christchurch is a walkers' city but it does have a tramline and a good bus network with a new terminal, the Bus Exchange, on the corner of Lichfield and Colombo streets.**

### BUS

» Nearly all Christchurch buses serve the central Bus Exchange. An exception is the Orbiter, which provides a useful link between suburban hubs and shopping malls.

» Bus fares use a three-zone system, with all the central city in zone 1 (NZ$2.80). Buy your ticket from the driver, or get a Metrocard smart card from the Bus Exchange.

» The hybrid electric, free, yellow City Shuttle takes in a north–south route from the Casino through Cathedral Square and down Colombo Street and back, and operates every 10–15 minutes, Mon–Fri 7.30am–10.30pm, Sat 8am–10.30pm and Sun 10–8.

» The Best Attractions Express Shuttle links the Christchurch Gondola, Christchurch Tramway, International Antarctic Centre and Willowbank Wildlife Reserve and departs at 90-minute intervals from Cathedral Square, directly opposite the tram stop. An all-day pass (with bonus second day free) allows you to visit each venue as often as you wish (adult NZ$15, child NZ$10).

### TRAM

Between 1905 and 1954 Christchurch had a thriving tram system. Since 1995 the restored trams have followed a 2.5km (1.5-mile) loop around the heart of the city, passing various sights of interest on the way (commentary provided).

» Trams operate Apr–end Oct daily 9–6 and Nov–end Mar daily 9–9. A restaurant car offers a daily dining tour at 7.30pm.

» The trams stop at or near many of the main attractions, including the Botanic Gardens and Cathedral Square.

» For more information tel 03-366 7830, www.tram.co.nz.

## GETTING AROUND IN WELLINGTON

**Wellington's transportation system is efficient and extensive, with buses, trolley buses, trains, ferries and a vintage cable car. Information on all services is available from Ridewell, tel 0800-801 700.**

### BUS

» Metlink buses operate daily 7am–11pm. City and suburban coverage is good and there is a 10-trip ticket system available. Services depart from the main city bus stop at the Railway Station and Courtenay Place.

» A free shuttle service runs to the Interislander ferry terminal from the rail station.

» If you intend to visit the Kapiti Coast or Hutt Valley it's worth considering the Metlink Explorer Pass, which allows a day of unlimited travel on regional buses and trains (NZ$15).

» Valley Flyer operates regular daily services to Hutt Valley. GOWellington operates express services aboard the Flyer, which goes from Wellington Airport to Wellington City and Upper Hutt. The Wellington–Airport fare is NZ$6.50 adult, NZ$3.50 child.

» The Daytripper ticket (adult NZ$5) is valid on all Metlink buses. The STARPass (adult NZ$10) is valid on GOWellington buses and also on Valley Flyer and Airport Flyer services.

### CABLE CAR

The cable car terminus is on Lambton Quay, and the car runs every ten minutes (Mon–Fri 7am–10pm, Sat 8.30am–10pm, Sun 9am–10pm) to the Botanic Garden at Kelburn, via Victoria University. One-way journey NZ$2.50 (child NZ$1), both ways NZ$4.50 (child NZ$2, family NZ$12).

### FERRY

» The Dominion Post ferry sails from Queens Wharf to Matiu (Somes) Island and Days Bay, and to Petone and Seatoun on weekends.

» For information tel 04-499 1282, www.eastbywest.co.nz.

### TRAIN

» Tranz Metro operates suburban trains to Johnsonville, Melling, Paraparaumu and Upper Hutt, as well as trains to Masterton and Palmerston North.

## DRIVING

**Although it is possible to negotiate the country by train or bus, for sheer convenience driving is the best choice. Many of the country's attractions are off the beaten track and a long walk from the nearest bus stop. You will also free yourself from organized schedules.**

Beyond the cities, parking and traffic congestion are rarely problematic. In some remote areas of the country, especially in the South Island, the roads are single track and unpaved, so a little more driving skill is required. Keep the speeds and gears low on these roads. There may well be sheep or cattle along the verges in rural areas, so take extra care. There are very few wild mammals in New Zealand, but you might well encounter the cat-sized, brush-tailed possum, of which there are 70 million or so (▷ 23).

Insurance is generally offered by car rental companies. If you are planning to visit for several months, they may offer temporary purchase or long-term rental (▷ 42).

### RULES AND REGULATIONS

» Traffic drives on the left.

» Speed limits are generally 100kph (62mph) on the open road (although they may be lower in some places) and 50kph (31mph) in built-up areas. Be aware that police patrol cars and speed cameras are omnipresent.

» Police operate random breath and blood tests. The alcohol limit for drivers is 80mg (0.003oz) in 100ml (0.2 pints) of blood; for drivers under 21 no alcohol at all is allowed.

» When you are turning, give way to the right—the oncoming car has right of way. Check your way is clear in all directions before turning.

» If you are turning left, give way to vehicles coming towards you that are turning right.

» If you are turning right, you should give way to vehicles on your right that are turning right.

» Seatbelts must be worn in front seats at all times, and in rear seats where fitted.

» Turn on your headlights from dusk until dawn, or at any other time when you can't see vehicles clearly at a distance of 100m (110 yards) away.

» Dip your headlights when other vehicles are coming towards you, when following other vehicles, when police are directing traffic and when you stop.

**Above** *Busy Lambton Quay, Wellington*
**Opposite** *A trolley bus in Wellington*

| LING TIMES AND DISTANCES FROM AUCKLAND | DISTANCE | CAR | BUS | TRAIN | AIR |
|---|---|---|---|---|---|
| TON | 647km | 9hrs 15mins | 10hrs 30mins | 12hrs | 1hr |
| ISTCHURCH | 1,000km | 2 days | 2 days | 2 days | 1.5hrs |
| DUNEDIN | 1,358km | 2–4 days | 3 days | Not available | 2.5hrs |
| QUEENSTOWN | 1,484km | 2–4 days | 3 days | Not available | 2hrs 35mins |
| BAY OF ISLANDS | 241km | 4hrs 15mins | 4hrs 30mins | Not available | 50mins |
| ROTORUA | 235km | 3hrs 30mins | 4hrs | Not available | 45mins |

## DOCUMENTS

You need a valid driver's licence from your own country. This must be produced if you rent a vehicle (⊳ 42).

## FUEL

» Petrol (gas) comes in 91, 95 or 98 octane (all unleaded). LPG (liquified petroleum gas) and diesel are also available. CNG (compressed natural gas) is available only in the North Island.

» Challenge is New Zealand's own brand of fuel, with a network of service stations throughout the country. For a list of locations go to www.challenge.net.nz.

## CAR BREAKDOWN

Most rental companies include a free breakdown service in the deal.

» Members of the the AA in the UK, AAA in the US or driving organizations affiliated to the AIT receive six months' free reciprocal membership of the New Zealand Automobile Association (AA), including breakdown assistance (tel 0800-500 222).

## AT THE SCENE OF AN ACCIDENT

» If you are involved in an accident in which someone is hurt, you must inform the police as soon as possible, and no later than 24 hours after the accident.

» If no one is hurt, you must give the owner or driver of any damaged vehicle or property your name and address (and the name and address of your vehicle's owner) as soon as possible and no later than 48 hours after the accident.

» If this isn't possible, report the incident to the police as soon as you can and no later than 60 hours afterwards.

» If your vehicle is insured, tell your insurance company as soon as possible.

**Below** *The Otira Viaduct at Arthur's Pass took less than two years to complete*

» If you injure an animal, tell its owner; if this isn't possible, tell the police or the SPCA (Royal New Zealand Society for the Prevention of Cruelty to Animals, tel 09-256 7300) no later than 48 hours after the accident.

**PARKING**

» Parking in the cities can be very expensive. Do not risk parking in restricted areas or exceeding your time allotment on meters.

» Note that you must park with the flow of traffic, never against it.

» At night, a car parked on the road must show two tail lights and one front light on the side of the car nearest the middle of the road, unless it's under a street light and visible to other vehicles at a distance of 50m (55 yards) in a 50kph area or 100m (110 yards) in an area with a higher limit.

**BUYING A CAR**

Although by no means essential, buying a car is a cost-effective option if you are intending to visit for a long time. Second-hand cars are inexpensive and readily available.

**BUYING PROCEDURE AND LEGALITIES**

» A current international or accepted driver's licence is essential.

» All cars need a safety certificate to be legally on the road and to obtain registration. Most garages and specialist 'drive in, drive out' Vehicle Testing Stations do a Warrant of Fitness (WOF) test for about NZ$35. If passed, this is valid for six months. If you buy a car with a WOF make sure it is not more than 28 days old.

» Registration can be gained (for a fee) with legal ownership and a valid WOF certificate for six months (about NZ$100) or twelve months (NZ$200).

» The buyer and seller must fill in an MR13A form, which can be bought and submitted at any Post Shop (NZ$10).

» Insurance is not compulsory in New Zealand but a minimum of third party coverage is highly recommended.

» The New Zealand AA offers good insurance rates, emergency breakdown help (tel 0800-500 222), free maps and information (tel 0800-500 444, www.aa.co.nz).

» To have the car's credentials checked before you purchase, contact AA Auto Report on the New Zealand AA's website (NZ$25) or tel 0800-500 333 and quote the chassis and licence plate number of the vehicle.

» The New Zealand AA provides vehicle inspections, as do other companies found in the Yellow Pages (www.yellowpages.co.nz).

| | Auckland | Cape Reinga | Gisborne | Hamilton | Napier | New Plymouth | Palmerston North | Rotorua | Tauranga | Wellington |
|---|---|---|---|---|---|---|---|---|---|---|
| Auckland | | 440 | 507 | 127 | 422 | 366 | 530 | 235 | 208 | 656 |
| Cape Reinga | 440 | | 943 | 566 | 861 | 805 | 967 | 672 | 645 | 1100 |
| Dargaville | 185 | 285 | 685 | 312 | 605 | 554 | 713 | 420 | 390 | 845 |
| Gisborne | 507 | 943 | | 394 | 215 | 600 | 390 | 292 | 300 | 540 |
| Hamilton | 127 | 566 | 394 | | 295 | 242 | 402 | 109 | 108 | 533 |
| Hicks Bay | 508 | 945 | 180 | 398 | 396 | 600 | 574 | 289 | 302 | 730 |
| Kaitaia | 325 | 114 | 827 | 450 | 748 | 692 | 853 | 560 | 535 | 982 |
| Masterton | 638 | 1077 | 448 | 511 | 233 | 343 | 109 | 444 | 530 | 100 |
| Napier | 422 | 861 | 215 | 295 | | 412 | 178 | 227 | 312 | 320 |
| New Plymouth | 366 | 805 | 600 | 242 | 412 | | 234 | 315 | 308 | 355 |
| Paihia | 241 | 220 | 745 | 368 | 664 | 610 | 773 | 476 | 447 | 900 |
| Palmerston North | 530 | 967 | 390 | 402 | 178 | 234 | | 340 | 420 | 145 |
| Rotorua | 235 | 672 | 292 | 109 | 227 | 315 | 340 | | 86 | 460 |
| Taupo | 280 | 720 | 335 | 153 | 143 | 296 | 259 | 84 | 165 | 378 |
| Taumarunui | 295 | 726 | 450 | 162 | 264 | 183 | 240 | 172 | 230 | 360 |
| Tauranga | 208 | 645 | 300 | 108 | 312 | 308 | 420 | 86 | | 545 |
| Thames | 115 | 554 | 413 | 106 | 360 | 348 | 470 | 200 | 114 | 586 |
| Waiouru | 423 | 819 | 446 | 267 | 261 | 288 | 145 | 195 | 279 | 264 |
| Wanganui | 454 | 893 | 466 | 328 | 252 | 160 | 74 | 305 | 439 | 195 |
| Wellington | 656 | 1100 | 540 | 533 | 320 | 355 | 145 | 460 | 545 | |
| Whangarei | 170 | 270 | 680 | 295 | 597 | 540 | 700 | 405 | 381 | 818 |

**HOW TO NAVIGATE A ROUNDABOUT (TRAFFIC CIRCLE)**

Slow down on the approach to a roundabout and give way to all vehicles that will cross your path from your right. Most multi-laned roundabouts are marked with lanes and arrows, to guide you into the correct lane—but note that not all are marked the same way. If you need to cross lanes near an exit, give way to any vehicles in the lane that you want to enter.

If you're continuing straight ahead (across the roundabout) don't signal on the approach, but signal left before your exit.

| | Blenheim | Christchurch | Dunedin | Greymouth | Invercargill | Kaikoura | Mount Cook | Nelson | Queenstown | Timaru |
|---|---|---|---|---|---|---|---|---|---|---|
| Alexandra | 775 | 455 | 190 | 661 | 202 | 641 | 242 | 870 | 93 | 307 |
| Arthur's Pass | 440 | 150 | 451 | 100 | 668 | 308 | 408 | 385 | 645 | 250 |
| Blenheim | | 318 | 675 | 324 | 900 | 132 | 645 | 116 | 798 | 475 |
| Christchurch | 318 | | 362 | 255 | 579 | 186 | 331 | 425 | 487 | 163 |
| Collingwood | 251 | 509 | 871 | 384 | 1088 | 383 | 840 | 135 | 961 | 672 |
| Dunedin | 675 | 362 | | 565 | 217 | 548 | 331 | 790 | 283 | 199 |
| Franz Josef Glacier | 502 | 410 | 563 | 179 | 575 | 518 | 498 | 469 | 404 | 493 |
| Gore | 825 | 513 | 151 | 705 | 66 | 699 | 378 | 941 | 169 | 350 |
| Greymouth | 324 | 255 | 565 | | 760 | 339 | 510 | 290 | 583 | 352 |
| Haast | 645 | 554 | 421 | 321 | 433 | 660 | 356 | 611 | 262 | 418 |
| Hokitika | 370 | 270 | 570 | 41 | 700 | 380 | 520 | 337 | 530 | 360 |
| Invercargill | 900 | 579 | 217 | 760 | | 765 | 444 | 1007 | 187 | 416 |
| Kaikoura | 132 | 186 | 548 | 339 | 765 | | 517 | 248 | 673 | 349 |
| Milford Sound | 1085 | 773 | 411 | 860 | 278 | 959 | 550 | 1145 | 291 | 610 |
| Mount Cook | 645 | 331 | 331 | 510 | 444 | 517 | | 756 | 271 | 211 |
| Nelson | 116 | 425 | 790 | 290 | 1007 | 248 | 756 | | 910 | 590 |
| Oamaru | 560 | 247 | 115 | 445 | 332 | 433 | 216 | 675 | 319 | 84 |
| Queenstown | 798 | 487 | 283 | 583 | 187 | 673 | 271 | 910 | | 335 |
| Te Anau | 964 | 652 | 290 | 739 | 158 | 838 | 434 | 1025 | 170 | 489 |
| St Arnaud | 100 | 352 | 710 | 222 | 932 | 232 | 682 | 119 | 839 | 514 |
| Timaru | 475 | 163 | 199 | 352 | 416 | 349 | 211 | 590 | 335 | |

## WHERE TO BUY A CAR

» Auto magazines are available at newsagents. Daily newspapers (such as the *New Zealand Herald*, on Wednesday and Saturday) and auctions are recommended sources of information.

» Car fairs are held at:
Ellerslie Racecourse, Greenlane (Sun 9–noon), tel 09-529 2233, www.carfair.co.nz;
Manukau Car Market, Manukau City Centre Car Park (Sun 9–1), tel 09-358 5000;
Sell It Yourself, 1106 Great South Road, Otahuhu (daily 8–6.30), tel 09-270 3666;
60 Wairau Road, Glenfield (daily 7–7), tel 09-443 3800.

» Car auctions are held at:
Turners Car Auctions, corner of Penrose and Leonard roads, Penrose (Thursday, Saturday), tel 09-525 1920, www.turnersauctions.co.nz;
Hammer Auctions, corner of Neilson and Alfred streets, Onehunga (Monday, Thursday, Saturday), tel 09-579 2344, www.hammerauctions.co.nz.

» Sale and guaranteed buy-backs are offered by:
Budget Car Sales, 12 Mount Eden Road, Mount Eden, tel 09-379 4120;
Downtown Rentals, 31 Neilson Street, Onehunga, Auckland, tel 09-625 6469;
Rex Swinburne, 825 Dominion Road, Mount Roskill, tel 09-620 6587.

**Above** *A stretch of road on the scenic drive at Waitakere Ranges*

## BUSES AND TAXIS

National bus travel in New Zealand is generally well organized, with high standards of comfort, efficient networks and reliable daily schedules. Several shuttle companies serve the South Island. There are also many local operators and independent companies providing shuttles to accommodation establishments, attractions and activities.

» The two main long-distance bus brands, Intercity (www. intercity. co.nz) and Newmans (www. newmanscoach.co.nz), are operated by the same organization.

» For information and reservations about bus travel call the following regional offices:
Auckland tel 09-623 1503
Wellington tel 04-385 0520
Christchurch tel 03-365 1113
Dunedin tel 03-471 7143.

» In Northland, Northliner Express (tel 09-623 1503, www.northliner. co.nz) runs in cooperation with Intercity.

» Other companies in North Island include White Star (tel 06-759 0197, www.yellow.co.nz/site/whitestar/), which serves the route between New Plymouth and Wellington, taking in Wanganui and Palmerston North; and the Pavlovich Express (tel 09620 5490, www.pavlovichexpress. co.nz), operating between Auckland, Rotorua, Tauranga and Taupo via Hamilton. Coromandel Explorer Tours (tel 07-866 3506, www. coromandeltours.co.nz) operates around Coromandel.

» The principal backpacker bus companies (▷ 50) are:
Kiwi Experience, tel 09-366 9830, www.kiwiexperience.com;
Magic Travellers, tel 09-358 5600, www.magicbus.co.nz;
Stray, tel 09-309 8772, www.straytravel.com; and
Flying Kiwi, tel 0800-693 296, www.flyingkiwi.com.

» Bottom Bus (tel 03-437 0753, www.bottombus.co.nz) runs around the Southern Scenic Route between Dunedin and Milford Sound, via Queenstown.

**Below** *Taxis generally offer good value and are a comfortable option for short trips*

### CONCESSION FARES

All bus companies offer a variety of concession fares.

» Infants younger than three travel free and children younger than twelve travel at 33 per cent discount on Intercity and Newmans.

» Passengers over the age of 60 travel at 20 per cent discount, backpackers (YHA, VIP, BBH, Nomads cardholders) and students at 15 per cent.

» Saver fares of 25 per cent discount and supersaver fares of 50 per cent discount are available, but these must be reserved in advance.

» Intercity and Newmans operate a Club Free-Way Card. This accrues points that can later be redeemed for discounts or free tickets.

### BUS PASSES

Intercity/Newmans Countrywide bus passes can be bought for a choice of four 'hop on–hop off' routes throughout the North and South islands, ranging from an Auckland-to-Christchurch trip from NZ$565 to an Auckland- and-back deal from NZ$729, both driving the length of the South Island.

### INTERCITY/NEWMANS NORTH ISLAND BUS PASSES

» The Pacific Coast Highway runs from Auckland to Thames (via the Coromandel Peninsula), through Tauranga and Rotorua, and then rejoins the coast at Whakatane before continuing to Gisborne and Napier to Wellington; adult NZ$209, child NZ$140.

» The North Island Value Pass is a flexi-plan ticket between Auckland and Wellington, taking in either Coromandel or Waitomo; adult NZ$156, child NZ$105.

» The Bay of Islands Pass is valid on services between Auckland and Kerikeri; adult NZ$105, child NZ$70.

#### INTERCITY/NEWMANS SOUTH ISLAND BUS PASSES

» The Milford Bound Adventurer is available on services from Christchurch via Mount Cook to Queenstown and then onto Milford Sound; adult NZ$235, child NZ$157.

» The Southern Discovery departs from either Christchurch or Greymouth, taking in Mount Cook, Queenstown and Milford Sound; adult NZ$355, child NZ$238. This trip is best combined with the famous TranzAlpine rail journey between Greymouth and Christchurch (▷ 217).

» The West Coast Passport covers the whole of the West Coast, from Picton through Nelson and Greymouth to Queenstown; adult NZ$169, child NZ$113. Shorter options are available from Nelson (adult NZ$145, child NZ$97) and from Greymouth (adult NZ$125, child NZ$84).

#### BACKPACKERS AND NO-FRILLS TRAVEL

» An increasingly popular way to get round the country is to use services provided primarily for backpackers by companies like Stray (tel 09-309 8772, www.straytravel.com) and Kiwi Experience (tel 09-366 9830, www.kiwiexperience.com). This travel option is a cross between a bus service and backpacker-oriented coach tour.

» Different passes are offered: Stray's prices start with a NZ$35 Auckland day tour, or a tour round the bottom of the South Island from Dunedin for $330, and go up to a 22-day nationwide tour for NZ$1,200; Kiwi Experience passes range from NZ$95 for a one- or two-day Auckland–Paihia (Bay of Islands) trip or NZ$169 for Queenstown–Milford Sound, to NZ$1,969 for a 38-day comprehensive tour round the whole country.

» No-frills buses have also hit New Zealand roads, with fares on Nakedbus starting from just NZ$1.70, including booking fee (tel 0900-NAKED—calls cost at least $1.80 per minute—www.nakedbus.co.nz). This company doesn't have the comprehensive network of the more established operators, but its services are expanding in both main islands. Bookings must be made on the internet.

#### TAXIS

» You can take taxi cabs from ranks or hail one in the street.

» If there are three or more of you, taking a taxi can be less expensive than the bus, and no tip is expected.

» Long-distance fares should be negotiated in advance of the journey.

» Combined Taxis New Zealand runs a central service putting callers in touch with registered and approved taxi firms in different towns and cities. Call 0800-505555 and when prompted add:

11 for Auckland
13 for Christchurch
14 for Dunedin
36 for Greymouth
15 for Hamilton
31 for Nelson
34 for Queenstown
16 for Rotorua
18 for Tauranga
12 for Wellington or
21 for Whangarei.

Other destination numbers are listed in the phone prompts.

» Information on special needs, meet-and-greet packages and taxi tours is available from the New Zealand Taxi Federation (tel 04-499 0611, www.taxifederation. org.nz).

## BICYCLING

» For information on bicycle rental ▷ 42.

» In towns, some bicycle lanes are coloured to mark them out from the road—for instance, some Christchurch and Hamilton lanes are red; Auckland's bicycle lanes are green.

» Helmets are compulsory for all bicyclists.

» All bicyclists must have a rear reflector (preferably red) on the back of the bicycle; yellow pedal reflectors or reflective leg-straps, and good brakes on the front and back wheels.

» You must have lights (white in front, red behind) to cycle after dark.

» Bicyclists must follow the same rules as drivers, including giving way at intersections (▷ 45).

» Bicyclists can only ride beside another cyclist or a moped—not alongside a car or truck.

» Bicyclists passing another vehicle must ride in single file.

» For more information: Land Transport New Zealand, tel 0800 699 000, www.landtransport.govt.nz; Cycling Advocates' Network (CAN), tel 04-972 2552, www.can.org.nz.

**Right** *Cyclists travelling along tree-lined Kenepuru Road, Marlborough Sounds*

## TRAINS

**The rail network throughout the country is disappointing and in a seemingly incessant state of flux. New Zealand has struggled for years to maintain even a core network between its main hubs of population and the provincial towns.**

» Apart from commuter services in Auckland and Wellington, in the North Island Tranz Scenic (tel 0800 TRAINS, www.tranzscenic.co.nz) operates the Overlander between Auckland and Wellington daily in summer, Friday to Sunday in winter.
» In the South Island are Tranz Scenic's daily TranzCoastal services between Christchurch and Picton, connecting with the Interislander ferry to Wellington, and the daily TranzAlpine between Christchurch and Greymouth.
» The trains themselves are quite comfortable. Service is usually good and most trains have a viewing car at the rear, great for taking in the scenery.
» The tourist Taieri Gorge Limited (tel 03-477 4449, www.taieri.co.nz) runs daily between Dunedin and Pukerangi or Middlemarch, and weekly to Palmerston.

### FARES

Tranz Scenic fares range widely from Standard to Super Saver. Before purchasing a ticket be sure to check your entitlements and any available deals.
» All trains are single class.
» Reservations and timetables are available from Wellington and Christchurch rail stations, i-SITES and travel agents throughout New Zealand.
» Several specialist travel packages are on offer, including Great Train Escapes and Day Escapes, comprising a range of one- to six-day excursions, most of which include accommodation. Prices range from NZ$79 for a day excursion to NZ$545 for six days. Children travel for around 40 per cent of the adult fare.

**Above** *The TranzAlpine Railway travels through the scenic countryside of the South Island*

## DOMESTIC FLIGHTS AND FERRIES

**In addition to the principal international airports of Auckland, Wellington and Christchurch, New Zealand has many well-served provincial town airports. Air New Zealand Link is by far the dominant carrier. Qantas also flies from Auckland to Wellington and Christchurch. Services are highly professional and efficient, so you will rarely have problems with delays.**

### DOMESTIC FLIGHTS

Apart from the major domestic operators, there are many smaller companies with scheduled services. These include: Great Barrier Airlines (Great Barrier, Coromandel and Northland), Sounds Air (offering an alternative to the ferry between the North and South islands) and Stewart Island Flights (between Invercargill and Stewart Island).

Air2there (tel 04-904 5130, 0800 777 000, www.air2there.com), based at Paraparaumu just north of Wellington, offers services to Nelson, Blenheim and Wellington, bypassing the capital for people on the Kapiti Coast.

Mountain Air (tel 0800-922 812, www.mountainair.co.nz,) operates flights between Auckland, Whangarei and Great Barrier Island. Flying anywhere in New Zealand is, on a clear day, a scenic delight.

#### Domestic Discount Fares

If you can, reserve domestic flights well in advance via the internet or through a travel agent. Most discounted fares can be bought only in New Zealand.

There are many available deals that can make considerable savings, depending on the season and availability of flights. Air New Zealand offers the South Pacific Airpass, which works on a zone and coupon system and must be ticketed prior to arrival. For more information ask your travel agent or see www.airnewzealand.co.nz.

**Above** *Several small companies operate sightseeing tours of the remote areas, and charter services*

### DOMESTIC FERRIES

Other than a few small vehicle ferries and the short trip to Stewart Island from Bluff in Southland, the main focus of ferry travel is the inter-island route across Cook Strait. The two ports are Wellington, at the southern tip of the North Island, and Picton, in the Marlborough Sounds, northern South Island.

| DOMESTIC AIRLINES |
|---|
| **Air New Zealand** tel 0800-737 000 www.airnewzealand.co.nz |
| **Great Barrier Airlines** tel 0800-900 600 www.greatbarrier.co.nz |
| **Qantas** tel 0800-900 600 www.qantas.co.nz |
| **Sounds Air** tel 0800-505 005 www.soundsair.com |
| **Stewart Island Flights** tel 03-218 9129 www.stewartislandflights.com |

## FERRY CONTACTS

| | |
|---|---|
| **Bluebridge** tel 0800-844 844 www.bluebridge.co.nz | |
| **Campbelltown Passenger Services** tel 03-212 7404 | |
| **Interisland Line** tel 0800-802 802 www.interislander.co.nz | |
| **Stewart Island Experience** tel 0800-000 511 www.stewartislandexperience.co.nz | |

### Linking South and North

The scenic 85km (53-mile) journey across the Cook Strait takes up to three-and-a-half hours, depending on which vessel you take.

» In rough weather the crossing can be something of an ordeal. Sailings are stopped if considered too dangerous, but this does not happen often.

» Reserve tickets well in advance, especially in December and January. Most major visitor information centres and travel agents can organize reservations and tickets.

» On board the Interislander's *Arahua, Kaitaki* and *Aratere* ferries there are bars, food courts, cafés, movies, visitor information points, children's play areas and nurseries, and private work desks. The slightly higher-priced Club Class ticket gives access to a private lounge and complimentary tea, coffee, magazines and newspapers.

» A free shuttle bus to the terminal (2km/1 mile) runs from Wellington Rail Station 35 minutes before each scheduled ferry departure.

» Fares for passengers range from the standard NZ$65 (child NZ$33) to the saver NZ$45 (child NZ$31). Cars cost NZ$99–NZ$160. The vehicle fare does not include the driver. Motorcycles cost NZ$36–NZ$55, bicycles NZ$15. Best of New Zealand Pass and Travelpass New Zealand are accepted, and children under the age of four travel free.

» Various day/limited-excursion, family and group fares and standard discounted fares are available but must be reserved in advance and are subject to availability. At peak periods (particularly December/ January) discounts are rarely available.

» The latest operator making the crossing is the independent Bluebridge, with the ex-Mediterranean vessels *Monte Stello* and *Santa Regina*. Facilities are more basic, but adequate; the service is efficient and the staff friendly. The standard fare is NZ$49 for a passenger (child NZ$25), and NZ$120 for a vehicle.

### Getting to Stewart Island

» Stewart Island Experience sails October to May 9.30, 11.30 and 5, and May to September 9.30 and 4.30, from the port of Bluff. The crossing by fast catamaran takes about an hour and costs NZ$55–NZ$60 (child NZ$27.50–NZ$30) one way.

» Secure parking is available in Bluff for NZ$5 per day.

» Campbelltown Passenger Services offer a regular daily shuttle to and from Invercargill to coincide with the Stewart Island ferries (NZ$12 one way). Reservations are advised.

### Northland

» A car ferry operates across the Hokianga Harbour from Rawene (tel 09-405 2602, www.fndc.govt.nz), providing a useful link up the west coast of Northland. Fullers Bay of Islands (tel 09-402 7421, http://fboi.co.nz) operates car ferries linking the Russell area to Opua and passenger-only ferries to Paihia.

### Hauraki Gulf

» Passenger ferries operated by Fullers (tel 09-367 9111, www.fullers.co.nz) and Kawau Kat (www.360discovery.co.nz) criss-cross the Waitemata Harbour and the Hauraki Gulf, serving the North Shore and out to Great Barrier Island.

» Sealink (tel 09-300 5900, 0800 732 546, www.sealink.co.nz) operates frequent vehicle ferries to Waiheke Island from Half Moon Bay near Pakuranga, and from central Auckland, and daily (except Saturdays) from central Auckland to Great Barrier Island.

**Below** *Small ferries provide a shuttle service across Auckland's Waitemata harbour*

# VISITORS WITH A DISABILITY

For visitors with a disability, New Zealand can be frustrating. While the majority of public facilities are accessible to wheelchairs, older lodgings and some public transportation systems (especially rural buses) are not as well organized. However, the good news is that the situation is improving slowly, and it is now a legal requirement for new buildings to include facilities for people with disabilities.

## SPECIALIST TOUR COMPANIES

**Accessible Kiwi Tours Ltd**
1610 State Highway 30
RD4 Rotorua
Tel/Fax 07/362 7622
www.tours-nz.com,
Email info@accessible-tours.co.nz
Themed tours for individuals and groups, plus information for independent travel.

**Galaxy Motors**
PO Box 21985, Otahuhu,
Tel 0800 TO GALAXY
www.galaxyautos.co.nz
Email: f.hall@xtra.co.nz
Specially equipped cars and vans; tour guides and companions are also available.

**Physical Freedom and Manawatu Jet Tours**
PO Box 53, Ashhurst,
Tel/fax 06-329 4060
Email man-jet-tours@ inspire.net.nz
Range of activities, including jet-boat river rides, drift-rafting, four-wheel driving, clay-bird shooting. Bus accommodates five wheelchairs. Personalized tours available.

» Air New Zealand's International Boeing 747, 767 and 737-300 and Airbus A320 planes have onboard skychairs, which are designed to fit within narrow aisles. These are not available on domestic flights, but airports will provide skychairs for wheelchair-users for arrivals and departures.

» Facilities for people with disabilities at Auckland and Christchurch airports include automatic doors, elevators, wheelchair access, accessible toilets and showers, and ATMs with Braille keys. There are parking spaces for card-holders in front of the terminals and in airport parking areas.

» A useful sign to look for is the International Symbol of Access. It is awarded by local authorities to inspected properties that meet the needs of the mobility impaired.

» The Youth Hostels Association (YHA) runs 27 hostels in New Zealand, of which 11 are suitable for people with restricted mobility: Auckland International, Christchurch City Central, Franz Josef, Greymouth, Kaikoura, Lake Tekapo, Nelson, Queenstown, Te Anau, Tauranga and Wellington City.

» Visitors with disabilities often receive discounts on travel and some admission charges.

» Parking concessions are available and temporary cards can be issued on receipt of a mobility card or medical certificate.

» Accessible New Zealand, by Alexia Pickering, is a guide for visitors with restricted mobility. It covers a range of topics, including attractions, accommodation, shopping and parking, toilets, restaurants, transport and activities.

## USEFUL CONTACTS

**Disability Persons Assembly (DPA)**
Tel 04-801 9100
Fax 04-801 9565
www.dpa.org.nz
Email gen@dpa.org.nz
Umbrella organization for people with disabilities, covering the whole country from its offices in Wellington.

**Enable New Zealand**
69 Malden Street, PO Box 4547, Palmerston North
Tel 0800 ENABLE
www.enable.co.nz
This organization aims to help people with disabilities, as well as their families, employers and health professionals.

**New Zealand Federation of Disability Information Centres**
PO Box 24-042, Royal Oak, Auckland
Tel 0800 NZFDIC
www.nzfdic.org.nz
Provides information for people with disabilities via local (independent) information centres.

**Weka**
Tel 0800 171 981
www.weka.net.nz
New Zealand's disability information website, for people with disabilities, as well as their families and caregivers, health professionals and disability information providers.

# REGIONS

This chapter is divided into six regions of New Zealand (⊳ 8–9). Places of interest are listed alphabetically in each region.

**New Zealand's Regions (⊳ 56–258)**

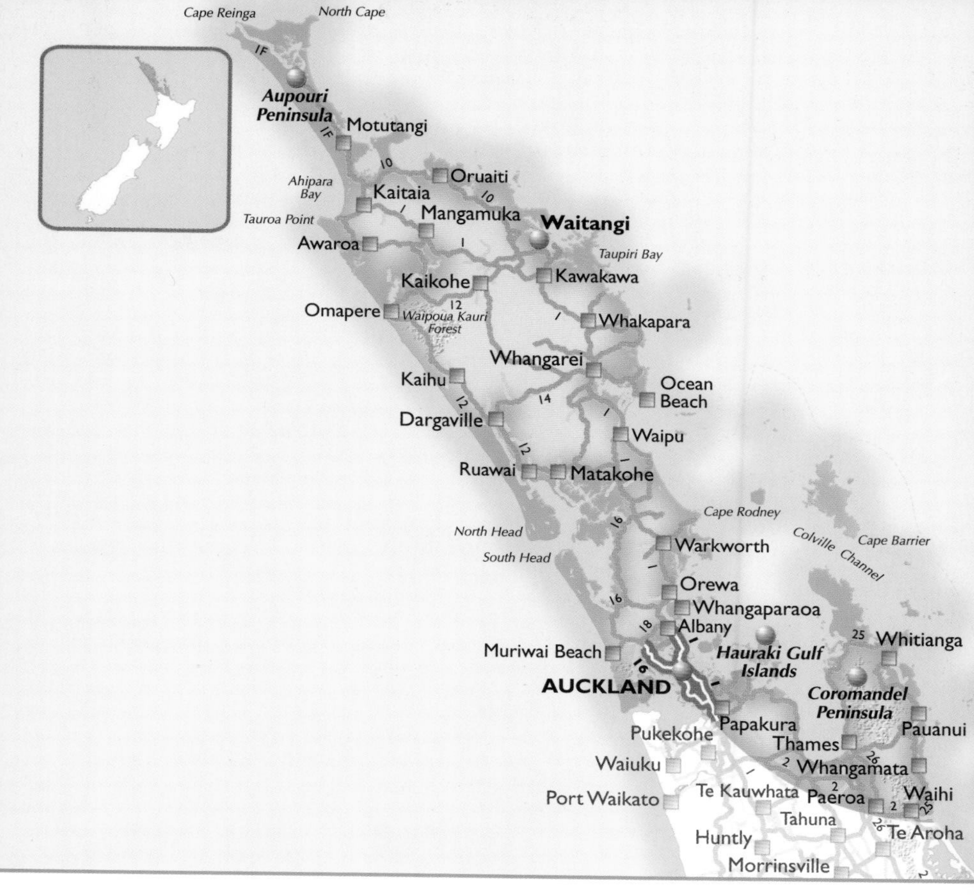




# AUCKLAND, NORTHLAND AND COROMANDEL

Auckland is New Zealand's biggest city and the hub for the country's intercontinental air traffic, so most visitors will find themselves spending some time there. Clean, green and spacious, the city sprawls across an isthmus with the Pacific Ocean to the east and the Tasman Sea to the west. Auckland subtitles itself 'City of Sails'. Boat ownership per capita is the world's highest, and with a balmy climate and the glorious Waitemata Harbour at its feet—Sea of Sparkling Waters in the Maori language—that's not surprising. Another distinguishing feature is volcanoes. Auckland sits squarely on the Pacific Ring of Fire. Within a 20km (12.5 mile) radius of the city there are 48 volcanic cones, the youngest of which is the 600-year-old Rangitoto, at the mouth of Auckland's harbour. Auckland is also the world's largest Polynesian city, thanks to a substantial Maori population, as well as sizeable numbers of immigrants from islands scattered around the South Pacific.

Beyond Auckland, Northland flings a long arm into the Pacific Ocean. This is the warmest part of the country, an undulating landscape of farms and forest with a rich Maori history. Its biggest drawcard is the Bay of Islands, the country's most popular holiday destination, a natural harbour with its 144 islands floating like green pillows on the sea. This was also where the history of modern New Zealand began. The town of Russell was the first European settlement on New Zealand soil, and nearby Waitangi was the scene for the treaty of Waitangi, signed between Maori chiefs and representatives of the British crown, and New Zealand's founding document.

Jutting out from the coast east of Auckland like a blunt thumb, the Coromandel Peninsula is a part of New Zealand that New Zealanders would rather keep to themselves. The centre of the peninsula is ridged by a spine of craggy volcanic peaks that rise to more than 800m (2,600ft), while the east coast has some of the country's best beaches.

# AUCKLAND

## INTRODUCTION

Auckland sits on a narrow strip of land between two attractive natural harbours: the Waitemata, to the east, and the Manukau, to the southwest. At its heart is the CBD (Central Business District) and the main thoroughfare of Queen Street. To either side, the jungle of high-rises occasionally gives way to older buildings such as the Auckland Art Gallery and the green sanctuaries of Albert Park and the Domain, with its crowning glory, the Auckland Museum. Immediately north, the sails and ferries of Waitemata Harbour herald the end of the concrete sprawl, and the 1912 Ferry Building is a sharp contrast to the modern tower blocks behind it.

Viaduct Basin, along the waterfront, was formerly the America's Cup Village and is the home of the New Zealand National Maritime Museum. The Harbour Bridge (1959) leads to the huge expanse of the North Shore, an area of modern suburbs and relatively calm beaches stretching along to the Whangaparaoa Peninsula and the edge of the city, 40km (25 miles) away. The small suburb of Devonport, across the Waitemata Harbour, has a more intimate, affluent atmosphere, with a marina, a lively beach culture and smart villas. Two volcanic cones at Devonport—Mount Victoria and North Head—give excellent views of the city.

Dominating the southern horizon are Mount Eden and One Tree Hill. South of these landmarks, the low-income suburbs of South Auckland spread to the southern edge of the built-up area at the Bombay Hills, and encompass the Botanic Gardens. In the inner western suburbs, the zoo and the Museum of Transport and Technology (MOTAT) border the lakeside park of Western Springs. Auckland's westward expansion is restricted by the Waitakere Ranges, a hilly recreational area which takes in Auckland Centennial Park.

The first Maori to settle in this area were thought to be hunters of the now extinct moa bird, who arrived before AD1000. From the 12th to the 14th century

**INFORMATION**

www.aucklandnz.com

299 J4 SKYCITY, corner of Victoria and Federal streets 0800 SKYCITY Daily 8–8 Britomart Transport Centre

**Above** *Looking across the Waitemata Harbour to Devonport and the volcanic cone of Rangitoto*

**Opposite** *Sky Tower looks over Hobson West Marina*

**TIPS**

» Get your bearings from the observation decks of the Sky Tower.

» The best time to visit Mount Eden is at dawn, especially on a misty winter morning, before the crowds arrive.

Maori tribes migrated here, and in the early 18th century Kiwi Tamaki's tribe rose to power, establishing *pa* (fortified Maori settlements) on almost every volcano in the district. A series of brutal conflicts with rival tribes, along with an epidemic of smallpox brought here by the early Europeans, subsequently decimated the area's Maori population.

In 1820 missionaries Samuel Marsden and John Gare Butler were the first white Europeans to pay an 'official' visit. Low-key European settlement followed, and 20 years later Lieutenant-Governor Captain William Hobson bought a triangular section of the isthmus from the Ngati Whatua for £55 and a few blankets. He called this area Auckland in tribute to George Eden, First Earl of Auckland, then Governor General of India.

As a result of the New Zealand Wars (▷ 32) and the discovery of gold in Otago and the nearby Coromandel Peninsula, Auckland entered a period of decline and, in 1865, lost its status as capital to Wellington. By the end of the 19th century its fortunes had revived, thanks to its fertile soils, good climate and a booming kauri industry. Growth continued during the 20th century and a combination of geography, climate, industry, agriculture, and sporting and business opportunities have encouraged its development as a vibrant, cosmopolitan city.

**Below** *Auckland's famous Harbour Bridge spans Waitemata Harbour*

## WHAT TO SEE

### AUCKLAND ART GALLERY (TOI-O-TAMAKI)

www.aucklandartgallery.govt.nz

The Auckland Art Gallery occupies two buildings in the middle of the city: one in Kitchener Street and the other on the corner of Wellesley and Lorne streets. Together they form the country's largest and most comprehensive collection of national and international art.

The original gallery in Kitchener Street is more than 100 years old and, although it has undergone major reconstruction over the years, it retains its handsome French Renaissance style, with steeply pitched roofs. Works from the permanent collections include international masters, focusing on the 17th century, but the most interesting are those by Charles Goldie (1870–1947) and Gottfried Lindauer (1839–1926), two early European settlers who specialized in oil landscapes and portraits of Maori elders.

The New Gallery, opened in 1995, is across the road. It houses temporary exhibitions and contemporary artists' installations, with a permanent exhibit by modern artist Colin McCahon (1919–87).

62 B2 Corner of Wellesley and Kitchener streets 09-307 7700 Daily 10–5. Free guided tours 2pm Adult Collection displays free; special exhibitions NZ$7 day pass, child (under 5) free

### AUCKLAND WAR MEMORIAL MUSEUM TAMAKI PAENGA HIRA

www.aucklandmuseum.com

Rising above New Zealand's oldest and biggest park, the Domain, the museum is a neoclassical building of 1929 housing the outstanding collections of the Auckland Museum. Among its displays are the Pacific and Maori Taonga (treasures), which combine to form the largest such collection in existence. Other attractions include a children's discovery centre with computers, games and interactive displays; social and settlement history sections; natural history galleries; and Scars on the Heart, the story of New Zealanders at war, from the New Zealand Wars of the 19th century to the campaigns in Gallipoli and Crete in the two world wars (▷ 34).

The highlight of the collection is Maori Gallery, He Taonga Maori, housing a variety of craftwork ranging from woven baskets to lethal hand weapons carved from bone and greenstone. Its focal points are the 25m (82ft) *Te Toki a Tapiri* (Tapiri's Battleaxe), last of the Maori war canoes *(waka)*, carved from a single tree trunk in 1836; and Hotunui, a beautifully carved meeting house dating from 1878. A Maori concert is staged daily at 11am, noon and 1.30 (additional performance Jan–Mar 2.30) by Manaia, the museum's cultural performance group.

The museum was built in tribute to the fallen of World War I; it houses a War Memorial Hall, and veterans gather on the forecourt at dawn every year on 25 April—Anzac (Remembrance) Day. Spread around the museum are the Domain's 80ha (198 acres) of fields, gardens and woods, protected as a reserve by Governor Hobson in 1840. Look for the Wintergarden, and the regular orchestral and operatic outdoor events in summer.

62 C3 Domain Drive 09-304 0443 Summer daily 9–5.30; winter daily 9–4.30 Adult NZ$5 donation, child (under 18) free. Maori Concert NZ$25, child NZ$12.50 Excellent gift shop with jewellery, knitwear, ceramics and books

### AUCKLAND ZOO

www.aucklandzoo.co.nz

New Zealand's premier wild animal collection is set in parkland near Western Springs, 4km (2.5 miles) west of the city's hub. The zoo has an active programme of conservation and captive breeding of native species including kiwi and tuatara, both of which are on display. Elephants are also on view, and are sometimes taken for walks around the zoo. Imaginative themed exhibits

**Above** *Sky Jump from the top of Sky Tower takes 16 seconds*

**Below** *Auckland War Memorial Museum*

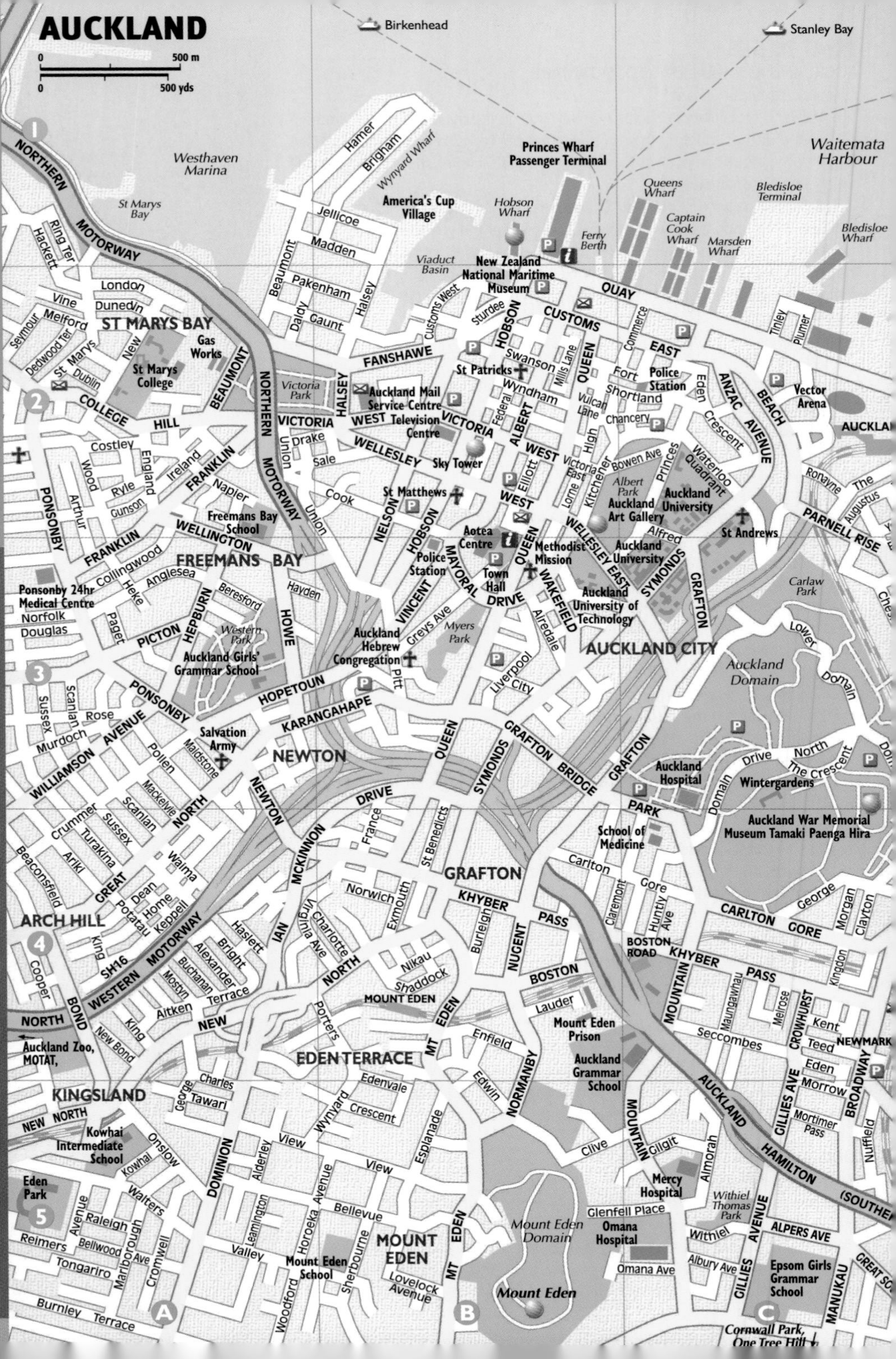

# AUCKLAND

0 500 m
0 500 yds

Birkenhead
Stanley Bay
Westhaven Marina
St Marys Bay
Waitemata Harbour
Princes Wharf Passenger Terminal
Hobson Wharf
Queens Wharf
Captain Cook Wharf
Marsden Wharf
Bledisloe Terminal
Bledisloe Wharf
Ferry Berth
America's Cup Village
Viaduct Basin
Wynyard Wharf
New Zealand National Maritime Museum
ST MARYS BAY
Gas Works
St Marys College
Victoria Park
Auckland Mail Service Centre
Television Centre
Sky Tower
St Patricks
Police Station
Vector Arena
St Matthews
Aotea Centre
Town Hall
Methodist Mission
Albert Park
Auckland Art Gallery
Auckland University
Auckland University of Technology
St Andrews
Carlaw Park
FREEMANS BAY
Freemans Bay School
Ponsonby 24hr Medical Centre
Western Park
Auckland Girls' Grammar School
Auckland Hebrew Congregation
Myers Park
AUCKLAND CITY
Auckland Domain
Auckland Hospital
Wintergardens
Auckland War Memorial Museum Tamaki Paenga Hira
School of Medicine
Salvation Army
NEWTON
GRAFTON
ARCH HILL
EDEN TERRACE
Mount Eden Prison
Auckland Grammar School
Auckland Zoo, MOTAT,
KINGSLAND
Kowhai Intermediate School
Eden Park
Mercy Hospital
Withiel Thomas Park
Mount Eden Domain
Omana Hospital
MOUNT EDEN
Mount Eden School
Mount Eden
Epsom Girls Grammar School
NEWMARKET
Cornwall Park, One Tree Hill

NORTHERN MOTORWAY
WESTERN MOTORWAY SH16
QUAY
CUSTOMS
FANSHAWE
VICTORIA
WELLESLEY
HOBSON
NELSON
ALBERT
QUEEN
MAYORAL DRIVE
KARANGAHAPE
PONSONBY
FRANKLIN
COLLEGE HILL
HOPETOUN
SYMONDS
GRAFTON BRIDGE
PARK
KHYBER PASS
BOSTON ROAD
CARLTON GORE
MOUNTAIN
MT EDEN
NEW NORTH
DOMINION
GILLIES AVENUE
BROADWAY
MANUKAU
AUCKLAND HAMILTON (SOUTHERN MOTORWAY)
ALPERS AVE
GREAT NORTH
NEWTON
MCKINNON
IAN
NORMANBY
NUGENT

A B C
1 2 3 4 5

# AUCKLAND STREET INDEX

include a huge walk-through aviary, and a rainforest where primates swing freely through the trees. Recent additions include Pridelands—a spacious home for the giraffes, lions and zebras; the adjoining Hippo River; and a state-of-the-art Sealion and Penguin Shores.

Off map 62 A4 Motions Road, Western Springs 09-360 3805 Sep–end May daily 9.30–5.30; Jun–end Aug daily 9.30–5 Adult NZ$19, child (4–15) NZ$9

### CORNWALL PARK

www.cornwallpark.co.nz

Just south of Mount Eden and 5km (3 miles) south of the Sky Tower, Cornwall Park offers a great escape from city life. Its main claim to fame is One Tree Hill, an extinct volcanic cone with well-preserved remains of Maori fortified settlements around the summit (the lone pine tree which gives the hill its name was cut down in 2000). Kiwi Tamaki, chief of the Wai O Hua tribe, lived here in the 18th century with thousands of his family and followers, and you can still see the ditches and ramparts that marked their dwellings. Scottish settler and Auckland mayor Sir John Logan Campbell bought the hill and surrounding land, and Huia Lodge, now the visitor office, was his gatekeeper's house. Directly across the road is restored Acacia Cottage (Dec–end Mar 7–dusk, Apr–end Nov 7–4), in which Campbell lived; the oldest house in Auckland, from 1841, it was relocated here from the city in the 1920s.

Off map 62 C5 Greenlane Road, Manukau Road, Campbell Road 09-630 8485 Daily 7–dusk Free

### DEVONPORT

A bronze sculpture on King Edward Parade marks the spot where the first Polynesians landed in their canoe, *Tainui*, in the 14th century. Devonport was later a European settlement and still has many splendid 19th-century buildings, including the restored Esplanade Hotel. Ferries dock at Devonport Wharf, at the end of the main street, Victoria Road, which is lined with cafés and shops selling books, crafts, souvenirs and antiques. A footpath from its far end leads up Mount Victoria, an extinct volcanic cone with traces of a Maori *pa* around the summit. The views of the Hauraki Gulf and offshore islands are magnificent. At the tip of the peninsula, North Head Historic Reserve is another volcanic cone, pocked with 19th-century gun emplacements and tunnels, evidence of a Russian invasion scare. Spring Street leads from the waterfront to the Royal New Zealand Navy Museum (daily 10–4.30).

Off map 63 D1 Every half hour from Ferry Building, Quay Street; 10-minute crossing

**Below** *Seahorses are one of the fascinating species to be seen at Kelly Tarlton's Antarctic Encounter and Underwater World*

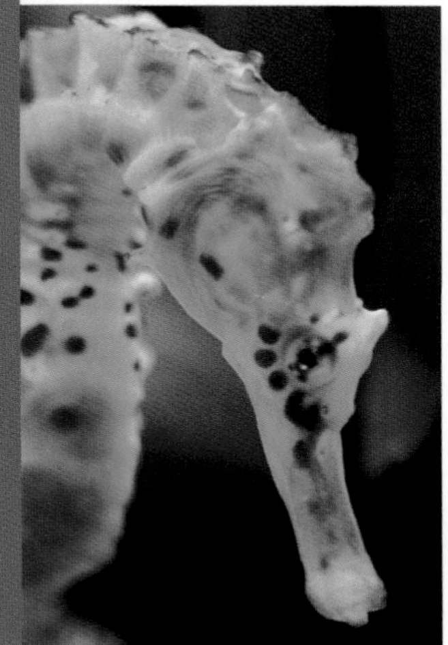

### KELLY TARLTON'S ANTARCTIC ENCOUNTER AND UNDERWATER WORLD

www.kellytarltons.co.nz

This hugely popular attraction, the brainchild of diver Kelly Tarlton, was set up in subterranean storage tanks behind Orakei Wharf. Visits are divided into two main parts. The Antarctic Encounter displays relate the story of early Antarctic exploration. Before entering a replica of Captain Scott's 1911 South Pole expedition hut, you are primed by a weather update from the modern base, citing barely imaginable sub-zero temperatures and wind speeds. From here a snow cat carries you through Penguin Encounter, where king and gentoo penguins breed in carefully maintained natural conditions.

Through Stingray Bay is the original Underwater World, where Tarlton pioneered the concept of viewing sea life through fibreglass tunnels. Stingrays and sharks glide directly above your head, and smaller tanks contain a host of species including seahorses, moray eels and poisonous scorpion fish. Open rock pools and an education facility provide a learning experience for children.

Off map 63 D2 23 Tamaki Drive, 6km (4 miles) from downtown 09-528 0603/0800 805050 Daily 9–6 (last entry 5) Adult NZ$26.55, child (4–14) NZ$12.60, under-4s free

## MUSEUM OF TRANSPORT, TECHNOLOGY AND SOCIAL HISTORY

www.motat.org.nz

The Museum of Transport, Technology and Social History (generally referred to as MOTAT) is near Auckland Zoo, on a site that once pumped water from Western Springs Lake to the city's houses. The original pumphouse and beam engine are part of a complex ranged over two sites and housing an eclectic 30,000-item collection that includes vintage cars, fire engines and motorcycles, telephone boxes and printing presses. MOTAT 2, on Motions Road, occupies the Sir Keith Park Memorial Site (named after New Zealand's most famous wartime aviator) and concentrates on aviation, rail and the military. Prize exhibits include the only Solent Mark IV flying boat in the world, and a World War II Avro Lancaster bomber. The two sites are connected by a vintage tram (NZ$2 round trip), which also stops at the zoo.

Off map 62 A4 · Great North Road, Western Springs, 4km (2.5 miles) west of downtown · 09-815 5800/0800 668 2869 · Daily 10–5 · Adult NZ$14, child (5–16) NZ$7, under-5s free, family NZ$30

## NEW ZEALAND NATIONAL MARITIME MUSEUM

www.nzmaritime.org

Ranged around the waterfront on Hobson Wharf, the New Zealand National Maritime Museum is as diverse and interesting as you might expect in the City of Sails. The layout is chronological, beginning with a video presentation of early Polynesian arrivals and replicas of their vessels, before moving on to European maritime history. The living quarters of an early immigrant ship are replicated, complete with moving floor and sound effects.

Next come the galleries of New Zealand's yachting history, tracing the nation's participation and triumphs in the Louis Vuitton Cup, the Whitbread Round the World Yacht Race and the America's Cup. Harbour cruises include a trip aboard the 17m (56ft), traditionally built scow *Ted Ashby*, and excursions aboard the *Pride of Auckland*.

Off map 62 B1 · Corner of Quay and Hobson streets · 0800-725897/09-373 0800 · Oct–end Apr daily 9–6; May–end Sep daily 9–5 · Adult NZ$16, child (5–17) NZ$7, family NZ$36. Cruises NZ$15, child NZ$7, family NZ$35 (Ted Ashby)

**Above** *The Auckland city skyline viewed from North Head, Devonport*

**Above** *The Sky Tower, likened to a hypodermic needle, dominates the city skyline*
**Below** *Glass floor panels in the Sky Tower's observation platform give vertiginous views*

### SKY TOWER

www.skycity.co.nz

In 1997 Auckland's skyline gained a dramatic addition in the concrete needle-shape of the Sky Tower, the southern hemisphere's tallest building, at 328m (1,076ft) high, and part of the SKYCITY casino, hotel and shopping complex. It takes a mere 40 seconds for the elevator to reach the main observation deck, and there are even more stunning views from the Sky Deck.

If admiring the view isn't quite exciting enough you can opt for Vertigo Climb—a two-hour guided tour up the interior of the tower's mast, culminating in an internal climb from the upper observation deck to the first crow's nest. For an even bigger adrenalin boost there's Sky Jump, a tethered base jump from 192m (630ft) with a 16-second fall time.

62 B2 Corner of Victoria and Federal streets 09-363 6000 Daily 8.30–11 (observation deck) Adult NZ$28, child (5–14) NZ$11, under-5s free, family NZ$61
Orbit revolves to give 360-degree views of the city; the Observatory gives diners access to the main deck

## MORE TO SEE

### AUCKLAND REGIONAL BOTANIC GARDENS

www.aucklandbotanicgardens.co.nz

A 64ha (158-acre), 10,000-plant collection is laid out 20 minutes south of downtown Auckland. Planting began in 1974 and consists mostly of New Zealand natives. There is also an ornamental lake, a nature trail and a fragrant display of New Zealand-bred roses.

Off map 63 D5 102 Hill Road, Manurewa 09-267 1457 Summer daily 8–8; winter daily 8–6; visitor office hours vary Free

### EWELME COTTAGE

Not far from Kinder House is Ewelme Cottage, built in 1863 as the Auckland home of the family of Archdeacon Vicesimus Lush (1817–82). It was altered in 1882 but has since remained largely unchanged, and contains colonial furniture and household effects.

63 D4 14 Ayr Street, Parnell 09-379 0202 Fri–Sun 10.30–12, 1–4.30
Adult NZ$7.50, child free

### KINDER HOUSE

This two-floor building was built in 1856 as the home of pioneer churchman and artist John Kinder (1819–1903). It now displays some of his art works.

63 D4 2 Ayr Street, Parnell 09-379 0202 Tue–Sun 11–3
Adult NZ$2, child 50c

### MOUNT EDEN

At 196m (643ft), the closest volcano to downtown Auckland (15 minutes' drive, or bus 274/275 from Customs Street East) provides a terrific view. At its southern base Eden Garden (daily 9–4.30) contains flowering shrubs and native New Zealand plants. Mount Eden village has a fine delicatessen, interesting shops and a number of good cafés and restaurants.

62 B5

### NEWMARKET

A modern commercial suburb best known for its shopping, quality restaurants, cafés and entertainment. The grand Highwic House at 40 Gillies Avenue (Wed–Sun 10.30–12, 1–4.30, enter from Mortimer Pass) was the 1860s home of 'colonial gentleman of property' Alfred Buckland (1825–1903). Lion Breweries at 380 Khyber Pass Road give tours of their facilities (tel 09-358 8366; Mon, Wed–Sat 9.30, 12.15, 3), with samplings included.

63 D4

## ONE TREE HILL

A single totara tree once stood on One Tree Hill and gave the area its original name: Te-Totara-a-Ahua (the totara that stands alone). Settlers cut this tree down in 1852, and to make amends a new totara and several Monterey pines were planted in its place. Most failed to flourish and by 1960 only one pine was left, providing Auckland's greatest landmark before the advent of the Sky Tower. In 1994 this tree was damaged by a pro-Maori activist, and after a further attack in 1999 it was decided that the pine must be removed for safety's sake. On the day of its felling hundreds of people gathered to say goodbye, and a Maori karakia (prayer service) was said at dawn.

✚ Off map 62 C5

## PARNELL

Parnell is a fashionably restored suburb 2km (1 mile) east of downtown, full of craft shops, galleries and restaurants. At the top of Parnell Rise is the modern Auckland Cathedral of the Holy Trinity (Mon–Sat 10–4, Sun 11–4); just behind it, the older St. Mary's (1888) is one of the world's largest wooden churches. Parnell Rose Gardens (daylight hours) bloom from November to March. Nearby St. Stephen's Chapel (1857) is a fine example of the Gothic style that evolved under Bishop Selwyn (1809–78).

✚ 63 D3

**Below** *North Head viewed from Devonport*

## AUPOURI PENINSULA

New Zealand's most northerly finger of land is bounded by Ninety Mile Beach to the west, and Great Exhibition Bay and Rangaunu Bay and Harbour to the east. At its tip are Cape Reinga and the North Cape—the northernmost point of the North Island. The whole peninsula was once covered in kauri forest; now it consists mainly of extensive dune systems and swamps, interspersed with commercial forestry such as Aupouri Forest.

### BEYOND KAITAIA

First stop after Kaitaia (▷ 72) is the Ancient Kauri Kingdom in Awanui, 8km (5 miles) north (daily 9–5), which sells kauri furniture and crafts and displays an imposing, 50-tonne (55-ton) log sculpture. About 17km (10 miles) farther north at Gumdiggers Park (daily 9–5), a reconstructed gumdiggers' village illustrates workers' lives, digging for fossilised kauri gum, around 1900. The route north passes Ninety Mile Beach, an uninterrupted sweep of empty white sand backed by impressive dunes. Join a tour—soft sands and quicksands make driving along it inadvisable, and forbidden by car rental companies.

In the small fishing village of Houhora there are guided tours of the Subritzky/Wagener Homestead, a 19th-century Polish settler's residence little changed since 1900 (11.30, 1.30 and 3.30).

### THE FARTHEST POINTS

From Te Kao the road leads north to the vast Te Paki Station and Recreation Reserve, covering 23,000ha (56,830 acres) in all and giving access to the two capes, about 21km (13 miles) away. Local Maori own almost a quarter of the land here, and regard areas around North Cape as sacred. The tip of North Cape is a scientific reserve and has limited public access.

Most visitors head for Cape Reinga and its lighthouse. Views from the hill above extend as far as the Three Kings Islands, 57km (35 miles) offshore. They were named by Abel Tasman, who first spotted them at Epiphany in 1643. The Northland coastline has claimed more than 140 ships since 1808, most foundering around the Cape. The lighthouse contains the lens of an older structure which stood on Motuopao Island, to the south.

### INFORMATION

www.fndc.govt.nz/infocentre
298 G1 Information Far North, Centennial Park, South Road, Kaitaia
09-408 0879 Daily 8.30–5
Daily tours from Kaitaia, Paihia and Mangonui

### TIPS

» Pukenui is the last major settlement on the way to the Cape, so it pays to buy fuel and provisions at the café and general store.

» The drive to the Cape from Kaitaia takes about an hour and a half. The road is sealed to Te Paki Station; beyond this point it is metalled and speeds should be kept low.

**Above** *Enjoying the sand dunes at Te Paki*
**Opposite** *The lighthouse at Cape Reinga dates from 1941*

**INFORMATION**
www.thamesinfo.co.nz
299 K4 206 Pollen Street, Thames 07-868 7284 Mon–Fri 8.30–5, Sat, Sun, public hols 9–4
Coromandel–Auckland flights Fri, Sun
Coromandel–Auckland ferries Tue, Thu, Fri, Sat

**Above** *Riding the waves at the surfing venue of Whangamata*

## INTRODUCTION

The Coromandel Peninsula's varied landscapes and laidback style make it the main attraction on the Pacific Coast Highway. The west coast, bounded by the Firth of Thames, is the least developed side, with a ragged coastline of islands and pebble beaches lined with pohutukawa trees. In contrast, the east coast is a stretch of beautiful bays, resort development and some of New Zealand's most popular beaches. Between the two coasts, a spine of bush-covered mountains makes up the Coromandel Forest Park.

First to set foot here was the Maori explorer Kupe, 1,000 years ago. Captain Cook paid a brief visit in 1769, and from 1795 ships landed regularly to load timber for the British navy. Nearly three-quarters of the kauri forests were felled, leaving just 5,000ha (12,355 acres). Coromandel is named after the timber ship HMS *Coromandel*, which called here in 1820. Charles Ring discovered gold in 1852; at the peak of the boom, around 1880, the peninsula's population topped 12,000.

## WHAT TO SEE

### COLVILLE AND THE CAPE ROAD

North of Coromandel town the Colville Road enters the most remote and scenic area of the peninsula. From the beach at Waitete Bay it climbs a hill and drops to the tiny village of Colville, with just a general store-cum-café and a fuel station. Beyond Colville the interior is dominated by 893m (2,930ft) Moehau. The road eventually climbs around the northern tip of the cape and descends to Port Jackson, where there are superb views of Great Barrier Island. Fletcher Bay marks the beginning of the three-hour Coromandel Walkway to Stony Bay, and thence the east coast road and all points south.
299 K4

### COROMANDEL

www.coromandeltown.co.nz
The township of Coromandel is 56km (35 miles) north of Thames (▷ 77), on the peninsula's west coast. It was built to serve the kauri timber trade, but

boomed when gold was discovered at nearby Driving Creek. During the peak gold-rush years of the 1860s and 1870s its population reached 12,000. Today its inhabitants number around 1,000, and it has a village atmosphere. Most of Coromandel's cafés and shops are on Kapanga Road, which runs at right angles to the port. The Coromandel School of Mines and Historical Museum on Rings Road (summer daily 10–4; winter Sat, Sun 1.30–4) is in the original School of Mines (1897) and includes New Zealand's first prison; the Coromandel Gold Stamper Battery on Buffalo Road (summer daily 10–5) lets you pan for gold.

A short drive north of town is the Driving Creek Railway and Potteries (daily). You can ride up to the ridge-top Eyefull Tower terminus, through tunnels and across viaducts and past potter and railway restorer Barry Brickell's sculptures.
299 K4 · 355 Kapanga Road · 07-866 8598

### NEW CHUMS BEACH

This is one of the best beaches in the Coromandel, accessible only on foot. Even in bad weather, this stunning beach is worth the walk.
299 K4 · Take the SH25 east from Coromandel town over the ranges to Te Rerenga and Whangapoua Harbour, then continue 4km (2.5 miles) north to Whangapoua village and take a 30-minute walk north from the road around the headland

### WHITIANGA

www.whitianga.co.nz
Whitianga is on glorious Mercury Bay, within walking distance of several fine beaches. There are plenty of leisure activities, but Whitianga is most famous as a sea- and big-game-fishing base. The Mercury Bay Museum (Dec–Easter daily 10–4), which traces the area's social history, faces the main wharf, where a passenger ferry shuttles across the narrows to Ferry Landing. This was the township's original site, and the stone wharf (built in 1837) is said to be the oldest in the country. The main waterfront beach is named after a timber ship, HMS *Buffalo*, wrecked here in 1840. Two smaller resorts lie within reach of Whitianga: Cooks Beach, on its southern edge (where Captain James Cook planted the British flag on 5 November 1769 and claimed the country for George III), and Hahei (▷ 86), 35km (22 miles) farther by road and accessible by ferry. Both have wonderful beaches. A track north of Hahei on Grange Road leads in half an hour to Cathedral Cove, a fabulous beach with a natural rock arch, guarding the Te Whanganui-A-Hei Marine Reserve (▷ 83).
299 K4 · 66 Albert Street · 07-866 5555

## MORE TO SEE

### OPOUTERE

Quiet and magical Opoutere, on the east coast, is one of the Coromandel's best-kept secrets. White-sand Ocean Beach is guarded by Wharekawa Harbour and a narrow tract of forest. At the tip of the sand spit is the Wharekawa Wildlife Refuge, where oystercatchers and rare New Zealand dotterels breed.
299 L5

### WAIHI

www.waihi.org.nz
Waihi once had 1,200 gold mines, producing half the country's gold. The Martha Mine (free guided tours most weekdays), was one of the first.
300 K5 · Seddon Street · 07-863 6715

### WHANGAMATA

The Coromandel's main surfing venue also has several good short coastal walks, and south of town the Wentworth and Parakiwai valleys offer longer trails, taking in waterfalls and remnants of the gold-mining industry.
300 L5 · 616 Port Road · 07-865 8340

**Below** *Gathering mussels on the seashore at Coromandel*

## BAY OF ISLANDS

www.visitnorthland.co.nz

A group of 150 islands huddled in their large bay on the east Northland coast has become a major draw for holidaymakers, who come for watersports and superb coastal scenery. This area is also of huge historic significance, as the site of the signing of the 1840 Treaty of Waitangi—the document that set in train New Zealand's bicultural society (▷ 29). You can explore the islands—now designated a Historic and Maritime Park—by kayak, yacht or sailing ship; you can also go fishing for marlin or shark, dive among shoals of blue maomao, swim with dolphins, bask on the beaches or jump out of a plane.

Most facilities are based in Paihia (▷ 76). From here a ferry crosses the bay to the small village of Russell (▷ 76). State Highway 11 runs to the bay, though a more interesting route is via the Old Russell Road, which leaves SH1 for the coast at Whakapara, about 26km (16 miles) north of Whangarei (▷ 79). You reach the coast at Helena Bay, which, along with Whananaki and Mimiwhangata to the south and the Whangaruru Peninsula to the north, offers remote and beautiful coastal scenery. From Whangaruru the road passes the neck of the beautiful Cape Brett Peninsula before turning inland and slowly negotiating its way to Russell.

299 J2 Marsden Road, Paihia 09-402 7345 Maritime Building, Paihia Ferry between Russell and Paihia; car ferry to Opua, 9km (5.5 miles) south of Paihia Bay of Islands airport, between Paihia and Kerikeri

## COROMANDEL PENINSULA

▷ 70–71.

## HAURAKI GULF ISLANDS

▷ 73–74.

## KAI IWI LAKES

www.kauricoast.co.nz

Located about 30km (19 miles) south of the Waipoua Kauri Forest (▷ 79), and only 10km (6 miles) from the coast, three freshwater lakes—Kaiiwi, Taharoa and Waikere—form part of the Taharoa recreation reserve. On their crystal clear waters you can enjoy sailing, windsurfing, water-skiing, jet-skiing and fishing, and you can explore the area along an extensive walking track. Note that, lacking cover and so close to the western coast, the lakes can be exposed to the elements.

298 H3 12 Otaika Road, Whangarei 09-438 1079

## KAITAIA

Kaitaia is the last significant outpost of the Far North, and a good start point for exploring Ninety Mile Beach (▷ 69). It frequently registers the hottest temperatures in the country. Its population is mainly Maori but includes a Croatian minority, whose forebears arrived during the kauri gum boom years of the late 19th century.

The Far North Regional Museum (daily 10–4) has a number of Maori treasures, including the Kaitaia Carving, one of the earliest Maori carvings in existence, and a 1,500kg (1.5-ton) anchor left by French navigator Jean-François de Surville in 1769. Other collections include moa remains and remnants from the Greenpeace ship *Rainbow Warrior* (▷ 36).

The Okahu Estate Winery, on the corner of Okahu Road and the Ahipara/Kaitaia highway, 3.5km (2 miles) from Kaitaia (daily 10–5, closed winter weekends), is New Zealand's northernmost winery and offers free tastings.

298 H2 Jaycee Park, South Road 09-408 0879 Kaitaia Travel Bureau, 170 Commerce Street Airport 6km (4 miles) north

## KARIKARI PENINSULA

This peaceful, beautiful T-shaped spur juts out on the northeastern coast, before it extends into the long, straight run of the Aupouri Peninsula (▷ 59). Its remote beaches separate Doubtless Bay from the mangrove swamps of Rangaunu Harbour and the broad, empty sweep of Karikari Bay to the north. Whales are frequently stranded here. In 1995 more than 100 pilot whales were refloated by locals and officials, only to beach themselves again the following day. Tokerau Bay is the main settlement on the peninsula.

298 H1

**Below** *A natural rock arch by Piercey Island, in the Bay of Islands*

## INTRODUCTION

The scattering of islands between the Coromandel Peninsula to the east and the mainland to the south and west provide an easy escape from the city for day trips or overnight stays. Most of the Hauraki Gulf lies within Hauraki Gulf Maritime Park, which takes in 47 islands and one mainland reserve (North Head in Devonport). Some are wildlife sanctuaries. The most densely populated island is Waiheke, a 35-minute ferry ride from Auckland.

Traces of Maori *pa* sites can still be seen on many hillsides. After the arrival of Europeans in the 19th century some of the islands were sold for gold, arms and ammunition.

## WHAT TO SEE

### GREAT BARRIER ISLAND

www.greatbarrier.co.nz

Rugged Great Barrier (or 'the Barrier') is the largest island in the gulf, with a population of around 1,000. This is the habitat for some rare and endangered species, including brown teal and New Zealand's largest skink (lizard), the cheveron. Over half of the island is conservation land.

Great Barrier earned its name from Captain Cook because it appeared to bar the entrance to the gulf. It was one of the first islands to be colonized by Europeans, who mined for gold and copper and plundered its extensive kauri forests. There are old kauri dams, the remains of whaling stations and tramping tracks to explore.

299 K3 Information: 09-367 6009 Sailings Apr–end Oct Sun–Tue, Thu, Fri; more frequent in summer; always check ahead (tel 09-300 5900) Daily flights from Auckland

### KAWAU ISLAND

www.warkworth-information.co.nz

Kawau, 8km (5 miles) off the Mahurangi Peninsula, was once the headquarters of Maori pirates. Europeans took possession in 1837, and the island was mined first for manganese, then for copper. Operations ceased in 1869, but remnants of copper mines can be found near the wharf. In 1862 Sir George Grey, Governor of New Zealand, bought the island for £3,500 and began a

### INFORMATION

www.aucklandcity.govt.nz

299 K4 Department of Conservation office, Ferry Building, Quay Street, Auckland 09-379 6476 Mon–Fri 9–5, Sat 10–3 Fleet of ferries run by Fullers, Quay Street, Auckland, tel 09-367 9111, www.fullers.co.nz: see individual islands for sailings Airfields at Waiheke (3km/2 miles east of Ostend) and Great Barrier (Claris, Okiwi)

### TIPS

» Take your own picnic to Rangitoto and Tiritiri Matangi as the shops there do not sell food.

» There is no mains electricity—or streetlight—on Great Barrier Island, so bring a torch: lights out at 10pm.

» Water, sun block and a hat are essential, as the black scoria (volcanic rock) can radiate a lot of heat.

**Above** *Boats moored in Matiatia Bay on Waiheke Island*

26-year stay in Bon Accord Harbour, where he created the Mansion House (daily 10–3.30). Grey amassed a small collection of exotic animals and plants here, unaware of the environmental damage he was unleashing on native flora and fauna. To this day, Australian wallabies and kookaburras inhabit the bush.
299 J4 1 Baxter Street, Warkworth 09 425 9081 From Sandspit at 10.30am, 2, 3.30

**RANGITOTO ISLAND**

Rangitoto's comparatively young volcanic cone (about 600 years old) dominates views of the Hauraki Gulf from almost every vantage point in Auckland. Of the island's many walks, most culminate at the summit (two hours). The island's vegetation is of international importance, with 200 species of native tree and flowering plants, 40 kinds of fern, and orchids and lichens. Underfoot are mounds of loose laval scoria.
299 J4 Rangitoto Island Heritage Conservation Trust 09-634 1398 From Ferry Building daily at 9.15, 12.15, 3.15

**TIRITIRI MATANGI ISLAND**

Visitors can wander freely on a network of walkways on this open bird sanctuary 4km (2.5 miles) off the Whangaparaoa Peninsula. The 220ha (544-acre) island has become a haven for rare and endangered species including the takahe, little spotted kiwi, kokako, whitehead, saddleback, North Island robin, kakariki and stitchbird.
299 J4 Ferries from Pier 3, Ferry Building Wed–Sun at 9am; or the same ferry from Z Pier, Gulf Harbour on the Whangaparaoa Peninsula, 45 min later

**WAIHEKE ISLAND**

The busiest island has a thriving arts and crafts community. Its main village is Oneroa, at the western end of the island. Behind the visitor information office, in the Artworks Complex, Whittakers Musical Museum (daily 10–4) displays instruments dating back 500 years. Live performances are staged at 1.30pm (except on Tuesday and Friday). Waiheke enjoys average temperatures 5°C (9°F) warmer than the mainland, and has many vineyards and wineries. The island is fringed with beaches, and inland there are walkways through native bush and farmland. One of the most popular is the track to Stony Batter, where an underground complex is linked by a series of tunnels built in World War II as defence against a possible Japanese invasion.
299 K4 Korora Road, Oneroa 09-372 1234 Auckland Ferry Building, daily

**Below** *The familiar shape of Rangitoto Island, viewed from Auckland*

## KAWAKAWA

Bizarre as it might seem, the main attraction in this town 17km (10.5 miles) south of Paihia is the public toilet. The Hundertwasser public toilets are the imaginative creation of Austrian artist Friedensreich Hundertwasser (1928–2000). The interior uses tiles of all sizes and shades and stained glass to produce a cheerfully chaotic effect, and the whole building is topped with a grass roof.

South of Kawakawa, local Maori guides give tours of the Kawiti Caves (daily 8.30–4.30), a series of subterranean passages originally occupied by a Maori woman fleeing from her tribe.

298 H2

## KERIKERI

www.kerikeri.co.nz

North of Paihia, rolling hills give way to corridors of windbreaks hiding trees of citrus, grape and kiwifruit, for which the area is famous. Keri means 'dig', and it was here that the first plough cut into New Zealand soil in 1820. Kerikeri is rich in Maori and early European history; the Kerikeri Historic Basin, 2km (1 mile) northeast of the present town, was the nucleus of New Zealand's first European colonization.

Where the road meets the Kerikeri River stands the Stone Store (Nov–end Apr daily 10–5; May–end Oct daily 10–4), the country's first stone building, completed in 1836 and used by the first Anglican bishop, George Selwyn, as a library in the early 1840s. It later housed ammunition during conflicts with Ngapuhi chief Hone Heke, before assuming its intended purpose as a general mission store. A museum occupies the top floor.

Almost immediately next door is the two-floor Mission Station or Kemp House (Nov–end Apr daily 10–5; May–end Oct daily 10–4), the oldest surviving wooden building in New Zealand. The Reverend John Gare Butler had it built in 1821 on land offered by the great local Maori warlord Hongi Hika, who accepted 48 felling axes in return. In 1832 it became the home of lay missionary and blacksmith James Kemp, whose family lived in the house until 1974, when it was given to the nation. The house now contains Kemp family relics.

Overlooking both buildings is the ancient Kororipo *pa*, which was chief Hongi Hika's territory until the 1820s, when he had a European-style house built near by. A stroll across the river leads to Rewa's Village (Dec–end Mar daily 9–5; Apr–end Nov daily 10–4), a re-created pre-European Maori fishing settlement, or *kainga*, named after Hongi Hika's successor. Its reed-and-thatch huts have beds of bracken and fern; traditional cooking areas occupy separate shelters.

In addition to its fruit, Kerikeri is also famous for its arts and crafts. Among many venues are Origin Art and Craft Co-op at 128 Kerikeri Road (daily 9.30–5), which displays and sells pottery, stained glass and other crafts; and the Kauri Workshop, at 500 Kerikeri Road (daily 9–5), where kauri and other native wood products are made.

The Aroha Island Ecological Centre, on Rangitane Road 12km (7 miles) northeast of town (Tue–Sun 9.30–5.30; also overnight visits), and the nearby Rangitane Scenic Reserve are important remnant habitats of the brown kiwi. The island is kept predator-free and offers a small but valuable sanctuary for a few birds. As the kiwi is nocturnal, daytime visitors can only see interpretive material, but if you stay overnight you may see and hear the birds on a guided tour.

298 H2 Airport between Paihia and Kerikeri

**Below** *Stone-built warehouse at Kerikeri, known as 'Kemp's Folly'*

## MATAKOHE KAURI MUSEUM

www.kauri-museum.com

Highly imaginative displays in this museum in the village of Matakohe, 45km (28 miles) south of Dargaville, give a detailed account of the natural history of the kauri tree and its exploitation. The Volunteer Hall contains a 22.5m (74ft) kauri slab, a local specimen which was felled by lightning. On the wall at its base are the circumference outlines of larger recorded trees, the largest having a diameter of 8.5m (28ft).

Around the hall are exquisite examples of kauri furniture, and models of kauri scows that used to ply the Kaipara Harbour. Other sections include a working Steam Sawmill, monstrous moving equipment and saws, and a superb kauri gum display, with carvings, busts and ornaments fashioned from the tree's resin or sap, some of it hundreds of thousands of years old. Restored kauri buildings in the museum grounds include the 1867 Pioneer Church and the Post Office which dates from 1909.

298 J3 Church Road, Matakohe 09-431 7417 Nov–end Apr daily 8.30–5.30; May–end Oct daily 9–5 Adult NZ$15, child (5–15) NZ$3, family NZ$30 SH12 at Brynderwyn; all Twin Coast Discovery Highway routes stop here

## MATAURI BAY

www.matauribay.co.nz

The views above Matauri Bay, studded with the Cavalli Islands, are sublime. Captain Cook named the islands after buying travally (a species of fish) from local Maori. The Samuel Marsden memorial church in Matauri Bay commemorates the missionary who first preached the gospel in the Bay of Islands, on Christmas Day 1814.

This prime venue for deep-sea fishing and diving is probably more famous as the site of the remains of the *Rainbow Warrior*. This flagship of the environmental movement Greenpeace was bombed by French secret service agents in Auckland in 1985 to prevent her leading a protest flotilla to the French nuclear test grounds on the Pacific atoll of Mururoa. Matauri Bay's local Maori tribe, the Ngati Kura, offered the ship a final resting place, and her sunken hull now lies 3km (2 miles) offshore. A memorial on the hill overlooking the islands near the beach pays tribute to the ship, her crew (one of whom was killed) and the campaign for establishing a nuclear-free region.

The Maori *waka* (war canoe) *Mataatua II*, nearby, was built in 1990 to commemorate the Pacific migration from Polynesia in about AD1100.

298 H2

## MURIWAI BEACH

www.muriwai.com

Muriwai, 45km (28 miles) west of Auckland, is the west coast's most visited beach. During summer weekends, locals and visitors flock to its black sands to soak up the sun, enjoy the surf, fish, or look over the gannet colony. Gannets have taken up residence on the flat rock outcrops at its southern end to breed, forming a small seabird city. In spring you can witness at close range the fluffy white chicks being fed by their angry-looking parents. Muriwai boasts the only major North Island colony, after Cape Kidnappers (▷ 101).

Muriwai itself is well equipped for visitors and has a fine golf course. If Muriwai beach is too busy, you can try another surf spot, Maori Bay, just south of Muriwai and reached via Waitea Road.

299 J4

## PAIHIA

www.paihia.co.nz

Paihia is the most convenient base for cruises or other activities in the Bay of Islands Historic and Maritime Park (▷ 72), and for visiting Russell (see below), Kerikeri (▷ 75) and Waitangi (▷ 78). It has a wide range of motels, hotels and other places to stay, as well as plenty of restaurants, cafés and shops. At the Maritime Building on the quayside there are several booking and information offices, including the visitor office. Behind it, Paihia wharf is busy with charter vessels, dolphin-watch boats and the Russell ferries. Next to the wharf, Aquatic World aquarium (daily 9.30–6; extended hours in summer) provides an insight into marine life in the Bay of Islands.

298 H2 Maritime Building, Marsden Road 09-402 7345 Maritime Building

## RUSSELL

www.russell.gen.nz

About 2km (1 mile) across the water from Paihia is the settlement of Russell, which has a village feel and a rich history.

Soon after the signing of the Treaty of Waitangi (▷ 29), Captain William Hobson purchased a block of land at nearby Okiato—renamed Russell after Lord John Russell, then British Colonial Secretary—with the aim of establishing the country's capital there. Nine months later, in March 1841, the capital was transferred to Auckland, and in 1844 the notoriously rowdy whaling port of Kororareka was given the name Russell.

The economic decline that followed the shift of the capital to Auckland provoked resentment among local Maori, who sacked the town in 1845. It was rebuilt the following year, and by the turn of the century had become a quiet summer resort. In 1930 a road was laid between Whangarei and Russell, allowing access by car for the first time.

The Russell Museum (Jan daily 10–5; rest of year 10–4) has a collection of early settler relics and a lot of information about Captain Cook, including a 1:5 scale model of his ship *Endeavour*.

A short distance south along the shore from the museum is Pompallier House (Dec–Apr daily 10–5; May–Nov tours at 10.15, 11.15, 1.15, 2.15, 3.15), a French-style dwelling set up in 1842 by early Roman Catholic missionaries as a printing works. It later served as a tannery and a private home, and became a museum in 1990.

The 1836 Anglican Christ Church on the corner of Church and Robertson streets was one of the few buildings to survive the 1845 sacking and ensuing Maori war (bar a few visible musket ball holes), and is the oldest church in New Zealand.

A steep climb up Flagstaff Hill (Maiki) gives grand views. The flagstaff itself was raised after the signing of the Treaty of Waitangi. It was cut down several times by local Maori chief Hone Heke Pokai (▷ 31) and replaced in the 1850s as a gesture of conciliation.

A farther 1km (0.6 miles) north, the earth terraces of the ancient *pa* on the Tapeka Point Reserve make an interesting walk. Long Beach, 1km (0.5 miles) behind Russell, is a pleasant venue on a summer's day.

298 J2 Paihia Wharf every 20–30 min Oct–Mar 7.30–10.30; Apr–Sep 7.30–7.30

## THAMES

www.thamesinfo.co.nz

The historic town of Thames is at the western base of the Coromandel Peninsula (▷ 70–71), at the mouth of the Waihou River and on the fringe of the Hauraki Plains. Behind the town rise the hills of the Coromandel Forest Park.

The best place to start exploring is the War Memorial Monument Lookout on Waiotahi Creek Road, at the northern end of the town, where the panorama takes in the Hauraki Plains and Firth of Thames. Also at the northern end of town, on attractively preserved Pollen Street, is the Thames Gold Mine and Stamper Battery (daily 10–4). Regular tours take in the impressive ore-crushing stamper and horizontal tunnels, with an informative commentary about the process and history of gold mining along the way. On the same theme, the Thames School of Mines and Mineralogical Museum (daily 11–4) has a collection of rocks and minerals from around the world.

Other places of interest include the Matatoki Cheese Farm (weekdays 9–4.30, weekends 10–4.30), and the Piako Ostrich Farm (tours daily 11 and 2; closed Tue, Wed, Oct–end Jun). There are also several notable gardens in the area, including Lyndell and Stony Creek Gardens. Every Saturday the town's popular market is held in Grahamstown, at the north end of Pollen Street.

299 K5 206 Pollen Street 07-868 7284 From Auckland, Tauranga

## TUTUKAKA COAST

www.whangareinz.org.nz

The Tutukaka coastline's ruggedly scenic bays are best known for their safe access to some of the best deep-sea fishing and diving in the world. Tutukaka itself has a large, sheltered marina, and the village of Ngunguru, 5km (3 miles) away, has most of the visitor amenities.

Accessed from Tutukaka, the Poor Knights Islands are a popular diving venue, which lie 25km (15.5 miles) offshore—the remnants of a large volcano which erupted more than 10 million years ago. They provide a predator-free refuge for land animals such as the tuatara (a reptile that has changed little in 60 million years), native lizards, giant weta (the largest insect in the world—around the size of a mouse), flax snails, giant centipedes and a wide variety of rare seabirds. They are also home to several species of plants, including the Poor Knights lily, found only here and on the Hen and Chickens Islands off Whangarei Heads (▷ 79). Landing on the Poor Knights Islands is forbidden without a permit.

299 J2 Otaika Road, Whangarei 09-438 1079 Coastal shuttle from Walton Street supermarket, Tutukaka

**Opposite** *Diving off Poor Knights Islands*
**Below** *Tranquil Russell was once a rowdy whaling port*

## WAITANGI

The haunting sound of piped Maori song draws you into the visitor complex of the Waitangi National Reserve, where an audiovisual display outlines the events that led to the signing of the Treaty of Waitangi in 1840 (▷ 29), and highlights the significance of the document to this day. A daily 30-minute Maori *kapa haka* performance takes place in the visitor centre's theatre (10.30, 11.30, 1.30, 3).

The main focus of the reserve is the beautifully restored wooden Treaty House, built between 1833 and 1834 and once the home of British resident James Busby, who played a crucial role in the lead-up to the signing. The house is full of detailed and informative displays that help clarify the confusing series of events surrounding the creation of the treaty.

### AROUND TREATY HOUSE

Near Treaty House is perhaps the most visited Maori meeting house in the country—Whare Runanga. The word 'house' is misleading; Maori meeting houses are essentially works of art, and this is a magnificent example, erected in 1940 and incorporating carved panels contributed by major tribes.

In front of the Treaty House and Whare Runanga a spacious lawn overlooks the bay to Russell. A flagstaff marks the actual spot where the treaty was signed. From the lawn it is a short walk down to the shore where the war canoe *(waka) Ngatokimatawhaorua* is housed. This impressive craft, 35m (115ft) long, is named after the canoe in which Kupe, the great Maori ancestor and navigator, discovered Aotearoa (New Zealand). It was commissioned, along with the Whare Runanga, as a centennial project to commemorate the signing of the treaty. The *Ngatokimatawhaorua* continues to be launched every year as part of the Waitangi Day ceremonies hosted on and around the reserve.

The Huia Creek Walkway, which begins near Treaty House, is an easy two-hour walk through the reserve to the Haruru Falls, taking in a good example of mangrove habitat on the way.

### INFORMATION

www.waitangi.net.nz
298 H2 Waitangi Treaty Grounds, 1 Tau Henare Drive, Waitangi 09-402 7437 Daily 9–6 Adult NZ$12, child (under 14) free; tours extra (see below); *kapa haka:* NZ$12, child (under 5) free Services from Auckland Self-guided Discovery (NZ$12, child free); Embrace Waitangi (NZ$10, child NZ$5), 9.15, 10.30, noon, 1.30, 3 Waikokopu café/restaurant: breakfast, snacks, lamb, beef, seafood (9–5) Traditional local arts and crafts

### TIP

» The 75-minute Maori Sound and Light Show is staged on Monday, Wednesday, Thursday and Saturday at the Whare Runanga.

**Above** *Elaborately carved native woods decorate the interior of Whare Runanga*

## WAIPOUA KAURI FOREST

www.doc.govt.nz

On the west coast within the 15,000ha (37,065-acre) Waipoua Forest is Waipoua sanctuary, of which 2,639ha (6,521 acres) contain mature kauri trees. Walking tracks at the northern end of the forest, immediately next to the highway, give access to the two largest known kauri specimens: Tane Mahuta, or Lord of the Forest, and Te Matua Ngahere, Father of the Forest. Tane Mahuta is an awesome sight, 51.5m (169ft) high, with a girth of 13.8m (45ft). It is estimated to be more than 1,500 years old.

From a parking area 2km (1 mile) south, a 20-minute walk leads to Te Matua Ngahere; a shorter path reaches the Four Sisters, a stand of trees growing together.

298 H2 · Off SH12 towards southern end of the park · 09-439 3011

## WAIPU

A party of 120 Scottish settlers founded Waipu in 1853, and its ethnic origins are reflected in names such as Braemar Lane, Argyll Street and Caledonian Park. The war memorial in the square is made of Aberdeen granite and was shipped from Scotland in 1914 to commemorate the 60th anniversary of the town's founding. The community's heritage is explored in the Waipu House of Memories (daily 9.30–4), which has cases full of early settlers' personal effects.

Every New Year's Day since 1871 the Waipu Highland Games have been celebrated, with highland dancers, pipe bands and kilted, caber-tossing men (Waipu Caledonian Society, www.highlandgames.co.nz).

At the Waipu Caves, 13km (8 miles) west via Shoemaker Road, you can see glow-worms through a 200m (656ft) passage, part of an extensive limestone cave system. You'll need to take a torch and have sturdy footwear.

299 J3 · 36a The Centre · 09-432 0746 · Whangarei–Auckland routes (reserve in advance)

## WARKWORTH

www.warkworth-information.co.nz

This former kauri-milling town is now a farming and tourism service base on the banks of the Mahurangi River. The Warkworth and District Museum (daily 9–4), in the shadow of two 600- to 800-year-old kauri trees within the Parry Kauri Park, uses reconstructed rooms to illustrate the life of early pioneers.

About 4km (2.5 miles) north of Warkworth is Sheepworld (daily 9–5, show 11–2), where you can feed the lambs and get involved in some shearing. A farther 3km (2 miles) north, at the Dome State Forest, walks range from 40 minutes to 3 hours, the best climbing to the Dome Summit, from where you can spot the Auckland Sky Tower (▷ 66) on a clear day.

299 J3 · 1 Baxter Street · 09-425 9081 · Outside visitor office, Baxter Street

## WHANGAREI

www.whangareinz.org.nz

Whangarei is the Northland district's biggest city. Mount Parahaki, on Memorial Drive (off Riverside Drive), once the site of one of the largest Maori *pa* (fortified site), is a good place for an overall view of the city and the bay. You can also walk up via the Mair Park, which has remains of an old gold mine and of further Maori fortifications.

Town Basin is a lively waterfront development with museums, art galleries and craft shops. Its most unusual attraction is Claphams Clocks (daily 9–5), a collection of timepieces gathered from around the world.

In the suburb of Maunu, 6km (4 miles) west of town, the Whangarei Museum, Clarke Homestead and Kiwi House (daily 10–4) is a colonial farming complex with a modern gallery housing Maori treasures, including a musket that belonged to the great warrior Hone Heke.

A Scot, William Carruth, was the first to buy land from the Maori in 1839 and settle at the mouth of the Hatea River. The quest for kauri gum and the building of a shipyard in the 1860s brought prosperity, and in the 1930s road and rail links with Auckland were completed.

299 J3 · Tarewa Park, Otaika Road · 09-438 1079 · Rose Street and outside visitor office · Onerahi, 9km (5.5 miles) southeast; shuttle bus

## WHATIPU

Solitude and wilderness are the attractions of Whatipu, 45km (28 miles) southwest of downtown Auckland, at the southernmost tip of the Waitakere ranges. Its huge expanse of sand forms part of the narrow mouth of Manukau Harbour.

At the terminus of the winding, unpaved road a small cluster of buildings called Whatipu Lodge is the last sign of habitation and last chance of accommodation before the beach stretches 6km (4 miles) north to Karekare.

Hidden inland among the dune grasses and cabbage trees are extensive wetlands that are home to paradise shelduck, pied stilts and black swans.

299 J4

**Below** *The war memorial, made of Aberdeen granite, was shipped to Waipu from Scotland to mark the town's founding*

# WEST COAST BEACHES AND THE WAITAKERE RANGES

**This circular tour explores Auckland's wild west-coast beaches and the Waitakere Ranges, with their memorable city views.**

**THE DRIVE**
**Distance:** 95km (59 miles)
**Time:** 6–8 hours
**Start/end at:** Sky Tower, SKYCITY, Auckland
299 J4

★ From SKYCITY take Hobson Street south to the motorway on-ramps. Take the Northwestern motorway, SH16 (signposted). After 3km (2 miles) take the Great North Road exit (exit 8) onto urban route 11, then 19 southwest to Titirangi Road (urban route 24).

❶ The suburban village of Titirangi is considered the gateway to the Waitakeres and has a number of laid-back cafés, interesting shops and a good art gallery, Lopdell House (daily 10–4.30), on the corner of Titirangi and South Titirangi roads. Titirangi is part of Waitakere City, known for its liberal attitudes, art, vineyards and orchards, and its spectacularly wild unspoiled bush and beaches. As a result, it has attracted many seeking an alternative lifestyle, and is home to artists and craftspeople. On the last Sunday of the month the market is held in the Memorial Hall (10–2).

From the middle of Titirangi continue west to the roundabout (traffic circle) and turn onto Scenic Drive, signposted to Piha (urban route 24). Take care on this road as it has many blind corners and connecting residential driveways. Follow Scenic Drive for another 5km (3 miles) to the Arataki Information Centre, which is on the left.

❷ The information centre is an impressive modern building with a vast amount of information and interesting interpretive and audiovisual displays, which provide the perfect introduction to the region and its natural history. There is also a short nature trail from here with

spectacular views south over the Nihotupu Reservoir and Manukau Harbour. An impressive Maori *pou* (guardian post) dominates the entrance to the centre. It lost its not insignificant 'manhood' a few years ago through vandalism, but thankfully for this great warrior another was duly carved, and the glint in his little paua-shell eye has been restored.

From the information centre continue north along Scenic Drive for 4km (2.5 miles), then turn left onto Piha Road to Piha (11km/7 miles).

❸ Piha has been luring dreamers and surfers for years, and is one of the west coast's most popular beaches and coastal enclaves. If you swim at Piha you can do so in relative safety, but always stay between the flags and under the vigil of the lifesavers. When you are weary of sunbathing, swimming or trying to hold on to your surfboard in the fierce surf, there are two things you must do. The first is to climb Lion Rock, the guardian of the beach, via the steep track (allow 30 minutes to reach the top). The second, especially when the surf is high, is to take the Tasman Lookout Track at the south end of the beach to The Gap, where breakers crash into the narrow rock crevice.

There is also an interesting, if less dramatic, walk at the northern end of Piha Beach, which leads to the isolated and beautiful Whites Beach. If you have time, also try to see the Kitekite Falls—they're reached via the Kitekite Track, up Glenesk Road behind the main camping ground in the middle of the village.

From Piha drive back up the hill and look for Karekare Road to Karekare Beach (on the right). Descend to the parking area.

❹ Karekare is another fine west coast beach and was used as a backdrop to the hugely successful New Zealand film *The Piano* (1993). There are a number of short walks and tracks around Karekare, some of which head inland or south to join the network of tracks in the Waitakeres. The short walk up the Taraire Track to Karekare Falls is worthwhile, especially if you intend to swim in the pool beneath it. Another is the Colmans Track from the end of Watchmans Road (signposted on the right before the parking area), where the path creeps up the hill at the northern point of Karekare Beach and terminates with a magnificent view. Looking south you can see well past Karekare

**Right** *The community centre at Titirangi*
**Opposite** *Part of the scenic drive through the Waitakere Ranges*

Beach to the huge expanse of Whatipu Beach beyond, as well as the tiny, inaccessible Mercer Bay, immediately below and north.

Return to Piha Road and the junction with Scenic Drive (urban route 24). Turn left towards the TV mast. After 1km (0.6 miles) look for signs to Rose Hellaby House (on the right).

❺ The Scenic Drive (28km/ 17 miles long) winds along the eastern fringe of the Waitakeres, offering stunning views across Auckland, but one of the best viewpoints is the garden of Rose Hellaby House. Its owner, Rose, who loved these hills, donated the property to the city.

Continue north along Scenic Drive, taking care when negotiating blind corners. There are a number of other viewpoints across the city along the way. Descend back to the fringe of the city and the intersection with Swanson Road. Turn right along Swanson Road (urban route 24) to the roundabout, and then continue straight across onto Universal Drive. At the end of Universal Drive turn left onto Lincoln Road to rejoin SH16 Northwestern Motorway (signposted) back into the city centre and SKYCITY (exit 4B).

## WHERE TO EAT

### HARDWARE CAFÉ

Light, healthy meals with a traditional Kiwi edge—and good coffee are served here.

✉ 404 Titirangi Road (in the heart of Titirangi) ☎ 09-817 5059 🕐 Mon–Tue 9–5, Wed–Sun 7am–10pm

## INFORMATION

### TOURIST INFORMATION

www.aucklandnz.com

✉ Auckland Visitor Centre, Atrium, Sky City, corner of Victoria and Federal streets, Auckland ☎ 09-363 7184 🕐 Daily 9–5

### ARATAKI INFORMATION CENTRE

www.arc.govt.nz

✉ 333 Scenic Drive, Titirangi ☎ 09-366 2000 🕐 Sep–end Apr daily 9–5; May–end Aug daily 10–4

## PLACES TO VISIT

### ROSE HELLABY HOUSE

✉ 515 Scenic Drive ☎ 09-366 2000 🕐 Gardens: daily 8–5. House: Sat, Sun 1–4 Free

**Below** *Karekare Beach was one of the film locations of* The Piano *(1993)*

# HAHEI AND CATHEDRAL COVE

**The highlight of this walk is Cathedral Cove, where secluded beaches are connected by a natural arch and guarded by bizarre rocky stacks.**

**THE WALK**
**Distance:** 6km (4 miles)
**Time:** 3 hours
**Start/end at:** Kotare Domain car park, Pa Road, Hahei 299 K4

**HOW TO GET THERE**
Hahei is 35km (22 miles) by road from Whitianga. Go Kiwi offers shuttle services from Ferry Landing, Whitianga (book at the information centre). In summer, the five-minute, passenger-only ferry crossing operates 7.30am–6.30pm, 7.30pm–8.30pm, 9.30pm–10.30pm. In winter hours may be reduced.

★ On entering Hahei village turn right onto Pa Road. Park in the Kotare Domain car park on the left, 200m (220 yards) from the end of Pa Road. Walk to Te Pare Point.

❶ The Te Pare Point Historic Reserve is the site of a *pa* occupied by the Ngati Hei people. This tribe and the settlement are named after Maori chief Hei, a *tohunga* (priest) who arrived around 1350. He settled his people here because of its resources and beauty. Hei's descendants, as *tangata whenua*, retain a strong spiritual attachment to the site, and proudly continue their role as guardians, or *kaitiaki*.

From Te Pare Point descend the steps to the beach—only possible at low tide. At high tide, walk back along Pa Road for 100m (110 yards) to the grass walkway on the right (marked) and cross the bridge. Steps are signposted. At the north end of the beach steps and a walkway lead uphill to Cathedral Cove Lookout (signposted). From the lookout take the track to Cathedral Cove.

❷ The scenic jewel in the region's crown, Cathedral Cove guards the Te Whanganui-A-Hei (Cathedral Cove) Marine Reserve. Cathedral Cove is actually two coves and two beaches connected by a natural limestone arch (▷ photograph above), negotiable at low tide. There are sandstone pinnacles on both beaches, the highest is Sail Rock. The snorkelling opportunities in Te Whanganui-A-Hei Marine Reserve are also outstanding, especially at Gemstone Bay and the western side of Mahurangi Island.

Return to the lookout and take Grange Road back into Hahei and the small shopping centre. From here, turn right onto the main road. Head south back to Pa Road and return to Kotare Domain car park.

**WHERE TO EAT**
**LUNA CAFÉ**
1 Grange Road, Hahei 07-866 3016
Daily in summer from 9am until late, with reduced hours in winter

**THE CHURCH**
www.thechurchhahei.co.nz
87 Beach Road, Hahei 07-866 3533
Wed–Sun

**INFORMATION**
**TOURIST INFORMATION**
www.whitianga.co.nz
Whitianga i-SITE, 66 Albert Street, Whitianga 07-866 5555

# DEVONPORT AND NORTH HEAD

**Escape the city bustle by ferry to experience the history and village feel of Devonport, and the views from North Head, one of Auckland's most iconic (extinct) volcanoes.**

**THE WALK**
**Distance:** 5km (3 miles)
**Time:** 3 hours
**Start/end at:** Devonport Wharf, Devonport
299 J4

**HOW TO GET THERE**
Fullers ferry from the Ferry Building, Quay Street, Auckland, operates every 30 minutes, from NZ$10 return. Crossing: 15 minutes.

Located at the southernmost tip of the North Shore and named after the naval base in Plymouth, England, the suburb of Devonport was one of the first areas to be settled in Auckland and is home to the Royal New Zealand Navy. Long before the first Europeans dropped anchor there in the early 1800s, the Maori used the two small but distinct volcanic mountains as *pa* (fortified settlements). They would almost certainly have witnessed the dramatic eruption of Rangitoto (▷ 74), the most recent and least modified volcano of the Auckland volcanic field and an unmistakable natural feature that dominates the view from North Head.

★ From the Devonport Wharf and ferry terminal, facing towards the middle of Devonport, turn right and walk along the waterfront (King Edward Parade), then turn left into Cheltenham Road. Turn right off Cheltenham Road onto Takarunga Road and climb North Head.

❶ North Head (Maungauika) is one of about 50 dormant volcanoes within Greater Auckland, and at 65m (213ft) offers some of the most memorable views of the city and Waitemata Harbour. From here it is easy to see why Auckland is dubbed the City of Sails and is renowned as one of the most desirable sailing venues in the world. During international yachting events, including the Whitbread Round the World in 1993 and America's Cup campaigns in 2000 and 2003, this was a prime viewpoint for locals cheering on the New Zealand crews. Today huge cargo ships and cruise liners are also a common sight.

In the days when tall ships brought the first European settlers to New Zealand, a small gun was sited on North Head to signal the much-anticipated arrival of mail ships.

The activity on North Head has not always been so celebratory in its mood. In response to the fear of a Russian invasion in the 1880s and of a possible Japanese invasion in World War II, the mound was heavily fortified and a maze of tunnels, bunkers and gun emplacements were constructed. Convicts built tunnels with nothing more than a

**Opposite** *The ferry terminal at Devonport*

pick, a shovel and their bare hands. The remnants of these tunnels, along with gun emplacements and lookouts, can be explored today (torch/flashlight recommended).

Take time to explore and walk around North Head. Then, from the northern slope, descend the steps onto Cheltenham Beach, the first of the northern beaches and considered by many to be the best on the North Shore. Walk to the top end of the beach onto Vauxhall Road. Head south along Vauxhall Road back towards Mount Victoria, looking for signs on the right for the Mount Cambria Reserve.

❷ The Mount Cambria Reserve was once a volcanic mount in its own right, and named Takaroro by Maori. Quarried for scoria in the late 1800s, it is now an attractive landscaped garden and home to the Devonport Museum. A relatively low-key affair, the museum showcases the early days of the historic suburb with objects and photographs.

Walk through Mount Cambria Reserve onto Church Street, turning left past the old power station to the Mount Victoria Walkway steps (signposted right). Climb round the mount on the spiral walkway to reach the summit.

❸ At 881m (2,890ft), Mount Victoria (Takarunga) commands superb views across the harbour, city and surrounding suburban streets. From here you can see the wooden villas and colonial architecture that characterize the suburb.

Steeped in history and intrigue, Mount Victoria still has remnants of the Maori Kawerau tribe fortifications. At its foot, on the northern edge, there is an old cemetery where some of the North Shore's first settlers are buried.

From the Mount Victoria summit parking area follow the summit road onto Flagstaff Lane, then Victoria Road, Devonport's main thoroughfare.

❹ Victoria Street is the commercial and social heart of Devonport. Here you will find a range of tourist-oriented shops selling everything from secondhand books or antiques to local art. Alternatively, relax and enjoy a cappuccino in one of several streetside cafés. If you have an interest in naval tradition and antiquity you may also want to visit the Devonport Navy Museum in the dockyard, which forms the principal base for the Royal New Zealand Navy (▷ 64). Opened in 1888, its Calliope dry dock was once the largest dry dock in the southern hemisphere. Although often seconded for peacekeeping missions overseas, some fleet vessels may be in evidence.

Walk down Victoria Street past the visitor information centre and Esplanade Hotel back to the Devonport Wharf and ferry terminal.

### WHERE TO EAT

There is plenty of choice in Devonport, from streetside cafés for coffee or light snacks to à la carte restaurants. For a good coffee, healthy light meals and great atmosphere try Manuka, 49 Victoria Road. For a buffet dinner or Sunday brunch (from NZ$16), try the Watermark on the waterfront (33 King Edward Parade). For fish and chips it's hard to resist the Cod Piece, 26 Victoria Road, or the more traditional Catch 22, 19 Victoria Road.

### TIP

» Take binoculars, and a torch if you plan to explore the tunnels on North Head.

### PLACES TO VISIT

#### DEVONPORT MUSEUM

www.devonportmuseum.org.nz
✉ Mount Cambria Reserve ☎ 09-445 2661 🕐 Sat, Sun 2–4 or by arrangement

#### NAVY MUSEUM

www.navymuseum.mil.nz
✉ Spring Street ☎ 09-445 5186
🕐 Daily 10–4.30

### INFORMATION

#### TOURIST INFORMATION

www.tourismnorthshore.org.nz
✉ 3 Victoria Road, Devonport
☎ 09-4460677

**Below** *The Devonport ferry makes the crossing from Auckland every 30 minutes*

# COROMANDEL COUNTRYSIDE AND COAST

**A circular tour exploring the rugged hills, townships and spectacular coastal scenery of the Coromandel Peninsula.**

**THE DRIVE**
**Distance:** 135km (84 miles)
**Time:** 8 hours (or two days)
**Start/end at:** Coromandel Township
299 K4

★ From the old gold-mining township of Coromandel (▷ 70–71) take SH25 south for 3km (2 miles), then turn left onto The 309 Road. This is unsealed in places, but manageable with care. The first stop is the Waiau Waterworks.

❶ Waiau Waterworks is a garden full of whimsical water sculptures and gadgets. You are greeted by a metal stick figure who operates a waterwheel hung, not with wooden boards, but with pots, pans and other kitchenware. There are many more interactive water-powered inventions, including an old bicycle that you peddle furiously to squirt a hose of water across a lily pond.

Continue south on The 309 Road, keeping an eye open (left) for the aptly named Castle Rock (526m/1,725ft), a knobbly volcanic plug that can be seen from many points on the peninsula.

❷ The stiff climb to the top of Castle Rock takes up to two hours. To reach the summit track (signed) take the forest road left 2km (1mile) south of the Waiau Waterworks. The track is more like a stream for much of the year, but the view is well worth the effort.

Just over 7km (4 miles) south from the Coromandel end of The 309 are the Waiau Falls, with a drop of 6m (20ft). View them from a lookout by the road, or via an access track.

Less than a kilometre (0.6 miles) south of the falls you will come to Kauri Grove.

❸ Kauri Grove is a small stand of ancient kauri trees that survived the rapacious logging at the end of the 19th century. Now fully protected, they offer a glimpse of what much of the upper North Island must once have looked like. The walk (signed) takes 20 minutes.

From Kauri Grove continue southeast on The 309 to the intersection with SH25. Turn right and drive through the settlement of Coroglen. Eight kilometres (5 miles) beyond Coroglen turn left, signed to Hahei and Hot Water Beach. Turn right to the beach.

❹ At Hot Water Beach, about two hours each side of low tide you can dig a hole in the sand to access natural hot water (the local store rents out spades for NZ$5). The beach is very pleasant, but it is also very dangerous for swimming, with

**Opposite** *As the sun sets, Coromandel Harbour is bathed in glorious tones of pink and orange*

notorious rips. Once suitably boiled in your own hot spa, pop your head into the Moko Artspace at 24 Pye Place, just opposite the car park.

About 10km (6 miles) north of Hot Water Beach is Hahei, signposted to the right.

❺ Hahei is an unspoiled coastal settlement surrounded by some of the best coastal scenery on the peninsula. Dramatic Cathedral Cove is the highlight (▷ 83).

From Hahei return to SH25 and head back north to Whitianga.

❻ The peninsula's most popular holiday spot, Whitianga (▷ 71) presents the perfect opportunity for a lunch stop, or an overnight stay (book ahead October–March). There's plenty of accommodation in the town, with Villa Toscana one of the top bed-and-breakfasts in the region.

North from Whitianga, SH25 straddles bush-clad hills before descending towards the coast again at Kuaotunu.

❼ The small beachside hamlet of Kuaotunu is a lovely spot, especially for swimming, but it also acts as the gateway to Otama and Opito bays via the scenic Black Jack Road (this is unsealed but manageable for standard vehicles). Both bays have lovely beaches and magnificent views across to the Mercury Islands. This is a great spot if you want to escape the crowds.

Back on SH25 and a little farther west (signposted 1km off SH25) is the sterile real-estate settlement of Matarangi. Although it's usually bypassed by visitors, you may like to spend time enjoying its 5km (3-mile) sweep of beach, or perhaps book a tee time at its well-groomed golf course (tel 07-866 5394). From Matarangi continue west on SH25 to Te Rerenga. On a clear day you will see Castle Rock straight ahead. At Te Rerenga turn right, following signs to Whangapoua.

❽ Whangapoua is little more than a conglomeration of baches (holiday homes) that come alive in summer. The village is the gateway to one of the most idyllic beaches on the peninsula—New Chums Beach (▷ 71), reached only by foot. From the northern end of Whangapoua, cross the river (at low tide) and follow the edge of the beach, where you will find a track. Follow this to the headland, where it ducks left through bush, soon revealing the beach. The slopes surrounding the headland are noted for their pohutukawa trees, which flower crimson in December, earning it the label New Zealand's Christmas tree.

From Whangapoua return to SH25 at Te Rerenga then turn right. From here SH25 winds its way over the ranges, offering views of the Hauraki Gulf before descending steeply to the west coast and Coromandel township. On a clear day, with binoculars, you should be able to see the needle-sharp Sky Tower in Auckland (▷ 66), just beyond the volcanic cone of Rangitoto.

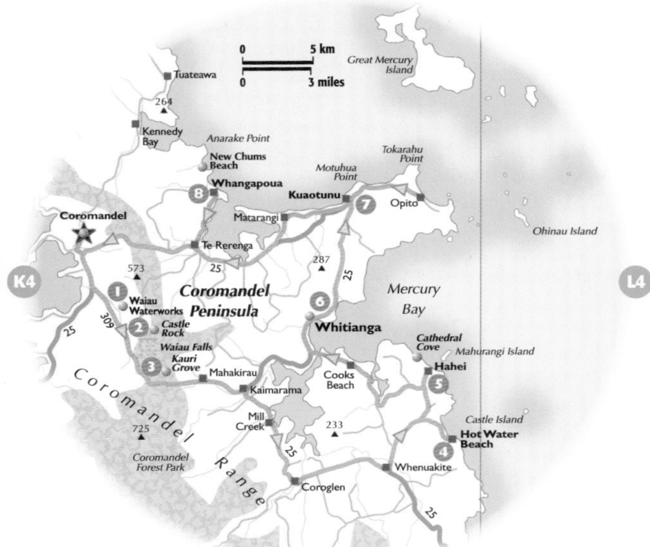


### WHERE TO EAT
**CAFÉ NINA**

Café Nina offers an imaginative menu and a fine cup of coffee.
✉ 20 Victoria Street, Whitianga
☎ 07-866 5440 🕓 Daily 8–4.30

### WHERE TO STAY
**VILLA TOSCANA**

www.villatoscana.co.nz
A grand villa offering superb views.
✉ Ohuka Park, Whitianga ☎ 07-866 2293

### INFORMATION
**TOURIST INFORMATION**

www.coromandeltown.co.nz
✉ Coromandel Visitor Centre, 355 Kapanga Road, Coromandel ☎ 07-866 8598

### PLACES TO VISIT
**WAIAU WATERWORKS**

www.waiauwaterworks.co.nz
✉ The 309 Road, Coromandel ☎ 07-866 7191 🕓 Oct–end Mar daily 9–dusk; Apr–end Sep daily 9–5 Adult NZ$12, child NZ$6

## AUCKLAND

### AOTEA SQUARE MARKET

In the heart of downtown Auckland, this market sets up under sun umbrellas in Aotea Square on Fridays and Saturdays. The stalls are a mix of arts and crafts, Pacific culture, funky fashion and ethnic food, with the added fun of street entertainers.
✉ Aotea Square, Queen Street, Auckland ☎ 09-307 5493 ⏱ Fri–Sat 10–6

### AUCKLAND BRIDGE CLIMB

www.aucklandbridgeclimb.co.nz
Walkways provide a safe, not-too-demanding experience, lasting 1.5 hours, with great views. It can be combined with bungy jumping. No children under 7, and children 7 to 15 must have written parental consent. Night trips are available on Saturday in summer on request.
✉ Westhaven Reserve, Westhaven Marina, Auckland ☎ 09-361 2000 ⏱ Daily 9, 11.30, 2.30 💰 NZ$65

### AUCKLAND THEATRE COMPANY

www.atc.co.nz
The company performs at various venues. Shows are listed on the company website.
✉ Level 2, 108 Quay Street, Auckland ☎ 09-309 0390

### CLASSIC COMEDY AND BAR

www.comedy.co.nz
Comedians entertain from Wednesday to Saturday. The venue also hosts cabaret, films and music. Events are listed on the website.
✉ 321 Queen Street, Auckland ☎ 09-373 4321 ⏱ Daily 7–late 💰 NZ$10–NZ$20 🍸 Two bars

### DOGS BOLLIX IRISH BAR

www.dogsbollix.co.nz
This bar pulls in the crowds with gigs featuring New Zealand bands, jam sessions and Irish music nights.
✉ 2 Newton Road, Auckland ☎ 09-376 4600 ⏱ Mon–Wed 3–late, Thu–Sun 11.30–late 💰 NZ$5 cover charge for some performances

### DOLPHIN AND WHALE SAFARI

www.dolphinexplorer.com
Trips lasting 4 to 5 hours with a marine research team in the Hauraki Gulf Marine Park viewing dolphins, whales and a variety of seabirds. You can also swim with the dolphins (conditions apply).
✉ Booking kiosk, Viaduct Harbour, Auckland ☎ 09-359 5987 ⏱ Daily 9.30am (weather permitting) from Pier 3 on the waterfront 💰 Adult NZ$140, child (5–15) NZ$100, family NZ$380

### THE EDGE

www.the-edge.co.nz
Several venues make up The Edge: the multipurpose Aotea Centre, built in 1990 and adjoining Aotea Square; the Auckland Town Hall, built in 1911 and favoured as a concert hall; and the opulent Civic Theatre, built in 1929 as a cinema, and now popular for music theatre.
✉ Aotea Square, Queen Street, Auckland ☎ 09-309 2677

### ELEPHANT HOUSE

www.nzcrafts.co.nz
A co-operative operated by local craftspeople, Elephant House carries only items handmade in New Zealand and the range is huge: wood, mobiles, leather, greenstone, clothing, honey and kiwifruit products, ceramics, Maori carving, paua, glass, souvenirs and gifts.
✉ 237 Parnell Road, Parnell, Auckland ☎ 09-309 8740 ⏱ Mon–Fri 9.30–5.30, Sat, Sun 10–5 🚌 On the Link bus route

### ELLERSLIE RACECOURSE

www.ellerslie.co.nz
Ellerslie is the home of the Auckland Racing Club, which hosts 26 horse-racing events a year. Details of dates are listed on the website. A highlight

**Opposite** *A photography outlet in Victoria Park Market*

is the Auckland Cup, held in March. It is also the venue for other events. ✉ 80–100 Ascot Avenue, Greenlane East, Auckland ☎ 09–524 4069 🚗 Take Greenlane off-ramp (exit 433) from SH1

### FORMOSA COUNTRY CLUB

www.formosa.co.nz

Best known for its 160ha (395-acre), 18-hole golf course designed by Bob Charles with views over the Hauraki Gulf, there is also villa accommodation and dining at this sports stadium with heated pool. ✉ 110 Jack Lachland Drive, Beachlands, South Auckland ☎ 09–536 5895 🕐 From 7am 🎫 Green fees with cart from NZ$100

### FULLERS

www.fullers.co.nz

Fullers operates ferry services to Devonport, Rangitoto and Waiheke Island, and cruises including a 90-minute Harbour Cruise. The day trip to Tiritiri Matangi (▷ 74) is particularly recommended.
✉ Fullers Cruise Centre, Ferry Building, 99 Quay Street, Auckland ☎ 09-367 9111 🕐 Harbour cruise daily 10.30, 1.30 🎫 Harbour cruise adult NZ$30, child NZ$15, family NZ$76

### HOWICK HISTORICAL VILLAGE

www.fencible.org.nz

Life in Auckland's colonial past is re-created in this museum of living history, with characters in 19th-century costume and authentic public buildings and settlers' houses. ✉ Bells Road, Lloyd Elsmore Park, Pakuranga, Auckland ☎ 09-576 9506 🕐 Daily 10–4 🎫 Adult NZ$14, child NZ$7 (under 5 free), family NZ$36

### LIONZONE

www.lionzone.co.nz

Interactive tour of New Zealand's largest brewery, home of Steinlager and Lion Red, with tastings.
✉ Lion Breweries, 380 Khyber Pass Road, Auckland ☎ 09-358 8366 🕐 Wed–Sat 9.30, 12.15, 3, Tue 12.15, 3 🎫 Adult NZ$18, child NZ$7, family NZ$48 🚌 On the Link bus route

### MAIDMENT THEATRE

www.maidment.auckland.ac.nz

This twin theatre complex is on the University of Auckland city campus. Events are listed on the website.
✉ 8 Alfred Street, Auckland ☎ 09-308 2383

### MOUNT SMART STADIUM

www.mountsmartstadium.co.nz

The main venue for rugby league matches and other sports events, the stadium also hosts concerts.
✉ Beasley Avenue, Penrose, Auckland ☎ 09–571 1603 🚗 Take Mount Wellington off-ramp (exit 438) from SH1

### OTARA MARKET

On Saturday mornings the Otara shopping centre car park is crammed with stalls serving Auckland's Pacific Island communities, with fruit and vegetables, clothing, Island music, crafts and prepared foods.
✉ Newbury Street, Otara, Auckland ☎ 09-274 0830 🕐 Sat 6–noon 🚌 Bus 487,497 🚗 20km (12 miles) south of Auckland CBD. Take the East Tamaki off-ramp (exit 444) from the Southern Motorway (SH1)

### RAINBOW'S END

www.rainbowsend.co.nz

This theme park has wild rides like the corkscrew roller coaster and tame rides for the little ones, as well as dodgems, go-karts, bumper boats, mini golf, a pirate ship and interactive games. Refreshments and free parking are available.
✉ Corner of Great South and Wiri Station roads, Manukau City, Auckland ☎ 09-262 2030 🕐 Daily 10–5 🎫 Adult NZ$44, child (4–13) NZ$34, (2–3) NZ$31, under 2 free. Family discounts 🚌 Bus 471 or 472 from 55 Customs Street East 🚗 Take Manukau off ramp (exit 448) from SH1

### SAILNZ

www.sailnz.co.nz

Experience life on America's Cup racer *NZL40* or *NZL41*. You can become the crew and take the helm, pump the grinders or sit back and enjoy the action.
☎ 09-359 5987 🕐 Daily, usually 2pm 🎫 Adult from NZ$140, child NZ$110

### SKYCITY CASINO

www.skycity.co.nz

Part of the SKYCITY complex, the casino has table games and 1,200 gaming machines.
✉ Corner of Federal and Victoria streets, Auckland ☎ 09-363 6010 🕐 Daily 24 hours

### SKYCITY METRO

This futuristic building bordering Aotea Square has a six-level atrium and houses an entertainment complex including a 13-screen cinema, Time Out games, Borders bookstore and a food hall.
✉ 291–297 Queen Street, Auckland ☎ 09-369 2411 🕐 Cinema: Mon–Thu, Sun 10–9.30, Fri, Sat 10am–11.30pm 🎫 Adult NZ$9–NZ$14, child (3–15) NZ$7–NZ$8.50

### SKYCITY THEATRE

www.skycity.co.nz

Part of the SKYCITY complex, this hosts live shows and concerts.
✉ Corner of Federal and Victoria streets, Auckland ☎ 09-363 6010

### SKY JUMP

www.skyjump.co.nz

Harness jump from just above the restaurant of the Sky Tower (▷ 66); maximum weight 120kg (265lbs). No children under 10; written parental consent is required for children aged 10 to 13.
✉ SKYCITY, corner of Victoria and Federal streets, Auckland ☎ 0800-SKYJUMP 🕐 Daily 10–5.15 🎫 NZ$195

### SMITH AND CAUGHEY'S

www.smithandcaughey.co.nz

This 1880s department store sells accessories, clothing, cosmetics, household items, perfume, shoes, stationery and food. Also at 225 Broadway, Newmarket.
✉ 253–261 Queen Street, Auckland ☎ 09-377 4770 🕐 Mon–Thu 9.30–6.30, Fri 9.30–7, Sat 10–6, Sun 10.30–5.30

### TWO DOUBLE SEVEN

www.westfield.com/newmarket

Shopping complex with smart international and local fashion boutiques such as Oroton, Polo Ralph Lauren, Esprit, Country Road,

Scarpa, Barkers, Max and Keith Matheson. Also food, accessories, CDs, leisure and household items.
277 Broadway, Newmarket, Auckland 09-978 9400 Mon–Wed, Thu, Fri 9–6, Sat 9–6, Sun 10–5 On the Link bus route From downtown Auckland, exit SH1 at Gillies Avenue (exit 431), turn left then first right into Mortimer Pass

### VICTORIA PARK MARKET

www.victoria-park-market.co.nz

Recognizable by its brick chimney, this shopping mall is housed in the workshops of the furnace that burned the city's rubbish in the early 1900s. Shops sell crafts, clothing and souvenirs; there is a food court.
210 Victoria Street, West Auckland 09-309 6911 Daily 9–6 On the Link bus route Several cafés

### WESTFIELD DOWNTOWN SHOPPING

More than 60 speciality stores are here, including fashion, crafts and souvenirs, America's Cup clothing, sheepskins, jewellery and an international food court.
11–19 Customs Street West, Auckland 09-978 5265 Mon–Fri 8–6, Sat 10–6, Sun 10–4

### ZAMBESI

www.zambesi.co.nz

Zambesi is one of New Zealand's leading fashion labels, that of designer Elisabeth Findlay. Also found at 2 Teed Street, Newmarket (tel 09–523 1000), the shops carry other designer fashion too. Zambesi Man carries international and local men's fashion (10 O'Connell Street).
Corner of Vulcan Lane and O'Connell Street, Auckland 09-303 1701 Mon–Thu 9–6, Fri 9–8, Sat 9–5, Sun 11–4

## CLEVEDON

### CLEVEDON COAST OYSTERS

www.clevedonoysters.co.nz

Buy live oysters direct from the farm and watch them being processed. You can also buy mussels and wines from the owner's vineyard.
914 Clevedon–Kawakawa Bay Road, Clevedon 09-292 8017 Mon–Fri 7–4.30, Sat 9–2

### CLEVEDON GALLERY

www.countryknits.co.nz

In this gallery you'll find local arts and crafts, especially knitwear, sheepskins and mohair rugs made from wool, mohair and possum/merino blend yarns. The local information centre is also here.
9 North Road, Clevedon 09-292 8660 Daily 10–5

### VIN ALTO

www.vinalto.com

A hillside vineyard inland from Clevedon specializes in Italian grape varieties and traditional wine-making methods, including Retico, made from grapes dried in the Amarone style. Enjoy cellar-door tastings, a wine museum, shop and wine-tasting lunches (NZ$50).
424 Creightons Road, Clevedon 09-292 8845 Sep–end Jul Sat, Sun 11–4.30

## COROMANDEL TOWN

### COROMANDEL ARGO ADVENTURE TOURS

The Coromandel's mussel farms are a popular recreational fishing ground. Mussel Barge Snapper Safaris take you there on a traditional flat-bottomed wooden scow. Rods are available for hire. If you prefer to stay on land, the same operator takes tours of old gold-mine workings on eight-wheel-drive all-terrain vehicles.
PO Box 132, Coromandel 07-866 7667 Daily From NZ$35

### THE COROMANDEL SMOKING COMPANY

www.corosmoke.co.nz

Coromandel seafood is smoked daily over native manuka sawdust at this smokehouse and deli. Specialities include mussels, oysters, kingfish, trevally, tarakihi and kahawai. They'll also smoke the fish you catch.
70 Tiki Road, Coromandel Town 07-866 8793 Daily 9–5.30

## HAHEI

### CATHEDRAL COVE KAYAKS

www.seakayaktours.co.nz

Explore the dramatic volcanic coastline of the Coromandel Peninsula by kayak in half- or full-day tours, with all equipment provided. The scenery is spectacular and cappuccino is served on the beach to revive you.
88 Hahei Beach Road, Hahei 07-866 3877 Daily Oct–end May, otherwise on demand From NZ$75

## KAITAIA

### HARRISONS CAPE RUNNER

www.ahipara.co.nz/caperunner

These bus tours to Cape Reinga via Ninety Mile Beach include a break for some sand-dune tobogganing, and a picnic lunch is included in the cost. Harrisons also offer a more personalized 4X4 Reef Runner tour, which includes sand tobogganing.
123 North Road, Kaitaia 09-408 1033 Daily 9am Adult NZ$45, child NZ$25

## KAWAKAWA

### BAY OF ISLANDS ADVENTURE COMPANY

www.adventurecompany.co.nz

Guided tours of a 62ha (153-acre) cattle farm on either horseback or quad bikes explore farmland, native bush and the Tirohanga River. No experience is necessary, and the horse treks are suitable for all abilities. Families can opt for a 4X4 safari, and the children can meet the farm animals.
Tirohanga Road, Kawakawa 09-404 1142 Daily Adult from NZ$55, child NZ$25 3km (2 miles) north of Kawakawa

## KERIKERI

### MAHOE FARMHOUSE CHEESE

www.mahoecheese.co.nz

Bob and Anna Rosevear make Dutch-style cheese out of milk from the cows on their dairy farm. You can buy the cheeses from the shop.
SH10, Oromahoe, Kerikeri 09-405 9681 Mon–Sat 8.30–5, Sun 10–5 12km (7 miles) south of Kerikeri on SH1

### MAKANA CONFECTIONS

www.makana.co.nz

A viewing window allows you to watch chocolates being made by hand, often using local ingredients such as macadamia nuts. The shop is elegant, the quality of the

chocolates excellent, and you can taste before you buy.
504 Kerikeri Road, Kerikeri 09-407 6800 Daily 9–5.30

## MATAKANA

### MORRIS AND JAMES

www.morrisandjames.co.nz
Clay dug from the banks of the Matakana River is the inspiration for Morris and James pottery. The showroom, filled with their vibrant ware, has become a popular attraction on the Matakana wine trail. The restaurant is an added draw, serving food on their ceramic ware with local wines.
Tongue Farm Road, Matakana 09-422 7116 Mon–Fri 8–4.30, Sat, Sun 10–5 Mon, Tue 9–3, Wed–Sun 9–3, 6–9

## MATAURI BAY

### KAURI CLIFFS GOLF COURSE

www.kauricliffs.com
Aimed at the luxury market, this spectacularly sited golf course overlooks the ocean and is designed to use the natural features of the site. You can stay in beautifully appointed, secluded cottages and dine at the lodge, which also has tennis courts, a swimming pool and fitness centre.
Kauri Cliffs, Matauri Bay Road, Matauri Bay 09-407 0010 From NZ$300 a round Turn off SH10 at Matauri Bay Road

## MERCER

### MERCER CHEESE

The shelves in this shop are stacked with fine Dutch-style cheeses, made at the nearby farm, which can be cut to order.
Old Great South Road, Mercer 09-232 6778 Daily 10–5

## MIRANDA

### MIRANDA HOT SPRINGS

www.mirandahotspring.co.nz
Don't miss a visit to what is reputedly the largest naturally heated mineral pool in the southern hemisphere. The hot springs complex also has a toddlers' pool, private spa, barbecue area and a holiday park next door.
East Coast Road, Miranda 07-867 3055 Daily 9am–9.30pm Adult NZ$14, child (5–13) NZ$7, (1–4) NZ$4.50 12km (7 miles) off SH2

### MIRANDA SHOREBIRD CENTRE

www.miranda-shorebird.org.nz
More than 60 species of shorebirds congregate here, including the rare wrybill and the New Zealand dotterel, which flock on the tidal flats at the Firth of Thames. Some species fly 12,000km (7,455 miles) from Arctic breeding grounds to over-winter from October to March. The centre has displays, information, birdwatching and accommodation.
283 East Coast Road, Miranda 09-232 2781 Daily 9–5 Donation 20km (12 miles) off SH2

## MURIWAI

### MURIWAI GOLF CLUB

www.muriwaigolfclub.co.nz
This links course is located in a bird sanctuary, on naturally rolling fairways with views of the sea and forests. Book well in advance. ▷ 76
Coast Road, Muriwai 09-411 8454 Daily 7am–4pm From NZ$35 Take Muriwai Road off SH16

## PAIHIA

### THE CABBAGE TREE

www.thecabbagetree.co.nz
With three outlets in Paihia, the Cabbage Tree has a comprehensive range of New Zealand men's and women's fashion clothing, All Black merchandise, possum-fur products, knitwear, bone and jade carving, wood, jewellery and paintings.
Williams Road and the Maritime Building, Paihia 09-402 7318 Mon–Sat 9–6, Sun 9.30–6

### FULLERS BAY OF ISLANDS

www.fboi.co.nz
Fullers runs ferry services between Paihia and Russell, Opua and Okiato, and catamaran tours around the islands, including the famous Hole in the Rock at Cape Brett. Choose from lunch cruises, swimming with the dolphins, an island stopover, or land tours to Cape Reinga, Russell and Kerikeri.

**Above** *Chocolate by Makana Confections*

Maritime Building, Waterfront, Paihia 09-402 7421 Daily Adult from NZ$77, child from NZ$38.50

### THE ROCK

www.rocktheboat.co.nz
Dubbed 'the backpackers' cruise ship', this 24-hour trip combines sightseeing with activities such as snorkelling and mussel diving, fishing for your dinner, night kayaking, dolphin- and penguin-watching, and island walks. You sleep in dormitories or double cabins. Meals are included.
Corner of Marsden and Williams roads, Paihia 0800 762 527 From NZ$178

### SALT AIR

www.saltair.co.nz
If you want to see a lot in a short time, Salt Air's half-day trip to Cape Reinga combines scenic flights with a 4X4 driving tour. You can also choose from a number of scenic flights around the Bay of Islands by Cessna aircraft or helicopter.
PO Box 293, Paihia 09-402 8338 Daily from 8am From NZ$195

## PAKIRI BEACH

### PAKIRI BEACH HORSE RIDES

www.horseride-nz.co.nz
Horseback-riding on the beach is the speciality here. Choose from a one-hour ride to a seven-day trek, taking in the beach, pine forest and native bush. There are horses to suit

all ages and skill levels, with tuition available. Overnight accommodation is in cabins with farmhouse cooking. ✉ Rahuikiri Road, Pakiri Beach ☎ 09-422 6275 Daily From NZ$50 SH1 to Warkworth, turn right, follow signs to Leigh and Goat Island Marine Reserve. Continue over the hill to Pakiri. At the village turn second right into Rahuikiri Rd

## RUSSELL

### CAPE BRETT WALKWAYS

www.capebrettwalks.co.nz

This gives access to walking tracks on the Cape Brett peninsula on both DoC and Maori Trust land, with spectacular seascapes and forested ridges. Walks take from two hours to two days over easy to moderate terrain, and are suitable for people of all ages as long as you are fit. ✉ PO Box 149, Russell, Bay of Islands ☎ 09-403 8823 From NZ$30 independent, NZ$250 guided

## TUTUKAKA

### DIVE TUTUKAKA

www.diving.co.nz

Diving around the Poor Knights Islands is the main attraction here, with underwater caves, tunnels and archways, and shipwrecks to explore. You can also snorkel, kayak or whale- and dolphin-watch. ✉ Poor Knights Dive Centre, Marina Road, Tutukaka ☎ 09-434 3867 From NZ$130

## WAIHEKE ISLAND

### ANANDA TOURS

www.ananda.co.nz

Visit Waiheke artists in their studios, tour the island's vineyards, do coastal walks (moderate fitness required), or take an eco-tour in Whakanewha Regional Park. Other options include garden tours and overnight stays. ✉ 20 Seaview Road, Ostend, Waiheke Island ☎ 09-372 7530 Daily From NZ$100

### STONYRIDGE VINEYARDS

www.stonyridge.co.nz

Stephen White aims to make the highest quality Cabernet blend in the world. His flagship Larose is one of New Zealand's most sought-after wines, with a price tag to match. Vineyard tours and tastings are held at 11.30am on weekends. Olives are also grown on the estate, and the café serves Mediterranean food. ✉ 80 Onetangi Road, Waiheke Island ☎ 09-372 8822 Sat, Sun 11.30–5 Tours NZ$10

### WAIHEKE WINE CENTRE

This impressive wine store in Oneroa specializes in Waiheke wines. For NZ$15 you can taste four local wines and sample Waiheke olive oil. ✉ 153 Ocean View Road, Oneroa, Waiheke Island ☎ 09-372 6139 NZ$15

## WAIMAUKU

### BEESONLINE HONEY CENTRE AND CAFÉ

www.beesonline.co.nz

A working honey centre with a bee theatre, a range of honey products, tastings, a retail outlet and a café serving indigenous and organic food. ✉ 791 State Highway 16, Waimauku ☎ 09-411 7953 Mon–Fri 9–4, Sat, Sun 9–5

### BUSH AND BEACH

www.bushandbeach.co.nz

Coach tours tailored to fitness and age explore the black-sand beaches and lush native bush within 30km (18 miles) of Auckland. Half-day, full-day and overnight tours are available. ☎ 09–837 4130 Daily From NZ$125

### CORBAN ESTATE ARTS CENTRE

www.ceac.org.nz

Former winery buildings on the original Corban's Wine Estate have been turned into studios for artists and artisans. The Pacific Island community holds regular markets. ✉ 426 Great North Road, Henderson ☎ 09-838 4488/4455 Daily 10–4.30 Free Near the intersection of Lincoln Road and Mount Lebanon Lane

## WAITANGI

### COASTAL KAYAKERS

www.coastalkayakers.co.nz

Choose to explore the outer islands, lagoons, natural rock caves and

**Above** *Galloping on sands at Pakiri Beach*

beaches, or challenge the Haruru Falls on these guided kayaking and canoeing trips, which last from half a day to several days. All equipment and refreshments provided. ✉ Te Karuwha Parade, Ti Bay, Waitangi ☎ 09-402 8105 Daily From NZ$55

### CULTURE NORTH SOUND AND LIGHT SHOW

www.culturenorth.co.nz

This show gives a Maori perspective on events right through from the story of Kupe, the first Maori chief to discover New Zealand, to the signing of New Zealand's founding document and the present day. ✉ Waitangi ☎ 09-402 5990 Oct–end Apr, Mon, Wed, Thu, Sat 7.30pm–9.30pm NZ$55

## WAIWERA

### WAIWERA INFINITY SPA

www.waiwera.co.nz

This complex of 26 indoor and outdoor thermal pools has waterslides for the children, facial and body treatments for adults, spa packages and a fitness centre. ✉ 21 Main Road, Waiwera ☎ 09-427 8800 Daily 9am–10pm Adult NZ$25, child NZ$15, family NZ$60

## WHANGAMATA

### KIWI DUNDEE ADVENTURES

www.kiwidundee.co.nz

Personalized walks and nature tours, from easy day walks to challenging hikes, taking in native bush, beaches and former gold mines. ✉ PO Box 198, Whangamata ☎ 07-865 8809 From NZ$220

# FESTIVALS AND EVENTS

## JANUARY

### ASB CLASSIC AND HEINEKEN OPEN

www.asbbankclassic.co.nz
www.heinekenopen.co.nz
These annual international tennis tournaments are held consecutively over two weeks.
ASB Tennis Centre, 1 Tennis Lane, Parnell, Auckland 09-373 3623

## FEBRUARY

### DEVONPORT FOOD AND WINE FESTIVAL

www.devonportwinefestival.co.nz
This beachside food, wine and music festival in the picturesque village of Devonport has two stages, with non-stop entertainment and 30 stalls of New Zealand's wine and food.
Winsor Reserve, Devonport 09-378 9031 NZ$35 via www.iticket.co.nz and door sales From the Auckland ferry terminal

## FEBRUARY–MARCH

### AUCKLAND FESTIVAL

www.aucklandfestival.co.nz
This biennial arts festival is held over three weeks in venues all over the city. Book through Ticketek, tel 09-307 5000.
PO Box 3787, Shortland Street, Auckland 09-309 0101

## MARCH

### AUCKLAND WINE AND FOOD FESTIVAL

www.aucklandwineandfoodfestival.com
This popular wine and food festival takes place over a weekend in late March. The entry fee includes a tasting glass, free tastings from some of the region's leading wineries and entertainment.
Eastern Viaduct parking area, corner Quay and Hobson streets 09-489 1460 Adult NZ$20, child (5–12) NZ$5

### PASIFIKA

www.aucklandcity.govt.nz
This annual one-day festival is New Zealand's largest Pacific Island celebration, with contemporary arts and music, traditional food, craft and cultural performances. Parking is limited, but public transport goes to the venue.
Western Springs Lakeside and Stadium, Great North Road, Auckland 09-379 2020 Free Bus 045 from Downtown

## EASTER

### ROYAL EASTER SHOW

www.royaleastershow.co.nz
As well as the traditional agricultural competitions such as sheep shearing, dog trials and equestrian events, there are carnival rides, children's stage shows and Farmworld 'petting pens'. At the same venue are artworks from the Royal Easter Show Art Awards.
ASB Showgrounds, 217 Greenlane West, Epsom, Auckland 09-623 7728 Adult NZ$15, child (2–12) NZ$5, family NZ$30 Buses 302–312, 327–359 from Midtown Exit Southern Motorway at Greenlane (exit 433)

### WAIHEKE ISLAND OF JAZZ

www.waihekejazz.co.nz
Concerts featuring local and international performers are held over five days at pubs, cafés and vineyards around Waiheke Island, linked by a shuttle bus. Book your accommodation well ahead.
PO Box 170, Oneroa, Waiheke Island 09-372 5301 From the Auckland ferry terminal

## SEPTEMBER

### AIR NEW ZEALAND FASHION WEEK 2004

www.nzfashionweek.com
This is aimed at fashion buyers and the media, but the public can get close with shows such as ANZFW 4 U public access day (tickets available through Ticketek, tel 09-307 5000), and big-screen coverage of the event at Viaduct bars.
PO Box 147240, Auckland
09-377 8033

## NOVEMBER

### ELLERSLIE INTERNATIONAL FLOWER SHOW

www.ellerslieflowershow.co.nz
The largest flower show in the southern hemisphere, Ellerslie showcases New Zealand horticulture, landscape design and garden art, with food, wine and entertainment.
Auckland Regional Botanic Gardens, Manukau City 09-579 6260 Adult NZ$28, child (5–14) NZ$4 Manukau Station and shuttle bus Exit the Southern Motorway (SH1) at Manukau (exit 433) and follow signs

## NOVEMBER–DECEMBER

### POHUTUKAWA FESTIVAL

www.pohutukawafest.com
Timed to coincide with the flowering of the 'New Zealand Christmas tree', this 17-day festival is an umbrella for many different events in the area, including swimming and diving competitions, an adventure run, outdoor expo, food and wine festival and jazz brunch.
PO Box 592, Thames, Coromandel Peninsula 07-867 9077 Reservations at Ticketek, tel 09-307 5000, www.ticketek.co.nz

**Below** *The country's wine is celebrated at Devonport and Auckland festivals*

# EATING

## PRICES AND SYMBOLS

The restaurants are listed alphabetically. The prices given are the average for a two-course lunch (L) and a three-course dinner (D) for one person, without drinks. The wine price (W) is for the least expensive bottle. All the restaurants listed accept credit cards unless otherwise stated.

For a key to the symbols, ▷ 2.

## AUCKLAND

### KERMADEC

www.kermadec.co.nz

This seafood complex in the Viaduct Basin combines a casual brasserie and bar with a classy restaurant. You can order Japanese or modern New Zealand dishes such as seared snapper on corn risotto and chervil beurre blanc.

✉ Viaduct Quay, Auckland ☎ 09-309 0412 ⌚ Brasserie daily 10–late; restaurant Mon–Fri 6–late ✋ Brasserie L NZ$45, D NZ$55, W NZ$29; restaurant D NZ$70, W NZ$36

### LAVA

www.lavanz.co.nz

Opposite the beach, with great views over the harbour, Lava is known for its modern New Zealand food, such as lamb rump with goat's cheese and thyme crust served on kumara and pine nut risotto.

✉ 425 Tamaki Drive, St. Heliers, Auckland ☎ 09-575 9969 ⌚ Mon–Fri 11.30am–late, Sat, Sun 10am–late ✋ L NZ$30, D NZ$60, W NZ$34

### OH CALCUTTA

www.ohcalcutta.co.nz

Oh Calcutta's dishes are a mixture of northern and southern Indian. Seafood marinated, skewered and smoke-roasted in the tandoor is a speciality. A bustling place popular with expatriate Indians and families, it has indoor and outdoor seating.

✉ 151 Parnell Road, Parnell, Auckland ☎ 09-377 9090 ⌚ Daily 5.30–11.30, also Wed–Fri 12–2 ✋ L NZ$30, D NZ$40, W NZ$29

### ORBIT AND THE OBSERVATORY

www.skycityauckland.co.nz

Up the Sky Tower, the Orbit à la carte restaurant serves modern New Zealand brasserie food, such as cold-smoked Akaroa salmon with salsa verde. Reservations are required. The Observatory, above the main level, serves buffets at a fixed price.

✉ Sky Tower, corner of Victoria and Federal streets, Auckland ☎ 09-363 6000 ⌚ Daily 5.30–9.30; also Orbit Mon–Fri 11.30–2.30, Sat, Sun 10–3; Observatory Fri–Sun 12–2 ✋ Orbit L NZ$45, D NZ$53, W NZ$32; Observatory L NZ$39.50, D NZ$59, W NZ$32

### SOUL BAR AND BISTRO

www.soulsearch.co.nz

Strong on seafood, the menu is a blend of Mediterranean and Eastern cooking. Dishes include tuna tartar with black sesame seeds, tempura soft shell crab and squid ink mayonnaise, and pan fried snapper, sautéed chorizo and squid with saffron potatoes.

✉ Viaduct Harbour, Auckland ☎ 09-356 7249 ⌚ Mon–Fri 11am–late, Sat, Sun 10am–late ✋ L NZ$55, D NZ$70, W NZ$39

### WHITE

www.whiterestaurant.co.nz

For views, classy atmosphere, food and service, White is hard to beat. Surrounded on three sides by the sea, it serves the best of local seafood and regional produce in a modern style. The wine list is vast. It is within the Hilton Hotel, ▷ 96.

✉ Hilton Hotel, Princes Wharf, 147 Quay Street, Auckland ☎ 09-978 2000 ⌚ Mon–Fri 6.30am–10.30am, 12–3, 6pm–11pm, Sat, Sun 11–3 ✋ L NZ$39, D NZ$80, W NZ$60

**Above** *The revolving Sky Tower restaurant*

## COLVILLE

### COLVILLE GENERAL STORE AND CAFF

This classic Kiwi rural store has a café attached and is the daytime hub of social contact in these parts. It has the usual café fare, including cakes, pastries, pies and coffee.

✉ Main Road, Colville, Coromandel Peninsula ☎ 07-866 6805 ⌚ Daily 9.30–4, also Fri–Sun 6–8pm From NZ$6

## COROMANDEL TOWN

### PEPPER TREE

www.coromandeltown.co.nz

Pepper Tree is a community meeting place, with a big-screen TV and music jam sessions. The menus focus on oysters, mussels, snapper, smoked fish and crayfish. You can also get hearty country fare. On summer evenings book in advance.

✉ 31 Kapanga Road, Coromandel Town ☎ 07-866 8211 ⌚ Daily 10–9 L NZ$35, D NZ$50, W NZ$25

## KERIKERI

### MARSDEN ESTATE

www.marsdenestate.co.nz

Beside a lake among the vines, the menu includes dishes such as black pudding with blue cheese, pear and blueberry sauce. Dishes are designed to complement the wines.

✉ Wiroa Road, Kerikeri ☎ 09-407 9398 ⌚ Aug–end May daily 10–5; Jun, Jul daily 10–4 L NZ$25, W NZ$19.50

## MATAKANA

### OAK GRILL BISTRO

www.ascensionvineyard.co.nz

The house speciality is dishes prepared over a grill fuelled by French oak barrel shavings. Ascension wines are served. The restaurant regularly hosts live music.

✉ 480 Matakana Road, Matakana ☎ 09-422 9601 ⌚ Mon–Fri 11–4, Sat, Sun 11–9 L NZ$40, D NZ$55, W NZ$25

## PAIHIA

### ONLY SEAFOOD

Located on the waterfront above its companion restaurant Bistro 40, you get a fine view across the bay. Game fish is typically served seared in a light soy sauce. Other dishes include chargrilled hapuka, scallops and local Orongo Bay oysters.

✉ 40 Marsden Road, Paihia ☎ 09-402 6066 ⌚ Daily from 5pm Main and veg NZ$30

## POKENO

### HOTEL DU VIN

www.hotelduvin.co.nz

This restaurant is part of a luxury retreat at Firstland Vineyard, with dishes such as roasted quail stuffed with apple and fennel, wrapped in bacon and parsnip purée with pistachio and pomegranate relish and cider jus. On Sundays you can combine a three-course lunch (NZ$45) with use of the hotel's leisure facilities. Reserve in advance.

✉ Lyons Road, Mangatawhiri Valley, Pokeno ☎ 09-233 6314 ⌚ Mon–Sat 12–2.30, 6–9.30, Sun 11.30–2.30, 6–9.30 L NZ$55, D NZ$70, W NZ$49

## RAWENE

### BOATSHED CAFÉ

A welcome refreshment stop before or after the ferry crossing, the Boatshed Café serves a varied selection of snacks and good coffee, with views of Hokianga Harbour.

✉ Clendon Esplanade, Rawene ☎ 09-405 7728 ⌚ Daily 8.30–4, closed mid-Sep to mid-Oct L from NZ$10

## RUSSELL

### DUKE OF MARLBOROUGH

www.theduke.co.nz

It's hard to think of a more romantic place to dine than this old waterfront hotel. You can order local fish and seafood, including Orongo Bay oysters, but the menu is also strong on chargrills and game.

✉ Duke of Marlborough Hotel, The Waterfront, Russell ☎ 09-403 7829 ⌚ Daily 7.30am–9pm L NZ$50, D NZ$63, W NZ$30

## WAIHEKE ISLAND

### MUDBRICK RESTAURANT

www.mudbrick.co.nz

The earth-brick restaurant and winery is in a spectacular location. The food has a Mediterranean theme, with Waiheke Pacific oysters, home-baked foccacia, and dishes such as saffron and spinach ravioli, set off by local wines. Advance booking is essential.

✉ Church Bay Road, Oneroa, Waiheke Island ☎ 09-372 9050 ⌚ Daily 11–5, 6–late L NZ$52, D NZ$75, W NZ$41

## WAITANGI

### WAIKOKOPU CAFÉ

www.waitangi.net.nz

This attractive café overlooks a bush walk and pond, and the coastline. You can choose from snacks or dishes such as corn and coriander fritters served with guacamole, sour cream and tomato salsa.

✉ Treaty Grounds, Waitangi ☎ 09-402 6275 ⌚ Daily 9–5 L NZ$20, W NZ$22

## WHANGAREI

### A DECO

www.a-deco.co.nz

The signature dish here is braised oxtail and wild mushroom tart with porcini polenta and Parmesan crumble, but the menu ranges widely, from chilled mushroom soup to pina colada crème brulée.

✉ 70 Kamo Road, Kensington, Whangarei ☎ 09-459 4957 ⌚ Tue, Sat 6–late, Wed–Fri 11–2.30, 6–late L NZ$25, D NZ$50, W NZ$28

## WHENUAKITE

### COLENSO COUNTRY CAFÉ & SHOP

Surrounded by herb gardens, you can sit on a shady veranda or indoors. The food is simple but good home baking. Freshly squeezed juice from the café's organic orchard is a treat.

✉ Main Road, Whenuakite, Coromandel Peninsula ☎ 07-866 3725 ⌚ Sep–end Jul daily 10–5 L NZ$30, W NZ$25

## WHITIANGA

### THE FIRE PLACE

www.thefireplace-restaurant.com

The food follows the fireplace theme, with pizza from the wood-fired oven. Book ahead, or be prepared for a long wait.

✉ 9 The Esplanade, Whitianga, Coromandel Peninsula ☎ 07-866 4828 ⌚ Daily 5pm–9.30pm (also 11am–2pm in summer) L NZ$40, D NZ$60, W NZ$30

**PRICES AND SYMBOLS**

The prices are the lowest and highest for a double room for one night including breakfast, unless otherwise stated. All the hotels listed accept credit cards unless otherwise stated. Note that rates can vary widely throughout the year.

For a key to the symbols, ▷ 2.

## AUCKLAND

### AACHEN HOUSE BOUTIQUE HOTEL

www.aachenhouse.co.nz

Aachen House is a five-star luxury B&B hotel in the chic suburb of Remuera. The grand 1904 house is superbly furnished with antiques and porcelain. Guest rooms look out on tranquil gardens and are decorated in period style, with king-size or twin beds.

39 Market Road, Remuera, Auckland 09-520 2329 NZ$310–NZ$590, including pre-dinner drinks 5 rooms, 3 suites Take Market Road exit (exit 432) signposted from SH1 Southern Motorway

### CITY CENTRAL HOTEL

www.citycentralhotel.co.nz

A no-nonsense hotel, the City Central is well placed, clean and comfortable. Some rooms sleep up to five people, but all have TV, tea-making facilities and telephone. The standard rooms are very small.

Corner of Wellesley and Albert streets, Auckland 09-307 3388 NZ$99–NZ$160, excluding breakfast 104 rooms (25 non-smoking) Except standard rooms

### ESPLANADE HOTEL

www.esplanadehotel.co.nz

This boutique hotel is one of Auckland's oldest, built in 1903. It has fine harbour views. Rooms are spacious, with tea-making facilities. A penthouse apartment has two bedrooms, two bathrooms, a lounge and fully equipped kitchen. The restaurant and the Mecca café both serve meals throughout the day.

1 Victoria Road, Devonport, Auckland 09-445 1291 NZ$350–NZ$840 15 rooms, 2 suites, 1 apartment On main bus route from Takapuna Ferries (10 min) half-hourly from Auckland

### GREAT PONSONBY BED AND BREAKFAST

www.greatpons.co.nz

The Great Ponsonby is a stylish, century-old villa in a quiet cul-de-sac, a short stroll away from 'funky' Ponsonby Road. Brightly decorated rooms and self-contained studios are equipped with phones, modems, coffee plungers, CD players, irons and de-mist mirrors—among other thoughtful touches. Bicycles, laundry facilities and beach towels are available on request.

30 Ponsonby Terrace, Ponsonby, Auckland 09-376 5989 NZ$220–NZ$380 5 rooms, 6 studios, 1 penthouse Near main bus route from CBD

### HILTON HOTEL

www.hilton.com

The Hilton occupies a wharf in the harbour close to the heart of the city. The accommodation is first class, with contemporary furniture and spacious bathrooms. Rooms have king-size or twin beds, private decks and internet access. Luxury suites have 180-degree views. There are also serviced apartments, a stylish restaurant, White (▷ 94), a cocktail bar, fitness facility and shops. Breakfast costs NZ$25–NZ$35.

Princes Wharf, 147 Quay Street, Auckland 09-978 2000 NZ$480–NZ$1,210 160 rooms, 6 suites, 35 apartments Outdoor

**Above** *The Esplanade Hotel in Auckland*

## COROMANDEL TOWN

### COROMANDEL HOLIDAY PARK

www.coromandelholidaypark.co.nz

Coromandel Holiday Park is set in parkland, five minutes' walk from the town. You can camp in a tent or caravan, or stay in a basic cabin or in a motel room. Facilities include barbecues, a playground, trampolines and a games room.

636 Rings Road, Coromandel 07-866 8830 Tent sites from NZ$26, powered sites NZ$26, cabins NZ$55, motel units NZ$75 40 tent sites, 26 powered sites, 10 cabins, 6 motel units Outdoor

### KARAMANA HOMESTEAD

www.karamanahomestead.com

One of the oldest homes on the Coromandel Peninsula, dating from 1872, Karamana has three guest rooms, named French, Victorian and Colonial and furnished accordingly. There is also a two-bedroom cottage. Devonshire teas are a speciality. Breakfast includes fresh fruit and pancakes.

84 Whangapoua Road, Coromandel Town 07-866 7138 NZ$175–NZ$225 3 rooms, 1 cottage

## GREAT BARRIER ISLAND

### OASIS LODGE

www.barrieroasis.co.nz

Set in a vineyard, this homestead offers spacious, open-plan rooms with modern décor, TV and video, a bar and fridge, and outdoor decks. There is also a self-contained chalet sleeping up to six. Diving, fishing, kayaking and horse-riding are available close by. A small restaurant serves international dishes.

Tryphena, Great Barrier Island 09-429 0021 NZ$270 3 rooms, 1 chalet Ferry (4.5 hours) from Auckland

## HAHEI

### THE CHURCH ACCOMMODATION

www.thechurchhahei.co.nz

This former village church has been turned into a restaurant. Accommodation is in separate studio units or self-contained cottages, all with french doors leading onto verandas. Studios and cottages have a queen-size bed and window-seat bed, refrigerator and tea-making facilities. Self-contained cottages also have a separate living area and kitchen; two have an open fire.

87 Beach Road, Hahei, Coromandel Peninsula 07-866 3533 Closed Aug NZ$105–NZ$175; additional adults NZ$20 extra 4 studio units, 11 cottages 37km (23 miles) southeast of Whitianga: turn off SH 25 at Whenuakite. No public transport

## KERIKERI

### THE SUMMER HOUSE BED AND BREAKFAST

www.thesummerhouse.co.nz

Subtropical gardens and a citrus orchard add to the appeal of this popular B&B. The two rooms have antique beds, while the self-contained suite is contemporary in style, with a South Pacific theme, including Maori weavings.

424 Kerikeri Road, Kerikeri 09-407 4294 NZ$240–NZ$240 2 rooms, 1 suite 2km (1 mile) off State Highway 10 on Kerikeri Road. Airport pick-up available

## MANGONUI

### CARNEVAL

www.carneval.co.nz

This modern B&B is on a hill overlooking Doubtless Bay. The rooms, with king-size beds, refrigerators, ironing and tea-making facilities, and private bathrooms, have either garden or ocean views. A sauna and log-burning fire add to the appeal.

360 State Highway 10, Cable Bay, Mangonui 09-406 1012 NZ$150–NZ$190 2 suites Just after Mangonui on SH10

## OHAEAWAI

### LUDBROOK HOUSE

www.ludbrook.co.nz

The Ludbrook family welcomes visitors for dinner and B&B at the 1920s homestead. Decorated in period style, Ludbrook House has four simple but comfortable guest rooms with private bathrooms.

State Highway 1, Ohaeawai 09-405 9846 NZ$500–NZ$760 4 rooms On SH1 near the junction with SH12

## PAIHIA

### COPTHORNE HOTEL AND RESORT BAY OF ISLANDS

www.millenniumhotels.co.nz

Right on the waterfront, within the Waitangi National Reserve, this hotel has modern rooms with standard facilities. There is an in-house café restaurant serving Pacific Rim food. The hotel is well set up for children.

Tau Henare Drive, Paihia 09-402 7411 NZ$144–NZ$530 102 rooms (88 non-smoking), 7 suites 2km (1 mile) past Paihia town centre. Follow signs on Marsden Road to the Waitangi Reserve; hotel is immediately right after the bridge

## PUKENUI

### PUKENUI LODGE

www.pukenuilodge.co.nz

Overlooking Houhora Harbour, Pukenui Lodge has tidy, self-contained motel units with their own kitchen and bathroom.

Corner of Main Highway North and Wharf Road, Pukenui 09-409 8837 NZ$94–NZ$121, excluding breakfast (NZ$8.50) 9 motel units, hostel Outdoor

## RUSSELL

### PUKEMATU LODGE

www.pukematulodge.co.nz

Perched on the hill, this B&B has spectacular views to Waitangi and Paihia. The stylish suites have fresh flowers, robes, fruit and organic bathroom products. Breakfast is served on the deck. Evening meals are available on request.

Flagstaff Hill, Russell 09-403 8500 NZ$295 2 suites 10km (6 miles) from Opua vehicle ferry and 1km (0.5 miles) from the middle of Russell

## WAIHEKE ISLAND

### ONETANGI BEACH APARTMENTS

www.onetangi.co.nz

On the 2km-long (1-mile) Onetangi Beach, close to all facilities, the complex has spa pools and a sauna, and kayaks are available. There are studios and beachfront and courtyard options.

27 The Strand, Onetangi 09-372 0003/0800-663 826 NZ$120–NZ$370 8 units Ferry from Auckland

# CENTRAL NORTH ISLAND

One of the most remarkable parts of the country, this region has been shaped by natural cataclysm. Much of this area sits on top of the Taupo Volcanic Zone, and the evidence of its power is all around. Its centrepiece is the city of Rotorua, one of the most popular visitor attractions in the country, a hissing, spurting, gushing, thermal wonderland, where bubbling mud pools, steam vents and sulphurous smells intrude into the very heart of the city. Rotorua also has a prominent Maori community. This is an ideal place to take a Maori-guided tour and to sample a *hangi*, a traditional feast cooked in an earth oven, followed by a Maori concert.

A one-hour drive south, Lake Taupo is a giant crater lake, formed by one of the largest volcanic eruptions that the world has ever seen. Today, the lake and the rivers that feed it are renowned for their trout fishing. This is one of the few places in New Zealand open for fishing all year round.

South of Lake Taupo is Tongariro National Park, home to volcanic peaks that still belch fire and brimstone, surrounded by a scorched, eerie, lunar landscape that became the backdrop for Mordor in the *Lord of the Rings* films.

The east coast city of Napier was almost completely destroyed by an earthquake in 1931, and rebuilt in the art deco style that was in vogue at the time. Napier is also the centre of the Hawkes Bay winegrowing region, source of some of New Zealand's finest Chardonnays, Cabernet Sauvignon and Merlot wines.

## CAPE KIDNAPPERS

This remote and jagged white peninsula marks the southern boundary of Hawke's Bay. Its name recalls the 'rescue' in 1769 of a young Tahitian servant on Captain Cook's ship by local Maori, who mistakenly believed he was being held captive.

In summer up to 15,000 gannets gather here to breed, forming New Zealand's biggest mainland colony (visits Oct–late Apr). An 8km (5-mile) walk leads to the colony from Clifton Motorcamp, but since tides restrict the access times it's best to join one of the many available tours.

301 M8 100 Marine Parade, Napier 06-834 1911 Cape Shuttle between Napier and Clifton or Te Awanga; subject to season and tides

## EAST CAPE

Most of the wild East Cape—the heel of New Zealand's upturned boot—is sparsely populated and mountainous, and much of the Raukumara mountain range, which dominates the interior, remains impenetrable by road. Early European settlers here were few, and the population remains predominantly Maori.

The 343km (213-mile) Pacific Coast Highway (SH35) follows the coast from Opotiki around the mouth of the Motu River and passes near Potala, at the northern edge of the East Cape. It continues to Hicks Bay, which has a wild surf beach and is a popular viewing point for the planet's earliest sunrise. Look out here for the Tuwhakairiora Marae (1870), one of the grandest meeting houses in the area. A beautiful stretch of road passes beaches and rivers on its way to East Cape lighthouse and the North Island's most easterly point.

On the more populous, east side of the cape, a turn-off before the Mata River crossing leads to 1,752m (5,748ft) Mount Hikurangi, the North Island's highest non-volcanic mountain. The mountain is sacred in Maori myth, as the first point of land to appear when Maui fished the North Island from the sea—a statue depicting Maui's canoe faces the rising sun today.

The road continues to Tolaga Bay—a coastal town with a wharf that is 660m (720 yards) long—to Gisborne. At the tiny junction settlement of Nuhaka, south of Gisborne, a scenic coastal road leaves SH2 towards the barren, windswept Mahia Peninsula, which marks the boundary between the Pacific and Hawke's Bay.

301 P6 District Council Building, Te Puia 06-864 6853. See also Gisborne, below; Opotiki ▷ 105 Opotiki and Gisborne; services between Hick's Bay and Whakatane or Gisborne Mon–Sat Gisborne airport 2km (1 mile) west of town

## GISBORNE

www.gisbornenz.com

This small city is set in an area of fertile land, with fruit growing and vineyards its main staples—it labels itself the Chardonnay capital of the country. Gisborne was the first place that Captain Cook set foot in on his return to New Zealand in 1769, before retreating from hostile Maori. Cook's Landing Site (marked by a statue of the explorer) and National Historic Reserve are next to the main port and the base of Titirangi (Kaiti Hill). To the west is Te Poho-O-Rawiri Marae (1930), one of the largest carved meeting houses in the country.

A statue standing on the southern bank of the Turanganui River commemorates Captain Cook's cabin boy, Nicholas Young, who was the first member of the crew to sight land in 1769 and gave his name to the promontory Young Nicks Head, which forms the southern edge of Poverty Bay.

The Tairawhiti Museum on Stout Street (Mon–Sat 10–4, Sun 1.30–4) has regional displays. In the adjacent Te Moana Maritime Museum is the restored wheelhouse of *The Star of Canada*, which foundered at the base of Kaiti Beach in 1912.

301 N7 209 Grey Street 06-868 6139 Grey Street

## HAMILTON

www.hamiltoncity.co.nz
www.visithamilton.co.nz

New Zealand's fourth largest city grew out of an 1864 military settlement on the Waikato River. Garden Place lies on Victoria Street, at the heart of the downtown area, which was modernized in the 1990s.

The Waikato Museum (daily 10–4.30) overlooks the river on the corner of Victoria and Grantham streets and contains an impressive collection of Maori treasures, including the exquisitely decorated war canoe *Te Winika*, presented to the museum in 1973 by Te Arikinui Dame Te Atairangikaahu, the late Maori Queen.

South of the city are the 58ha (143-acre) Hamilton Gardens (daily 7.30am–sunset), a conglomerate of Japanese, Chinese and English flower gardens. Hamilton Zoo (daily 9–5, extended hours Jan), 8km (5 miles) away on SH23, mixes native New Zealand species with others important to international conservation breeding projects, and has a vast walk-through, free-flight aviary.

300 K5 Transport Centre, corner of Bryce and Anglesea streets 07-839 3580 Transport Centre Fraser Sreet, Frankton Airport 15km (9 miles) south of city

**Opposite** *An Italian Renaissance setting in Hamilton Gardens*

**Below** *Remote Cape Kidnappers*

**INFORMATION**

www.hawkesbay.com

301 M8 Central Hawke's Bay Visitor Information Office, Railway Esplanade, Waipukurau 06-858 6488 Mon–Fri 9–5, Sat 9–1 Services link all main towns and suburbs

**TIPS**

» The Hawke's Bay Wine Trail is outlined in the free leaflet of the same name, and gives details of each vineyard's facilities.

» Tours with exclusive access to the 252m (827ft) summit of Taumata's hill are available through Airlie Mount Farm Walks (tel 06-858 7601).

## HAWKE'S BAY

Bleached cliffs embrace this scenic bay on the east coast between Havelock North and the Mahia Peninsula. Its fertile soils prompted early European settlers to plant vines, using the wine primarily for religious services; the Catholic Society founded its Mission in Taradale in 1851 and since then the wine industry has boomed, with its capital at Napier (▷ 106–107). Hawke's Bay's diverse 'sub regions'—such as Bay View and the Esk Valley—produce a wide range of wines, and there are more than 25 vineyards in all, most offering sales and tastings. Some have additional attractions—notable architecture, for instance, or fine restaurants and cafés. Chardonnay and Cabernet Sauvignon are two of the region's top wines (for wine tours contact Napier's visitor information office).

### ALONG SH2

South of the wine region, SH2 winds its lonely way through the little-visited but stunning region of the Wairarapa (▷ 141), before arriving in Wellington (▷ 144–149). On SH2 there are a number of small towns including Waipawa, Waipukurau, Dannevirke and Norsewood (the last two having strong Scandinavian links). Activities available in the area include ballooning and hiking (▷ 126–131). The wild Kaweka and Ruahine Ranges are good for tramping, but you should plan carefully and go well prepared. The Department of Conservation at 59 Marine Parade, Napier (Mon–Fri 9–4.15) has all the necessary information.

### A CURIOSITY

There is one other place worth visiting (if only for the novelty value) on a minor route into the back country. The point of this diversion is to see an unremarkable hill called Taumatawhakatangihangakoauauotamateaturipukaka-pikimaungahoronukupokaiwhenuakitanatahu, and a sign declares this 85-letter place name the longest in the world. Roughly translated, it means 'the place where Taumata (known as Land Eater), the man with the big knees, who slid, climbed and swallowed mountains, played his flute to his loved one'. To reach the hill from Waipukurau, take the coast road towards Porangahau. After about 40km (25 miles) turn right and follow the AA Historic Place sign.

**Below** *There is plenty to do and see in the varied scenery around Hawke's Bay*

## HASTINGS

www.hastings.co.nz

Hastings is a lively agricultural town 20km (12 miles) south of Napier (▷ 106–107), lined with hanging baskets during the summer flower festival. Like Napier, Hastings was devastated by the earthquake of 1931. In rebuilding the town the architects echoed Napier's art deco and Spanish Mission styles, the best examples of which are the Westerman's Building on Russell Street and the Municipal Theatre on Hastings Street. The art deco clock tower in the middle of town was built in 1935 to house the bells from the Post Office tower, which collapsed in the quake.

301 L8 · Westerman's Building, corner of Russell and Heretaunga streets · 06-873 0080 · Weekday services from Napier

## HAVELOCK NORTH

Vineyards and orchards surround this prosperous village, which sits in the shadow of the 399m (1,309ft) Te Mata Peak. There are tremendous views from the top of the peak.

Arataki Honey Ltd, on Arataki Road (daily 9–5), is one of the largest beekeeping enterprises in the southern hemisphere, with a staggering 17,000 hives and 40,000 very busy bees.

301 M8

## HAWERA

Hawera is the largest of the south Taranaki townships, near the coast at the junction of SH45 and SH3. Its most obvious landmark is the water tower, built in 1914 at the request of insurance underwriters who were dismayed at the town's propensity to catch fire, which it did in 1884, 1895 and 1912. The Historic Hawera heritage trail leaflet, available at the visitor office, details other major buildings in the town.

Realistic life-size wax exhibits and scale models to depict Taranaki's past are made on site and shown at the privately owned Tawhiti Museum, on Ohangai Road (Boxing Day–end Jan daily 10–4; Feb–end May, Sep–end Dec Fri–Sun 10–4; Jun–end Aug Sun 10–4). A narrow gauge railway runs on the first Sunday of each month, bringing to life the history of logging in the area.

Equally unusual is the Elvis Presley Memorial Record Room, at 51 Argyle Street (call for an appointment, tel 06-278 7624), where avid collector and fan Kevin Wasley has amassed memorabilia and approximately 2,000 of the King's records.

300 J8 · 55 High Street · 06-278 8599 · Daily from Wellington and New Plymouth

**Above** *Sunset bathes the hills around Te Mata Peak in scarlet*

## KAWHIA

www.kawhia.co.nz

Outside the summer, when the population almost trebles, Kawhia (pronounced Kafia) is a sleepy village southwest of Hamilton on the shores of Kawhia Harbour. Most of its points of interest are on the shoreline, extending around to the port entrance and Ocean Beach. This is the most popular beach, best reached through the Tainui Kawhia Forest Track, southwest of central Kawhia.

At the Te Puia Hot Springs on Ocean Beach you can dig your own spa bath, but it's difficult to know exactly where to start unless you join a local tour.

When the Tainui people first landed here some 750 years ago they tied their canoe to a pohutukawa tree and named it Tangi-te-Korowhiti. The tree (unmarked) is one of a small grove at the northern end of Kaora Street, and the canoe's burial site is marked with two stones, Hani and Puna, behind the Maketu *marae*, about 500m (545 yards) south of the landing site (ask for permission to view the site at the *marae*).

300 J6 · Kawhia Regional Museum and Gallery · 07-871 0161

## MATAMATA

Large ranches and farmsteads sprawl over this fertile agricultural landscape, which was never a visitor hotspot—until the *Lord of the Rings* movie trilogy came along. A plot of private farmland near Matamata was transformed into the village of Hobbiton (daily tours from visitor office 9.30, 10.45, 12, 1.15, 2.30, 3.45). Director Peter Jackson was obliged to clear away all traces of his sets, including this one, so other than a hobbit hole with a plywood frontage the only real attraction is the spectacular view across the Kaimai Ranges.

East of the town on Tower Road, Firth Tower is the main focus of the district's local history museum (Thu–Mon 10–4).

300 K6 · 45 Broadway · 07-888 7260 · Broadway

## MOUNT EGMONT NATIONAL PARK

www.taranakinz.org.nz

At the heart of Mount Egmont National Park is a 2,518m (8,261ft), beautifully symmetrical dormant volcano with two names: Taranaki, the original Maori name, and Egmont, the name given by Captain Cook in 1770. It was formed by numerous eruptions over 12,000 years—most recently about 350 years ago. Experts believe another may be due any time. The mountain vegetation is called 'goblin forest' due to its diminutive appearance at higher altitudes.

There are 140km (87 miles) of walks in the park, with a duration ranging from 30 minutes to four days. Many people have lost their lives here: in winter the slopes are covered in snow and ice, so climbing boots, crampons and an ice axe are essential. Even in summer crampons are advised on the summit. Visitor offices here and in New Plymouth can advise on routes, hut stays and weather.

300 H8 16km (10 miles) from North Egmont Village, end of Egmont Road 06-756 0990 Shuttle services from New Plymouth

## MOUNT MAUNGANUI

Dominated by its namesake mountain and graced by golden beaches, the town of Mount Maunganui, 6km (4 miles) north of Tauranga, is inundated with sunbathers every summer. The Hot Salt Water Pools, on Adams Avenue (Mon–Sat 6am–10pm, Sun 8am–10pm), are a popular attraction.

A network of pathways criss-crosses the mountain's wooded slopes, once an important Maori refuge and defensive site. The summit climb, best started south of the motor camp, takes about 45 minutes one-way. From the narrow neck of the Mount, Ocean Beach begins a stretch of sand that sweeps east around the Bay of Plenty. Just offshore are two small islands: Moturiki, noted for fishing, and Motuotau, important for its wildlife.

**Above** *A walkway spans the steaming silica terraces at Orakei Korako Thermal Reserve on the shores of Lake Ohakuri*

301 L5 Salisbury Avenue 07-575 5099 Services from Tauranga

## NAPIER

▷ 106–107.

## NEW PLYMOUTH

www.newplymouthnz.com

Prosperous New Plymouth, the main population hub of the Taranaki region, is a good base for exploring Mount Egmont National Park. It has an excellent modern art gallery, the Govett-Brewster Gallery, at the corner of Queen and King streets (daily 10.30–5). Puke Ariki, on Ariki Street (Mon–Fri 9–6, Sat, Sun 9–5), has a collection of Maori items, and includes Richmond Cottage (daily 11–3.30), on Ariki Street, a colonial cottage of 1853.

Other notable sites include the oldest stone church in the country, St. Mary's, on Vivian Street, built in 1846, and the Pou Tutaki (Fitzroy Pole), on the corner of Devon Street East and Smart Road, erected by Maori in 1844 to commemorate Governor Fitzroy's clamp-down on settler acquisitions. The 45m (148ft) Wind Wand, created for the 2000 millennium celebrations on the waterfront by local artist Len Lye, sways gently in the breeze, and lights up at night.

New Plymouth is famous for its parks and gardens, the oldest and finest of which are Pukekura and Brooklands, best reached at Fillis Street, south of the heart of town. Pukekura, opened in 1876, is a well-maintained tract of lakes and gardens, and nearby Brooklands has an outdoor amphitheatre, ponds and gardens, and a historic colonial hospital museum/gallery.

Boats sail from West Quay to the volcanic Sugar Loaf Island's Marine Park, near the port and power station, home to fur seals and seabirds. The shore is part of a 7km (4-mile) Coastal Walkway, culminating in a strenuous climb up Paritutu Rock, which involves pulling yourself up by a cable.

300 H7 Puke Ariki Museum and Library 06-759 6080 Corner of Queen and King streets 10km (6 miles) north of town

## NGARUAWAHIA

The Maori capital of New Zealand, set at the confluence of the Waipa and the mighty Waikato, 19km (12 miles) north of Hamilton, is home of the Maori King, Tuheitia Paki, and of one of the country's most significant *marae*, Turangawaewae. The *marae*, on River Road, is open just once a year, in March during the annual regatta, when *waka* (war canoes) are raced on the river. The Mahinarangi House, built in 1929, is beautifully carved both inside and out. Next door is the King's official residence.

300 K5 Pharos Corner

## OPOTIKI

www.opotiki.co.nz

Opotiki, 60km (37 miles) east of Whakatane on the Bay of Plenty, near the mouths of the Waioeka and Otara rivers, is a small town with fine beaches. It was once the base of the Hauhau—a revivalist sect of Maori rebels who were fierce enemies of the early Pakeha.

The Hukutaia Domain, signed about 6km (4 miles) from town, is 1ha (2.5 acres) of bush with many native trees, including a sacred 2,000-year-old puriri tree called Taketakerau, with a girth of about 22m (72ft) and standing over 23m (75ft) high. Its hollow was used by the local *iwi* to store the bones of their dead. The Church of Hinoa (St. Stephen's Anglican Church, 1864), at the north end of Church Street, was built for the Church Missionary Society and the Lutheran missionary Karl Volkner, who was suspected of being a government spy and beheaded by Hauhau emissaries in 1865.

301 M6 · Corner of St. John and Elliot streets · 07-315 3031 · Hot Bread Shop, 43 St. John Street

## ORAKEI KORAKO THERMAL RESERVE

www.orakeikorako.co.nz

One of the best thermal parks in the country occupies a tranquil lakeside spot behind the Ohakuri Dam. Jet-boats carry visitors across the Waikato River to the colourful algae-covered silica terraces, boiling pools, geysers and bubbling mud. There's also the subterranean Ruatapu Cave to explore, with the warm Waiwhakaata pool (pool of mirrors) at its 40m (131ft) base, where it's said your wishes will come true if you dip your hand in the water. Look for silver ferns—the national emblem of New Zealand—in the surrounding bush and scrub.

300 L6 · 494 Orakei Korako Road, 40km (25 miles) north of Taupo · 07-378 3131 · Daily from 8am; last boat leaves 4.30pm Nov–end Mar, 4pm Apr–end Oct · Adult NZ$31, child (16 and under) NZ$12 · Shuttle from Taupo

## OTOROHANGA

www.otorohanga.co.nz

This small town is the main point of access to the Waitomo caves (▷ 116–117) and the site of the Otorohanga Kiwi House and Native Bird Park, on Alex Telfer Drive (daily 9–5). It was established in 1971, and is one of the oldest native bird and reptile parks in the country. More than 50 species are housed here, including three of the four known species of kiwi.

300 K6 · 21 Maniapoto Street · 07-873 8951 · Corner of Maniapoto and Tuhoro streets · Services from Wellington, Hamilton and Auckland

## RAGLAN

www.raglan.co.nz

Raglan, on the coast west of Hamilton, is the Waikato's main seaside resort and is internationally renowned for its surfing. The most convenient and safest beach for swimming is Te Kopua, reached from the end of Bow Street. Ocean Beach has good views across the bar (port entrance); access is off Wainui Reserve Road. Manu Beach is next, and then Whale Bay—which can only be reached over rocks. Remote Ruapuke Beach has wild coastal scenery and is reached along the old coast road and Ruapuke Beach Road. Safe and child-friendly beaches near town include Coxs Bay (accessed from the walkway on Government Road) and Puriri Park (Aro Aro Bay) at the end of Wallis Street.

The 756m (2,480ft) summit of Mount Karioi can be climbed from Te Toto Gorge, 12km (7 miles) southwest, in around six hours.

300 J6 · 4 Wallis Street · 07-825 0556 · Services from Hamilton

**Below** *Looking down the main street at Raglan, a popular holiday resort for families*

## ROTORUA

▷ 108–111.

## TAURANGA

www.bayofplentynz.com

Busy Tauranga, on the Bay of Plenty, has enjoyed enormous growth in recent years, and cruise liners as well as merchant ships now negotiate the narrow entrance to its superb natural port. Its proximity to Rotorua (▷ 108–111) and Mount Maunganui (▷ 104) are a significant part of the town's appeal.

The main historical attraction is the Elms Mission House on Mission Street (Wed, Sat, Sun 2–4), site of the original mission, established here in 1834. Nearby, in Robbins Park on Cliff Road, on the eastern side of the peninsula, are the remnants of the Monmouth Redoubt (daily 9–6), built by government forces during the New Zealand Wars of the 1860s. At the base of the hill, on The Strand, is *Te Awanui Waka*, a Maori war canoe carved in 1973.

A series of superb beaches stretches from Mount Maunganui east to Papamoa.

300 L5 · 95 Willow Street · 07-578 8103 · Corner of Wharf and Willow streets · Spirit Harbour Ferry, Coronation Wharf to Mount Maunganui daily 7–5.30 (winter hours vary) · 4km (2.5 miles) east

**INFORMATION**
www.isitehawkesbaynz.com
301 M8 100 Marine Parade
06-834 1911 Mon, Tue, Thu, Fri 8.30–5, Wed, Sat, Sun 9–5 Travel Centre, Munroe Street Munroe Street
Airport north of town; shuttles

**Above** *Tree-lined Marine Parade is Napier's busy main street, with art deco buildings and gardens*

## INTRODUCTION

Napier is a bright, dynamic coastal community with a relaxed atmosphere. At first glance it seems to enjoy a perfect relationship with nature; its fertile surroundings and the warm climate have made it the capital of the wine-producing region (▷ 103) of Hawke's Bay.

Nature has not always been kind to Napier, however, and on 3 February 1931 an earthquake almost razed the town to the ground. The inhabitants set about its rebuilding with a collection of art deco buildings now considered among the finest in the world. Much of the city is negotiable on foot and, given its architectural appeal, is best appreciated from the street. Many of Napier's chief attractions line the long waterfront promenade, Marine Parade.

When Captain Cook first mapped Hawke's Bay in 1769, Maori were already well established here. In the 1830s seasonal whalers arrived from Australia, and the first significant group of European settlers arrived 20 years later. In 1854 the town was named after British general Charles Napier.

During the New Zealand Wars of the 1860s the residents, with the help of local Maori, defended themselves against aggressive northern tribes. With the development of agriculture, the settlement flourished. The earthquake of 1931 destroyed everything, but as a result of the earth movement, the land surrounding Bluff Hill had risen several feet and huge tracts of land, previously underwater or covered in swamp, were now available for use. Earthquake-resistant concrete buildings with art deco designs reflecting the optimism of the jazz era gave the town a new face within a decade, thanks largely to architect Louis Hay (1881–1948).

## WHAT TO SEE

### ART DECO ARCHITECTURE

Napier's two central streets, Emerson and Tennyson, have many impressive art deco buildings. The ASB Bank, on Emerson Street, incorporates Maori designs and a fine doorway, while on Tennyson Street the highlights are (from east to west) the *Daily Telegraph* Building, the restored Municipal Theatre and the Desco Centre (art deco heritage society and shop).

Farther afield is perhaps the most attractive building of all, the 1932 Rothmans Pall Mall Building, at the corner of Bridge and Osian streets, in the port area of Ahuriri. The façade and entrance are worth the diversion—especially at night, when they are imaginatively lit. During the day it is possible to have a look at the interior, which shows exquisite attention to detail. A more modern example of art deco architecture is the pharmacy at the southern end of Emerson Street.

**TIPS**

» The view from Bluff Hill, at the northern tip of town, is worth the climb.

» A good view down Marine Parade and across the city can also be enjoyed from Lighthouse Road, above the Centennial Gardens (reached via Lucy Road, off Coote Road).

### MARINE PARADE

Marine Parade creates an impressive perspective, its long promenade lined with Norfolk pines and old wooden houses (the few that survived the earthquake). At its northern end are elegant gardens, including the Centennial Gardens, at the base of Bluff Hill. Farther south the renovated Ocean Spa (Mon–Sat 6am–10pm, Sun 8am–10pm) has hot pools, private spas, health and beauty therapies and a café. More gardens are laid out immediately to the south of the spa complex, dominated by a floral clock, the Tom Parker Fountain (which becomes an aquatic light show after dark) and a statue called *Pania of the Reef*, depicting a Maori maiden.

Heading south you reach the art deco Colonnade and Sound Shell. Once a dancing and skating hall, the Colonnade now houses a bell and memorial dedicated to the crew of HMS *Veronica*, which was in port at the time of the earthquake. Members of the crew were among the first to come to the city's aid and pull victims from the rubble. Every New Year the bell is rung to commemorate their brave efforts. Opposite the Sound Shell, which is occasionally used for open-air concerts, are the Art Deco Tower (A&B building), which is also lit at night, and the Masonic Hotel.

Past the modern visitor office and Mini Golf Park are the Sunken Gardens, complete with water-lily ponds and a lazy waterwheel. Beyond them, seal and dolphin displays are combined with a project aimed at wild penguin and gannet rehabilitation at Marineland (Apr–Nov daily 10–4.30; rest of year Mon, Thu 10–4.30, Tue, Wed, Fri, Sat, Sun 10–5.30). In daily sessions you can feed and swim with the dolphins. Continuing southwards you encounter the intriguing Millennium Sculpture, a work using reflective steel discs, by local artist David Trubridge.

### HAWKE'S BAY MUSEUM

www.hbmag.co.nz

A wide range of exhibits set in modern surroundings relates to the history and art of the Hawke's Bay region. Nga Tukemata (The Awakening) presents the art and *taonga* (treasures) of the local Maori and rare evidence that dinosaurs once existed in New Zealand—remains unearthed in the Maungahouanga Valley of northern Hawke's Bay. Special attention is given to the earthquake of 1931, when 100 fires raged over 30 hours after the initial shock, and 258 people lost their lives.

✉ 9 Herschell Street ☎ 06-835 7781 🕒 Daily 10–6 ✋ Adult NZ$10, child (under 16) NZ$5

**Below** *The art deco Tom Parker Fountain in gardens off Marine Parade*

## MORE TO SEE

### NATIONAL AQUARIUM OF NEW ZEALAND

www.nationalaquarium.co.nz

The newest of Napier's waterfront attractions hosts an eclectic mix of native and non-native water and land creatures, including seahorses and kiwis. Divers enter the tanks to feed the fish at 10am and 2pm. At other times they also act as guides to the aquarium, conducting informative tours behind the scenes (an extra charge applies).

✉ Marine Parade ☎ 06-834 1404 🕒 Daily 9–5 ✋ Adult NZ$15.50, child (up to 14) NZ$8

**INFORMATION**
www.rotoruanz.com
301 L6 1167 Fenton Street
07-348 5179 Daily 8–6
i-SITE, Fenton Street Eastern shores of Lake Rotorua, about 10km (6 miles) from town; shuttle service

## INTRODUCTION

Rotorua—alias Sulphur City—is the thermal and volcanic resort capital of New Zealand, and is often smelt before it's seen. In addition to exploring the geysers, pools and vents of bubbling mud in its immediate vicinity, you can enjoy a Maori *hangi* (feast), throw yourself down a waterfall in a raft, jump out of a plane or shop until you drop—preferably into one of the city's many restorative hot thermal pools. Rotorua sprawls on the southern shores of the lake of the same name, its half-timbered, mock-Tudor buildings recalling its development as a European-style health spa at the start of the 20th century.

The shores of Lake Rotorua and Whakarewarewa were first settled by Maori from the Arawa canoe in the 14th century. By the 1840s the first missions had been established. When inter-tribal war broke out the Te Arawa sided with the government. After the end of the New Zealand Wars, European settlement began. The population rapidly expanded, drawn by the aesthetic and therapeutic qualities of the thermal waters, and tourism flourished.

## WHAT TO SEE

### HELL'S GATE AND WAI ORA SPA

www.hellsgate.co.nz

The aptly named Hell's Gate thermal reserve is one of the most active, with two levels separated by a tract of bush and connected by a warm thermal stream, complete with steaming waterfall. The pools of bubbly mud and water on the lower levels hiss menacingly. The upper level has steaming lakes and tiny steaming vents, scattered with mini mud volcanoes and cauldrons of boiling water. Best of all is the Devil's Cauldron, a pit where a lively, globular mud pool makes wonderfully disgusting noises. Services include massage, sulphur spas, therapeutic mud facials, scrubs and private mud baths.
301 L6 15km (9 miles) from Rotorua on SH30 07-345 3151 Daily 8.30–8.30
Adult NZ$25, child (under 16) NZ$10. Spa only NZ$15, child NZ$10

**Above** *The crater rim of Tarawera shows geological upheaval*

## LAKE ROTORUA

This flooded volcanic crater is the largest of the 17 lakes in the Rotorua thermal region, covering an area of 89sq km (34 square miles) and sitting 279m (915ft) above sea level. Boat trips from the city take in the nature reserve of Mokoia Island. Recreational activities include boating, water-skiing and trout-fishing. On the northern shores are the Hamurana Gardens, at 733 Hamurana Road, where a spring erupts with beautiful clarity and a volume of more than 3,780,000 litres (831,600 gallons) an hour.

301 L6

## OHINEMUTU

Narrow streets lined with steaming drains lead to the former Maori settlement and thermal area of Ohinemutu, on the city's lakefront. The focal point is the Tamatekapua Marae, a beautifully carved meeting house, renovated in 1939 but containing 19th-century carvings. Facing it is St. Faith's Church (daily 8–5), built in 1910. The interior pillars, beams, rafters and pews are carved with Maori designs, and on a window overlooking the lake a Maori Christ is sandblasted, as if walking on the lake, dressed in a *korowai* (chief's cloak). Members of the Arawa tribe are buried in the graveyard, among them the only European to be admitted to full chieftainship: Captain Gilbert Mair (1843–1923), who twice saved the Arawa from inter-tribal attacks.

## POLYNESIAN SPA

www.polynesianspa.co.nz

Rain or shine, this luxury spa complex is a delight. Among the treats are hot springs and pools, private spa pools, a family spa—and massage treatments are also available. Outside, in timber-style tubs, therapeutic adult hot springs overlook the lake and range in temperature from 33°C (91.4°F) to 43°C (109.4°F). The best times to go are at lunch and dinner, when the tour buses are elsewhere.

Hinemoa Street · 07-348 1328 · Daily 8am–11pm · Adult NZ$13, child NZ$6

## ROTORUA MUSEUM OF ART AND HISTORY

www.rotoruamuseum.co.nz

People used to come from all over the world to the 1908 red-and-white half-timbered Bath House, which now houses this museum, to take advantage of the thermal water's therapeutic and curative powers. In one wing you can see some of the original baths, changing rooms and equipment used by the early visitors. A superb collection of Te Arawa *taonga* (treasures) contrasts with modern Maori artworks. An excellent audiovisual display, Rotorua Stories, introduces the area's history and legends—complete with shuddering pews during the dramatic account of the 1886 eruption.

Government Gardens · 07-349 4350 · Oct–end Mar daily 9–8; Apr–end Sep daily 9–5 · Guided tours daily 11, 2 · Adult NZ$12, child NZ$5.50

## WAI-O-TAPU

www.geyserland.co.nz

Wai-O-Tapu is the best thermal park in the region, with an almost surreal range of volcanic features, from mud pools and silica terraces to the beautiful Champagne Pool. If you can, time your arrival with the daily 10.15am eruption of the Lady Knox Geyser, which is signposted on the Wai-O-Tapu Loop Road (off SH5). A self-guided walk around the park takes about two hours, passing the Artist's Palette—a steaming silica field in pastel yellow, green and blue, and the Champagne Pool—an orange-rimmed pool which heats the water to a surface temperature of around 74°C (165°F).

301 L6 · 29km (18 miles) south of Rotorua off SH5 · 07-366 6333 · Daily 8.30–5 · Adult NZ$27.50, child (5–15) NZ$9

**TIP**

» The visitor office has an in-house travel section administering local and national bus, air and rail ticketing.

**Below** *Demonstrating the traditions of Maori cooking*

## WAIMANGU

www.waimangu.co.nz

The volcanic features of the Waimangu volcanic valley were created as a result of the 1886 eruption of Tarawera (▷ 33). Lake Rotomahana is a water-filled crater which, before the eruption, was the site of the famous Pink-and-White Terraces. Both silica terraces were obliterated by the eruption, replaced by the Waimangu Cauldron—the world's largest boiling lake; the Inferno Crater Lake, which rises and falls up to 10m (33ft); steaming cliffs, and boiling springs and steaming fumaroles.

301 L6 · 26km (16 miles) south of Rotorua, off SH5 · 07-366 6137 · Daily 8.30–5 · Adult from NZ$32.50, child (6–16) NZ$10

## TE PUIA, WHAKAREWAREWA

www.nzmaori.co.nz

This is the most famous of the region's thermal reserves, and includes within its grounds the Rotowhio Marae, the Mai Ora Village (a replica of the former Te Arawa Maori settlement) and the modern Te Puia arts and crafts institute. There are two geysers here: Pohutu, or Big Splash, which goes off 10 to 25 times a day (more recently for days on end), achieving a height of more than 30m (98ft), and Prince of Wales Feathers, which is less spectacular. Tracks negotiate other small mud pools and volcanic features and lead back to the Rotowhio Marae, which has a banquet and weaving house, and hosts daily cultural performances. A longer performance in the evening includes a *hangi* (feast).

3km (2 miles) south of downtown along Fenton Street · Maori Arts and Crafts Institute 07-348 9047 · Daily 8–5; Maori guided tours hourly 9–5; cultural performances 10.15, 12.15, 3.15 · Tours NZ$50, child (5–15) NZ$25; evening performance NZ$85, child NZ$50

**Above** *The sacred Green Lake*
**Below** *A natural steam-cloud engulfs the Rotorua Museum*

## MORE TO SEE

### AGRODOME

www.agrodome.co.nz

The Agrodome Complex has a wide array of attractions, from bungy jumping to farm activities. The principal attraction is the Sheep Show, at which you are introduced to 19 different breeds of sheep.

300 L6 · 10km (6 miles) north of Rotorua on SH5 · 07-357 1050 · Daily 8.30–5; shows 9.30, 11, 2.30 · Show NZ$24, child (5–15) NZ$12

## BLUE AND GREEN LAKES

Mount Tarawera Road leads to Blue Lake (Tikitapu), used for boating and swimming, and Green Lake (Rotokakahi), which is sacred and off limits. Beyond them the road enters the Te Wairoa Valley, home of the Buried Village, where the Pink-and-White Terraces, the village and its hotel were laid waste by the 1886 eruption.

301 L6 Southeast of city, off SH30

## BLUE BATHS

www.bluebaths.co.nz

Built in the Spanish Mission style during the Great Depression of 1933, the pools flourished as a major social and recreational venue, and were one of the first public baths to have mixed bathing. Restored and reopened in 1999, today they offer hot pools and a museum.

Government Gardens 07-350 2119 Dec–end Mar Mon–Thu 10–7, Fri–Sun 10–8; Apr–end Nov Mon–Thu 10–6, Fri–Sun 10–7 Adult NZ$11, child (5–14) NZ$6

## MOUNT TARAWERA

Tarawera is 1,111m (3,645ft) high, with a 6km (4-mile) converging gash of craters. It is a conglomerate of three mountains: Wahanga to the north, Ruawahia in the middle and Tarawera to the south. Helicopter flights and 4X4 tours give access to the interior. Independent access is discouraged.

301 L6

## SKYLINE SKYRIDES

www.skylineskyrides.co.nz

Visitors travel up the mountain in gondolas and return on the infamous luge, which involves riding down a concrete course on a plastic tray with wheels and primitive brakes. A family course provides a gentler version.

Fairy Springs Road 07-347 0027 Daily 9–late Gondola only, adult NZ$24, child (14 and under) NZ$12, gondola and 5 luge rides NZ$30

## TARAWERA FALLS

In the heart of the Tarawera Forest, the Tarawera River flows from the eastern shores of Lake Tarawera and northern slopes of Mount Tarawera. A walkway leads to the point where the river disappears underground before emerging from a sheer cliff face.

301 L6 70km (43 miles) from Rotorua on SH30

**Below** *Meeting the sheep at the Agrodome's Sheep Show*

**INFORMATION**

www.mtruapehu.com
300 K8 Department of Conservation office, Whakapapa Village, SH48 07-892 3729; www.doc.govt.nz Daily 8–5 All surrounding townships. Local shuttles to Whakapapa Village and walk drop-off/pick-up points Services from Auckland and Wellington to Ohakune and National Park At intersection of SH47 and SH48

## INTRODUCTION

In 1887 Horonuku Te Heuheu Tukino, chief of Ngati Tuwharetoa, gave the sacred volcanoes of Ruapehu, Ngauruhoe and Tongariro to the nation to preserve, creating the heart of Tongariro National Park—the fourth oldest in the world. The park covers an area of 75,250ha (185,940 acres), taking in forest, tussock country and volcanic desert. Dominating everything are the majestic active volcanic peaks of Tongariro, Ngauruhoe and Ruapehu. Whakapapa and Turoa offer some of the best skiing in the country (Jul–Oct).

On Christmas Eve of 1953 the wall of Mount Ruapehu's crater collapsed and a mighty lahar (a wash of volcanic rock debris and water) rushed down the Whangaehu River, destroying the rail bridge at Tangiwai. The night train to Auckland arrived moments later, and 151 lives were lost in the disaster. The mountain erupted in September 1995, and again a year later.

## WHAT TO SEE

### MOUNT NGAURUHOE

The youngest of the three volcanoes lies 3km (2 miles) south of Tongariro and reaches 2,287m (7,503ft). Its classic symmetrical cone shape is due to its relative youth and the fact that it has only one vent. In recent years, Ngauruhoe has been the most continuously active, frequently venting steam and gas, and occasionally ash and lava. Its last significant eruption occurred in 1954.
300 K7

### MOUNT RUAPEHU

www.mtruapehu.com
About 16km (10 miles) south of Ngauruhoe is the truncated cone of Ruapehu, with its snow-covered summit peaks and azure crater lakes. This is the North Island's highest mountain, at 2,797m (9,176ft). In the last century it saw the most violent activity of the three volcanoes, last errupting in 1995/6. Thousands of visitors come to ski, climb on its slopes or enjoy its walking tracks—the longest of these, the Round-the-Mountain Track, takes five to six days. Ruapehu has three ski fields: Whakapapa, serviced by Whakapapa and Iwikau villages; Turoa, serviced by Okahune; and Tukino, the smallest of the three.
300 K8 54 Clyde Street, Ohakune 06-385 8427

**Above** *Mount Ngauruho, viewed from the balcony of Chateau Tongariro hotel*

### NORTHERN CIRCUIT

The Tongariro Northern Circuit walking trail winds its way over Mount Tongariro and around Mount Ngauruhoe, passing lakes, craters and glacial valleys. The walk takes three to four days to complete. The track starts from Whakapapa Village and finishes at the Mangatepopo Road, just off SH47.

Visitor Centre, SH48, Whakapapa Village 06-892 3729

### TONGARIRO CROSSING

www.tongarirocrossing.co.nz

When the weather is clear, the views and volcanic features on this one-day hike are unforgettable. The 16km (10-mile) trail involves steep climbs and the occasional scramble, and can take up to 10 hours. In winter it can be impassable and even in summer it may be dangerous. Most hikers walk from Mangatepopo to Ketetahi to minimize the climbing.

Visitor Centre, SH48, Whakapapa Village 07-8923729

## MORE TO SEE

### OHAKUNE

www.ohakune.info

The pretty little ski resort of Ohakune sits near the southern edge of the park. Turoa ski field is 17km (10.5 miles) up the Ohakune Mountain Road. The Department of Conservation field centre, at the base of the road (Mon–Fri 9–12.30, 1–3), shows a video of the 1995/6 Ruapehu eruption.

300 K8 Clyde Street 06-385 8427 Holiday Shoppe

### WHAKAPAPA VILLAGE

www.mtruapehu.com

Whakapapa is the headquarters and information base for the national park, and gives access to the Whakapapa Skifield and several good shorter walks. Its main landmark is the magnificent Chateau Tongariro Hotel, built in 1929. The Department of Conservation field centre (daily 8–5) has excellent displays and a seismograph monitoring the moods of Ruapehu.

300 K8 Visitor Centre, SH48, Whakapapa Village 07-892 3729 Shuttles to village and ski field

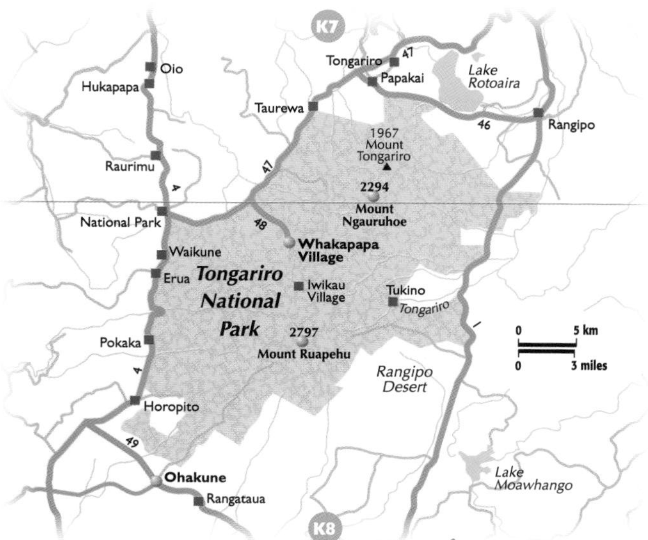


### TIPS

» If you're walking the Tongariro Crossing get to the Ketetahi Hut early, as it operates on a first come, first served basis.

» For the latest update on volcanic activity log on to www.geonet.org.nz.

**Above and opposite** *Lake Taupo is famed for its fishing and its Maori rock carvings*

## TAUPO

www.laketauponz.co.nz

Massive volcanic eruptions formed the Taupo region's landscape over 250,000 years. The latest occurred in AD186, spewing out ash and debris at up to 900kph (560mph). Its effects were visible from China and Rome, and it was one factor in the creation of the vast and now placid 619sq km (239 square-mile) expanse of Lake Taupo.

The busy resort town of Taupo sits on the northern lakeshore and offers a multitude of activities—principally trout-fishing in the lake, but also bungy jumping, tandem skydiving, mountain biking, golf, sailing and walking. Longer lake cruises take in a remarkable set of Maori carvings, showing a huge tattooed face and covering an entire rockface. These relatively recent creations, can only be seen from the water, at Mine Bay.

The Taupo Museum and Art Gallery at Story Place (daily 10.30–4.30) focuses on the early days of the region. West of the museum, the Waikato River begins its 425km (264-mile) journey to the Tasman Sea, winding north behind the town towards Wairakei Park. Mid-river just before the park is Cherry Island (daily 9–5), which is a small wildlife visitor attraction.

300 L7 Tongariro Street (SH1) 07-376 0027 Gascoigne Street 10km (6 miles) south of town

## TE PUKE

www.tepuke.co.nz

Te Puke, 31km (19 miles) southeast of Tauranga, claims to have launched New Zealand's kiwifruit industry. Take a Kiwikart tour at Kiwi360 (daily 9–5), 5km (3 miles) east of the town on SH2. Next door, at the Vintage Auto Barn (daily 9–5), there are more than 90 classic and vintage vehicles on display.

301 L6 130 Jellicoe Street 07-573 6772

## TE UREWERA NATIONAL PARK

Te Urewera is a daunting and mysterious place of almost threatening beauty. The national park, northwest of Wairoa, encompasses the largest block of native bush in the North, home to rare kiwis, kakas and kokakos. The focus is Lake Waikaremoana—the Sea of Rippling Waters, created 2,000 years ago, when the Waikaretaheke River was dammed by a huge landslide.

301 M7 SH38, Aniwaniwa, Lake Waikaremoana 06-837 3803

## TONGARIRO NATIONAL PARK

▷ 112–113.

## TURANGI

www.taupodc.govt.nz

This small village on the scenic Tongariro River is famous for trout-fishing, and makes a good base for exploring the Tongariro National Park to the south (▷ 112–113). At the Tongariro National Trout Centre, 3km (2 miles) south of the village on SH1 (daily 9–5), you can see a trout hatchery in operation, with adult fish in a large pool and an underwater viewing area.

300 K7 Ngawaka Place, off SH1 07-386 8999

## WAIRAKEI PARK

In the heart of the Wairakei Park, north of Taupo, is one of the country's most spectacular waterfalls. Huka Falls, reached via Huka Falls Road, start as the sedately flowing Waikato River before being forced through a cleft of solid rock 15m (49ft) wide and 100m (328ft) long. From here they emerge to fall 7m (23ft) into a foaming cauldron. Depending on the flow (regulated at Lake Taupo for electricity generation), the falls vary from 9m to 10m (29ft to 33ft) high.

Wairakei Terraces, north of Taupo (daily 9–5), are the region's latest thermal attraction. About 1km (0.5 miles) farther on is the Wairakei Thermal Valley.

300 L7

## WAITOMO

▷ 116–117.

## WHAKATANE

www.whakatane.com

The principal town in the eastern Bay of Plenty sits at the mouth of the Whakatane River and has a rich Maori history dating back to 1150, when the Polynesian explorer Toi te Hauatahi landed here. This historic town is a departure point to the active volcano of Whakkaari/White Island, which on a clear day can be seen steaming 50km (31 miles) offshore. Other major activities include swimming with dolphins and fishing. The island closest to shore is Moutohora (or Whale) Island, a wildlife refuge.

Pohaturoa is a large rock outcrop at the corner of The Strand and Commerce Street, used for 600 years as a Maori meeting place. The summit was a sacred place for the bones of early chiefs, and newborns were dedicated to the gods in a stream at its foot. More local history is related in the Whakatane Museum and Gallery on Boon Street (Tue–Fri 10–4.30, Sat, Sun 11–3).

301 M6 Corner of Quay and Kakahoroa Drive 07-308 6058 Intercity services and East Cape shuttle Northwest of town

**INFORMATION**

www.waitomo-museum.co.nz
300 K6 Waitomo Museum of Caves, Main Street, Waitomo 07-878 7640 Daily 8–5 Services from Hamilton and Rotorua; shuttles to caves from Otorohanga and Waitomo village Services from Auckland to Otorohanga

**Above** *Blackwater rafting tours of the Ruakuri caves are for the adventurous*

## INTRODUCTION

Visitors come in droves to the district of Waitomo and its underground world of limestone caves. Above ground, the typical farmland and the resort village itself give no clue to what lies below. Many of the region's features can be enjoyed along the three-hour Waitomo Walkway, which begins opposite the Glow-worm Caves and follows the Waitomo Stream to the Ruakuri Scenic Reserve. A short circular track in the reserve takes in caves and natural limestone bridges, hidden among lush native bush.

The limestone around Waitomo was once a seabed, formed about 30 million years ago. Over the ages its layers have been raised by the action of the earth's plates, bending and buckling and creating a maze of cracks and joints. As rainwater drains into these cracks it mixes with small amounts of carbon dioxide in the air and soil, forming a weak acid. This slowly dissolves the limestone, widening its faults. Over time small streams flow through converging cracks and create underground caves. The caves themselves have a finite lifespan—as is evident at the Lost World, near Waitomo, where part of a cave system has collapsed in on itself.

## WHAT TO SEE

### ARANUI CAVE

Just 2km (1 mile) away, Aranui is a less frenetic, more sedate experience than the Glow-worm Caves at Waitomo. It was discovered by chance by Maori hunter Ruruku Aranui, in 1910, while he was hunting pigs. Effective lighting brings out the hues and variety of the formations.

3km (2 miles) west of Glow-worm Caves, in Ruakuri Scenic Reserve Half-hourly tours 9–5 Adult NZ$32, child (5–14) NZ$14; under-5s free. Combined Glow-worm and Aranui ticket NZ$45, child NZ$22

## GLOW-WORM CAVES

www.waitomocaves.co.nz

This cave network is Waitomo's biggest attraction, and the most commercial, drawing almost 250,000 visitors annually. The network was first extensively explored in 1887 by a local Maori, Tane Tinorau, and an English surveyor, Fred Mace, and the caves were opened to visitors in 1889. Despite the crowds, the highlight of the 45-minute tour—the silent trip to the glow-worm colony by boat—is still magical. The glow-worm *Arachnocampa luminosa* emits light to attract its prey and is unique to New Zealand. It is the larval stage of a two-winged insect.

Waitomo Caves Road, off SH3 07-878 8227 Tours half-hourly 9–5 Adult NZ$32, child (5–14) NZ$14; under-5s free. Combined Glow-worm and Aranui ticket NZ$45, child NZ$22; Shuttle from Waitomo and Otorohanga

## MANGAPOHUE NATURAL BRIDGE SCENIC RESERVE

A short streamside walk on the route between Waitomo and Te Anga leads to an impressive natural limestone arch with some unusual stalagmites. This was once part of an enormous cave, and it is hard to imagine that the now rather inconspicuous little stream created it all.

About 5km (3 miles) farther on are the Piripiri Caves, reached by a short but strenuous climb up a boardwalk. These caves are in stark contrast to the well-lit, visitor-friendly offerings in Waitomo: They are dark and forbidding, and the path into them is steep and quite dangerous. If you are alone do not venture far, and take a torch (flashlight).

Marokopa Road Free

## MUSEUM OF CAVES

www.waitomo-museum.co.nz

A thorough introduction to the area is presented at this museum, considered the best of its kind in the world. Displays cover cave formation, the history surrounding the local caves and the natural history, including the spectacular glow-worms. There's a small collection of everyday implements and treasures once belonging to the Tainui Maori, who lived in this valley for 500 years. These include *toki* (adzes), *waka kereru* (bird traps) and an exquisite oyster-shell necklace discovered in a local cave. There are also fascinating exhibits relating to early tourism in the area.

In the visitor office, Main Street, Waitomo 07-878 7640 Dec–end Mar daily 8–8; Apr–end Nov daily 8–5 Adult NZ$5, child (4–14) NZ$3, under-4s free

# MORE TO SEE

## THE SHEARING SHED

Large, fluffy Angora rabbits are cuddled to within an inch of their lives at this unusual venue, and then shorn for their highly prized, fine hair. Angora products—yarn, duvets, underlay and sweaters—are on sale, and there are guided tours to tell you about it all.

Waitomo Caves Road, Waitomo 07-878 8371 Shows daily at 12.45 Free

## WOODLYN PARK

www.woodlynpark.co.nz

This is the main above-ground attraction in Waitomo, if not the whole region—a show hosted by ex-shearer Barry Woods, giving an informative, interactive and very funny interpretation of old and modern-day Kiwi country life. The production is an eccentric affair involving a clever pig, a not-so-clever pig, an axe, an ingenious home-made computer, dogs, sheep, a 'Kiwi bear' and items of underwear.

1177 Waitomo Valley Road, Otorohanga 07-878 6666 Shows daily, 1.30; reserve tickets Adult NZ$22, child (school age) NZ$13, under-5s NZ$6, family NZ$68

## TIPS

» No specialist clothing is required to explore the Aranui and Waitomo caves, which have walkways and handrails, but flat-heeled shoes are recommended.

» If possible, arrive well before the scheduled tour time for the Glow-worm Caves.

» For the claustrophobic, the Museum of Caves offers an audiovisual display and a fake cave to crawl through.

**Below** *Stalactites hang above the walkway in the softly lit Aranui Cave*

# AROUND LAKE ROTORUA

**Drive around Lake Rotorua to sample just a few of the natural and manmade features that first spawned tourism in New Zealand and made the region the tourism capital of the North Island.**

**THE DRIVE**
**Distance:** 85km (53 miles)
**Time:** 8 hours
**Start/end at:** Rotorua Visitor Information Centre 301 L6

Rotorua is where tourism began in New Zealand. The Government's Department of Tourist and Health Resorts took over the spa in 1901, and in 1902 appointed the first official balneologist. For more than a century the diverse volcanic and geothermal features of the region have lured visitors with the hope of both drama and cure: Drama in the form of gushing geysers, bubbling mud, or the former pink silica terraces (▷ 110), and cure in the form of therapeutic pools and curative treatments. From its inception in 1908, the town's world-famous Bath House was the main focus for many making the journey to the Bay of Plenty. The Bath House now forms part of the Rotorua Museum of Art and History (▷ 109).

★ From Fenton Street head south, following signs for the airport (east) and SH30. After 2km (1.5 miles) turn right onto Tarawera Road. On the right is the northern fringe of the Whakarewarewa Forest Park.

❶ Whakarewarewa Forest Park has a good network of tracks that are mostly used for mountain biking. The park is said to be one of the best venues in the country, and if you have never tried the sport this presents a perfect opportunity. A small visitor centre and gift shop on Long Mile Road provides all the details, including advice on bicycle hire and organized tours.

❷ At the eastern fringe of the park (8km/5 miles along Tawarewa Road) are Lake Rotokakihi (the Green Lake) and Lake Tikitapu (the Blue Lake; ▷ 111). The difference in colour between the two lakes is a result of the effects of subterranean minerals.

From Lake Tikitapu the road veers east towards Lake Tarawera and the partly excavated Maori Buried Village. Here you can gain an insight into the eruption of Mount Tarawera in 1886. Tarawera Landing is a little farther east; boat trips are available on MV *Reremoana* (▷ 130).

From Tarawera Landing return to SH30 and head east (right) around the lake, past the airport to the intersection between SH30 (Whakatane) and SH33 (Tauranga). Remain on SH30 as it heads east away from the lake, following signs to Hell's Gate (3km/2 miles).

❸ After your thermal experience at Hell's Gate (▷ 108), return to the lake and turn right onto the Tauranga Road (SH33).

Cross over the Ouau Channel (that connects Lake Rotorua with Lake Rotoiti) and continue north to Okere (2km/1 mile). At Okere turn left, following signs to the Okere Falls Scenic Reserve, just before the river bridge.

❹ The Okere Falls Scenic Reserve offers an excellent opportunity for a short bush walk and to watch the rafting and whitewater action on the tempestuous Kaituna River. It is one of the best venues for the sport in the North Island, and the 7m (23ft) drop from the Tutea Falls is a dramatic highlight. There is a viewing platform just a short distance from the main track (signposted) where you can watch the rafters plummeting over the edge with trepidation, or glee. If you are tempted, trips can be arranged through the visitor centre in Rotorua (from NZ$85).

From Okere return south and turn right just before the lake and Ohau Channel. This road hugs the northern fringe of Lake Rotorua and offers pleasant views back towards Rotorua. Take a brief stop at the crystal-clear Hamurana Springs. (Look for the golf course on the right and park your car in the golf course parking area.)

❺ Hamurana Springs are the largest in the North Island, and erupt at a volume of more than 1 million gallons per hour, creating a beautifully clear river that flows the short distance into Lake Rotorua. The head of the springs can be reached via a 10-minute walk through a glade of giant redwood trees that fringe the river. Access is from the former Hamurana Gardens parking area (which doubles as the Hamurana Golf Course parking area) beside the main road. Cross the bridge at the car park and follow the path upstream.

From Hamurana Springs continue west through Ngongotaha to join SH5 towards Rotorua. Continue south for 3km (2 miles), stopping at the Skyline Skyrides (▷ 111) on the left. Rainbow Springs (▷ 129) is opposite.

From Skyline Skyrides continue south on SH5, bearing left on Lake Road into the city to return to the visitor information centre on Fenton Street. Alternatively, a perfect end to your tour would be a soak in the thermal pools at the Polynesian Spa (▷ 109) at the southern end of Government Gardens, off Fenton Street. The best bet is to go at lunchtime, when the tour buses are elsewhere.

### WHERE TO EAT

**SKYLINE SKYRIDES COMPLEX**

Enjoy traditional Kiwi fare with views across the city and lake.

☒ On the slopes of Mount Ngongotaha, SH5 ☎ 07-347 0027 🕒 Jan–end Mar daily 9–8.30; Apr–end Dec daily 9–6
✋ Entry fee applies for gondola: adult NZ$24, child (5–14) NZ$12 (▷ 111)

### INFORMATION

**TOURIST INFORMATION**

www.rotoruaNZ.com
☒ Rotorua Visitor Centre, 1167 Fenton Street, Rotorua ☎ 07-348 5179
🕒 Daily 8–5.30

**WHAKAREWAREWA FOREST PARK VISITOR INFORMATION CENTRE**

☒ Long Mile Road, off Tarawera Road
☎ 07-346 2082 🕒 Mon–Fri 8.30–5, Sat–Sun 10–4

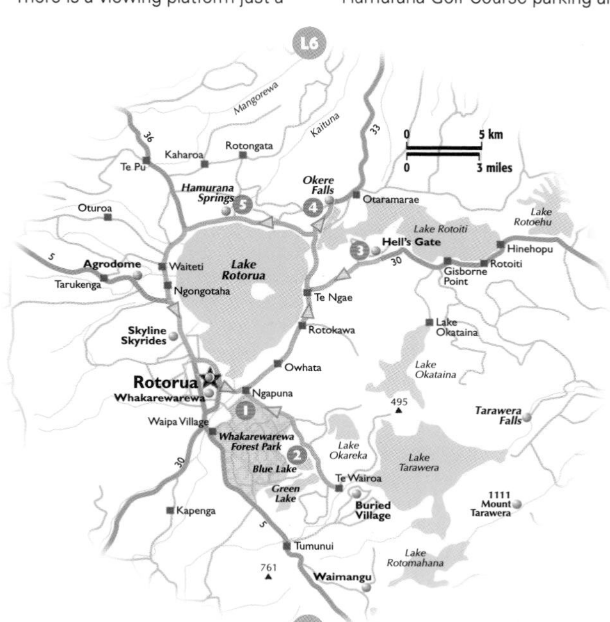


**Opposite** *A pall of fog cloaks the volcanic landscape near Rotorua*

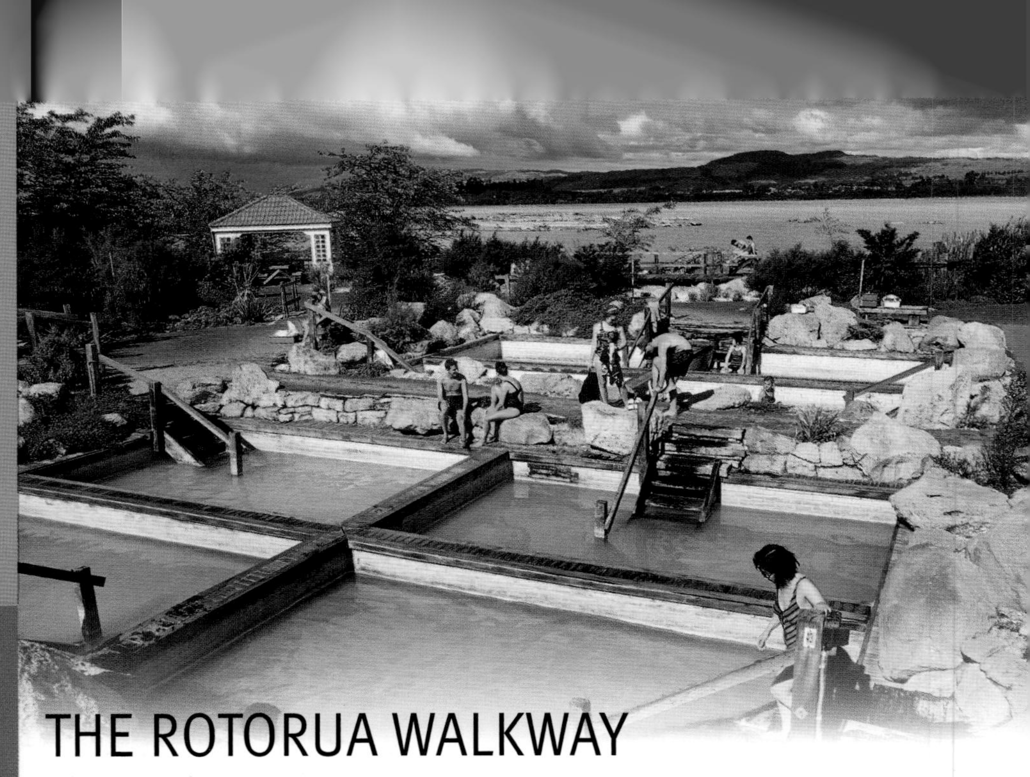

# THE ROTORUA WALKWAY

**This easy circular walk through the heart of the city and around the lakefront offers a great introduction to Rotorua's intriguing natural and human history.**

**THE WALK**
**Distance:** 2km (1 mile)
**Time:** 2–3 hours
**Start/end at:** Polynesian Spa car park, lake end of Hinemoa Street

As the North Island's most popular tourist destination, and host to almost 2 million visitors a year, there is no doubting Rotorua's commercialism, or its ability to entertain. But amid all the hype and adrenalin-pumping activities, one of the best ways to get a feel for the place (if not to escape the crowds) is to explore part of the 26km (16-mile) Rotorua Walkway. The short section described below concentrates on the heart of the city and the lakefront and offers a mix of local history, architecture and—of course—a sample of the region's celebrated and unpredictable geothermal features.

★ From the Polynesian Spa (▷ 109) car park head west through the heart of the city along Hinemoa Street to the intersection with Ranolf Street. Turn right and enter Kuirau Park at the intersection of Pukuatua and Ranolf streets. Head north through the park.

❶ With your nose assailed by the pungent smell of sulphur, you quickly realize that Kuirau Park is not your average town park. It is pock-marked with fenced-off craters and steaming hot pools, and you could be forgiven for thinking you were on another planet. Once a dangerous swamp, the 30ha (74-acre) Kuirau Park was endowed as a reserve by the local Maori, Ngati Whakaue, and first developed during the Depression of the 1930s.

Although all the pools in Kuirau Park are now out of bounds to the public, for many decades locals and visitors used the more temperate among them for bathing and relaxation. Maori legend has it that a local girl, Kuiarau, who used to bathe in the biggest lake (originally known as Taokahu), was seized by a despicable *taniwha* (spirit) who inhabited a lair beneath the waters. This was noticed by the gods, who decided to boil the lake in order to destroy the *taniwha*. From that time on the lake was known as Kuiarau, or Kuirau, in memory of the girl.

From the northern fringe of Kuirau Park head right up Pukeroa Hill on Lake Road.

❷ Pukeroa Hill (also known as Hospital Hill) was a *pa* site used by the local Maori, Ngati Whakaue, who adapted the small hilltop for their defences. There are still some burial

**Opposite** *Bathing outdoors in the thermal luxury of Rotorua's Polynesian Spa*

sites *(urupa)* present on the hill. In 1961 the hill became the site for a military hospital, later developed into the King George V Hospital.

From Lake Road turn left down Haukotuku Street, then right along Tunohopu Street.

❸ The historic Maori settlement of Ohinemutu is home to St. Faith's Church and the magnificent Tamatekapua Meeting House (⊳ 109).

Continue round the lake, and the fringe of Government Gardens.

❹ A short distance from the Rotorua Museum of Art and History is another Rotorua icon, the Blue Baths (⊳ 111).

From the museum, return to the lakefront and head east to the Motutara Point and Sulphur Bay.

❺ From beyond Motutara Point Lake, Rotorua (⊳ 108) is laid out before you, with Mokoia Island dominating the horizon. Among the waterbirds you may see here are brown teal, along with black swans and a colony of pied shags.

From Motutara Point continue south on the marked walkway to Sulphur Point.

❻ The view of Sulphur Bay, the southernmost bay on Lake Rotorua, is dominated by a steaming, sulphurous crust that sits above an active geothermal field. Although a hostile and unproductive habitat for wildlife, it still provides sanctuary for both roosting and nesting birds, including the omnipresent and handsome red-billed gulls. It was officially designated as a wildlife refuge in 1967.

Local Maori also made use of the thermal features and the small islands of Sulphur Bay, particularly Moturere Island—which before lake levels rose had a thermal pool known for its therapeutic properties. The soft rock and warm waters also made it a perfect site to sharpen greenstone tools and weapons.

From Sulphur Point continue south to return to the Polynesian Spa car park.

### WHERE TO EAT

#### THE FAT DOG CAFÉ

Something of a local institution, this café has an imaginative blackboard menu and plenty of character.
✉ 1161 Arawa Street, Rotorua
☎ 07-347 7586

### INFORMATION

#### TOURIST INFORMATION

www.rotoruanz.com
✉ Rotorua Visitor Centre, 1167 Fenton Street, Rotorua ☎ 07-348 5179

**Above** *The former Bath House is now the city's museum*
**Left** *Natural steam vents in front of the Tamatekapua Marae*

# A CIRCUIT OF TONGARIRO NATIONAL PARK

**Throughout this tour you'll have the company of two large and unpredictable landmarks—Ruapehu and Ngauruhoe—the North Island's most celebrated volcanoes.**

**THE DRIVE**
**Distance:** 328km (203 miles)
**Time:** 8 hours
**Start/end at:** Taupo ✚ 300 L7

★ From Taupo (▷ 114) follow SH1 south along the eastern shore of Lake Taupo.

❶ Given the sheer expanse of water and its apparent serenity, it is hard to imagine that Lake Taupo is a volcanic crater. It was formed after a massive eruption that occurred around AD230.

At the southeastern edge of the lake, near the mouth of the Tongariro River, is the small resort of Turangi (▷ 114).

❷ The Tongariro is renowned for its excellent trout-fishing, and is also popular for whitewater rafting and canoeing.

At the southern fringe of Turangi turn right onto SH41. Follow this for 3km (2 miles), then turn left onto SH47, which climbs to a viewpoint looking back towards Lake Taupo before straddling a pass between Pihanga (1,325m/4,347ft) on the left and Kakaramea (1,301m/4,268ft) on the right. If you feel like a break, you might consider the relatively easy two-hour walk around Lake Rotopounamu, which is hidden in the bush on the western flank of Pihanga. The car park and track are clearly signposted.

❸ Just south of the Lake Rotopounamu car park, Lake Rotoaira comes in to view. Beyond this you will see the northern slopes of Mount Tongariro (1,967m/6,455ft) and the volcanic cone of Ngauruhoe (2,287m/7,501ft). Lake Rotoaira is another good place for trout-fishing, and is frequented by hundreds of black swans. If you look carefully, about two-thirds of the way up the slopes of Mount Tongariro (to the south), you may be able to see the Ketetahi Hut. This 'sanctuary in the clouds' has been a welcome sight to many a tired soul undertaking the Tongariro Crossing (▷ 113), considered one of the best day hikes in New Zealand.

Continue south on SH47 and enjoy the spectacular views on the left over the Tongariro National Park (▷ 112–113). The dominant features are Mount Ngauruhoe, with its classic volcano shape, and Mount Ruapehu, also a volcano and at 2,797m (9,176ft) the highest mountain in the North Island. At the foot of Mount Ruapehu you will see the historic Chateau Tongariro hotel (▷ 135), another icon of the national park. Turn left onto SH48 following signs to the Chateau and Whakapapa Village (7km/4 miles).

❹ Park in the middle of Whakapapa Village (▷ 113) to explore, then continue up the main road (Bruce Road) to reach the Whakapapa Ski Field (Top o' the Bruce). The dramatic rocky outcrops around the main skiing complex were used in the *Lord of the Rings* movies as Mount Doom in Mordor.

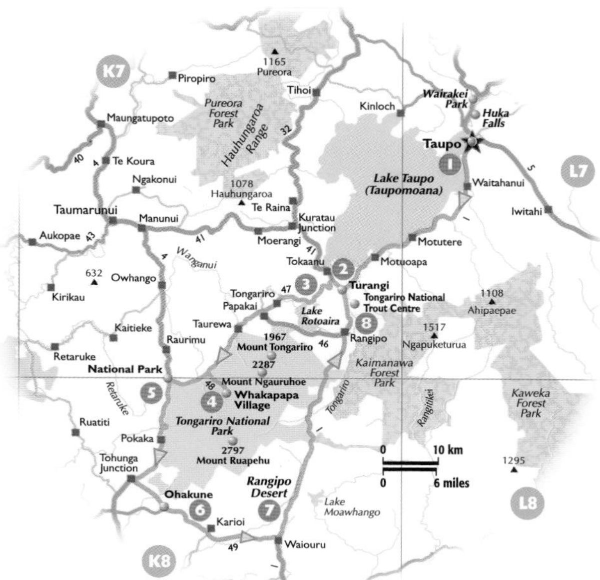


**Opposite** *Snow-capped volcanic peaks line the shore of Lake Taupo*

From Whakapapa, return via SH48 to SH47 and continue left (west) to the village of National Park (9km/ 6 miles).

❺ A drab-looking place, National Park is an accommodation base for the ski fields.

Turn left again onto SH4 and continue south for 26km (16 miles) before turning left onto SH49 to Ohakune (▷ 113), the halfway point on the tour.

East of the heart of the village and signposted off SH49, the 17km (11-mile) drive up Mountain Road to the Turoa ski fields is well worth the journey in good weather, providing fine views to the west. If it is a particularly clear day you may be able to see the snow-capped volcanic peak of Mount Taranaki/ Mount Egmont (▷ 104). According to Maori legend, there was a feud between the mountains of Tongariro and Taranaki after both fell in love with the beautiful Pihanga. A mighty battle ensued. Taranaki lost the fight and, wild with grief and anger, ripped himself from his roots and tore a path towards the coast, where he now stands alone. Perhaps through indifference or appeasement, Tongariro created the waters that filled Taranaki's path of destruction, and the Whanganui River was born.

From Ohakune follow SH49 east as it circles the southern fringe of Ruapehu. Twelve kilometres (7 miles) beyond Ohakune on the left are two lakes collectively known as Lake Rotokura (signposted). Access is on foot only.

❻ The tranquil upper lake reflects the peak of Ruapehu, and can be reached with an easy 30-minute walk from the car park, located just off SH49.

A little farther east on SH49 is the Whangaehu River, straddled by a new road bridge. Alongside it is the Tangiwai Memorial.

On Christmas Eve 1953, the walls of the crater lake of Ruapehu collapsed without warning and a mighty lahar rushed down the Whangaehu River, wiping out the rail bridge at Tangiwai. The night train to Auckland arrived moments later—151 lives were lost.

A further 7km (4 miles) brings you to Waiouru and a intersection. Turn left, heading north on SH1.

❼ Just north of Waiouru, SH1 cuts through a barren, flat expanse of grassland known as the Rangipo Desert, in the rain shadow of Ruapehu. This stretch, dubbed the Desert Road, is often temporarily closed in winter due to snow.

Continue on SH1 back to Turangi. Three kilometres (2 miles) south of Turangi, pass the Tongariro National Trout Centre.

❽ At this trout hatchery you can observe wild trout in the Waihukahuka stream through a viewing window. The visitor centre showcases the history of fishing in the region, and how to catch your own fish on Lake Taupo.

From Turangi return on SH1 to Taupo, where you can enjoy a dip at the Taupo Hot Springs.

### WHEN TO GO

Snow sometimes causes road closures.

### WHERE TO EAT/STAY

The Chateau Tongariro (▷ 135)

### INFORMATION

#### TOURIST INFORMATION

www.LakeTaupoNZ.com
✉ Taupo Visitor Centre, 30 Tongariro Street, Taupo ☎ 07-376 0027
🕐 Daily 8.30–5

#### DOC WHAKAPAPA VISITOR INFORMATION CENTRE

www.doc.govt.nz
✉ Whakapapa Village ☎ 07-892 3729
🕐 Daily 8–6

### PLACES TO VISIT

#### TONGARIRO NATIONAL TROUT CENTRE

✉ Turangi ☎ 07-386 9254 🕐 Dec–Apr daily 10–4; rest of year 10–3 🎫 Free, but donations appreciated

# THE WAITOMO WALKWAY

**Often described as one of the finest short walks in the North Island, the Waitomo Walkway follows the meandering course of the Waitomo Stream, culminating in a 40-minute loop to take in the major limestone features within the Ruakuri Scenic Reserve.**

**THE WALK**
**Distance:** 12km (7 miles)
**Time:** 3 hours
**Start/end at:** Waitomo Glow-worm Caves car park 300 K6

**HOW TO GET THERE**
The Waitomo turn-off is 16km (10 miles) south from Otorohanga on SH3; Waitomo is 7km (4 miles) west of SH3 on SH37.

The limestone around Waitomo was once the sea-bed, and formed about 30 million years ago from the layered remains of countless marine animals. Over millennia these layers have been raised by the action of the earth's plates; in some places the limestone is 200m (656ft) thick.

Through its gradual uprising the limestone bends and buckles, creating a network of cracks and joints. As rainwater drains in to these cracks it mixes with small amounts of carbon dioxide in the air and soil, forming a weak acid. Over thousands of years this acid slowly dissolves the limestone and the cracks and joints widen. Yet more time sees small streams flow through converging cracks, to create the features we see within the Ruakuri Scenic Reserve. Eventually these streams disappear underground, where they can scour out dramatic underground caves such as Waitomo and Aranui.

Within these caves the acidic water continues to seep from the walls or drips from the roof, leaving a minute deposit of limestone crystal. Gradually these deposits form stalactites, stalagmites and other features. The size and rate of their formation depends on the rate of flow. In time, the caves collapse, forming gorges, holes or arches.

★ From the Waitomo Glow-worm Caves (▷ 117) car park follow the signposted walking track (Waitomo Walkway) southwest to the Ruakuri Scenic Reserve and Aranui Cave car park.

❶ According to local tradition, the Aranui Cave was inhabited by a pack of wild dogs—hence its name, *'rua'*, which means cave and *'kuri'*,

**Opposite** *Blackwater rafting on inner tubes through caves*
**Right** *Stalactites and stalagmites fused into columns in the Glow-worm Caves*
**Below** *The lofty interior of Cathedral Cave*

the name for a Maori dog. There are burial caves in the cliffs along the track, making this a place of special significance for Maori. The entrance to Ruakuri Cave, marked by karaka trees with a burial cave above, is *waahi tapu* (sacred).

From the car park begin your circuit of the Scenic Reserve.

❷ The Ruakuri Scenic Reserve encompasses typical karst landscape, characterized by caves, natural arches, tunnels, gorges, depressions and sculpted rock outcrops, the presence and formation of which are explained and outlined on information boards along the way. The first 50m (55 yards) of the walk are fringed with damp walls and small overhangs that are inhabited by glow-worms (obviously best seen if you return after dark, but take a torch/flashlight).

One of the highlights of the walk is the Ruakuri natural bridge tunnel, which is home to a colony of native long-tailed bats. They are an endangered species and one of only two land mammals native to New Zealand (both of which are species of bat).

After completing the Ruakuri circuit return via the Waitomo Walkway to the Waitomo Glow-worm Caves car park.

## WHERE TO EAT

### MOREPORK CAFÉ

Morepork is a congenial pizza café with a spacious deck.

✉ Kiwipaka Hostel, School Road, Waitomo Caves Village ☎ 07-878 3395
🕓 Daily 8am–9pm

## INFORMATION

### TOURIST INFORMATION

www.waitomo-museum.co.nz
✉ Waitomo Museum of Caves Visitor Information Centre, 21 Waitomo Caves Road, Waitomo ☎ 0800-474839/07-878 7640

## TIP

» Take a tour to the Waitomo Glow-worm Caves (▷ 117) before or after your walk.

# WHAT TO DO

## CAMBRIDGE

### CAMBRIDGE THOROUGHBRED LODGE

www.cambridgethoroughbredlodge.co.nz

An hour-long New Zealand Horse Magic Show on a 40ha (100-acre) farm showcases various horse breeds, which perform with audience participation. Afternoon tea and a horse ride are included.

SH1, Karapiro, Cambridge 07-827 8118 Daily 10–3, shows at 10.30 or 11.30. Check for times and dates. Bookings are essential Adult NZ$12, child NZ$5 6km (4 miles) south of Cambridge

## GISBORNE

### ANIMAL KRACKERS PET PARK

www.oaklandtruffles.com

Children can feed the rabbits, miniature horses, deer, llama and kunekune pigs at this little pet park. Their parents may also be interested in visiting the *truffière*, New Zealand's first commercial producers of prized Périgord black truffles. A trained dog sniffs out the delicacies from May to the end of August.

Oakland Truffière, Ferry Road, Waerenga-a-hika, Gisborne 06-862 5597 Daily 1–4; *truffière* visits by appointment Adult NZ$5, child NZ$2 Turn off SH2 at the Bushmere Arms

### BULMER HARVEST CIDER

You can taste and buy a range of ciders made on site by New Zealand's largest cider producer. They also make honey mead and a liqueur.

Customhouse Street, Gisborne 06-868 8300 Mon–Fri 10–4

### CHALET SURF LODGE

www.chaletsurf.co.nz

Surfing is the theme of this lodge, 8km (5 miles) north of Gisborne, which combines with a local surf retailer, The Boardroom, to provide an experience of the region's surf beaches. Surf coaching, accommodation and board rental are also available.

62 Moana Road, Wainui 06-868 9612 From NZ$22

### MILLTON VINEYARDS

www.millton.co.nz

The Millton vineyards were the first in New Zealand to have full organic certification. Wines here are grown biodynamically, mixing organics with the theories of Rudolf Steiner. The flagship Clos de Ste. Anne Pinot noir and Chardonnay from Naboth's Vineyard are both particularly highly regarded.

119 Papatu Road, Manutuke, Gisborne 06-862 8680 Dec daily 10–5; Oct, Nov, Jan–end Apr Mon–Sat daily 10–5; otherwise by appointment Off SH2

### NEW ZEALAND SAFARI ADVENTURES

www.nzsafari.co.nz

Hunting is the focus of this operation, spread over 6,667ha (16,474 acres) at Tangihau Station, where you can pursue big game such as red stag and fallow buck, or water fowl, turkeys and ducks in season. Non-hunters can experience station life with farm tours, rock sliding, swimming at the Rere Falls, golf and wine trails.

Tangihau Station Enterprise, Rere 06-867 0872 NZ$100–NZ$1,000 44km (27 miles) from Gisborne

### SMASH PALACE

A bar, barbecue and museum of eccentricities in the heart of Gisborne's industrial area, Smash Palace hosts DJs and live bands, particularly in summer. It also has a reputation in Gisborne for its delicious flaming pizza.

24 Banks Street, Gisborne 06-867 7769 Mon–Thu 3pm–late, Fri, Sat 12pm–3am, Sun 3pm–late

**Opposite** *The gannet colony is the big draw on Cape Kidnappers tours*

## HAMILTON

### DONOVANS CHOCOLATES

www.donovanschocolates.co.nz

A family firm specializing in European-style chocolates, Donovans has a factory shop selling 40 kinds of confectionery.

137 Maui Street, Hamilton 07-847 5771 Mon–Sat 9.30–5, Sun 10–4 Serves espresso and snacks

### EXSCITE

www.exscite.org.nz

Standing for Explorations in Science and Technology, Exscite is an interactive science exhibit aimed at children, attached to the Waikato Museum (▷ 101).

1 Grantham Street, Hamilton 07-838 6553 Daily 10–4.30 Adult NZ$6, child NZ$5, under-3s free, family NZ$20

### FOUNDERS THEATRE

Hamilton's major performance venue, this 1,250-seat auditorium is located in Boyes Park and hosts international acts, musicals and concerts, opera, dance and cultural events. More intimate concerts and plays are staged at the Clarence Street Theatre (59 Clarence Street), and alternative theatre and dance at The Meteor (1 Victoria Street).

221 Tristram Street, Hamilton 07-838 6600

### THE GOUDA CHEESE SHOP

www.goudacheese.co.nz

Ben and Fieke Meyer make Dutch-style cheeses using the milk from their farm outside Hamilton. You can buy the cheeses cut to order at this retail outlet in the suburb of Hillcrest, which also carries a selection of Dutch foods.

245 Cambridge Road, Hillcrest, Hamilton 07-856 6633 Mon–Fri 9–5, Sat 9–4

### HAMILTON GARDENS

www.hamiltongardens.co.nz

Hamilton's most famous attraction, this is a collection of themed gardens with river walks, lakes and exotic pavilions. Guided tours are available. The Gardens Pavilion hosts a full schedule of shows and events.

Cobham Drive, State Highway 1, Hamilton 07-856 6782 Oct–end Apr daily 7.30am–8pm; May–end Sep 7.30–5.30

### MV *WAIPA DELTA*

www.waipadelta.co.nz

Replica 'paddleboat' cruises explore the Waikato River, with lunch, afternoon tea or a buffet dinner. There is a bar on board.

Memorial Park Jetty, Memorial Drive, Hamilton 07-854 7813 Thu–Sun 12, 2.45, 6.30 From NZ$25 adult, child (under 15) half price

### RIVERSIDE ENTERTAINMENT CENTRE

www.skycityhamilton.co.nz

This complex houses SKYCITY Hamilton Casino, with 23 gaming tables and 339 gaming machines. On level two, The Bowlevard has 10-pin bowling, laser games, a sports bar and nightclub. Minimum age 20, smart casual dress required.

346 Victoria Street, Hamilton 07-834 4900 (Sky City) Sky City: Sun–Wed 9am–3am, Thu–Sat 9am–5am. The Bowlevard: Mon 4pm–10pm, Tue, Wed 10am–11pm, Thu–Sat 10am–2am, Sun 10am–11pm

### WATERS DAY SPA

www.waters.net.nz

Spa treatments are offered in premises overlooking the Waikato River. There is also an infrared sauna.

1226a Victoria Street, Hamilton 07-838 2202 Tue–Sat 9–5 From NZ$45

## HASTINGS

### EARLY MORNING BALLOONS

www.hotair.co.nz

Hot-air balloon flights over Hawke's Bay last approximately an hour, but allow four hours' total excursion time—launch sites vary according to the conditions. The flight fee includes a picnic. Minimum four people, maximum six, and not recommended for children under 10.

71 Rosser Road, RD4, Hastings 07-879 4229 Adult NZ$290, child (under 12) NZ$240

### HAWKE'S BAY FARMERS' MARKET

Local growers and artisan food producers sell their wares here. Stalls include fruit and vegetables, meat, poultry, eggs, herbs, coffee, ice cream, preserves, confectionery and flowers.

Hawke's Bay Showgrounds, Kenilworth Road, Hastings 06-974 8931 Sun 8.30–12.30

### ON YER BIKE WINERY TOURS

www.onyerbikehb.co.nz

Visit the wineries of the Ngatarawa area on these self-guided bicycle tours. Comfortable mountain bikes, maps and a picnic lunch are provided, as well as a mobile phone for back-up (such as arranging to have your wine purchases collected). Routes up to 28km (18 miles) long cater for various levels of fitness. Minimum age 18.

129 Rosser Road, RD4, Hastings 06-879 8735 Oct–end Apr daily 10–5.30; May–end Sep daily 11–4 From NZ$50

### RUSH MUNRO'S ICE CREAM GARDENS

www.rushmunro.co.nz

Rush Munro's have been making handcrafted natural ice creams to their own traditional recipes since 1926. They use no colourings or additives, and their fruit ice creams contain real fruit. The choice of flavours offered is huge, ranging from passionfruit to hokey pokey.

704 Heretaunga Street West, Hastings 06-878 9634 Dec–end Feb Mon–Fri 11–8, Sat, Sun 10–9; Mar–end Nov Mon–Fri 12–5, Sat, Sun 11–5

### SPLASH PLANET

www.splashplanet.co.nz

There's something for the whole family to enjoy at this themed water park, with 15 rides and attractions including the Sky Castle Screamer, Master Blaster and Never-Ending River ride. For the less adventurous there are land-based activities such as mini-golf and a toddlers' pool.

Grove Road, Hastings 06-873 8033 Mid-Nov to end Feb daily 10–6 Adult NZ$25, child (4–13) NZ$18

## HAVELOCK NORTH

### AIRPLAY

www.airplay.co.nz

Specialists in foot-launched paragliding, Airplay fly from a variety of graded sites. Tandem paragliding flights range from 15 minutes over the cliffs of Te Mata Peak to cross-country flights lasting up to four hours. Courses are also available.
Te Mata Peak, Havelock North
0274 512 886 From NZ$140

### VILLAGE GROWERS' MARKET

www.blackbarn.com

This delightful small market takes place on Saturday mornings in the summer months in the heart of the vineyard. Local growers and producers sell their seasonal wares, along with artisan breads, coffee, flowers, meat, pickles, olive oil and lavender products.
Black Barn Vineyards, Black Barn Road, Havelock North 06-877 7985 Late Oct–end Apr Sat 9–12

## HAWERA

### DAM DROPPING

www.damdrop.com

This three-hour trip on water sledges on the Waingongoro River includes an 8m (26ft) drop over a dam. It differs from whitewater rafting as you control of your own sledge.
Kaitiaki Adventures, Surf Highway, Hawera 06-752 8242 Oct–end Mar daily 9, 12, 3.30; Apr–end Sep 9, 12
From NZ$100

### HAWERA WATER TOWER

Climb to the top of the 54m (177ft) tower, built in 1914 for fire-fighting, for views over the whole of South Taranaki, and to the mountain.
55 High Street, Hawera 06-278 8599
Mon–Fri 8.30–5, Sat, Sun 10–2
Adult NZ$2

## NAPIER

### ART DECO SHOP

www.artdeconapier.com

The shop stocks a wide range of art deco products, including books, posters, clothing, writing paper, needlepoint, place mats, coasters and table napkins.
Deco Centre, 163 Tennyson Street, Napier 06-835 0022 Daily 9–5

### ART DECO TOURS

www.artdeconapier.com

Enjoy a guided or self-guided art deco tour of the city, by car or on foot. A 2.5-hour tour, starting at 2pm at the Art Deco shop (▷ above), includes a two-hour guided walk and video screening with refreshments. Shorter morning walks start at 10am from the visitor information office, or you can pick up an *Art Deco Walk* booklet (NZ$5) for a self-guided tour. Self-drive touring maps (NZ$5) are available, or tour in a vintage Buick (NZ$130 for up to three people).
Art Deco Trust, 163 Tennyson Street, Napier 06-835 0022 Daily From NZ$14, children free

### CHURCH ROAD WINERY

www.churchroad.co.nz

Founded in 1897, the Church Road winery is one of the oldest in New Zealand and is known particularly for the work of pioneering wine-maker Tom McDonald, after whom the winery's top red wine and cellar are named. The winery also houses New Zealand's only wine museum.
150 Church Road, Taradale, Napier
06-844 2053 Daily 9–5 Tours daily at 10, 11, 2 and 3, NZ$10

### GANNET BEACH ADVENTURES

www.gannets.com

Tours leave from Clifton Beach on trailers pulled by vintage tractors, following the Cape Kidnappers coastline to the gannet colonies. Stopping for 90 minutes allows time to swim or get a close view of the birds. Departure times depend on the tides.
PO Box 1463, Hastings 06-875 0898
Oct–early May daily Adult from NZ$38, child NZ$23

### NAPIER MUNICIPAL THEATRE

www.venues.co.nz

An art deco building that has been sensitively extended to create a modern performing space, this theatre seats 970 and is regularly used for concerts, drama, dance and international acts. The website gives performance details.
119 Tennyson Street, Napier
06-835 1087

### OCEAN SPA

Built on the site of the original Hot Sea Water Baths, the complex has pools of differing depths and temperatures, spas, sauna, steam room, massage and beauty therapies. The stylish Soak café is licensed and has good food.
Marine Parade, Napier 06-835 8553
Mon–Sat 6am–10pm, Sun 8am–10pm
Admission adult NZ$6, child (2–14) NZ$4, private spa NZ$8, massage from NZ$35

## NEW PLYMOUTH

### FUN HO! NATIONAL TOY MUSEUM

www.funhotoys.co.nz

For more than 50 years Fun Ho! miniature vehicles and toys could be found in New Zealand's playgrounds. This collection contains more than 3,000 of them, made between the 1930s and 1980s, as well as other New Zealand-made toys. Replica toys are also made at the museum.
25 Rata Street, Inglewood (Inglewood is around 20km/12 miles southeast of New Plymouth) 07-756 7030 Daily 10–4
Adult NZ$6, child NZ$3, family NZ$15

### KINA

www.kina.co.nz

Kina is located in the 1894 Exchange Chambers and specializes in New Zealand-made arts and crafts, including turned wood, flax weaving and paua. Monthly local exhibitions are held in the adjacent art space.
101 Devon Street West, New Plymouth
07-759 1201 Mon–Fri 9–5.30, Sat 9.30–4, Sun 11–4

### TARANAKI MINERAL POOLS

www.windwand.co.nz/mineralpools

Incorporating the original Tarawhata Mineral Baths, the Bonithon Spa Health company has transformed the artesian mineral well into a modern healing facility. Communal and private pools are available. Advance booking is essential.

**Above** *A walking tour of Napier is a great way to see this art deco city*

✉ 8 Bonithon Avenue, New Plymouth ☎ 06-759 1666 🕐 Mon, Wed–Fri 9am–8pm, Tue 9–5, Sat, Sun 12–9 💰 From NZ$5

### TSB BOWL OF BROOKLANDS

www.bowl.co.nz

Attractively set in parkland, with a lake, this natural amphitheatre seating up to 15,000 is a popular summer venue for Christmas in the Bowl, ballet, concerts, international acts and events such as the WOMAD world music festival.

✉ Pukekura Park, New Plymouth ☎ 07-759 6080 🕐 Events listed on the www.newplymouthnz.com website

### YARROW STADIUM

Major local and national sporting events are held in the 25,000-seater stadium, including rugby, cricket and soccer.

✉ Maratahu Street, New Plymouth ☎ 07-759 6060 🕐 Events listed on the www.newplymouthnz.com website

## OHAKUNE

### CANOE SAFARIS

www.canoesafaris.co.nz

Guided canoeing trips lasting from one to five days can be taken on the Whanganui and Rangitikei rivers. Rafting trips are also available on the Mohaka River. Most trips are suitable for families with children aged five upwards. Guides go ahead to set up campsites and lunches.

✉ Tay Street, Ohakune ☎ 06-385 9237 🕐 Oct–end Apr 💰 From NZ$105, child NZ$75

### TUROA SKIFIELD

www.mtruapeu.com

On the Ohakune side of Mount Ruapehu, with reputedly the biggest vertical drop of all ski fields in Australasia, Turoa is popular with both skiers and snowboarders. It covers 500ha (1,200 acres) and has 11 lifts, equipment hire and cafés. Ski passes are also valid at Whakapapa on the other side of Mount Ruapehu.

✉ Ohakune ☎ 07-385 8456 🕐 Usually mid-Jun to end Oct 💰 From NZ$83, youth NZ$48

## ORAKEI KORAKO THERMAL RESERVE

### NZ RIVERJET

www.riverjet.co.nz

Jet-boat trips take in lovely scenery on the Waikato River for one hour, or head to the hidden valley of Orakei Korako Thermal Reserve.

✉ Vaile Road, Reporoa ☎ 07-333 7111 🕐 Daily 10.30 💰 From NZ$125, child NZ$50, family NZ$300 🚗 37km (23 miles) north of Taupo, off SH5

## RAGLAN

### RAGLAN SURFING SCHOOL

www.raglansurfingschool.co.nz

Learn to ride Raglan's famed 'Endless Summer' breaks at Raglan Surf School, which offers three-hour lessons and two- to five-day surf adventure packages, including equipment and accommodation.

✉ 5 Whaanga Road, Whale Bay, Raglan ☎ 07-825 7873 🕐 Daily 10am 💰 From NZ$89

## ROTORUA

### JADE FACTORY

www.jadefactory.com

Visit the workshop to watch jade carvers create pendants and sculptures in traditional and contemporary designs, many of which have symbolic associations—as the carvers will explain. The adjacent gift centre sells their works as well as souvenirs, woollen products, clothing, jewellery and items made from native wood.

✉ 1288 Fenton Street, Rotorua ☎ 07-349 3968 🕐 Daily 9–6

### MOKOIA ISLAND TOURS

www.mokoiaisland.co.nz

Paddleboat cruises on the lake are combined with breakfast, lunch, afternoon tea or dinner and dancing. A trip to Mokoia Island Nature Reserve includes a Maori cultural experience related to the history of Hinemoa and Tutanekai.

✉ Memorial Drive, Lakefront, Rotorua ☎ 07-345 7456 🕐 Daily 10, 12, 2, 4 💰 Adult from NZ$95, child NZ$47–NZ$50

### MOUNT TARAWERA NZ LTD

www.mt-tarawera.co.nz

A choice of six tours is available from one of the few operators licensed to take visitors to the crater left by the eruption of 1886. You can travel by 4X4 or helicopter, walk the crater rim or scree slide, and combine Tarawera visits with other Rotorua attractions.

✉ 171 Fairy Springs Road, Rotorua ☎ 07-349 3714/0274 963083 🕐 Daily 8, 1 💰 From NZ$133, child (under 12) NZ$78

### THE PIG AND WHISTLE

www.pigandwhistle.co.nz

Housed in a former police station, this lively bar sells micro-brewed beers with names like Swine Lager. Live bands play on Thursday, Friday and Saturday nights, and a guitarist on Wednesday and Sunday. There's also a big screen in the garden bar with Sky Sport.

✉ 1182 Tutanekai Street, Rotorua ☎ 07-347 3025 🕐 Daily 11.30am–late

### RAINBOW SPRINGS

www.rainbowsprings.co.nz

This nature park sets out to be family friendly, with bush walks, kiwi and other native birds, and trout that can be fed. An entertaining farm show also gives an insight into life on a New Zealand farm.

✉ Fairy Springs Road, Rotorua ☎ 07-350 0440 🕐 Daily 8am–9.30pm 💰 Adult NZ$24.50, child (5–15) NZ$14.50, under-5s free, family NZ$65

### TAMAKI MAORI VILLAGE

www.maoriculture.co.nz

Maori life in pre-European times is re-created at this village, which gives

an insight into *marae* protocol with demonstrations of culture and crafts, a concert party and a *hangi* (food cooked in an earth oven, ▷ 278). You can also buy carvings, flax weaving, foods, Maori medicines and clothing.
✉ 1220 Hinemaru Street, Rotorua ☎ 07-349 2999 🕐 Oct–end Apr daily 5.30, 6.30, 7.30; May–end Sep 5.30, 7.30 ✋ Adult NZ$90, child (5–15) NZ$50

### THE TARAWERA LANDING

A morning cruise on Lake Tarawera retraces the route of Maori canoes that visited the famed Pink and White Terraces before the 1886 Mount Tarawera eruption, with a stop to walk to Lake Rotomahana. Afternoon scenic cruises are also available. Advance booking essential.
✉ The Landing, Lake Tarawera ☎ 07-362 8595 🕐 Daily 10.30 ✋ From NZ$38, child NZ$23

### TE PUIA MAORI ARTS AND CRAFTS INSTITUTE

www.tepuia.com
Part of the Whakarewarewa complex (▷ 110), the institute preserves the arts of wood carving *(whakairo)* and weaving *(raranga)*. You can walk around the carving school, visit a greenstone jeweller's studio, watch women weaving flax or a Maori cultural performance.
✉ Hemo Road, Whakarewarewa, Rotorua ☎ 07-348 9047 🕐 Daily 8–5 ✋ General admission adult NZ$50, child (5–15) NZ$25

### WET 'N' WILD

www.wetnwildrafting.co.nz
Depending on the level of adrenalin rush desired, you can choose from whitewater rafting at various grades on five rivers. Trips last anything from 45 minutes to a highly recommended multi-day trip down the remote Motu River.
✉ 2 White Street, Rotorua ☎ 07-348 3191 ✋ From NZ$100

### ZORB ROTORUA

www.zorb.co.nz
Zorbing is rolling downhill in an inflated ball at up to 50kph (30mph). You can choose to go harnessed in a dry Zorb, or loose in a Hydro Zorb (known as the 'wash cycle'), or try the zigzag track. The Hydro Zorb can be done with friends, which reduces the cost. There's a children's Zorb for playing on flat ground.
✉ Agrodome Adventure Park, Western Road, Ngongotaha, Rotorua ☎ 07-357 5100 🕐 Dec–end Mar 9–5; Apr–end Nov 9–8 ✋ NZ$45

## TAUPO

### CHRIS JOLLY OUTDOORS

www.chrisjolly.co.nz
Chris Jolly offers scenic cruises, lake fishing, fly fishing, hunting, water-skiing, jet-skiing, self-drive boats, guided walks and scenic flights. One option is to take a two-hour guided bush walk, be met by boat, and fish and cruise back to Taupo (NZ$1,040 for 2–4 people).
✉ Taupo Boat Harbour, Taupo ☎ 07-378 0623 ✋ From NZ$40, child NZ$16

### KURA GALLERY

www.kura.co.nz
This small gallery specializes in contemporary New Zealand ethnic art and craft, including jewellery, carving, wood turning, paintings and flax weaving.
✉ 47A Heu Heu Street, Taupo ☎ 07-377 4068 🕐 Mon–Fri 10–6, Sat, Sun 10–4

### THE MERCHANT OF TAUPO

www.themerchant.co.nz
The Merchant provides all the ingredients for a slap-up picnic: cheese, pâté, olives and cured meats, salmon, sauces, biscuits and chocolates, wines, beers and spirits. He also does glassware and gifts.
✉ 14 Spa Road, Taupo ☎ 07-378 4626 🕐 Daily 9–6

**Left** *Rent a craft to get a close-up view of the Maori rock carvings on Lake Taupo*

### TAUPO HOT SPRINGS SPA

www.taupohotsprings.com
This thermal complex has hot pools, private spas and an interactive warm-water children's playground with hydroslide. Spa treatments include therapeutic massage and beauty treatments.
✉ SH5, Taupo ☎ 07-377 6502 🕐 Daily 7.30am–9.30pm ✋ From NZ$15, child (3–12) NZ$4; treatments from NZ$65

### WAIRAKEI INTERNATIONAL GOLF COURSE

www.wairakeigolfcourse.co.nz
Designed as a green-fee course rather than a club, this internationally recognized golf course welcomes visitors and has a driving range, pro shop, bar and restaurant.
✉ State Highway 1, Taupo ☎ 07-374 8152 ✋ From NZ$150 🚗 9km (6 miles) north of Taupo on SH1

## TAURANGA

### BAYCOURT ENTERTAINMENT CENTRE

www.baycourt.co.nz
Baycourt supports Tauranga's lively performing arts scene, with a modern 590-seat theatre hosting local and touring shows, and a 1926 Wurlitzer theatre organ.
✉ Durham Street, Tauranga ☎ 07-577 7198

### BUTLER'S SWIMMING WITH DOLPHINS

www.swimwithdolphins.co.nz
*Gemini Galaxsea*, an eco-friendly 20m (65ft) sailing boat, takes you on a leisurely trip to watch and swim with dolphins. It leaves from either Tauranga or Mount Maunganui. The boat has a swim bar for hanging onto when the dolphins swim faster than you can. Whales, seals and seabirds are also plentiful.
☎ 0508 BUTLER 🕐 Daily 9am Tauranga Marina, 9.30 Salisbury Wharf, Mount Maunganui ✋ Adult NZ$125, child (under 13) NZ$90

## TE AROHA

### TE AROHA MINERAL POOLS

www.tearohapools.co.nz

Established in 1883 to take advantage of mineral soda hot springs, Te Aroha is in a landscaped domain (park) and retains many Edwardian buildings. You can choose from modern or Edwardian private bath houses or outdoor spas.

✉ Te Aroha Hot Springs Domain, Te Aroha ☎ 07-884 4498 🕐 Spa daily 10–10; pool Mon–Fri 10–6, Sat, Sun 10–7 🖐 From NZ$17, child NZ$8

## WAIPUKURAU

### AIRLIE MOUNT WALKS

Itineraries lasting from half a day to three days combine walks on private farms with visiting grand 1800s homesteads not otherwise open to the public. The walks take in native bush, bird and marine life, beaches and *pa* sites.

✉ PO Box 368, Waipukurau ☎ 06-858 7601 🕐 Daily 🖐 From NZ$90

## WAITOMO

### THE LEGENDARY BLACK WATER RAFTING COMPANY

www.blackwaterrafting.co.nz

Best known for its underground cave-tubing experience, Black Labyrinth, this company also offers Black Abyss abseiling (rappelling). Reasonable fitness is required. Minimum age 13.

✉ PO Box 13, Waitomo Caves ☎ 07-878 6219 🕐 Black Labyrinth daily 9, 10.30, 12, 1.30, 3; Black Abyss daily 9.30, 2.30 🖐 Black Labyrinth NZ$95; Black Abyss NZ$185

## WHITE ISLAND

### PEEJAY WHITE ISLAND TOURS

www.whiteisland.co.nz

Enjoy an 80-minute launch trip to White Island's active volcano, and a guided walk (with hard hat and gas mask provided) through the remains of a sulphur factory to the rim of the volcano.

✉ 15 The Strand East, Whakatane ☎ 07-308 9588 🕐 Daily 9.15 (more trips Dec–end Feb) 🖐 From NZ$175, child (1–13) NZ$120 (child rates not available Nov–end Mar)

# FESTIVALS AND EVENTS

## FEBRUARY

### BREBNER PRINT ART DECO WEEKEND

www.artdeconapier.com

This not-too-serious celebration of Napier's art deco heritage has become so popular it now runs into several days, with walks and tours, events on stage and screen, a vintage car cruise, street jazz and a seaside ball.

✉ Deco Centre, 163 Tennyson Street, Napier ☎ 06-835 11911

### HARVEST HAWKE'S BAY

www.hawkesbaynz.com

Around 30 Hawke's Bay vineyards open their doors to show off their wines in this festival of tastings, tours, concerts, art exhibitions and workshops.

✉ Hawke's Bay Wine Country ☎ 0800-442 946 🖐 Adult NZ$15

## MARCH

### WOMAD NEW ZEALAND

www.womad.co.nz

This three-day biennial celebration of world music, arts and dance is held in odd years, with concerts, workshops, storytellers, crafts and Kidzone for children.

✉ TSB Bowl of Brooklands, New Plymouth ☎ 06-759 8412

## EASTER

### NATIONAL JAZZ FESTIVAL

www.jazz.org.nz

Concerts at Baycourt span the decades from New Orleans, Chicago and Latin America, with a New Zealand spin, while Tauranga holds a Mardi Gras celebration of wine, food and music.

✉ Baycourt, corner of Durham and Wharf streets, Tauranga ☎ 07-577 7018

## JUNE

### MATARIKI

www.matarikifestival.co.nz

This celebrates the Maori New Year, the first new moon after the rising of Pleiades star cluster in the eastern sky at dawn. There are feasting and fun activities here, and in other parts of the country.

✉ Hawke's Bay Showgrounds ☎ 06-873 3526

### NEW ZEALAND NATIONAL AGRICULTURAL FIELDAYS

www.fieldays.co.nz

The biggest agricultural trade show in the southern hemisphere, Mystery Creek attracts 1,000 exhibitors and more than 115,000 visitors. It is also famous for its Rural Bachelor of the Year contest.

✉ Mystery Creek, Mystery Creek Road, Hamilton ☎ 07-843 4499 🖐 Adult NZ$15, child (5–14) NZ$6

## SEPTEMBER

### HASTINGS BLOSSOM FESTIVAL

www.blossomfestival.co.nz

The apple orchards are in full bloom for this celebration of spring in one of New Zealand's leading fruit-growing regions. The 10 days of concerts and events include a blossom parade.

✉ 106 Russell Street South, Hastings ☎ 06-878 9447

## OCTOBER

### GISBORNE WINE AND FOOD FESTIVAL

www.gisbornenz.com

This one-day event showcases the best of the region's food and wine. About a dozen venues participate, each one dispensing its own food, wine and music.

✉ Showgrounds Park, Main Road, Gisborne ☎ 0800 447 267 🖐 Adult NZ$60

# EATING

**PRICES AND SYMBOLS**

The restaurants are listed alphabetically. The prices given are the average for a two-course lunch (L) and a three-course dinner (D) for one person, without drinks. The wine price (W) is for the least expensive bottle. All the restaurants listed accept credit cards unless otherwise stated.

For a key to the symbols, ▷ 2.

## GISBORNE

### THE COLOSSEUM CAFÉ & WINE BAR

Matawhero is regarded as the cradle of Gewürztraminer in New Zealand, and its winemaker Denis Irwin is a great character, producing fine and unusual wines since 1970. You can taste his wines and have brunch, lunch, evening meals and casual snacks at his vineyard café. The antipasto platter (NZ$35) is a generous introduction to the menu.
✉ 4 Riverpoint Road, Matawhero, Gisborne ☎ 06-867 4733 🕐 Sep–end May daily 10.30–7 L NZ$25, D NZ$38, W NZ$20

### THE WHARF CAFÉ

www.wharfbar.co.nz

Set in a wharf building, the café looks over the marina. Inside the styling is simple, with sails stretched across the ceiling. The food is mainly modern New Zealand, such as fresh crayfish with salad greens, roast gourmet potatoes, smoked salmon and roquette butter.
✉ The Wharf, 60 The Esplanade, Gisborne ☎ 06-868 4876 🕐 Daily 9am–late L NZ$38, D NZ$65, W NZ$36

### THE WORKS

This harbourside winery and café houses the cellar door for several local wineries. The brick building is cleverly converted into a casual restaurant, where you can have anything from coffee and a snack to lunch or dinner. The food has a regional focus; seafood and paua (abalone) are among the specialities.
✉ The Wharf, 60 The Esplanade, Gisborne ☎ 06-863 1285 🕐 Daily 10–10 L NZ$25, D NZ$60, W NZ$28

## HAMILTON

### CANVAS

www.canvas.net.nz

Modern art on the walls, lots of plants, muted lighting and jazz on the sound system give Canvas a sophisticated atmosphere, and the food and service are both highly regarded. The menu is modern New Zealand, with dishes such as cervena loin on kumara and thyme dauphinoise, or lamb on quinoa and potato mash.
✉ Grantham Street, Hamilton ☎ 07-839 2535 🕐 Mon–Fri 11.30–2.30, 6–late, Sat 6–late L NZ$35, D NZ$65, W NZ$35

### IGUANA

www.iguana.net.nz

Spacious and popular, Iguana serves a Pacific Rim menu, including steak, chicken, lamb and pizzas. Cook-your-own hot rocks are a speciality—a mini barbecue of heated granite with your choice of ingredients. Sit on the street or in a booth.
✉ 203 Victoria Street, Hamilton ☎ 07-834 2280 🕐 Mon–Fri 10am–late, Sat, Sun 9am–3am L NZ$23, D NZ$55, W NZ$32

## HAVELOCK NORTH

### TERRÔIR

www.craggyrange.com

This stunning stone-built winery restaurant looks over vines to Te Mata Peak. The restaurant specializes in rôtisserie and wood-fired oven cooking, and showcases Craggy Range wines. There is an outstanding international wine list. For a specifically New Zealand experience, try the paua sausage with potatoes and fern fronds.

**Opposite** *Pizzas at the Iguana, Hamilton*

✉ Craggy Range Vineyards, 253 Waimarama Road, Havelock North ☎ 06-873 0143 🕐 Late Oct to mid-Apr Mon–Sat 11– 3, 6–late, Sun 11–3; mid-Apr to late Oct Tue–Sat 11–3, 6–late, Sun 11–3 L NZ$48, D NZ$63, W NZ$38

## LAKE TARAWERA

### THE LANDING CAFÉ

www.purerotorua.com

At this café beside Lake Tarawera, have a drink in the Old Trout Bar or take a veranda table overlooking the lake, but protect yourself from sandflies. The menu includes open sandwiches, salads and pasta.
✉ Spencer Road, The Landing, Lake Tarawera ☎ 07-362 8595 🕐 Daily 9.30–4.30, evenings by arrangement L NZ$30, D NZ$45, W NZ$30

## MOUNT MAUNGANUI

### ASTROLABE

www.astrolabe.co.nz

Astrolabe is laid out in separate but interrelated areas with a bar, café, courtyard and formal dining room. It's popular for brunch/ lunch, casual drinks or more serious meals, with standards like poached eggs and smoked salmon or Pacific Rim dishes such as beef salad with cashew, coriander, chilli and lime.
✉ 82 Maunganui Road, Mount Maunganui ☎ 07-574 8155 🕐 Daily 9am–10pm L NZ$30, D NZ$45, W NZ$29

## NAPIER

### CAUTION AND SHED 2

www.shed2.com

Converted from a 19th-century wool store, Shed 2 makes the most of its waterfront location, with large quayside decks. On cold days there's a welcome open fire. The menu has an Eastern orientation with dishes such as a seafood broth with wasabi and lime calamari. The nextdoor Caution dining lounge provides a retreat from big-screen TVs with a more formal menu, local wine list and brunch at weekends.
✉ West Quay, Ahuriri, Napier ☎ 06-835 2202 🕐 Mon–Fri 11.30am–late, Sat, Sun 9am–late L NZ$25, D NZ$40, W NZ$33

### CHAMBERS RESTAURANT

www.countyhotel.co.nz

On the Napier waterfront in the Edwardian County Hotel (▷ 134), Chambers is one of the few silver-service restaurants in the city. It is noted for its elegant décor, attentive service and extensive wine lists. The menu is international, with dishes such as paella, a plate of sushi and sashimi, lamb shanks in a red wine stock and white chocolate tiramisu.
✉ County Hotel, 12 Browning Street, Napier ☎ 06-835 7800 🕐 Daily 6.30pm–late D NZ$62, W NZ$39

### MISSION ESTATE

www.missionestate.co.nz

New Zealand's oldest winery, Mission Estate is on a hillside overlooking Napier. The restaurant is in a restored seminary building, and offers a seasonally focused menu. Specialities are Aoraki salmon fillet panfried medium rare, in puff pastry with smoked salmon, spinach and summer greens and drizzled with salmon caviar butter sauce; and loin of venison with a peppercrust on potato mash.
✉ 198 Church Road, Taradale, Napier ☎ 06-845 9350 🕐 Daily 10am–late L NZ$35, D NZ$65, W NZ$25

## NEW PLYMOUTH

### ANDRÉ L'ESCARGOT

www.andres.co.nz

L'Escargot's 1870s premises give the place a timeless quality. The menu is unashamedly French, with classics such as steak au poivre, goat's cheese soufflé and tarte tatin. A platter of seasonal dishes for two is NZ$39.50 per person. The wine list includes French as well as New Zealand and Australian wines.
✉ 37–43 Brougham Street, New Plymouth ☎ 06-758 4812 🕐 Mon–Sat from 5pm D NZ$65, W NZ$40

## OHAKUNE

### FAT PIGEON GARDEN CAFÉ

This bright café has a wood fire to snuggle up to in winter, and tables in the garden for warm weather. The coffee is good and the deli cabinet is full of snacks, such as filled panini.
✉ Mountain Road, Ohakune ☎ 06-385 9423 🕐 Jul–end Oct daily 9am–10pm; Nov–end Jun Thu–Sun 9am–10pm L NZ$20, D NZ$50, W NZ$22

## ROTORUA

### AORANGI PEAK

www.aorangipeak.co.nz

Chefs produce dishes such as smoked salmon in a sushi roll served with aioli dressing, followed by chicken breast wrapped with prosciutto and flaky pastry, served with prawn and escargot butter.
✉ Top of Mountain Road, Rotorua ☎ 07-347 0036 🕐 Daily noon–late L NZ$30, D NZ$65, W NZ$33

### BISTRO 1284

www.bistro1284.co.nz

Often voted Rotorua's best restaurant, here the menu is minimalist but carefully considered. A speciality is twice cooked pork with hoisin sauce on coriander rice cakes. Reservations are essential.
✉ 1284 Eruera Street, Rotorua ☎ 07-346 1284 🕐 Tue–Sat 6–9 D NZ$65, W NZ$34

### FAT DOG

Fat Dog combines quirky décor with a casual atmosphere, a wide-ranging menu and good coffee. Choose from a menu of snacks or light meals. In the evening there are main dishes such as venison and sirloin steaks. Portions are generous.
✉ 1161 Arawa Street, Rotorua ☎ 07-347 7586 🕐 Sun–Wed 8am–9pm, Thu–Sat 8am–9.30pm L NZ$25, D NZ$40, W NZ$25

## TAURANGA

### HARBOURSIDE BRASSERIE AND BAR

www.harbourside-tga.co.nz

The Harbourside's menu features Pacific Rim dishes and seafood. Choices include sushi and sashimi, with Asian pickled vegetables, wasabi and ponzu, and Whangamata scallops, pan seared with a potato blini, citrus salad and turmeric broth.
✉ The Strand, Tauranga ☎ 07-571 0520 🕐 11.30am–late L NZ$30, D NZ$60, W NZ$23

Above *Maungatautari Lodge, Cambridge*

**PRICES AND SYMBOLS**
The prices are the lowest and highest for a double room for one night including breakfast, unless otherwise stated. All the hotels listed accept credit cards unless otherwise stated. Note that rates can vary widely throughout the year.

For a key to the symbols, ▷ 2.

## CAMBRIDGE

### MAUNGATAUTARI LODGE

www.malodge.com
Spacious, sumptuously furnished suites have super-king beds, double spa baths and private balconies or terraces with views of the gardens and Lake Karapiro. The four-course dinner features home-grown and organic produce. Horseback-riding and massage are available.
844 Maungatautari Road, Lake Karapiro, Cambridge 07-827 2220 NZ$680–NZ$1,060, including pre-dinner drinks and dinner 5 suites, 3 villas Outdoor 9km (6 miles) south of Cambridge

## DAWSON FALLS

### DAWSON FALLS TOURIST LODGE

www.mountainhouse.co.nz
The Alpine-Swiss style lodge is set in native bush on the slopes of Mount Taranaki/ Egmont, in the heart of Egmont National Park. There is a bar, log fire and a restaurant.
Manaia Road, Dawson Falls 06-765 5457 NZ$200–NZ$230 11 Accessed from the north via Opunake (SH45) or Stratford (SH3), or from the south via Manaia (SH45)

## HAMILTON

### NOVOTEL TAINUI HOTEL

www.accorhotels.co.nz
Centrally located, on the banks of the Waikato River, the four-star Tainui is Hamilton's premier hotel. Some rooms have river views, and all have internet access. The restaurant has indoor and outdoor dining.
7 Alma Street, Hamilton 07-838 1366 NZ$145–NZ$349 177 rooms (130 non-smoking), including 4 suites

## HAVELOCK NORTH

### MANGAPAPA PETIT HOTEL

www.mangapapa.co.nz
This luxury hotel in a grand country home 3km (2 miles) from Havelock North, is surrounded by orchards and manicured gardens. The rooms are opulently furnished, with meticulous attention to detail. Guests can indulge in a four-course dinner matched with local wines, play tennis and rent bicycles.
466 Napier Road, Havelock North 06-878 3234 NZ$612–NZ$2,300 12 rooms, 5 suites Outdoor

## NAPIER

### COUNTY HOTEL

www.countyhotel.co.nz
This Edwardian hotel was one of the few buildings to survive the 1931 earthquake. It has 18 spacious suites named after New Zealand birds, ranging from standard double to two bedrooms with private lounge, spa bath and balcony. All rooms have internet connection. The hotel also has a popular restaurant, Chambers (▷ 133) and bar.
Browning Street, Napier 06-835 7800 NZ$270–NZ$880 18 suites (all non-smoking)

## NEW PLYMOUTH

### THE NICE HOTEL

www.nicehotel.co.nz
Art and history are the themes of this offbeat boutique hotel in the 1850s former Redcoats Hospital building. In addition to stylish design and contemporary artworks,

the rooms include luxuries such as double spa baths and comfy armchairs. The award-winning Table restaurant serves good Pacific Rim cuisine. Complimentary airport transfers are available.
71 Brougham Street, New Plymouth 06-758 6423 NZ$230–NZ$290 7 rooms, 1 suite

## OHAKUNE

### POWDERHORN CHATEAU

www.powderhorn.co.nz

The Alpine-style hotel is a popular base for skiing. Each of the 30 suites has a queen-size bed, a double sofa bed and a lounge suite. The Mansion apartment can sleep up to eight. There is babysitting, a small casino and internet access. Two restaurants are lively après-ski venues.
Corner of Mangawhero Terrace and Thames Street, Ohakune 06-385 8888 NZ$198–NZ$215 30 suites, 1 apartment Indoor At the northern end of the village, at the start of Mountain Road

## RAGLAN

### SOLSCAPE

www.solscape.co.nz

Renovated railway guard's vans are arranged as dormitories or self-contained units. Two cottages with open fires are also available. The property enjoys fabulous views across the Tasman Sea and there is also a menagerie of animals.
611 Wainui Road, Raglan 07-825 8268 NZ$58–NZ$135 17 cabooses, 2 cottages From Raglan follow the Wainui Road for 5.5km (3.5 miles)

## ROTORUA

### MILLENNIUM HOTEL ROTORUA

www.millenniumhotels.co.nz

This popular chain hotel is close to the Polynesian Spa. The modern rooms and suites have direct-dial phones and modem points. There is a nightly Maori cultural performance and *hangi* (feast). The restaurant is considered one of the city's best.
Corner of Eruera and Hinemaru streets, Rotorua 07-347 1234 NZ$230–NZ$390 227 rooms (120 non-smoking) Indoor

### REGAL PALMS MOTOR LODGE

www.regalpalmsml.co.nz

Of the dozens of motels in Rotorua, the Regal Palms is one of the best, with a five-star rating. It has one- and two-bedroom suites and three serviced apartments, all with kitchen facilities and a spa pool. Facilities also include a sauna, internet access, a bar, mini-golf, children's playground and barbecue area.
350 Fenton Street, Rotorua 07-350 3232 NZ$195–NZ$285 41 suites, 3 apartments Outdoor On the main bus route 2km (1 mile) south of the CBD

### SOLITAIRE LODGE

www.solitairelodge.co.nz

This celebrated hideaway is on the shores of Lake Tarawera. There are nine spacious, luxurious suites some with spa, deck and lake views.
Lake Tarawera, Rotorua 07-362 8208 NZ$1,440–NZ$1,957, including dinner 9 suites Helicopter access 20km (13 miles) south of the CBD

## TAUPO

### CABOOSE LODGE

www.taupocaboose.co.nz

Built in log-cabin style with African rail safari theme, this hotel has spas, internet access, a lounge with open fire and a restaurant. Fishing safaris are a speciality.
100–102 Lake Terrace, Taupo 07-376 0116 NZ$189–NZ$259 22 compartments, 28 sleepers, 1 suite Outdoor 1km (0.5 mile) from Taupo CBD

### HUKA LODGE

www.hukalodge.com

Huka Lodge is the most popular luxury lodge. Hidden in parkland beside the Waikato River, it regularly hosts royalty seeking privacy. The complex has a classic lodge feel, a library, roaring fire and deep armchairs. The suites offer every comfort, and cuisine is first-class.
Huka Falls Road, Taupo 07-378 5791 NZ$1,480–NZ$8,400, including cocktails, dinner, airport transfer 20 suites Helicopter access 3km (2 miles) from Taupo CBD

### WAIRAKEI RESORT

www.wairakei.co.nz

The resort, in the Wairakei Thermal Park, offers tennis, golf, squash and a gym, plus a spa, pool and sauna in which to relax afterwards. There is a wide variety of accommodation available from rooms to villas.
State Highway 1, Wairakei 07-374 8021/0800 RESORT NZ$99–NZ$170 157 rooms, 9 suites and 15 villas (most non-smoking) Outdoor 7km (4 miles) north of Taupo

## TAURANGA

### HARBOUR CITY MOTEL

www.taurangaharbourcity.co.nz

This classy motel is ideally located in the heart of Tauranga's shopping and café district. All rooms have spa baths. Children are catered for, with free cots and high chairs.
50 Wharf Street, Tauranga 07-571 1435 NZ$145–NZ$180 16 studios, 4 one-bedroom units 4km (3 miles) southwest of the airport

## WHAKAPAPA

### THE CHATEAU TONGARIRO

www.chateau.co.nz

Chateau Tongariro provides luxury in Tongariro National Park. It offers elegance in keeping with its age (built in 1929), including a restaurant, bar, café, pool and golf course. It's worth paying for a mountain view.
Whakapapa Village, State Highway 48, Mount Ruapehu 07-892 3809 NZ$215–NZ$1,180 95 rooms, 5 suites. Family units in separate building Indoor 45km (28 miles) south of Turangi on SH48

### SKOTEL ALPINE RESORT

www.skotel.com

Skotel will appeal to visitors on a budget. With a restaurant and bar, lounge, games room, spa pools, drying room, ski shop and tramping gear rental, it provides a comfortable base for park activities. A hostel and family chalets are also available.
Whakapapa Village, State Highway 48, Mount Ruapehu 07-892 3719 NZ$2130–NZ$219 22 deluxe, 7 standard rooms 46km (28 miles) south of Turangi

# SOUTHERN NORTH ISLAND

This region extends from the city of Wanganui to the southern tip of North Island. Wanganui's river, the Whanganui, is the longest navigable river in the country, carving a passage through steep-sided green hills and terraced fields that were once cultivated by Maori, and both the river and the city of Wanganui remain strongholds of Maori culture.

Dominating this region is Wellington, New Zealand's capital. Many visitors find themselves in Wellington by necessity rather than choice. Sited at the southern end of North Island, the city is the terminus for the vehicle and passenger ferries that cross Cook Strait to South Island. Those who linger for a day or two will discover a likeable and cultured capital city. As well as the political centre of the nation, it's a showcase for national excellence and the base for some of New Zealand's leading cultural institutions including Te Papa, the national museum. Built around a series of bays on the western side of Port Nicholson, the city is backed by the steep slopes of the Tararua Ranges. The lack of level ground for building has forced the city to squeeze itself into the relatively narrow platform along its reclaimed waterfront, while its suburbs have expanded into the nearby Hutt River Valley. Wellington is sometimes subtitled 'the windy city', and although locals might protest, it's a fact that this is New Zealand's breeziest metropolis. Cook Strait, immediately to the south, is the only major gap between the mountains of North and South islands and air currents increase in velocity as they funnel between the two islands. Wellington prides itself on its restaurant, bar and nightlife scene. The city has an outstanding choice of top-end restaurants in particular.

**CAPE PALLISER**

The road to the North Island's most southerly point passes the eroded rocky spires and turrets of the Putangirua Pinnacles, and the fishing village of Ngawihi, where tractors and bulldozers wait on the beach to launch the boats. The road ends at the Cape Palliser lighthouse, where a climb up the 250 steps is rewarded with outstanding views towards the South Island. A colony of New Zealand fur seals live on the bluff year-round—keep your distance, especially during the breeding season (Nov–Jan).

Be aware, the drive to Cape Palliser and back takes a day.

303 K11

**CASTLEPOINT**

www.wairarapanz.com

Castlepoint is the highlight of the Wairarapa's wild coastline. At the eastern end of the main beach the weather-beaten Castlepoint Lighthouse perches on a stark, rocky headland, that sweeps south to enclose a large lagoon. Just below it is a cave that can be explored at low tide, but take care: a small memorial stone commemorates those who have drowned while exploring the offshore reef.

303 L10 316 Queen Street, Masterton 06-370 0900

**KAPITI ISLAND**

Kapiti Island lies 5km (3 miles) offshore from Paraparaumu, and with its adjunct marine reserve is administered by the Department of Conservation. The 10km (6-mile) long, 2km (1-mile) wide island has been cleared of possums, rats and other predators, and after numerous plant and animal reintroductions is now a haven to native New Zealand species. You can follow tracks through native bush, while inquisitive robins, saddlebacks and stitchbirds flit about your head, and weka and takahe poke about for insects disturbed by your feet. Other occupants include kiwi, little blue penguins and the endangered kokako, which has one of the loveliest bird songs ever to grace the air.

The island has a rich history as the 19th-century stronghold of the Maori warrior Te Ruaparaha, and in the 20th century as a whaling hub. The resorts that line the stretch of mainland between Otaki and Paekakariki, known as the Kapiti Coast, are popular weekend destinations for the residents of Wellington.

303 J10 DoC, Government Buildings, Lambton Quay, Wellington 04-472 7356 Access by arrangement with DoC, tel 04-472 5821 Landing permits from DoC NZ$9, child (5–15) NZ$4.50 Boats depart from Paraparaumu Beach, 9–9.30, return 3–4 From Wellington to Paraparaumu

**MARTINBOROUGH**

This attractive, busy little town at the hub of the Wairarapa region (▷ 141) was founded in the 1880s by British settler John Martin, who laid out the village square and its radiating streets in the form of the Union Jack flag. Today there are no fewer than 20 vineyards within walking distance of the square, most of which offer tastings, and a wine centre in the heart of the village (daily 10–5) can advise on tours and hours. The Colonial Museum on the square (Sat, Sun, 2–4) occupies the former library, built in 1894.

A limestone gorge, the Patuna Chasm, with stalactites, fossils and waterfalls, can be visited on Patuna Farm, Ruakokopatuna Road (Oct–Easter, guided tours only). The nearby Ruakokopatuna glow-worm caves can be accessed with permission from Blue Creek Farm (tel 06-306 9797); be sure to take a torch (flashlight) and try to wear sturdy footwear.

303 K10 18 Kitchener Street, Martinborough 06-306 5010 Services from Featherston

**OTAKI**

www.naturecoast.co.nz

Otaki is a small town steeped in Maori history. It has several *marae*, including the finely carved 1910 Te Pou O Tainui Marae on Te Rauparaha Street, as well as the Maori Rangiatea Church, rebuilt after it was destroyed by arsonists in 1995. Otaki is the main eastern base for exploring the Tararua Forest Park: Otaki Gorge Road, 2km (1 mile) south of town, leads to Otaki Forks, where several tracks wind up into the mountains.

303 K10 Centennial Park, SH1 04-364 7620 Services from Wellington

**PAEKAKARIKI**

Train enthusiasts flock to this tiny seaside village on the Kapiti Coast to appreciate the restored vintage trains—some are still running—at the Steam Inc Engine Shed (Sat 11–3), by the rail station. More examples of vintage transport are shown at the Wellington Tramway Museum (Sat, Sun, 11–5), 5km (3 miles) north of here in Queen Elizabeth Park, where four trams are currently in operation.

303 J10 Services from Wellington

**Opposite** *Castlepoint Lighthouse*

**Right** *Martinborough's Wine Centre lies at the heart of town, close to 20 vineyards*

**Above** *Tower blocks mark the heart of modern Palmerston North*

## PALMERSTON NORTH

www.manawatunz.co.nz

A university town, Palmerston North is a gateway to the south and west of North Island, and a place of pilgrimage for rugby fans.

This agricultural and university community is set on the Manawatu River, and makes a good base for exploring the southern sector of the North Island. It also gives access through the impressive Manawatu Gorge to the Wairarapa (▷ 141) and Hawke's Bay (▷ 102). The heart of the city is the vast green, tree-lined Square. Because the town topography is so flat, you can easily get lost. It is advisable to not stray too far from the central square and visible tall buildings without a street map from the tourist office.

Other than Massey University (second in size only to Auckland's university, and named after former prime minister William Massey), the town is perhaps most famous for the New Zealand Rugby Museum at 87 Cuba Street (Mon–Sat 10–12, 1.30–4, Sun 1.30–4). It has a huge collection of memorabilia, and an archive resource of videos with accounts of every All Black game since 1870.

The excellent Te Manawa Science Centre, Museum and Art Gallery, at 396 Main Street (daily 10–5), integrates social, cultural and artistic heritage with hands-on science displays. In the museum are Maori *taonga* (treasures) and several significant artworks by contemporary figures such as Colin McCahon and Ralph Hotere. There is also a hands-on science section.

In the Manawatu flatlands north of Palmerston sits Feilding. It is a pretty place on the banks of the Oroua River, relatively prosperous and particularly well known for its gardens. These have played a key role in the town's success in the nation's Most Beautiful Small Town Awards, which it has won a remarkable 12 times. Feilding has a scattering of small museums (traction engines being a local speciality), craft outlets and gardens, and it is a tranquil place to explore on foot, or by horse and cart. It's also fun to watch local farmers bidding at the stock sales on Friday.

✚ 303 K9 ℹ The Square ☎ 06-350 1922 🕐 Daily 9–5 🚌 Corner of Pitt and Main streets 🚆 Services from Auckland and Wellington ✈ 4km (2.5 miles) northwest of city

## PARAPARAUMU

www.naturecoast.co.nz

Paraparaumu is the principal township on the Kapiti Coast and has two main beaches: Raumati Beach, to the south, and Paraparaumu Beach, to the north. The latter is also the base for trips to Kapiti Island (▷ 139).

North of town, off SH1, Southward Car Museum (Nov–Easter daily 10–5; Easter–end Oct daily 10–4.30) has an outstanding collection of 250 vehicles dating from 1895, including cars, traction engines, motorbikes, bicycles and a model railway. Highlights include a Rolls Royce that once belonged to film star Marlene Dietrich.

✚ 303 J10 ℹ Coastlands shopping centre, off SH1 ☎ 04-298 8195 🚆 Services from Wellington

## PUKAHA MOUNT BRUCE WILDLIFE CENTRE

www.mtbruce.org.nz

Pukaha Mount Bruce is the flagship of the Department of Conservation's endangered species breeding policy, where you can see rare species such as takahe, stitchbird and kokako. Wild indigenous eels live in the stream running through the reserve and gather beneath the bridge at feeding time (1.30pm) in a swirling mass. Cheeky kaka (bush parrots), bred here and now living wild in the area, will happily nibble your ear before cracking open a peanut. They are fed by staff at 3pm.

✚ 303 K10 ✉ 30km (18 miles) north of Masterton on SH2 ☎ 06-375 8004 🕐 Daily 9–4.30 ✋ Adult NZ$8, child (5–17) NZ$2 ☐

## WAIRARAPA

www.wairarapanz.com

Wild coastal scenery, relaxed rural towns like Martinborough (▷ 139), vineyards and the North Island's southernmost point (Cape Palliser, ▷ 139) all make this little-visited region worth getting to know.

From Masterton, the chief town, SH2 leads south to Carterton. Here, at the Paua World factory (▷ 152) on Kent Street, you can watch jewels being crafted from exquisite paua (abalone) shells, which are subject to strict quotas and harvesting rules. One of the best views in the Wairarapa can be enjoyed from Mount Dick, 14km (9 miles) along Dalefield Road, at the southern end of the town.

At the Waiohine Gorge, 22km (14 miles) south of Carterton, walks lead high above the river and negotiate the heart-stopping, 40m-high (130ft) swing bridge. Greytown, farther along SH2, is best known for its antiques and craft shops housed in a row of beautifully restored wooden-fronted buildings on Main Street. The Cobblestones Museum on Main Street (daily 9–4.30) is a collection of buildings and memorabilia from early settler days.

Featherston is the Wairarapa's southern point of access, set in the shadow of the Rimutaka Range. In the 1870s this was the base during construction of the Wairarapa–Wellington rail link. Its main attraction now is the Fell Locomotive Museum on the corner of State Highway 2 and Lyon Street (daily 10–4), housing the beautifully restored engine that used to climb the 265m (870ft) rise of the Rimutaka Incline. The incline is now part of the Rimutaka Rail Trail, starting at the end of Cross Creek Road, 10km (6 miles) south of Featherston, and leading in a day to Summit and back or to Kaitoke.

303 K10 316 Queen Street, Masterton 06-370 0900 Services from Wellington to Masterton

**Right** *Castlepoint Lighthouse stands proud on the rugged Wairarapa seaboard*

## WANGANUI

www.wanganuinz.com

Wanganui lies at the mouth of the Whanganui River, once a vital north–south supply route. Formerly a bustling port, Wanganui is now the southern gateway to Whanganui National Park. The area of Queen's Park, east of the central thoroughfare of Victoria Avenue, with its restored Victorian and Edwardian houses, is the city's cultural heart. It's also home to the modern Whanganui Regional Museum (daily 10–4), which contains a fine collection of Maori canoes and illustrates ingenious Maori methods of catching fish and birds. Crowning Queens Park hill is the domed Sarjeant Gallery (daily10.30–4.30), with more than 4,000 artworks.

Sailings of the restored Waimarie paddlesteamer, which worked the river for 50 years before sinking in 1952, leave from Wanganui Riverboat Centre on Taupo Quay (Nov–Apr daily 2pm; May–Oct Sat, Sun 1pm).

Within Cooks Gardens, on St. Hill Street, are the colonial-style Opera House (1899); a stadium and wooden velodrome; and the 1901 Ward Observatory (Fri 8–9.30).

Across the city bridge from Taupo Quay a tunnel takes you 200m (656ft) into the hillside to ride the Durie Hill Elevator (1919) to the top (Mon–Fri 7.30–6, Sat 9–6, Sun 10–5), where you can climb Durie Hill War Memorial Tower, built of shellrock.

303 J9 101 Guyton Street 06-349 0508 Ridgeway Street, Ingestre Street

## WELLINGTON

▷ 144–149.

## WHANGANUI NATIONAL PARK

www.doc.govt.nz

From its source high on the volcanic slopes of Tongariro National Park, the Whanganui River travels 290km (180 miles) to the sea, carving through some of the North Island's least accessible country. At its most remote parts it cuts deep into the soft sand and mudstone and is joined by tracts of forest, which form the heart of the Whanganui National Park. The entire area is difficult to reach, but there are walking tracks and jet-boat and kayak trips along the river itself. Be aware that slips and flooding are real dangers; consult the Department of Conservation before an excursion.

The windy and scenic Whanganui River Road branches off SH4 15km (9 miles) north of Wanganui and follows the river to Pipiriki before turning inland to Raetihi, where it rejoins SH4. The 106km (66-mile) round trip, passes a number of mission settlements that were created in the 1840s by the Reverend Richard Taylor.

300 K8 74 Ingestre Street, Wanganui 06-349 2100 Cherry Grove, Taumarunui 07-8958201 Owairua Road, Pipiriki 06-385 5022

# TE PAPA TONGAREWA-MUSEUM OF NEW ZEALAND

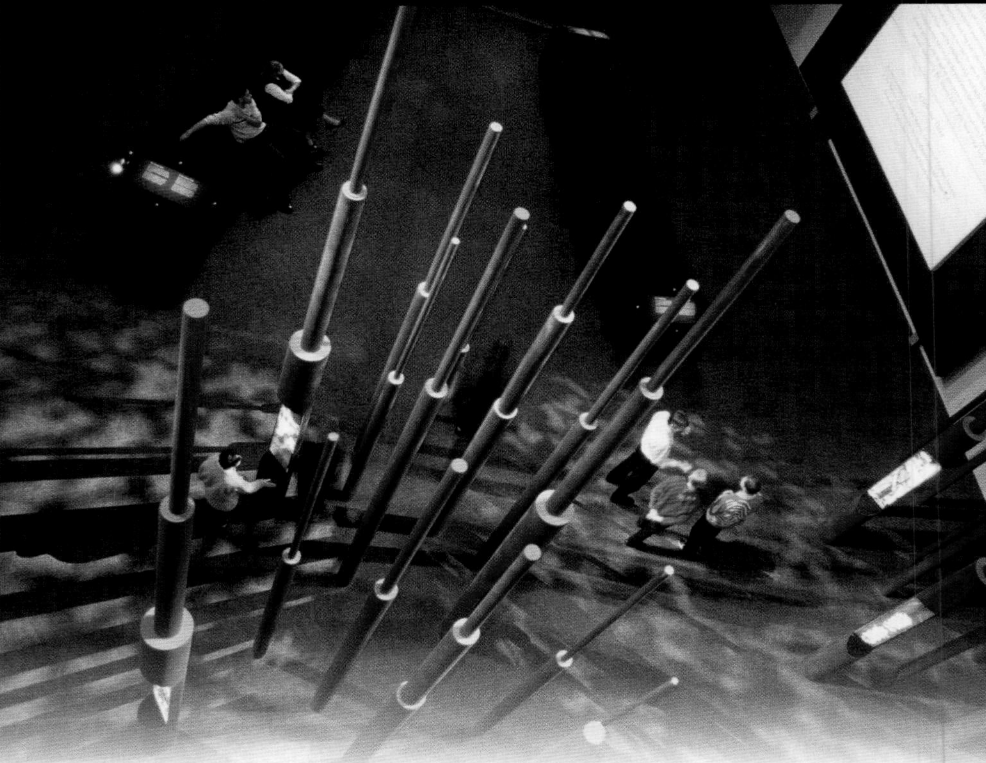

### INFORMATION

www.tepapa.govt.nz
146 C4 Cable Street, Wellington 04-381 7000 Fri–Wed 10–6, Thu 10–9 Free; charge for visiting exhibitions; Time Warp rides from NZ$8, child (4–14) from NZ$6, family from NZ$19 City Circular Daily introductory tour Nov–end Mar 10.15, 11.15, 12, 1, 2, 3; Apr–end Oct 10.15, 2; NZ$11, child NZ$5.50 Level 1: excellent collection of museum merchandise, books, gifts, crafts, jewellery; Level 2 for toys Licensed café (level 1) and espresso bar (level 4) Te Papa Explorer, NZ$2 (on sale at information desk, Level 2)

**Above** *Signs of a Nation (Level 4) explores the Treaty of Waitangi*

## INTRODUCTION

One of the largest new museums in the world, covering more than 36,000sq m (387,500sq ft), Te Papa has an ambitious mission—to explore New Zealand's bicultural heritage, natural history and environment. NZ$317 million has been spent achieving this end since its opening in 1998.

Te Papa sprawls on the waterfront and uses its setting to great effect, incorporating gardens, waterways, outdoor exhibits and performance areas on the bayside. A vast lobby on ground level gives a wonderful view out over the harbour. From this space, 20m (66ft) high, there is access to the exhibition areas. Te Papa holds a staggering variety of items, including the largest Maori collection held by any museum in the country—almost 16,000 *taonga*, from woodcarvings, personal ornaments and musical instruments to sections of meeting houses, canoes and storehouses, weapons, woven raincapes and feather and dogskin cloaks, and a contemporary *marae*. European history is represented by 23,500 items, including costume, fine furniture and a major archive of 19th-century photographs (all Level 4).

Among other sections are the world's biggest collection of marine mammal skeletons; the national fish collection; 230,000 dried plant specimens; 65,000 specimens of birds, most from New Zealand (all Level 2); artworks from the late 19th century to the present day by artists including Charles Frederick Goldie, Rita Angus and Colin McCahon (Levels 5–6), and much, much more. Don't miss the underground Quake Braker exhibition, outside the entrance to the museum, which shows how the museum building is designed to reduce the effects of earthquakes.

## WHAT TO SEE

### GOLDEN DAYS (LEVEL 4)

Golden Days re-creates a cluttered junkshop, where the drama of New Zealand's landmark historical events is played out in a 12-minute movie. The absorbing Made in New Zealand, on the same level, showcases the creativity and ingenuity behind 300 years of Kiwi visual arts and culture.

### MANA WHENUA (LEVEL 4)

This fabulous display of Maori art treasures and objects is a great introduction to Maori culture, with personal genealogical histories brought to life on audiovisual screens, and stories and legends told in the *marae* carved meeting house. Learn about the myth of the sacred *pounamu* (greenstone), and admire the feathered cloaks and other ornaments.

### STORYPLACE (LEVEL 2)

Children aged from 18 months to 5 years old can settle down here, an interactive space where carers are at hand to play and tell stories (tickets cost NZ$2 for a 45-minute session). Discovery Centres on Levels 2 and 4 also give children the chance to make their own animated films, read, have a go at weaving or study the world's largest flower.

### TIME WARP (LEVEL 2)

The Time Warp section is about information through entertainment. Blastback and Future Rush are two high-tech simulated rides—the former taking you back in time to show the creation of New Zealand from both Maori and geological perspectives (15 minutes), and the latter whisking you to Wellington of 2055, where you'll visit a super-modern house and fly around in a futuristic car (18 minutes). In the Present Zone you can make a virtual bungy jump or shear a virtual sheep.

### TIPS

» You will need at least half a day to make the most of the museum; if possible pay more than one visit.

» The information desk on Level 2 can advise you on the latest events and exhibits.

**Below** *The museum building is a landmark on Wellington's waterfront*

# WELLINGTON

**INFORMATION**
www.wellingtonnz.com
303 J11 101 Wakefield Street (Civic Square) 04-802 4860 Mon–Wed, Fri 8.30–5, Thu 9–5, Sat, Sun 9.30–4.30 Bunny Street Bunny Street Daily services to Picton, South Island Rongotai, 6km (4 miles) southeast; Stagecoach Flyer bus and shuttles to downtown

**Above** *Native timbers including totara, matai and kauri were used in the construction of Old St. Paul's*

## INTRODUCTION

Wellington is New Zealand's capital, and the port for ferries from the South Island. The city is sandwiched between green hills and the waterfront, and anyone arriving by road or rail is delivered right into its high-rise heart. Lambton Quay, the main business and shopping street, leads to Molesworth Street, Thorndon and the Parliamentary district. The harbour, with its bordering main roads of Waterloo Quay, Customhouse Quay, Jervois Quay, Cable Street and Oriental Parade, sweeps south and east, encompassing the modern, revitalized waterfront. Here the main landmark is the Te Papa museum (▷ 142–143), the city's top visitor attraction, which explores New Zealand's bicultural heritage. Cuba Street leads towards funky Cuba Mall, and Courtenay Place, lined with restaurants and cafés. Behind the Central Business District (CBD) are the Botanic Garden and the hillside suburb of Kelburn. Dominating the view southeast is Mount Victoria, an ideal place to get your bearings.

According to Maori legend Kupe, the great Polynesian explorer, landed here in about AD950. The first European ships to arrive were the *Rosanna* and the *Lambton*, on a preliminary exploration for the first New Zealand Company in 1826, and the first settlers came in 1839 and 1840. The original community was in the area that is now Thorndon. A major earthquake in 1855 created new, flat land suitable for building, and Wellington began to prosper. It became the capital in 1865 and takes its name from Arthur Wellesley, the 1st Duke of Wellington (1769–1852).

## WHAT TO SEE

### BOTANIC GARDEN AND CABLE CAR

www.wellingtoncablecar.co.nz

Wellington's Botanic Garden is magnificent but excruciatingly hilly. The best way to get there is on the red cable car, an attraction in itself, which takes about five minutes to climb 121m (440ft). There are four stations on the way up, and from the summit station there's a splendid view across the city. Gracing the precarious slopes are 26ha (64 acres) of specialist gardens, flowerbeds, foreign trees and native bush. A crowning glory is the Carter Observatory (▷ 154), with static displays, planetarium shows and audiovisuals. The other highlight is the Lady Norwood Rose Gardens, an impressive circular display of more than 300 varieties found at the northern end of the garden, at the base of the hill. The rose gardens are seen at their best between November and April.

146 B3 Glenmore Street, Thorndon; cable car 280 Lambton Quay 04-499 1400; cable car 04-472 2199 Daily dawn–dusk; cable car Mon–Fri 7am–10pm, Sat, Sun 9am–10pm, every 10 mins Free; cable car NZ$2.50, child (school age) NZ$1, under-5s free 3, all buses along Lambton Quay Skyline Café has great views over the city

### CIVIC SQUARE AND THE WATERFRONT

A beautiful silver fern orb is suspended above the middle of this public space, which is often used for outdoor events. This is the setting for the excellent City Gallery (daily 10–5), which hosts regular shows of contemporary art in various media and has regular film screenings and performances. Also on the square is Capital E (daily 10–5), where children's events and exhibitions are staged; there's a large toyshop attached.

From Civic Square it's a short walk to the waterfront across the City-to-Sea Bridge, by artist Para Matchitt, which sprouts sculptures celebrating the arrival of the Maori in New Zealand. The waterfront itself is a major focus for the city's museums and recreational activities, and sunny weekends here are abuzz with visitors and locals.

146 C4 City Circular

### TIP

» Tourism Wellington promotes a 'four quarters' map system to help negotiate the city's streets. The quarters, mentioned on many maps and in brochures, run clockwise from Mount Victoria: Courtenay, Cuba, Willis and Lambton.

**Below** *A view over the city and the harbour from the Botanic Garden*

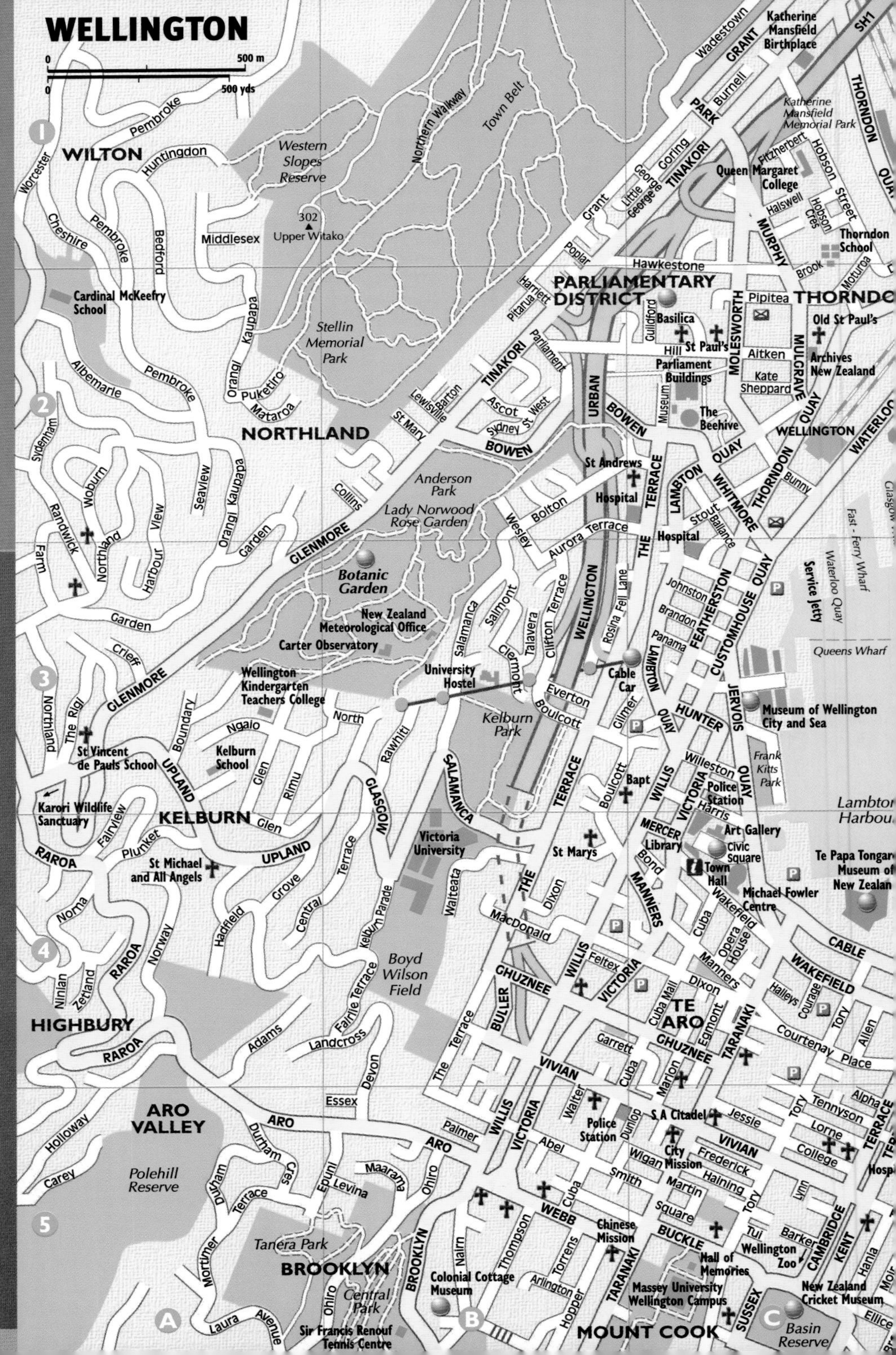
WELLINGTON
0
500 m
0
500 yds
WILTON
NORTHLAND
KELBURN
HIGHBURY
ARO VALLEY
BROOKLYN
TE ARO
MOUNT COOK
PARLIAMENTARY DISTRICT
THORNDON
Western Slopes Reserve
302
Upper Witako
Town Belt
Northern Walkway
Stellin Memorial Park
Anderson Park
Lady Norwood Rose Garden
Botanic Garden
New Zealand Meteorological Office
Carter Observatory
Wellington Kindergarten Teachers College
University Hostel
Kelburn Park
Kelburn School
Victoria University
Boyd Wilson Field
Polehill Reserve
Tanera Park
Central Park
Sir Francis Renouf Tennis Centre
Colonial Cottage Museum
Massey University Wellington Campus
Basin Reserve
New Zealand Cricket Museum
Wellington Zoo
Hall of Memories
Chinese Mission
City Mission
S A Citadel
Police Station
St Michael and All Angels
St Vincent de Pauls School
Karori Wildlife Sanctuary
Cardinal McKeefry School
Katherine Mansfield Birthplace
Katherine Mansfield Memorial Park
Queen Margaret College
Thorndon School
Basilica
St Paul's
Old St Paul's
Archives New Zealand
Parliament Buildings
The Beehive
St Andrews
Hospital
Cable Car
Museum of Wellington City and Sea
Frank Kitts Park
Lambton Harbour
Queens Wharf
Service Jetty
Waterloo Quay
Fast - Ferry Wharf
Art Gallery
Civic Square
Library
Town Hall
Michael Fowler Centre
Te Papa Tongarewa Museum of New Zealand
St Marys
Bapt
Wadestown
GRANT
PARK
Burnell
SH1
THORNDON QUAY
TINAKORI
Goring
George
Little George
Grant
Poplar
Hawkestone
Pitarua
Harriett
Guildford
Hill
MOLESWORTH
MULGRAVE
Aitken
Kate Sheppard
Pipitea
Fitzherbert
Hobson
Hobson Cres
Halswell
Hobson Street
MURPHY
Brook
Moturoa
URBAN
BOWEN
Museum
LAMBTON QUAY
WELLINGTON
WATERLOO
WHITMORE
Bunny
Stout
Ballance
Parliament
Ascot
Sydney West
Barton
Lewisville
St Mary
Collins
GLENMORE
Bolton
Wesley
Aurora Terrace
THE TERRACE
WELLINGTON
Rosina Fell Lane
Clifton Terrace
Talavera
Salmont
Clermont
Salamanca
Everton
Boulcott
Gilmer
Johnston
Brandon
Panama
FEATHERSTON
CUSTOMHOUSE QUAY
JERVOIS QUAY
HUNTER
Willeston
WILLIS
VICTORIA
Harris
MERCER
Bond
MANNERS
Wakefield
Cuba
Opera House
Manners
Dixon
CABLE
WAKEFIELD
Halleys
Courage
Tory
Allen
Courtenay Place
TARANAKI
Egmont
Cuba Mall
GHUZNEE
Garrett
Marion
VIVIAN
Jessie
Tennyson
Alpha
Lorne
College
TERRACE
Frederick
Haining
Martin
Square
Tui
Barker
CAMBRIDGE
KENT
Hania
Ellice
Lynn
BUCKLE
SUSSEX
Wigan
Smith
Abel
Dunlop
Walter
WEBB
Cuba
Torrens
Hopper
Arlington
Thompson
Nairn
BROOKLYN
Ohiro
Palmer
ARO
Feltex
BULLER
MacDonald
Dixon
THE TERRACE
The Terrace
Walteata
Kelburn Parade
SALAMANCA
Rawhiti
GLASGOW
Terrace
Central
Grove
Hadfield
UPLAND
Rimu
Glen
Ngaio
North
Boundary
Plunket
Fairview
RAROA
Norma
Norway
Ninian
Zetland
Adams
Fairlie Terrace
Landcross
Devon
Essex
Durham Cres
Durham
Terrace
Epuni
Levina
Maarama
Mortimer
Laura
Avenue
Holloway
Carey
Northland
The Rigi
Crieff
Garden
Farm
Randwick
Woburn
Northland
View
Harbour
Seaview
Orangi Kaupapa
Sydenham
Albemarle
Pembroke
Puketiro
Mataroa
Orangi
Kaupapa
Bedford
Middlesex
Cheshire
Worcester
Huntingdon
1
2
3
4
5
A
B
C

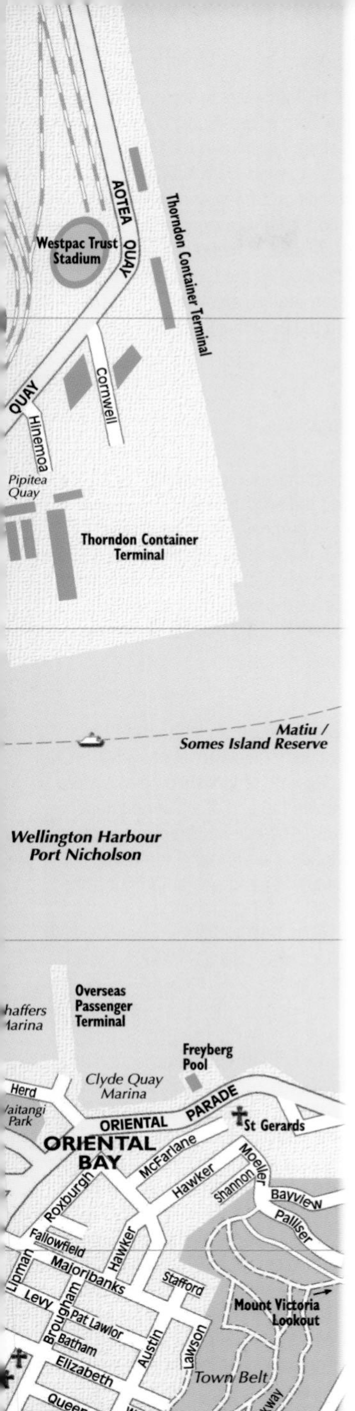


# WELLINGTON STREET INDEX

## MOUNT VICTORIA LOOKOUT

From a distance, the wooded slopes of 196m (643ft) Mount Victoria hardly seem in character with the movie trilogy the *Lord of the Rings*, but they provided a location for several scenes depicting the Shire in the first film, *Fellowship of the Ring*. Although it is not easy to miss from downtown, reaching the lookout is something of an expedition. The best route is by car, to Thane Road via Majoribanks Street, at the bottom of Courtenay Place. If you lose your way in the web of residential hillside streets, keep heading uphill. On foot, the summit is part of the Southern Walkway. At the top you can watch planes make the tricky landing into Wellington Airport, enjoy the city view and investigate the Byrd Memorial, a tribute to US-born aviator and Antarctic explorer Richard Byrd (1888–1957).

Off map 147 D5 · 20

## MUSEUM OF WELLINGTON CITY AND SEA

www.museumofwellington.co.nz

Housed in the former Bond Store, this superb museum competes very successfully with its much bigger neighbour, Te Papa. Its interior, multilevel design combines a modern and rustic feel; its emphasis is on local history, with a particular maritime slant. Of special note is the Wahine Disaster Gallery, using original film footage set to a dramatic score to recall the loss of 51 lives on the *Wahine* passenger ferry, which came to grief at the port entrance in 1968.

146 C3 · Queens Wharf · 04-472 8904 · Daily 10–5 · Free · City Circular

## NEW ZEALAND CRICKET MUSEUM

www.nzcricket.co.nz

Enthusiasts will love this small but well arranged museum in the old 1924 grandstand of the Basin Reserve cricket ground. It displays national and international memorabilia, dating back to 1743, with emphasis on encounters with arch-enemy Australia. The ground occupies the site of a planned dock, made impractical after the earthquake of 1855. The curious Grecian temple structure just inside the eastern boundary fence is a memorial to William Wakefield, leader of the New Zealand Company Wellington settlement from 1840 until 1848.

146 C5 · The Old Grandstand, Basin Reserve · 04-385 6602 · Nov–end Apr daily 10.30–3.30; May–end Oct Sat, Sun 10.30–3.30 · Adult NZ$5, child (13–16) NZ$2; 12 and under free if with an adult · 1, 3, 4, 22, 23, 43, 44

**Above** *The modern Byrd Memorial on top of Mount Victoria*

**Below** *Cuba Street is a good place to take a break in a café or restaurant*

## PARLIAMENTARY DISTRICT

A stroll around this district, focused on Molesworth Street, takes in several of Wellington's most interesting buildings. One is the aptly named Beehive, a city landmark which houses government offices. Designed by British architect Sir Basil Spence and built in 1980, it is hated and loved in equal measure. Tours of Parliament, including the 1922 Parliament House, start here (Mon–Fri 10–4, Sat 10–3, Sun 12–3), and you can watch the House of Representatives in session (times vary). Old Government Buildings on Lambton Quay, built in 1876 to house Crown Ministers, was designed to look like stone, but is actually the world's second largest wooden building (after Japan's Todaji Temple). It was restored in 1994, complete with fibreglass replica chimneys. On Mulgrave Street, Archives New Zealand (Mon–Fri 9–5, Sat 9–1) contains historical documents including the original Treaty of Waitangi (▷ 29). The neo-Gothic Old St. Paul's Cathedral, built in 1866, has impressive interior timberwork and stained-glass windows, and is well worth a look.

The Prime Minister's official residence, Premier House, is a much-enlarged 1843 building on Tinakori Road. Farther north on the same road at No. 25 is the Katherine Mansfield Birthplace (Tue–Sun 10–4), where New Zealand's best-known writer, born in 1888, lived until the age of five (▷ 35). The simple house

features in her short stories *Prelude* and *A Birthday*, and has been faithfully restored to resemble the house as it was when she lived there.
146 B2 04-471 9999 City Circular, 14

### TE PAPA TONGAREWA-MUSEUM OF NEW ZEALAND

▷ 142–143.

## MORE TO SEE

### COLONIAL COTTAGE MUSEUM

www.colonialcottagemuseum.co.nz
A restored and furnished Victorian interior is housed in one of the city's oldest buildings (1858), which belonged to the family of carpenter and timber merchant William Wallis for 119 years. Early settler life and Wellington's growth are charted.
146 B5 68 Nairn Street, Brooklyn 04-384 9122 Jan–Easter daily 10–4; Easter–end Dec Sat, Sun 12–4 Adult NZ$5, schoolchild free 7, 8, 9

### KARORI WILDLIFE SANCTUARY

www.sanctuary.org.nz
In 1994, 250ha (618 acres) in a valley of regenerating bush in the suburb and hills of Karori was set aside and protected with a predator-proof fence. The benefits are already apparent, as native species are reintroduced and birdsong returns to the bush. The area around the perimeter fence is popular for walking and mountain biking.
Off map 146 A3 Waiapu Road, Karori 04-920 9200 Dec–end Mar daily 10–5 Adult NZ$12, child (under 14) NZ$5, family NZ$29 3, 17, 18, 21, 22, 23

### MATIU/SOMES ISLAND RESERVE

www.eastbywest.co.nz
Once a quarantine station, this island now supports a number of protected native birds. Ferries travel here from Queen's Wharf three times a day on the way to Days Bay, near the coastal resort of Eastbourne.
Off map 147 D3 Wellington Harbour 04-499 1282 Daily 8.30–5 Ferry, adult NZ$18.50, child (3–15) NZ$10, under-3s free

### WELLINGTON ZOO

www.wellingtonzoo.com
Conservation projects are central to this zoo, whose residents include kiwi, tuatara and a wide variety of non-native species including Sumatran tigers, Malayan sun bears and a troupe of chimps—the second largest to be found in the southern hemisphere.
Off map 146 C5 Daniell Street, Newtown 04-381 6750 Daily 9.30–5 Adult NZ$15, child (3–16) NZ$7.50 10, 23

**Above** *The view from Mount Victoria Lookout is worth the expedition to reach it*

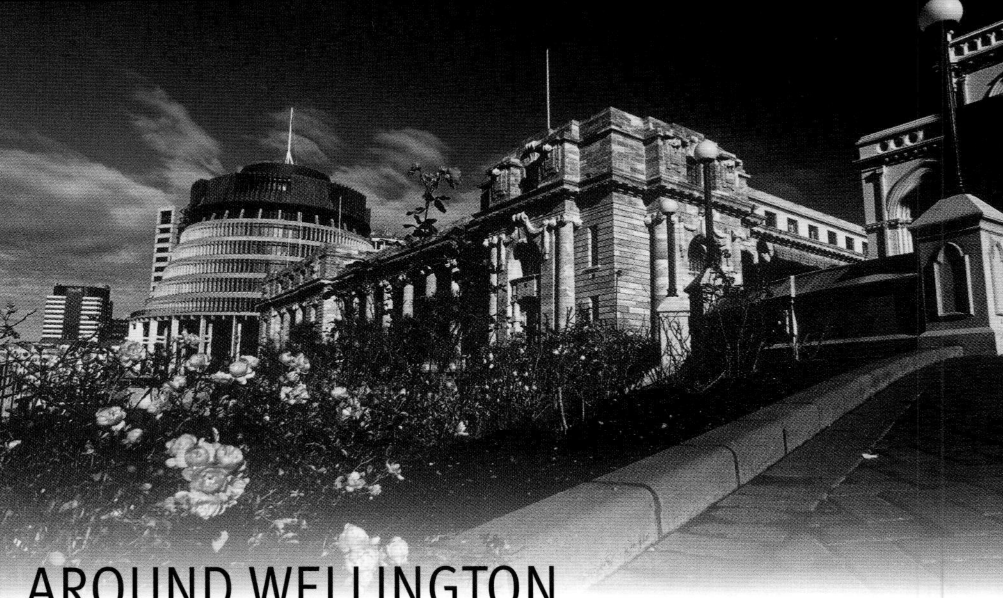

# AROUND WELLINGTON

**This walk begins with a cable car ride to the heights of the city then circles back to the harbour via the Wellington Botanic Gardens, historic Tinakori Road and the Parliamentary district.**

**THE WALK**
**Distance:** 5.5km (3 miles)
**Time:** 3 hours
**Start at:** Kelburn Cable Car 146 C3
**End at:** Te Papa Museum 146 C4

★ Begin at the Kelburn Cable Car (Cable Car Lane, near 280 Lambton Quay, $3 one way, every 10 minutes, Mon–Fri 7am–10pm, Sat 8:30am–10pm, Sun 9am–10pm) the funicular railway that whisks you to the top entrance of the Wellington Botanic Gardens, and a magnificent view across the city and Te Whanganui-a-Tara, The Great Harbour of Tara.

Turn right at the Cable Car Terminus to enter the Wellington Botanic Gardens. Take the first path that turns left, Grass Way—although after the dramatic ride from the city you might want to call in at the Cable Car Museum, on your left, which tells the story of the country's only remaining public cable car system.

❶ Established in 1868, the garden now covers 26ha (64 acres) of exotic forest, ponds, native species, floral displays and specialist gardens.

Continue along this path past the Children's Play Area and the Succulent Garden and head towards The Treehouse, the gardens' visitor centre. Off this section of the path to the right is the camellia garden while to the left are the vireya rhododendrons, both plantings well worth a detour when they're in flower. Continue past the Sound Shell Lawn and exit the gardens at the Founders Entrance, and turn right into Tinakori Road.

❷ In 1848, not long after it was founded, much of Wellington was devastated by the powerful Marlborough Earthquake. While the city's brick and stone buildings suffered substantial damage, its timber buildings were relatively unscathed. The message was not lost on the city's architects, and timber was used almost exclusively for Wellington's building in the second half of the 19th century. The row of six houses at 304–314 Tinakori Road illustrate another fact of Wellington life. Since level building ground was scarce, houses tended to be tall and slender. At No. 260, Premier House has been the official residence of the prime minister since 1865.

Just past Harriett Street, take a look at the houses in Torless Terrace, Calgary Avenue and Poplar Grove. These were built during the 1890s, and the streetscape remains largely intact from that era. No. 5 Torless Terrace is thought to date back to the 1850s, which would make it one of Wellington's oldest houses.

**Above** *The neoclassical Parliament House, flanked by The Beehive*

❸ Just past Hobson Street Bridge at No. 25 is the house where Kathleen Beauchamp, later known to the world as the writer Katherine Mansfield, was born in 1888 and lived the first five years of her life. In 1908 she left New Zealand for good, although several of her short stories were set in Wellington. The house, which has been restored as a typical Victorian family home, contains furnishings, photographs and audiovisual material from Mansfield's life and times.

Return to the Hobson Street overpass, cross the motorway and turn right to walk through Katherine Mansfield Memorial Park. Turn left into Murphy Street, which becomes Mulgrave Street, and continue to Old St Paul's Church.

❹ Consecrated in 1866, this is a splendid example of the Gothic Revival style in timber. Even the roof trusses are works of craftsmanship that transcend their mundane function. The church uses a variety of native timbers—totara, matai and rimu as well as kauri.

At No. 10 Mulgrave Street, Archives New Zealand houses the nation's most important historic documents including the Treaty of Waitangi, the nation's founding document, which is on permanent display in the archives' Constitution Room. It's not in good shape. After it was signed in 1840, the treaty was kept in a box and barely seen until 1908, by which time water, time and rodents had taken their toll. Early attempts at preservation caused yet more damage, however recent restoration has at least preserved what remains.

Walk along Aitken Street and cross Molesworth Street to the Parliament Buildings.

❺ The neoclassical Parliament House is flanked on the right by the Gothic-influenced Parliamentary Library, and on the left by the Executive Wing building. It's hard to imagine a more stark contrast than this building, commonly known as The Beehive. Free, daily, one-hour guided tours of Parliament depart from the Visitor Centre in the foyer of the Beehive.

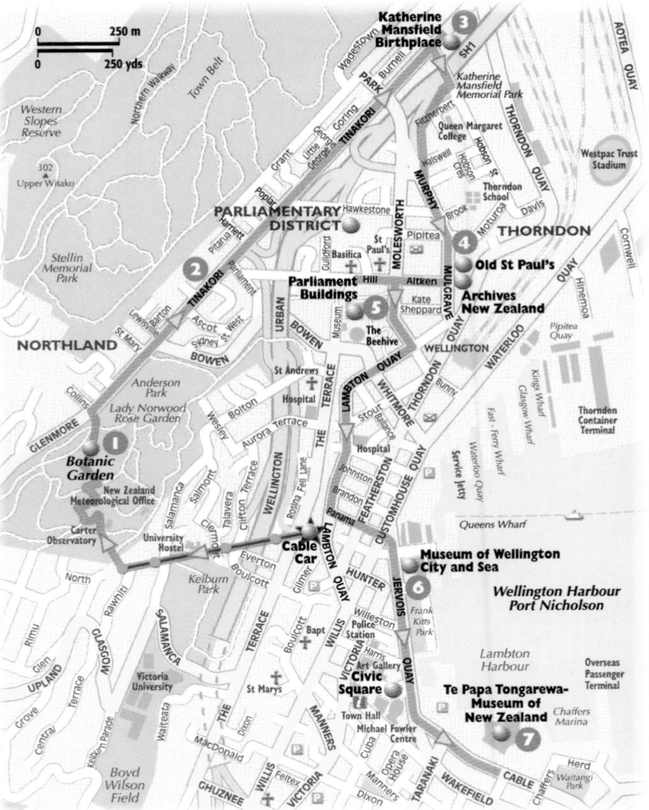

Turn right from Molesworth into Lambton Quay, left at Panama Street and cross to Queens Wharf.

❻ The Museum of Wellington City and Sea charts the city's history, with the emphasis on its strong maritime links. Mixing traditional museum displays with audiovisual effects, it provides an entertaining as well as an informative vision of Wellington's past, present and what may be its future.

Continue along the waterfront to Te Papa.

❼ The Museum of New Zealand is a rich and satisfying experience. Using a variety of storytelling techniques, it explores New Zealand's ecology, Maori and contemporary culture and sporting and intellectual achievements, often in a provocative style.

## WHEN TO GO

Just about any time when the sun is shining is ideal for this walk. Te Papa, at the end of this tour, closes at 6pm, 9pm on Thursday.

## WHERE TO EAT

**WORD OF MOUTH**

This bright and breezy café serves salads, bagels and well-stuffed sandwiches.

✉ Shop 10, 100 Molesworth Street, Thorndon, Wellington ☎ 04-472 7202
🕐 Mon–Fri 8–5

## CARTERTON

### BALLOONING NEW ZEALAND

Early-morning flights complete with a café 'champagne breakfast' are a speciality. Flights last an hour.
✉ 54B Kent Street, Carterton ☎ 06-379 8223 ⌚ Oct–end Apr daily 6am; May–end Sep daily 7am ✋ NZ$260 including breakfast

### PAUA WORLD

www.pauashell.co.nz

The iridescent bluey-green shell of the paua (abalone) is turned into all sorts of distinctive New Zealand souvenirs at this factory and outlet. Boggle at the paua hallway, watch a video about the life of this curious mollusc, and take the free factory tour for an insight into the processing of the shells. There's also a children's playground and a salt-water aquarium.
✉ 54 Kent Street, Carterton ☎ 06 379 6777 ⌚ Daily 9–5 ✋ Free

## GREYTOWN

### THE FRENCH BAKER MOÏSE CERSON

www.frenchbaker.co.nz

Croissants, palmiers, *réligieuse, pissaladière*—artisan baker Moïse Cerson bakes wonderful authentic French breads, savouries and pâtisserie at his bakery and espresso bar.
✉ 81 Main Street, Greytown ☎ 06-304 8873 ⌚ Tue–Sun 8.30–4

## MANAKAU

### SOO'S BROWN ACRES

Home-grown vegetables, fruit and berries ripened on the property are sold at Soo's stall on the main road near Levin. Tree-ripened apples of many varieties are a speciality. They also sell confectionery and ice cream.
✉ Main Road, Manakau, Levin
☎ 06-362 6029 ⌚ Daily 9–5.30

## MANGATAINOKA

### TUI BREWERY

www.tui.co.nz

Tui beer has been associated with the Tararua region since it was first brewed on this site in the 1880s. The building is known by some as the local equivalent of the Taj Mahal! Brewery tours are available (advance reservations are essential), and there is promotional clothing for those so inclined.
✉ State Highway 2, Mangatainoka
☎ 06-376 0615 ⌚ Tours daily 11 and 2 ✋ NZ$12.50, under-16s free 🏪 Mon–Fri 10–4 🚘 On SH2, 24km (15 miles) east of Palmerston North

**Above** *The Wairarapa wine trail, starting from Martinborough Wine Centre, takes in wineries with cellar-door tastings*

## MARTINBOROUGH

### ATA RANGI

www.atarangi.co.nz

Wines of international stature are made at Ata Rangi, known particularly for its Pinot noir, which is regarded as one of New Zealand's top wines. The Paton and Masters families who make the wines live on site, and you're likely to meet them if you visit their rustic cellar door for tastings and purchases.
✉ Puruatanga Road, Martinborough
☎ 06-306 9570 ⌚ Mon–Fri 1–3, Sat, Sun 12–4

### AU SPA BELGE

Yvette Françoise Bonfond brings European techniques to this women's day spa, offering facials, massage therapy, mud treatments, full body treatments, detoxification and hydrotherapy spa baths.
✉ 41 Strasbourge Street, Martinborough
☎ 06-306 8188 ⌚ Wed–Sun 9.30–5
✋ From NZ$60

### MARTINBOROUGH BEER AND ALES

Martinborough may be best known for its wine, but it also produces some fine craft beers. Martinborough Beer and Ales makes wheat beer, lager, ale and stout, which you can taste while you watch the beer being made.

Corner of New York and Princess streets, Martinborough 06-306 8310 Late Oct–end Mar Wed–Sun 11–7; Apr–late Oct Fri, Sat 11–7

### MARTINBOROUGH WINE CENTRE

www.martinboroughwinecentre.co.nz

A good starting point for the Wairarapa wine trail, the centre has information about local wineries and an excellent selection of wines to taste and buy. They also stock wine books and local products.

6 Kitchener Street, Martinborough 06-306 8814 Daily 9–5

### MCLEODS QUAD ADVENTURES

www.mcleodsadventures.co.nz

If you've ever wanted to experience the thrill of exploring by quad bike, then this could be your chance. Tours across farmland take in river crossings and fabulous views. No experience required, but advance booking is essential.

White Rock Road, Martinborough 06-306 8846 From NZ$120

### OLIVO

www.olivo.co.nz

Wander through the Wairarapa's first commercial olive grove, which is located in beautiful gardens. You can also taste and buy the oil and learn about its production.

Hinakura Road, RD4, Martinborough 06-306 9074 Sat, Sun 3km (2 miles) from Martinborough Town Square

### SUNDAY MARKET

www.martinboroughwinecentre.co.nz

Wairarapa food producers and craftspeople sell their wares at the weekly Sunday market. It's held in a rustic workshop at the back of the Martinborough Wine Centre.

6 Kitchener Street, Martinborough 06-306 9040 Sun 10–2

### TORA COASTAL WALK

www.toracoastalwalk.co.nz

This three-day, circular, 40km (25-mile) walk crosses the southern Wairarapa hills and drops down to the coast. The hosts are farmers who give you a warm welcome—you dine at their homes. You stay in well-equipped farm cottages and can opt for provisions or take your own food. Your baggage can also be carried.

Wairewa Farm, RD2 Martinborough 06-307 8115 Oct–end Apr Adult NZ$330

## MASTERTON

### KINGSMEADE CHEESE

www.kingsmeadecheese.co.nz

Kingsmeade specializes in sheep cheeses made from milk from its own flock. You can buy the cheeses, as well as jams, chutneys, crafts and local products, at their retail outlet. To find out more about how the cheese begins life, join a farm tour to watch the sheep-milking take place.

8b First Street, Masterton 06-378 7178 Mon–Fri 9–5, Sat 10–1

### WAIRAPAPA GOURMET WINE ESCAPES

www.tranzit.co.nz

Wine tours depart daily from Wellington (by train to Featherston), Masterton, Carterton, Greytown, Featherston and Martinborough, visiting four Martinborough wineries and the Martinborough Wine Centre, with lunch in a vineyard café.

Tranzit Coachlines, Masterton 06-377 1227 Daily From NZ$115

## PALMERSTON NORTH

### CENTREPOINT THEATRE

www.centrepoint.co.nz

One of the few theatres to have its own full-time professional theatre company, Centrepoint stages regular shows, from comedy to classic drama, with an emphasis on local New Zealand plays.

Corner of Pitt and Church streets, Palmerston North 06-354 5740 Tue 6.30, Wed–Sat 8, Sun 5 NZ$35

### EZIBUY

www.ezibuy.co.nz

The retail outlet of a well-known Palmerston North mail-order company, Ezibuy stocks clothing, footwear, homeware and gift lines. There is also a four-screen video wall and a children's play area.

170–178 John F Kennedy Drive, Palmerston North 06-952 2112 Mon–Wed, Fri 8.30–5.30, Thu 8.30am–8pm, Sat 9–5, Sun 10–5

### GO 4 WHEELS

www.go4wheels.co.nz

Two-hour trips to the Tararua Wind Farm are the main attraction on these rides—from the hilltops you can see both sides of the North Island. Expect it to be windy! One-hour trips are also available (NZ$80). Advance booking is essential.

Horne Road, Ballance, Pahiatua 06-376 7043 NZ$120

### REGENT THEATRE

www.regent.co.nz

Opened in 1930, the original picture palace of Palmerston North was restored in 1998. With a seating capacity of almost 1,400, the Regent Theatre hosts a variety of events such as ballet, musicals, orchestra concerts and comedy.

Broadway Avenue, Palmerston North 06-350 2100

## PARAPARAUMU

### LINDALE CENTRE

A complex of agricultural speciality shops, this is well worth stopping at for local Kapiti cheeses, honey, olive products, sheepskins, and a farm-kitchen restaurant.

State Highway 1, Paraparaumu 04-297 0916 Daily 9–5

### PARAPARAUMU BEACH GOLF CLUB

www.paraparaumubeachgolfclub.co.nz

An international-standard golf links ranked 73rd in the world, this club was graced by Tiger Woods at the NZ Open in 2001, and the venue for 12 New Zealand golf opens.

376 Kapiti Road, Paraparaumu 04-902 8200 NZ$90

## PIPIRIKI

### BRIDGE TO NOWHERE TOURS

www.bridgetonowhere-lodge.co.nz

You can hunt deer, pigs, goats or possums from this remote lodge, but it is also accessible to daytrippers with a four-hour jet-boat ride along the Whanganui River and a guided walk to the Bridge to Nowhere. Overnight accommodation can be arranged. Also trips to the Matemateaonga Track, and Tieke Marae, for an experience of Maori river culture.

✉ Pipiriki, RD6 Wanganui
☎ 06-348 7122 ✋ From NZ$105

## TAIHAPE

### MOKAI GRAVITY CANYON

www.gravitycanyon.co.nz

This company offers the North Island's highest bungy (80m/262ft) and New Zealand's longest Flying Fox (aerial cableway), stretching 1km (0.6 miles), on which you can reach 160kph (107mph)—not for the fainthearted! If you still have the nerve, a Giant Swing swoops into the Mokai Canyon.

✉ Mokai Bridge, Taihape ☎ 06-388 9109 ✋ From NZ$110 🚗 Off SH1, south of Taihape

## UPPER HUTT

### EFIL DOOG GARDEN OF ART

www.efildoog-nz.com

Explore 4ha (10 acres) of beautiful gardens full of quirky sculpture. There's also a small art gallery, which specializes in early New Zealand paintings. Guided tours are available.

✉ 1995 Akatarawa Road, RD 2, Upper Hutt ☎ 04-526 7924 🕐 Oct–end Mar Wed–Sun 10–4.30 ✋ Adult NZ$14, child (5–16) NZ$6

### SILVER STREAM RAILWAY

www.silverstreamrailway.org.nz

Take a Sunday afternoon ride on a vintage steam train, leaving from the site of the country's biggest collection of preserved historic railway engines.

✉ Silverstream, Upper Hutt ☎ 04-563 7348 🕐 Trains operate Sun 11–4 ✋ Adult NZ$10, child (5–15) NZ$5, family NZ$25

## WANGANUI

### ROYAL WANGANUI OPERA HOUSE

www.royaloperahouse.co.nz

Small but very grand, the opera house was built in 1899. It seats 800 and is used for touring shows, opera and rock bands.

✉ Saint Hill Street, Wanganui
☎ 06-349 0511

### WANGANUI RIVERCITY TOURS

www.rivercitytours.co.nz

No experience is needed for these escorted canoe adventures over four days in Whanganui National Park. The service includes hotel pick-up, safe vehicle storage, fresh food supplies and informed guides. Sleeping bags and mats are available for hire.

✉ PO Box 4224, Wanganui ☎ 06-348 7122 🕐 Nov to mid-Apr ✋ Adult NZ$545, child (under 16) NZ$272

### WHANGANUI RIVER CRUISES

www.riverboat.co.nz

New Zealand's last operating coal-fired passenger paddle steamer, PS *Waimarie*, was built in 1899 and restored in 2000, and now runs scheduled cruises along the Whanganui River.

✉ Whanganui Riverboat Centre, 1A Taupo Quay, Wanganui ☎ 06-347 1863 🕐 Late Oct–end Apr daily 2pm; May–end Jul, Sep–late Oct Sat, Sun 1pm ✋ Adult NZ$33, child (5–15) NZ$14, family NZ$94

## WELLINGTON

### BAR BODEGA

www.bodega.co.nz

Bar Bodega hosts local and occasional international music events, and is dedicated to real ale and good music.

✉ 101 Ghuznee Street, Wellington
☎ 04-384 8212 🕐 Daily 4pm–3am

### BASIN RESERVE

www.westpacstadium.co.nz

Arguably New Zealand's most famous sports ground, and the only one with heritage status, the Basin Reserve is maintained largely for regional and national cricket fixtures. It is also home to the New Zealand Cricket Museum (▷ 148). During the winter it is used for club rugby.

✉ Rugby Street, Wellington
☎ 04-384 3171

### BATS THEATRE

www.bats.co.nz

Alternative and experimental theatre and dance are regularly performed in this casual and intimate theatre, which specializes in New Zealand works. It is also a venue for the annual Fringe Festival (▷ 157).

✉ 1 Kent Terrace, Wellington
☎ 04-802 4176

### CAPITAL E

www.capitale.org.nz

A creative technology and performance facility for children, located in Civic Square, Capital E has professional theatrical shows, including puppets, masks and music. There are also events, exhibitions, activities, and workshops, which include a TV studio.

✉ Civic Square, Wellington ☎ 04-913 3720 🕐 Daily 10–5

### CARTER OBSERVATORY AND PLANETARIUM

www.carterobservatory.org.

The observatory is located in the Botanic Garden, close to the top terminal of the Cable Car (▷ 145), and includes a planetarium, several telescopes and a giftshop. Choose from two shows at the planetarium (one of which is always the current night sky), and enjoy solar viewing or night sky telescope viewing.

**Below** *Lilac-hued irises by a pool at Efil Doog Garden of Art*

✉ 40 Salamanca Road, Wellington ☎ 04-499 4444 🕐 Nov–end Feb Sun–Tue 10–5, open late Wed–Sat; Mar–end Oct Mon–Thu 11–4, open late Fri, Sat 🎁

### CIRCA THEATRE

www.circa.co.nz

Located next to Te Papa (▷ 142–143), Circa is a professional theatre which presents international drama and comedy as well as New Zealand works on two stages. The atmosphere in the theatre is casual but the standard of productions is always high.

✉ 1 Taranaki Street, Wellington ☎ 04-801 7992 🕐 Usually Tue–Wed 6.30, Thu–Sat 8, Sun 4 💳 From NZ$40 ☕

### DOWNSTAGE THEATRE

www.downstage.co.nz

Downstage, New Zealand's longest-running professional theatre, is an intimate venue which presents classic and contemporary drama, dance and comedy, as well as touring shows.

✉ 12 Cambridge Terrace, Wellington ☎ 04-801 6946 🕐 Mon–Thu 6.30, Fri, Sat 8 🍷

### EMBASSY THEATRE

www.deluxe.co.nz

A restored cinema with a giant screen, this is a popular venue during film festivals and hosted the world première of *Lord of the Rings—Return of the King*. The first-floor café, Blondini's, is also a venue for live jazz. Details of films and jazz concerts are published on the website.

✉ 10 Kent Terrace, Wellington ☎ 04-384 7657 💳 From NZ$12

### THE ESTABLISHMENT

www.theestablishment.co.nz

You can dance until late at this popular hangout on Courtenay Place, listen to jazz or watch the weekend's big match. The Establishment serves Southwest American food and tapas in its restaurant, and there's also a lounge bar.

✉ Corner of Courtenay Place and Blair Street, Wellington ☎ 04-382 8654 🕐 Mon–Fri 11–late, Sat, Sun 10–late

### FERGS ROCK 'N' KAYAK

www.fergskayaks.co.nz

Owned by Olympic champion Ian Ferguson, Fergs guides and coaches kayaking, climbing and in-line skating on the waterfront. You can have a paddle along the shore or a full guided tour, and the indoor rock wall caters for all levels of climbing.

✉ Shed 6, Queens Wharf, Wellington ☎ 04-499 8898 🕐 Mon–Fri 10–8, Sat, Sun 9–6 💳 From NZ$15

### FRUTTI

One of Cuba Street's many funky designer shops, Frutti has a lively mix of streetwear and party gear. Many items are made out of vintage fabrics, including one-off designs, bags and accessories.

✉ 166 Cuba Street, Wellington ☎ 04-384 6965 🕐 Mon–Thu 10.30–6, Fri 10–9, Sat 10–6, Sun 11–5

### HAPPY

www.happy.net.nz

A relaxed basement venue, Happy has nightly gigs featuring alternative live music and jazz. It is one of the venues in the Wellington Jazz Festival in March.

✉ Corner of Vivian and Tory streets, Wellington ☎ 04-384 1965 🕐 Gigs 8pm and/or 10pm

### HELIPRO

www.helipro.co.nz

Scenic helicopter flights give views over the city and harbour, or can take you farther afield on a wine tour to the Marlborough Sounds or lunch at Wharekauhau.

✉ Queens Wharf, Wellington ☎ 04-472 1550 💳 From NZ$95

### KIRKCALDIE AND STAINS

www.kirkcaldies.co.nz

Wellington's grand department store, founded in 1863, retains an elegant air, with a commissionaire still present. Originally a draper's store, Kirkcaldie and Stains still specializes in fashion for men and women, but also carries a wide range of cosmetics, stationery, lingerie, children's wear, household items, gifts and food.

✉ 165–177 Lambton Quay, Wellington ☎ 04-472 5899 🕐 Mon–Thu 9–5.30, Fri 9–6, Sat 10–5, Sun 11–4

### MOORE WILSON FRESH

www.moorewilson.co.nz

A must for food lovers, Moore Wilson Fresh is the leading fresh produce store in New Zealand, selling artisan breads, fresh meat, fresh chicken, fresh fish, a huge cheese selection and deli range, coffee and flowers. (There is also a branch at Porirua Masterton.)

✉ Corner of College and Tory streets, Wellington ☎ 04-384 9906 🕐 Mon–Fri 8–7, Sat 8–6, Sun 9–5

### MUD CYCLES

www.mudcycles.co.nz

Close to Makara Peak Mountain Bike Park, standard mountain bikes and 24-speed cycles are available for hire, with the option of central city drop-off and collection. Mud Cycles also offers instruction classes and tours, which range from easy sightseeing to advanced technical trails for eager and experienced thrill seekers.

✉ 338 Karori Road, Wellington ☎ 04-476 4961 💳 From NZ$30

### OLD BANK SHOPPING ARCADE

www.oldbank.co.nz

The arcade contains 27 shops, many of them exclusive to the Wellington region, including fashion, food and cosmetics. It occupies the former banking chamber of the heritage BNZ bank building, with the buried remains of the ship *Inconstant* on display in the basement.

✉ 223–237 Lambton Quay, Wellington ☎ 04-922 0600 🕐 Mon–Thu 9–6, Fri 9–7, Sat 10–4, Sun 11–3

### THE OPERA HOUSE

www.stjames.co.nz

The Opera House is the grand old lady of Wellington theatres—typical of lavish early 1900s architecture, and with a large stage. It is a popular venue for concerts, musicals and touring shows.

✉ 111 Manners Street, Wellington ☎ 04-802 4060

**READING CINEMAS COURTENAY CENTRAL**
www.readingcinemas.co.nz
A 10-screen complex located on level 3 of a shopping and entertainment mall, Reading Cinemas shows popular films and has good parking. Details of films are listed on the website.
✉ 100 Courtenay Place, Wellington ☎ 04-801 4601 ✋ From NZ$12, child NZ$10.50

**SCOTTIES**
www.fashionz.co.nz/scotties
Scotties sells high fashion womenswear by New Zealand designers such as Marilyn Sainty, Julia Fong and Beth Ellery. You'll also find international labels, including Issey Miyake, Lanvin and Comme des Garçons.
✉ 4 Blair Street, Wellington ☎ 04-384 3805 🕘 Mon–Fri 9.30–6, Sat 10–5

**SEAL COAST SAFARI**
www.sealcoast.com
Tours of Wellington's wild south coast take in the Red Rocks and the wind turbine, as well as the fur seal colony at Tongue Point and Sinclair Head. There is time to meet the seals, learn about their life cycle and have refreshments. Tours leave from the visitor information office.
✉ 32 Salamanca Road, Wellington ☎ 0800-732 527 🕘 Daily 10.30, 1.30 ✋ NZ$79, child (under 14) NZ$40

**SOMMERFIELDS**
www.sommerfields.net
Specializing in New Zealand-made gifts and souvenirs, this store carries many items made exclusively for them. The range includes Maori carvings, greenstone, native timber products, hand-blown glass and paua shell.
✉ 296 Lambton Quay, Wellington ☎ 04-499 4847 🕘 Mon–Thu 9–5.30, Fri 9–6, Sat 10–5, Sun 11–3

**STARFISH**
www.starfish.co.nz
Wellington designers Laurie Foon and Carleen Schollum create innovative clothing for men and women reflecting the New Zealand lifestyle and environment. The shop also stocks the luxury Laurie Foon range and other New Zealand designer labels, including Doris De Pont, Fix, Din and Sabatini. You can also buy national and international accessories. Samples, seconds and sale items are available at Star X (213 Left Bank, Cuba Mall, tel 04-384 7827).
✉ 128 Willis Street, Wellington ☎ 04-385 3722 🕘 Mon–Thu 9.30–6, Fri 9.30–8, Sat 10–5, Sun 11–4

**TAMARILLO**
www.tamarillonz.com
A dealer gallery and craft shop, Tamarillo holds monthly exhibitions and carries contemporary New Zealand works of art by established and emerging artists, including glass, ceramics, wood, sculpture and jewellery. Worldwide shipping is available.
✉ 102–108 Wakefield Street, Wellington ☎ 04-473 6095 🕘 Mon–Fri 9.30–6, Sat 10–4, Sun 12–4

**UNITY BOOKS**
www.unitybooks.co.nz
An excellent bookshop committed to New Zealand publishing, Unity is strong on fiction, politics, history and cookery. It has useful review boards and a knowledgeable staff.
✉ 57 Willis Street, Wellington ☎ 04-499 4245 🕘 Mon–Thu 9–6, Fri 9–7, Sat 10–5 Sun 11–4

**WALK WELLINGTON**
www.wellingtonnz.com/Walk-Wellington/
Knowledgeable locals take guided walks around the city, which can be personalized to suit your interests or focus on arts, heritage, shopping or nature. Book at least three days ahead. Scheduled Essential Wellington walks give a general introduction to the city. They leave from the visitor information office and you can book them there (tel 04-802 4860).
☎ 04-472 8280 🕘 Essential Wellington: Nov–end Mar daily at 10am; Apr–end Oct call ahead to find out times and days ✋ From NZ$20, child (5–16) NZ$10, under-5s free

**WELLINGTON CONVENTION CENTRE**
www.wellingtonconventioncentre.com
An umbrella for 19 venues around Wellington, this includes the modern Michael Fowler Centre (111 Wakefield Street), which stages opera and concerts and is home to the New Zealand Symphony Orchestra; the beautifully restored 1904 Wellington Town Hall next door, which is also a concert hall; and the modern TSB Bank Arena (Queens Wharf), used for sports and pop concerts, accommodating 5,000.
✉ 111 Wakefield Street, Wellington ☎ 04-801 4231 ✋ Tickets available through Ticketek ☎ 04-384 3840, www.ticketek.co.nz

**WELLINGTON ROVER TOURS**
www.wellingtonrover.co.nz
With these coach tours you can visit *Lord of the Rings* locations (including lunch at Rivendell), take a 'hop on hop off' day pass or search for glow-worms on a sunset drive around the south coast.
✉ PO Box 11167, Wellington ☎ 021-426211 ✋ From NZ$40, child NZ$25

**WESTPAC ST. JAMES THEATRE**
www.stjames.co.nz
The St. James was built in 1912 as a vaudeville and picture theatre, and extended and refurbished in 1998. Today it has one of the best stages in New Zealand. The ornate interior has been retained and a spacious foyer with a café added. It hosts musicals, dance and touring shows and is home to the Royal New Zealand Ballet.
✉ Courtenay Place, Wellington ☎ 04-802 4060

**WESTPAC STADIUM**
www.westpacstadium.co.nz
Seating 34,500, with seven food and beverage outlets, this is the main venue for national and international rugby fixtures, international rugby sevens tournaments and cricket. It also hosts events, such as Carols by Candlelight and rock concerts.
✉ Waterloo Quay, Wellington ☎ 04-473 3881

## JANUARY

### WELLINGTON CUP WEEK

www.trentham.co.nz

The highlight of the Wellington race calendar also marks Wellington's Anniversary Weekend. And high fashion is all part of the race-day fun.

✉ Trentham Racecourse, Upper Hutt

### WINGS OVER WAIRARAPA

www.wings.org.nz

Organized by the New Zealand Sport and Vintage Aviation Society, this biennial show (odd years) commemorates milestones in aviation, with displays of World War I and II warbirds and many other famous and interesting vintage aircraft.

✉ Hood Aerodrome, Masterton

☎ 027-477 417

## FEBRUARY–MARCH

### FRINGE FESTIVAL

www.fringe.org.nz

The Fringe started as an offshoot of the International Festival to cater for people with smaller pockets and alternative tastes. It has now become an annual festival in its own right, with comedy, dance, new media, parties, spoken word, music and free performances.

✉ 61 Abel Smith Street, Wellington

☎ 04-382 8015

### MARTINBOROUGH FAIR

www.martinboroughfair.org.nz

This country fair—the largest event of its type in New Zealand—is held on two days, one month apart, and includes arts, crafts and food from all over the country. It attracts around 480 stallholders and more than 40,000 visitors each year.

✉ The Square, Martinborough

☎ 06-304 9933 Free

### NEW ZEALAND INTERNATIONAL ARTS FESTIVAL

www.nzfestival.nzpost.co.nz

The city barely sleeps during this month-long biennial festival (held in even years) as Wellington hums with top international acts that would not normally come to New Zealand—cabaret, jazz, circus, classical music and avant-garde theatre—along with fresh, commissioned local work.

✉ PO Box 10113, Wellington

☎ 04-473 0149

## MARCH

### GOLDEN SHEARS

www.goldenshears.co.nz

Reckoned to be the world's premier shearing and wool-handling championship, this three-day event gives a unique insight into New Zealand's rural community as sheep are shorn at lightning speed.

✉ 12 Dixon Street, Masterton

☎ 06-378 8008

### WELLINGTON INTERNATIONAL JAZZ FESTIVAL

www.jazzfestival.co.nz

From jazz standards to avant-garde cabaret, free jazz to funky dance grooves, there is jazz to suit every taste in cafés, bars and venues all over the city during this annual two-week festival of international and local talent.

✉ PO Box 11981, Manners Street, Wellington ☎ 04-385 9602

From NZ$10; tickets from Ticketek

## SEPTEMBER

### WORLD OF WEARABLE ART

www.worldofwearableart.com

Art is taken off the wall to adorn the body in wildly wonderful ways in this annual show, which started in Nelson and has spread to the extent that it has had to make a home in Wellington. The WOW exhibition remains in Nelson (▷ 173).

✉ TSB Bank Arena, Wellington

☎ 03-548 9299

## NOVEMBER

### SCARECROW'S BIG DAY OUT

www.gladstone.org.nz

Scarecrows are scattered throughout the Gladstone district in this lighthearted fair, which includes a 'Scarecrow Scamper' 10km (6-mile) walk and fun run.

✉ Gladstone School, Gladstone

☎ 06-372 7601

### TOAST MARTINBOROUGH

www.toastmartinborough.co.nz

A highlight of the New Zealand wine calendar, this festival is so popular that the 10,500 tickets sell out fast. Festival-goers move from vineyard to vineyard, where local and Wellington chefs match food to the winemaker's selection, and there is top live entertainment. You also get the chance to sample vintages that have been saved for the festival, but have otherwise sold out. There is a free shuttle bus.

✉ Kitchener Street, Martinborough

☎ 06-306 9183 NZ$60

**Above** *A shearer demonstrates speed and skill in deftly working the fleece from a sheep at the Golden Shears championship*

# EATING

**PRICES AND SYMBOLS**

The restaurants are listed alphabetically. The prices given are the average for a two-course lunch (L) and a three-course dinner (D) for one person, without drinks. The wine price (W) is for the least expensive bottle. All the restaurants listed accept credit cards unless otherwise stated.

For a key to the symbols, ⊳ 2.

## GREYTOWN

### MAIN STREET DELI

www.mainstreetdeli.co.nz

A charming little café, snug inside and with a large outdoor eating area, the Main Street Deli serves breakfasts and lunches, along with home-cooked slices, quiches and cakes. The coffee is good, too.

88 Main Street, Greytown 06-304 9022 Daily 8–5 L NZ$30, W NZ$15

### THE WHITE SWAN

www.thewhiteswan.co.nz

Created from a former Railways building, the White Swan cleverly combines old and new. Meat is cooked on a hot stone grill, which locks in flavour without using additional fats or oil. The Lilac Dining Room also opens out onto the veranda and serves modern country food, such as chicken encrusted with basil pesto and pinenuts.

Main Street, Greytown 06-304 8894 Daily 10–4, 7.30–9.30 L NZ$36, D NZ$50, W NZ$27

## MARTINBOROUGH

### THE VILLAGE CAFÉ

www.martinboroughwinecentre.co.nz

Centrally located next to the Martinborough Wine Centre, the café serves breakfast, brunch, lunch and snacks. The focus is on local products, such as manuka-smoked bacon, and they make their own sausages, bread, cakes and biscuits. You can also get local wines, locally brewed beer, organic coffee and speciality teas.

6 Kitchener Street, Martinborough 06-306 8814 Daily 9–5 L NZ$20, W NZ$25

## MASTERTON

### CAFÉ CECILLE

www.cafececille.co.nz

Café Cecille is set in the pretty Queen Elizabeth Park, and its menu uses local ingredients such as Gladstone ham, Kilrae olive oil and Parkvale mushrooms. It's a café by day, serving brunch and lunch, and a restaurant/ wine bar in the evenings.

Queen Elizabeth Park, Masterton 06-370 1166 Tue 10–3, Wed–Fri 10–9, Sat 9–9, Sun 9–3 L NZ$30, D NZ$65, W NZ$35

## PAHIATUA

### BLACK STUMP CAFÉ AND HARROWS RESTAURANT

www.blackstump.tripod.com

On the road between Palmerston North and Masterton, this is worth a stop for its rustic barn setting, with 'wool press' tables, native wood flooring and exposed-beam ceilings. You can eat bar snacks or stay for dinner in the 1900s-themed dining room. The food is modern and interesting, with choices such as bacon, potato and roast pear salad with blue-cheese dressing, or seared beef with caramelized red onions and Parmesan.

106 Main Street, Pahiatua 06-376 7123 Tue–Sun 11.30–late L NZ$26, D NZ$45, W NZ$22

## PALMERSTON NORTH

### BELLA'S CAFÉ

www.bellas.co.nz

A popular café, Bella's mixes Italian with Thai and Pacific Rim dishes. For lunch, choose from tapas, home-made breads, salads or pasta. For

**Opposite** *Bella's Café, Palmerston North*

dinner you can get a range of grills and vegetarian dishes. For dessert, Bella's Blitz of confectionery, fruit and nuts, with chocolate cream and coulis, is made for sharing.
✉ 2 The Square, Palmerston North ☎ 06-357 8616 🕒 Tue–Sat 11.30–3, 6–10 🍴 L NZ$30, D NZ$65, W NZ$31

### DÉJEUNER

www.dejeuner.co.nz
Déjeuner's food is a fusion of European, Asian and Pacific cuisines. Twice-roasted lamb shanks are a speciality, but you can also get ostrich or tandoori beef salad. The 'Eat and Out by 8' option on Thursday to Saturday nights is good value at NZ$45 for two courses.
✉ 159 Broadway Avenue, Palmerston North ☎ 06-952 5581 🕒 Tue–Sat 6–late 🍴 D NZ$65, W NZ$32

## WANGANUI

### AMADEUS RIVERBANK CAFÉ

Overlooking the river, the Amadeus is a good place for breakfast, lunch or coffee. 'The Works' (NZ$12) is their signature breakfast, with eggs, bacon and all the trimmings. There's an all-day menu, with specials and snacks such as samosas, bagels and nachos, along with cakes and tarts.
✉ 69 Taupo Quay, Wanganui ☎ 06-345 1538 🕒 Daily 8.30–4 🍴 L NZ$20, W NZ$17

## WELLINGTON

### THE BACKBENCHER

www.backbencher.co.nz
In the heart of the Parliamentary district, the Backbencher assures you of a good pub lunch and a choice of tap ales, plus the satirical cartoons and three-dimensional caricatures on the walls.
✉ 34 Molesworth Street, Wellington ☎ 04-472 3065 🕒 Daily 11–late 🍴 L NZ$15, D NZ$25

### BOULCOTT STREET BISTRO AND WINE BAR

www.boulcottstreetbistro.co.nz
This is one of Wellington's top restaurants, occupying a Victorian house and headed by a celebrated chef, Chris Green. The menu mixes classics such as fillet béarnaise and crème brûlée with innovative dishes like corn risotto with morels or caramelized lemon tart with tamarillo ice cream.
✉ 99 Boulcott Street, Wellington ☎ 04-499 4199 🕒 Mon–Fri 12–2 (wine bar all day), 6–late, Sat 6–late 🍴 L NZ$50, D NZ$65, W NZ$35

### CAFFE L'AFFARE

www.laffare.co.nz
L'Affare is a thriving coffee business as well as a relaxed café. Tucked down a side street, it is worth searching out. It's a popular meeting place, and serves filled paninis, counter snacks and all-day breakfast. Seafood chowder is a speciality, and the coffee is excellent.
✉ 27 College Street, Wellington ☎ 04-385 9748 🕒 Mon–Fri 7–4.30, Sat 8–4 🍴 L NZ$20, W NZ$35

### THE DUBLINER

Located above Molly Malone's pub, the Dubliner restaurant gives its dishes pseudo-Irish names, but the food is fairly standard hotel fare: soup of the day, salads and pasta, grills and apple crumble. Value for money and hearty portions are the main attractions, with fine ales and a good head on the Guinness.
✉ 134 Courtenay Place, Wellington ☎ 04-384 2896 🕒 Daily noon–late 🍴 L NZ$25, D NZ$40, W NX$29

### KAI IN THE CITY

www.kaicity.co.nz
This *whare kai* (restaurant) in the heart of the city is based on traditional Maori culture. Maori names are given for all the foods and indigenous seasonings, such as piko piko ferns and miro berries, give a unique taste to the dishes. *Kaimoana* (seafood) is prominent. You are encouraged to ask the staff questions and there is entertainment on Saturday night. Reservations are essential.
✉ 21 Majoribanks Street, Wellington ☎ 04-801 5006 🕒 Mon–Sat 5pm–late 🍴 D NZ$50, W NZ$26

### LOGAN BROWN

www.loganbrown.co.nz
Logan Brown is located in grand premises in a neo-Grecian 1920s banking chamber. Booth seating gives diners privacy. The food is modern New Zealand, including dishes like duck with kumara (sweet potato) confit, or mango tarte tatin. A three-course bistro menu is available at lunch and pre-theatre. Reservations are essential.
✉ 192 Cuba Street, Wellington ☎ 04-801 5114 🕒 Mon–Fri 12–2, 6–late, Sat, Sun 6–late 🍴 L NZ$45, D NZ$90, W NZ$41

### MONSOON POON

www.monsoonpoon.co.nz
Monsoon Poon brings the tastes of India, South China, Vietnam, Thailand, the Philippines, Malaysia and Indonesia together under one roof. Chefs cook in full view of the dining room. You can sample different cooking styles by sharing dishes. There are no reservations.
✉ 12 Blair Street, Wellington ☎ 04-803 3555 🕒 Mon–Thu 11–11, Fri 11am–midnight, Sat 5pm–midnight, Sun 5–11 🍴 L NZ$25, D NZ$40, W NZ$28

### SHED 5

www.shed5.co.nz
Built in 1888 as a wool store, Shed 5 has been transformed into an elegant restaurant and bar. Indoors can get crowded and noisy, so take a table outdoors and watch the boats come and go. The menu is modern New Zealand with a focus on seafood. Main courses also include lamb, venison and poultry.
✉ Queens Wharf, Wellington ☎ 04-499 9069 🕒 Mon–Fri noon–late, Sat, Sun 10am–late 🍴 L NZ$40, D NZ$60, W NZ$39

### TULSI

www.tulsirestaurant.co.nz
Deservedly popular in lively Cuba Mall, Tulsi serves Indian cuisine at affordable prices. Butter chicken is a speciality. There are also Tulsi restaurants in Petone and Christchurch.
✉ 135 Cuba Street, Wellington ☎ 04-802 4144 🕒 Daily 11.30am–late 🍴 L NZ$20, D NZ$35, W NZ$30

**Above** *Wharekauhau Country Estate, Featherston*

**PRICES AND SYMBOLS**
The prices are the lowest and highest for a double room for one night including breakfast, unless otherwise stated. All the hotels listed accept credit cards unless otherwise stated. Note that rates can vary widely throughout the year.

For a key to the symbols, ▷ 2.

## CARTERTON

### DORNEYWOOD HOMESTAY BED AND BREAKFAST

Two private self-contained suites are on a 7ha (17-acre) small farm, with a lake for kayaking. The farm is 3km (2 miles) from Carterton. One room is wheelchair accessible.
✉ 170 Park Road, RD2, Carterton ☎ 06-379 5099 NZ$95 2 units

## FEATHERSTON

### LONGWOOD

www.longwood.co.nz
Longwood, reputedly New Zealand's largest private home, is surrounded by park-like grounds in the heart of the Wairarapa wine country. The lodge has magnificent reception rooms and four spacious bedrooms with canopied beds, private bathrooms and fireplaces. The tariff includes breakfast, afternoon tea on arrival and a four-course dinner. There is also a choice of self-contained accommodation in the 1850s former gamekeeper's cottage, coach house and groom's quarters.
✉ Longwood Road East, Featherston ☎ 06-308 8289 Cottages NZ$150–NZ$250; lodge NZ$495 per person, including dinner 4 rooms, 3 cottages

### WHAREKAUHAU COUNTRY ESTATE

www.wharekauhau.co.nz
Pronounced 'forry-coe-hoe', this is one of the country's top luxury lodges. Part of its appeal is its location on a 2,000ha (5,000-acre) working sheep station overlooking the ocean, where you can relish getting away from it all. Lodging is in self-contained cottages dotted round the estate, with four-poster beds, open fireplaces and a naturalistic décor of cotton, clay, hemp and wool. TV, newspapers, internet and activities are available. Dinner in the lodge features French/Italian cuisine matched with top local wines.
✉ Western Lake Road, Palliser Bay, Featherston ☎ 06-307 7581 NZ$1,220–NZ$3,050 per person, including cocktails and dinner 12 cottage suites, 2 houses

## MANGAWEKA

### MOUNT HUIA

www.mthuia.co.nz
You can join in farm activities, walk through pastureland and native bush, or enjoy river sports on this farm in the Rangitikei hill country. Self-contained Hodd Cottage has three bedrooms, two bathrooms, a kitchen, and an open fire. Breakfast ingredients can be provided. Bed-and-breakfast accommodation in the 1920s farmhouse has private access, and a private bathroom and spa pool on the deck. Dinner is available (from NZ$20).
✉ 906 Ruahine Road, RD 54 Kimbolton ☎ 06-382 5726 Farmstay NZ$180; cottage NZ$50 per adult (breakfast provisions NZ$10) 1 room, 1 cottage 9km (6 miles) from SH1

## MARTINBOROUGH

### AYLSTONE WINE COUNTRY RETREAT

www.aylstone.co.nz
A spacious homestead, built in the early 1900s, Aylstone is surrounded by vineyards. The guest rooms are individually designed, in keeping

with the house's colonial heritage, with a choice of super-king, queen or twin beds. All rooms have telephones, TV and internet facilities. Leisurely, seasonal breakfasts are a speciality, and there is a a restaurant in the summer. Bicycles are provided free of charge.
Huangarua Road, Martinborough
06-306 9505 NZ$260
6 rooms

## PALMERSTON NORTH

### AVENUE MOTEL

www.avenuemotel.co.nz
This modern motel in a quiet location is just a few minutes' walk from the heart of the city. There are private spa pools and the standard, family and two-bedroom units are all on the ground floor. A studio unit is wheelchair accessible.
116 Fitzherbert Avenue, Palmerston North 06-356 3330/0888 116 333
NZ$88–$123 13 units

### BENTLEYS MOTOR INN

www.bentleysmotorinn.co.nz
Bentleys has 22 modern, ground-floor units, including studios, one- and two- bedroom suites and a three-bedroom apartment with full kitchen and laundry. All suites have spa pools or spa baths, CD players and cooking facilities. The inn is quiet and within walking distance of shops and cafés, and there are on-site squash courts, a sauna and a gym. Breakfast is available.
Corner of Linton and Chaytor streets, Palmerston North 06-358 7074/0800 BENTLEYS NZ$135–NZ$280 22 rooms Close to the main square, off Fitzherbert Avenue

## PARAPARAUMU

### GREENMANTLE ESTATE

www.greenmantle.co.nz
Close to the site of the New Zealand Open, this was where champion golfer Tiger Woods stayed in 2001. A spacious, rambling 1940s mansion set in gardens full of native birds, it offers six beautifully appointed private rooms and suites, with king beds, oak furniture and double showers. Guests also have use of a gym, heated pool and hot tub hidden away in native bush.
214 Main North Road, Paraparaumu
04-298 5555 NZ$525–NZ$595 6 rooms Outdoor 3km (2 miles) north of Paraparaumu

## WANGANUI

### BRAEMAR HOUSE

www.braemarhouse.co.nz
Braemar House is an Edwardian villa which retains its period charm as a guest house, in a quiet location close to the Whanganui River. Backpacker accommodation is also available. The house has attractive formal dining and living rooms, a well-equipped kitchen, and centrally heated single, double and twin rooms, with shared bathroom.
2 Plymouth Street, Wanganui
06-348 2301 NZ$95 8 rooms
1km (0.5 miles) from Wanganui CBD

### RUTLAND ARMS INN

www.rutland-arms.co.nz
A heritage hotel centrally located in downtown Wanganui, the Rutland Arms has individually designed double, triple and twin suites. Some have spa baths. The first floor is non-smoking. A guest lounge is available, with large screen TV and reading material. A bar, restaurant, courtyard café and shops are attached.
Corner of Victoria Avenue and Ridgway Street, Wanganui 06-347 7677 NZ$140–NZ$175 8 suites
First-floor rooms 5km (3 miles) from the airport

## WELLINGTON

### HOTEL INTERCONTINENTAL

www.wellington.intercontinental.com
This striking, bronze-hued building is a city landmark, near Lambton Quay shops, Parliament and the major sports stadium. You are welcomed by the doorman, and the lobby gleams with marble. Rooms include luxury suites—queen, twin and standard. There is a fitness centre, and restaurants and bars.
Grey Street, Wellington 04-472 2722 NZ$280–NZ$1,824 231 rooms, 7 suites (187 non-smoking)
Indoor In the CBD

### THE LIGHTHOUSE

www.thelighthouse.net.nz
This replica lighthouse offers views across the harbour entrance and oozes character. There is a small kitchen and bathroom on one floor—the living and sleeping areas (two rooms, one main bedroom with spa) are above. The owners also offer B&B in a stone keep in Houghton Bay.
326 The Esplanade, Island Bay, Wellington 04-472 4177 NZ$180–NZ$200 2 rooms 6km (4 miles) south of the CBD

### SHEPHERD'S ARMS HOTEL

www.shepherds.co.nz
Established in 1870, this hotel is full of character. Rooms are decorated in keeping with their Victorian origins, some with four-poster king or queen beds. All double rooms have private bathrooms. There is a popular bar and dining room with an open fire.
285 Tinakori Road, Thorndon, Wellington
04-472 1320 NZ$165–NZ$215
14 rooms 2km (1 mile) from the CBD

### THE TERRACE VILLAS

www.terracevillas.co.nz
A collection of historic houses close to the Cable Car and Lambton Quay, the Terrace Villas are divided into 50 self-contained serviced apartments, from studios to three-bedroom units. All have modern kitchens.
202 The Terrace, Wellington 04-920 2020 NZ$225–NZ$245, excluding breakfast (NZ$9) 50 apartments
In heart of the CBD

### THE WELLESLEY HOTEL

www.thewellesley.co.nz
The 1920s neo-Georgian Wellesley is a heritage building offering furnished suites with character in the Lambton Quarter. Rooms have queen-size beds and spacious bathrooms. Facilities include a gymnasium, sauna and a popular restaurant, which features regular live music.
2–8 Maginnity Street, Wellington
04-474 1308 NZ$195–NZ$290
Luxury suites and rooms
Near the Parliamentary district

# NELSON AND MARLBOROUGH

While it might lack the strident postcard drama of some other parts of South Island, this slice of the north coast is a serene beauty, with rich rewards for anyone who enjoys wilderness walks, wines and boating.

Gateway to the region is the town of Picton, the terminal for ferries from Wellington. Picton sits deep in the Marlborough Sounds, a series of river valleys that drowned when seas rose at the end of the last Ice Age. What remains is a marine paradise, a filigree of broad waterways separated by forested peninsulas and islands, and a world of wonders for wilderness lovers. Rising sharply from the water's edge, the Sounds' steep terrain defies those who would tame it. Despite its 1,400km (870 miles) of coastline, beaches, roads and houses are few.

To the southwest of the Sounds is the Wairau Valley, the heart of the Marlborough region, source of New Zealand's most prestigious wines. The major producers such as Montana, Cloudy Bay and Stoneligh all have cellar-door tasting rooms, but visiting Marlborough is a prime opportunity to taste some of the wines from small producers that are rarely seen on the bottle shop shelves.

Set deep in the cup of Tasman Bay with the Tasman Mountains rising from the far shore, Nelson is a sprightly city of 40,000 inhabitants with a lively cultural calendar, and the home for some of New Zealand's leading artists and craftworkers. Even the climate is benign, with more hours of sunshine than any other city in the country.

A one-hour drive to the northwest, the coastline of Abel Tasman National Park is a series of sandy bays edged with forested granite headlands, rising steeply from the coast to an altitude of more than 1,000m (3,280ft). Although this is the smallest of New Zealand's national parks, Abel Tasman is also one of the most popular. One of the reasons is the Abel Tasman Track, an all-seasons' walk that threads through forest and along beaches. The shoreline of Abel Tasman has New Zealand's most popular sea kayaking. The bays and headlands of this scalloped coast are tailor-made for bobbing around with a paddle in your hands—often with seals and dolphins for company.

## BLENHEIM

www.destinationmarlborough.com

The Marlborough region's largest town is a resort known for its wineries—more than 50 of them, most clustered off SH6 near the village of Renwick, 10km (6 miles) west of town on the fertile soils of the Wairau Plains. Famous names include Montana, Cloudy Bay and Nautilus Estate, and tours and tastings are widely available (▷ 182). Blenheim's dry climate has its disadvantages: in recent years the whole region has suffered from a severe lack of rain.

The Marlborough Provincial Museum at Brayshaw Park, New Renwick Road, 3km (2 miles) south of town (daily 10–4), is a mainly open-air reconstruction of an early settlers' village. It is at the end of the narrow-gauge Blenheim Riverside Railway (tel 03-578 9442).

302 H11 Rail Station, SH1, Sinclair Street 03-577 8080 Services to Christchurch, Picton and Nelson Grove Road; services from Christchurch and Picton On Middle Renwick Road, 7km (4 miles) west; shuttles

## COLLINGWOOD

This tiny village on Golden Bay was once known as Gibbstown and—unlikely as it now seems—was once a booming gold-mining town promoted as a suitable capital for the nation. That dream turned to dust when the gold reserves ran out and a fire almost destroyed the village. Rebuilt and renamed Collingwood in tribute to Admiral Lord Nelson's second-in-command, the community was struck by fire again in 1904 and yet again in 1967, when the town hall, hotel and two shops were reduced to ashes. Despite its calamitous history, Collingwood retains a few historic buildings, including the courthouse, which is now a café.

South of the village, in the attractive Aorere River Valley, are the privately owned Te Anaroa and Rebecca Caves, on Caves Road, near Rockville (reservations essential, tel 03-525 6044). The Te Anaroa Caves are 350m (1,148ft) long and include stalactites and fossilized shells; the Rebecca Caves are known for their glow-worms.

If you have time, an exploration of the pretty Aorere River valley (Heaphy Track Road) is recommended, taking in the river gorge at Salisbury Bridge and the Bainham Store, an original store that has changed little in decades and is still open for business.

302 G10

## FAREWELL SPIT AND GOLDEN BAY

Countless tons of sand have been ejected into the northerly ocean currents from river-mouths scattered all the way up the west coast, forming this dynamic though desert-like landscape at the northwest tip of the South Island, with sparse vegetation struggling to take root in the dry and shifting sand. Both Cape Farewell and Farewell Spit were noted by Abel Tasman in 1642, and named by Cook when he left New Zealand in 1770. The lighthouse at the very tip of the spit was first erected in 1870, and relocated after the sea almost washed it away.

The majority of the spit is a nature reserve, and the mud flats that it creates along its landward edge are one of New Zealand's most important habitats for wading birds. More than 100 species have been recorded around the spit, but it is the sheer numbers of each species that are most notable. Migrating flocks of godwits and knots can run well into the thousands. Black swans are also found here.

The spit is remarkable for its powerful sense of isolation, but from afar and from sea level its extensive dune system appears no more than a coastal mirage. For an impression of its scale, the best viewpoint is around the Pillar Point Light Beacon, accessed from Wharariki Road and Puponga. A marked walk leads from the beacon along the cliffs to Cape Farewell, where you may see or hear (or smell!) fur seals.

From here you can descend to Wharariki Beach, one of the most beautiful in the country (you can also reach it from Puponga along Wharariki Road), where golden sands are punctuated with caves, dunes and rock arches.

302 G9–10 Freemans Access, Puponga 03-524 8454

**Above** *A gannetry occupies the tip of Farewell Spit*

**Opposite** *Abel Tasman National Park's rolling hills and native bush (▷ 166–167)*

**INFORMATION**

www.doc.govt.nz
302 G10 Wallace Street, Motueka 03-528 6543 Daily 8–7 Department of Conservation field centre, corner of King Edward and High streets, Motueka 03-528 1810 Mon–Fri 8–4.30 Services from Nelson to Kaiteriteri and Marahau via Motueka (southern entrance), and to Totaranui (northern sector) Water taxis from Motueka, Kaiteriteri and Marahau; can also be hailed within park Awaroa Bay (from Nelson or Motueka): Abel Tasman Air (tel 03-528 8290)

**Above** *A water taxi is a good way to explore Abel Tasman's beautiful coastal inlets and wetlands*

## INTRODUCTION

More than 150,000 visitors a year come to appreciate the Abel Tasman's rolling hills of native bush; its granite, limestone and marble outcrops; its clear, azure waters; and its 91km (56 miles) of coastline indented with more than 50 sandy beaches. Birds such as tui and bellbirds inhabit lush pockets of forest, and pukeko feed in the wetlands—outside the park's boundaries these are protected as the Tonga Island Marine Reserve.

On an average summer's day the park attracts up to 4,000 people, and you must reserve well in advance for all places to stay and most activities.

Maori communities have lived along this coast for at least five centuries but from 1855 European settlement got underway, which meant the clearing of forests and quarrying of granite. Fears that logging would strip the coast of its vegetation led to a campaign for the protection of this stretch of shoreline, and finally in 1942 the national park was opened.

## WHAT TO SEE

### AWAROA BAY

A 6km (4-mile), three- to six-hour walk makes the most of this glorious inlet south of Totaranui. Its starting point is reached from Takaka along the Totaranui Road, via Pohara, Wainui Inlet and the Pigeon Saddle, with tremendous views to be had along the way. From the Totaranui Road, a right turn takes you on to the Awaroa Road and the Awaroa parking zone.

To enjoy the walk you need to time your arrival with an outgoing tide, as it begins on the beach (this stage is best done barefoot). It ends at Awaroa Lodge, where you can buy beer, coffee or tea, before retracing your steps to the Awaroa parking zone, keeping a careful eye on the tide.

302 G10

### COAST TRACK

This world-famous two- to five-day, 51km (32-mile) walk requires medium fitness; the track itself is well maintained. The only obstacles and difficult sections are the two estuary crossings at Awaroa Inlet and Torrent Bay—the most scenic beaches on the route—which must be negotiated at low tide. There are several ways to tackle the track in whole or in part. The most popular routes are from the south (Marahau) to the north (Wainui), or from Totaranui in the north (by water taxi from Marahau) to Marahau in the south. There are plenty of campsites and huts along the way and a few independent lodges. The walk involves a lot of bush walking, where views of the sea and beaches are obscured for long periods of time.

#### INLAND TRACK

The Inland Track is a quieter but more energetic walk than the Coast Track, and leads away from the coast and its hordes of visitors. It provides a link between Marahau and Wainui via the Pigeon Saddle on the Takaka–Totaranui Road, and takes three to five days to cover 37km (23 miles). The main appeals here, other than the fact that the walk is far less popular than the coastal track, are the undisturbed regenerating bush and the occasional sublime views. You may also hear kiwis at night.

#### TORRENT BAY TO MARAHAU WALK

This 14km (8.5-mile) route takes from three to six hours to complete. From Marahau you can take an early morning water taxi to Torrent Bay (NZ$30; first taxi leaves 8.30), making sure that your arrival at Torrent Bay coincides with low tide. From here the route joins the Coast Track heading south, for which you need to take off your boots and follow the markers across the estuary, and continues via the lovely sands of Anchorage Bay Beach, intimate Watering Cove, and Stillwell and Appletree bays.

### MORE TO SEE

#### KAITERITERI

Scenic launches, water taxis and kayak trips set off from this very pretty village on the dead-end road to the southern boundary of the park. There are two exceptionally good beaches here. At the eastern end of the main beach is the Kaka Pa Point Lookout. Idyllic Breakers Beach, below, looks eastward.

302 G10 Services from Nelson

#### MARAHAU

Marahau is 6km (4 miles) east of Kaiteriteri, on the same southern approach road to the park. It offers a wide range of places to stay and activities, water taxis and a café. Controversy is raging about a NZ$15 million resort development given resource consent on the environmentally sensitive wetlands at the entrance to the park—a project that confirms the worst fears of conservationists about threats to the unspoiled beauty of the Abel Tasman.

302 G10 Services from Nelson

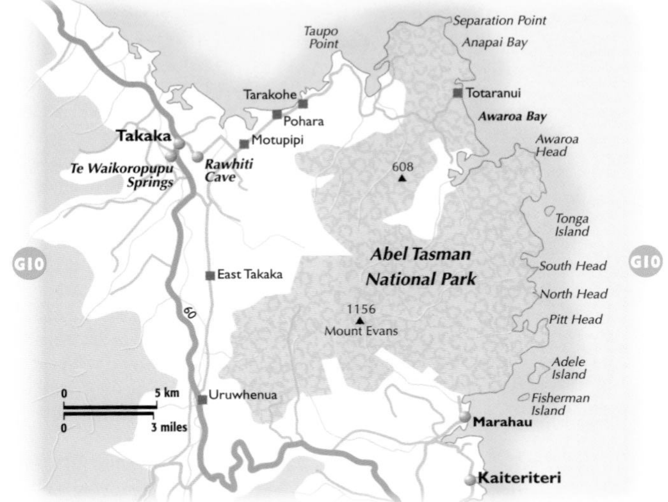


#### TIPS

» Visitor information and DoC offices in Motueka can help with reserving places to stay, passes, transportation, activities and tide times.

» General information, hut reservations, maps and leaflets are also available at the DoC office.

» Unmanned DoC information stations and intentions sheets are available at Marahau and Totaranui (seasonal).

## HAVELOCK

www.rutherfordtravel.co.nz

Travelling west from Blenheim (▷ 165), the SH6 passes through the small village of Renwick before winding through the rolling hills of the Inner Marlborough Sounds to Nelson. About 41km (25 miles) along, at the head of the Pelorus Sound, is the enchanting little fishing settlement of Havelock. The village has a fine café, a famous restaurant (Mussel Pot, ▷ 187), art and craft galleries, a pub and a small but interesting museum on Main Road (daily 9–5). It's also an ideal base for exploring the glorious Pelorus and other outer sounds. Takorika Hill, behind the town, offers panoramic views of the surroundings.

Havelock was once a thriving gold-mining town and was the boyhood home of one of New Zealand's most famous sons, atomic physicist Ernest Rutherford (1871–1937)—the man who split the atom. His former home is now the youth hostel, and a memorial stands on the main street. These days Havelock's gold is the green-lipped mussel, without doubt the finest-tasting thing in a shell, and a major export industry within the Sounds.

A network of old bridleways makes up the 27km (17-mile) Nydia Track, which begins near Havelock at Kaiuma Bay. The two-day walk takes in an old timber-milling site and magnificent forest on the way to Duncan Bay.

About 18km (11 miles) west of Havelock is the Pelorus Bridge Scenic Reserve, where the Rai and Pelorus rivers flow through bush-clad hills. You can walk in the area, and there's a great café by the bridge.

302 H10 46 Main Road 03-574 2104 Main Road Services from Blenheim and Nelson

## KAHURANGI NATIONAL PARK

www.doc.govt.nz

Kahurangi, opened as a national park in 1996, is a wide and remote landscape in the northwest of rugged alpine ranges and river valleys. The most notable of these is the Heaphy, which meets, in part, the park's most famous walking route, the 82km (51-mile) Heaphy Track—named for Major Charles Heaphy, the first to traverse the coastal section, in 1846. It takes four to six days to cover the whole route, which reaches its highest point of 915m (3,002ft) at Flannigan's Corner, near Mount Perry. The eastern Heaphy Track trailhead is reached via Collingwood (▷ 165), and Bainham (Aorere River Valley), at the end of the Heaphy Track Road. The route is signposted from Collingwood. The western trailhead starts about 15km (9 miles) north of Karamea. Book hut accommodation ahead in summer.

Some of the country's oldest rock landforms—spectacular limestone caves, plateaux, arches and outcrops—are contained within the park, and it provides a home for more than half New Zealand's native plant species (over 80 per cent of all alpine species) and more than 18 native bird species, including the New Zealand falcon and the great spotted kiwi, as well as the huge New Zealand land snail.

302 G10 DoC field centres: Millers Acre, 79 Trafalgar Street, Nelson 03-546 9339; corner of King Edward and High streets, Motueka 03-528 1810; Commercial Street, Takaka 03-525 8026 Services from Nelson, Takaka and Karamea

**Below** *Orchards and hop farms surround the sunny resort of Motueka*

## MOTUEKA

www.abeltasmangreenrush.co.nz

Motueka sits among sun-bathed hop farms and orchards, a short distance from several beautiful beaches. Many visitors pass through en route to the Abel Tasman National Park and Golden Bay, making this a bustling resort in summer and a sleepy service town in winter. The best beaches near Motueka (and before the national park) are in Kaiteriteri (▷ 167). For a short walk try the Motueka Quay, reached via the waterfront west of downtown. Motueka has a small museum (Dec–Apr daily 9–4; May–Nov Mon–Fri 10–4).

The route between Motueka and Richmond (SH60), known as Nelson's Coastal Way, is the place to go for arts and crafts and wineries, plus the Touch the Sea Aquarium (daily 9–5) and the Cool Store art gallery next door.

302 G10 Wallace Street 03-528 6543 Airport on College Street, 2km (1 mile) west

## KAIKOURA

The small town of Kaikoura sits on the spectacular northeast coast, in the shadow of the snow-capped Kaikoura mountains. South, a sea trough extends unusually close to the coastline, creating an upsurge of nutritious plankton soup and attracting an extraordinary variety of ocean inhabitants.

Modern Kaikoura was established as a whaling station in the early 19th century. Station manager George Fyffe built Kaikoura's oldest remaining house (Fyffe House) near the Old Wharf in 1860, and gave his name to the mountain immediately behind the township. The whaling industry was replaced by fishing, particularly for crayfish. Today Kaikoura's wildlife is hunted only by the camera, and the resident and migratory whales are the big draw.

### WATER-BASED ACTIVITIES

The sea around Kaikoura abounds with dolphins, from the common and bottlenose to the smaller, rare Hector's dolphin. You are most likely to encounter or swim with dusky dolphins; pods running into the hundreds, if not the thousands, are common. Kaikoura is home to its own pod of sperm whales. Whale-watching trips depart from the Whaleway Station off Beach Road, offering a chance to spot dolphins, seals and other wildlife. Other whale species that appear regularly include humpbacks, rights and orcas, and if you are very lucky you may see an enormous blue whale. For details of tours and availability, ▷ 183.

### LAND-BASED SIGHTS

Clifftop and shoreline walkways link the northern and southern settlements of Kaikoura, and cross the head of the Kaikoura Peninsula. A good spot to get an overall impression of the town, the peninsula and its mountain backdrop is the lookout just off Scarborough Terrace (off SH1 between the northern and southern settlements). See also the walk, ▷ 180.

There are three historical venues of note: the Kaikoura District Museum, at 14 Ludstone Road (Mon–Fri 12.30–4.30, Sat, Sun 2–4), offering an insight into early Maori and whaling activities; Fyffe House, on Avoca Street near the Old Wharf (Nov–end Apr daily 10–5; May–end Oct Thu–Tue 10–4); and the Maori Leap Cave, 2km (1 mile) south of Kaikoura, a sea-formed limestone cave, discovered only in the 21st century (daily tours).

### INFORMATION

www.kaikoura.co.nz
302 H12 West End, Kaikoura 03-319 5641 Mon–Fri 9–5, Sat, Sun 9–4 Services from Christchurch, Blenheim, Picton and Hanmer Springs. Shuttles to all main sights Clarence Street; services from Christchurch, Blenheim and Picton

### TIPS

» In midsummer it's advisable to reserve all activities ahead, and essential if you want to go whale-watching or dolphin-swimming.

» Kaikoura is subject to changeable weather. Trips may be cancelled at short notice, so be sure to request inclusion on alternative trips.

**Above** *Watching a sperm whale dive off the Kaikoura coast*

## MARLBOROUGH SOUNDS

A mosaic of tiny islets, coves and waterways, Marlborough Sounds can be enjoyed along coastal paths or from the water.

The Marlborough Sounds are the South Island's giant entrance foyer. This vast, convoluted system of drowned river valleys, wooded peninsulas and remote green islets has sublime coastal scenery and offers every opportunity for kayaking, wildlife-watching or just relaxation. From its base at Picton (▷ 171) it is only a short journey to Blenheim (▷ 165), the region's capital. On the map, the Sounds take up a relatively small area, but the myriad drowned river valleys create an astonishing 1,500km (932 miles) of coastline, known for seabirds and dolphins. The two main inlets are Queen Charlotte and Pelorus sounds.

### EXPLORING THE SOUNDS

There are two popular walking tracks in the sounds: the Nydia Track (Havelock ▷ 168) and the Queen Charlotte Track, a 71km (44-mile), coastal route which leads in three to five days from Ship Cove to Anakiwa. The track is suitable for most people of average fitness, and is open in part to mountain bicycles. It winds its way around sheltered coves, over skyline ridges and through native forest, fringing an extensive network of sunken river valleys.

Boat access in the Sounds is well organized and readily available. Other options include guided and self-guided walks, as well as kayaking trips and a ride on the Magic Mail Run (tel 03-573 6175, www.mailboat.co.nz). There is road access for drivers at Camp Bay (Punga Cove), Torea Bay (The Portage) and Mistletoe Bay (Te Mahia).

### EARLY VISITORS

There is evidence of Maori settlement here from as early as the 14th century. Captain Cook visited the Sounds on each of his voyages between 1770 and 1777. He was particularly fond of Ship Cove, near the mouth of Queen Charlotte Sound, which he visited five times: a monument there commemorates the occasions. Less celebrated visits by other early explorers include those of Abel Tasman (before Cook), and French navigator Jules Dumont d'Urville in 1827. In the same year, London whaler John Guard established Marlborough's first European settlement, and the country's first land-based whaling station, at Te Awaiti Bay in Tory Channel, on Arapawa Island.

#### INFORMATION

www.destinationmarlborough.com
302 J10 · Foreshore, near the ferry terminal, Picton · 03-520 3113 · Daily 8.30–5 · Services to Picton from Christchurch, Nelson and Blenheim · Daily service Christchurch–Picton: arriving 12.13pm, departing 1pm · Ferries to Picton from Wellington · Koromiko airport, 10km (6 miles) south of town

#### TIPS

» Marlborough Sounds can be explored on foot or by boat. Several water-based operators will drop off or pick up from a number of points along the Queen Charlotte walking track.

» Sea access is possible at Ship Cove, Resolution Bay, Endeavour Inlet, Camp Bay (Punga Cove), Bay of Many Coves, Torea Bay (the Portage), Lochmara Bay, Mistletoe Bay (Te Mahia) and Anakiwa.

**Below** *A coastline indented with appealing little bays characterizes Queen Charlotte Sound*

**MURCHISON**

www.nelsonnz.com

Murchison sits at the head of the Buller Gorge, where the Matakitaki and Buller rivers meet, and gives access to the west coast from the north. Although once an important gold-mining town—and nearly wiped out by a violent earthquake in 1929—it is now a quiet place, primarily of interest for activities such as fishing, white-water rafting, kayaking, caving and mountaineering.

The Murchison Museum, on Fairfax Street (daily 10–4), has exhibits on gold-mining and the town's past.

302 F11 · 47 Waller Street · 03-523 9350 · Services from Nelson and the West Coast

**NELSON**

▷ 172–173.

**NELSON LAKES NATIONAL PARK**

This somewhat underrated national park protects 102,000ha (252,042 acres) of the northernmost Southern Alps range. Dominating the park are two long, scenic and trout-filled lakes, Rotoroa and Rotoiti, which lie cradled in beech-covered alpine ranges, surrounded by beautiful tussock valleys and wildflower-strewn meadows.

The ranges and river valleys offer superb walking, notably the 80km (50-mile), four- to seven-day Travers-Sabine Circuit and the excellent two- to three-day Robert Ridge/Lake Angelus Track. The principal base for the park is the pretty little hamlet of St. Arnaud, at the northern end of Lake Rotoiti—ask at the visitor information office here about shorter walks in the vicinity.

302 G11 · St. Arnaud · 03-521 1806 · Services from Nelson to St. Arnaud

**PICTON**

www.picton.co.nz

After you have arrived on the modern ferry, with its comfy seats and state-of-the-art radar screens, you will thank your lucky stars for progress when you encounter the old hulk of the 1853 East India trading ship *Edwin Fox*, between the ferry terminal and the heart of town (daily 9–5). Ranked the ninth oldest ship in the world, she carried troops in the Crimean War before being commissioned to bring immigrants to Australia and New Zealand.

Next door is the Seashore World (daily 9–6), whose inhabitants include an octopus called Larry, seahorses and rays. Farther towards the town on London Quay is the Picton Community Museum (daily 10–4), which contains a cluttered but interesting range of items focusing mainly on the 1800s whaling operations in the sounds, as well as Maori taonga (treasures) and early pioneer settler pieces.

A short walk across the footbridge and the inlet leads to the eastern side of the waterfront and Shelley Beach. Here, the Echo Café and Bar (daily 10–late) is based around a scow, built in 1905 and gradually restored after her retirement in 1965. She was the last commercial trader under sail in New Zealand, and served in World War II. During her eventful life, Echo was stranded 15 times and damaged 16 times, had two new engines, propellers and shafts, suffered fires in 1911 and 1920, not to mention having seven collisions involving 75 different vessels and being sunk twice. She now has a quieter time as a restaurant.

For a comprehensive guide to the walks around Picton, get hold of the excellent broadsheet *Picton by Foot,* available free from the visitor information office.

302 H11 · Foreshore, near ferry terminal · 03-520 3113 · Daily 8.30–5 · Services from Christchurch, Nelson and Blenheim · Service from Christchurch · Ferries from Wellington · 10km (6 miles) south of town

**Above** *Inside the restored teak hull of the East India trading ship* Edwin Fox, *the ninth oldest ship in the world, at Picton*

**INFORMATION**
www.nelsonnz.com
302 G10 Corner of Trafalgar and Halifax streets 03-548 2304 Daily 9–5 Outside visitor information office; services from Christchurch, Blenheim, Picton, Golden Bay, Abel Tasman, Takaka and West Coast Airport 6km (4 miles) southwest of town off SH6

**Above** *A sunset stroll along the city's Tahunanui Beach*

## INTRODUCTION

Nelson is known as the sunniest place in the country—and this could apply to its atmosphere, its people and its surroundings, in addition to its Mediterranean climate. The city's colonial heart is around Trafalgar Street, and the Saturday market is a highlight (▷ 184). Within 100km (60 miles) of town are superb beaches and coastal scenery, as well as three diverse national parks: Abel Tasman (▷ 166–167), Nelson Lakes (▷ 171) and Kahurangi (▷ 168). Little wonder that Nelson is considered one of the top places to visit—and to live—in the country.

Maori tribes migrated to this area from the North Island in the 16th century. In the 1840s New Zealand Company agent Colonel William Wakefield negotiated a land purchase at Nelson. Subsequent disagreements about ownership of further land led to the Wairau Affray and the death of his brother, Captain Arthur Wakefield, and 27 others. In 1844 the NZ Company collapsed, leaving many destitute. Recovery began in 1857, when gold was discovered, and by the end of the 19th century Nelson's rich agricultural potential was finally being realized.

## WHAT TO SEE

### BEACHES

No visit to Nelson would be complete without a trip to the beach. The most popular stretch of sand is at the Tahunanui Beach Reserve, just southwest of downtown. It may not have the same scenic beauty (or solitude) of more remote beaches in the region, but it is a convenient place to relax. About 20km (12 miles) farther round Tasman Bay towards Motueka, off SH60, are the seemingly never-ending sands and forest swathe of Rabbit Island.

## BROADGREEN HISTORIC HOUSE

An 11-room cob house of 1855, made of clay, sand and straw, has been furnished in its original style and opened to the public. It was built for Englishman Edmund Buxton, following the model of a Devon farmhouse, and sits amid lawns and rose gardens.

276 Nayland Road, Stoke, 6km (4 miles) southwest of downtown · 03-547 0403 · Daily 10.30–4.30 · Adult NZ$4, child (school age) NZ$1, pre-school free · From Travel Centre, 27 Bridge Street

## NELSON MUSEUM PUPURI TAONGA O TE TAI AO

www.museumnp.org.nz

The new regional museum covers the natural and human history of the top of the South Island. Displays include photos of everyday life from an outstanding collection made in the 1860s, as well as Maori *taonga* (treasures), works of art and a range of domestic and technical objects.

Corner of Hardy and Trafalgar streets · 03-548 9588 · Mon–Fri 10–5, Sat, Sun 10–4.30

## SUTER TE ARATOI O WHAKATU

www.thesuter.org.nz

The Suter, next to Queen's Gardens, is foremost among several major galleries in this city known for its thriving arts and crafts. Four exhibition spaces showcase permanent and temporary historical and contemporary collections. There is also a theatre on the site.

208 Bridge Street · 03-548 4699 · Daily 10.30–4.30 · Adult NZ$3, schoolchild NZ$0.50 · From Travel Centre, 27 Bridge Street; Double-Decker Express

## WORLD OF WEARABLE ART AND CLASSIC CARS (WOW)

www.wowcars.co.nz

In 1987 Nelson sculptor Suzie Moncrieff created and directed a unique stage show called Wearable Art. Contributors were asked to create a piece of themed artwork in any medium in a form that could be worn in motion. The show became an annual event and has now shifted to Wellington (▷ 157), but the best entries can be seen in this gallery. A fully scripted moving parade of extreme costumes is displayed, reflecting an astonishing array of creative thought and eccentric wit—not to be missed. A second gallery in the same complex houses vintage cars.

Quarantine Road, Annesbrook · 03-547 4573 · Jan–Easter daily 10–6; Easter–end Dec daily 10–5 · Adult NZ$18, child (5–14) NZ$7, under-5s free, family from NZ$26 · From Travel Centre, 27 Bridge Street; Double-Decker Express

### TIPS

» Nelson's vineyards are overshadowed by the reputation and scale of those in Marlborough, but the wine they produce can be of excellent quality. For more information see www.nelsonwines.co.nz.

» A half-hour's climb to the viewpoint above the Botanical Gardens, off Milton Road or Maitai Road, gives a great view of the town from a site claimed as New Zealand's geographical mid-point.

**Left** *The Boatshed Restaurant overhangs the water*

**Below** *South Street's houses are among the oldest in the country*

**Above** *The clear waters of Te Waikoropupu springs give exceptional visibility and a home to many species of animal and plant life*

## RAWHITI CAVE

This ancient cave 7km (4 miles) east of Takaka has one of the largest cave entrances in the world, laden with thousands of multi-hued tufa stalactites. It can be accessed independently, but the best way to see it is on a three-hour guided walk with Kahurangi Walks (tel 03-525 7177, www.kahurangiwalks.co.nz), which takes you through the wonderful gorge of the Dry River. The ground is slippery, so you'll need to wear sturdy shoes.

302 G10 Clifton Road, Golden Bay

## TAKAKA

www.nelsonnz.com

Takaka was founded in 1854 and is the principal business and shopping area for Golden Bay (▷ 165). Particularly busy during summer, it has a life of its own all year as a cosmopolitan art and crafts hub. It is also the main base for visits to the northern sector of the Abel Tasman National Park (▷ 166–167), the vast Kahurangi National Park, and the remote 35km (22-mile) Farewell Spit (▷ 165). The small seaside village of Pohara, about 10km (6 miles) northeast of Takaka on the road to the northern boundary of the Abel Tasman National Park, boasts the best local beach and provides safe swimming.

In the town itself the Golden Bay Museum and Gallery (daily 10–4, closed Sun in winter) displays local treasures and a special feature on explorer Abel Tasman's unfortunate first encounter with the local Maori (when four of his crew were killed). The gallery next door showcases the cream of local arts and crafts talent. There are many other independent studios and galleries in the area, listed in the free *Arts of Golden Bay* leaflet, available at the visitor information office.

The odd and shapely karst features of the Labyrinth Rocks (daily 1–5) form an intriguing sight 3km (2 miles) outside the town on Labyrinth Lane. More interesting land formations can be seen at the Grove Scenic Reserve at Clifton. Here a short 10-minute walk brings you to a spot where massive rata trees grow out of curiously shaped limestone outcrops. There are fine views to be had and a fabulous summer flowering of begonias at nearby Begonia House on Richmond Road (Nov–end May daily 10–5; Jun–end Oct Mon–Fri 10–3).

The Abel Tasman Memorial on the headland just beyond Tarakohe, on Totaranui Road, was erected in 1942 to commemorate the tercentenary of the Dutch explorer's arrival. Drive on towards Totaranui and at the base of Wainui Bay is an easy 40-minute walk to the pretty Wainui Falls. The same road can also take you to the northern beaches and walking access points of the Abel Tasman National Park.

302 G10 Willow Street 03-525 9136 Willow Street; services from Abel Tasman and Kahurangi Airfield 6km (4 miles) west of town on SH60

## TE WAIKOROPUPU SPRINGS

The biggest attraction in the Takaka area is the beautiful, crystal-clear Te Waikoropupu, or Pupu Springs. Turquoise waters bubble out of the ground to create the clearest freshwater lake outside Antarctica, with an extraordinary 62m (203ft) of horizontal visibility. It provides a habitat for a wide range of aquatic plants and fish, including brown trout. The main spring has a basin 40m (131ft) across, and there are several smaller springs, identifiable by the white sand thrown up to the surface by water action. The spring is a sacred Maori site, and bathing in its chilly waters is not permitted.

The source of the water is the Takaka River and its tributaries, which flow over karstified marble to the south, entering swallow holes and flowing through a massive underground cave system until it reaches this outlet.

To get to this peaceful place follow SH60 north of Takaka, turning left just after the bridge over the Takaka River. Follow Pupu Valley and Pupu Springs Road to the parking zone. There are well-maintained paths and boardwalks through forest and swamp, and the reserve can be explored thoroughly in about 45 minutes (access is free). Nearby the Pupu Walkway, which starts at the end of Pupu Valley Road, retraces an old gold-mining water race.

302 G10 North of Takaka, Golden Bay Daily Free

## WAIRAU VALLEY

More than 50 wineries operate in the sunbaked Marlborough region, concentrated in the fertile Wairau Valley and producing highly acclaimed Chardonnay, Riesling, Cabernet Sauvignon, Merlot, Pinot noir, sparkling *méthode champenoise* and some of the best Sauvignon blanc in the world. Montana sowed the first seeds of success in the early 1970s and is now the largest winery in the country, joined by a host of other international names and providing a major national export industry.

Like Hawke's Bay in the North Island, the wineries have been quick to take advantage of the influx of summer visitors. Most offer tours, tastings (free or inexpensive) and good restaurants. The vineyards may lack the architectural splendour or variety of Hawke's Bay (▷ 103), but the wine itself is outstanding.

### TOURING THE AREA

Several excellent tours offer full- or half-day overviews of the whole Wairau Valley area, taking in the pick of the crop and the widest variety of wine types. There is always an informative commentary on offer—and often a lunch stop, too. If you have particular tastes, many tour operators will create a personal itinerary; and if you wish to explore by yourself there are plenty of maps and leaflets available at the visitor information office. Most of the wineries are located off SH6, west of Blenheim, and the best time of year to visit them is in April, when the vines are ripe for the picking.

Montana Brancott Winery, at Riverlands on Main South Road (SH1) just south of Blenheim (▷ 165), started it all and is well worth visiting (daily 9–5). It is the central venue for the famous Wine Marlborough festival, held in February (▷ 185), where you can sample more than 150 wines.

In addition to wineries there are distilleries, breweries and orchards in the Wairau Valley, producing everything from liqueurs and fruit wines to olive oil. Prenzel Distillery on Sheffield Street, Riverlands Estate is the country's first commercial fruit distillery, with a whole range of products including fruit liqueurs, schnapps and brandies. The Mud House on Rapaura Road (daily 10–5) has an olive shop, crafts, a coffee house and a restaurant.

### INFORMATION

www.winemarlborough.net.nz
302 H11 · Blenheim Railway Station, Blenheim · 03-577 8080 · Summer daily 8.30–6.30; winter Mon–Fri 9–5.30, Sat, Sun 9–4 · Services to Blenheim from Christchurch, Nelson and Picton · Services to Blenheim from Christchurch and Picton · Airport on Middle Renwick Road, 7km (4 miles) west of Blenheim

### TIPS

» The visitor information office produces a *Wines and Wineries of Marlborough* wine trail map and a broadsheet called *The Marlborough Wine Region*.

» Detailed information about New Zealand wines can be found in the magazine *Cuisine Wine Country*, available in most bookshops and magazine outlets.

**Below** *Shingle Peak vineyard lies at the foot of the Richmond Range, in the Wairau Valley*

# A TASTE OF THE ABEL TASMAN

**This section of the Abel Tasman Coast Track, from Bark Bay to Anchorage, includes dense native bush, turquoise bays, golden beaches and idyllic swimming spots.**

**THE WALK**
**Distance:** 12km (7 miles)
**Time:** 7 hours; 4 hours of walking
**Start/end at:** Marahau, 67km (42 miles) northwest of Nelson 302 G10

It takes up to five days to walk the entire Abel Tasman Coast Track (▷ 166), but water taxis make it easy to walk this delicious one-day taster. The walking track is in excellent condition, the climbs are gentle and there's plenty of time to relax and enjoy the beauty.

Abel Tasman is New Zealand's smallest and most popular national park. It was named after Dutch explorer Abel Janszoon Tasman (1603–*c*1659), who managed to upset the Maori without actually setting foot on land. His two ships moored off the northern coast of the South Island in 1642, watched warily by the Ngati Tumatakokiri tribe. A small boat, ferrying sailors between the ships, was rammed by one of eight Maori canoes. A skirmish erupted and four of Tasman's crew were killed. Tasman heatedly named the beach Murderers' Bay; it was later renamed Golden Bay.

★ Meet the water taxi at its Marahau base for the 9am departure to Bark Bay.

❶ The hour-long trip takes you past Split Apple Rock, a huge ball of porous granite from Separation Point that, at some unknown time, broke clean in half. It is stained red by the iron oxide that gives the beaches their golden tone and the oysters an interesting tang.

As you step off the boat at Bark Bay, the track is at the south (left-hand) end of the beach. There are toilets here: it's 8km (5 miles) to the next ones, and the Department of Conservation does not encourage bushland emergencies.

❷ Bark Bay was home to a family of European settlers—Timothy Huffam and his sons, who arrived in 1870. One of their money-earning activities

**Opposite** *Sailing past Split Apple Rock*

was to gather beech and rimu bark to sell in Nelson for the tanning process. They stayed until 1904. The DoC hut at the north end of Bark Bay beach is built on the site of their homestead, and the redwoods they planted are still there.

Follow the track as it meanders away from the coast and through native bush, which includes tree ferns, kanuka and beech. After 1km (0.6 miles), a signposted track on the left points to South Head. The short track gives views over the sea and Pinnacle Island. Once back on the main track, take your time crossing the Falls River swingbridge—seals often cruise for fish here at high tide.

❸ Descend into Torrent Bay and walk down the two sandy 'streets' of holiday baches. At the south end of the beach a picturesque jetty gives a superb view of the bay and is a good spot for lunch. Toilets are another 500m (550 yards).

Stay on the main track. (It is possible to get to Anchorage across the bay at low tide; this route is 3km/2 miles shorter, but be sure of the tides.)

❹ The bush in this section of the walk is lush compared with other areas. From Bark Bay to Onetahuti Beach, the next beach to the north, there is a lot of scrubby manuka and kanuka, while visitors to the park's northwestern entrance at Wainui Bay pass a stretch of invasive, prickly gorse. It's all part of an experiment in land recovery. This land was leased to European settlers on the condition that it was cleared for productive use, and sawmills, granite quarries, boatyards and farms appeared. None were sustainable: Farmland was quickly drained of nutrients and stock failed to thrive. Through the 1930s Nelson conservationist Perrine Moncrieff led a vigorous campaign to have 15,000ha (37,000 acres) made into a national park. It opened in 1942. The track follows a series of picturesque coves.

❺ Birdlife is prolific and seals often come up the rivers to play and forage. The seals that frequent these coves are New Zealand fur seals. Sealers decimated the population in the 19th century, but now they are fully protected, numbers are crawling back by around 2 per cent a year. The marine reserve around Tonga Island, north of Bark Bay, attracts them with a plentiful supply of squid and fish. Pups are born in early summer, and learn to swim at about four weeks old. As teenagers, they are playful and curious, and may climb aboard sea kayaks. As adults they can be fierce if disturbed.

In 2km (1 mile) look for a sign to Cleopatra's Pool, 1km (0.6 miles) inland from the main track. This detour follows a stream to a freshwater swimming hole and picnic area.

Return to the main track and continue south towards Anchorage. After 1.5km (1 mile) the path rises; at the brow of the hill is a signpost. Turn left down the hill and it's 500m (550 yards) to the broad curve of Anchorage Beach. Relax until 4pm, when the water taxi will pick you up and take you back to Marahau.

### WHEN TO GO

Spring and autumn are more peaceful in the Abel Tasman, though the weather can be cool. December and January are very busy, while Christmas/ New Year is plain crazy.

### WHERE TO EAT

Have a picnic at Torrent Bay. Supplies can be ordered the day before from Hooked on Marahau at the Marahau Beach Camp (tel 03-527 8176; summer daily 8am–9pm; winter daily 8–6). Take ample drinking water with you, and a spare bag for rubbish.

### INFORMATION

#### TOURIST INFORMATION

www.AbelTasmanGreenRush.co.nz
✉ Wallace Street, Motueka
☎ 03-528 6543

#### DEPARTMENT OF CONSERVATION

www.doc.govt.nz
✉ Corner of King Edward and High streets, Motueka ☎ 03-528 1810

### TIP

» For a water taxi, book with Aqua Taxi at least one day ahead (tel 800-278 282; www.aquataxi.co.nz). The Beaches and Bays trip costs around NZ$60.

**Below** *Water taxis, booked ahead, enable you to walk sections of the track*

# QUEEN CHARLOTTE DRIVE

**This route combines the Queen Charlotte scenic drive between Havelock and Picton with exploring the wine-making region of Marlborough.**

**THE DRIVE**
**Distance:** 100km (62 miles)
**Time:** 2.5 hours
**Start/end at:** Picton Visitor Centre, near the ferry terminal 302 H11

Beyond the towns of Blenheim and Picton, Marlborough is one of the country's least populated regions. Even the gorgeous coastline is underwhelmed by human inhabitants, and holiday homes far outnumber permanent residences. It could have been so different—in the 1860s Picton had high hopes of becoming New Zealand's capital city. Now it is most famous for being the South Island port for the interisland ferries (▷ 52–53), and more than a million travellers pass through every year.

★ From the visitor centre in Picton (▷ 171), drive south down Auckland Street to the intersection with Broadway. Continue on the southeast fork, Wairau Road. The road goes around Nelson Square and continues out of Picton as SH1 towards Blenheim.

❶ The Para Wetlands, a signposted area, is frequented by duck-shooters in season. Mount Richmond Forest Park rises up 4km (2.5 miles) to the west.

This road wiggles comfortably south.

❷ The Wairau Plains—the flat area north of Blenheim—is superb farmland. The river valley soil is fertile, the sunshine hours are long, and it's all sheltered by the Richmond Ranges. Grapes grow marvellously well, but so do apples, cherries and berries.

After 21km (13 miles) reach the small township of Spring Creek. At Spring Creek, turn right into Rapaura Road and within 1km (0.6 miles) you are deep in vineyard country. Rows and rows of vines make up the vista on both sides of the road, while mountains rise up to the north. In 7km (4 miles) you reach the acclaimed Hunter's Estate.

❸ Hunter's, with its pleasant winery, garden, restaurant and resident artist's studio, is well worth a stop. The estate has one of the highest international profiles of any in New Zealand. Its founder, Ernie Hunter, was a pioneer of Marlborough wine-making, putting grapes down in 1983 and winning major UK awards just three years later. The estate is now run by his wife, Jane Hunter, herself a viti-culturalist. In 2004 she won the inaugural Women in Wine award at the International Wine and Spirits Awards, held in London.

In another 4km (2.5 miles) you reach the Mud House.

❹ The Mud House offers regional and local specialities such as olive oil, gifts and Prenzel liqueurs, as well as a range of Mud House boutique wines.

Around 2km (1 mile) after the Mud House, take SH6 to Havelock. The highway crosses the mighty Wairau River after 2km (1 mile), then follows the Kaituna River. After 25km (16 miles) there is a clearly signposted turn-off for Queen Charlotte Drive.

If you would like to buy fresh green-shell mussels, continue ahead for a detour into Havelock (▷ 168, try the Four Square supermarket or Mussel Pot restaurant on the main street).

From Queen Charlotte Drive there's a view of Havelock's marina to the north, then the road starts winding upwards through Mahakipawa Scenic Reserve. For 8km (5 miles) the road tracks the Mahakipawa Arm of Mahau Sound. The picnic area at the end of this stretch, developed by Linkwater locals, is the best place to stop and absorb the views. The next 6km (4 miles) are relatively straight with farmland on both sides, but it gives access onto Kenepuru Road, which leads to the Queen Charlotte Track.

**Above** *Lush vegetation lines much of the drive route*
**Opposite** *A stretch of road follows the southern shoreline of Queen Charlotte Sound*

❺ The Queen Charlotte Track is notable among New Zealand walking tracks for its accessibility. The long sliver of land offers 55km (34 miles) of ridge and coastal walking and mountain biking. Apart from the beautiful bays and bush sections, the joy is the number of points connecting with boats or cars, so walkers can do as much or as little as they fancy. The other bonus is the amount of accommodation en route, from campsites to luxury rooms, so heavy packs aren't required.

The final 17km (11 miles) of Queen Charlotte Drive are the most rewarding. This tight stretch of road passes pretty marinas at Momorangi and Ngakuta bays, enclaves of secluded housing, cool tracts of native bush and views of the jagged inlets of Queen Charlotte Sound. Governor's Bay is a good place to stop, with safe parking and a lookout a couple of metres from the road, and a sandy swimming beach 1km (0.6 miles) down the hill.

Port Shakespeare's logging wharf is the first sign of Picton, 5km (3 miles) away. Before your final descent, there's a large roadside car park overlooking the ferry terminal and Picton township. In 1km (0.6 miles) reach a major roundabout (traffic circle), and turn east into Dublin Street. The next left (northward) turn is Auckland Street, which leads back to the visitor centre.

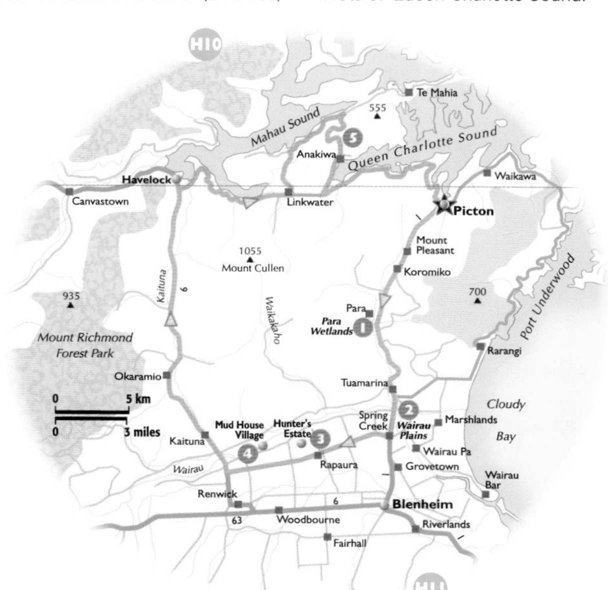


## WHERE TO EAT

### HUNTER'S WINERY AND GARDEN RESTAURANT

www.hunters.co.nz
Local gourmet produce such as lamb, venison, seafood and salmon are presented here. There is outdoor dining in summer and an open fire in winter. Reservations advised.
✉ 603 Rapaura Road, Blenheim ☎ 03-572 8489 🕒 Mon–Fri 11–3, Thu–Sat 6–late

### MUD HOUSE VILLAGE CAFÉ

Simple counter food plus cakes, coffee and ice cream are served here. A pleasant patio is by a pond.
✉ 193 Rapaura Road, Blenheim
☎ 03-572 7170 🕒 Daily 10–5

## INFORMATION

### TOURIST INFORMATION

www.destinationmarlborough.com
✉ Foreshore, near ferry terminal, Picton
☎ 03-520-3113

# CLIFFS OF KAIKOURA

**This waymarked walk takes you from the seal colony to the cliff-tops, where you can look over colonies of birds to the same ocean vista as the early whalers.**

**THE WALK**
**Distance:** 8.5km (5.5 miles)
**Time:** 2 hours
**Start/end at:** Peninsula car park at the northeast end of the Kaikoura Peninsula
302 H12

★ The Peninsula car park overlooks a large (and pungent) fur seal colony and tidal rock pools. Start at the eastern end, following a sign to the Cliff-Top Walk. A 200m (220-yard) climb is rewarded with a view of the Seaward Kaikoura Ranges and the ocean. Take the southwest path over the stile and past the squat, yellow lighthouse. After 500m (550 yards), the fence line turns at a right-angle. Walk right to the corner.

❶ In spring, you'll see the busy comings and goings of a red-billed seagull colony below this point—but don't lean on the fence, it may be electrified. Around 12,000 of these gulls nest on the peninsula, which is also popular with black-backed gulls, white-fronted terns and shags. The tidal platforms attract wading birds such as turnstones, oystercatchers and herons.

After another 200m (220 yards), a stile leads you onto the cliff-side of the fence, but the track is still clear and secure. In another kilometre (0.6 miles), you reach Whalers' Bay Lookout. There's a bench here, or in another 300m (330 yards) you can take a seat above the rocky white hump known as Sugar Loaf.

❷ These points are where whalers sat in the 1840s, looking out to sea for spouting whales. Once they were spotted, a signal was sent to boats on the shore below and the oarsmen set to work. The preferred quarry was the southern right whale, which would rise to the surface when dead and usually yielded vast

**Above** *The Kaikoura peninsula proved a good defensive site for Maori* pa
**Below** *Fur seal pups are a familiar sight along this route*

**Right** *Whalewatch Kaikoura's headquarters is housed in the old railway station off Beach Road*

quantities of oil. The animal was hauled back to shore and butchered on the beach. The oil was generally sent to England for lamp fuel and as a lubricant, while the pliable bone of the whale's jaw was used in corsets, stays and horsewhips. Demand dropped with the increased use of electricity. The last whale commercially killed in New Zealand was caught off Kaikoura in 1964.

Shortly, green signposts turn you inland towards South Bay, and soon you have a view of the wharves. White posts with orange triangles lead you down the hill, heading northwest. At the stile before Atia Point, turn north and follow the fence line straight down the hill. After a cliff-edge walk along a wider dirt track, pass through a double gate and walk beside pine trees, then along a stony beach until you enter South Bay Recreation Reserve.

❸ The name Atia Point alludes to one of the Cook Islands. Such names are thought to be very old, as they hark back to the Maori homelands. Oral tradition testifies that Kaikoura's first Maori settlers, the Waitaha, arrived a thousand years ago with Chief Rakaihautu.

At the end of the grassy area, turn west onto Kaka Road to reach Moa Point, site of a whale-processing factory that closed in 1922. Now it shelters the boats of today's commercial whaling industry—Whalewatch Kaikoura (▷ 183).

Shortly turn inland up Tui Drive, then eastwards along South Bay Parade for 1km (0.6 miles). Houses on the seaward side give way to reserve land; beyond this, white fences mark a stream bed and a green sign points inland to Kaikoura township (▷ 169). Follow this route across the grassy reserve towards a stile. Follow the white marker post to a steep climb heading north, with pine trees to the east. This brings you to a viewpoint overlooking South Bay. Continue north and cross two stiles onto Scarborough Street.

❹ Across Scarborough Street is the site of Nga Niho *pa*. This terrace-edged village was fortified with defensive earthworks that still stand more than 2m (7ft) tall. It was probably built in the 1820s, one of 15 *pa* known to have stood on the peninsula. Its position was ideal—easy to defend with a plentiful food source nearby.

Walk eastwards up Scarborough Street, turn north up Austin Terrace, then east onto Cromer Terrace at the corner. Where Cromer Terrace meets Ward Street there's a green signpost for Fyffe Quay. Cross the stile and follow the southern fence line until you see a track winding down the hill. In the northeast corner, a yellow triangle sign and stile lead onto a back road. Walk westwards and descend onto Jimmy Armer's Beach on Fyffe Quay. Continue east along the road for 1km (0.6 miles) to return to the car park.

### WHERE TO EAT
### WHITE MORPH RESTAURANT

www.whitemorph.co.nz

The dining room of the seafront White Morph Motor Inn is one of the best places in town to sample Kaikoura's legendary crayfish, in a modestly polished setting.

✉ 92–94 The Esplanade, Kaikoura
☎ 03-319 5014 🕒 Daily from 5.30pm

### INFORMATION
### TOURIST INFORMATION

www.kaikoura.co.nz

✉ West End, Kaikoura ☎ 03-319 5641

**Below** *A sperm whale breaches off the coast of Kaikoura*

## ABEL TASMAN NATIONAL PARK

### ABEL TASMAN WILSON'S EXPERIENCES

www.abeltasman.co.nz

Depending on your budget and the time you have available, you can choose from half-day to five-day experiences of the Abel Tasman Coast Track (⊳ 166), cruising, walking and/or kayaking, with or without a guide. There's also the opportunity to stay overnight in beachfront accommodation, with food provided.

✉ 265 High Street, Motueka ☎ 03-528 2027 Adult from NZ$57, child NZ$27

### KAITERITERI KAYAKS

www.seakayak.co.nz

As well as kayaking trips lasting from two hours to five days, this company offers the option of swimming with the seals at the Tonga Island Marine Reserve. Swimming is combined with kayaking, water taxi trips or, on dry land, exploring the Abel Tasman Coast Track.

✉ Sandy Bay Road, Kaiteriteri ☎ 03-527 8383 Adult from NZ$80, child NZ$65

**Above** *Strapped in for the Skywire ride at Happy Valley Adventures*

## BLENHEIM

### CLOUDY BAY

www.cloudybay.co.nz

New Zealand's most internationally acclaimed Sauvignon blanc is made here, and so are some other less well known but equally interesting wines, including barrel-fermented Chardonnay, Pinot noir, Pelorus *méthode traditionelle* and Te Koko, an oak-aged Sauvignon blanc fermented with wild yeasts.

✉ Jacksons Road, Blenheim ☎ 03-520 9140 Daily 10–5

### MARLBOROUGH TRAVEL

www.marlboroughtravel.co.nz

Insights into many interesting and varied aspects of Marlborough life are offered in these land- and sea-based tours. The signature Greenshell Mussel Cruise visits a mussel farm in the Sounds, and serves mussels cooked on board with a glass of locally made Sauvignon blanc. A gourmet tour focuses on wine and food matching. Other tours visit gardens, olive groves, vineyards and craftspeople. Tours can be personalized to your particular interests.

✉ PO Box 1000, Blenheim ☎ 03-577 9997 From NZ$99

## COLLINGWOOD

### FAREWELL SPIT TOURS

www.farewellspit.com

This company has more than 50 years' experience of taking people out onto Farewell Spit. The tours go to the lighthouse, the gannet colony, Cape Farewell, and to see the wading birds (⊳ 165). Trips last from 3 to 6.5 hours.

✉ Tasman Street, Collingwood ☎ 03-524 8257 Adult from NZ$100, child (under 16) NZ$50

## KAIKOURA

### DOLPHIN ENCOUNTER AND ALBATROSS ENCOUNTER

www.dolphin.co.nz; www.oceanwings.co.nz

You can swim with dolphins or watch rare seabirds on launch trips by these sister companies. Wetsuits and snorkelling equipment are provided for swimmers, and there are hot showers on board.

✉ 96 Esplanade, Kaikoura ☎ 03-319 6777 Adult from NZ$80, child NZ$40 Oct–end May daily 5.30, 8.30, 12.30; Jun–end Sep 8.30, 12.30

### KAIKOURA KAYAK

www.seakayakkaikoura.co.nz

Kayaking is a good way to encounter seals and watch ocean-going birds

such as albatrosses, while keeping the impact on the environment to a minimum. You can Freedom Hire or take a half-day guided tour, with diving and snorkelling. Kayak training is also available.
☎ 021-462 889 🕐 Oct–end Apr daily 8.30, 12.30, 4.30; May–end Sep daily 9, 1 💳 Adult from NZ$80, child (under 12) NZ$60. Freedom Hire from NZ$65

**MAORI TOURS KAIKOURA**
www.maoritours.co.nz
A good introduction to local culture and protocol, these tours visit local *pa* sites and a Maori home, and explore native bush to see how the Maori used plants. Tours leave from the Kaikoura Information Office.
✉ 10 Churchill Street, Kaikoura ☎ 03-319 5567 🕐 Daily 9, 1.30 💳 Adult NZ$99, child (under 15) NZ$55

**WHALEWATCH KAIKOURA**
www.whalewatch.co.nz
You need to book well in advance for these boat trips. As well as whales, you may see dolphins, seals and albatrosses (there is an 80 per cent refund if no whales appear). An on-board computer animation explains the marine geography of the Kaikoura Canyon. Trips are weather dependent. Children under 3 years old are not permitted.
✉ Whaleway Station, off Beach Road (SH1), Kaikoura ☎ 03-319 6767 🕐 Mar–end Oct daily 7.15, 10, 12.45; Nov–end Feb 7.15, 10, 12.45, 3.30 💳 Adult NZ$140, child NZ$60

**WINGS OVER WHALES**
www.whales.co.nz
Sightseeing flights give you a bird's-eye view of whales, dolphins and seals, as well as the spectacular Kaikoura scenery.
✉ Kaikoura Airfield, 6km (4 miles) south of Kaikoura ☎ 03-319 6580/0800-226629 🕐 Daily 9–4 💳 Adult from NZ$145, child (4–13) NZ$75

## MAPUA

**COOL STORE GALLERY**
www.coolstoregallery.co.nz
The works of more than 70 artists and craftspeople from the Nelson and West Coast regions are displayed here.
✉ 7 Aranui Road, Mapua ☎ 03-540 3778 🕐 Daily 10–5

**MAPUA ADVENTURES**
www.mapuaadventures.co.nz
Jet-boating, mountain biking, birdwatching and kayaking are among the diversions available, with options for individuals, families and children. Trips explore the Mapua estuary, coastline and forests.
✉ 8 Aranui Road, Mapua ☎ 03-540 3833 💳 From NZ$40

## MOTUEKA

**ABEL TASMAN AIR**
www.abeltasmanair.co.nz
If you are short of time and want to see a lot, this may be the way to go. Tours fly to Abel Tasman National Park for lunch at Awaroa Lodge, to the West Coast for part of the Heaphy Track, or head to Kaikoura for whale-watching and a crayfish lunch. The company also operates scenic flights and connecting flights for trampers.
✉ PO Box 125, Motueka ☎ 0800 304 560 💳 From NZ$90

**BUSH AND BEYOND**
www.naturetreks.co.nz
Bush and Beyond is a conservation-based guiding business specializing in flora and birds. Treks last from one to eight days in Kahurangi National Park. Itineraries cater for all ages and fitness levels and can be personalized. You can stay in comfortable lodges, walk the Heaphy Track or go off-track wilderness back-packing.
✉ 35 School Road, RD3 Motueka ☎ 03-528 9054 💳 From NZ$150, family NZ$425

**MOTUEKA SUNDAY MARKET**
This eclectic market mixes food, New Zealand crafts, Asian and Peruvian clothing, collectables, second-hand items, plants, seasonal fruits and vegetables with live music and street drama.
✉ Decks Reserve Carpark, Motueka ☎ 03-540 2709 🕐 Sun 8–1

## MURCHISON

**ULTIMATE DESCENTS**
www.rivers.co.nz
Despite the name, this company arranges family-friendly rafting trips on the Buller River, as well as adrenalin-pumping whitewater kayaking and rafting, camp-outs, and one- to five-day heli-journeys. Minimum ages apply to all trips.
✉ 51 Fairfax Street, Murchison ☎ 03-523 9899 🕐 Adult from NZ$105, child NZ$88

## NELSON

**FOUNDERS HISTORIC PARK**
www.founderspark.co.nz
This collection of buildings from the late 1800s houses several businesses, including a bone carver and a café. There are also displays of vintage transport, and train rides daily between 26 December and 10 January. Children can enjoy the playground and 3-D maze, and their parents can sample the excellent organic brews produced on-site by Founders craft brewery.
✉ 87 Atawhai Drive, Nelson ☎ 03-548 2649 🕐 Daily 10–4.30 💳 Adult NZ$5, child NZ$2, family NZ$13

**HAPPY VALLEY ADVENTURES**
www.happyvalleyadventures.co.nz
This 650ha (1,600-acre) farm offers eco-tours on 4X4 motorcycles, taking in a native forest valley with a 2000-year-old matai tree. Other attractions include bushwalks, Skywire rides reaching up to 100kph (60mph), and rides on an amphibious all-terrain vehicle.
✉ 194 Cable Bay Road, Nelson ☎ 03-545 0304 💳 From NZ$75, child (under 16) NZ$1 per year of age

**NATURELAND**
www.naturelandzoo.co.nz
This little family-oriented zoo has exotic, domestic and native wildlife, a walk-through aviary and an aquarium. Families can feed the animals and picnic.
✉ Tahunanui Beach, Tahunanui (southwest of downtown Nelson) ☎ 03-548 6166 🕐 Daily 9–4 💳 Adult NZ$5, child (2–14) NZ$2

### NELSON MARKET

www.nelsonmarket.com

On Saturday mornings a dreary car park in central Nelson is transformed into a marketplace, with a flea market mix of clothes and crafts and a fine selection of food. Look for local organic fruit and vegetables, speciality breads, local sheep's cheese, bratwurst made from local pork, and the Blackbird Valley Forge's knives which are made from recycled materials.

✉ Montgomery Square, Nelson ☎ 027-270 2600 🕐 Sat 8–1

### POMEROY'S COFFEE AND TEA CO.

www.pomeroys.co.nz

An old-fashioned boutique coffee roaster, Pomeroy's sells 25 blends of coffee and a huge variety of speciality teas. It also serves excellent coffee to drink on the spot, and stocks Nelson olive oils and deli items.

✉ 80 Hardy Street, Nelson ☎ 03-546 6944 🕐 Mon–Fri 9–5, Sat 9.30–12.30

### VERTICAL LIMITS

www.verticallimits.co.nz

Even if you have no previous experience you can join a rock-climbing expedition, or learn the principles indoors on a climbing wall.

✉ 34 Vanguard Street, Nelson ☎ 03-545 7511 🕐 Mon–Thu 3–9, Fri 12–5, Sat 10–6, Sun 12–4 ✋ From NZ$16

### VICTORIAN ROSE

www.victorianrose.co.nz

A firm supporter of local music, the Victorian Rose pub has regular Tuesday night gigs with the Nelson Jazz Club, Wednesday and Thursday nights devoted to freewheeling jazz, and weekends get feet dancing with jazz-rock blends of local and imported bands. There's a blackboard menu, Mac's beers and local wines.

✉ 281 Trafalgar Street, Nelson ☎ 03-548 7631 🕐 Daily 11am–late

## PICTON

### THE COUGAR LINE

www.cougarlinecruises.co.nz

Scheduled trips around the Marlborough Sounds visit various bays to drop off and take on passengers. Short cruises are also available, taking in up to 80km (50 miles) of coastline in three hours, with a commentary on the way. A popular option is the day trip to Ship Cove, with the opportunity to walk for five hours on the Queen Charlotte Track to Furneaux Lodge.

✉ The Waterfront, Picton ☎ 03-573 7925 ✋ From NZ$63

### DOLPHIN WATCH ECOTOURS

www.naturetours.co.nz

As well as the popular swimming with dolphins, this company takes trips to Motuara Island bird sanctuary, to walk a section of the Queen Charlotte Track, and do some birdwatching for species such as king shags (found only in the Sounds), New Zealand robins, little blue penguins and saddlebacks.

✉ The Waterfront, Picton ☎ 03-573 8040 ✋ From NZ$90

### MARLBOROUGH SOUNDS ADVENTURE COMPANY

www.marlboroughsounds.com

Adventures of all kinds are on offer in trips that combine kayaking, mountain biking and walking on the Queen Charlotte Track. One of the most popular is the Ultimate Sounds Adventure, a guided one-day hiking, one-day sea kayaking, one-day mountain biking adventure. There is an overnight stay at Portage Resort Hotel, either backpacker-style or in twin-share ensuite accommodation.

✉ London Quay, Picton ☎ 0800-283283 ✋ From NZ$65

### SOUNDS CONNECTION

www.soundsconnection.co.nz

Choose from launch and coach tours, or fishing or wine tasting on scheduled and private half- to full-day tours.

✉ 10 London Quay, Picton ☎ 03-573 8843 ✋ From NZ$70

## RICHMOND

### CRAFT HABITAT

www.crafthabitat.co.nz

Watch the makers at work at Nelson's arts and crafts village, buy their work or commission them to make something for you. There is also a specialist food shop.

✉ Champion Road, Richmond ☎ 03-544 1488 🕐 Daily 9–5 ☕ Courtyard café

### HÖGLUND ART GLASS

www.hoglund.co.nz

Ola Höglund and Marie Simberg-Höglund have an international reputation as hot-glass blowers and their gallery is a treasure trove of brilliant hues and design. Their International Glass Centre includes a glass-blowing studio, exhibition

**Left** *Dolphins swim alongside a Dolphin Watch boat trip*

hall, engraving studio, and cold-work studio for cutting, sandblasting and polishing. Guided tours show you the artists at work.
✉ Landsdowne Road, Richmond ☎ 03-544 6500 ⓘ Daily 9–5; tours 10.30, 1.30, 3 ✋ Tours: adult NZ$15, child (under 14) free

## STOKE

### MAC'S BREWERY

www.macs.co.nz
Nelson's local brewery, Mac's makes naturally brewed lagers, ales and innovative limited-release beers. You can tour, sample the beers and browse in the shop.
✉ 660 Main Road, Stoke ☎ 03-547 0526 ⓘ Daily 10–5.30; tours daily 11, 2

## TAKAKA

### ANATOKI SALMON

www.anatokisalmon.co.nz
Catch your own salmon here and tour the salmon farm on the banks of the Anatoki River. Fishing rods and tackle are supplied, and you can hire a barbecue to cook your fish.
✉ McCallums Road, Takaka ☎ 03-525 7251 ⓘ Nov–end Apr daily 9–5; May–end Oct 9–4.30

### BENCARRI NATURE PARK

www.bencarri.co.nz
Feeding the Anatoki eels has been a popular holiday pastime here since 1914, and Bencarri has plenty of other friendly farm animals to feed, touch and interact with. Horse-riding and mini-golf are among the other attractions, and the gallery sells knitwear and alpaca/llama yarns.
✉ McCallums Road, Takaka ☎ 03-525 8261 ⓘ Sep–end Apr daily 10–6 ✋ Adult NZ$12, child (5–15) NZ$6

## WAIRAU VALLEY

### LEIGHVANDER

www.leighvandercottage.co.nz
A collection of 140 varieties of lavender grows in this lovely garden, which surrounds a restored 1859 cob cottage. Products made from lavender are sold in the studio, which also offers gifts, including ribboned lace and candle wicking.
✉ RD1 Wairau Valley ☎ 03-572 2851 ⓘ Nov–end Mar by appointment

# FESTIVALS AND EVENTS

## JANUARY

### NELSON JAZZFEST

www.nelsonjazzfest.co.nz
A wide variety of jazz bands from the Nelson region and around the country perform in this week-long festival, with events on the streets and at various venues around the town. There's a grand finale on New Year's Day at Fairfield Park.
✉ Nelson Jazz Club, PO Box 7188, Nelson ☎ 03-547 7211 ✋ Tickets from Everyman Records, 249 Hardy Street, Nelson

## JANUARY–FEBRUARY

### MARLBOROUGH 4 FUN SUMMER CONCERTS

www.marlborough4fun.co.nz
Free outdoor concerts are held in various locations during the summer holiday season.
✉ Various locations ☎ 03-577 8935

## FEBRUARY

### WINE MARLBOROUGH FESTIVAL

www.wine-marlborough-festival.co.nz
This showcase for Marlborough wines, held in a vineyard on the second Saturday and Sunday in February, provides an opportunity to sample around 150 wines from more than 40 wineries. The event includes wine workshops, entertainment and music.
✉ Brancott Vineyard, Brancott Road, Blenheim ☎ 03-577 9299 ⓘ 10–6 ✋ NZ$40 from Ticket Direct, tel 0800-224 224 🚌 Shuttle buses from Blenheim

## EASTER

### CLASSIC FIGHTERS MARLBOROUGH

www.classicfighters.co.nz
Aircraft are displayed as part of a theatrical spectacle, where battle scenes from both world wars are re-enacted on the ground as well as in the air.
✉ Omaka Aerodrome, Blenheim ☎ 03-579 1305 ⓘ From 7.30am ✋ Gate sales: adult from NZ$45, child (5–14) free

## OCTOBER

### KAIKOURA SEAFEST

www.kaikoura.co.nz/seafest
Held on the first Saturday of October, Seafest is a celebration of the abundance of the ocean. It combines live entertainment with cooking demonstrations and food, wines and beverages from the Kaikoura, Marlborough and North Canterbury regions. Beforehand, you can dance at the Big Top Bash.
✉ Takahanga Domain, Kaikoura ☎ 03-319 5641 ⓘ 10–5 ✋ Adult NZ$35, child (5–17) NZ$15

### NELSON ARTS FESTIVAL

www.nelsonfestivals.co.nz
Entertainment of all kinds is provided in this annual two-week festival, which includes a mask carnival, sculpture symposium, street fun and cultural events.
✉ Nelson City Council, 110 Trafalgar Street, Nelson ☎ 03-546 0212

## NOVEMBER

### HUNTER'S GARDEN MARLBOROUGH

www.garden-marlborough.com
Green-fingered enthusiasts gather in Blenheim for this annual six-day celebration of gardening, which includes garden tours, seminars, workshops and a market day with 200 stalls in Seymour Square.
✉ PO Box 1180, Blenheim ☎ 03-577 5500

## DECEMBER

### KAHURANGI ENDURANCE TRIATHLON AND MOUNTAIN CLASSIC RUN

www.nelsontriclub.co.nz
One-day multi-sport events in New Zealand started here in 1984, and this is still one of the best, combined with a classic off-road run. An endurance test strictly for the super fit, combining cycling, kayaking and running.
✉ Golden Bay

**PRICES AND SYMBOLS**

The restaurants are listed alphabetically. The prices given are the average for a two-course lunch (L) and a three-course dinner (D) for one person, without drinks. The wine price (W) is for the least expensive bottle. All the restaurants listed accept credit cards unless otherwise stated.

For a key to the symbols, ⊳ 2.

## APPLEBY

### SEIFRIEDS VINEYARD RESTAURANT

www.seifried.co.nz

The Seifried family are particularly noted for their Riesling, Chardonnay and dessert wines. The restaurant is surrounded by vineyards, with indoor and outdoor dining. They serve seasonal local produce, including popular antipasto platters, and home-made breads and desserts.

✉ Corner of SH60 and Redwood Road, Appleby ☎ 03-544 1555 🕐 Daily 10–5, and evenings in summer 🖐 L NZ$20, W NZ$20

## BLENHEIM

### BELLAFICO CAFFE AND WINE BAR

www.bellafico.co.nz

A casual café by day and serious restaurant at night, Bellafico has excellent coffee, a German chef enthusiastic about local produce, and an outstanding list of local and international wines. Havelock mussels may come steamed either in a coconut cream and ginger broth, or battered in Marlborough Moa Noir beer. Wild venison cutlet is served with a kumara and bacon mash.

✉ 17 Maxwell Road, Blenheim ☎ 03-577 6072 🕐 Mon–Fri 10am–late, Sat 6pm–late 🖐 L NZ$30, D NZ$50, W NZ$29

### HERZOG'S WINERY AND RESTAURANT

www.herzog.co.nz

One of the top restaurants in the country, Herzog's has been created as a gourmet destination. When Hans and Therese Herzog came to Marlborough from Switzerland to establish a vineyard, they brought their chef and their outstanding collection of wines with them. The restaurant is furnished with Limoges china, Riedel crystal and French silverware. The three or five-course *degustation* menu is highly recommended.

✉ 81 Jeffries Road, Blenheim ☎ 03-572 8770 🕐 Mid-Oct to end Apr Tue–Sun 7–late; Dec–end Feb Tue–Sun 12–4 🖐 L NZ$80, D NZ$110, W NZ$50

### TWELVE TREES RESTAURANT

www.allanscott.com

This garden restaurant is constructed from rammed earth, with a walled courtyard and picnic area. The menu is simple and fresh, reflecting local seasonal specialities such as mussels and strawberries. There is usually a pasta dish and a salad, and the vineyard platter is always popular.

✉ Allan Scott Wines and Estates, Jacksons Road, Blenheim ☎ 03-572 7123 🕐 Daily 9–4.30 🖐 L NZ$25, W NZ$20

## COLLINGWOOD

### COURTHOUSE CAFÉ

This is the place to be found guilty of gluttony with intent to demolish three-fruit smoothies. The old colonial building, which was once the district courthouse, is a remnant of busier times, when Collingwood was the focus of a gold boom. Alas m'lud, now the only case in session revolves around the levels of relaxation, the menu (with some criminally good vegetarian options) and the quality of the coffee.

✉ Corner of Gibbs Road and Elizabeth Street, Collingwood ☎ 03-524 8025 🕐 Dec–end Jun daily 8am–late; Jul–end Nov 11–4 🖐 L NZ$20, D NZ$40, W NZ$22

Opposite *Courthouse Café, Collingwood*

### MUSSEL INN

www.musselinn.co.nz

People come to the Mussel Inn for the mussels, the beer and the atmosphere. Local mussels are served simply steamed with bread. The beer is brewed on site, using home-grown hops, the most unusual being Captain Cooker manuka beer. In the evening, it hosts regular gigs.

✉ Onekaka, Golden Bay ☎ 03-525 9241 🕒 Sep–end Jul daily from 11 L NZ$20, D NZ$40, W NZ$22

## HAVELOCK

### MUSSEL POT

www.themusselpot.co.nz

The distinctive restaurant, with outsize mussels on the roof, has spawned a franchise, and it would be hard to find fresher or tastier mussels. Choose from chowder, steamers or flats grilled with a choice of toppings (and there are also meats and salads).

✉ 73 Main Road, Havelock ☎ 03-574 2824 🕒 Daily 10.30–8 L NZ$20, D NZ$43, W NZ$28

## KAIKOURA

### HISLOPS CAFÉ

www.hislops-wholefoods.co.nz

Hislop's is a pleasant place to stop for refreshments or lunch. The café specializes in wholefoods, using organically grown ingredients where possible. Most vegetables come from the family farm. The beverage list also includes organic wines and beers. The cakes are a treat, notably the apricot and chocolate cream cheese slice.

✉ 33 Beach Road, Kaikoura ☎ 03-319 6971 🕒 Summer daily 10–9; winter Tue, Wed 10–4, Thu–Mon 10–9 L NZ$30, D NZ$50, W NZ$26

## KEKERENGU

### THE STORE AT KEKERENGU

Dramatically located on the coast, the Store is a must-stop for refreshments or lunch. The café has indoor seating around a double-sided fireplace, and tables on the deck outdoors with spectacular views over the thundering surf. The décor is rustic with massive wharf piles supporting the hessian-draped roof. The food is made on site, with light meals including venison pies through to sophisticated dishes of crayfish and blue cod.

✉ State Highway 1, Kekerengu ☎ 03-575 8600 🕒 Oct to mid-Apr daily 7.30–7; mid-Apr to end Sep 8–6.30 L NZ$23, D NZ$45, W NZ$33

## MAPUA

### FLAX RESTAURANT AND BAR

Looking over the Mapua estuary, Flax is one of the Nelson region's finest restaurants. Run by chef Tim Greenhough and *maître d'* Karen Hannan, it has an extensive wine list that also features Greenhough wines made by brother Andrew. The style of food is modern New Zealand, with dishes such as lambs' brains with balsamic roast cherry tomatoes, ricotta pesto and bacon. The pork belly is a popular choice.

✉ Mapua Wharf, Mapua ☎ 03-540 2028 🕒 Tue–Sun 11–10.30 L NZ$25, D NZ$45, W NZ$30

### THE SMOKEHOUSE CAFÉ

www.smokehouse.co.nz

You can buy smoked fish or eat in the restaurant overlooking the water. The menu is based on locally supplied fish, mussels and vegetables hot-smoked on site, using a traditional brick kiln, manuka wood shavings and no artificial additives. Try the warehou, hake or trevally, as well as the snapper and salmon. Smoked mushrooms and smoked tomato soup are also good.

✉ Shed 2, Mapua Wharf, Mapua ☎ 03-540 2280 🕒 Daily 11–late L NZ$28, D NZ$50, W NZ$32

## MARAHAU

### PARK CAFÉ

www.parkcafe.co.nz

Hikers finishing the Abel Tasman Coast Track stop here for the menu, bar, good coffee and internet access. It's popular with daytrippers and hikers starting from Marahau, too. You can get anything from breakfast to evening meals or snacks and cakes, from soups and salads to steaks, fish and vegetarian dishes.

✉ Harveys Road, Marahau ☎ 03-527 8270 🕒 Daily 8am–9pm L NZ$20, D NZ$40, W NZ$28

## NELSON

### BOATSHED CAFÉ

www.boatshedcafe.co.nz

This converted boatshed has water lapping at the piles. The view over the harbour is stunning. Seafood is a speciality, particularly Nelson white fish and scallops, Golden Bay crabs and locally farmed salmon, oysters and green-lipped mussels.

✉ 350 Wakefield Quay, Nelson ☎ 03-546 9783 🕒 Daily 9am–10.30pm L NZ$35, D NZ$65, W NZ$36

### LAMBRETTA'S CAFÉ-BAR

www.lambrettascafe.co.nz

Devoted to all things Italian, this café has scooters bolted to the walls, along with Lambretta paraphernalia. The pizzas, pastas and antipasti challenge the heartiest appetite.

✉ 204 Hardy Street, Nelson ☎ 03-545 8555 🕒 Daily 9am–late L NZ$20, D NZ$40, W NZ$22

## RICHMOND

### CAFÉ IN THE VINEYARD

www.waimeaestates.co.nz

Café in the Vineyard is the cellar door and café for Waimea Estates. You can sample and purchase the wines, and lunch in the extensive dining area, which flows out to the vines. Fresh, local ingredients are used in dishes.

✉ Appleby Highway, Hope, Richmond ☎ 03-544 4963 🕒 Sep–end Mar daily 11–5; Apr–end Aug Wed–Sun 11–4 L NZ$30, W NZ$24

## TAKAKA

### WHOLEMEAL CAFÉ

www.wholemealcafe.co.nz

In the old Takaka Theatre, the mood is bohemian. It has good coffee, fresh juices and organic beers, and a daytime menu of free-range egg dishes, salads and cakes.

✉ Commercial Street, Takaka ☎ 03-525 9426 🕒 Daily 7.30am–9.30pm L NZ$15, D NZ$35, W NZ$25

**PRICES AND SYMBOLS**

The prices are the lowest and highest for a double room for one night including breakfast, unless otherwise stated. All the hotels listed accept credit cards unless otherwise stated. Note that rates can vary widely throughout the year.

For a key to the symbols, ▷ 2.

## ABEL TASMAN NATIONAL PARK

### AWAROA LODGE

www.awaroalodge.co.nz

Awaroa Lodge combines wilderness experience with sophisticated accommodation and dining. The lodge is set in native bush, close to the beach and the Abel Tasman Track, and offers suites with private deck, deluxe and family rooms. All units are designed with natural materials. Local seafood and organic garden produce are staples on the café menu.

✉ Awaroa Bay, Abel Tasman National Park ☎ 03-528 8758 NZ$255–450 12 suites, 10 deluxe, 4 family Tasman Helicopters, Abel Tasman Air and Flightcorp fly to Awaroa airstrip from Nelson, Motueka and Wellington No road access. On foot from the Abel Tasman Track or 1.5 hours by water taxi from Marahau

## BLENHEIM

### HOTEL D'URVILLE

www.durville.com

A boutique hotel has been created in the old bank vaults of the grand Public Trust Building. The individually themed suites have lofty ceilings, native wood floors, and an eclectic mix of four-poster beds, exotic fabrics and antiques—from African textiles to a Javanese daybed. The central vault has been converted into a lounge. The hotel is also known for its lively bar and restaurant.

✉ 52 Queen Street, Blenheim ☎ 03-577 9945 NZ$195–NZ$335 11 suites 7km (4 miles) from the airport

### OLD SAINT MARY'S CONVENT

www.convent.co.nz

This century-old two-storey convent has been transformed into a retreat, surrounded by vineyards and olive groves. Seven spacious rooms have expansive views, and access to the balcony or garden. The original character of the building has been retained. There is a billiard room, and a chapel in the garden.

✉ Rapaura Road, Blenheim ☎ 03-570 5700 NZ$550–NZ$750 5 rooms, 2 suites 15km (9 miles) from Blenheim

**Above** *Fyffe Country Lodge, Kaikoura*

## COLLINGWOOD

### THE INNLET

www.goldenbayindex.co.nz

A good base for bush walks, kayaking, horseback-riding, cycling and trips to Farewell Spit, this backpackers' hostel has double and twin rooms (with shared bathroom), a rustic hut and a self-contained cottage in a lovely bush setting. The simply furnished cottage sleeps up to seven. Guests have access to a streamside barbecue and hot tub, and nearby sandy swimming beach.

✉ Main Road, Pakawau ☎ 03-524 8040 NZ$70 2 cottages, backpacker rooms 11km (7 miles) north of Collingwood

## KAIKOURA

### FYFFE COUNTRY LODGE

www.fyffecountrylodge.com

A striking building made of rammed earth and native timber, Fyffe Country Lodge is surrounded by English-style gardens. Seafood chowder is a speciality of the in-house restaurant, which has an open fire, and the bar leads onto a pretty courtyard. Courtesy mountain bikes are available.

State Highway 1, Kaikoura 03-319 6869 NZ$189–NZ$750 6 studios, 1 suite 6km (4 miles) south of Kaikoura on SH1

### THE OLD CONVENT

www.theoldconvent.co.nz

A former convent, built for French nuns in 1911, has become an unusual B&B. The cells are now bedrooms with private bathrooms, and the former chapel is the guest lounge. An added attraction is the four-course French-style dinner (NZ$50 or NZ$75 with Kaikoura's famous crayfish). Bicycles, croquet, pétanque and tennis are available.

Mount Fyffe Road, Kaikoura 03-319 6603/0800-365 603 NZ$120–NZ$195 16 rooms Outdoor Signposted 5km (3 miles) north of Kaikoura

## MARAHAU

### ABEL TASMAN MARAHAU LODGE

www.abeltasmanmarahaulodge.co.nz

Close to the start of Abel Tasman Coast Track, this attractive lodge offers self-contained, two-room units and studios. Local wine is provided in the fridge and there is a communal kitchen. The complex includes a sauna and spa. Evening meals are available.

Marahau Beach, RD2 Motueka 03-527 8250 NZ$150–NZ$205 8 suites, 4 self-contained units 16km (10 miles) north of Motueka

## MARLBOROUGH SOUNDS

### HOPEWELL

www.hopewell.co.nz

You get an ideal blend of isolation, relaxation, value and comfort at this waterfront accommodation. Five cottages provide shared rooms and doubles with bathrooms. A self-contained, two-bedroom cottage sleeps up to six. Linen is supplied, but not food. The well-equipped kitchen and lounge has a wood fire, TV, stereo and library. Other attractions include an outdoor spa, bush walks, kayaking, mountain biking, fishing, golf and water-skiing.

Kenepuru Sound 03-573 4341 NZ$98–NZ$120 8 double/twin rooms, 1 cottage Soundsair flies from Wellington to the local airfield 85km (53 miles) from Picton, via Linkwater and Te Mahia. Water taxi from Picton or Havelock recommended

## MOTUEKA

### MOTUEKA RIVER LODGE

www.motuekalodge.co.nz

This luxury fishing lodge in the picturesque Motueka Valley has an elegant, country-style interior with spectacular views in every direction. Anglers are offered guided trout-fishing in local rivers and streams. In the farmhouse kitchen the chef uses local produce to give a 'taste of Kiwi' with a touch of class. There is a minimum two-night stay.

Motueka Valley Highway, Ngatimoti, Motueka 03-526 8668 NZ$1,100–NZ$1,430, including dinner 5 rooms 30km (19 miles) southwest of Motueka

## NELSON

### THE HONEST LAWYER COUNTRY PUB

www.honestlawyer.co.nz

Located near the airport in the Waimea estuary, the Honest Lawyer is a popular English-style pub. It also has good food, king and twin rooms, a honeymoon suite, and a self-contained cottage. All rooms have internet connections, and a guest pantry has complimentary drinks and snacks.

1 Point Road, Monaco, Nelson 03-547 8850/0800-921 192 NZ$170–NZ$230 8 rooms, 1 suite, 1 cottage 6km (4 miles) from Nelson CBD. Turn right off Nayland Road into Songer Street which leads to Monaco

### RUTHERFORD HOTEL

www.rutherfordhotel.co.nz

The principal hotel in the city has a view of the cathedral gardens. It has spacious double rooms and two executive suites. Executive rooms have an internet connection for laptops. The Japanese Miyazu restaurant is highly regarded.

Trafalgar Square, Nelson 03-548 2299/0800-437 227 NZ$165–NZ$219 113 rooms Outdoor

## PICTON

### BROADWAY MOTEL

www.broadwaymotel.co.nz

The four-star Broadway is on the edge of town and handy for the ferry terminal. Its top-range units have a private balcony or courtyard, super-king and queen beds, and kitchens with microwave ovens.

113 High Street, Picton 03-573 6563/0800 101 919 NZ$115–NZ$215 18 units 1km (0.5 miles) from the Interislander Ferry Terminal

## ST. ARNAUD

### ALPINE LODGE

www.alpinelodge.co.nz

The Alpine Lodge offers self-contained two-bedroom apartments and spa bath suites, double rooms, family units sleeping up to six, and a chalet for budget-conscious visitors which has double and shared rooms. The Lodge has a bar, a café and a licensed restaurant.

Main Road, St. Arnaud 03-521 1869/0800-367 377 NZ$98–NZ$140 28 rooms (8 non-smoking), 4 studios and 4 apartments in the lodge

## RAPAURA

### CRANBROOK COTTAGE

www.cranbrook.co.nz

Surrounded by vines and fruit trees, this 135-year-old cottage is romantic, with breakfast delivered to your door on a tray with fresh flowers. The cottage is self-contained, with queen and twin bedrooms, cooking facilities, lounge and dining area and private bathroom.

Giffords Road, Rapaura RD3, Blenheim 03-572 8606 NZ$195 1 cottage Giffords Road is off Rapaura Road, reached from SH6 or SH1

## TAKAKA

### SANS SOUCI INN

www.sanssouciinn.co.nz

This environmentally friendly inn has adobe-brick bungalows in its garden. Rooms have king-size futons. The restaurant serves home-style meals.

Richmond Road, Pohara, Takaka 03-525 8663 NZ$95 Single, twin, double and family bungalow rooms 8km (5 miles) northeast of Takaka

# CANTERBURY AND THE WEST COAST

The capital of the Canterbury region and South Island's largest city, Christchurch is an enigma. Polite, genteel and lavishly green, Christchurch often seems under the delusion that it is somewhere in southern England. At its heart, instead of the usual boulder-leaping New Zealand torrent, there burbles the placid Avon, an ankle-deep brook where one may take a punt out for an excursion between banks lined with willows and chestnut trees. Compact and calm, the city centre is easily explored in a half-day stroll.

To the east is the Banks Peninsula, where the wild, fretted coastline is dominated by knobby volcanic peaks. Its main source of fame is the town of Akaroa, which was chosen as the site for a French colony in 1838. Within 10 years of its foundation, the French abandoned their attempt at colonization, but the settlers remained and Akaroa still has a lingering Gallic air.

North of Christchurch, the town of Kaikoura is one of the best places in the world to see sperm whales, the largest toothed mammal. The reason is the abundance of squid, the whale's favourite main course, in the deep trench barely a kilometre (half a mile) off Kaikoura. Another Kaikoura speciality is swimming with the playful, fast and sociable dusky dolphins that live in big pods just off the coast.

Canterbury also includes the Southern Alps, the tallest peaks in the country, a mountainous spine that rises to 3,500m (11,500ft) within 50km (30 miles) of the coast. These mountains are best seen from Mount Cook National Park or from the west coast, where some of the world's most accessible glaciers dribble down into rainforest, to end just a few kilometres from the coast.

**Above** *The TranzAlpine scenic rail route heading towards the Southern Alps*
**Opposite** *Arthur's Pass*

## ARTHUR'S PASS

www.doc.govt.nz

At the northern edge of Craigieburn Forest Park, road and rail penetrate the vast, open-braided Waimakariri River valley before entering Arthur's Pass National Park. From there it is a short drive to the tiny alpine outpost of Arthur's Pass, 924m (3,031ft) above sea level.

Arthur Dudley Dobson, a pioneer surveyor, first explored the route to the west coast via the east Waimakariri and west Otira river valleys in 1864. A road based on his observations was built within a year; a rail link for the coal and timber trade took another 60 years to complete. To the north, the impressive Otira Viaduct gives a sense of the scale of the engineering challenges.

305 F13 · SH73 · 03-318 9211 · Services from Christchurch and Greymouth · TranzAlpine service from Christchurch and Greymouth

## ARTHUR'S PASS NATIONAL PARK

This area of 114,500ha (282,930 acres) extends from Harpers Pass in the northern Southern Alps, to the mountains around the head of the Waimakariri and Otira rivers. Designated a national park in 1929, it embraces mountain ranges, gorges and braided river valleys. One of the highest mountains is 2,270m (7,447ft) Mount Rolleston, southwest of Arthur's Pass. In the eastern part of the park the forests are almost entirely made up of mountain beech, while to the west, on the other side of the Great Divide, the vegetation is more complex, with a variety of podocarp species, beech, kamahi and kaiwakawaka. Many indigenous alpine plant species thrive above the treeline. The most notable native bird is the green mountain parrot, the kea, which may well fly down to greet you and relieve you of your sandwiches (and your vehicle of anything flexible, from window seals to wipers).

The park has a network of tracks. Braided rivers and their tributaries are notorious for flash floods, so take extra care.

305 F13 · See Arthur's Pass, left

## BANKS PENINSULA

▷ 194.

## CHRISTCHURCH

▷ 196–201.

## GERALDINE

Set among the Four Peaks and Peel Forest Mountain ranges, this pleasant country town has a lively arts and crafts community and two museums. The Vintage Car Club and Machinery Museum on Talbot Street (daily 10–4) houses cars and tractors dating back to 1900, and some notable aircraft. A small town museum is on Cox Street (Mon–Sat 10–12, 1.30–3.30, Sun 1.30–3.30) in the 1885 former Town Board office. The town's most unusual attraction is found in the back room of a sweater shop. The shop, called the Giant Jersey, claims to have the biggest sweater in the world: a faithful copy of the Bayeux Tapestry made from a glittering mosaic of more than two million tiny pieces of spring steel, the on-going work of enthusiast Michael Linton. There are good walks in the Talbot Forest Scenic Reserve.

305 E15 · Corner of Cox and Talbot streets · 03-693 1006

## GREYMOUTH

www.greydistrict.co.nz

Greymouth is the west coast terminus of the spectacularly scenic TranzAlpine rail journey from Christchurch across the Great Divide and the northern ranges of the Southern Alps. The town was founded during the gold rush, and continued to prosper thanks to the coal and timber industries and its status as the west coast's principal port. The region's mining and nautical past is explored at the History House Museum on Gresson Street (Mon–Fri 10–4).

The Grey River was a famous source of greenstone *(pounamu)*, or New Zealand jade, which the Maori sought out. The interesting Jade Boulder Gallery on Guinness Street (Oct–end Apr daily 8.30am–9pm; May–end Sep daily 8.30–5) displays a fascinating range of crafted greenstone jewels and sculptures, a Jade Discovery Walk, master sculptors at work and a huge, river-polished jade boulder. Also worth a look is the Left Bank Art Gallery on Tainui Street (Nov–end Apr Mon–Fri 10–5, Sat, Sun 10–3; May–end Oct Tue–Sat 10–4), showing the work of west coast artisans in a variety of media.

Shantytown, off SH6 (Rutherglen Road) 11km (7 miles) south of Greymouth (daily 8.30–5), is a re-created 1880s gold-mining settlement complete with shops, bank, saloon, jail, a working sawmill and a steam train which runs daily (9.45–4). You can also try your hand at gold-panning or even tie the knot in the original church.

Lake Brunner (Moana), 37km (23 miles) east of Greymouth, is the west coast's largest lake and one of the most attractive, offering fishing and other water-based activities. Watch for the beautiful white herons *(kotuku)*, which visit the lake outside the summer breeding season.

305 E12 · Corner of Mackay and Herbert streets · 03-768 5101 · Mackay Street · TranzAlpine service from Christchurch

## BANKS PENINSULA

Like the bulb on a jigsaw piece, Banks Peninsula juts out into the Pacific Ocean from Christchurch (⊳ 196–201). Its largest harbours are Lyttelton to the north and Akaroa to the south. Akaroa is its main settlement. It has refreshing hill and coastal scenery, historic sites and activities that include cruising and looking for the world's smallest and rarest dolphin, the Hector's dolphin. Captain Cook was the first European to discover the peninsula, but he charted it as an island, naming it after his ship's naturalist, Sir Joseph Banks.

### LYTTELTON

Lyttelton, on the opposite side of the volcanic crater of Lyttelton Harbour, is only 12km (7 miles) from Christchurch via the Lyttelton Tunnel. Explorers Robert Falcon Scott and Ernest Shackleton used the port as a base during their Antarctic expeditions, and relics from these heroic times can be seen in the Lyttelton Museum on Gladstone Quay (Tue, Thu, Sat, Sun 2–4). The Lyttelton Timeball Station, high on the hillside off Sumner Road (Wed–Sun 10–5), is the only survivor of three timing contraptions built in New Zealand to aid mariners' calculations of longitude.

Rapapa Island was originally a Maori *pa* and subsequently the base of Fort Jervois, built in 1886 to repel a feared Russian invasion. There are daily sailings (Dec–end Mar 10.20, 12.20; Oct–end Nov, Apr 12.20) to Quail Island, a former leper colony and now a refuge for native birds.

### AKAROA

Sprinkled with attractive old colonial wooden houses and picket fences, the pretty village of Akaroa has distinctly French roots. In 1835 Jean Langlois established a whaling station at French Bay and, seeing its potential for settlement, made a down-payment on the land with the local Ngai Tahu Maori. French settlers arrived, knowing nothing of the Treaty of Waitangi (which had placed New Zealand under British sovereignty only 13 days before), and were obliged to sell their claims and integrate. The community's rich history is traced at the Akaroa Museum, on the corner of rue Lavaud and rue Balguerie (Nov–end Apr daily 10.30–4.30; May–end Oct daily 10.30–4).

While you are exploring Akaroa, try not to miss Barry's Bay Cheese. They offer factory tours (Oct–end Apr daily).

**INFORMATION**

www.akaroa.com
305 G14 · 80 rue Lavaud, Akaroa · 03-304 8600 · 20 Oxford Street, Lyttelton · 03-328 9093 · Daily 9–5 · Lyttelton: 28 from the Bus Exchange, Christchurch; Akaroa: daily shuttles from Christchurch

**TIP**

» Staff at the Akaroa information office have local knowledge and can direct you to the peninsula's more remote places.

**Above** *Sheep graze the hill pastures of the peninsula*

## HAASST

The Haast region of South Westland contains some of New Zealand's purest ecosystems, taking in mountains, coastal plains and wetlands, dense tracts of forest, swamps, hidden lakes and beaches. From the north, a lush corridor of coastal forest and the 750m (2,460ft) Haast River Bridge brings you to the splintered settlement of Haast, named after German geologist Julius von Haast, who explored the coast in 1863. Several tiny conglomerations make up the community: Haast Junction, Haast Beach, and the remote village of Jacksons Bay. Haast township is inland on SH6.

South of Haast, the unsealed Cascade Road follows the Jackson River valley (a tributary of the Awawata) to tranquil Lake Ellery, then rises to a high point in the valley, where views take in the Cascade Valley and the dramatic glacial sweep of hills to the coast. Inland, the Olivine Range and Red Hills (coloured by magnesium and iron) mark the boundary of Mount Aspiring National Park (▷ 237).

At Jacksons Bay is the iron-framed grave of Claude Morton Ollivier, who died of pneumonia just weeks after arriving in 1875. The oldest known European grave on the West Coast, it commemorates the first, disastrous attempts at European settlement.

✚ 304 C14 ℹ SH6 beyond Haast River Bridge ☎ 03-750 0809 🚌 North and southbound services

## HAAST PASS

From Haast township SH6 turns inland and follows the bank of the Haast River before being enveloped by mountains and surmounting the 563m (1,847ft) Haast Pass, an ancient Maori greenstone trail plagued by floods and landslips. The first of three waterfalls, Roaring Billy, can be viewed on a short loop walk, and about 25km (15.5 miles) farther on, Thunder Creek Falls drop 28m (92ft) into the Haast River. Beyond are the boulders and precipitous rock walls of the Gates of Haast gorge, which foiled road-building attempts until 1960. Above it, Fantail Falls tumble over a series of rocky steps. From here it is a short distance to the Haast Pass and the boundary of Westland and Otago.

✚ 304 C15

## HANMER SPRINGS

Hanmer's biggest attraction is its Thermal Reserve on Amuri Avenue (daily 10–9). The natural hot springs were first discovered by Europeans in 1859 and became a commercial venture in 1907. Steaming streams connect a series of pools, and the mineral-rich waters range in temperature from a lukewarm 32°C (89.6°F) to a balmy 42°C (107.6°F). The alpine resort is a popular base for mountain bicycling and walking, and in winter for skiing.

✚ 305 G12 ℹ Amuri Avenue ☎ 03-315 7128 🚌 Services from Kaikoura and Christchurch

## HOKITIKA

www.hokitika.org

More gold passed through Hokitika in the 1860s than through any other town on the West Coast. From 1865 to 1867, 37,000 prospectors poured in. Today this is the West Coast's craft capital, attracting crowds to watch glass-blowers and greenstone-carvers and to browse in its galleries, concentrated on Tancred Street. To the south the mountain ranges climb steadily towards the peaks of the Westland Tai Poutini National Park and Mount Cook/Aoraki. Hokitika Gorge, 25km (15.5 miles) east of Hokitika, is crossed via a swinging footbridge—an exciting experience when the river becomes a raging torrent.

✚ 305 E13 ℹ Carnegie Building, corner of Hamilton and Tancred streets ☎ 03-755 6166 🚌 Tancred Street ✈ 1km (0.6 miles) east

## KARAMEA

This former frontier settlement, perched on its namesake river estuary and overshadowed by the peaks of the Kahurangi National Park, is the northernmost town on the West Coast. It is a good base for walkers tackling the Heaphy Track (▷ 168).

The limestone caves and arches of the Oparara Basin, 26km (16 miles) north and east of Karamea, are some of the South Island's most remarkable karst scenery. A thick veil of rainforest covers the bizarre formations, creating the eerie mood of a lost world. Bones found in the caves include those of the now extinct New Zealand eagle, with a 3m (10ft) wingspan. Residents include the gradungula spider, the country's biggest, with a leg span of 10cm (4in).

✚ 302 F10 ℹ Bridge Street ☎ 03-782 6652 🚌 Services from Westport and Heaphy Track ✈ Karamea airstrip

**Below** *A log cabin nestles among trees near the thermal resort of Hanmer Springs*

**INFORMATION**

www.christchurchnz.net
305 G14 Old Chief Post Office, Cathedral Square 03-379 9629
Mon–Fri 8.30–5, Sat, Sun 8.30–4
Corner of Lichfield and Colombo streets Troup Drive, Addington, 3km (2 miles) from downtown. Services to Kaikoura, Blenheim, Picton and TranzAlpine scenic journey to West Coast (▷ 217) 12km (7.5 miles) northwest of city

**Above** *Roses flourish in the Botanic Gardens, Hagley Park*

## INTRODUCTION

Christchurch, the largest city in the South Island, has a winning combination of cosmopolitan vivacity, quiet charm and a proud cultural and architectural heritage. Its heart is around Cathedral Square, to the west of the immense, tree-lined Hagley Park, and its borders are known as the Four Avenues: Rolleston Avenue, on the eastern fringe of Hagley Park; Moorhouse Avenue to the south; Fitzgerald Avenue to the east; and Bealey Avenue to the north. One of the most attractive features of the city is the River Avon, which winds its way gently through Hagley Park and downtown from west to east. The city is essentially flat, and has a grid system of streets extending in all directions from Cathedral Square, with most good shopping on the north–south Colombo Street. The central area is easily negotiable on foot.

Given Christchurch's strong and obvious English links, it is ironic that the first European settlers on the Canterbury Plains were Scottish. Brothers William and John Deans settled here in 1843, calling it Riccarton. Five years later the government bought this and surrounding land for more concerted settlement.

In 1849 Robert Godley founded the Canterbury Association (mainly worthies from his old university college of Christ Church, Oxford) to establish a new Anglican settlement. In 1850 the first four ships brought 782 colonists to the whaling base of Lyttelton. Despite the collapse of the Association in 1855, the colony flourished and much of its founding English influence prevails.

## WHAT TO SEE

### ARTS CENTRE

The lively Arts Centre on Worcester Boulevard occupies the original site of the University of Canterbury. The Gothic-revival buildings now house arts and crafts workshops, galleries, sales outlets, theatres, cinemas, cafés, restaurants and bars. There is a weekend craft market and local entertainment, including buskers. Historical features include the 'den' of physicist Ernest Rutherford (1871–1937), the Great Hall, with its stained-glass windows, and the Townsend Observatory.

198 D3

### AVON RIVER

This pretty river meanders from the northwest tip of the Four Avenues through Hagley Park, the Botanic Gardens and downtown, before continuing through the city's eastern suburbs to the sea. You can feed the ducks, and go punting from the eastern bank, just beyond Cathedral Square and beside the Worcester Street Bridge (summer daily 9–6; winter daily 10–4). Across the bridge and on the right, farther up Worcester Street, is the Christchurch Art Gallery Te Puna O Waiwhetu (Thu–Tue 10–5, Wed 10–9), designed to evoke the river—but dubbed by locals 'a warehouse in a tutu'. More than 3,000sq m (32,292sq ft) of exhibition space are devoted to New Zealand artists such as Charles Goldie and Ralph Hotere, as well as contemporary artworks and national and international shows.

198 C3

### CATHEDRAL SQUARE

Dominated by its Gothic-revival Anglican cathedral, Christchurch's main square underwent a facelift in the late 1990s, resulting in a profoundly controversial display of sharp angles and steel-and-concrete façades. The cathedral itself (tours Mon–Fri 11, 2, Sat 11, Sun 11.30) has an unusual interior design combining Maori and European styles, and its spire can be climbed in part, offering a panoramic view of the city.

Two notable characters inhabit the square, one permanently and the other between November and March. The former is the statue of founding father John Robert Godley; the latter is the Wizard, a local eccentric who wears a pointed hat and has been entertaining the masses with his views on life, the universe and everything for decades. The Four Ships Court, a memorial to the first four immigrant ships, stands outside the 1879 Old Chief Post Office (now the i-SITE visitor information office). The tall cone sculpture was commissioned for the millennium celebrations. Guided walks of the city leave from the southeast corner of the Square (Oct–end Apr 10am, 1pm; May–end Sep 1pm).

198 E3 12, 20, 33

**TIP**

» If you're driving it's a good idea to park free south of Moorhouse Avenue (the old rail station and Hoyts 8 Cinema), then catch the free shuttle to the heart of the city.

**Below left** *The grand Edwardian mansion of Riccarton House*

**Below** *Stained glass in Christchurch's Anglican cathedral*

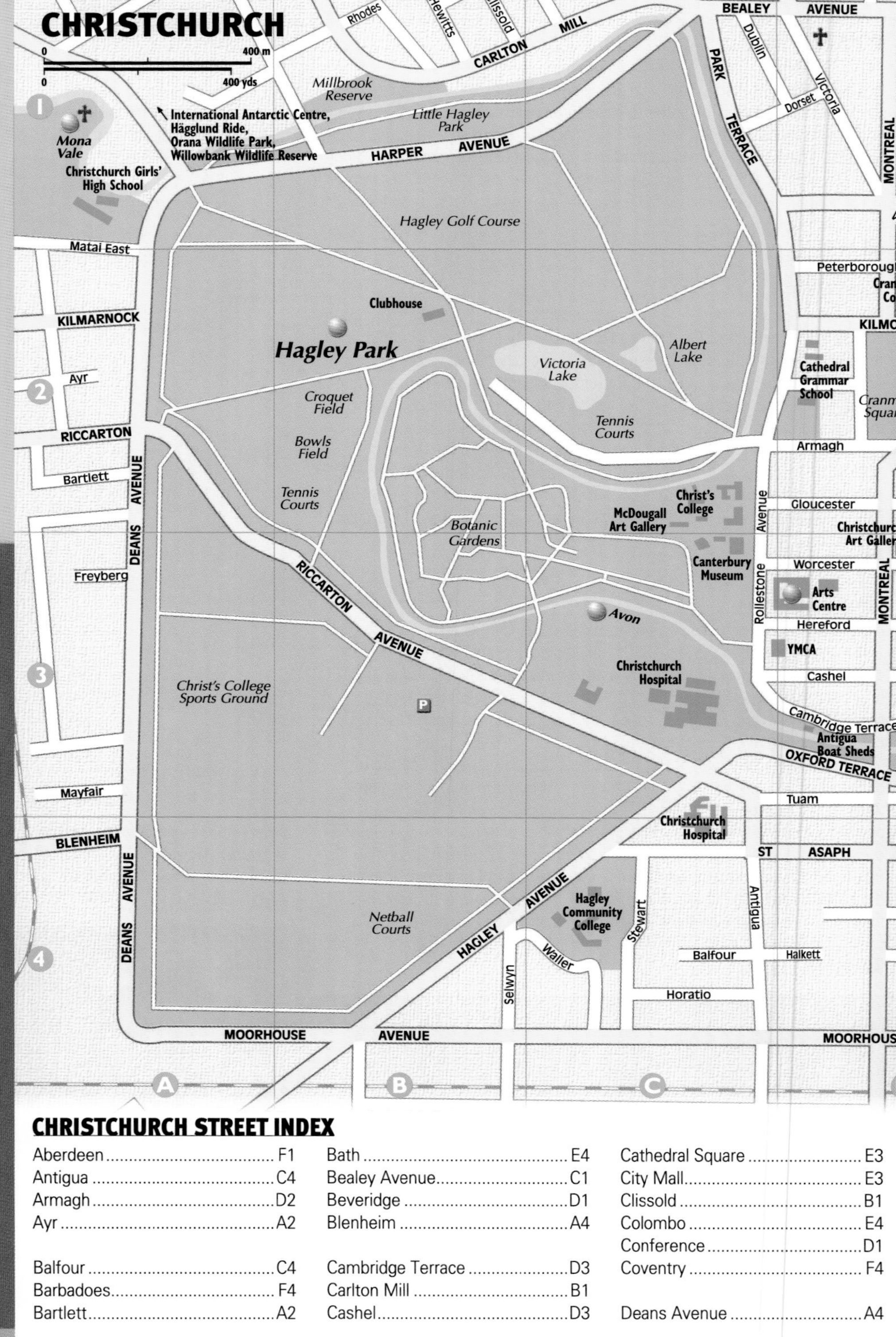


## CHRISTCHURCH STREET INDEX

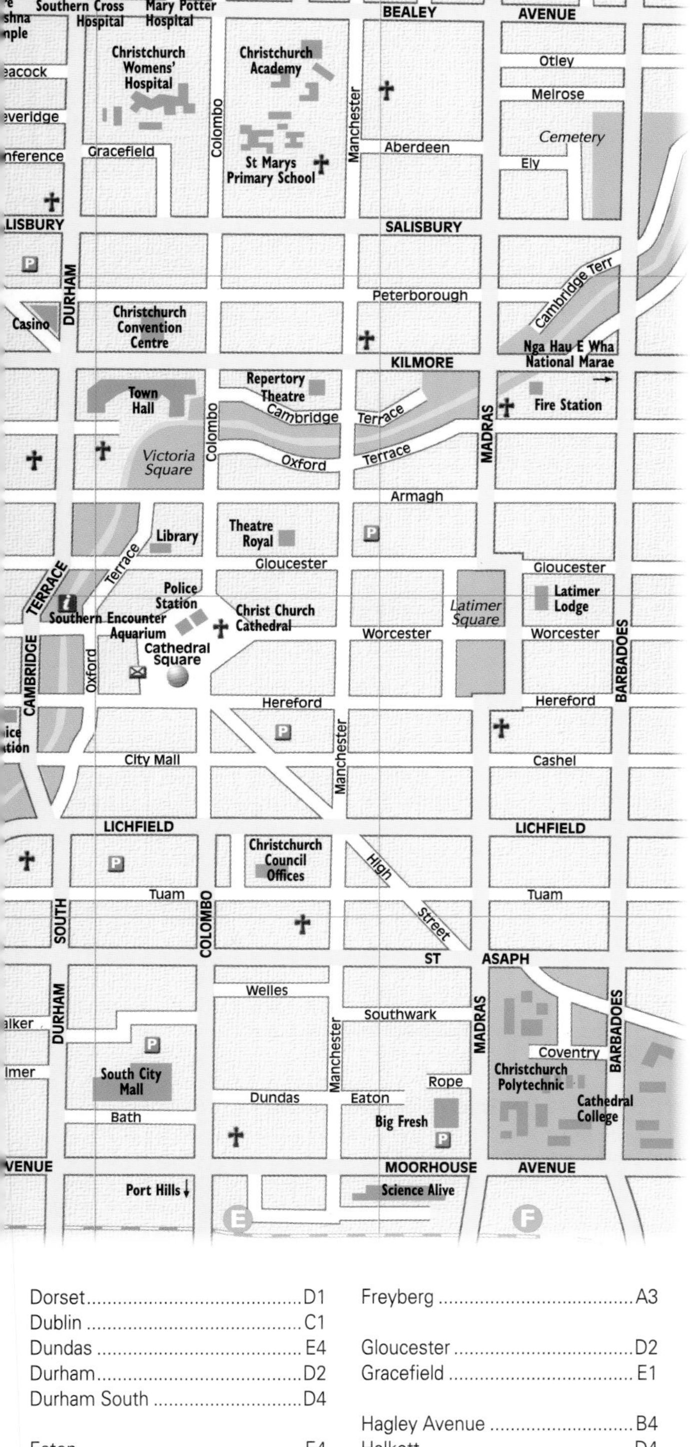
Southern Cross Hospital
Mary Potter Hospital
BEALEY
AVENUE
Christchurch Womens' Hospital
Christchurch Academy
Otley
Melrose
Cemetery
Colombo
Manchester
Gracefield
Aberdeen
Ely
St Marys Primary School
SALISBURY
Peterborough
Cambridge Terr
DURHAM
Casino
Christchurch Convention Centre
KILMORE
Nga Hau E Wha National Marae
Repertory Theatre
Town Hall
Cambridge
Terrace
Fire Station
MADRAS
Victoria Square
Oxford
Terrace
Armagh
Library
Theatre Royal
Gloucester
Gloucester
TERRACE
Terrace
Police Station
Southern Encounter Aquarium
Christ Church Cathedral
Latimer Square
Latimer Lodge
Worcester
Worcester
CAMBRIDGE
Oxford
Cathedral Square
BARBADOES
Hereford
Hereford
City Mall
Cashel
LICHFIELD
LICHFIELD
Christchurch Council Offices
High
Tuam
Tuam
SOUTH
COLOMBO
Street
ST
ASAPH
Welles
Southwark
DURHAM
Coventry
Christchurch Polytechnic
South City Mall
Rope
Dundas
Eaton
Cathedral College
Bath
Big Fresh
MOORHOUSE
AVENUE
Port Hills
Science Alive
E
F

## HAGLEY PARK

This enormous swath of parkland, covering more than 200ha (495 acres), is divided in two by Riccarton Avenue, and comprises tree-lined walkways, sports fields and, in its central reaches, the well-maintained and varied Botanic Gardens (daily 7–dusk; Conservatory Complex: daily 10.15–4).

At the entrance to the Botanic Gardens, on Rolleston Avenue, is the Canterbury Museum (daily 9–5), founded in 1867 and housed in an 1870 neo-Gothic building. The museum's highlights are the impressive Maori collection and the Hall of Antarctic Discovery.

Just north of the museum is Christ's College (tel 03-366 8705; guided tours Oct–end Apr), New Zealand's most famous public school, built in 1850. At the southern end of Rolleston Avenue you can hire a punt at the Antigua Boat Sheds, a former boatbuilders' premises dating from1882.

198 B2 A, 5, 7, 14, 27, 33

## INTERNATIONAL ANTARCTIC CENTRE AND HÄGGLUND RIDE

Since the turn of the 20th century and the days of polar explorers Scott and Shackleton, Christchurch has been an important point of access to the Antarctic (Scott is also commemorated with a statue by his widow Kathleen on Worcester Boulevard). The Antarctic Centre is a working campus occupied by Antarctica New Zealand (managers of New Zealand's scientific activities in the Antarctic), the Antarctic Heritage Trust and other official groups. The visitor centre gives an excellent introduction to the great white continent, with displays including the Snow and Ice Experience—a chill-inducing room kept at -15°C (-5°F) and decked with manufactured snow and ice to allow less adventurous visitors a taste of the Antarctic conditions.

The Hägglund is a tracked vehicle originally used by the US and New Zealand Antarctic programmes at Scott and McMurdo bases. A 15-minute ride takes you to see some of the centre's main facilities before giving you a taste of the vehicle's all-terrain abilities on an adventure course.

**Above** *The 19th-century Gothic-revival Anglican cathedral, topped by its copper-sheathed spire, dominates tree-lined Cathedral Square*

Off map 198 A1 Airport (signposted), Orchard Road 03-358 9896 Oct–end Mar daily 9–7; Apr–end Sep daily 9–5.30 From NZ$30, child (3–15) NZ$20; combination ticket NZ$48, child NZ$36 A, 10 from Bus Exchange

### RICCARTON BUSH AND RICCARTON HOUSE (PUTARINGAMOTU)

www.riccartonhouse.co.nz

The Riccarton Estate, set in 12ha (30 acres) of parkland, was the home of Scottish pioneers and brothers William and John Deans, the first European settlers on the Canterbury Plains. You can see the faithfully restored original 1843 Deans cottage, in which they first lived, and the grand Victorian-Edwardian homestead built by the next generation between 1856 and 1874. Riccarton Bush reserve, Canterbury's sole remnant of kahikatea floodplain forest, has survived for 3,000 years.

Off map 198 A2 3km (2 miles) west of downtown; entrance to reserve 16 Kahu Road 03-341 1018 Deans cottage daily; homestead Mon–Fri 1–4; tours Sun–Fri Adult NZ$10, child NZ$5, family NZ$25 24

**Above** *Punting on the Avon reveals the city's English origins*

**Below** *Christ's College school was built around an open quadrangle*

## MORE TO SEE

### MONA VALE

In 1905 a beautiful Elizabethan-style homestead was built in 5ha (12 acres) of landscaped grounds by Annie Townend, who named it after her mother's birthplace in Australia. The original homestead now houses a restaurant and café, and the surrounding gardens include a lily pond, vibrant rhododendrons and azaleas, and exotic trees, all pleasantly set on the River Avon and accessible by punt.

198 A1 63 Fendalton Road 03-348 9660 Summer daily 9.30–5; winter daily 9.50–4. Gardens: daily dawn–dusk Free Airport bus, 9

### NGA HAU E WHA NATIONAL MARAE

The Marae of the Four Winds is the country's largest *marae*, a beautifully constructed meeting house complete with greenstone-inlaid steps, which should be rubbed for good luck. Guided tours introduce you to facets of Maori culture, and you can stay to experience the evening performance and take part in the *hangi* (feast).

Off map 199 F2 250 Pages Road 03-388 7685 Mon–Fri 9–4.30; evening performance and *hangi* 6.45 Free, or by donation; performance from adult NZ$65 5, 51

### ORANA WILDLIFE PARK

www.oranawildlifepark.co.nz

New Zealand's largest wildlife reserve for captive animals is set in 80ha (198 acres) of parkland and has a mix of native and international wildlife, with an emphasis on African animals. Giraffes and rhinos are among the many inhabitants, along with the ever-popular inquisitive meerkats, and there is a nocturnal kiwi house.

Off map 198 A1 743 McLeans Island Road, near airport 03-359 7109 Daily 10–5 Adult from NZ$21, child (5–14) NZ$7, under-5s free, family NZ$49 Sunshine Shuttle from Cathedral Square, 10 and 1

### WILLOWBANK WILDLIFE RESERVE

www.willowbank.co.nz

Native wildlife and farm animals are the focus at Willowbank, with daily guided tours and night and day kiwi-viewing. The reserve has a very successful kiwi-breeding programme. You can also see the cheeky kea (mountain parrots) being fed.

Off map 198 A1 60 Hussey Road, off Gardiners Road 03-359 6226 Daily 10–10 Adult NZ$25, child (5–15) NZ$10, under-5s free, family NZ$60 Best Attractions from Cathedral Square

### LAKE KANIERE

Swimming, water sports, picnicking and walking are all popular at this summer haven about 14km (9 miles) inland from Hokitika. The surroundings of the lake, which is the heart of the Lake Kaniere Scenic Reserve, can be explored on foot or by car, boat or bicycle. The two best short walks are the Kahikatea Walk at Sunny Bight (10 minutes) and the Canoe Cove Walk (15 minutes)—both include good beaches. If you are feeling more energetic, the Lake Kaniere Walkway (four hours), which also starts at Sunny Bight, follows the western shore of the lake to Slip Bay at its southern edge. The road on the eastern edge gives access to the hardest walk (seven hours): the ascent of Mount Tuhua.

305 E13 Carnegie Building, corner of Hamilton and Tancred streets, Hokitika 03-755 6166

**Above** *Lake Kaniere is home to a wide variety of waterfowl species including crested and little grebes, scaup and teal*

### LAKE OHAU

www.twizel.com

Lake Ohau provides a pleasant diversion off SH8 between Omarama and Twizel. In winter it becomes a ski resort, known for its views and quiet atmosphere. Most activity focuses on Lake Ohau Alpine Village, above the southern shores just west of Lake Middleton, a small sub-lake separated from Ohau by a strip of land. In summer the lake and its surroundings are popular for walking, fishing and mountain bicycling. Six forests lie around its shores, with a number of tracks, access points and campsites.

304 D15 Northern entrance to Market Place, Twizel 03-435 3124 Twizel: services from Christchurch and Queenstown Omarama

### LAKE TEKAPO

Between Lake Tekapo and Twizel (▷ 205) is the heart of the Mackenzie Country, where lake and mountain ranges give way to the tussock grasslands of the Tekapo River basin. The SH8 delivers you to the southern shores of Lake Tekapo and the settlement of the same name, where the most famous landmark is a solitary stone church overlooking the lake. The Church of the Good Shepherd was built in 1935 in memory of the Mackenzie Country pioneers, who cleared this land of matagouri and speargrass for Merino sheep. Close by is a statue of a sheepdog—a moving tribute to the high-country shepherd's best friend and helper.

If you have time and a robust vehicle it's worth exploring the unpaved roads on either side of Lake Tekapo. The road to the west passes lakes Alexandria and McGregor before winding its way north to terminate at the Godley Peak Station. On the eastern side the road travels along the lake's edge past the Mount Hay and Richmond stations before continuing up into the wilds of Macaulay and Godley river basins.

There are plans to open a Mackenzie Heritage Centre in Tekapo in the future.

304 E14 Kiwi Treasures, Main Street 03-680 6686 Services from Christchurch and Queenstown

### LEWIS PASS

From Hanmer Springs, SH7 crosses the northern ranges of the Great Divide (Southern Alps) to the West Coast via the Lewis Pass, Maruia Springs, Springs Junction and Reefton. At the top of the Hope River Valley the road skirts the borders of the Lake Sumner Forest Park and begins to follow the Lewis River to its headwaters and the saddle known as the Lewis Pass, 864m (2,834ft) high.

In pre-European times the Ngai Tahu Maori of Canterbury used this route to access the west coast in search of greenstone. Having negotiated the pass on their return, they are said to have killed their slaves and feasted on their bodily parts. A valley known as Cannibal Gorge immortalizes this rather grim tale.

The pass itself was named in 1860 in tribute to pioneer surveyor Henry Lewis. The Lewis Pass offers excellent walks, ranging from one hour to several days, and its lichen-covered beech forests are superb. The five-day St. James Walkway begins near the Lewis Pass summit parking area and is best negotiated in summer or autumn.

Just beyond The Lewis Pass, heading west, is the oasis of Maruia Springs, an attractive Japanese-themed thermal resort.

305 G12

## MOUNT COOK/AORAKI NATIONAL PARK

The breathtaking array of mountain peaks in Aoraki National Park is crowned by Mount Cook/Aoraki. This spectacular 70,696ha (174,690-acre) park backs onto the Westland Tai Poutini National Park (⊳ 206–207). The 3,754m (12,316ft) peak of Mount Cook/Aoraki—New Zealand's highest mountain—sits at its heart, towering over lower peaks such as Tasman, at 3,498m (11,476ft), and Mount Sefton, 3,157m (10,361ft), and surrounded by another 19 peaks reaching more than 3,000m (9,840ft). Tipping down from this great chancel are the vast and impressive Hooker and Tasman glaciers. The area is considered sacred by Maori, who see Aoraki as a powerful symbol of being, an ancestor from whom the Ngai Tahu people, the *tangata whenua*, are descended, and a link between the supernatural and natural world.

### MOUNT COOK VILLAGE AND BEYOND

The village is the hub for all activities in the region, including scenic flights and heli-skiing. The only distinctive building is the Hermitage Hotel—the third version to have been built. The original, erected in 1884 farther down the valley, was destroyed by floods in 1913; a second, on the present site, was gutted by fire 44 years later.

In addition to the gargantuan vista of Mount Cook/Aoraki and Mount Sefton, the associate glacier valleys are worthy of investigation. Directly north of the Hermitage is the Hooker Valley. To the east, dwarfing the Wakefield Range, is the vast Tasman Valley, with its own massive glacier—the longest in New Zealand. Both act as watersheds that feed Lake Pukaki, and were once full of ice, hence the incredible expanse of boulder fields that precede the lake waters. Fine glacial moraine (rock flour) gives the glacial lakes their exotic azure shade.

### WALKING IN THE PARK

Walks within the park take in every variation, from a strenuous climb to the Muller Hut, 1,768m (5,800ft) up on the ridge of Mount Oliver (the first peak in the region climbed by Edmund Hillary, who conquered Everest in 1953), to the 10-minute Bowen Bush Walk, which starts from behind the Alpine Guides Centre in Mount Cook Village and takes you through classic totara forest. Other tracks lead to the Hooker Valley, Muller Glacier and the Tasman Valley.

### INFORMATION

www.mtcooknz.com
304 D14 Bowen Drive, Mount Cook Village 03-435 1186 Oct–end Apr daily 8.30–6; May–end Sep daily 8.30–4.30 Services to Mount Cook Village from Christchurch and Queenstown 3km (2 miles) south of Mount Cook Village, sightseeing flights

### TIP

» Always seek up-to-date information on track and weather conditions before embarking on walks in the park, and beware of rock falls.

**Below** *Icy chunks of the Tasman Glacier float in Terminal Lake*

## MOUNT SUNDAY

Mount Sunday dominates the Rangitata valley, in stark contrast to the mountainous skyline of the Southern Alps, and was used as the set for Edoras and King Theoden's grand hall in *The Two Towers*, the second of the *Lord of the Rings* movies. From Mount Somers the road leads west through the Ashburton Gorge towards lakes Camp and Clearwater, before opening into a wide tussock valley. A route west towards the end of the valley and the edge of the Mount Harper Range (Harpers Knob) gives a sudden and dramatic view down into the Rangitata valley and, in the far distance, Mount Sunday's prominent outcrop, 611m (2,004ft) high. Direct access to the hill is forbidden.

305 E14

## PAPAROA NATIONAL PARK

www.doc.govt.nz

Paparoa National Park covers 30,000ha (74,130 acres) on the West Coast, with a predominantly karst (limestone) topography. Its most famous features are the pancake rocks and blowholes of Dolomite Point at the small settlement of Punakaiki. Erosion has produced fluted vertical columns here known as karren, and a 20-minute track loops around lookout points and blowholes. At high tide the spectacle can be amazing, with the ground physically shaking to the thunderous pounding of the waves, and sea spray hissing through the cracks.

Tiromoana, 13km (8 miles) north of Punakaiki, is the northern trailhead for the Inland Pack Track, a 27km (17-mile), two- to three-day route that takes in the Fox River gorge. This is a system of caves including one 100m (328ft) long, and the 100m-by-30m (328ft by 98ft) Ballroom Overhang, which sits like half an umbrella embedded in the river bed.

Closer to Punakaiki is the Bullock Creek valley, which leads to Cave Creek—a deeply incised limestone gorge. In 1995 a viewing platform set high above the cavern collapsed, killing 15 students, and as a result there was a complete review of similar structures countrywide.

The area is also home to rare wildlife, such as the Westland black petrel, which nests only on Paparoa's mountains.

305 F12 SH6, Punakaiki 03-731 1895 Services from Greymouth and Nelson

**Below** *Layers of limestone at Punakaiki, on the northern West Coast, laid down 30 million years ago now stand exposed*

## PUKEKURA

www.pukekura.co.nz

The population of this tiny west-coast settlement is two: Peter Salter and Justine Giddy. The township was originally a stagecoach stop; a saw mill opened in the 1950s and shut down in the 1980s, and in 1993 Salter and Giddy established the Bushman's Centre here. In later years they bought the pub, houses and helipad, which lie within the scenic forest reserve. At the heart is an interactive museum, where you can learn about bushcraft and stroke a pig. Other activities based here include horse-trekking, gold-panning and Canadian canoe safaris (▷ 220).

304 E13 18km (11 miles) south of Ross 03-755 4144

## REEFTON

www.reefton.co.nz

In 1888 this former gold town at the head of the Lewis Pass (▷ 202) became the first town in the southern hemisphere to receive a public electricity supply and street lighting. Today Reefton has fine fishing in the local rivers and a wealth of walking and mountain bicycling opportunities, mainly within the 180,000ha (444,780-acre) Victoria Conservation Park, the largest forest park in the country.

On the Strand is the Single Fairlie R28 locomotive, the sole survivor of its type. An easy 40-minute walk crosses the river to the former powerhouse that once proudly lit up the town. Blacks Point Museum, just beside SH7 in Blacks Point (summer, Wed–Fri, Sun 9–noon, 1–4, Sat 1–4), has displays about aspects of the region's goldfields.

302 F12 Broadway 03-732 8391

## TIMARU

Timaru, halfway between Christchurch and Dunedin, is New Zealand's second biggest fishing port and makes an enjoyable and interesting stop. The South Canterbury Museum, on Perth Street (Tue–Fri 10.30–4.30, Sat, Sun 1.30–4.30), contains exhibits on local maritime history and Maori rock art, of which hundreds of examples can be seen in the area. It also traces the exploits of aviator Richard Pearse (1877–1953), said to have made the first manned flight in 1903, nine months before the Wright brothers of America (▷ 35). A full replica of his impressive flying machine is on display.

The Aigantighe Art Gallery on 49 Wai-iti Road (Tue–Fri 10–4, Sat, Sun 12–4, gardens dawn–dusk), founded in 1956 in a 1908 building surrounded by a sculpture garden, is one of the best art galleries in the country, with works dating back to the seventh century.

At Caroline Bay, to the north of the town centre, there's a beach formed in 1877 by land reclamation and harbour development, which provides the focus for the popular Summer Carnival.

305 E15 Landing Service Building, 2 George Street 03-688 6163 Services from Christchurch and Dunedin

**Above** *The busy main street of Westport, the oldest town on the West Coast*

## TWIZEL

www.twizel.com

Right in the heart of the Mackenzie Basin stands the rather featureless holiday centre of Twizel, a former hydroelectric-scheme construction town built in the 1970s. Pioneer surveyor John Thompson bestowed the name in tribute to the Twizel Bridge, which crosses the River Tweed on the border between England and Scotland. Twizel's most famous residents are the endangered kaki, or black stilts, which, along with the town's proximity to the Mount Cook National Park, are its biggest draw. Once common in the heartlands and braided-river beds throughout New Zealand, kaki are now one of the rarest wading birds in the world, currently numbering fewer than 100 in the wild. Guided visits to a viewing hide on Lake Ruataniwha, 3km (2 miles) south of Twizel, allow you to view the stalwart survivors and a captive population of 66, bred in enclosed aviaries (late Oct to mid-Apr, daily; winter by prior arrangement only).

304 D15 Northern entrance to Market Place 03-435 3124 Outside information office; services from Christchurch and Queenstown

## WAITAKI VALLEY

From Oamaru, SH83 turns through this pretty valley on its way to Omarama, Mackenzie Country and Mount Cook/Aoraki. Its lakes and the Waitaki River are regulated by an extensive system of hydroelectric dams, and activities include fishing and water sports on lakes Benmore and Aviemore, gliding from Omarama airfield and winter skiing at Lake Ohau (▷ 202). The Clay Cliffs, between Omarama and Twizel, echo the bizarre eroded rock and gravel formations of the Pinnacles in the Wairarapa, North Island (▷ 141).

Travelling from east to west the first settlement of any significance is Duntroon. With the discovery of gold in 1868, the town enjoyed a very brief boom before the diggings proved a failure, earning them the label 'poor man's field'. After a return to relative obscurity, there was more excitement with the discovery of a quartz reef between the Maerewhenua and Otekaike rivers in 1870, but, like the gold, its extraction was short-lived.

Duntroon is now a small farming settlement with a number of amenities, activities and scenic attractions. The Elephant Rocks, reached from Livingstone Road, near the Maerewhenua River Bridge, are unusual limestone outcrops, and there are Maori rock drawings at Takiroa, on the other side of the Maerewhenua valley, dating back more than 1,000 years.

West of Duntroon are Lake Aviemore, whose dam has a 1km-(0.6-mile) long fish-spawning race used by up to 3,000 adult trout at a time; and Lake Benmore, with the biggest dam in New Zealand.

307 E16

## WESTLAND TAI POUTINI NATIONAL PARK

▷ 206–207.

## WESTPORT

www.westport.org.nz

The West Coast's oldest town has a long main street fed by a flat expanse of orderly blocks of buildings and wide roads. Westport is most often used by visitors as an overnight base before heading northwards to Karamea and the Heaphy Track or south towards the town of Greymouth.

The excellent Coaltown Museum on Queen Street South (daily 9–4.30) has a range of displays with an emphasis on coal mining, but also including gold, pioneer and maritime exhibitions. Of note are the simulated walk-through mine and the massive brake drum from the Denniston Incline, with a coal wagon pitched at the incline's 47-degree angle.

Cape Foulwind, 11km (7 miles) south of Westport, is a buttress of land where a fur seal colony thrives on beautiful Tauranga Bay.

302 F11 1 Brougham Street 03-789 6658 Services from Greymouth and Nelson

**INFORMATION**
www.doc.govt.nz
304 D13–14 DoC Franz Josef Glacier, southern end of Franz Josef 03-752 0796 Summer daily 8.30–12, 1–6, winter 8.30–noon, 1–4.45 DoC Fox Glacier, SH6, northern end of Fox 03-751 0807 Mon–Fri 9–noon, 1–4.30 Services to Franz Josef and Fox from Queenstown and Greymouth

**Above** *Sunset reflected in the perfectly still waters of Lake Matheson*

## INTRODUCTION

Westland Tai Poutini National Park is separated from Mount Cook/Aoraki National Park (▷ 203) by the jagged summits and peaks of the Southern Alps. To the west of the Alpine Fault the forests and ravines of the Southern Alps are crowned with permanent snowfields. Among the glaciers they feed are the two most famous: Franz Josef (Ka Roimata o Hine Hukatere) and Fox (Te Moeka o Tuawe), which flow from a height of 3,000m (9,840ft) at more than 1m (3ft) a day, down into forest. Each has its own access village, offering a variety of walking opportunities and scenic flights.

Franz Josef Glacier was documented by both Abel Tasman in 1642 and Captain Cook in 1770, but the first thorough exploration of the glacier was carried out in 1865 by geologist Julius von Haast, who named it after the Austrian emperor.

## WHAT TO SEE

### BRUCE BAY AND LAKE PARINGA

From Fox Glacier township SH6 winds its scenic way to the most remote region of the west coast—South Westland. South of the heavily forested Copeland Valley, Bruce Bay is a quiet coastal spot. SH6 continues south, crossing the Paringa River before arriving at Lake Paringa. The river is the farthest point south that explorer Thomas Brunner reached during his epic 18-month journey from Nelson and the Buller Gorge in 1848—a feat marked by a plaque.

304 C14–D14 Atomic Shuttle and Intercity services to Copeland Valley entrance

### FRANZ JOSEF GLACIER

New Zealand's steepest and fastest-moving glacier is a dazzling landscape of ice crevasses, pinnacles, caves and ravines descending almost to sea level through dense rainforest. The juxtaposition of ice and greenery provides an ecosystem found nowhere else in the world. The road runs alongside the cold, grey Waiho River, which appears dramatically from beneath the glacier's face. From the parking area you can walk along the riverbed to within 500m (1,640ft)

of the glacier, but to walk on the glacier itself you must join a guided trip (⊳ 218). The viewpoint on Sentinel Rock is reached from the main parking area.
✚ 304 D14 ✉ 5km (3 miles) south of Franz Josef village along Glacier Access Road

### FOX GLACIER

Many visitors head for Franz Josef and neglect Fox Glacier, but it is no less impressive. Fox Glacier valley and the chilly Fox River, which surges from the glacier terminus, create a significantly different mood, with precipitous, ice-carved cliffs looming over the village parking area. Like nearby Franz, Fox can be explored at its terminus independently, or climbed with a guide.
✚ 304 D14 ✉ 5km (3 miles) southeast of Fox Glacier village

### KNIGHTS POINT AND SHIP CREEK

On the coastline south of the National Park, Knights Point gives spectacular views of sea stacks and virtually inaccessible beaches, and beyond the viewpoint you may see fur seals dozing. At the base of the hill, about 3km (2 miles) south, a small parking area gives access to Murphys Beach, where, when the tide is out, you can explore the sweep of golden sand and the rugged coast.

Farther south is the more popular beach at Ship Creek, where short walks explore the beach, the coastal forest and a lake between the dunes. In summer it is not unusual to see Fiordland crested penguins coming ashore. Ship Creek was named in memory of a shipwreck on the Australian coast at Cape Otway in Victoria. The *Schomberg* ran aground on her maiden voyage in 1854, and pieces of the vessel washed up here, more than 1,500km (930 miles) away.
✚ 304 C14 ✉ South of Lake Moeraki

## MORE TO SEE

### LAKE MOERAKI AND MUNROE BEACH

The waters of Lake Moeraki are popular for swimming, kayaking and birdwatching, and its outlet river leads to a wonderful west coast beach and pounding surf. In the breeding season (Jul–Dec) or during their late summer moult, rare Fiordland crested penguins fight their way into the bush.
✚ 304 C14 ✉ 18km (11 miles) south of Lake Paringa 🚘 The parking area and trailhead are 200m (220 yards) north of Moeraki River bridge. A path takes you through forest to the sands

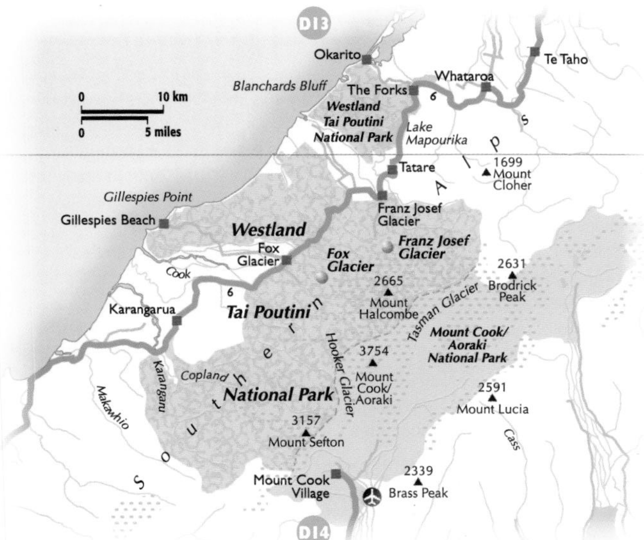


### TIPS

» Scenic flights over the glaciers from above and below are completely dependent on good weather conditions, though guided walks are rarely cancelled.
» Activities can be reserved and transportation arranged at the DoC Information Centre on Main Road, Franz Josef (tel 03-752 0288).
» Up-to-date weather forecasts and maps of the area are available at the DoC information centre.

# LAKE KANIERE AND HOKITIKA GORGE

**Easy walking detours enable you to explore the bush and a tumbling waterfall around the lake, then it's a short trek across farmland to the swingbridge across the Hokitika Gorge.**

**THE DRIVE**
**Distance:** 95km (60 miles)
**Time:** 3 hours
**Start/end at:** Junction of Stafford Street and SH6, Hokitika, West Coast 305 E13

★ Stafford Street is the more southerly of two roads heading inland from Hokitika (▷ 195). After 5km (3 miles) it forks; take the left arm signposted Lake Kaniere Road. In another 8km (5 miles) enter Lake Kaniere Scenic Reserve. The surroundings become markedly more lush and the Southern Alps dominate the horizon. In another 4km (2.5 miles) pass the Hokitika Angling Club. About 500m (550 yards) after this the road forks. In the middle is the start of a water-race known as The Landing, and your first view of Lake Kaniere.

❶ The Landing was built in 1875 to bring water to the Kaniere goldfield. By 1907 it had been reconstructed to feed the powerhouse 7km (4 miles) west on Lake Kaniere Road. This is now the smallest hydro-power station in Westland, supplying about 40 houses in Hokitika. The lake also provides Hokitika's drinking water. Lake Kaniere was gouged out by glaciers some 12,000 years ago. It is 195m (640ft) deep and home to trout, eels and freshwater mussels, and attracts birds such as teal, scaup and crested and little grebes.

Turn south into Sunny Bight Road and drive for 1km (0.6 miles), passing a row of holiday baches. Park the vehicle at Sunny Bight picnic area and take the Kahikatea Forest Walk.

❷ This 1km (0.6-mile) loop track begins on a boardwalk over wetland for 200m (220 yards) and continues on a wide, well-formed path. Kahikatea trees grow up to 60m (197ft) high, distinctively straight with branches that start high on the trunk. These characteristics make it ideal for milling, so stands of mature trees are few and far between. Kahikatea are hosts to epiphytes—mosses, lichens and ferns.

Drive back up Sunny Bight Road and turn east into Dorothy Falls Road. In 1km (0.6 miles) there's a small parking area for Canoe Cove walk. Take your picnic and stroll through podocarp forest to a secluded beach. It's a great spot to enjoy the lake, the mountains and perhaps a quick dip.

Continue along Dorothy Falls Road. In 1.5km (1 mile) you'll pass through Hans Bay, a quiet holiday village. The road then becomes unsealed and narrow in places. After 4.5km (2.5 miles) there's a car park for Dorothy Falls.

❸ You can see Dorothy Falls from the road, but for the full impact walk down and stand on the rocks near the bottom. The waterfalls are most dramatic from autumn to spring. If you didn't swim at Canoe Cove, now's your chance.

The gravel road continues for another 5km (3 miles), most of it on fair surface through farmland. After 3km (2 miles), pass the western end of Lake Kaniere walkway, a 13km (8-mile) path through bush and lakeside that emerges near the Kahikatea loop. At the Mark Wallace Bridge over Styx River the road becomes sealed again. This marks the edge of the Kaniere Reserve and you continue through open farmland. Mount Lathrop, at 1,905m (6,250ft), is the highest of the ranges to the east. In a further 13km (8 miles) from Mark Wallace Bridge reach Kokatahi. At the eastern end is the Hokitika junction. Continue straight on towards Hokitika Gorge. After 1km (0.6 miles) the road turns southeast, so you have excellent views of the Southern Alps. The road takes five right-angle turns, all well signposted. Sixteen kilometres (10 miles) beyond Kokatahi, the road is unsealed again and you enter the Hokitika Gorge Scenic Reserve. The car park is in another 1.5km (1 mile).

**Above** *Grabbing a photo opportunity on the Hokitika Gorge swingbridge*
**Opposite** *Canoeing on a river near Hokitika*

❹ To see the gorge, walk from the car park down steep, rough steps. Once over the bridge, the track on your left (upriver) takes you down a difficult track to a view of the bridge. The original was built in the late 19th century, and marked the start of the Westland farmers' long journey across the Southern Alps into Canterbury, to the nearest sale yards. In 2004, the bridge became the focus of new controversy. An Australian company planned to surround it with an 'airwalk'—platforms enabling visitors to walk a loop around the tree tops, up to 21m (69ft) above ground. The 'pro' crowd claimed it would bring road improvements and economic spin-offs; the 'anti' group argued that the tranquillity and views would be disturbed.

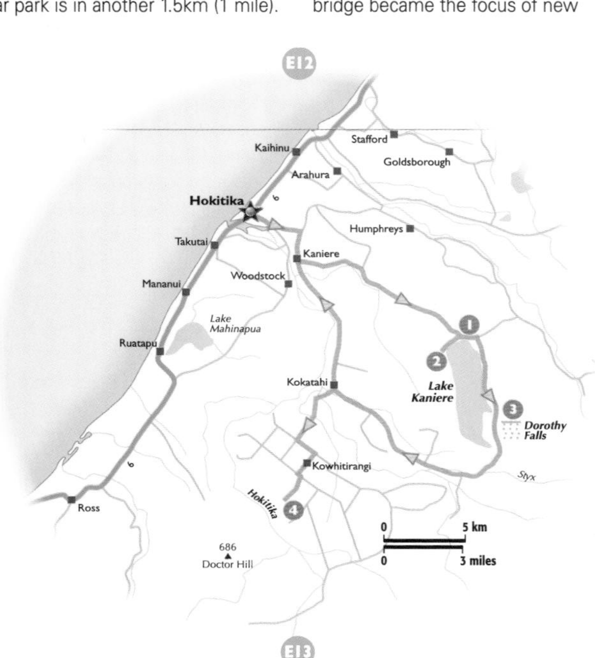


Return to your car and retrace your path to Kokatahi. At the junction, turn north for the road back to Hokitika. It's 10km (6 miles) to the Stafford Street/Lake Kaniere Road junction, and another 5.5km (3 miles) to SH6.

## WHEN TO GO

On damp days with low cloud you won't see the mountains, but the lake and bushwalks are still magical.

## WHERE TO EAT

Picnic at Canoe Cove. Supplies can be bought from Café de Paris, 19 Tancred Street, Hokitika (tel 03-755 8933; daily 7.30am–11pm).

## INFORMATION

### TOURIST INFORMATION

✉ Carnegie Building, corner of Hamilton and Tancred streets, Hokitika
☎ 03-755 6166

# OVER THE PORT HILLS

**This route climbs into the Port Hills and follows an impressive course along the historic Summit Road. The hilltop lookouts contrast the ragged inlets of Lyttelton Harbour with Christchurch's rambling flatness, while the dramatic Southern Alps rise up in the distance.**

**THE DRIVE**
**Distance:** 40km (25 miles)
**Time:** 2.5 hours
**Start/end at:** Ferrymead Heritage Park, Christchurch 305 G14

In 1849, Sumner, a beach town southeast of Christchurch, was expected to become a bustling business hub, buoyed by Evans Pass traffic between Lyttelton and Christchurch. It only happened on paper—the Lyttelton rail tunnel was built in 1867 and by the 1870s there was little more to Sumner than a hotel. Then, in 1888, a tramline opened between Sumner and Christchurch. It started the trend for day-trippers.

★ From Ferrymead Heritage Park, drive east to the end of Ferrymead Park Drive and turn left (north) along Bridle Path Road. At the T-junction opposite the estuary, turn right onto Main Road. It's an easy drive past Mount Pleasant, Balmoral Hill, Redcliffs and Moncks Bay. After 4km (2.5 miles), Shag Rock marks the western end of Sumner Beach. Once you pass the Clifton turn-off (south) and the surf club (north), turn left (northeast) into the Esplanade.

❶ On the seaward side of the Esplanade, Cave Rock can be climbed for a lifeguard's lookout, or walk right through it at low tide. Opposite Cave Rock is the broad entrance to a cave where moa bones were found.

Drive 1km (0.6 miles) to the playground at the end of the Esplanade. Turn right (south) up Heberden Avenue and cross the speed bump at the Nayland Street intersection. After 1km (0.6 miles), turn left (south) onto Evans Pass Road and begin your climb into the Port Hills countryside. After 2km (1 mile), a viewing area looks over Sumner. Straight after this, turn west, following yellow signs for The Sign of the Kiwi and Summit Road.

❷ Summit Road is linked with the life of Harry G. Ell (1863–1934), maverick MP and conservationist. Ell envisaged a continuous network of paths along the Port Hills and across Banks Peninsula to Akaroa with 14 rest stations. By the time he died only four had been built—but even this was a feat. He had a knack of upsetting authorities from the Prime Minister down, and repeatedly brought his Summit Road trust to the brink of bankruptcy, only to be bailed out by friends.

The next 12km (7 miles) follow the winding Summit Road. At regular intervals on either side there are parking bays to enjoy the fabulous views over Christchurch, Lyttelton Harbour and Banks Peninsula. Good spots to stop are the Memorial to Pioneer Women, 1km (0.6 miles) after you pass under the Christchurch Gondola cables, and the Sugar Loaf Scenic Reserve car park, 7km (4 miles) after the memorial. By this point you will also have a good view of the 120m (394ft) television transmitter.

Summit Road is crisscrossed with walking tracks. For a break, stop at Tihiokahukura (Castle Rock), 1km (0.6 miles) after the memorial. It's a 500m (550-yard) track with unhindered views across the Canterbury Plains. In 2km (1 mile) you'll reach The Sign of the Kiwi restaurant.

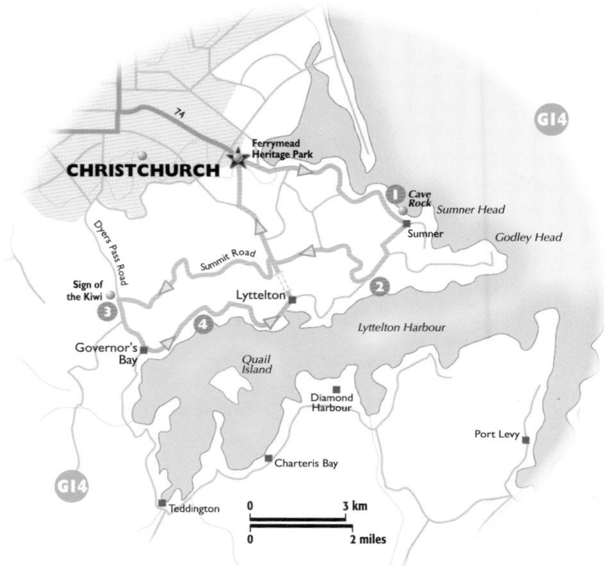


❸ Compared to Ell's fanciful masterpiece, The Sign of the Takahe (finished 1939), The Sign of the Kiwi is modest—a stone cottage with a warm, wooden interior and pleasant views towards Christchurch. It was opened in 1916 but, true to Ell's form, did not operate without controversy. When the Summit Road and Reserves Association publicly disowned Ell in 1920 (due to a NZ$5,000 debt), Ell moved into the Kiwi and refused to leave. His wife, Ada, came to the rescue by running the tearooms at a profit each year until 1926, when she suffered a nervous breakdown.

As you leave the Kiwi car park, turn south onto Dyers Pass Road, signposted Lyttelton. After 3km (2 miles) and some nerve-racking switchbacks, turn east to skirt Governor's Bay and follow the road to Lyttelton. Drive through the scenic hamlets of Rapaki and Cass Bay. As you leave Corsair Bay you will see the yachts of Lyttelton Harbour. At the T-junction of Simeon Quay, turn right (east). About 300m (330 yards) farther is the SH74 Lyttelton Tunnel roundabout.

❹ Governors Bay Road gives clear views of Quail Island. Now an attractive destination for walkers and daytrippers, it held a leper colony from 1907 to 1925, when the remaining sufferers were moved to Fiji. There are scant remnants of its huts, nurses' quarters and the small hospital.

For a jaunt through Lyttelton, continue east towards the heart of town. After 500m (550 yards), turn left (north) into Oxford Street. Pass the visitor office, then turn left (west) into London Street. After 250m (275 yards), turn left (south) into Dublin Street and arrive back at the roundabout. Turn north through the tunnel on SH74. Exit SH74 immediately after the tunnel, following signs for the gondola and Ferrymead.

## WHEN TO GO

This is a popular Sunday drive route for all Christchurch, so go during the week if possible.

## WHERE TO EAT

### SIGN OF THE KIWI

Friendly arts and crafts-style bungalow with an all-day menu. Three-course set-lunch menu NZ$20; morning and afternoon teas a speciality.

✉ Corner of Dyers Pass and Summit roads ☎ 03-329 9966 🕓 Jan–end Mar daily 10–6; Apr–end Dec daily 10–4

## INFORMATION

### TOURIST INFORMATION

www.christchurchnz.net

✉ Old Chief Post Office, Cathedral Square (West), Christchurch ☎ 03-379 9629

## PLACES TO VISIT

### FERRYMEAD HERITAGE PARK

www.ferrymead.org.nz

✉ Ferrymead Park Drive, off Bridle Path Road, Christchurch ☎ 03-384 1970

🕓 Daily 10–4.30

**Opposite** *A stretch of the long and winding Summit Road*

**Below** *Sailing in Lyttelton Harbour*

# MOUNT COOK/AORAKI NATIONAL PARK

**The Hooker Valley Track is Mount Cook/Aoraki National Park's most popular route, offering perfect views of Mount Cook and the smaller giants around it. The linear track takes you past a glacier terminal lake via two dramatic swingbridges and ends at Hooker Lake.**

**THE WALK**
**Distance:** 12km (8 miles) return; ascent 140m (460ft)
**Time:** 4 hours
**Start/end at:** Visitor information centre, Mount Cook Village 304 D14

★ From the visitor centre in the village (▷ 203), 760m (2,493ft) above sea level, take the cobblestone path by the Hermitage Hotel, heading north. Cross the road to a green Department of Conservation sign for White Horse Hill Campground and Kea Point Track.

❶ The gravel track is fairly flat for this section (1.5km/1 mile) and winds through scrub and scree. The landscape was formed in 1913, when heavy rains caused the outwash stream of the Mueller Glacier to burst through the moraine wall, pushing a mass of boulders before it and destroying the original Hermitage. West is the Mueller range, 1,200m (3,936ft) above the track. North are the Footstool (2,764m/ 9,066ft), Mount Sefton (3,158m/10,358ft) and a glimpse of Mount Cook/Aoraki.

Forty per cent of the national park's area (70,000ha/172,970 acres) is covered by glacial ice. Five glaciers fill the upper reaches of the main valleys, including the Tasman Glacier, which at 29km (18 miles) is the longest in New Zealand. The mountains are being forced up by the Alpine Fault at the same pace their tops erode—about 1cm (0.3 inches) a year.

Turn east, following a sign for the campground and the Hooker Valley Track. Just south of the campground is the old Hermitage's fireplace. In the northeast corner of the campground is the track's official start. In 200m (220 yards) you come across a 3m (10ft)-high stone pyramid just north of the track, a memorial to lives claimed by Mount Cook/Aoraki. Shortly after, the track climbs to a stone wall lookout over Mueller Glacier lake, Mount Sefton and the Footstool. In another 600m (656 yards) it zigzags downhill to the first swingbridge across the Hooker River. The milky-blue of the water is due to fine particles of rock crushed by the Hooker Glacier.

❷ The Mount Cook lily—actually the world's largest buttercup—is symbolic of this region, but hundreds of other alpine plants thrive, too. After the white buttercups in spring come the mountain daisies of early summer and the gentians of early autumn. Many other plants put on more subtle displays, so it's worth taking a patient look on hands and

**Above** *Crossing a swingbridge between snow-capped mountains on the Hooker Valley Track*

knees. Ninety-three per cent of New Zealand's alpine species are endemic and many have no close relatives anywhere else in the world. Once across the first swingbridge, the track skirts the eastern side of Mueller Glacier terminal lake. Uphill sections are made easier by stone steps. The trickiest part occurs at the bluff just before the second swingbridge, where the path is cut out of a rock face by the river. It may challenge the nerves, but a railing on the river-side means there is little real danger. Take special care in winter, when it may be icy.

❸ The dark green keas are the park's resident clowns. These protected alpine parrots are sociable and intelligent. They are notorious for roughing up climbing gear and windscreen wipers, but often engage in harmless fun—sliding down hut roofs, skidding across snowfields, gliding in storm winds and tumbling on the Hermitage lawn. They are easily identified by a flash of red under the wing.

After the bridge, the track narrows but it's easier underfoot. Here you find magnificent views of Mount Cook/ Aoraki, its south face framed by the rocky valley and underlined by the river. In summer there can be a profusion of Mount Cook lilies.

❹ After 1.2km (0.7 miles) you arrive at Stocking Stream, which has a shelter and toilets.

Despite serious attempts from 1882, Mount Cook/Aoraki remained unconquered until 1894, when the imminent attempt of an English climber and his Swiss guide spurred three young Kiwis—Tom Fyfe, George Graham and Jack Clarke—to have a go. They made it to the top on Christmas day, much to the pride and relief of New Zealanders, although they had no flag and had to fly an old sugar bag instead.

The final kilometre (0.6 miles) begins with a flat section and some boardwalks. It then rises slightly and as you reach the top, you see Hooker Lake in front of you. It's often sunny and sheltered, a good place to lunch before you retrace your steps to the village.

**WHERE TO EAT**

Picnic at Hooker Lake. Supplies from The Hermitage Hotel, Mount Cook Village (tel 03-435 1809, ▷ 225). Hampers (from NZ$21) can be provided at two hours' notice.

**WHEN TO GO**

Peak seasons are October to April and July to September. There's a quiet window between April and June. This popular track is often busy, so start early if you can.

**INFORMATION**

**TOURIST INFORMATION**

www.doc.govt.nz

✉ 1 Larch Drive, Mount Cook Village

☎ 03-435 1186

**Above** *Mount Cook lily, Hooker Valley*

**Below** *Stunning scenery is reflected in the Old Mountaineers' Café, Mount Cook Village*

**Above** *Action at Addington Raceway, Christchurch, home to the New Zealand Metropolitan Trotting Club*

## AKAROA

### AKAROA BLUE PEARLS

www.akaroabluepearls.com

Iridescent blue mabe (hemispherical) pearls are cultured in paua in Akaroa Harbour and Tory Channel. The Eyris Blue Pearl Centre tells the story of their creation and sells them.

✉ Main Wharf, Akaroa ☎ 03-304 7877 🕐 Oct–end Mar daily 10.30–5.30; Apr–end Sep 11–4.30

### AKAROA HARBOUR CRUISES

www.blackcat.co.nz

Two-hour scenic wildlife cruises at 11am and 1.30pm are on offer here. Although the highlight is the likely sighting of Hector's dolphins, you may also see little blue penguins, spotted shags and fur seals. You can also swim with dolphins and take a guided kayak trip.

✉ Main Wharf, Akaroa ☎ 03-304 7641 🕐 Nov–end Apr 11, 1.30; May–end Oct 1.30 ✋ Adult from NZ$60, child (5–15) NZ$25

### AKAROA SEAL COLONY SAFARI

www.sealtours.co.nz

The four-wheel-drive safari takes a crater-rim road and goes through sheep and cattle paddocks to the seal colony on the eastern bays of Banks Peninsula. You can observe the colony from a distance, or walk around the rocky coastline to see it at close quarters.

✉ PO Box 4, Akaroa ☎ 03-304 7255 🕐 Daily 9.30am, 1pm ✋ Adult NZ$70, child NZ$50, family NZ$190

### BANKS PENINSULA TRACK

www.bankstrack.co.nz

Leaving from Akaroa, the track takes in 35km (22 miles) of spectacular coastline, native bush, waterfalls and beaches. It can be done in two or four days, staying in farm cottages with hot showers and well-equipped kitchens. You can take your own food and some supplies are available on route. Pack cartage is available (at extra cost) for parts of the track.

✉ PO Box 54, Akaroa ☎ 03-304 7612 🕐 Oct–end Apr ✋ 2 days from NZ$135, 4 days from NZ$225

### BARRYS BAY CHEESE

www.barrysbaycheese.co.nz

At Barrys Bay, Don and Jeanette Walker are carrying on a cheese-making tradition going back more than 150 years. They are the only people in New Zealand still making traditional cloth-bound rinded cheddar, and also make a range of European cheeses. You can watch the cheese being made on alternate days during the season, and taste it in the shop, which also sells local wine and deli items.

✉ Main Road, Barrys Bay, Akaroa Harbour ☎ 03-304 5809 🕐 Daily 9–5

### LINTON ARTIST'S GARDEN VISITS

www.linton.co.nz

Surprises are everywhere in Josie Martin's enchantingly eccentric artist's garden, dotted with sculptures and mosaics, including an extraordinary sculptural wall mosaic. The house is a showcase for her paintings, and the venue for art workshops and concerts. You can also stay in the house on a bed-and-breakfast basis.

✉ 68 rue Balguerie, Akaroa ☎ 03-304 7501 🕐 Jan–end Apr daily 12–5; May–end Dec daily 2–4 ✋ House NZ$10; garden NZ$12

### LUMIÈRE

www.lumiere.co.nz

Therapeutic massage, exfoliation, body wraps, outdoor hot tubs and

reflexology are among the range of services offered at this 'private outdoor wilderness'.
✉ 8 rue Balguerie, Akaroa ☎ 03-304 7404 🕐 Daily 10–5 ✋ From NZ$50

**NATURALLY JADE**
www.naturallyjade.co.nz
You can watch the craftsman at work here, carving items from greenstone (*pounamu*, or New Zealand jade). The gallery has a superb collection of greenstone works, from large sculptures to jewellery—many show designs with symbolic associations, which he will explain. The shop also stocks gold, silver, paua and bone jewellery by other artists.
✉ 57 rue Lavaud, Akaroa ☎ 03-304 7781 🕐 Mon–Fri 9–5, Sat, Sun 10–5

**POHATU PENGUINS**
www.pohatu.co.nz
Pohatu is home to the largest white-flippered penguin colony on the South Island. The best time to visit the colony is during the breeding season, from September to January. Guided evening walks are conducted through the colony; because the road is accessible only to four-wheel-drive vehicles or mountain bicycles, the recommended option is to join the tour at Akaroa. Scenic day tours of the area as well as kayak rental are available.
✉ Pohatu Flea Bay, Akaroa ☎ 03-304 8552 ✋ Adult from NZ$66, child (under 12) NZ$50

## CHRISTCHURCH

**ADDINGTON RACEWAY**
www.addington.co.nz
The New Zealand Metropolitan Trotting Club offers harness racing all year round, including the popular Christchurch Casino and New Zealand Trotting Cup. Advance booking is required.
✉ Jack Hinton Drive, Christchurch ☎ 03-338 9094

**ADVENTURE CANTERBURY**
www.adventurecanterbury.com
Whether it's golf or skiing, Akaroa or Mount Cook/Aoraki, rafting or horse-trekking, farm visits, a wine trail or fishing, this company has a tour on offer.
✉ PO Box 1259, Christchurch ☎ 03-358 5991 ✋ From NZ$45

**ARTS CENTRE**
www.artscentre.org.nz
Take a guided retail therapy tour or browse around the 40 art and craft outlets, many of which are working studios (▷ 197). Try to catch the weekend market, when up to 70 stalls put up their awnings and the smell of cooking from many countries fills the air. Several performance venues are clustered on the Arts Centre site (▷ 197), including the Court Theatre (tel 03-963 0870, www.courttheatre.org.nz), one of New Zealand's leading professional theatre companies, which presents local and international drama, musicals and comedy. Occasional performances are also given at the University Theatre (tel 03-374 5483) and the Southern Ballet and Dance Theatre (tel 03-379 7219). The Academy Cinema and Cloisters Cinemas (tel 03-366 0167) screen art-house films. Plays and concerts, including Friday lunchtime concerts, are performed in the Great Hall.
✉ Worcester Boulevard, Christchurch ☎ 03-366 0989 🕐 Daily 9.30–5

**BALLANTYNES**
www.ballantynes.co.nz
A Christchurch institution, this traditional, family-run department store stocks everything from perfume to household items, bed linen to toys, and furniture to fashions for men, women and children. Branches at Christchurch Airport and Timaru.
✉ City Mall, Christchurch ☎ 03-379 7400 🕐 Mon–Thu 9–6, Fri 9–8, Sat 9–5, Sun 10–5

**BIVOUAC OUTDOOR**
www.bivouac.co.nz
Bivouac specializes in mountaineering and alpine sports equipment, including clothing, tents and packs, sleeping bags, ski gear and climbing equipment.
✉ Corner of Lichfield and Colombo streets, Christchurch ☎ 03-366 3197 🕐 Mon, Wed, Thu 9–5.30, Tue 9.30–5.30, Fri 9–8, Sat, Sun 10–4

**CENTENNIAL LEISURE CENTRE**
www.centennial.org.nz
This leisure centre is less than 10 minutes' walk from Cathedral Square in the heart of the city. Centennial has both a leisure pool and a lap pool, sauna, steam and spa facilities, and a fitness centre.
✉ 181 Armagh Street, Christchurch ☎ 03-941 6853 🕐 Mon–Thu 6am–9pm, Fri 6am–7pm, Sat, Sun 7–7 ✋ Fitness centre NZ$10, pool NZ$5, child (under 16) NZ$2.50

**CHRISTCHURCH BIKE TOURS**
www.chchbiketours.co.nz
Billed as the country's only guided city bicycle tours, the two-hour route takes you through Hagley Park to Riccarton Bush and Mona Vale, taking advantage of the flatness of the city's topography and its excellent bicycle facilities. Bicycles are provided.
✉ 24A Achilles Street, Dallington, Christchurch ☎ 03 366 0337 🕐 Nov–end Mar daily 2pm ✋ NZ$30

**CHRISTCHURCH CASINO**
www.chchcasino.co.nz
The casino has 350 gaming machines as well as blackjack, baccarat, Caribbean stud poker, American roulette, keno and *tai sai*. The dress code is smart casual and the minimum age is 20. There are several restaurants and bars within the casino complex.
✉ 30 Victoria Street, Christchurch ☎ 03-365 9999 🕐 Daily 24 hours

**CHRISTCHURCH PERSONAL GUIDING SERVICE**
Daily two-hour walks leave from a kiosk in Cathedral Square, with trained guides providing informative commentary about historic and modern buildings.
✉ 1/28 Packe Street, Christchurch ☎ 03-365 8480 🕐 Oct–end Apr daily 10am, 1pm; May–end Sep 1pm ✋ NZ$10

## CHRISTCHURCH TOWN HALL

www.convention.co.nz

The 2,000-seat auditorium, noted for its acoustics, is a regular venue for concerts by the Christchurch Symphony Orchestra and Christchurch City Choir, as well as touring orchestras, musicians and performers. The smaller proscenium-arch James Hay Theatre hosts chamber music, opera and various theatrical productions.

✉ 95 Kilmore Street, Christchurch
☎ 03-366 8899

## CRUZ

www.cruz.co.nz

A gay bar and nightclub is located upstairs in the Ministry nightclub. Cruz provides a relaxed lounge environment with a free pool table early on weeknights, before becoming a nightclub at 11pm.

✉ 90 Lichfield Street, Christchurch
☎ 03-379 2910 ⌚ Wed–Sun 7–late

**Above** *Top-class rugby and cricket fixtures are held at Christchurch's Jade Stadium, such as this floodlit rugby match*

## DUX DE LUX

www.thedux.co.nz

A restaurant and pub in the Arts Centre, the Dux hosts regular gigs by local and visiting performers. The venue is tiny and noisy, but the large outdoor courtyard acts as a popular meeting place. The attached restaurant serves vegetarian dishes and seafood, but the pub is most highly regarded for its boutique brewery. The beers are available only on tap, and are given quirky local names such as Nor'Wester (after Canterbury's famous wind). Ginger Tom ginger ale is recommended.

✉ 41 Hereford Street, Christchurch
☎ 03-366 6919 ⌚ Daily 11am–late

## EXPLORE NEW ZEALAND BY BICYCLE

www.cyclehire-tours.co.nz

You can go bicycling almost anywhere in the South Island with this company, from short-term hire of family bicycles for an excursion in Hagley Park to taking the gondola up into the Port Hills and mountain biking down, or touring even farther afield.

☎ 03-339 4020 From NZ$25

## HAGLEY GOLF CLUB

www.hagley.nzgolf.net

Located in Hagley Park, in the heart of Christchurch, the golf course caters for players of all abilities. The regular Friday morning 12-hole tee-off is a feature, and non-members are welcome.

✉ Hagley Park, Christchurch ☎ 03-379 8279 ⌚ Daily, open to green-fee players after 10.30am NZ$20 for 18 holes

## ISAAC THEATRE ROYAL

www.isaactheatreroyal.co.nz

The grand old lady of Christchurch theatres, the Theatre Royal opened in 1908. It retains its ornate interior, and refurbishments backstage in 2005 brought it up to international standards. It hosts ballet, drama and musicals.

✉ 145 Gloucester Street, Christchurch
☎ 03-366 6326

## JADE STADIUM

www.jadestadium.co.nz

Major rugby fixtures and test cricket attract huge crowds here. Check events on the website and book tickets through Ticketek (tel 03-377 8899).

✉ Wilsons Road, Christchurch
☎ 03-379 1765

## MAPWORLD

www.mapworld.co.nz

Mapworld has a wide range of digital and topographical maps; also atlases and accessories such as binoculars.

✉ Corner of Manchester and Gloucester streets, Christchurch ☎ 03-374 5399
⌚ Mon–Thu 8–6, Fri 8–8, Sat, Sun 9–5

## MERIVALE MALL

www.merivalemall.co.nz

Serving a smart residential suburb, Merivale Mall has more than 40 speciality shops, many of them devoted to New Zealand and international fashion labels. It also houses several stylish restaurants and wine bars and a particularly good supermarket.

✉ 189 Papanui Road, Christchurch
☎ 03-355 9692 ⌚ Mon–Wed, Fri 9–6, Thu 9–8, Sat 10–5, Sun 10–4

## NIMBUS PARAGLIDING

www.nimbusparagliding.co.nz

The Port Hills above Christchurch make a good take-off spot for paragliders. You can do a tandem

paraglide without training, or Nimbus will instruct you until you are able to do a solo flight. Flying at Taylors Mistake, Scarborough Cliffs or Castle Rock, you get great views over the Canterbury Plains.
✉ PO Box 17712, Sumner, Christchurch ☎ 03-326 7373 ✋ From NZ$160

**QEII PARK**
www.qeiipark.co.nz
Built for the 1974 Commonwealth Games, QEII is a multi-sport and leisure complex. The aquatic facility includes a 40m (131ft) wave pool, lazy river and children's play zone with interactive water toy features. Spa, sauna and café facilities are available poolside. QEII also has a modern fitness centre and aerobic studio, squash courts, Olympic weight-lifting gym, athletic stadium and cricket wicket.
✉ Travis Road, New Brighton ☎ 03-941 6849 🕒 Mon–Fri 6am–9pm, Sat, Sun 7am–8pm ✋ Adult from NZ$5, child NZ$2.50

**RICCARTON PARK RACECOURSE**
www.riccartonpark.co.nz
The Canterbury Jockey Club holds 20 race days through the year, including the New Zealand Cup, New Zealand Grand National and Easter Racing Carnival.
✉ Racecourse Road, Christchurch ☎ 03-342 0000

**RICCARTON ROTARY MARKET**
A community project operated by the local Rotary Clubs, this popular weekly market has more than 300 stalls selling crafts, food, clothing, jewellery and bric-à-brac. There are also outlets for local produce.
✉ Riccarton Park Racecourse, Racecourse Road, Christchurch ☎ 03-339 0011 🕒 Sun 9–2

**SAMMY'S JAZZ REVIEW**
www.sammys.co.nz
Sammy's has live jazz seven nights a week, and supports local musicians with regular weekly gigs, as well as hosting visiting groups. There's also a good à la carte menu, so you can dine while you listen.
✉ 14 Bedford Row, Christchurch ☎ 03-377 8618 🕒 Mon–Sat 5–late, Sun 10.30–1.30, 5–late

**SCIENCE ALIVE!**
www.sciencealive.co.nz
The whole family can be entertained while learning about science through hands-on experiences and shows in this interactive exhibit. There is also a well-stocked science shop.
✉ 392 Moorhouse Avenue, Christchurch ☎ 03-365 5199 🕒 Daily 10–5 ✋ Adult NZ$14, child (5–16) NZ$10 🎁

**SOUTHERN BLUES BAR**
www.bluesbar.org
Smooth blues is the daily diet for this small but friendly bar, with just enough room to shimmy and shake if the sounds move your soul.
✉ 198 Madras Street, Christchurch ☎ 03-365 1654 🕒 Daily 7pm–late

**SWANNDRI CONCEPT STORE**
www.swanniestore.com
Best known for its famous bush shirts of checked wool—much loved by hunters, farmers and trampers needing rugged protection from the elements—Swanndri also produces a range of more fashion-conscious lightweight merino garments for men, women and children.
✉ 123 Gloucester Street, Christchurch ☎ 03-379 8674 🕒 Mon–Fri 9–5.30, Sat 10–5

**TASTE CANTERBURY**
www.goodthings.co.nz
Tailor-made food and wine tours take you to meet the makers, see them at work, and taste their wares. Half-day and full-day tours explore Christchurch city and plains, Akaroa and Banks Peninsula, West Melton, Ellesmere and Waipara.
✉ 3 Scarborough Road, Christchurch ☎ 03-326 6753 ✋ From NZ$100

**TRANZALPINE HIGH COUNTRY EXPLORER TOUR**
www.high-country.co.nz
Enjoy a variety of Canterbury attractions on this tour, with a coach trip across the Canterbury Plains, morning tea, a jet-boat trip, a four-wheel-drive safari, lunch and then a scenic rail trip back to Christchurch from Arthur's Pass on the TranzAlpine train.
✉ 6 Fraser Place, Rangiora (north of Christchurch) ☎ 03-377 1391 ✋ Adult NZ$340, child (4–14) half price

**TRANZALPINE RAILWAY**
www.tranzscenic.co.nz
This 4.5-hour rail trip from Christchurch to Greymouth takes in spectacular mountain, farm and rainforest scenery, including areas not seen from the road, such as the Waimakariri Gorge. An open-air viewing deck adds to the experience, and there is a buffet car. You can do the return trip in a day.
✉ Christchurch Railway Station, Troup Drive, Addington ☎ 0800 872467 🕒 Daily 8.15am ✋ Adult day return NZ$152, child (2–14 NZ$85

**THE TWISTED HOP**
http://thetwistedhop.co.nz
The Twisted Hop brews its own English-style cask-conditioned Golding, Challenger and Twisted Ankle ales year-round, and India Pale Ale in summer. There's a quiz night every other Sunday, and live jazz on Wednesday and Thursday.
✉ 6 Poplar Street, Lichfield Lanes, Christchurch ☎ 03-962 3688 🕒 Daily noon–late

**UNTOUCHED WORLD**
www.untouchedworld.com
Located not far from the airport, Untouched World is a stylish modern store specializing in high-quality New Zealand lifestyle products, including its own-label merino-opossum blend knitwear, leisure and fashion clothing, skincare, art and food. A courtesy bus is available.
✉ 155 Roydvale Avenue, Christchurch ☎ 03-357 9399 🕒 Mon–Fri 8–5, Sat, Sun 9–5 🍴 Restaurant and wine bar

**UP UP AND AWAY**
www.ballooning.co.nz
Early-morning balloon flights over the Canterbury plains give spectacular views of the Southern Alps. You can help with preparations

for take-off and, after landing, celebrate with a glass of bubbly. ✉ PO Box 36-308, Merivale, Christchurch ☎ 03-381 4600 Adult NZ$290, child (5–11) NZ$250

## FOX GLACIER

### ALPINE GUIDES

www.foxguides.co.nz

Trips leave throughout the day to suit various fitness levels, from a gentle walk to the glacier terminal or a half-day hike on the lower reaches of the glacier to heli-hikes, ice climbing or multi-day mountaineering. Ice-climbing instruction days are a speciality. Some equipment is provided, including crampons. ✉ Main Road, Fox Glacier ☎ 03-751 0825 Adult from NZ$85, child NZ$49

## FRANZ JOSEF

### AIR SAFARIS

www.airsafaris.co.nz

A 30-minute scenic flight gives overviews of the Franz Josef and Fox glaciers, rainforest and Westland Tai Poutini National Park. The popular 50-minute Grand Traverse also takes in the Southern Alps, Aoraki/Mount Cook and the Tasman and Murchison glaciers. ✉ Main Road, Franz Josef ☎ 03-752 0716 Adult from NZ$280, child NZ$195

### FRANZ JOSEF GLACIER GUIDES

www.franzjosefglacier.com

A choice of trips is available, ranging from an easy 2km (1.2-mile) walk to the glacier terminal or a half-day hike on pre-cut steps, to a full-day climb on spectacular icefalls and overnight trips staying in alpine huts. Popular heli-hikes combine a scenic flight with a two-hour guided trip around the ice pinnacles of the middle glacier. Some equipment is provided, including crampons. Minimum ages and numbers apply. ✉ Main Road, Franz Josef ☎ 03-752 0763 Adult from NZ$60, child (6–16) NZ$45

## GERALDINE

### BARKER'S BERRY BARN

www.barkers.co.nz

Barker's fruit processors make juices, jams, toppings, spiced fruit sauces and condiments from local and Central Otago fruit. You can taste before you buy at this retail outlet, which also sells gift baskets, fruit smoothies and sundaes. ✉ Te Moana Road, Geraldine ☎ 03-693 8969 Daily 9–5.30

### TALBOT FOREST CHEESE

A remarkable range of cheeses is produced at this little factory in the heart of Geraldine's shopping complex. You can watch stages in the cheese production process and sample the cheeses at the attached retail outlet, which also sells a variety of food-related gift items. ✉ 16 Talbot Street, Geraldine ☎ 03-693 1111 Daily 9–5.30

## GREYMOUTH

### ECO-RAFTING

www.ecorafting.co.nz

Relaxing river excursions, fly-fishing trips and extreme whitewater adventures are offered in half-day to multi-day trips on the Arnold, Grey and Buller rivers. ✉ 108 Mawhera Quay, Greymouth ☎ 0580 669 675 From NZ$100

### MONTEITH'S BREWING COMPANY

www.monteiths.co.nz

The Monteiths name has been associated with brewing on the West Coast since the 1850s, and this is the only brewery in New Zealand where the beer is made in open fermenters by coal-fired boilers. Tours fill you in on the history, show the brewing process, explain the different beer styles and include a formal tasting. Advance booking is essential. ✉ Corner of Turumaha and Herbert streets, Greymouth ☎ 03-768 4149 Tours Mon–Fri 10, 11.30, 2, Sat, Sun 11.30, 2 NZ$10

## HANMER SPRINGS

### HANMER FOREST CONSERVATION PARK

www.doc.govt.nz

Some of New Zealand's oldest exotic forest can be accessed in self-guided walks, ranging from easy trails taking less than an hour to hill climbs taking between one and five hours. Trail maps of the park are available from the park's visitor information office. ✉ Hanmer Springs ☎ 03-315 7128

### HANMER SPRINGS ADVENTURE CENTRE

www.hanmeradventure.co.nz

You can rent mountain bikes of all kinds from this store, as well as in-line skates, motorized scooters, skis and snowboards, and fishing rods—with local fishing information and licences. Transport to the Hanmer Springs Ski Area is also available. The shop sells outdoor clothing, swimwear, camping, fishing, mountain biking and ski gear. Quad-bike trips are available (minimum age 12), plus rental of mountain bikes (one hour NZ$14, full day NZ$28), scooters, motorbikes, ATVs, fishing tackle and ski equipment. ✉ 20 Conical Hill Road, Hanmer Springs ☎ 0800 3687 386 Daily 8.30–5.30 Mountain bike hire from NZ$19

### THRILLSEEKERS CANYON ADVENTURE CENTRE

www.thrillseekerscanyon.co.nz

Bungy jumping off the 135-year-old Waiau Ferry Bridge, jet-boat rides and rafting are organized on this spectacular stretch of the Waiau River gorge near the Hanmer turn-off from SH7. You can recover from your exertions at your leisure at the on-site café. ✉ Waiau Ferry Bridge, Main Road, Hanmer Springs ☎ 03-315 7046 Adult from NZ$85, child NZ$50 9km (6 miles) south of Hanmer

## HAWARDEN

### ALPINE HORSE SAFARIS

www.alpinehorse.co.nz

Lawrie and Jenny O'Carroll are best known for their high-country trail rides lasting up to 11 days. They also offer two-hour and half-day treks, and the opportunity to take part in farm life by joining a sheep or cattle round-up. ✉ Waitohi Downs, Hawarden ☎ 03-314 4293 From NZ$50

## HOKITIKA

### JUST JADE EXPERIENCE

www.jadeexperience.co.nz

Gordon Wells combines jade carving with a backpacker's stop in Hokitika. Spend a day learning how to carve and polish greenstone, then create a piece of your own.

✉ 197 Revell Street, Hokitika ☎ 03-755 7612 ✋ From NZ$20

### NATIONAL KIWI CENTRE

This is a kiwi house and indoor marine aquarium on the outskirts of Hokitika, which displays sea life unique to the West Coast. Watch sharks being fed by divers, as well as giant eels, crayfish, seahorses and octopuses. You can also catch a salmon in the lake and have it cooked in the restaurant.

✉ Sewell Street, Hokitika ☎ 03-755 5251 ⏲ Daily 9–5 ✋ Adult NZ$12, child NZ$6, family NZ$30

### SCENIC WATERWAYS PADDLE BOAT CRUISES

www.paddleboatcruises.com

*Takutai Belle*, a stern-drive paddleboat, takes trips through rainforest along the Mahinapua Creek as far as Lake Mahinapua, on the old Gold Trail Waterway route. Tours can be arranged to suit—ask to make a refreshment stop at the Mahinapua pub, an authentic West Coast tavern.

✉ Main South Road, Hokitika ☎ 03-755 7239 ⏲ Dec–end Apr daily 2pm ✋ Adult NZ$30, child NZ$15

## LAKE TEKAPO

### EARTH AND SKY

www.earthandsky.co.nz

Day and evening tours run to Mount John Observatory.

✉ PO Box 112, Lake Tekapo ☎ 03-670 6960 ⏲ Daily 11–3. Also 10pm in summer and 8pm in winter ✋ Adult from NZ$15, child NZ$5

### LAKE TEKAPO ADVENTURES AND CRUISES

www.laketekapo.co.nz

An attractive combination tour includes a cruise around Motuariki Island on Lake Tekapo with optional fishing plus a 4X4 trip up Mount John, giving spectacular views over the Mackenzie Basin and Southern Alps. Another option is a day's fly fishing with lessons and lunch.

✉ PO Box 129, Lake Tekapo ☎ 03-680 6629 ✋ Combination NZ$120 with fishing, NZ$70 without; fly fishing NZ$600, for up to 3 people

### MOUNT COOK ALPINE SALMON

www.mtcooksalmon.com

At 677m (2,221ft) above sea level, with a stunning view of the mountain after which it is named, Mount Cook Alpine Salmon is reckoned to be the highest salmon farm in the world. The farm makes use of the hydro canal, growing 70,000 salmon in cages. You can take a self-guided tour and feed the fish, catch your own fish (rod supplied), or buy one at the shop and barbecue it on the spot.

✉ Tekapo-Pukaki Canal Road, Lake Tekapo ☎ 03-435 0085 ⏲ Daily, daylight hours ✋ Tour: 2 adults NZ$5, child free 🚗 From SH8, take Hayman Road at Lake Pukaki, or the Heritage Trail at Irishman Creek

## LITTLE RIVER

### LITTLE RIVER GALLERY

www.littlerivergallery.com

A popular stop halfway between Christchurch and Akaroa, this gallery shows the work of local artists in sculpture, painting and jewellery. The adjacent café and general store sells excellent country food.

✉ Main Road, Little River, Banks Peninsula ☎ 03-325 1944 ⏲ Daily 9.30–5.30

## LYTTELTON

### SEA CRUISES

www.sea-cruises.co.nz

Combine city sightseeing with dolphin-watching on the Scenic Lyttelton Tour, which includes pick-up, a scenic coach tour and dolphin cruise. Other cruises go to Ripapa and Quail islands.

✉ B Jetty, Lyttelton ☎ 03-328 7720 ⏲ Daily ✋ Adult NZ$50, child (5–15) NZ$17.50, family NZ$117.50

## METHVEN

### BLACK DIAMOND SAFARIS

www.blackdiamondsafaris.co.nz

These skiing enthusiasts take people to Canterbury's club fields for a special New Zealand skiing or boarding experience on ungroomed slopes, with rope tows and no tow queues. Tours include one-day and multi-day trips. Safety equipment is included.

✉ PO Box 60, Methven ☎ 0274-508 283 ✋ From NZ$150

### MOUNT HUTT SKI AREA

www.nzski.com

Canterbury's largest commercial ski area, Mount Hutt has nine lifts and a vertical drop of 675m (2,214ft), with snowmaking equipment, and slopes suitable for everyone from beginners to advanced skiers. It has a ski shop, gear for rent, and a restaurant.

✉ Mount Hutt, Methven ☎ 03-302 8811 ⏲ Jun–end Oct ✋ Adult from NZ$87, child NZ$47

**Below** *Barker's Berry Barn in Geraldine sells the produce of Barker's, processors of fruit from the Central Otago area*

**Above** *A whitewater rafting tour of the breathtaking Buller Gorge*

## MOUNT COOK

### ALPINE GUIDES

www.alpineguides.co.nz

The only resident guiding company in the national park, Alpine Guides can take you on anything from half- and full-day walks to full-scale mountaineering trips and heli-skiing on the Tasman Glacier.

✉ Bowen Drive, Mount Cook ☎ 03-435 1834 💰 From NZ$130, child NZ$60

### HELICOPTER LINE

www.helicopter.co.nz

Three flights are offered in the park: a 20-minute trip landing on either Fox or Franz Josef glaciers, a 30-minute trip to the Richardson Glacier, and a 45-minute Mountains High adventure which takes you over the Tasman Glacier, makes a snow landing and flies over Main Divide and Franz Josef and Fox glaciers.

☎ 03-435 1801 💰 From NZ$185

## OKARITO

### OKARITO NATURE TOURS

www.okarito.co.nz

Kayaking is a good way to explore Okarito Lagoon, New Zealand's largest unmodified wetland (3,240ha/8,000 acres). It's the main feeding ground for kotuku (white herons), and visited by more than 70 other bird species.

✉ PO Box 89, Franz Josef ☎ 03-753 4014 💰 From NZ$35

## PUKEKURA

### PUKEKURA BUSHMAN'S CENTRE LODGE

www.pukekura.co.nz

While staying in this tiny settlement, you can browse in the museum, try gold panning, or fish in a Canadian canoe, then revive yourself with a plate of possum pie at the Puke Pub and soak in the hot pools before retiring to the Lodge.

✉ Pukekura, Lake Ianthe, South Westland ☎ 03-755 4144 🕐 Daily

## STAVELEY

### TUSSOCK AND BEECH ECOTOURS

www.nature.net.nz

The 'In the Hobbits' Footsteps' tour includes a visit to Mount Sunday, site of Edoras in *The Lord of the Rings: The Two Towers*. The trip includes lodging in a heritage-registered cottage, meals, a tour through the spectacular glaciated landscape, a beech forest walk along a mountain stream, and lunch beside a lake. You can also join nature tours.

✉ Staveley, RD1, Ashburton ☎ 03-303 0880 💰 From NZ$305

## WAIPARA

### ATHENA OLIVE GROVES AND MILL HOUSE

www.athenaolives.co.nz

Producers of Canterbury's first olive oil, Athena presses its olives on a traditional Tuscan press within hours of picking them, producing extra virgin olive oil of high quality. You can watch the process in season or see a video, and taste the olive products in the shop.

✉ 164 Mackenzies Road, Waipara ☎ 03-314 6774 🕐 Daily 9–4

### THE MUD HOUSE WINERY AND CAFÉ

Separated from the ocean by the Teviotdale Hills, the 20-plus wineries located in the Y-shaped Waipara Valley produce some fine Pinot noirs and Rieslings in particular. This statuesque winery offers a fine introduction and window on the world of Waipara wineries.

✉ 780 Glasnevin Road, Waipara ☎ 03-314 6900 🕐 Daily 9–4

## WESTPORT

### BULLER ADVENTURES

www.adventuretours.co.nz

You can choose from several adventures in and around the spectacular Buller Gorge, with rafting graded from family to whitewater and heli-rafting, as well as jet-boating, horse-trekking and eight-wheel-drive Argo tours.

✉ Buller Gorge Road, Westport ☎ 03-789 7286 💰 From NZ$75, child NZ$65

# FESTIVALS AND EVENTS

## JANUARY–FEBRUARY

### WORLD BUSKERS FESTIVAL

www.worldbuskersfestival.com

Street performers from around the world converge on Christchurch for 10 days in the summer. They come in many forms—acrobats, comedians, contortionists, escapologists, fire-eaters, jugglers, 'living statues', magicians, mime artists, sword swallowers and street artists. Performances are generally free.

✉ PO Box 845, Christchurch
☎ 03-377 2365

## FEBRUARY

### CANTERBURY WINE AND FOOD FESTIVAL

Around 40 local wine producers, food producers and restaurants set up stalls under the trees in Hagley Park, and families gather on the grass to listen to live music.

✉ North Hagley Park, Christchurch
☎ 03-343 5953

## MARCH

### ELLERSLIE INTERNATIONAL FLOWER SHOW

New Zealand's premier gardening event brings a crowd of thousands to Christchurch's Hagley Park to see the latest in plants, colours, implements and garden designs. Sustainable gardening is a focus of the five-day event, which also showcases some of New Zealand's striking endemic plants.

✉ Hagley Park, Christchurch
☎ 03-379 4581

### HOKITIKA WILDFOODS FESTIVAL

www.wildfoods.co.nz

Hokitika has become famous for its annual Wildfoods Festival, on the second weekend of March, which attracts 18,000 visitors eager to sample 'bushtucker' such as huhu grubs, worms, grasshoppers, eels, mussels, snails, and the famous West Coast whitebait, washed down with local beer. There's a dance in the evening. Reserve accommodation well in advance.

✉ Cass Square, Hokitika ☎ 03-756 9048 ⏲ 11–5 💰 Adult NZ$30, child (5–18) NZ$5

### WAIPARA WINE AND FOOD CELEBRATION

Started as a European-style church and community celebration of grape-gathering and wine-making, the Waipara festival remains an appealingly small community event, which includes organ concerts in the church, and food and wine stalls and music outdoors.

✉ Glenmark Church, Waipara ☎ 03-314 6088 💰 NZ$25

## JULY–AUGUST

### CHRISTCHURCH ARTS FESTIVAL

www.artsfestival.co.nz

This two-week biennial winter festival is held in odd years, with live performances including opera, classical music, jazz, cabaret, drama and dance.

✉ PO Box 705, Christchurch
☎ 03-365 2223

## OCTOBER

### HERITAGE WEEK

www.heritageweek.co.nz

Plenty of heritage-related activities in the Christchurch area, including events, tours, quizzes and fairs.

☎ 03-941 8688

### REEFTON WILD WEST HUNT

The quality and variety of local wild foods are celebrated in this weekend hunt for the heaviest deer, pig and trout. There's a special section for children, too.

✉ Visitor Centre, 67 Broadway, Reefton
☎ 03-732 8391

## NOVEMBER

### CANTERBURY A&P SHOW

www.theshow.co.nz

The country comes to town in New Zealand's largest agricultural and pastoral show, attended by more than 100,000 people each year. In addition to livestock competitions, showjumping, dressage, dog trials and wood-chopping, there are 350 trade exhibitors and a Canterbury food pavilion. Look for local 'A&P' shows all over the country, too.

✉ Canterbury Agricultural Park, Christchurch ☎ 03-343 3033

### TIMARU FESTIVAL OF ROSES

www.festivalofroses.co.nz

The largest annual community event in the central South Island, this three-day festival attracts around 15,000 gardening enthusiasts and others with seminars, workshops, displays, competitions, shows, demonstrations, tours and 150 stalls and exhibits from across New Zealand. There is also a range of children's activities.

✉ Caroline Bay, Timaru
☎ 03-688 5531

## DECEMBER

### WAIMATE STRAWBERRY FARE

Waimate celebrates its berryfruit-growing tradition on the first or second Saturday in December—timed to coincide with the peak of the strawberry season. The festival is a mix of stalls, strawberry-picking competitions, free all-day family entertainment—and of course, lots of strawberries and ice cream.

✉ Seddon Square, Waimate
☎ 03-689 7771

## DECEMBER–MARCH

### SUMMERTIMES

www.summertimes.org.nz

Organized annually by the City Council, this festival of free outdoor entertainment includes musical, sporting, children's and community events, including the Classical Sparks orchestral concert with fireworks. The festival takes place for two months some time between December and March.

✉ Christchurch City Council Leisure
☎ 03-941 8999

# EATING

**Above** *The Bay House Café Restaurant Gallery in Westport*

**PRICES AND SYMBOLS**

The restaurants are listed alphabetically. The prices given are the average for a two-course lunch (L) and a three-course dinner (D) for one person, without drinks. The wine price (W) is for the least expensive bottle. All the restaurants listed accept credit cards unless otherwise stated.

For a key to the symbols, ▷ 2.

## AKAROA

### HARBOUR 71

Harbour 71 has great views over the water, and is set in a waterfront building. Pizzas are the daytime speciality. The evening menu turns Pacific Rim, serving dishes such as mussels infused with coconut, lime and coriander.

✉ 71 Beach Road, Akaroa ☎ 03-304 7656 🕐 Daily 10–late 💳 L NZ$30, D NZ$60, W NZ$32

## CHRISTCHURCH

### ANNIE'S WINE BAR AND RESTAURANT

www.annieswinebar.co.nz

Annie's, in the heart of the Arts Centre, has outdoor dining in the cloisters or indoors where the furniture is recycled wood. The atmosphere is casual, with a menu of modern New Zealand food. The platter of breads and spreads is popular. Annie's is well known for its wine list, and knowledgeable staff. Reservations are recommended.

✉ Arts Centre, Christchurch ☎ 03-365 0566 🕐 Daily 11–late 💳 L NZ$25, D NZ$60, W NZ$30

### COOK'N' WITH GAS

www.cooknwithgas.co.nz

A quirky restaurant opposite the Arts Centre, Cook'n' with Gas has a garden courtyard. The restaurant concentrates on New Zealand cuisine, serving, for example, Canterbury duck, local grilled venison, beef and Canterbury lamb. They have local beers.

✉ 23 Worcester Boulevard, Christchurch ☎ 03-377 9166 🕐 Mon–Sat 6pm–late 💳 D NZ$60, W NZ$35

### HAY'S

www.foodandwine.co.nz

Located opposite the Casino, this restaurant specializes in lamb grown on the Hay family's farm. The menu is modern New Zealand, with dishes such as lamb rack with Dijon mustard, parsley and tarragon crust, redcurrant and red wine jus and dauphinoise potatoes.

✉ 63 Victoria Street, Christchurch ☎ 03-379 7501 🕐 Nov to mid-Apr daily from 5pm; mid-Apr to end Oct Tue–Sat from 5pm 💳 D NZ$65, W NZ$42

### OXFORD ON AVON

www.oxfordonavon.co.nz

This popular carvery and buffet operates on two floors, with a courtyard overlooking the Avon River. The Old English Breakfast (NZ$15) is available until 11am, when the queues form for the set-price carvery lunch and buffet of European, Asian and Indian dishes. Children under 12 are charged NZ$1 for each year of their age.

✉ 794 Colombo Street, Christchurch ☎ 03-379 7148 🕐 Daily 6.30am–10.30pm 💳 L NZ$19, D NZ$25, W NZ$23

### PESCATORE

www.thegeorge.com

The George Hotel's classy restaurant triumphs in seafood. The style is Pacific Rim executed in exquisitely presented dishes, either à la carte or in *degustation* menus showcasing regional specialities matched with local wines. Typical dishes include

big eye tuna with red onion confit, kumara and ginger dauphinoise. Fang au Chocolat is the signature dessert.
✉ The George Hotel, 50 Park Terrace, Christchurch ☎ 03-371 0257 ⏲ Oct–end Apr daily from 6pm; May–end Sep Thu–Sun from 6pm ✋ D NZ$77, W NZ$45

## DUNSANDEL

### DUNSANDEL STORE

On the main road south of Christchurch, the Dunsandel Store is an appealing combination of rustic café, deli, country store and shop selling local produce. There's a pretty courtyard planted with herbs, and the food is fresh and interesting. Typical dishes include old-fashioned pork pie, and rabbit and prune terrine. Apples feature strongly, as the owner makes juices and cider.
✉ Main South Road, Dunsandel
☎ 03-325 4039 ⏲ Daily 7am–8pm
✋ L NZ$20, D NZ$35, W NZ$29

## FAIRLIE

### THE OLD LIBRARY CAFÉ

The Old Library Café has made the small town of Fairlie a must-stop for visitors on the road to Mount Cook/Aoraki and the Southern Lakes. The 1912 building has been converted into a sophisticated restaurant and friendly café, retaining the character of the building. Local Mackenzie Country lamb and beef are specialities.
✉ 7 Allandale Road, Fairlie ☎ 03-685 8999 ⏲ Daily 10am–late ✋ L NZ$27, D NZ$51, W NZ$20

## FOX GLACIER

### CAFÉ NEVÉ

Café Nevé is small and friendly. You can have breakfast, lunch or an evening meal. Pizzas are served from 11am in various sizes, to eat in or take away, or choose from West Coast treats such as whitebait, venison, salmon and fresh seafood. Espresso coffee is the speciality; hot chocolate and herbal teas are available too.
✉ Main Road, Fox Glacier ☎ 03-751 0110 ⏲ Daily 8am–late ✋ L NZ$20, D NZ$45, W NZ$25

## FRANZ JOSEF

### BLUE ICE CAFÉ

Downstairs an à la carte restaurant serves local specialities such as whitebait patties and venison. Upstairs is a bar—the late-night party venue with regular DJs.
✉ Main Road (SH6), Franz Josef
☎ 03-752 0707 ⏲ Oct–end Apr daily 2–10; May–end Sep daily 4–10
✋ D NZ$45, W NZ$29

## GREYMOUTH

### THE SMELTING HOUSE CAFÉ

In a former bank building, this café is run by a dietitian, who cooks home-style food and serves good coffee. Enjoy a full Farmer's Breakfast, and lunch dishes such as pasta.
✉ 102 Mackay Street, Greymouth
☎ 03-768 0012 ⏲ Daily 8.30–4.30
✋ L NZ$19, W NZ$26

## HANMER SPRINGS

### THE OLD POST OFFICE

This country restaurant has flowery décor, lush drapes, deep-pastel walls and heavy linen. The menu is strong on beef, lamb and game, and portions are generous.
✉ 2 Jacks Pass Road, Hanmer Springs
☎ 03-315 7461 ⏲ Daily 6–9pm
✋ D NZ$60, W NZ$32

## HOKITIKA

### CAFÉ DE PARIS

French cuisine with a Kiwi accent features in the menu here. An airy café during the day, it serves coffee, pastries and lunches. In the evening enjoy classics like French onion soup and profiteroles, or wild boar baked in pastry with mushrooms and wine.
✉ 19 Tancred Street, Hokitika ☎ 03-755 8933 ⏲ Daily from 7.30am ✋ L NZ$20, D NZ$40

## METHVEN

### STEEL-WORX RESTAURANT AND BAR

www.steel-worx.co.nz
Steel is the principal material used in this 1910 building. It's popular in the ski season, when the bar hosts party nights. The restaurant is warmed by a log-burning stove and serves après-ski dishes.
✉ 36 Forest Drive, Methven ☎ 03-302 9900 ⏲ May–end Nov daily 5pm–late
✋ D NZ$50, W NZ$30

## MOUNT COOK VILLAGE

### OLD MOUNTAINEERS' CAFÉ AND BAR

www.mtcook.com
The Old Mountaineer has a casual atmosphere, great views, an open fire and a wide-ranging menu. You can have breakfast until 12.30, then lunch on paninis or a selection of steaks, curries and pizzas.
✉ Mount Cook Village ☎ 03-435 1890
⏲ Nov–end Mar daily 9am–late; Apr–end Oct 11am–late ✋ L NZ$25, D NZ$43, W NZ$22

## OMARAMA

### CLAY CLIFFS ESTATE VINEYARD AND CAFÉ

www.claycliffs.co.nz
This Tuscan-style vineyard café overlooks a pond and vine-covered hills. The restaurant serves snacks, as well as substantial meals such as rack of lamb.
✉ Pinot Noir Court, Omarama ☎ 03-438 9654 ⏲ Jul–end May daily 11am–late
✋ L NZ$30, D NZ$60, W NZ$21

## WAIPARA

### PEGASUS BAY WINERY

www.pegasusbay.com
A grand vineyard restaurant in landscaped gardens, Pegasus Bay is a place for leisurely dining. The menu is seasonal and created around the wine list.
✉ Stockgrove Road, Waipara ☎ 03-314 6869 ⏲ Daily 12–4 ✋ L NZ$45, W NZ$37

## WESTPORT

### THE BAY HOUSE CAFÉ RESTAURANT GALLERY

www.bayhousecafe.co.nz
The waves roll into rugged Tauranga Bay by this café, where you can have excellent coffee, admire the art exhibitions and dine on Aotearoa fare. A typical dish is the Bay House Platter, which reflects seasonal West Coast produce.
✉ Tauranga Bay, Cape Foulwind
☎ 03-789 7133 ⏲ Daily 9am–late
✋ L NZ$30, D NZ$55, W NZ$32

# STAYING

**Above** *Rainforest Retreat, Franz Josef*

**PRICES AND SYMBOLS**

The prices are the lowest and highest for a double room for one night including breakfast, unless otherwise stated. All the hotels listed accept credit cards unless otherwise stated. Note that rates can vary widely throughout the year.

For a key to the symbols, ▷ 2.

## AKAROA

### WILDERNESS HOUSE

www.wildernesshouse.co.nz

This charming 1878 villa, on a quiet street is surrounded by gardens and a vineyard. Bedrooms are appointed with wool duvets, fresh flowers and New Zealand-made toiletries. A lounge has TV and complimentary refreshments. Dinner is available by arrangement. No children under 14.

✉ 42 rue Grehan, Akaroa ☎ 03-304 7517 NZ$260 4 rooms Rue Grehan is on the left as you enter Akaroa

## ARTHUR'S PASS

### THE TRANS ALPINE LODGE

www.arthurspass.com

Designed to look like a Swiss lodge, the Chalet combines alpine lodge accommodation with a European-influenced restaurant. Rooms are simply furnished, with en suite or shared bathrooms. There is an outdoor spa pool.

✉ Main Road, Arthur's Pass ☎ 03-318 9236 NZ$150 14 rooms (2 with shared bathroom)

## CHRISTCHURCH

### CROWNE PLAZA

www.crowneplaza.co.nz

A stylish building beside the Avon River, the Crowne Plaza has a choice of standard rooms and suites, with views over Victoria Square or the city and Alps. The hotel has a sports bar, a café, a highly regarded restaurant and authentic Japanese restaurant.

✉ Corner of Kilmore and Durham streets, Christchurch ☎ 03-365 7799/0800-154 181 NZ$185–NZ$735 298 rooms (177 non-smoking), 19 suites

### STONEHURST ACCOMMODATION

www.stonehurst.co.nz

Stonehurst—best known as a top-end backpackers'—now includes a motel annex with one- to three-bedroom units and apartments. These are well appointed, with fully equipped kitchens. The backpackers' also has single and double/twin rooms, some en suite.

✉ 241 Gloucester Street, Christchurch ☎ 03-379 4620 NZ$140–NZ$210 19 motel units, 9 apartments, 22 double/twin en suites Outdoor 1km (0.5 miles) from Cathedral Square

### SUMNER BAY MOTEL AND APARTMENTS

www.sumnermotel.co.nz

Every unit has a private balcony or courtyard, and two have spa baths. The motel is metres from Sumner Beach, with surfboards and bicycles available for hire.

✉ 26 Marriner Street, Sumner, Christchurch ☎ 03-326 5969, 0800 496 949 NZ$145–NZ$195 12 units

## FOX GLACIER

### TE WEHEKA INN

www.weheka.co.nz

Te Weheka Inn is a purpose-built, two-storey small hotel, four-star rated, with spacious bedrooms and a choice of en suite bath or shower. The lounge has a balcony, a small library and internet connection, and there is a laundry. Full or continental breakfast is included, and dinner is served during summer months.

✉ Main Road, Fox Glacier ☎ 03-751 0730 NZ$324–NZ$400 20 rooms Opposite Visitor Information Office

## FRANZ JOSEF

### RAINFOREST RETREAT

www.rainforestretreat.co.nz

Log cabins nestle among the trees in this quiet bush setting. Standard tree houses have bathrooms and heating. Tree lodges upgrade to a full kitchen. The complex also has motel units, a spa, sauna, internet access, bar, café and restaurant.

Cron Street, Franz Josef 03-752 0220 NZ$129–NZ$209 6 tree lodges, 2 tree houses, 9 tree hut motel units One block from shopping centre

## GREYMOUTH

### THE BREAKERS SEASIDE BED AND BREAKFAST

www.breakers.co.nz

Stunning ocean views and beach access add to the friendly welcome at this four-star lodge. The rooms, inspired by the traditional Kiwi bach (holiday home), have a large bedroom and lounge area, and a balcony. Dinner is available.

Nine Mile Creek, State Highway 6 03-762 7743 NZ$195–NZ$325 4 rooms 14km (8 miles) north of Greymouth

## HAAST

### MCGUIRES LODGE

www.mcguireslodge.co.nz

On a deer farm, the 19-unit complex comprises standard, studio and family rooms. There is also a spa pool, barbecue and laundry. The restaurant serves local specialities. Breakfasts are available.

State Highway 6, Haast Junction 03-750 0020/0800-624847 NZ$125–NZ$240 19 rooms 700m (760 yards) southeast of Haast River Bridge on SH6, by the DoC office at the Haast junction

## HOKITIKA

### SHINING STAR BEACHFRONT ACCOMMODATION

www.accommodationwestcoast.co.nz

This beachfront motel has log cabin lodging, studios and family chalets. Chalets have a kitchen and bathroom. Executive spa chalets have mezzanine floors, satellite TV, DVD and CD players. Breakfast (Continental) can be delivered.

11 Richards Drive, Hokitika 03-755 8921/0800-744 646 NZ$75–NZ$130 20 rooms Turn onto Richards Drive off SH6 at the northern end of town; 1km (0.5 miles) from downtown

## KARAMEA

### KARAMEA HOLIDAY PARK

www.karamea.com

This campground, beside an estuary and surrounded by native bush, has transport to the Heaphy and Wangapeka tracks.

Maori Point Road, Karamea 03-782 6758 Tent sites NZ$10, power sites NZ$22, cabins NZ$28–NZ$38, motel NZ$65–NZ$70, all excluding breakfast 70 tent sites, 32 power sites, 20 cabins, 3 motel units

### LAST RESORT

www.lastresort.co.nz

The Last Resort is an imaginatively designed complex with lodge-style blocks interconnected by a walkway, with a large bar/café and restaurant. Room service and internet access are available.

71 Waverley Street, Karamea 03-782 6617 NZ$69–NZ$140 Cottages, 13 studio en suites, 12 double lodge rooms (6 with en suite) Charter flights available from Karamea to Nelson and Takaka. Helicopter access On SH67

## LAKE TEKAPO

### LAKE TEKAPO LUXURY LODGE

www.laketekapolodge.co.nz

The four rooms here have super-king or queen/single beds with en suites, one with spa bath. Most have lake and mountain views. Bathrobes and slippers are provided. The lounge has an open fire, and internet access and satellite TV are available.

Aorangi Crescent, Lake Tekapo 03-680 6566/0800 LAKE TEKAPO NZ$250–NZ$430 4 rooms 1km (0.5 miles) from Tekapo village

## MOUNT COOK VILLAGE

### THE HERMITAGE

www.mount-cook.com

Spectacularly situated at the foot of the Alps, The Hermitage is one of New Zealand's most famous hotels, its isolation being part of the mystique. The complex includes hotel rooms, a luxury wing, self-contained motels and chalets. There is a shop, sauna, tennis courts and a choice of bars and restaurants, including a buffet and the fine-dining Panorama Room in summer.

Mount Cook Village 03-435 1635 Chalets closed May–end Sep NZ$128–NZ$530 221 rooms, 32 motels, 19 chalets 3km (2 miles) from Mount Cook airstrip 56km (35 miles) north of SH8

## PUNAKAIKI

### PUNAKAIKI ROCKS HOTEL AND VILLAS

www.punakaiki-resort.co.nz

Only 400m (435 yards) from the Pancake Rocks and Blowholes, the resort has studio units with private decks facing the ocean or eco, solar-powered rooms set farther back in bush. Rooms have cooking facilities, outdoor seating and satellite TV. The villas are linked by suspended boardwalks, and a walk-through underpass gives easy beach access.

State Highway 6, Punakaiki 03-731 1168/0800-786 2524 NZ$253–NZ$316 35 rooms 400m (435 yards) south of Paparoa National Park Visitor Information Office

## WAIPARA

### CLAREMONT COUNTRY ESTATE

www.claremont-estate.com

Claremont blends five-star accommodation in a heritage building on a sheep station with stunning scenery. The suites and rooms have spacious bathrooms and are furnished with antiques, but also have central heating, satellite TV and internet access. There is a tennis court, and a spa and sauna. Families are accommodated in a separate self-contained cottage. Note that Claremont Country Estate is closed from July to September.

828 Ram Paddock Road, Waipara Gorge 03-314 7559 NZ$430–NZ$928 5 suites, 1 cottage Private airstrip 55km (34 miles) north of Christchurch. Turn off SH1 at Georges Road opposite Waipara Hills Winery and follow the road for 12km (7 miles)

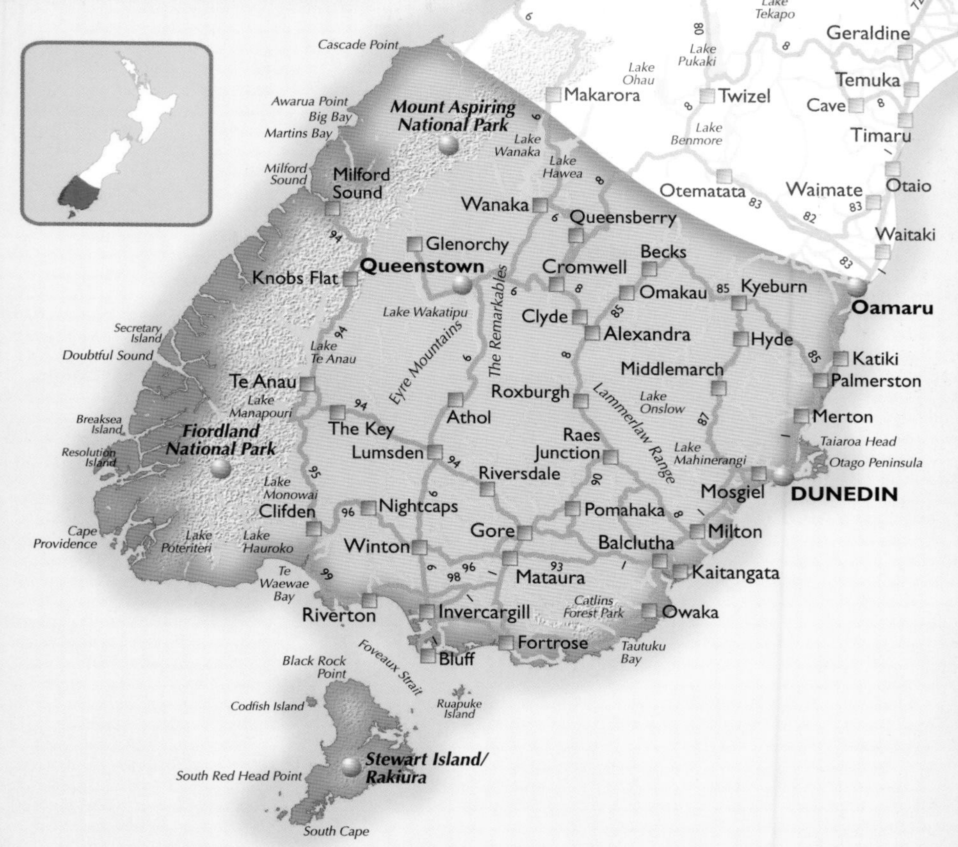


# OTAGO AND THE FAR SOUTH

This is a wild and majestic part of the country, home to some of its most flagrantly gorgeous scenery. Towering head and shoulders above every other facet of this region is Queenstown. Snuggled into the base of soaring peaks, clinging to the rim of its glacier-carved lake, it's only natural that Queenstown is New Zealand's adventure capital. Three of the country's best ski resorts are close at hand, several famous alpine hiking trails lace through the adjacent peaks and the town has become the launch pad for weird and wonderful adventure sports. The commercial sport of bungy jumping has its roots here, and its menu of extreme adventures includes giant swings, whitewater rafting with an inner tube, tandem parachuting, paragliding, hang-gliding and several variations on the bungy jump theme. It's a rich feast for the adrenal gland and despite the seeming death-defying nature of the action, the industry has an exceptional safety record.

Easily accessible from Queenstown, Fiordland includes the tattered coastline at the southwest corner of New Zealand, where glaciers have carved valleys between the mountain ranges that have been infiltrated by the sea. The most famous of all is Milford Sound, where cruise boats look like toys dwarfed by mountains and waterfalls that plunge from the clouds into the sea.

South Island's second largest city, Dunedin brings a handsome Victorian townscape to the western end of Otago Harbour. Dunedin flourished on the huge fortunes won during the Otago gold rush, and for a time it was considered the obvious choice for the country's capital. The city pays homage to its Scottish roots with a kilt shop, the country's only whisky distiller and an enormous statue of poet Robbie Burns at its heart. Dunedin also has a remarkable attraction in the albatross colony at Taiaroa Head, the only mainland breeding colony for this majestic bird.

## ARROWTOWN

www.arrowtown.org.nz

This is the best known of New Zealand's former gold-mining settlements, beautifully set beneath the foothills of the Crown mountain range, with pretty tree-lined streets and historic miners' cottages. The Lakes District Museum, on Buckingham Street (daily 9–4.30), depicts the area's chaotic and feverish gold-mining boom (1861–65), and even rents out gold pans for you to try your luck. At the far end of leafy Buckingham Street, reconstructed mud-walled huts illustrate the hardship suffered by Chinese miners.

306 C16 Lakes District Museum, 49 Buckingham Street 03-442 1824 Services from Queenstown

## BLUFF

The small port of Bluff heralds the end of the road in the South Island, and is dominated by its aluminium smelter—a jointly run New Zealand-Japanese project. Most visitors come here on their way to or from Stewart Island/ Rakiura (▷ 242), or to photograph the windblasted signpost at the terminus of SH1, which tells them they are several thousand miles from anywhere. En route to the signpost is the quirky Paua Shell House on Marine Parade (daily 9–5), which has become something of a New Zealand legend. Its former owners, Myrtle (who died in 2000) and Fred (who died in 2002) Flutey lined the interior walls with paua shells and amassed a huge collection of other shells.

306 C18 Services from Invercargill

## CATLINS COAST

www.southland.org.nz

The almost impenetrable coastal forests of the Catlins Coast were thought by the Maori to be the home of a race of hairy giants known as Maeroero. Timber-millers began their relentless destruction of the forest from the 1860s, but a few tracts of podocarp and silver woods have survived and this southeast tip, bordered by the Clutha and Mataura rivers, is still a wonderfully remote area with glorious scenery and rich flora and fauna.

Slope Point, the South Island's southernmost point, can be reached from a roadside parking area and has impressive views of the dramatic headlands. Beautiful Porpoise Bay is a superb place to try to spot Hector's dolphins. At Curio Bay, about 500m (545 yards) west, the petrified stumps of a fossilized forest more than 160 million years old scatter the rock platform.

Both Surat Bay, across the Owaka River 2km (1 mile) south of Owaka, the Catlins' largest town, and Cannibals Bay, north of Owaka, are good places to see Hookers sealions. About 3km (2 miles) east of Owaka is Tunnel Hill Scenic Reserve: the tunnel was dug in 1895 as part of the Catlins River branch railway line, which ran between Balclutha and Tahakopa and closed in 1971.

Just beyond the hill is the turn-off to Nugget Point, best visited at sunrise, when the spectacular rock pillars and outcrops take on an orange glow. The islets and rocky, inaccessible coastline are home to seals, yellow-eyed and blue penguins, sooty shearwaters and gannets.

306 C18 4 Clyde Street, Balclutha 03-418 0388 Services to Balclutha and Gore from Queenstown, Dunedin and Invercargill

## CLYDE

The pretty and historic village of Clyde, backed by Clyde Dam and Lake Dunstan (a reservoir), has several notable buildings dating from the 19th century. On Fraser Street, the Clyde Historical Museum and Briar Herb Factory (Dec–end Apr Tue–Sun 2–4), which began processing local thyme in the 1930s, now displays the original machinery and exhibits on early settler life. The Clyde Stationary Engine Museum, at the former railway station on Fraser Street (Sun 2–4), shows stationary steam engines.

306 C16 Services from Queenstown and Dunedin

## CROMWELL

www.cromwell.org.nz

A sculpture of giant pieces of fruit gives a clue to Cromwell's status as 'the fruit bowl of the south'. Its main point of interest is the Old Cromwell Town Precinct, at the end of Melmore Place, where many restored or reconstructed houses are open for viewing (daily 10–4.30). Former gold-mining sites in the area include the Goldfields Mining Centre, 6km (4 miles) west along SH6 (daily 9–5). It lets you explore historic gold workings, a Chinese settlers' village, gold stamper batteries and a sluice gun.

306 C16 47 The Mall 03-445 0212 Services from Queenstown, Christchurch and Invercargill

**Opposite** *The reservoir of Lake Dunstan generates hydroelectricity*

**Below** *The former postmaster's house in Arrowtown is now a top-notch B&B*

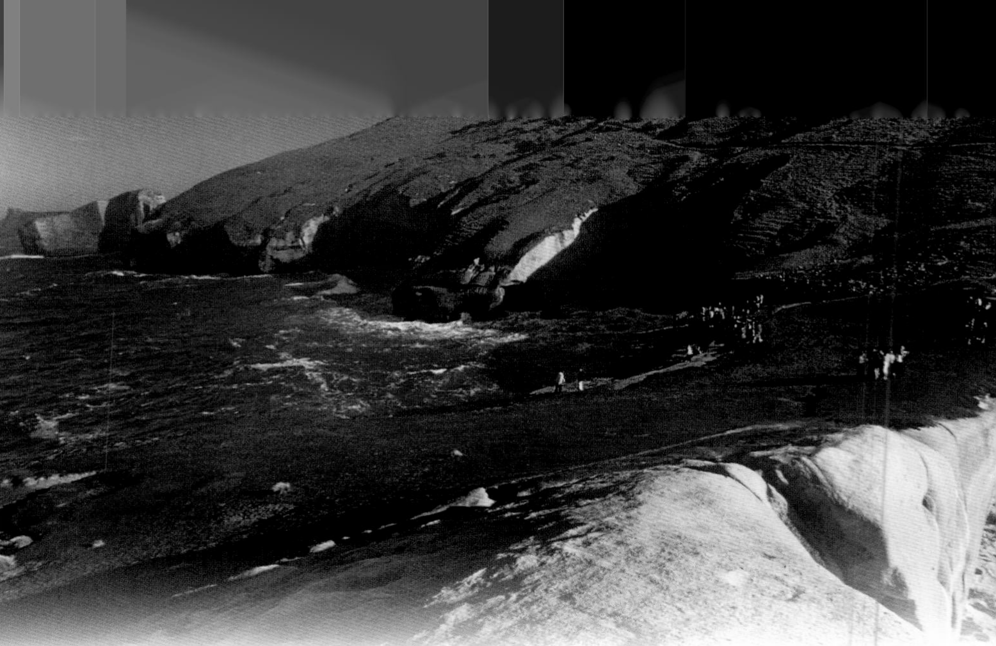

**INFORMATION**
www.dunedinnz.com
www.cityofdunedin.com
307 E17 48 The Octagon, below Municipal Chambers Building 03-474 3300 Mon–Fri 8–6, Sat, Sun 8.45–6 Services from Christchurch, Invercargill, Queenstown and Te Anau 27km (17 miles) south of city

**Above** *The extraordinary Tunnel Beach, southwest of St. Clair*

## INTRODUCTION

The influence of Scottish architecture is everywhere in this lively and attractive city: grand buildings of stone, built to last and to defy inclement weather. Its streets share the names of Edinburgh's most famous thoroughfares, and presiding over the scene is a statue of one of Scotland's greatest sons, the poet Robert Burns—his nephew Thomas (1796–1871) was one of the city's founding fathers. Princes Street and George Street combine to form the main downtown route, with the open square of the Octagon, surrounded by grand public buildings, at its heart. During term time, Dunedin's population is boosted by 18,000 students at New Zealand's oldest seat of learning, founded in 1869. Dunedin's beautiful backyard, the Otago Peninsula, is where the only mainland breeding colony of albatrosses thrives, along with rare yellow-eyed penguins and Hooker's sealions (⊳ 239).

The largest Maori *pa* in this area was on the Otago Peninsula. Following on the trail of the whalers and sealers, Dunedin's permanent settlement was begun in 1842 by Scot George Rennie, who planned a Presbyterian colony in a New Edinburgh of the South. With the discovery of gold the population exploded, growing by 500 per cent between 1861 and 1865. Dunedin was the largest city in New Zealand by the late 1860s—and its grandest buildings date from this period.

## WHAT TO SEE

### ARCHITECTURE

The 1906 railway station at the end of Lower Stuart Street is probably the most famous and most photographed building in the country, with stained-glass windows, Royal Doulton tiles, mosaics and brass fittings. The New Zealand Sports Hall of Fame, on the first floor (daily 10–4), celebrates the legacy of more than a century of New Zealand champions. Otago University's grand administration building and clock tower on Leith Street (modelled on Glasgow University) is another fine building. Dunedin's churches are worth more than a passing glance, particularly the Gothic First Church of Otago (1873), on Moray Place, and St. Paul's Cathedral (1915), in the Octagon, which contains the only stone-vaulted celing in the country.

### BOTANIC GARDEN

There are many New Zealand firsts in Dunedin, including the Botanic Garden, first laid out in 1914. The 28ha (69-acre) site is split into upper and lower gardens that straddle Signal Hill and specialize in rhododendrons, plants from Asia, the Americas and Australia, native species, and winter and wetland gardens. Access to the Lower Garden is via Cumberland Street; the Upper Garden via Lovelock Lane.

✉ Opoho Road ☎ 03-477 4000 ⌚ Daily dawn–dusk ✋ Free

### OLVESTON HOUSE

This Edwardian time capsule was built in 1906 and bequeathed to the city in 1966 by the last surviving member of the wealthy and much-travelled Theomin family. The Jacobean-style 35-room mansion had been left unaltered since the death of its first owner, David Theomin, in 1933, and its library, oak gallery and billiard room give a vivid glimpse of prosperous family life in the early 20th century. Contents include ceramics, carpets, arms, antiques, silverware and art acquired by the family during their travels in Asia and Europe.

✉ 42 Royal Terrace ☎ 03-477 3320 ⌚ Daily guided tours 9.30, 10.45, 12, 1.30, 2.45, 4 ✋ Adult NZ$15, child (school age) NZ$6 🚌 Moana Pool

### OTAGO MUSEUM

www.otagomuseum.govt.nz

Established in 1868, this museum is one of the oldest in the country, housing a staggering 1.7 million items. Its primary themes are culture, nature and science. The Southern Land–Southern People exhibit, the museum's centrepiece, is designed to reflect the beauty and diversity of southern New Zealand, and there is a hands-on Discovery World for children (fee payable).

✉ 419 Great King Street ☎ 03-474 7474 ⌚ Daily 10–5 ✋ Free; donation of NZ$5 suggested. Tours (daily 11.30) from NZ$10 🎁

### OTAGO SETTLERS MUSEUM

www.otago.settlers.museum/

The emphasis here is firmly on people and transport. Among the permanent exhibits are a couple of monstrous steam engines, and the temporary exhibitions cover unexpected topics such as Scotland's second national drink—tea. There is also an extensive archive.

✉ 31 Queens Gardens ☎ 03-477 5052 ⌚ Daily 10–5 ✋ Adult NZ$4, child (5–18) free 🎁

## MORE TO SEE

### CHURCHES

Dunedin's churches are worth a look, particularly the Gothic First Church of Otago (1873) on Moray Place, and St. Paul's Cathedral (1915) in The Octagon, which contains the only stone-vaulted ceiling in the country.

### DUNEDIN PUBLIC ART GALLERY

www.dunedin.art.museum

Traditional and contemporary art are shown in the country's oldest gallery, including an interesting collection of New Zealand works from 1860 to the present day.

✉ 30 The Octagon ☎ 03-474 4000 ⌚ Daily 10–5 ✋ Free

### TAIERI GORGE RAILWAY

The four-hour Taieri Gorge Railway journey encompasses the history and superb scenery of Otago's hinterland. Completed in 1891, the line negotiates the Taieri Gorge, with 12 viaducts, and leads to the Otago Central Rail Trail.

✉ Departs from train station, Anzac Avenue ☎ 03-477 4449 ⌚ Oct–end Apr daily 2.30, also Fri, Sun 9.30; rest of year daily 12.30 ✋ Adult from NZ$69

### TIPS

» Centennial Lookout and Lookout Point have grand views of the bay and city—reach them via Signal Hill Road, beyond Lovelock Avenue.

» Baldwin Street, off North Road, is said to be the world's steepest street, with a gradient of nearly 1 in 3—a 19-degree angle.

## INTRODUCTION

Fiordland National Park, in the remote southwest corner of South Island, covers 1.25 million ha (3,088,750 acres) and is the largest of New Zealand's 14 national parks. Even when this wettest part of the country is under heavy rain (more than 7,500mm/ 300 inches are recorded each year), Fiordland has a moody magnificence, with its high mountains, forested hills and deep inlets. Although the vast majority of the park remains inaccessible, there are more than 5,000km (3,100 miles) of walking tracks. The most accessible of the park's 14 fiords and one of the country's biggest visitor attractions is Milford Sound. For details of cruises on the sound ▷ 250. See also Lake Manapouri (▷ 236) and Te Anau (▷ 239).

Fiordland was gouged out by glaciers in the last Ice Age. Flora and fauna that once lived on the ancient supercontinent of Gondwana still thrive. In 1986 its role in evolutionary history, along with its outstanding natural features, earned the park the status of a World Heritage Area. In 1990 Fiordland and three other national parks—Mount Aspiring, Westland and Mount Cook/Aoraki—were linked to form the UNESCO World Heritage Area of Te Wahipounamu—South West New Zealand, its Maori name meaning place of greenstone.

## WHAT TO SEE

### DOUBTFUL SOUND

www.realjourneys.co.nz

Fiordland's mountain topography is generally lower the farther south you go, and its fiords become longer and more indented with coves, arms and islands. Captain Cook named this Doubtful Harbour in 1770, and did not explore beyond the entrance to the sound. It was not until 23 years later that Italian explorer Don Alessandro Malaspina, leading a Spanish expedition, sent a small crew into the fiord.

Doubtful Sound, though not as steep as Milford Sound, offers a sense of space and wilderness, and is the deepest of the fiords at 421m (1,381ft). It has three distinct arms and several superb waterfalls, including the 619m (2,031ft)

### INFORMATION

www.doc.govt.nz

306 A17–B16 · Lakefront Drive, Te Anau · 03-249 8900 · Daily 8.30–5.30 · DoC, Lakefront Drive · 03-249 0200 · Services from Queenstown and Te Anau to Milford Sound · Te Anau airfield between Te Anau and Manapouri; airfield in Milford

**Above** *A helicopter flight offers access into remote Doubtful Sound*

**Opposite** *Cruise boats make the remote sounds accessible to visitors*

**TIPS**

» About 30 tour buses regularly make the 12-hour journey to Milford Sound from Queenstown; most run daily in summer from 11am.

» Remember to take insect repellent: the sandflies at Milford are legendary.

Browne Falls. At the entrance to Hall Arm is an impressive 900m (2,953ft) cliff. Tours take in the dripping beech forests and a hydroelectric plant, and the sound has its own pod of about 60 bottlenose dolphins.

324 A16 Excursions by boat then bus from Pearl Harbour, Manapouri

## DUSKY TRACK

Remote Dusky Sound, at the very heart of Fiordland, is a true wilderness that has changed little since Captain Cook first set foot there. The Dusky Track offers the widest range of experiences of any track in Fiordland, from glacial valleys and densely forested mountains to the possibility of complete immersion in icy water. Both its location and grade of difficulty make it a challenge that should be attempted only by serious walkers and only in summer.

Shuttle services from Te Anau to Manapouri and Tuatapere Boat access to southern trailhead from Tuatapere and Manapouri Floatplane and helicopter services to Supper Cove and Lake Hauroko from Te Anau and Tuatapere

## HUMP RIDGE TRACK

Opened in late 2000 and privately owned, the Hump Ridge Track is a 60km (37-mile), three-day, moderate-grade circuit track at the southeastern end of Fiordland National Park, reached from the western end of Bluecliffs Beach. Its main attractions are a mix of coastal and podocarp and beech forest landscapes. It also takes in four viaducts, including the 125m (410ft) Percy Burn Viaduct, reputedly the largest wooden viaduct in the world. Wildlife to look for includes keas, bellbirds, fur seals and Hector's dolphins. Boardwalk is laid through the areas most subject to flooding, but always check on track conditions before departure.

Services to trailhead from Tuatapere

## KEPLER TRACK

This 60km (37-mile), three- to four-day tramp combines lake, mountain and river valley scenery. After skirting the edge of Lake Te Anau the track climbs to the Luxmore Hut, with one of the best views in Fiordland. From here it negotiates the open tops of the Luxmore Range before descending through silver beech and podocarp forest to the Iris Burn Valley, and back to civilization via Shallow Bay on Lake Manapouri. At night the forest sometimes echoes with the cries of kiwis.

Services to trailhead (Lake Te Anau outlet control gates) from Te Anau Boat services from Brod Bay

**Below** *The Fiordland National Park is noted for its rainfall—all the better for spectacular waterfalls*

## MILFORD SOUND

The approach to majestic Milford Sound is an exciting experience, with the mountains closing in on either side of Milford Road as you enter the Homer Tunnel, an amazing 1,200m (3,937ft) feat of engineering. You emerge in the spectacular Cleddau Canyon, where in heavy rain the water gushes from the steep outcrops in all directions, and where the Cleddau River has, over the millennia, sculpted round shapes and basins in the rock. Presently, Mitre Peak, at 1,683m (5,552ft), and Mount Tutoko, Fiordland's highest peak at 2,723m (8,934ft), are in view. Facing Mitre Peak is The Lion (1,302m/ 4,272ft), and behind it is Mount Pembroke (2,045m/6,709ft).

The fiord itself is 15km (9 miles) long and about 290m (951ft) at its deepest, and its mouth is only about 120m (394ft) wide. Cruises along the sound take about two hours. In heavy rains the whole sound can seem like one great waterfall, but by far the most impressive at any time or in any weather conditions are the powerful 160m (525ft) Lady Bowen Falls, a 10-minute walk from the cruiseboat terminal.

The Milford Deep Underwater Observatory (visits only as part of cruise packages or by prior arrangement, tel 0800-326969) opened in 1995 in the sheltered waters of Harrison Cove, about a third of the way out of the sound on its eastern edge. From its interpretive centre you descend 8m (26ft) into a circular viewing chamber, where you can see at close quarters the very rare black coral (which is actually white)—a species that can live for more than 300 years.

✚ 306 B15 ℹ Boat Terminal ☎ 03-249 8110

## MILFORD TRACK

www.doc.govt.nz

Often spoken of as the world's greatest walk, this four-day, 53km (33-mile) walk must be pre-booked (Apr–end Oct). Numbers are limited to no more than 100 people entering the track each day either as an independent or a guided walker, and everyone goes in the same direction from south to north to maintain the integrity of the environment. Highlights include the awesome vista from the top of the McKinnon Pass at 1,073m (3,520ft), the Sutherland Falls (New Zealand's highest at 580m/1,903ft), and walking through lush rainforest and beside Milford Sound at the end of the track.

It rains a lot here—more than 6m (235 inches) a year on average, and winter conditions can be treacherous. Always consult the Department of Conservation (tel 03-249 7924) before setting off. Reservations to walk the track are essential and should be made well in advance.

☎ Independent reservations: 03-249 8514. Guided walks: 03-441 1138/0800 659255
🚌 Services to Te Anau Downs from Te Anau ⛴ Boat services from Te Anau and Te Anau Downs to Glade House (south); from Te Anau and Milford Sound to Sandfly Point (north)
✈ Floatplane services from Te Anau

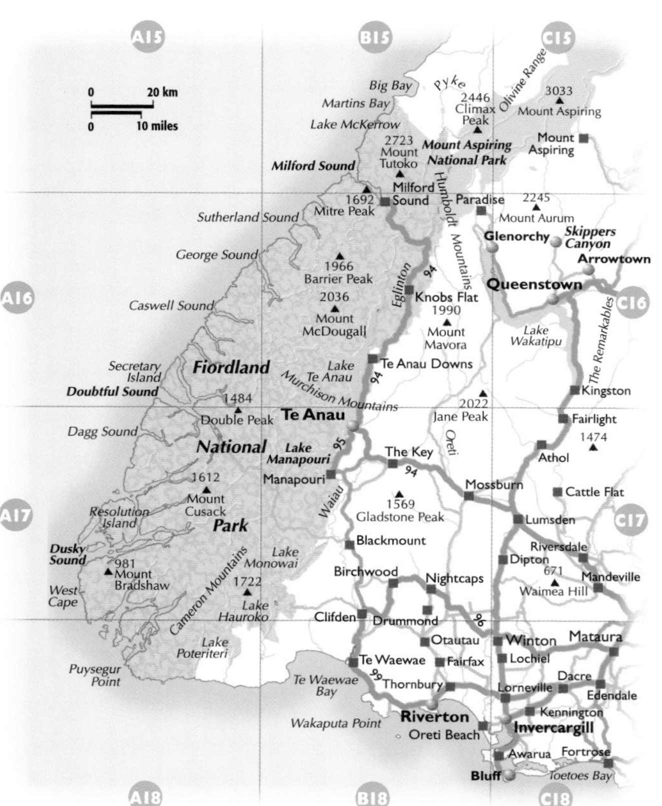

**Above** *Cruise boats make the most of day trips through the fiords*

**Below** *Admiring the view and the reflections at Mirror Lake*

## GLENORCHY

The tiny former frontier village of Glenorchy lies 48km (30 miles) northwest of Queenstown via the superb Lake Wakatipu scenic drive, and is surrounded by the rugged peaks of the Fiordland and Mount Aspiring national parks, the glacier-fed Rees and Dart rivers and ancient beech forests. A little settlement aptly named Paradise, 20km (12 miles) farther north in the Dart River valley, became a principal filming venue for the *Lord of the Rings* movies as Isengard. Activities in Glenorchy include jet-boating and horse-trekking, and the village is the main access point for the Routeburn, Greenstone/Caples and Rees-Dart walking tracks.

306 B16 DoC Visitor Centre, corner of Mill and Oban streets 03-442 9937 From Queenstown

## GORE

Gore, on the banks of the Mataura River, is the Southland region's second-largest town and is most famous for its unusual mix of trout-fishing, country music and its once illegal whiskey-distilling. Attractions include the Hokonui Moonshine Museum and the Gore Historical Museum (Oct–May Mon–Fri 8.30–4.30, Sat, Sun 9.30–3.30; Jun–Sep Mon–Fri 8.30–4.30, Sat, Sun 1–3.30), both in the Hokonui Heritage Centre and revealing Gore's days of prohibition and bootlegging. The Reservation (daily 10–5.30), at the top of Coutts Road, has a small menagerie including chinchillas and miniature horses.

306 C18 Corner of Hokonui Drive and Norfolk Street 03-203 9288 Services from Dunedin, Invercargill and Queenstown

## INVERCARGILL

www.visit.southlandnz.com

Though not much to look at and sandblasted by the worst extremes of the southern weather, Invercargill is the capital of the richest agricultural region in the South Island. Founded by Scots from Dunedin in 1856 on reclaimed swamp, it is the country's southernmost city, serving a wide farming district. Its main highlight is the Southland Museum and Art Gallery (Mon–Fri 9–5, Sat, Sun 10–5), housed in a large white pyramid on Victoria Avenue, which includes the excellent tuatara display and breeding project. This reptilian species, older than the land on which you stand, can be seen face-to-face in the Tuatarium; its oldest resident, Henry, is more than 120 years old. Beyond the museum is Queen's Park—80ha (198 acres) of trees, flowerbeds and duck ponds. For a fine view over the city head for the 1889 redbrick Water Tower (Sun 1.30–4.30) on the corner of Gala Street and Queen Drive. The 30km (19-mile) expanse of Oreti Beach lies 10km (6 miles) west of the city past the airport, and nearby Sandy Point, reached from Sandy Point Road, offers a range of short walks and other recreational activities.

306 C18 Gala Street 03-214 6243 Leven Street station 2km (1 mile) south of city; shuttles

## LAKE HAWEA

www.lakewanaka.co.nz

North of Wanaka on SH6 towards the west coast is Lake Hawea and the small resort settlement of Hawea. Lake Hawea—like nearby Lake Wanaka (▷ 239)—occupies an ancient glacial valley, and only a narrow strip of moraine known as the Neck separates the two. Lake Hawea is noted for its fishing and delightful scenery, with mountain reflections that disappear towards its remote upper reaches, 35km (22 miles) north of Hawea. The lake level was raised by 18m (59ft) in 1958 as part of the Clutha River hydropower system. Hawea itself nestles on the southern shore on the former site of an important and strategic Maori *pa*.

304 C15 100 Ardmore Street, Wanaka 03-443 1233 11km (7 miles) east of Wanaka

## LAKE MANAPOURI

Thirty-five islands disguise the boundaries of Lake Manapouri, which is a forbidding 420m (1,378ft) deep. To appreciate its size and complexity you have to get out on the water, which is on the route to Doubtful Sound. Hidden away on the west arm, right in the heart of Fiordland National Park (▷ 233–235), is the country's largest hydroelectric power station, the source of much controversy and around 10 per cent of the country's electricity. A 2,040m (6,693ft), 1:10 tunnel carved into the hillside allows access to the underground machine hall, where seven turbines and generators are fed by the water penstocks from 170m (558ft) above. The most impressive part is the 9.2m (30ft) diameter tailrace tunnel that expels used water at the head of Doubtful Sound, 10km (6 miles) away.

306 B17 Real Journeys, Pearl Harbour 03-249 7416 Services from Te Anau and Invercargill

## MOERAKI BOULDERS

According to Maori legend, these strange and much-photographed spherical boulders littering the beach at Moeraki, between Oamaru and Dunedin, are *te kai hinaki*, or food baskets and sweet potatoes, washed ashore after a shipwreck. The scientific explanation is that they are septarian concretions—massive rocks left behind from the eroded coastal cliffs. Their formation is described at the Moeraki Boulderpark Visitor Centre, in a building shaped like the boulders themselves, and in an interpretive panel at the parking area, where the path to the boulders starts.

Other, smaller boulders can be seen at Katiki Beach and Shag Point, beyond the village of Moeraki, 3km (2 miles) from the boulders. The village can be reached along the beach by foot or via SH1; it offers fishing, swimming, wildlife cruises (to see the rare Hector's dolphin) and pleasant coastal walks, as well as a historic lighthouse.

307 E16 Corner of Itchen and Thames streets, Oamaru 03-434 1656 Tours from Oamaru, Dunedin and Invercargill

## MOUNT ASPIRING NATIONAL PARK

New Zealand's third-largest national park has towering peaks, more than 100 glaciers and unique wildlife. Like most of New Zealand's majestic national parks, Mount Aspiring has an impressive list of vital statistics. Designated in 1964, the park has been extended to cover 355,000ha (877,205 acres), stretching for about 140km (87 miles) from the Haast Pass to the Humbolt Range at the head of Lake Wakatipu. At its widest point it is 40km (25 miles), and it contains five peaks over 2,600m (8,530ft), including Aspiring itself—at 3,027m (9,931ft) the highest outside the Mount Cook Range.

### AWESOME TERRAIN

Glaciers include the Bonar, the Therma and the Volta, and among the wildlife are the New Zealand falcon, the kea and the giant weta. The names associated with the area speak volumes about its terrain: Mount Awful, Mount Dreadful, Mount Chaos, The Valley of Darkness, Solitude Creek and Siberia River are just a few. Wanaka is the main base for trips into the park, and the small settlement of Makarora, about 67km (42 miles) away (almost on the border of the Otago and West Coast regions), acts as the portal to its northern trails and activities.

### WALKING IN THE PARK

Mount Aspiring National Park offers endless opportunities for walking and tramping. The 33km (20-mile) Routeburn Track crosses Mount Aspiring and Fiordland national parks between the head of Lake Wakatipu and SH94, the Te Anau–Milford Road.

The walk to Rob Roy Glacier takes one day from the Raspberry Creek parking area in the West Matukituki Valley, along the river and up into the Rob Roy Valley. From here the track follows the chaotic Rob Roy River through beautiful rainforest, revealing occasional views of the glacier above. After about an hour and a half it reaches the treeline and enters a hidden valley rimmed with solid rock walls and falls of water and ice.

Farther along this road, past Glendhu and before the entrance to the Treble Cone ski field, is the Rocky Mountain and Diamond Lake Walk, with grand views of Mount Aspiring and the Matukituki River Valley, Lake Wanaka, and rocks that form unusual mounds and folds across the landscape. It is a stiff climb for most people, but the path is marked clearly and it is definitely worth taking the three-hour round trip.

### INFORMATION

www.doc.govt.nz

304 C15 · 100 Ardmore Street, Wanaka · 03-443 1233 · Summer daily 8.30–6.30; winter 9.30–4.30 · DoC office, Upper Ardmore Street, Wanaka · 03-443 7660 · Daily 8–4.45 · Services to Wanaka from Christchurch, Dunedin and Queenstown; Mount Aspiring Express trailhead connections to Raspberry Creek, Mount Roy and Diamond Lake · Wanaka region airfield 11km (7 miles) east of Wanaka

### TIPS

» The park's alpine areas are suitable only for experienced trampers and mountaineers.

» Jet-boat trips are available on the park's larger rivers, such as the Dart and the Wilkin (▷ 250).

**Below** *Diamond Lake is a highlight of the national park*

## INFORMATION

www.tourismwaitaki.co.nz
307 E16 Corner of Itchen and Thames streets 03-434 1656 Dec–Easter Mon–Fri 9–6, Sat, Sun 10–5; Easter–end Nov Mon–Fri 9–5, Sat, Sun 10–4 All major east coast services; summer service (Mon, Wed, Fri) from Mount Cook

## TIPS

» For local crafts and produce visit Harbour and Tyne Market, 2 Tyne Street (Saturday, Sunday in summer; Sunday in winter).
» The Janet Frame Heritage Trail (▷ 19) starts from the Oamaru i-SITE.

**Above** *Yellow-eyed penguins come ashore to their burrows at night*

# OAMARU

Oamaru is an intriguing town on the east coast shores of Friendly Bay. Thanks to the prosperity of the 1860s to 1890s and the discovery of limestone that could easily be carved and moulded, the early architects of Oamaru created a settlement rich in imposing, classic buildings, earning it the reputation of New Zealand's best-built town. Styles range from Venetian to Victorian, and antiques shops, craft outlets, secondhand book stores and cafés add to the appeal.

The Oamaru steam train (Sun), operated by the Oamaru Steam and Rail Restoration Society, is worth a look, too. The shiny engine hisses into action beside the visitor office at the Harbourside Station and runs to Quarry Siding. The North Otago Museum on Thames Street (Mon–Fri 10.30–4.30, Sat, Sun 10–4) has interesting displays about Oamaru stone.

## SEEING THE PENGUINS

No visit to Oamaru would be complete without seeing its penguin colonies. The town has two species in residence: the little blue (the smallest in the world) and the larger, yellow-eyed penguin. There are two colonies and observation points—one at Bushy Beach, where you can watch the yellow-eyed penguins from a hide for free; and the official harbourside Oamaru Blue Penguin Colony (tel 03-443 1195), which charges a fee for access.

If you know nothing about penguins the best option is to join a tour, or to visit the official colony, before venturing out alone. The only time to view the penguins is from dusk (specific times are posted at the colony reception)—at other times they are at sea. There is a large covered stand from which you are given a brief talk before watching the penguins come ashore and waddle to their burrows.

## OTAGO PENINSULA

The beautiful Otago Peninsula extends 33km (20 miles) northeast from Dunedin into the Pacific Ocean. Its star attraction is the breeding colony of royal albatrosses on Taiaroa Head, at the very tip—the world's only mainland breeding albatross colony. The first egg was laid here in 1920; the colony now numbers almost 100 and can be seen from the Royal Albatross Centre observatory (Oct–end Mar daily 9–dusk; Apr–end Sep Wed–Mon 10–4, Tue 10.30–4). Rare Stewart Island shags also breed on the headland. Watch one of the rarest penguin species in the world from the Yellow-eyed Penguin Conservation Reserve or Penguin Place at Harington Point (Oct–end Apr daily from 10.15; May–end Sep daily 3.15– 4.45). You also can visit the Department of Conservation hide at Sandfly Bay at dawn or dusk.

Larnach Castle (daily 9–5), a Scottish-style Baronial mansion perched on the highest point of the peninsula off Castlewood Road, is the former residence of William Larnach (1833–98), a politician and financier renowned for his many personal excesses.

307 E17 48 The Octagon, Dunedin 03-474 3300 Tour buses from Dunedin

## QUEENSTOWN

▷ 240–241.

## RIVERTON

Riverton—or Aparima, to use its former Maori name—is the oldest permanent European settlement in Southland and one of the oldest in the country, established in the 1830s. The Riverton Museum, at 172 Palmerston Street (Nov–Easter daily 10–4.30; Easter–Oct daily 11–3.30), houses displays and photos of the early Maori, whaling and gold-mining days, with more than 500 portraits of the early pioneers.

The Riverton Rocks and Howell's Point, at the southern edge of Taramea Bay, provide safe activities such as swimming and fishing, and offer fine views across to Stewart Island (▷ 242).

306 B18 127 Palmerston Street 03-234 9991 Services from Invercargill

**Above** *A meadow full of bright yellow and orange Californian poppies at the foot of Mount Iron, Wanaka*

## SKIPPERS CANYON

Drivers of rented cars are warned at the entrance to the Skippers Canyon road that their insurance does not cover this route. No wonder, given its rough, pot-holed surface and vertiginous 120m (394ft) drops to the Shotover River below—but it's well worth joining a tour from Queenstown to be driven along this spectacular valley.

The road was funded by taxes raised on gold found in the river, and the remains of the gold-mining town of Skippers can be seen at the head of the canyon. The area's majestic mountains and valleys, terraced by the gold-mining process, were used as backdrops in the *Lord of the Rings* movies.

306 C16 Corner of Shotover and Camp streets, Queenstown 03-442 4100

## STEWART ISLAND/RAKIURA

▷ 242.

## TE ANAU

Every summer the township of Te Anau, on the shores of New Zealand's second-largest lake at the edge of Fiordland National Park (▷ 233–235), is inundated by crowds of trampers eager to visit its magnificent surroundings. Lake Te Anau is 61km (38 miles) long and 10km (6 miles) at its widest point. Along its western edge, between the Middle and South Fiords, are the 200m (656ft) Te Anau Caves, whose rock formations, whirlpools, waterfalls and glow-worms can be accessed only on boat trips from Te Anau wharf, which last around two hours (several times daily).

306 B17 Lakefront Drive 03-249 8900 Services from Christchurch, Invercargill, Dunedin and Queenstown Between Te Anau and Manapouri

## WANAKA

www.lakewanaka.co.nz

The quiet service town of Wanaka borders the very pretty Roy's Bay, which opens out beyond Ruby Island into the southern and indented bays of Lake Wanaka. The lake occupies an ancient glacier bed more than 45km (28 miles) long. The town becomes a popular ski venue during the winter months.

One of the most immediate ways to get acquainted with the Wanaka area is to make the 45-minute ascent up Mount Iron (240m/787ft), along a well-marked track starting shortly before the township on the main road.

On SH6, by Wanaka airfield, is the Wanaka Transport and Toy Museum (daily 8.30–5), with more than 15,000 items on display. The NZ Fighter Pilots Museum (daily 9–4) gives a fascinating insight into general aviation history, with a good collection of World War II fighters and trainers.

306 C15 100 Ardmore Street 03-443 1233 Services from Christchurch, Dunedin and Queenstown 11km (7 miles) east of town

**INFORMATION**
www.queenstown-nz.co.nz
306 C16 Corner of Shotover and Camp streets 03-442 4100 Daily 7–7 DoC, 37 Shotover Street 03-442 7935 Services from Christchurch, Invercargill, Dunedin, Wanaka, Greymouth, Mount Cook, Te Anau and Franz Josef 8km (5 miles) east in Frankton

**Above** *Boutiques and restaurants flourish around Steamer Wharf*

## INTRODUCTION

Queenstown is the biggest tourist draw in New Zealand, as one of the top adventure venues in the world. More than a million visitors a year partake in a staggering range of activities, from sedate steamboat cruises to heart-stopping bungy jumps. In winter the walking boots are simply replaced by skis. The town is compact and easily negotiable on foot. The main street for information and activity bookings is Shotover Street; the Mall is the principal shopping and restaurant area.

The first European to visit the area was Scotsman Donald Hay, who explored Lake Wakatipu in 1859. Gold was found in the Shotover River Valley in 1862, and within a year some 2,000 hopeful prospectors were camped here. The Shotover is the richest gold-bearing river of its size in the world, but after a decade the gold was exhausted. By the mid-20th century tourism was already taking hold.

## WHAT TO SEE

### A.J. HACKETT BUNGY AND SHOTOVER JET

www.AJHackett.com; www.shotoverjet.com

The Station is the main pick-up point for these two longest established activity operators. A. J. Hackett started professional bungy jumps at Kawarau Bridge, 43m (141ft) over the river east of Queenstown, in 1988. Since then he has created the 102m (335ft) Pipeline Bungy over the Shotover River and the 134m (440ft) Nevis Highwire, among others.

Shotover Jet are the only operators to ply the lower reaches of the Shotover River. A 70kph (43mph) jet down the river includes thrilling 360-degree turns.
The Station, corner of Shotover and Camp streets Bungy 0800-286 495, jet-boat 0800-SHOTOVER Summer daily 7am–9pm; winter daily 8am–10pm Bungy from NZ$165; jet-boat adult NZ$109, child NZ$69

### QUEENSTOWN GARDENS

Founded in 1867 on a small promontory pointing out into Lake Wakatipu, the gardens offer some respite from the crowds. There are oaks, sequoias and 1,500 roses planted in 26 named rosebeds. At the entrance is the restored 1865 Williams Cottage.

Marine Parade Free

### REMARKABLES LOOKOUT

Although it takes a rugged drive and a scramble to get there, the view of Lake Wakatipu and Queenstown from the Remarkables Lookout is worth every rut and step. Check that the weather is clear, wear warm clothes and sturdy walking boots and make sure that your car will survive the 1,500m (4,920ft) climb up the unsealed road to the ski fields; in winter you may need chains. If the ski field is open you can take a shuttle from Queenstown, and in winter you can use the Shadow Basin Chair Lift from the parking area. In summer, follow the path up the slopes behind the main building to Mid-Station, and from here continue roughly in line with the chairlift to its terminus. The lookout is about 200m (656ft) behind and farther up from this point.

Ski field road off SH6, 2km (1 mile) south of Frankton

### SKYLINE GONDOLA

www.skyline.co.nz

A cable car soars up to Bobs Peak, more than 450m (1,476ft) above town, where there's a world-class view and a host of activities, including the Ledge Bungy, the Luge, the Sky-Swing, paragliding and helicopter flightseeing. There are also Maori cultural shows (daily from 5.30).

Brecon Street 03-441 0101 Daily 9am–dusk Adult from NZ$21, child (5–14) NZ$10, under-5s free, family NZ$49

### TSS EARNSLAW

It won't take you long to spot the delightful twin-screw steamer *Earnslaw* plying the waters of Lake Wakatipu from Queenstown Bay. The steamer is named after the highest peak in the region, Mount Earnslaw (2,819m/9,249ft), and was launched at Kingston in 1912. Options include dinner cruises and trips to Walter Peak Station for an insight into farming life.

Steamer Wharf 0800-656 501 Oct–end Apr daily every 2 hours, 10–10; winter 12, 2, 4 Adult from NZ$42, child NZ$15

### TIP

» Despite the wide range of places to stay it is essential to reserve a room two or three days in advance in mid-summer and during the ski season, particularly in mid-July.

**Left** *Lake Wakatipu and Queenstown*
**Below** *Jumping from the original bungy site in Queenstown*

**INFORMATION**

www.stewartisland.co.nz
www.doc.govt.nz
306 B19 DoC Visitor Information and Field Centre, Main Road, Oban 03-219 0009 Mon–Fri 8–5, Sat, Sun 9–4 Shuttle services from Invercargill to coincide with ferries Foveaux Express ferries from Bluff Sep–end Apr 9.30–5; May–end Aug 9.30–4.30; Stewart Island Adventures ferries from Bluff 10am daily Flights from Invercargill to Halfmoon Bay, Masons, Doughboy, West Ruggedy and Little Hellfire

**TIP**

» Only 15kg (33lb) of personal baggage can be flown to Stewart Island/Rakiura, but additional baggage can be taken on subsequent flights.

**Above** *Golden sands in Post Office Bay*
**Opposite** *Bottle-nose dolphins swimming off Stewart Island*

## STEWART ISLAND/RAKIURA

Rakiura National Park is one of the country's most unspoiled and ecologically important areas—and New Zealand's newest national park. Lying 20km (12 miles) southwest of Bluff, across the Foveaux Strait, Stewart Island/Rakiura is known as the land of the glowing skies. In 2002, 85 per cent of the island was designated a national park.

The island is home to 21 threatened plants, some of which are indigenous or occur only on the island. Thanks to the absence of trout, there are 15 native fish species, and birds include mollymawks (a kind of albatross), petrels and shearwaters (muttonbirds), many of which breed on the offshore islets in vast numbers. Even on the main island (and fighting to survive the ravages of introduced vermin), breeding birds include two of the rarest and most unusual in the world: an odd and enchanting flightless parrot called a kakapo (of which only about 60 remain), and—perhaps most famous of all—*Apteryx australis lawryi*, better known as the Stewart Island brown kiwi, the largest and the only diurnal kiwi in New Zealand. Other inhabitants include the rare yellow-eyed penguins and Hookers sealions.

### OBAN AND AROUND

Oban, on Halfmoon Bay, is the island's principal settlement. A short, steady climb to Observation Rock, up Ayr Street at its southern end, gives great views of Paterson Inlet and the impenetrable forests that deck its southern shores. Oban's Rakiura Museum (Mon–Sat 10–12, Sun 12–2) traces a history of Maori occupation, whaling, saw-milling, gold-mining and fishing. The beach on the waterfront (Elgin Terrace) is a fine place to sit and watch the world go by, play industrial-size chess, or contemplate the many water-based trips available.

### WALKS

Stewart Island/Rakiura has 245km (152 miles) of walking tracks, ranging from short walks around Oban to the Northwest Circuit, a mammoth 125km (78-mile), 10- to 12-day tramp around the island's northern coast with a side trip to climb Mount Anglem (980m/3,215ft), the island's highest peak. All tramping on Stewart Island/Rakiura presents challenges, as the island is so undeveloped and wet underfoot. Information is available from the Department of Conservation.

# DIAMOND LAKE AND WANAKA VIEWS

**A clear track takes you through bush and tussock farmland to the summit of Rocky Mountain (775m/2,542ft), where a 360-degree view reveals Lake Wanaka and surrounding mountain ranges in full splendour.**

**THE WALK**
**Distance:** 7km (4 miles); ascent 400m (1,312ft)
**Time:** 2.5 hours
**Start/end at:** Diamond Lake Walking Track car park, near Wanaka, Central Otago

**HOW TO GET THERE**
From the information centre on the Wanaka lakefront, drive 18.5km (11 miles) west along Mount Aspiring Road. You will find the car park is 6km (4 miles) after Glendhu Bay motor camp.

★ From the car park, cross the cattle grid and follow the gravel farm road up the hill. At the top, there's a toilet to eastward (right) and a wooden sign marked 'track' on the left. Walk to this signpost and you will see another sign indicating the start of the track proper, and a donation box—NZ$2 per adult is asked for track maintenance. The next 300m (330 yards) of the track follow the edge of Diamond Lake.

❶ Diamond Lake, surrounded by willows and raupo rushes, is an alpine tarn. It was formed some 10,000 years ago by the same receding glaciers that carved out Lake Wanaka. Minerals leaching out of the soil cause its dark appearance. It often freezes over in winter and was popular for ice-skating in the days before health and safety regulations took hold.

The track narrows and the ascent begins. The next kilometre (0.6 miles) takes you through bush, climbing on a series of flat rocks and wooden staircases before you emerge into open farmland. After 500m (550 yards), a hand-painted sign shows your place on the route, at the bottom of the figure-of-eight. For the first emergency exit, take the eastern branch. A signposted view of Lake Wanaka is 1km (0.6 miles) up this track. For Rocky Mountain, continue along the western branch.

❷ Like much farmland in Central Otago, this area is speckled with wiry brown bracken, which prohibits sheep from grazing and sticks in their wool, depreciating its quality. To combat this, sections of the hillside are burned between August and October. A specialist makes sure the fire is hot enough to burn bracken but not grasses or native flora.

After a glimpse of Lake Wanaka, the path turns west towards Mount Aspiring and returns to bush. In another 800m (875 yards), a stile leads you back into farmland. Soon you reach a large flat rock on which to sit and admire the lake. If you've had enough, the next emergency exit is only 300m (310 yards) farther, at the middle of the figure-of-eight.

For both routes, turn west towards the hills and follow two

**Above** *Diamond Lake is fringed by hilly grasslands, its shoreline thick with willows and raupo rushes*

marker poles for 200m (220 yards). Shortly after a wooden bridge, you'll find another handpainted sign. Continue uphill if you want to leave the walk via the second emergency exit, or turn westwards to push for Rocky Mountain.

❸ You are approaching large schist rock-faces that are part of the area's attraction for climbers. The land on the opposite side of Wanaka Mount Aspiring Road is also popular. Its name—Hospital Flat—relates to its historic use as a recuperation spot for horses, rather than any association with climbing accidents.

The next 2km (1 mile) are a hard slog through tussocky farmland. The path zigzags steeply beneath large rocky overhangs, then turns east so you walk above them.

❹ After a tantalizing glimpse of the lake, you burst over the brow of the hill to a wonderful view of Lake Wanaka, its islands and peninsulas, the Matukituki River and bridge. At the western end of the valley is Mount Aspiring (▷ 237).

Much of this vista could have been lost but for a chance meeting in 1968. Plans were afoot to dam the outlet, at the east side of Lake Wanaka, for hydro-electricity; the community had been assured the water level would not rise significantly. Marion Borrie, a minister's wife, was walking up Mount Iron when she met a couple and stopped to talk about the plans. She was talking to the manager of the New Zealand Electricity Department, who admitted the plan would raise the lake by 6m (20ft), drowning land between Cromwell and Wanaka and parts of Wanaka township (▷ 239). Mrs Borrie raised the alarm, and after political furore the plans were shelved.

The descent starts north of the viewpoint—look for two red metal poles. The path becomes very steep and rocky; it can be slippy, so take care. The distinctive Piggyback Rock marks the end of this section. After 400m (440 yards) the path flattens to a dirt track. In another 100m (110 yards), there's an option to turn east and walk 500m (550 yards) for another view over the lake. Another 1,500m (1,640 yards) takes you back to the first painted signpost and you retrace your steps to Diamond Lake.

### WHEN TO GO

Summer heat can make the walk more challenging—an early morning start is recommended. The track may be closed in winter if conditions are not suitable—check with the Department of Conservation (DoC) office (tel 03-443 7660).

### WHERE TO EAT

The lake viewpoints are perfect for a picnic. Supplies can be bought from Kai Whaka Pai, at the corner of Helwick and Ardmore streets (tel 03-443 7795, daily 7am–late).

### INFORMATION

**TOURIST INFORMATION**

✉ 100 Ardmore Street, Wanaka
☎ 03-443 1233

### TIP

» For a half-day's effort, this walk offers exceptional rewards. Be prepared—the route is steep and a good level of fitness is required. However, its figure-of-eight structure provides two 'emergency exits'.

**Left** *Lake Wanaka, surrounded by hills*
**Below** *A profusion of California poppies*

# AROUND THE OTAGO PENINSULA

**Discover the inlets and beaches of the southeastern corner of the Otago Peninsula. The steeply rolling hills and sandy beaches belong to sheep, seals and wading birds. It's utterly remote, but just a short drive away from the friendly attractions of the northern side.**

**THE DRIVE**
**Distance:** 32km (20 miles)
**Time:** 2.5 hours
**Start/end at:** The parking bay at the southern end of Portsmouth Drive, 3km (2 miles) from The Octagon, in the heart of Dunedin 307 E17
It's marked by an information board and signposts to the peninsula.

Before you set off, look south to the opposite side of Portsmouth Drive, where Shore Street meets Portobello Road. There you will see a rock with 'Rongo' carved into it. This is a memorial to the Taranaki Maori prisoners of war held in Dunedin from 1869 to 1872 and from 1879 to 1881. They—and fellow European prisoners—built the seawall that runs all the way to Portobello. Rongo is the Maori god of peace.

★ From the car park turn east and cross Portobello Road's causeway. Continue straight on, following a blue sign for the peninsula. On your seaward side, pass Vauxhall yacht club. Take the first inland turn up Doon Street. Stay on Doon Street as it turns abruptly left. At the end of Doon Street, turn right into Connell Street, then left into Larnach Road (a main road). This turns into McKerrow Street after 500m (550 yards). When you reach the T-junction, turn left onto Highcliff Road.

After 200m (220 yards), Rotary Park lookout gives a dramatic view of Dunedin city and harbour. From here, the road narrows and enters countryside. After 1.5km (1 mile) pass a parking bay; just beyond is a well-marked track to the Soldier's Memorial, a 700m (765-yard) climb. Continue for another 5km (3 miles) and you come to Pukehiki, with its white, rectangular church tower and tiny public library to the north. The next intersection signposts Larnach Castle (▷ 239) to the north, but stay on Highcliff Road.

❶ Peninsula farms are distinctive for their use of drystone walls, rather than the ubiquitous No. 8 fencing wire (▷ 14). It shows skill and thrift by the early Scottish farmers—while neatly divvying up their paddocks, they cleaned up the volcanic stones that littered the ground. Look for the skewed macrocarpa trees, which tell tales about the southerly wind. Sandfly Bay did not get its name from the insects, but the gales that batter the coast.

After 2km (1 mile) pass the modern stone wall of Gatesheath bed-and-breakfast. At this corner, turn south down Sandymount Road. This marks the end of the tourist trail and after 600m (656 yards) the road is unsealed. To the north there are good views of Harbour Cone; to the south, the Pacific Ocean, beaches and rolling sheep country.

After 2km (1 mile) reach a triangular intersection. For a detour,

**Opposite** *Larnach Castle contains fine crafts and antique furniture*
**Right** *Oystercatchers are regular visitors to Hoppers Inlet*

continue up the steep road to Sandymount Recreational Reserve.

❷ From the reserve, well-marked tracks lead to the cliff known as Lovers Leap (2km/ 1 mile), and the high dunes of Sandfly Bay (5km/ 3 miles). Note that they are closed during the lambing season, from August to October.

To continue the tour, turn north onto Hoopers Inlet Road. After 1km (0.6 miles), the inlet is before you.

❸ The tidal mudflats of Hoopers Inlet (and Papanui Inlet to the northeast) offer good feeding for wading birds. Pied stilts, godwits, black and variable oystercatchers and spur-winged plovers are regular visitors, and spoonbills occasionally drop by.

Turn west and drive 2km (1 mile) around the inlet to a yellow signpost for Portobello. Follow this sign left (northwards) along Allan's Beach Road for 1.5km (1 mile), which brings you over the hill and into Portobello. From here, the Royal Albatross Centre (▷ 239) is a farther 11km (7 miles) out from the city, while Westpac Aquarium is 1.5km (1 mile) down Hatchery Road. Turn left (west) onto Portobello Road and take the 'low road' 14km (9 miles) back to Portsmouth Drive. The Portobello Coffee Shop is on Highcliff Road, to the south, opposite the inlet.

❹ Thematically painted bus shelters punctuate the drive back to Dunedin. These concrete caves were brightened up in 1989 by Broad Bay artist John Noakes. There are 12 of them along the route, often with designs relating to local names—a flock of chooks (chickens) are near the Happy Hens shop, four-leaf clovers (shamrocks) enliven Dublin Bay, while popular comic characters Wallace and Grommit appear for good measure.

The road is tightly snaking, with excellent views towards the city and north across the harbour towards Port Chalmers. It passes a number of well-signposted and worthwhile attractions such as the 1909 Fletcher House, Macandrew Bay beach and Glenfalloch Gardens. Take your time, especially as you go around Burns Point, 11km (7 miles) from Portobello. Despite the railings, cars sometimes end up in the harbour.

## WHERE TO EAT

### PORTOBELLO COFFEE SHOP

You'll get homestyle fare here, including traditional kiwi slices. Highlights are the craft gallery at the back featuring local knitting and pottery, and outdoor seating overlooking the bay.
699 Highcliff Road, Portobello
03-478 1055 Daily 9–5

## INFORMATION

### TOURIST INFORMATION

www.cityofdunedin.com
48 The Octagon, Dunedin
03-474 3300

## PLACES TO VISIT

### FLETCHER HOUSE

727 Portobello Road 03-478 0180
Daily 11–4, Boxing Day–Easter
Adult NZ$3, child free

### GLENFALLOCH WOODLAND GARDENS

430 Portobello Road 03-476 1775
Daily dawn–dusk Adult NZ$3, child NZ$1

### NZ MARINE STUDIES CENTRE AND WESTPAC AQUARIUM

www.marine.ac.nz
03-479 5826 Daily noon–4.30; tours 10.30am NZ$12; guided tour NZ$21

**Above** *Souvenirs of Otago and the Far South range from local crafts to gourmet food and fine wines*

## ALEXANDRA

### BLACK RIDGE VINEYARD AND WINERY

www.blackridge.co.nz

A wild, rocky ravine makes a dramatic and unusual location for this vineyard, where bulldozers had to reshape the schist to allow pockets of vines to be planted. The resulting wines are distinctive, in particular a highly regarded, flinty Gewürztraminer. You can purchase cheese and cured meats to complement the wine tastings. Cheeseboard and nibbles are available alfresco from 27 December to mid-January, and there is often live music at weekends.

✉ Conroys Road, Alexandra
☎ 03-449 2059 🕑 Daily 10–5

## ARROWTOWN

### AMISFIELD

www.amisfield.co.nz

Just outside Arrowtown, Amisfield is the closest winery to Queenstown. It has vineyards at picturesque Lake Hayes, and extensive plantings on the shores of Lake Dunstan. Specialists in Pinot noir and *méthode traditionelle*, it also produces Pinot gris, Sauvignon blanc, Riesling and an excellent rosé. The attractive stone winery has a spacious cellar door facility, which hosts art exhibitions, and an underground barrel hall.

✉ Lake Hayes Winery, 10 Lake Hayes Road, Arrowtown ☎ 03-442 0556
🕑 Daily 10–8

### THE GOLD SHOP

www.thegoldshop.co.nz

The Gold Shop reflects Arrowtown's gold-mining heritage in jewellery fashioned from gold bought from local miners. Gold flakes are shown off in lockets, and nuggets fashioned into pendants and bracelets.

✉ 29 Buckingham Street, Arrowtown
☎ 03-442 1319 🕑 Daily 8.30–5.30

### MILLBROOK

www.millbrook.co.nz

The resort is based around one of New Zealand's most beautiful and well-appointed golf courses, designed by Sir Bob Charles. Casual players can pay green fees and rent clubs, and packages are available (from NZ$200) that include green fees, golf clubs and shoes, golf cart, balls, tees, and a taxi to and from your accommodation. You can also stay on site. Millbrook has extensive facilities, including tennis courts, a swimming pool, a gymnasium, spa pools and sauna. It also has an associated day spa (tel 03-441 7017) offering massage, hydrotherapy, facials and body treatments.

✉ Malaghans Road, Arrowtown ☎ 03-441 7000 🎫 Green fees from NZ$90

### OUT THERE CLOTHING

www.otclothing.co.nz

Two local sisters design this relaxed, easy-to-wear but trendy clothing for men and women who want to be 'out there' doing things.

✉ 27 Beach Street, Queenstown
☎ 03-441 3029 🕑 Daily 10–5

## THE CATLINS

### CATLINS WILDLIFE TRACKERS ECOTOURS

www.catlins-ecotours.co.nz

These very informative two- and four-day tours give an in-depth look at the area's flora and fauna, geology, history and conservation. Small groups are taken to remote places to walk and appreciate rare wildlife, such as Hooker's sealions and yellow-eyed penguins.

Accommodation is provided, and connections from Balclutha can be made.
✉ Papatowai, RD2, Owaka
☎ 03-415 8613 ✋ From NZ$650

## CROMWELL

### THE BIG PICTURE

www.wineadventures.co.nz

The Big Picture offers 'the essential wine adventure', combining an interactive wine and film experience with an adjoining restaurant where you can sample the local Central Otago wines as you dine. There's an 'aroma room' featuring up to 60 different aromas associated with wine, and an auditorium where you are taken on a virtual flight over the region while wine-makers from various vineyards lead you through a tutored tasting.
✉ Corner of Sandflat Road and SH6, Cromwell ☎ 03-445 4052 🕓 Dec–end Feb 9am–11pm; Mar–end Nov 9–6 ✋ NZ$15

## DUNEDIN

### ARC CAFÉ

www.arc.org.nz

The Arc is an interesting and successful combination of arts venue, recording studio and vegan/vegetarian café, and is popular with local artists, musicians and students. It's run by a non-profit trust, and holds regular live gigs.
✉ 135 High Street, Dunedin ☎ 03-477 7200 🕓 Mon–Sat noon–late

### CADBURY WORLD

www.cadbury.co.nz

Cadbury World combines a visitor centre with heritage and interactive displays, a theatre presentation and a guided tour of the factory showing how various products are made. Reduced tours are available when the factory is not operating. A gift shop on site sells chocolates, clothing, hats, bags, toys, novelty items and souvenirs.
✉ 280 Cumberland Street, Dunedin ☎ 03-467 7967 🕓 Jan–end Apr daily 9am–7pm; May–end Dec daily 9–3.30 ✋ Mon–Sat adult NZ$16, child (under 15) NZ$10, family NZ$42; Sun, public holidays adult NZ$10, child NZ$5 🎁

### CARISBROOK SPORTING COMPLEX

www.orfu.co.nz

Carisbrook, home of the Otago Rugby Football Union and the venue for international rugby and cricket matches, is known locally as 'the house of pain'—because visiting teams find it so difficult to be successful here.
✉ Burns Street, Dunedin ☎ 03-466 4010

### DUNEDIN CASINO

www.dunedincasino.co.nz

This chic casino in the boutique Southern Cross Hotel aims for a sophisticated atmosphere, with a dress code of smart attire. Play blackjack, roulette, baccarat, *tai sai*, poker, or gaming machines. There is also a restaurant. Minimum age 20.
✉ Southern Cross Hotel, 118 High Street, Dunedin ☎ 0800-477 4545 🕓 Daily 10am–3am

### FORTUNE THEATRE

www.fortunetheatre.co.nz

Dunedin's professional theatre operates from a converted 1870 church, staging regular acclaimed productions of both local and international drama in two venues: the Mainstage and Studio. Bookings can be made at the theatre or via the website.
✉ Corner of Moray Place and Stuart Street, Dunedin ☎ 03-477 8323 🕓 Tue 6, Wed–Sat 8, Sun 4

### NEW ZEALAND SPORTS HALL OF FAME

www.nzhalloffame.co.nz

New Zealand's great sporting moments are relived in this exhibit, in the splendidly grandiose heritage Railway Station. A shop sells sporting paraphernalia.
✉ Dunedin Railway Station, Anzac Square, Dunedin ☎ 03-477 7775 🕓 Daily 10–4 🎁

### OTAGO FARMERS' MARKET

www.otagofarmersmarket.org.nz

Up to 4,000 people visit this Saturday market on a fine day, to buy fruit and vegetables, venison, free-range eggs, free-range pork, fresh fish, organic lamb and beef direct from the growers. Artisan producers also bring speciality breads, pies, pastries and chocolates. In season you can also find wild mushrooms, quinces, artichokes, hazelnuts and chestnuts.
✉ Dunedin Railway Station, Anzac Square, Dunedin ☎ 03-477 6701 🕓 Sat 8–1.30

### REGENT THEATRE

www.regenttheatre.co.nz

The beautifully restored Regent Theatre combines the spacious elegance of a classic 1920s movie palace with state-of-the-art projection and sound. It hosts live theatre, cinema, musicals and special events, including the annual film festival.
✉ 17 The Octagon, Dunedin ☎ 03-477 6481 🕓 Booking office Mon–Fri 9–5, Sat 10.30–1

### THE SCOTTISH SHOP

www.scottishshop.co.nz

Trading on Dunedin's Scottish heritage, this shop sells products made in Scotland alongside New Zealand-made items in a Scottish style. From tartan kilts, ties and stockings to oatcakes and shortbread—if it's Scottish, they'll stock it.
✉ 17 George Street, Dunedin ☎ 03-477 9965 🕓 Mon–Fri 9–5.30, Sat 10–3

### SPEIGHT'S BREWERY

www.speights.co.nz

Still on the site it has occupied since 1876, Speight's Brewery has become synonymous with the 'Southern Man' image of rural Otago and Southland. The Heritage Centre takes tours through the gravity-fed working brewery and museum, ending with a tasting session. You can also bottle, label and cap your own beer to take away in a wooden gift pack. The Ale House Bar and Restaurant (tel 03-471 9050) is a popular meeting place and open until late.
✉ 200 Rattray Street, Dunedin ☎ 03-477 7697 🕓 Brewery tours: Mon–Thu 10, 12, 2, 6, 7; Fri, Sun 10, 12, 2, 4, 6 ✋ Tours: adult NZ$17, child (5–15) NZ$6

## GLENORCHY

### DART RIVER SAFARIS

www.dartriver.co.nz

The safaris focus on the Dart River, involving a bus ride from Queenstown to Glenorchy, 4X4 drive through Paradise (taking in *Lord of the Rings* film locations on the way), walks through beech forest and a jet-boat trip back to Glenorchy. Horseback-riding and kayaking options are also available.

✉ Mull Street, Glenorchy ☎ 03-442 9992 ✋ Adult from NZ$199, child (5–15) NZ$99

## GIBBSTON

### GIBBSTON VALLEY WINES AND GIBBSTON VALLEY CHEESERY

www.gvwines.co.nz
www.gvcheese.co.nz

Gibbston Valley is a popular spot with visitors, not just because of the fine wines—notably its flagship Pinot noir and Chardonnay—but also for the educational tours it offers of the vineyard, winery and barrel cave; the food, featuring local produce in its restaurant; and the adjacent cheesery. Here you can learn how the handcrafted cow, goat and sheep cheeses are made.

✉ State Highway 6, Gibbston, RD1 Queenstown ☎ 03-442 6910 (winery); 03-441 1388 (cheesery) 🕒 Daily 10–5; tours: 10–4 on the hour ✋ NZ$9.50

## INVERCARGILL

### CIVIC THEATRE

A fine Renaissance-style Victorian theatre, the 1,000-seat Civic was built in 1906 as a cinema and to host opera, musicals, comedies and ballets. It is now the home of the Invercargill Repertory Society, and is also used by some professional touring companies.

✉ Tay Street, Invercargill ☎ 03-211 1777

### EMBASSY THEATRE

www.bdlhire.co.nz

Originally a cinema, the Embassy was revamped and reopened in 1999 as a performance and production venue with high-tech facilities. It is operated by an audio, lighting and DJ company and hosts functions and rock concerts.

✉ 112 Dee Street, Invercargill ☎ 03-214 0050

### THE SERIOUSLY GOOD CHOCOLATE COMPANY

www.seriouslygoodchocolate.com

Jane Stanton specializes in handmade chocolates with special fillings, such as branded wines, and is best known for her truffles made with local produce, such as Bluff oyster cinnamon truffles and tuatara chocolate eggs. Buy them direct from her shop or in stores in Invercargill and nationwide.

✉ 20 Windsor Street, Invercargill ☎ 03-217 5107 🕒 Mon–Wed, Thu 9–6.30, Fri–Sun 9–5.30

## KINGSTON

### KINGSTON FLYER

www.kingstonflyer.co.nz

The Kingston Flyer was originally a passenger service that operated between Kingston and the main railway line at Gore, from 1878 through to the mid-1950s. It provided a passage to Queenstown and the surrounding areas by meeting the lake steamers at Kingston Wharf. Today it puffs along a 14km (9-mile) track while passengers listen to 1920s music.

✉ Kingston Railway Station, Kingston ☎ 03-248 8848 🕒 Oct–end Apr daily 10, 1.30 ✋ Adult NZ$45, child NZ$22.50, family NZ$112.50 🚗 47km (29 miles) south of Queenstown

## MANAPOURI AND DOUBTFUL SOUND

### REAL JOURNEYS

www.realjourneys.co.nz

High tech and wild nature are combined in these trips to the Manapouri Power Station and Doubtful Sound. The Wilderness Day Cruise crosses Lake Manapouri by launch, takes a bus over the Wilmot Pass, and then a launch cruise on Doubtful Sound. You visit the hydro station on the way back. An overnight option lets you stay in Doubtful Sound on the *Fiordland Navigator*, designed along the lines of a trading scow. A shorter option visits only the power station.

✉ Pearl Harbour, Manapouri ☎ 03-249 7416 🕒 Daily 7.45 (Te Anau 8.45) ✋ Adult from NZ$185, child NZ$41

## MILFORD SOUND

### MILFORD SOUND RED BOAT CRUISES

www.redboats.co.nz

Cruises explore the sound to the Tasman Sea, taking in the majestic scenery, waterfalls, seal colonies and an optional underwater observatory (there is an additional charge, ▷ 234).

✉ Milford Wharf Visitor Centre, Milford Sound ☎ 0800-264536 🕒 Daily ✋ Adult from NZ$55, child NZ$15

### ROSCO'S MILFORD SOUND SEA KAYAKS

www.kayakmilford.co.nz

Choose from a variety of day, twilight or full-moon trips, as well as fly/kayak combinations, or paddle and walk part of the Milford Track.

✉ Deep Water Basin, Milford Sound ☎ 03-249 8500 ✋ From NZ$98

## OTAGO PENINSULA

### ELM WILDLIFE TOURS

www.elmwildlifetours.co.nz

These informative guided nature tours of the Otago Peninsula include Hooker's sea lions, fur seals, albatrosses and yellow-eyed penguins. The five- to six-hour trip takes in the Albatross Centre, a New Zealand fur seal colony and their own yellow-eyed penguin-breeding beach at the remote Cape Saunders. Other options include kayaking, a cruise around the heads, and the Catlins. You can stay at the backpackers' lodge or be picked up from elsewhere.

✉ Elm Backpackers Lodge, 19 Irvine Road, The Cove, Dunedin ☎ 03-454 4121 ✋ From NZ$79

### E-TOURS

www.etours.net.nz

Packages are available for doing the Otago Central Rail Trail at your own pace, including accommodation, transport, maps and gear.

✉ 67 Stuart Street, Dunedin ☎ 03-476 1960 ✋ From NZ$75

## QUEENSTOWN

### APPELLATION CENTRAL WINE TOURS

www.appellationcentral.co.nz

Philip Green has a Diploma of Wine and has been a wine collector for 15 years. He organizes small group tours (up to nine people) which depart daily, and customizes tours for wine enthusiasts. Afternoon tours visit four wineries in the Gibbston and Bannockburn areas and Cromwell, and include lunch. Full-day tours include a wine cave tour, cheese tasting, lunch and a wine experience at The Big Picture.

✉ Queenstown ☎ 03-442 0246 🕘 Daily 9.30, noon ✋ From NZ$145

### BODY SANCTUM

www.bodysanctum.co.nz

A soothing place to recover from the rigours of the day's activities, Body Sanctum is in a new building, with fine views from the treatment rooms. There is an outdoor spa, steam room and sauna, and treatments include skier's, snowboarder's or tramper's foot revival, aromatic body wraps, massage, reflexology, facials and water therapies.

✉ 50 Stanley Street, Queenstown ☎ 03-442 8006 🕘 Daily 9–9 ✋ From NZ$40

### CORONET PEAK/ REMARKABLES SKI AREAS

www.nzski.com

The original commercial ski field—and still one of the best when it gets a good covering of snow—Coronet Peak (1,649m/5,410ft) has excellent facilities and the added advantage of being an easy drive (18km/11 miles of sealed road) from Queenstown. Not surprisingly, it gets very busy. Its sister field across the valley, the Remarkables, is reached by a longer and more tortuous road (28km/17 miles of gravel road) but often has more snow as it goes higher (1,935m/6,348ft).

✉ Queenstown Snow Centre, corner of Camp and Shotover streets, Queenstown ☎ 03-442 4640 🕘 Late Jun to mid-Oct ✋ Lift passes from NZ$85

### EMBASSY CINEMA

www.readingcinemas.co.nz

Three screens show first-release movies and host the International Film Festival. Details of screenings are carried on the movie line, tel 03-442 9990.

✉ 11 The Mall, Queenstown ☎ 03-442 9994 ✋ Adult from NZ$11, child NZ$9

### EXTREME GREEN RAFTING

www.nzraft.com

Whitewater rafting on the spectacular Shotover and Kawarau rivers can be combined with jet-boating, helicopter flights, skydiving or bungy jumping, and the can be done on different days.

✉ 39 Camp Street, Queenstown ☎ 03-442 8517 ✋ From NZ$165

### FLYFISHING NEW ZEALAND

www.wakatipu.co.nz

Queenstown and the surrounding area offers great opportunities for fly fishing, lake trolling, drift-boat fishing and heli-fishing. The high-country stream fishing season opens on 1 October and runs to 30 May. Lake Wakatipu and the Kawarau River are open all year round.

✉ Queenstown Bay, Queenstown ☎ 03-442 5363 ✋ From NZ$115, plus NZ$18 fishing licence

### GLENORCHY AIR

www.glenorchy.net.nz
www.trilogytrail.com

Capitalizing on its experience of flying the *Lord of the Rings* cast and crew, this company does Trilogy trips to the locations used to represent Lothlorien, Amon Hen, Nen Hithoel, Amon Lhaw, Parth Galen, Ford of Bruinen, The Pillars of the King on the River Anduin, and the site of Gandalf's ride to Isengard. There is also a road trip to local filming sites (NZ$130 adult, NZ$65 child).

✉ Queenstown Airport, Queenstown ☎ 03-442 2207 ✋ From NZ$335, child NZ$167.50

### HAKA PA MAORI VILLAGE

www.hakapa.com

The cultural experience here starts with a traditional welcome and viewing of the Maori village, followed by a performance of traditional action songs and dances, *haka* (warrior dance) and *poi* (performed by the women). Dinner is a four-course feast, or *hangi*, based around meat and vegetables steamed in an earth oven. Pick-ups and drop-offs in Queenstown can be arranged.

✉ Waterfall Park, 345 Lake Hayes Road, Queenstown ☎ 03-442 1534 🕘 *Pa* daily 9–5; dinner 7–10 ✋ Cultural experience: adult NZ$89, child (5–15) NZ$40

**Above** *The Kingston Flyer re-creates the passenger service of the 1920s, on a 14km (9-mile) track*

### MILFORD SOUND SCENIC FLIGHTS

www.milfordflights.co.nz

The quickest and easiest way to see Milford Sound, this flight affords spectacular views of the fiord and dramatic scenery. You can choose from a combination of tours, including a launch trip on the sound and the option of going one way by coach or helicopter.

☎ 03-442 3065 ✋ Adult from NZ$325, child NZ$195

### SURREAL

One of Queenstown's popular nightspots, this nightclub is gay-friendly and has great DJs and sounds. It starts getting busy around 10.30pm. When the party swings, it's open until 5am.

✉ 7 Rees Street, Queenstown ☎ 03-441 8492 🕘 Daily 11am–late

## STEWART ISLAND/ RAKIURA

### RUGGEDY RANGE WILDERNESS EXPERIENCE

www.ruggedyrange.com

Former Department of Conservation guide Furhana Ahmad organizes a comprehensive itinerary of day and overnight guided walks, sea kayaking, kiwi-spotting and birdwatching trips on Stewart and Ulva islands. Packages are available and she assists with travel and accommodation bookings. Outdoor clothing and equipment is available for rent or sale. Some trips are suitable for children.

✉ 170 Horseshoe Bay Road, Stewart Island ☎ 03-219 1066 Adult from NZ$60, child NZ$45

## TE ANAU

### FIORDLAND BIKE AND HIKE

www.bikefiordland.co.nz

Offering an appealing way of making the journey from Te Anau to Milford Sound, these trips combine mountain biking on the downhill sections of the Milford Road with nature walks and a cruise on the sound, and the option of hiking part of the Routeburn Track. All equipment is provided, including wet weather gear. Suitable for children 14 and over.

✉ Sinclair Road, Te Anau ☎ 03-249 7098 Oct–end Apr daily 7.30am From NZ$99

### SINBAD CRUISES

www.sinbadcruises.co.nz

Help sail the 11m (36ft) gaff ketch *Little Ship Manuska*, or just sit back and enjoy the scenery. Trip options include day, afternoon, evening and overnight cruises, or combine cruising with a helicopter trip and/or walking at Mount Luxmore.

✉ 15 Fergus Square, Te Anau ☎ 03-249 7106 From NZ$20

## WANAKA

### ALPINE AND HELI MOUNTAIN BIKING

www.mountainbiking.co.nz

These folk put the mountain back into biking, with a choice of seven trips to some of the country's highest and most scenic track trailheads, including Mount Pisa, Mount Alpha and the Treble Cone. You can travel by four-wheel drive or helicopter. The most extensive range of options is available in summer, but some winter rides are also available. You can also do multi-day rides, staying overnight in old goldminers' cabins.

☎ 03-443 8943 From NZ$150

### LAKELAND ADVENTURES

www.lakelandadventures.co.nz

From their lakeside log cabin, Lakeland Adventures organize jet-boat trips on the Clutha River, guided fishing trips on Lake Wanaka, and cruises to the islands. They also rent aqua bikes, kayaks, mountain bikes, fishing rods and boats.

✉ The Log Cabin, Waterfront, Wanaka ☎ 03-443 7495 Adult from NZ$50, child NZ$25

### PARADISO CINEMA AND CAFÉ

www.paradiso.net.nz

A one-of-a-kind cinema, Paradiso shows first-release and art-house movies, but is best known for its quirky style. Seating includes a motley collection of old sofas and three seats in an old Morris Minor. A café and bar serves meals before, during or after the movie, and home-made ice cream and hot cookies during the intermission.

✉ 3 Ardmore Street, Wanaka ☎ 03-443 1505 Mon–Fri 3.30pm, Sat, Sun 1.30pm NZ$12

### RIPPON VINEYARD

www.rippon.co.nz

One of the most stunningly located vineyards in New Zealand, Rippon was planted in 1981. Known for its Pinot noir, it also makes other wines, including a *méthode traditionelle*, Riesling, Gamay rosé and a Merlot Syrah blend. Picnic lunches are served in summer, and a rock festival is held on Waitangi weekend in even years.

✉ 246 Mount Aspiring Road, Wanaka ☎ 03-443 8084 Dec–end Apr daily 11–5; Jul–end Nov daily 1.30–4.30

**Above** *Mountain biking through the waters of Long Gully towards Skippers Road, near Queenstown*

### TREBLE CONE SKI AREA

www.treblecone.com

Treble Cone is one of the top skiing and snowboarding areas in New Zealand, with more skiable terrain than anywhere else, plus great views of Lake Wanaka and Mount Aspiring. Equipment rental and tuition are available, and there is a childcare facility. The area is open in high summer for walking and mountain biking.

✉ Wanaka ☎ 03-443 7443 Late Jun to early Oct for skiing; 30 Dec to mid-Jan for summer activities Lift passes from NZ$90, child NZ$50, family NZ$235 20km (12 miles) northwest of Wanaka via Matukituki Valley Road

### WANAKA PARAGLIDING

www.wanakaparagliding.co.nz

Paragliders like the conditions in Wanaka so much they come here for the New Zealand championships. You can tandem paraglide from Treble Cone all year round, for magnificent views over Wanaka and the mountains. Short summer Eco Flights are also available from Mount Iron (but you walk up first).

✉ PO Box 118, Wanaka ☎ 0800 359 754 From NZ$180

# FESTIVALS AND EVENTS



## JANUARY–FEBRUARY

### CENTRAL OTAGO WINE AND FOOD FESTIVAL

The Central Otago Wine and Food Festival is held annually in the lovely setting of Queenstown Gardens, on the shores of Lake Wakatipu. It's a small but high-quality event. Foods of the region, prepared by members of the local Chefs Association, are matched with wines from 18 local wineries, and there is a farmers' market for small producers.

✉ Queenstown Visitor Centre, PO Box 253, Queenstown ☎ 03-442 4100 ⌚ 11–5 NZ$25

## APRIL

### BLUFF OYSTER AND SOUTHLAND SEAFOOD FESTIVAL

www.bluffoysterfest.co.nz

Bluff's famous oysters are celebrated at the annual Bluff Oyster and Southland Seafood Festival, where restaurants and community groups from Invercargill and Bluff have stalls featuring fresh local seafood, and chefs create dishes matching wines from a regional winery. A formal Southern Seas Ball is held the night before.

✉ Bluff Events Centre, Gore Street, Bluff ☎ 03-211 1400 ⌚ 11–5 Adult NZ$20, child NZ$10

## APRIL–MAY

### ARROWTOWN AUTUMN FESTIVAL

www.arrowtownautumnfestival.org.nz

Arrowtown celebrates its brilliant autumn hues in a 10-day community festival of arts and crafts, talks and tours, with tournaments, markets and a street parade.

✉ PO Box 148, Arrowtown ☎ 03-442 0809

## JUNE

### COUNTRY MUSIC FESTIVAL GORE

www.goldguitars.co.nz

Gore has established itself as the country music capital of New Zealand, hosting a 10-day country music festival each June, culminating in Gold Guitar Awards.

✉ PO Box 382, Gore ☎ 03-208 1978

## JUNE–JULY

### AMERICAN EXPRESS QUEENSTOWN WINTER FESTIVAL

www.winterfestival.co.nz

This annual 10-day celebration of the mountains takes place at three venues—Coronet Peak, Earnslaw Park and Queenstown Bay—and is a great excuse to party. As well as concerts, music and arts events, it includes the Classic Challenge of wild and wacky events. Some events are ticketed, others—such as the opening party, the parade and Mardi Gras—are free.

✉ Destination Queenstown, PO Box 353, Queenstown ☎ 03-441 2453

## SEPTEMBER

### GAY SKI WEEK

www.gayskiweeknz.com

A national gay and lesbian event, the ski week takes advantage of Queenstown's proximity to four major ski resorts. For those who are neither skiers nor boarders, the adventure capital of New Zealand still has plenty of off-piste activities.

✉ Queenstown

## SEPTEMBER–OCTOBER

### ALEXANDRA BLOSSOM FESTIVAL

www.blossom.co.nz

The fruit-growing district of Alexandra has been celebrating spring with this festival since the 1950s. Now held over two weeks, it includes crowning the Blossom Queen, a shearing competition, vintage car rally, motocross, boat races, a charity ball and the Grand Festival Parade with floats, bands, classic cars, floral princesses and animals. There is also a fair with arts and crafts, entertainment, wine and food (adult NZ$25, child (5–15) NZ$10, family NZ$40).

✉ PO Box 370, Alexandra ☎ 03-440 2097

## OCTOBER

### DUNEDIN RHODODENDRON FESTIVAL

www.rhododunedin.com

Dunedin's famous Botanic Garden's planting of 3,500 rhododendrons is regarded as one of the most significant in the world. The annual four-day celebration involves events for families and visitors as well as gardening enthusiasts, including garden tours, golf and a fête.

✉ PO Box 980, Dunedin ☎ 03-453 5521

## NOVEMBER

### BANNOCKBURN GUTBUSTER MOUNTAIN BIKE RACE

www.cromwell.org.nz

The Gutbuster is a pub-to-pub cycle race over a distance of 75km (47 miles) across the precipitous heights of the Nevis Pass. It starts from the Garston Hotel and finishes at the Bannockburn Hotel; many participants raise money for charity.

⌚ Entry from NZ$30

### OAMARU VICTORIAN HERITAGE CELEBRATIONS

Oamaru celebrates its Victorian heritage in five days of festivities, when local people dress in period costume and take part in a fair, street parade, Penny Farthing races, a ball and other activities.

✉ Visitor Information Office, Oamaru ☎ 03-434 1406

**Below** *April sees a seafood festival in Bluff*

# EATING

**Above** *South Sea Hotel, Stewart Island*

**PRICES AND SYMBOLS**
The restaurants are listed alphabetically. The prices given are the average for a two-course lunch (L) and a three-course dinner (D) for one person, without drinks. The wine price (W) is for the least expensive bottle. All the restaurants listed accept credit cards unless otherwise stated.

For a key to the symbols, ▷ 2.

## ARROWTOWN

### SAFFRON

www.saffronrestaurant.co.nz

A quality restaurant in Arrowtown's heritage precinct, Saffron uses wild local ingredients whenever possible: Lindis Pass hare, West Coast boar, porcini and rosehips. The menu shows Mediterranean and Asian influences. Central Otago wines head the wine list. The more casual Pesto restaurant next door is run by the same people, and serves a simple menu of pasta and pizza.

✉ 16 Buckingham Street, Arrowtown ☎ 03-442 0131 ⏲ Daily 11–4, 6.30–late 💳 L NZ$35, D NZ$90, W NZ$35

## CLYDE

### THE POST OFFICE CAFÉ AND BAR

Housed in Clyde's original post office (established in 1862), the restaurant retains much of the building's character. It's a pleasant place to have lunch; on a sunny day you can sit in the garden. The food is simple but tasty, with a menu featuring anything from venison to blue cod. The pies are a speciality.

✉ 2 Blyth Street, Clyde ☎ 03-449 2488 ⏲ Daily 10am–late 💳 L NZ$20, D NZ$40, W NZ$25

## CROMWELL

### LAZYDOG CAFÉ AND WINE BAR

www.akarua.com

This attractive restaurant is attached to Akarua Vineyard. Lamb and beef dishes are a strength, along with the produce of local orchards and Stewart Island salmon. Rack of lamb is a signature dish, served with kumara (sweet potato) and butternut squash and fettucine.

✉ Akarua Winery, Cairnmuir Road, Bannockburn ☎ 03-445 3211 ⏲ Summer daily 11–3, 6–late; winter Wed–Sun 11–3, 6–late 💳 L NZ$25, D NZ$50, W NZ$34

## DUNEDIN

### BELL PEPPER BLUES AND THE CHILE CLUB

www.bellpepperblues.co.nz

Chef Michael Coughlin takes inspiration from many cuisines. Cervena venison is a signature dish, which may be served as a grilled Denver leg cut with smoked venison sausage, kumara and leek hash cake. Both the service and presentation show meticulous attention to detail. The Chile Club offers a lunch menu.

✉ 474 Princes Street, Dunedin ☎ 03-474 0973 ⏲ Mon–Sat 6.30pm–late; also Wed–Fri 12–3 💳 D NZ$65, W NZ$34

## INVERCARGILL

### THE CABBAGE TREE

www.thecabbagetree.com

On the way to the beach, The Cabbage Tree has been rebuilt from the old Beach Store, with lots of native planting. The menu includes giant sandwiches, all-day breakfast and high tea: a speciality is the 'Chatter Platter' of blue cheese, salami, brie, pâté, smoked salmon, squid rings, ham strips, stuffed mushrooms, olives, guacamole, basil pesto, gherkins, sun-dried tomatoes, marinated vegetables with bread and crackers.

✉ 379 Dunns Road, Otatara, Invercargill ☎ 03-213 1443 ⏲ Daily 11am–late 💳 L NZ$30, D NZ$55, W NZ$22

**HMS KING'S**

A traditional fish restaurant decked out like a ship, King's is popular with families and serves fresh, locally caught seafood such as Bluff oysters, crayfish and whitebait. The cooking style is simple, and seafood chowder is a speciality.

✉ 80 Tay Street, Invercargill ☎ 03-218 3443 🕐 Mon–Fri 11.30–3, Sat–Sun 5–10 ✋ L NZ$18, D NZ$43, W NZ$25

## MANDEVILLE

**THE MOTH RESTAURANT AND BAR**

www.themoth.co.nz

Next to an air museum, The Moth is adorned with aviation memorabilia. The food is fresh, with home-made bread, and the menu includes roast chicken breast, lamb rump seared in mint oil, spicy BBQ pork loin and poached blue cod. Leave space for desserts such as dessert pizza of the day and berry jelly pannacotta.

✉ Old Mandeville Airfield, SH94, Mandeville ☎ 03-208 9662 🕐 Nov–end Apr daily 10am–late; May–end Oct Tue–Sun 10am–late ✋ L NZ$30, D NZ$50, W NZ$25

## MOERAKI

**FLEURS PLACE**

www.fleursplace.com

This quirky waterfront restaurant specializes in fresh fish. The menu offers blue cod, dory, moki, blue nose, gurnard, grouper, crayfish, mussels and titi (muttonbird). Reservations are essential.

✉ The Old Jetty, Moeraki ☎ 03-439 4480 🕐 Daily 9am–late ✋ L NZ$28, D NZ$50, W NZ$28

## OAMARU

**CRITERION HOTEL**

www.criterion.net.nz

In the historic heart of town, this restored Victorian pub has hand-pumped ales and boutique beers. The food is traditional, with beef hotpot, pies, roasts and sausage and mashed potato. You can also stay overnight in Victorian-themed rooms.

✉ Corner of Tyne and Harbour streets, Oamaru ☎ 03-434 6247 🕐 Mon–Wed 12–9.30, Thu 12–11, Fri, Sat 12–12, Sun 12–8 ✋ L NZ$15, D NZ$50, W NZ$18

## QUEENSTOWN

**THE BATHHOUSE CAFÉ AND RESTAURANT**

www.bathhouse.co.nz

This was the original Victorian bath house on the beach, and it retains its period charm. You can come for breakfast, lunch, afternoon tea or dinner. The menu is small. You can eat simply with an omelette, miso soup or waffles. For lunch there is moussaka and lamb shanks; for dinner there's venison, wild boar, beef pasta and rack of lamb.

✉ 15 Marine Parade, Queenstown ☎ 03-442 5625 🕐 Tue–Sun 10am–late ✋ L NZ$40, D NZ$80, W NZ$36

**THE COW**

The Cow—formerly a milking shed—is cramped but full of character. A Queenstown institution, it specializes in pizza and pasta, and serves up simple, hearty fare at reasonable prices.

✉ Cow Lane, Queenstown ☎ 03-442 8588 🕐 Daily 12–late ✋ L NZ$25, D NZ$35, W NZ$25

## ST. BATHANS

**THE VULCAN HOTEL**

When gold fever was at its height, there were 14 hotels in St. Bathans. Now there is only one: the Vulcan, a mudbrick building dating from 1882. The walls are thick and the place is full of charm. You can get bar snacks here and 'Devonshire' teas, and the hotel bistro serves a blend of traditional New Zealand with Polynesian, French, Italian and local ingredients. You can also stay the night in basic accommodation.

✉ 1670 Loop Road, St. Bathans, Oturehua ☎ 03-447 3629 🕐 Daily 8am–11pm ✋ L NZ$15, D NZ$35, W NZ$28

## STEWART ISLAND

**SOUTH SEA HOTEL**

www.stewart-island.co.nz

On the Oban waterfront, this is a country hotel and a popular meeting place for the locals. You can get a good taste of the island from the restaurant, which serves locally sourced oysters, mussels, salmon and scampi. The chowder is a speciality and the titi (muttonbird) is baked to order.

✉ Half Moon Bay, Oban, Stewart Island ☎ 03-219 1059 🕐 Daily 7am–9pm ✋ L NZ$25, D NZ$35, W NZ$21

## TE ANAU

**REDCLIFF CAFÉ AND BAR**

The Redcliff is a casual and intimate café with a convivial bar, set in a rustic cottage a block from the lake. It's also a popular venue for live entertainment. The menu focuses on fresh produce, with as much attention paid to the vegetables as the meat dishes. You can eat as simply as breads with spreads and pasta to hearty lamb and venison dishes, and finish with crème brûlée.

✉ 12 Mokonui Street, Te Anau ☎ 03-249 7431 🕐 Daily 5–9.30pm ✋ D NZ$45, W NZ$25

## WANAKA

**CARDRONA HOTEL**

www.cardronahotel.co.nz

The Cardrona Hotel and the adjoining buildings are all that remain of gold-rush Cardrona. The pub is full of atmosphere and you can stay in the modernized units. It's a great place to stop for an après-ski mulled wine, and in summer there's a garden with a children's playground. The restaurant serves an à la carte menu and regional and local wines.

✉ Crown Range Road, Wanaka ☎ 03-443 8153 🕐 Daily 11.30am–late ✋ L NZ$30, D NZ$52, W NZ$25

**MISSY'S KITCHEN**

www.missyskitchen.co.nz

Missy's has expansive views over the lake and mountains and a sophisticated city atmosphere. The Pacific Rim menu takes its inspiration from the Mediterranean kitchen with Cajun and Oriental overtones. The choices are relatively few but well considered. The beverage list includes a good range of wines, beers, whisky and speciality teas, and the sommelier is knowledgeable.

✉ Level 1, 80 Ardmore Street, Wanaka ☎ 03-443 5099 🕐 Daily 4pm–late ✋ D NZ$70, W NZ$30

**Above** *Corstorphine House Private Hotel in Dunedin*

**PRICES AND SYMBOLS**

The prices are the lowest and highest for a double room for one night including breakfast, unless otherwise stated. All the hotels listed accept credit cards unless otherwise stated. Note that rates can vary widely throughout the year.

For a key to the symbols, ▷ 2.

## ALEXANDRA

### ROCKY RANGE

www.rockyrange.co.nz

Set on a hill above Alexandra township, this purpose-built guest lodge provides luxury accommodation, tranquillity and marvellous views. The four guest rooms are spacious and beautifully decorated in a warm, country style featuring quality furnishings throughout. A range of spa treatments is available in-house, and there is a spa pool. Trout fishing is a local speciality and the lodge can provide a local guide.

✉ 159 The Half Mile, Alexandra ☎ 03-448 6150 NZ$375 4 rooms Spa pool 1.2km (0.8 miles) south of the Clutha River Bridge on the east side of SH8, between Alexandra and Roxburgh

## CROMWELL

### GOLDEN GATE LODGE

www.goldengate.co.nz

Smart and spacious, the lodge is designed to reflect the region's gold-mining heritage. Accommodation is in twin, double and king studios, suites (some with spa) and units, all with tea-making facilities. There are also a sauna and spa, licensed restaurant, café and wine bar. The Lodge is located at the entrance to the town, opposite the shopping mall and by the golf course.

✉ Barry Avenue, Cromwell ☎ 03-445 1777 NZ$135 47 rooms 500m (550 yards) from Cromwell Visitor Information Office

## DUNEDIN

### CORSTORPHINE HOUSE PRIVATE HOTEL

www.corstorphine.co.nz

A listed 1863 heritage building, this five-star Edwardian-style private hotel sits in a 5ha (12-acre) estate and commands fine views across the city. The house is beautifully appointed throughout, with stylish themed suites, from Scottish to art deco or a French boudoir. The estate produces flowers, vegetables, herbs, fruits, nuts and eggs for the house restaurant.

✉ 23A Milburn Street, Corstorphine, Dunedin ☎ 03-487 6676/6672 NZ$530–NZ$790 7 rooms 6km (4 miles) south of downtown

### HULMES COURT

www.hulmes.co.nz

Hulmes Court B&B is in a turreted 1860s Victorian mansion located two blocks from the Octagon. It is quiet, comfortable and friendly. Together with Hulmes Too, an Edwardian house next door, it has 14 bedrooms decorated in keeping with the period, with harbour and garden views, some with shared bath.

✉ 52 Tennyson Street, Dunedin ☎ 03-477 5319 NZ$70–NZ$165 14 rooms 1km (0.5 miles) from Dunedin Visitor Information Office

### MOTEL MORAY PLACE

www.97motel.co.nz

This modern, centrally located motel has quiet standard and executive

units with comfortable beds and tiled bathrooms. Executive units come with spa baths. The units do not have full cooking facilities, but continental breakfast is available and each unit has a TV, a microwave oven, tea-making facilities, a toaster, a fridge and an iron.
97 Moray Place, Dunedin 03-477 2050 NZ$115–NZ$170 40 unit 200m (220 yards) from the Octagon and Dunedin Visitor Information Office

**SOUTHERN CROSS**
www.scenic-circle.co.nz
Dunedin's premier hotel, located in the heart of the city, the Southern Cross dates back to 1883 when it was the original Grand Hotel. It has three in-house restaurants and two bars. The boutique casino is an added attraction for some guests. Rooms all have satellite TV, ironing facilities, hair dryers, tea-making facilities and internet access.
Corner of Princes and High streets, Dunedin 03-477 0752 NZ$281–NZ$534 170 rooms, 8 suites 1km (0.5 miles) from the Octagon and Dunedin Visitor Information Office

## INVERCARGILL

**ASCOT PARK HOTEL**
www.mainstay.co.nz
Ascot Park is in peaceful, park-like surroundings on the outskirts of Invercargill, and is the city's top hotel. Large and modern, it has a mix of deluxe, superior and standard rooms and motel units. It also has a restaurant, bar and tavern complex.
Corner of Tay Street and Racecourse Road, Invercargill 03-217 6195/0800-272 687 NZ$100–NZ$220 72 rooms, 24 motel units 4km (2.5 miles) from the CBD

## KAKA POINT

**NUGGET VIEW, KAKA POINT AND CATLINS COAST MOTELS**
www.catlins.co.nz
As the name suggests, this complex has a variety of accommodation options, from economy to five-star luxury, all with ocean views. Open-plan studios have double beds; two-room apartments are suitable for families; superior spa units have a king bed and double spa bath. Kayaks and body boards are provided. The owners also operate fishing trips and eco-tours to The Nuggets (▷ 229).
11 Rata Street, Kaka Point 03-412 8602/0800-525 278 NZ$85–NZ$305 14 rooms 23km (14 miles) from Balclutha and SH1 via Highway 92. Turn off Highway 92 at Romahapa

## MANAPOURI

**BEECHWOOD LODGE**
www.beechwoodlodge.com
A modern, deservingly popular boutique B&B that overlooks the lake and mountains, Beechwood accommodates guests in two spacious en suites, which have their own private entrance and kitchen. The entire floor can also be booked as a suite. The real drawcard is the lounge, from which you can sit and muse upon the ever-changing moods of the lake. Not suitable for children.
40 Cathedral Drive, Manapouri 03-249 6993 NZ$350–NZ$550 2 rooms 20km (13 miles) south of Te Anau

## MILFORD SOUND

**MILFORD SOUND LODGE**
www.milfordlodge.com
For the independent visitor, this backpackers' lodge is a great choice in Milford Sound. It can be very cosmopolitan and in midsummer, outside the local pub's opening hours, forms the hub of Milford's leisure activity. Single, double/twin and shared rooms are available, with shared bathrooms. The restaurant serves breakfast and pub meals. There's a kitchen, a large lounge and a store.
Milford Road, Milford Sound 03-249 8071 NZ$80–NZ$225 8 double/twin units On Milford Road, 1km (0.5 miles) east of Milford Sound airfield

## OAMARU

**KINGSGATE HOTEL BRYDONE**
www.millenniumhotels.co.nz
Oamaru's oldest and largest hotel, in the heart of town, the Brydone has an elegant Historic Wing, built in 1881 and furnished in period style, and a Pacific Wing, built in the 1970s. Despite the odd creaking floorboard, it's worth trying to book the former and soak up the atmosphere. The hotel has doubles or suites, some with spa baths, and there is a popular bar and restaurant.
115 Thames Street, Oamaru 03-434 0011 NZ$120–NZ$286 50 rooms 1km (0.5 miles) from Oamaru Visitor Information Office

## OTAGO PENINSULA

**LARNACH LODGE**
www.larnachcastle.co.nz
Larnach Lodge has beautifully appointed themed rooms, from the tartan Scottish Room to the Goldrush Room, with a king-size bed made from an old cart found on the property. The views across the harbour and peninsula are superb. Breakfast is served in the former stables. Dinner is optional (NZ$50) in the castle. Less expensive rooms with shared bathrooms in the former coach house are also available. It's essential to book ahead.
145 Camp Road, Otago Peninsula 03-476 1616 NZ$250–NZ$280 12 rooms 12km (8 miles) from Dunedin CBD via Highcliff and Camp roads

## QUEENSTOWN

**EICHARDT'S PRIVATE HOTEL**
www.eichardts.co.nz
This centrally located, historic hotel was founded in 1866. Refurbished since the 1990s Queenstown floods, it now caters for the luxury boutique market. It has elegantly appointed suites with antiques and an open fire, and a guest parlour with overstuffed chairs and sofas against a backdrop of exquisite antiques.
Marine Parade, Queenstown 03-441 0450 NZ$1,375–NZ$1,595 5 suites 200m (220 yards) from Queenstown Visitor Information Office

**HERITAGE QUEENSTOWN**
www.heritagehotels.co.nz
The Heritage is on the western edge of town in a quiet position, with great views. Bedrooms include luxury suites, some self-contained

with kitchen and laundry facilities, dishwasher and a full complement of crockery and glassware. There is a restaurant with open fire.
91 Fernhill Road, Queenstown
03-442 4988/0800-368 888
NZ$140–NZ$960 197 rooms
2km (1 mile) west of Queenstown Visitor Information Office

**MATAKAURI LODGE**
www.matakauri.co.nz
This is a magnificent place, set in private bush with uninterrupted views across Lake Wakatipu. Accommodation is in modern villas and fully self-contained suites. The spacious lodge has a library and four fireplaces, and the spa pavilion in the grounds is perfect for après-ski. Dinner is served with top quality local wines.
Glenorchy Road, Queenstown
03-441 1008 NZ$1,265–NZ$1,991, including dinner 6 suites and villa suites
5km (3 miles) west of Queenstown

**QUEENSTOWN HOUSE**
www.queenstownhouse.co.nz
Refurbished in 2002, this well-established modern upper-range B&B is in a central location overlooking the town. Accommodation comprises elegant en suites and new villa suites with fireside sitting rooms. The pre-dinner hospitality hour is a speciality—you can sample NZ wine, cheeses and seasonal treats, while exchanging experiences and sharing restaurant recommendations. The full cooked or Continental breakfasts are excellent. There is internet access.
69 Hallenstein Street, Queenstown
03-442 9043 NZ$295–NZ$595
13 rooms 500m (550 yards) from Queenstown Visitor Information Office

## STEWART ISLAND/ RAKIURA

**PORT OF CALL BOUTIQUE ACCOMMODATION**
www.portofcall.co.nz
In an idyllic spot overlooking the entrance to Halfmoon Bay, surrounded by 8ha (20 acres) of native bush and abundant bird life, this B&B has a charming double en suite, with great breakfasts and views from the deck. There are also two self-contained cottages. The friendly hosts also have an eco-guiding operation.
Jensen Bay, Stewart Island 03-219 1394 NZ$385, cottage NZ$170–NZ$300
1 guest room, 2 cottages 1km (0.5 miles) east of the village

**SOUTH SEA HOTEL**
www.stewart-island.co.nz
This is a great place to stay if you wish to mix with the locals and experience Stewart Island life. There are traditional hotel rooms (some with sea views) and self-contained motel units on a nearby property. There is a bar, and a restaurant where you can sample the local delicacy—muttonbird.
Main Road, Oban 03-219 1059
NZ$95–NZ$145 30 rooms, 9 motel units 100m (110 yards) from the ferry

## TE ANAU

**FIORDLAND LODGE**
www.fiordlandlodge.co.nz
A purpose-built luxury lodge in the classic style, this has stunning views across the lake and mountains. Facilities include smart guest rooms, two self-contained log cabins and a restaurant. The high ceilings, full tree-trunk pillars and huge picture windows add to the appeal and sense of space.
472 Te Anau–Milford Highway
03-249 7832 Cabins NZ$440–NZ$640; suites NZ$680–NZ$1,080, including dinner 10 rooms, 2 cabins 5km (3 miles) north of Te Anau

## WANAKA

**CARDRONA HOTEL**
www.cardronahotel.co.nz
The Cardrona may be a little out of the way, but is well worth the journey. The hotel is more than 140 years old and retains much of its character. Double rooms in the old stables look out over a beautiful garden and courtyard. There is a great rustic restaurant and bar. Advance booking is essential.
Crown Range Road (SH89), Cardrona
03-443 8153 NZ$135–NZ$185
16 rooms On the Crown Range Road, 26km (16 miles) south of Wanaka

**THE MOORINGS**
www.themoorings.co.nz
This modern, classy boutique apartment and motel block overlooks the lake, and is only metres from the lakeshore and the heart of town. Stylish motel rooms have underfloor heating and balcony views, and the spacious apartments have log burners and individual carports. Satellite TV and a ski-drying room are available.
17 Lakeside Road, Wanaka
03-443 8479 NZ$160–NZ$345
14 motel units, 8 apartments
100m (110 yards) from Wanaka Visitor Information Office

**Below** *Port of Call Boutique Accommodation on Stewart Island/Rakiura*

# PRACTICALITIES

Practicalities gives you all the important practical information you will need during your visit from money matters to phone numbers.

## WEATHER

### CLIMATE

New Zealand has what is called an ocean temperate climate—that is, generally agreeable. As the country is fairly elongated and lies at a north-to-south angle, the weather varies considerably. The north is consistently a few degrees warmer than the south; the warmest region is usually Northland and the coldest Southland. However, especially in recent years, uncommon weather patterns have seen the reverse to be true, sometimes lasting for days on end.

» In Auckland average temperatures for winter (June–August) are 8°C to 15°C (46°F to 59°F) and for summer (December–March) 14°C to 23°C (57°F to 74°F).

» In Dunedin winter temperatures average at 4°C to 12°C (39°F to 53°F) and summer temperatures at 9°C to 19°C (48°F to 66°F). But this can be misleading. Inland from Dunedin, Alexandra is often the hottest spot in the country.

» Nelson and Marlborough, in the South Island, have won the competition for sunniest place for several years running. Next year, though, it could just as easily be Napier, on the relatively dry and sunny east coast of the North Island, or even Whakatane in the Bay of Plenty.

» Wellington and Auckland also boast a lot of sunshine, Auckland being far more humid and Wellington notoriously windier.

» The west coast and Fiordland also have extremes of wind and rain, but even in winter the rain in New Zealand doesn't last for long periods.

### WHEN TO GO

The summer, or high season, lasts from November to March and is the busiest time, when New Zealanders are themselves taking a break. At these times, especially over Christmas and the whole of January, a large proportion of the population heads for the beach or the mountains. Accommodation is at a premium and the roads to major

### TIME ZONES

| CITY | TIME DIFFERENCE IN HOURS | TIME AT 12 NOON IN NZ |
|---|---|---|
| Amsterdam | -11 | 1am |
| Berlin | -11 | 1am |
| Brussels | -11 | 1am |
| Cairo | -10 | 2am |
| Chicago | -18 | 6pm (previous day) |
| Dublin | -12 | midnight |
| Johannesburg | -10 | 2am |
| London | -12 | midnight |
| Madrid | -10 | 2am |
| Montréal | -17 | 7pm (previous day) |
| New York | -17 | 7pm (previous day) |
| Paris | -11 | 1am |
| Perth, Australia | -4 | 8am |
| San Francisco | -20 | 4pm (previous day) |
| Sydney | -2 | 10am |
| Tokyo | -3 | 9am |

New Zealand is one of the first countries in the world to see the dawn. Standard time is 12 hours ahead of Greenwich Mean Time, and New Zealand Daylight Saving Time (summer time) runs from 2am on the first Sunday in October to 2am on the third Sunday in March. During this period clocks go forward one hour.

resorts can be busy—though in some areas, particularly the remoter parts of the South Island, 'busy' can mean a car passing every five or ten minutes.

» The months of late spring (September–October) or early autumn (March–April) are good alternatives. At these times the weather is still pleasant, accommodation easier to find and prices lower. The winter, or low season, sits between April/May and August/ September.

» Some places close in winter but generally New Zealand serves its visitors well year-round. Places such as Queenstown, where skiing is a major activity, can be busier in winter than they are in summer.

### NATURAL HAZARDS

Be aware that the sun in New Zealand is dangerous. Ozone depletion is heavy in the southern latitudes and the incidence of melanoma and other skin cancers is above average. Burn times, especially in summer, are greatly reduced: always wear a hat and appropriate sun block.

» If you are climbing, tramping or going into the bush, note that the weather is particularly changeable at higher elevations and can sometimes be deadly. Make sure you are properly clothed and shod and take maps, a first-aid kit and a compass. Above all, inform someone of your intentions.

» Major volcanic eruptions and earthquakes are rare but they do happen and can prove fatal. In the event of an earthquake stand in a doorway, get under a table or, if you are in the open, get indoors or keep away from loose rock formations and trees.

» Advance weather reports and safety information can be found on the Department of Conservation's website, www.doc.govt.nz.

## DOCUMENTS

### PASSPORTS AND VISAS

All visitors must be in possession of a passport that is valid for three months beyond the date of intended departure. Australian citizens or holders of an Australian returning resident visa do not need a visitor's visa and can stay in New Zealand indefinitely. Citizens of some countries, including the UK and the US, do not need visas for stays of up to three months (six months for UK citizens).

» For detailed visa information consult the Visiting section of the Immigration New Zealand (INZ) website, www.immigration.govt.nz or contact them at NZIS, Private Bag, Wellesley Street, Auckland (tel 09-914 4100/0508-558 855).

» Entry requirements can change: Always check before you travel.

### LONGER STAYS/WORK VISAS

It is illegal to work on a visitor's permit. Non-residents (with the exception of Australian citizens) must obtain a work visa, which allows entry to the country, and then a work permit, which allows the holder to work on arrival. Applications for both should be made well before arrival. The INZ website has details and application forms that can be downloaded.

» One exception to the rule is the working holiday visa, which is available for those aged 18 to 30 from countries including Argentina,



## WELLINGTON

### TEMPERATURE

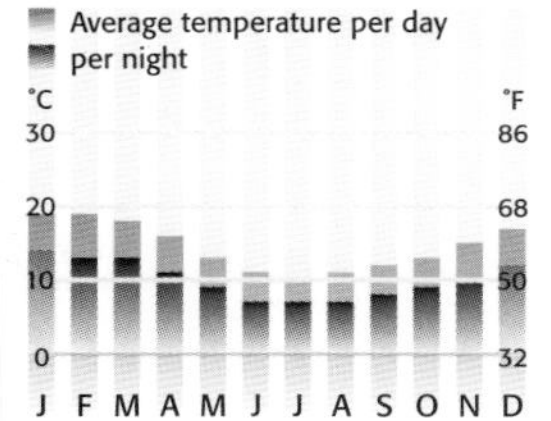


### RAINFALL

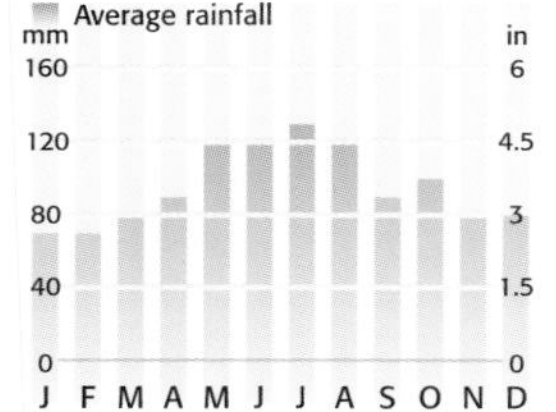


## AUCKLAND

### TEMPERATURE

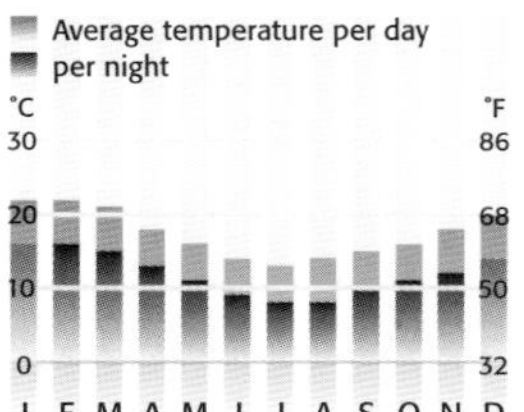


### RAINFALL

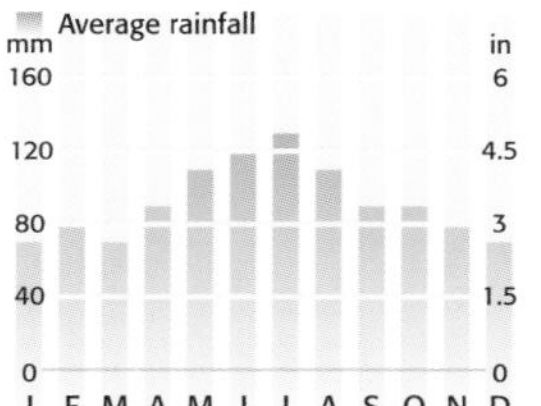


## CHRISTCHURCH

### TEMPERATURE

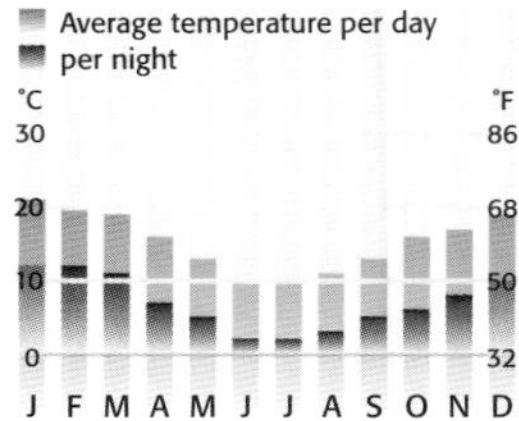


### RAINFALL

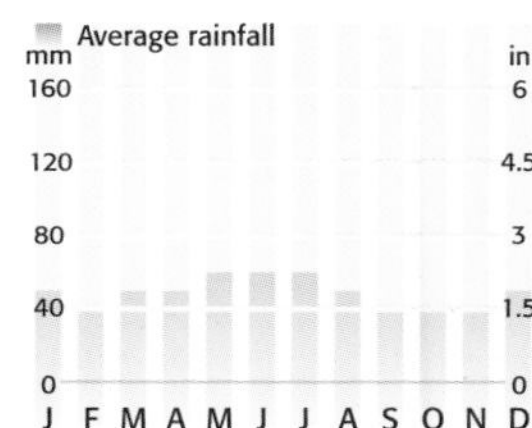

## CUSTOMS AND DUTY-FREE ALLOWANCES

New Zealand's environment and unique biodiversity have been decimated by non-native flora and fauna. Not surprisingly, therefore, the country has strict bio-security laws. You must not bring with you any fruit, animal or plant matter of any kind without prior permission. Heavy fines are imposed on those breaking the rules. Comprehensive advice for visitors is available on the New Zealand Customs Service website, www.customs.govt.nz.

If you are over 17 years of age you may import the following:

» 200 cigarettes or 250g of tobacco or 50 cigars or a combination of all three weighing no more than 250g

» 4.5 litres of wine or beer and one 1.125l bottle of spirits, liqueur or other alcoholic drink

Goods of value up to NZ$700 are duty- and tax-free.

Canada, Chile, Denmark, France, Germany, Hong Kong, Ireland, Italy, Japan, Korea, Malaysia, Netherlands, Singapore, Sweden, Taiwan, UK and Uruguay. This allows holders to work for 12 months.

» Student visas are needed for anyone (other than Australian citizens) planning to study a course of more than three months; anyone studying shorter courses will need a valid visitor's permit.

### TRAVEL INSURANCE

Full travel insurance is recommended, covering at least medical care and personal effects.

» The New Zealand accident compensation scheme (ACC) covers visitors to New Zealand for personal injury by accident. Benefits include some emergency medical expenses, but do not include loss of earnings.

» Healthline gives free 24-hour health advice and tells you how best to access the New Zealand health system, tel 0800 611 116.

» There is a wide variety of policies from which to choose, so shop around. Always read the small print carefully and check that the policy covers any activities you may intend to pursue, such as whitewater rafting or bungy jumping. Also check exactly what the medical cover includes—for example, ambulance, helicopter rescue or emergency flights home. You may have to pay before being reimbursed by the insurance company, so check the payment protocol.

### WHAT TO TAKE

New Zealand is a well-developed nation and all you are likely to need, from pharmaceuticals to camping equipment, is readily available throughout the country.

» If you are backpacking, bring a good sleeping bag and a sheet, items not always provided in hostels and which are certainly not available in backcountry tramping huts.

» Other items to remember are a compatible electrical adaptor plug, binoculars, a sun hat, sunscreen, insect repellent and sunglasses.

**Below** *Backpackers in Abel Tasman park*

## NEW ZEALAND EMBASSIES ABROAD

| COUNTRY | ADDRESS | WEBSITE |
|---|---|---|
| Australia | High Commission: Commonwealth Avenue, Canberra, ACT 2600, tel 02-6270 4211 | www.nzembassy.com |
| Canada | High Commission: Suite 727, Metropolitan House, 99 Bank Street, Ottowa, Ont K1P 6G3, tel 613/238-5991 | www.nzembassy.com |
| France | 7ter, rue Leonard de Vinci, 75116 Paris, tel 01 45 01 43 43 | www.nzembassy.com |
| Germany | Atrium, Friedrichstrasse 60, 10117, Berlin, tel 30 206 210 | www.nzembassy.com |
| Ireland | Consulate, PO Box 999, Dublin 6, tel 01 660 4233 | www.nzembassy.com |
| Netherlands | Carnegielaan 10, 2517 KH, Den Haag, tel 703 469324 www.nzembassy.com | |
| UK | High Commission: New Zealand House, Haymarket, London SW1Y 4TQ, tel 020 7930 8422 | www.nzembassy.com |
| USA | 37 Observatory Circle NW, Washington DC 20008, tel 202/328-4800 | www.nzembassy.com |

## MONEY

### BANKNOTES AND COINS

» The New Zealand currency is the dollar (NZ$), which is divided into 100 cents (c). Coins are in denominations of 10c, 20c, 50c, NZ$1 and NZ$2. Notes come in NZ$5, NZ$10, NZ$20, NZ$50 and NZ$100 denominations.

» Banknotes feature people important to New Zealand: Sir Edmund Hillary, conqueror of Everest (NZ$5); Kate Sheppard, pioneer of female emancipation (NZ$10); The Queen (NZ$20); Sir Apirana Ngata, Maori statesman (NZ$50); and Lord Rutherford, who split the atom (NZ$100).

### CREDIT CARDS, ATMS AND EFTPOS

» All major credit cards (Visa, MasterCard, Amex, JCB, Diners) are widely accepted. New Zealand operates an EFTPOS (Electronic Funds Transfer at Point of Sale) system, which effectively means that there are mini-ATMs at points of sale throughout the country. Most hotels, shops, retail outlets and fuel stations have EFTPOS. Debit and credit cards may be used with the relevant PIN numbers.

» Standard ATMs are available in almost all towns and accept non-host bank cards, though there may be hidden fees. Some banks are linked internationally via such networks as Cirrus and Plus.

» New Zealand's banks include the ANZ National Bank, ASB Bank, Bank of New Zealand, Kiwibank, TSB Bank and Westpac. Most are represented in all main towns, and branches or ATMs operated by one or more of the banks can be found in smaller places. Internet banking facilities are also popular. For a full list see www.rbnz.govt.nz/nzbanks/.

» Bank opening hours are Monday to Friday 9–4.30; some city branches also open on Saturday until 12.30.

» Exchange offices such as Travelex and American Express sometimes stay open until 9pm in the cities.

### TRAVELLERS' CHEQUES

The safest way to carry money is in travellers' cheques. These are available for a small commission from all major banks. American Express (Amex), Visa and Thomas Cook cheques are widely accepted.

» Most banks do not charge for changing travellers' cheques and they usually offer the best exchange rates.

» Be sure to keep a record of your cheque numbers and keep the cheques you have cashed separate from the cheques themselves, so that you can get a full refund of all uncashed cheques should you lose them.

» It is best to bring NZ$ cheques to avoid exchange costs.

### WIRING MONEY

If you need money quickly or in an emergency, you can have it wired to you via any major bank with Western Union (through New Zealand Post, tel 0800-005 253) or via Travelex and moneygram (tel 0800-200 232, www.travelex.co.nz). This transfer can be completed in less than an hour or may take up to a week depending on how much is being

wired and how much you are willing to pay (about NZ$30–NZ$80).

### TAXES

A 12.5 per cent GST (Goods and Services Tax) is placed on almost every bought item in New Zealand. Prices quoted almost always include GST, but on bigger items or services it pays to check. On leaving New Zealand there is a departure charge of NZ$20–NZ$25, depending on which airport you use. This is not included in your ticket price.

### TIPPING

Tipping is at the customer's discretion and is not generally expected in New Zealand.

| 10 EVERYDAY ITEMS AND HOW MUCH THEY COST | |
|---|---|
| Sandwich | NZ$4 |
| 50cl bottle of water | NZ$2 |
| Cup of tea or coffee | NZ$3 |
| Pint of beer | NZ$6–NZ$7 |
| Glass of wine | NZ$5 |
| Daily newspaper | NZ$1.20 |
| Roll of camera film | NZ$7–NZ$14 |
| 20 cigarettes | NZ$10 |
| Ice cream | NZ$2.50 |
| Litre of fuel | NZ$1.50 |

| LOST OR STOLEN CREDIT CARDS |
|---|
| **Visa International** |
| 0800-443 019 |
| **MasterCard International** |
| 0800-449 140<br>or any bank displaying the VISA or MasterCard trademark |
| **American Express** |
| 0800-656 660<br>or any American Express Travel Service Office |

## HEALTH

### VACCINATIONS

No vaccinations are officially required for entry into New Zealand. You are, however, advised to get a tetanus shot or ensure that your booster is up to date.

### TREATMENT COSTS

If you are injured in an accident while in New Zealand you are covered for treatment, regardless of fault, under the national personal injury insurance scheme, run by the Accident Rehabilitation and Compensation Insurance Corporation (ACC): PO Box 242, Wellington (tel 04-918 7700/0800 101 996, www.acc.co.nz); there are also 31 branch offices spread all over the country—details are available on the website. The provider of your treatment will help you complete the appropriate form.

» If you see a doctor or another healthcare professional for treatment for a personal injury, you may be asked to pay part of the cost.

» ACC does not cover illness, so health insurance is highly recommended—visits to a doctor cost from about NZ$50 excluding prescription charges, and dental and hospital services are expensive. See also Travel Insurance, ▷ 262.

### WHAT TO TAKE

» It's advisable to take photocopies of your insurance documents and to keep these separately from the originals, or scan them onto an email address that can be reached from abroad, in case they are lost in an accident or stolen.

» If you are on unusual medication take supplies with you in case they are not easily available locally, and bring your prescription certificate in case of difficulties at customs.

» New Zealand's sun is dangerous due to ozone depletion, so be sure to bring a hat, sunglasses and the strongest possible sunblock to protect against the damage caused by ultraviolet rays. Be prepared to cover up, and be sure to wear this protection even on overcast days.

» Bring an insect repellent, especially to ward off the common and very annoying sandflies. The size of a pinhead, they are found in some coastal and wetter inland areas, and their bite can produce unpleasant spots on the skin that may itch for weeks. Repellents come in two forms: chemical-based—which are toxic and should be used only in the lowest concentrations (5–10 per cent)—and natural. If you are unable to find natural repellent at home, New Zealand manufacturers offer a wide range of natural creams and oils using ingredients such as eucalyptus or citronella.

### HAZARDS

» New Zealand is a great outdoors destination for visitors. Make sure you match your chosen activities to your level of fitness and skill, and that you are fully equipped for sudden changes in the weather.

» When tramping (hiking) be aware that water levels in streams and rivers can change swiftly. On coastal walks such as the Abel Tasman (▷ 166–167) be aware of local tides and their likely impact on your route and schedule.

» If you are planning a serious hike or an overnight trip, make sure someone knows your intentions and when to raise the alarm if you are missing. You can sign in at the start of your trip at a Department of Conservation (DoC) visitor centre—but make sure you remember to sign out again on your safe return. Unless you are very experienced, tramping alone on the more remote and quieter tracks is not advisable.

» There are very few dangerous creatures in New Zealand. One exception is the katipo spider, about 25mm (0.9in) from leg tip to leg tip and found on beaches, under stones and in driftwood throughout the North Island and in parts of the South. Its bite inflicts agonizing localized pain and can be fatal. Antivenom is available in hospitals.

### HEALTHY FLYING

» Visitors to New Zealand from as far as the US, UK and other parts of Europe may be concerned about the effect of long-haul flights on their health. The most widely publicized concern is Deep Vein Thrombosis, or DVT. Misleadingly called 'economy class syndrome', DVT is the forming of a blood clot in the body's deep veins, particularly in the legs. The clot can move around the bloodstream and could be fatal.

» Those most at risk include the elderly, pregnant women, those using the contraceptive pill, smokers and the overweight. If you are at increased risk of DVT see your doctor before departing. Flying increases the likelihood of DVT because passengers are often seated in a cramped position for long periods of time and may become dehydrated.

**To minimize risk:**

Drink water (not alcohol)
Don't stay immobile for hours at a time
Stretch and exercise your legs periodically
Do wear elastic flight socks, which support veins and reduce the chances of a clot forming

**Exercises**

**1 ankle rotations**
Lift feet off the floor. Draw a circle with the toes, moving one foot clockwise and the other counterclockwise

**2 calf stretches**
Start with heel on the floor and point foot upward as high as you can. Then lift heels high, keeping balls of feet on the floor

**3 knee lifts**
Lift leg with knee bent while contracting your thigh muscle. Then straighten leg, pressing foot flat to the floor

Other health hazards for flyers are airborne diseases and bugs spread by the plane's air-conditioning system. These are largely unavoidable but if you have a serious medical condition seek advice from a doctor before flying.

» Sharks are a common sight around New Zealand shores, but shark attacks on humans are rare. The last fatal attack occurred in Eastland in 1976.

» Giardia is a water-borne parasite which, if it enters your system, causes severe vomiting and diarrhoea and rapid weight loss. The best safeguard is not to drink water from lakes, ponds or rivers without boiling it first.

» Tap water is safe to drink throughout New Zealand; city supplies are chlorinated and most are also fluoridated.

### HOSPITALS

» There are public hospitals throughout the North and South Islands of New Zealand. Most, but not all, of these have emergency facilities—details can be found in the front of every white pages telephone directory.

### AMBULANCES

» In an emergency dial 111 anywhere in the country for an ambulance.

» Ambulances in most of the country are provided by organizations like St. John Ambulance, which charge patients for their use—this cost should be covered by medical insurance.

» The exception is Wellington, where the Wellington Free Ambulance makes no charge for its services, and is supported by public donations.

» In remoter areas and offshore islands, rescue helicopters and fixed-wing air ambulances are used where necessary.

### DOCTORS

» There are about 10,000 doctors in New Zealand. The Medical Council of New Zealand supplies a list of registered doctors and updates it weekly:
The Medical Council of New Zealand, Level 13, Mid City Tower, 139–143 Willis Street, PO Box 11 649, Wellington (tel 04-384 7635, www.mcnz.org.nz).

» Many cities and towns have private after-hours clinics and pharmacies, which treat non-emergency cases for a fee. Details are in the telephone directory.

### DENTISTS

» Emergency dentists can be found in the telephone directory Yellow Pages.

### PHARMACIES

» New Zealand pharmacists are known as chemists, and their shops sell a selection of cosmetics and other products, as well as drugs.

» Chemist shops open during normal shopping hours, and in most large towns and cities emergency dispensaries are open outside these hours as well. These are listed in the front of the phone book, under Hospitals.

» Some drugs sold over the counter in pharmacies in other countries may be available in New Zealand only with a prescription.

### ALTERNATIVE MEDICINE

» The New Zealand Charter of Health Practitioners is the biggest organization representing complementary and alternative health (CAM) practitioners in New Zealand. Members of its signatories must meet a set level of competence and are entitled to advertise as chartered health practitioners:
New Zealand Charter of Health Practitioners, Private Box 302 305, North Harbour, Auckland, tel 09-414 5501, www.healthcharter.org.nz.

» The New Zealand Register of Complementary Health Professionals (NZRCHP) provides a directory of practitioners who have trained and qualified in their discipline and who abide by their field's code of ethics:
NZRCHP, PO Box 337, Christchurch.

### EMERGENCIES

» Contact details for hospital Accident and Emergency departments are listed in the front of the white pages telephone directory.

» In an emergency, dial 111 for an ambulance.

## BASICS

### ELECTRICITY

The New Zealand supply is 230/240 volts (50 hertz).

» Plugs are either two- or three-pronged with flat pins.

» North American appliances require both an adaptor and a transformer.

» UK appliances need an adaptor only, and Australian appliances are the same.

» Adaptors and transformers are available at local hardware stores or at the airport.

### LAUNDRY

Most towns, villages and places to stay have laundry services.

» Washing and drying machines tend to operate with NZ$1 or NZ$2 coins.

» A full wash and dry costs approximately NZ$6.

### MEASUREMENTS

New Zealand uses the metric system. Distances are measured and signed in kilometres and fuel is sold in litres. However, if you ask for 'a pint' in a pub or restaurant you will be understood.

### PUBLIC TOILETS

Public toilets are available in towns and large villages and at visitor attractions, parks and fuel stations. They are usually clean and well maintained. You may be able to use toilets at libraries or visitor offices.

**CONVERSION CHART**

| From | To | Multiply by |
|---|---|---|
| Inches | Centimetres | 2.54 |
| Centimetres | Inches | 0.3937 |
| Feet | Metres | 0.3048 |
| Metres | Feet | 3.2810 |
| Yards | Metres | 0.9144 |
| Metres | Yards | 1.0940 |
| Miles | Kilometres | 1.6090 |
| Kilometres | Miles | 0.6214 |
| Acres | Hectares | 0.4047 |
| Hectares | Acres | 2.4710 |
| Gallons | Litres | 4.5460 |
| Litres | Gallons | 0.2200 |
| Ounces | Grams | 28.35 |
| Grams | Ounces | 0.0353 |
| Pounds | Grams | 453.6 |
| Grams | Pounds | 0.0022 |
| Pounds | Kilograms | 0.4536 |
| Kilograms | Pounds | 2.205 |
| Tons | Tonnes | 1.0160 |
| Tonnes | Tons | 0.9842 |

**Above** *A bewildering range of activities makes New Zealand an excellent destination for children*

» Public toilets are usually free of charge and are operated by local councils. Find out about them on www.govt.nz.

» Many lavatories have two press-button flushes: one (usually marked with a circle) gives a full flush and the other (marked with a semi-circle) gives a half-flush to save water.

### SMOKING REGULATIONS

New Zealand is increasingly smoke-free, and since December 2004, all bars, clubs, restaurants, cafés, casinos and gaming machine venues have been required to be entirely smoke-free indoors if they are workplaces, serve alcohol or have a gambling licence.

» Budget Rent-a-Car have declared themselves a smoke-free company (0800-283 438, www.budget.co.nz).

### VISITING WITH CHILDREN

Children will love the smelly springs, steaming vents, sandy beaches—not to speak of the set locations to be tracked down from the *Lord of the Rings* movies.

» There are discounts for children on public transport and at most attractions, and many offer family tickets as well. Very young children are often allowed free admission.

» Several companies specialize in organizing trips and tours tailored for families: try www.familytravel.co.nz.

» Information on family activities throughout New Zealand is available on www.familystophere.com.

» Most hotels offer or can recommend a babysitting service, but don't be afraid to ask about the qualifications of the babysitter or the conditions applied to the service.

» Make sure children are well protected against the New Zealand sun, as their skin is more vulnerable than adult skin. Hats, sun-screen and long-sleeved shirts can all help to avoid painful sunburn.

» Baby-on-the-Move is a company renting out and selling baby products to overseas visitors. Products include lightweight frames for prams or pushchairs (strollers), newborn and toddler seats for cars, detachable cots and child-carrying backpacks (tel 0800 222 966, www.babyonthemove.co.nz).

## VISITORS WITH A DISABILITY

For visitors with disabilities New Zealand can be a frustrating place. While most public amenities are well equipped for wheelchair use, older hotels and some public transport systems (particularly rural buses) are not well adapted. However, it is now a requirement by law to have adequate facilities in new buildings.

» Larger airlines such as Air New Zealand and Qantas are well equipped and this applies both to international and to domestic flights.

» Visitors with disabilities usually receive discounts on travel and some admission charges, and parking concessions are also available, with temporary cards issued on receipt of a mobility card or medical certificate.

» Full details on local services are available from regional Disability Information Centres; a list of contacts can be obtained from the head office at PO Box 24-042, Royal Oak, Auckland (tel 09-625 8069/0800 693 342, www.weka.net.nz).

» Some tour operators specialize in providing itineraries and equipment for visitors with disabilities: for more details ▷ 54, On the Move: Visitors with a Disability.

## PLACES OF WORSHIP

Most large urban centres in New Zealand have Anglican, Presbyterian, Baptist, Methodist and Catholic places of worship.

» Some useful websites are:
www.baptist.org.nz
www.rcnz.org.nz
www.methodist.org.nz
www.presbyterian.org.nz
www.anglican.org.nz
www.catholic.org.nz

» There are several mosques in Auckland, Hamilton, Palmerston North, Wellington, Christchurch and Dunedin. Full addresses are available on www.nzmuslim.net.

» There are synagogues in Auckland, Hamilton, Christchurch, Wellington and Dunedin; details of addresses are listed on the website www.haruth.com.

» The Auckland Buddhist Centre is run by the Western Buddhist Order and has a shrine room at 381 Richmond Road, Grey Lynn, Auckland (tel 09-378 1120, www.aucklandbuddhistcentre.org).

» The largest Maori religious movements are Ringatu and Ratana, now both regarded as Maori Christian churches. Ratana has more than 49,000 members and Ringatu over 8,000. The Ratana Church is based at Ratana, Taranaki province, in the North Island, and Ringatu membership is largely concentrated in the northern half of the island.

**Below** *Christ Church in Russell is the oldest surviving church in New Zealand*

## FINDING HELP

### PERSONAL SECURITY

New Zealand has its fair share of crime, and while visitors are rarely targeted for anything other than petty crime, it pays to be careful.

» Theft is rife, especially in Auckland, and tourist hotels, hostels and other accommodation are not exempt.

» Cars and campervans and their contents are regularly targeted, and are especially vulnerable when left at isolated but well-known beauty spots. Carry all money and valuables with you, and lock anything else safe and out of sight in the boot (trunk). Keep your vehicle locked at all times, and make sure your insurance covers theft.

» Hitching is still quite heavily practised in New Zealand but is not entirely safe, and is inadvisable for those travelling alone. If you do decide to hitch, keep to the main highways and restrict your hitching to the daylight hours; and never take off a rucksack and put that or a bag in the car first.

### LOST PROPERTY

Report any lost property to the local police station; www.police.govt.nz has a list of all station addresses.

» For numbers to contact regarding lost or stolen credit cards, ▷ 263.

### POLICE

The New Zealand police force is a national service responsible for enforcing criminal and traffic laws.

» Police wear light blue shirts with epaulettes and insignia on the arms; darker blue trousers; often a dark blue tie; and dark blue peaked caps with a chequerboard design around the band.

» The police organization is divided into 12 districts, each of which has a central station. Contact details for some of the major police stations are listed in the table below. For a list of all police stations, see www.police.govt.nz

### WHAT TO DO IF YOU'RE ARRESTED

If you are taken to a police station because the police suspect you might have committed a crime, give your name, address, occupation and date and place of birth.

» The police have the right to search, fingerprint and photograph you, and you are entitled to see a lawyer privately without delay. There should be a list of lawyers at the station; ask for the list and pick one. If you use a lawyer from the roster it will not cost anything.

» For legal advice contact the local Citizens Advice Bureau. A full list of branches is available on www.cab.org.nz.

**Above** *Police in New Zealand do not routinely carry firearms*

| EMERGENCY PHONE NUMBER | |
|---|---|
| Police, Fire or Ambulance | 111 |

**MAIN CITY CENTRAL POLICE STATIONS**

| CITY | ADDRESS | TELEPHONE |
|---|---|---|
| Auckland | Corner of Cook and Vincent streets | 09-302 6400 |
| Christchurch | Corner of Hereford Street and Cambridge Terrace | 03-363 7400 |
| Dunedin | 25 Great King Street | 03-471 4800 |
| Palmerston North | 400 Church Street | 06-351 3600 |
| Wellington | Corner of Victoria and Harris streets | 04-381 2000 |

**EMBASSIES AND CONSULATES IN NEW ZEALAND**

| COUNTRY | ADDRESS | TELEPHONE |
|---|---|---|
| Australia | 72–78 Hobson Street, Wellington | 04-473 6411 |
| | 7th Floor, 188 Quay Street, Auckland | 09-921 8800 |
| Canada | Level 11, 125 The Terrace, Wellington | 04-473 9577 |
| France | 34–42 Manners Street, Wellington | 04-384 2555 |
| Germany | Private Bag 92-093, Auckland | 09-375 8709 |
| | 90 Hobson Street, Wellington | 04-473 6063 |
| Ireland | 7th Floor, Citibank Building, 23 Customs Street West, Auckland | 09-977 2252 |
| UK | IAG House, 151 Queen Street, Auckland | 09-303 2973 |
| | 44 Hill Street, Wellington | 04-924 2888 |
| US | Level 3, Citibank Centre, 23 Customs Street East, Auckland | 09-303 2724 |
| | 29 Fitzherbert Terrace, Thorndon, Wellington | 04-462 6000 |

## OPENING TIMES AND TICKETS

### BANKS

Bank opening hours are Monday to Friday 9–4.30. Some branches in cities open Saturday until 12.30.

### CHURCHES

City churches are generally open to visitors Monday to Saturday 9 or 10–5 and to worshippers during church services.

### DOCTORS AND CHEMISTS

Pharmacies open Monday to Friday 9–5. Emergency services are provided outside these hours; dispensaries are listed under Hospitals in the front of the telephone directory.

Typical doctors' surgery hours are Monday to Friday 7.30–6.30, and Saturday 8–noon; each clinic will supply details and contact numbers for after-hours arrangements.

### FUEL STATIONS

Fuel stations in more populous areas open until about 11pm, and some open 24 hours a day; expect earlier closure in rural areas. Many sell a substantial range of supermarket-type items.

### MUSEUMS AND GALLERIES

Opening hours for museums and galleries vary widely according to their size and location. In major cities and resorts they may open any time between 8am and 10am and close some time between 4.30pm and 7pm during weekdays, and some have restricted hours during weekends or on Sunday. In remoter areas museums may open on a seasonal basis or by previous arrangement only; others close during weekends or for part of the week. See individual entries for details, and check ahead with the local visitor information centre if you are planning a special trip.

### RESTAURANTS, CAFÉS AND BARS

Opening hours vary and are often seasonal. Most cafés open for breakfast between 7am and 9am and remain open until at least 5pm. Many also remain open until late into the evening or into the small hours. This usually applies seven days a week, with special Sunday brunch opening times.

Most mid-range restaurants open their doors daily for lunch (11–2) and dinner (from 6pm). The more exclusive establishments usually open for dinner at about 6pm and some have restricted days or hours, especially in winter.

Pubs and bars are generally open from 11am until 11.30pm. Many places have extended licences and stay open until midnight or even 3am during weekends.

### SHOPS AND OFFICES

Most shops and businesses open Monday to Friday 9–5. Many shops also open on Saturday and Sunday. Large malls open daily and have at least one late shopping night a week. Larger supermarket chains open most evenings, and New Zealand dairies—convenience stores, found on main streets—are often open until 10 or 11pm.

### DISCOUNTS AND CONCESSIONS

Virtually all visitor attractions and transportation systems offer discounted entrance fees and fares to children, usually of school age, and many give free admission or travel to those under 5.

» Senior citizens are also offered discounts at most major attractions and on trains and buses. Savings can range from 30 per cent to 50 per cent of the full price.

» Many, though not all, attractions offer family tickets; the definition of 'family' varies from place to place. See individual attractions for details.

» Student discounts are not as widespread, but holders of YHA or VIP cards can save on accommodation and travel, and there are plenty of budget options for anyone backpacking around the country.

**Above** *Te Marae decoration in Te Papa Museum, Wellington*

### NATIONAL HOLIDAYS

Shops and banks shut on public holidays. During school vacations—particularly in January and February—you should book accommodation and activities well ahead. This also applies to the winter season at major ski resorts like Tongariro, Wanaka and Queenstown.

|  |  |
|---|---|
| **1–2 January** | New Year |
| **6 February** | Waitangi Day |
| **April (variable)** | Good Friday; Easter Monday |
| **25 April** | Anzac Day |
| **1st Mon in June** | Queen's Birthday |
| **4th Mon in October** | Labour Day |
| **25 December** | Christmas Day |
| **26 December** | Boxing Day |

## TOURIST INFORMATION

### VISITOR OFFICES

The official New Zealand Visitor Information Network is made up of around 100 accredited visitor information centres, nationally known as i-Sites.

» National i-Sites are based in Auckland and Christchurch and main visitor resorts such as Rotorua and Queenstown. They open seven days a week and provide a comprehensive information service, including advance hotel reservation and domestic airline, bus and train tickets. Souvenir shops and occasionally other retail outlets, currency exchange and cafés may be attached.

» Regional i-Sites are found throughout the country; there may be more than one in each region. They provide a general information and reservation service, usually seven days a week, and there is also a huge amount of free material available.

» Local i-Sites can be found almost anywhere, providing local information as well as assistance in lodging and transport reservations. They open at least five days a week, but are subject to varying hours during weekends and in low season.

### NATIONAL I-SITES

**Auckland**
Princes Wharf,
137 Quay Street,
tel 09-307 0612/ 0800 AUCKLAND,
www.aucklandnz.com

**Christchurch**
Old Chief Post Office,
Cathedral Square, PO Box 2600,
tel 03-379 9629,
www.christchurchnz.net

**Queenstown**
Corner of Shotover and Camp streets, tel 03-442 4100,
www.queenstown-vacation.com

**Rotorua**
1167 Fenton Street, tel 07-348 5179,
www.rotoruanz.com

### SELECTED REGIONAL AND LOCAL INFORMATION

**North Island**

**Auckland**
International Terminal,
Arrivals Lounge,
Auckland Airport,
tel 09-275 6467,
www.aucklandnz.com

SKYCITY, tel 09-363 7182,
www.aucklandnz.com

**Bay of Islands**
Marsden Road, Pahia, tel 09-402 7345, www.fndc.govt.nz/infocentre

**Coromandel**
355 Kapanga Road, tel 07-866 8598,
www.coromandeltown.co.nz

**Hamilton**
Corner of Bryce and Anglesea streets, tel 07-839 3580,
www.waikatonz.com

**Hastings**
Russell Street North,
tel 5526/ 0800 429 537,
www.hastings.co.nz

**Mount Maunganui**
Salisbury Avenue, tel 07-575 5099,
www.bayofplentynz.com

**Napier**
100 Marine Parade, tel 06-834 1911,
www.isitehawkesbaynz.co.nz

**Palmerston North**
The Square, tel 06-350 1922,
www.manawatunz.co.nz

**Taupo**
30 Tongariro Street, tel 07-376 0027,
www.laketauponz

**Thames**
206 Pollen Street, tel 07-868 7284,
www.thames-info.co.nz

**Wanganui**
101 Guyton Street, tel 06-349 0508,
www.wanganui.com

**Wellington**
101 Wakefield Street, Civic Square,
tel 04-802 4860,
www.wellingtonnz.com

**Whakatane**
Quay Street, tel 07-308 6058,
www.whakatane.com

**Whangarei**
Tarewa Park, 92 Otaika Road, tel 09-438 1079, www.whangareinz.org.nz

**South Island**

**Arthur's Pass**
Main Road, tel 03-318 9211,
www.doc.govt.nz

**Christchurch**
Domestic Terminal, Christchurch Airport, tel 03-353 7774,
www.travelinfo.co.nzz

**Dunedin**
48 The Octagon, tel 03-474 3300,
www.cityofdunedin.com

**Franz Josef**
Main Road, tel 03-752 0796,
www.doc.govt.nz

### MAIN TOURISM NEW ZEALAND OFFICES OVERSEAS

**www.newzealand.com**

| COUNTRY | ADDRESS | TELEPHONE |
|---|---|---|
| **Australia** | Suite 3, Level 24, 1 Albert Street, Sydney, NSW 2000 | 02-8220 9000 |
| **Canada** | Suite 1200, 888 Dunsmuir Street, Vancouver BC V6C 3K4 | 604/634-2117 |
| **UK** | New Zealand House, Haymarket, London SWIY 4QT | 020 7930 1662 |
| **US** | Suite 2510, 221 East 41st Street, New York, NY 10017 | 212/661-7088 |
| | Suite 300, 501 Santa Monica Boulevard, Los Angeles, CA 90401 | 310/395-7480 |

**Greymouth**
Corner of Mackay and Herbert streets, tel 03-768 5101, www.greydistrict.co.nz

**Haast**
Main Road, tel 03-750 0809, www.doc.govt.nz

**Hanmer Springs**
42 Amuri Avenue, tel 03-315 7128, www.hurunui.com

**Hokitika**
The Carnegie Building, tel 03-755 6166, www.hokitika.org

**Invercargill**
Queens Park, 108 Gala Street, tel 03-214 6243, www.invercargill.org.nz

**Kaikoura**
Westend, tel 03-319 5641, www.kaikoura.co.nz

**Mount Cook**
Bowen Drive, tel 03-435 1186, www.doc.govt.nz

**Nelson**
Corner of Trafalgar and Halifax streets, tel 03-548 2304, www.nelsonnz.com

**Picton**
The Foreshore, tel 03-520 3113, www.destinationmarlborough.com

**Stewart Island/Rakiura**
Halfmoon Bay, tel 03-219 0009, www.doc.govt.nz

**Te Anau**
Lakefront Drive, tel 03-249 8900, www.fiordland.org.nz

**Wanaka**
Ardmore Street, tel 03-443 1233, www.lakewanaka.co.nz

**Westport**
1 Brougham Street, tel 03-789 6658, www.westport.org.nz

## USEFUL WEBSITES

### VISITOR INFORMATION

**www.newzealand.com**
Official New Zealand visitor information

### ACCOMMODATION

**www.purenz.com**
National farmstay information

**www.stayyha.com**
Youth Hostels Association

**www.vip.co.nz**
Backpacker organization

**www.backpack.co.nz**
Budget Backpacker Hostels Limited website

**www.doc.govt.nz**
Information on Department of Conservation (DoC) campsites and huts

### RESTAURANTS

**www.time2dine.co.nz**
Online guide and reservation facility

### MAJOR SIGHTS

**www.doc.govt.nz**
Department of Conservation (DoC) site: information on national parks

**www.nzmuseums.co.nz**
Guide to museums nationwide

**www.tepapa.govt.nz**
Te Papa-Museum of New Zealand

**www.rotoruanz.com**
Rotorua information

**www.skycity.co.nz**
Sky Tower, Auckland

**www.mtcooknz.com**
Mount Cook/Aoraki National Park

**www.motuekaisite.co.nz**
Motueka visitor office website, with information on Abel Tasman National Park

### HISTORY

**www.enzed.com**
Links to history, from the arrival of Maori

**www.nzhistory.net.nz**
National history resource

**www.teara.govt.nz**
The encyclopedia of New Zealand

### ENTERTAINMENT

**www.nz-events.co.nz**
NZ AA's online guide to New Zealand

**www.ticketek.co.nz**
Listings of shows and events and ticketing information

### WEATHER AND CLIMATE

**www.metservice.co.nz**
Weather information and analysis

**www.nzcity.co.nz**
Regional news and weather satellite picture

### CULTURE AND SOCIETY

**www.gaytravel.net.nz**
**www.gaynewzealand.com**
Information for gay and lesbian visitors

**www.tpk.govt.nz**
Maori life and culture

**www.wwoof.co.nz**
Organic farm work in return for bed and board

### NEWS AND GENERAL INTEREST

**http://tvnz.co.nz**
National site with regional news links

### INFORMATION ON MAORI LIFE

Te Puni Kokiri (Ministry of Maori Development)
143 Lambton Quay, PO Box 3943, Wellington, tel 04-819 6000, www.tpk.govt.nz

| USEFUL NUMBERS |
|---|
| **National directory assistance** |
| 018 |
| **International directory assistance** |
| 0172 |
| **International operator** |
| 0170 |
| **Toll help desk** |
| 123 |

**Left** *Internet cafés can be found throughout the country*

## COMMUNICATION

### TELEPHONES

Payphones are colour-coded. Both coin (blue) and credit card (yellow) booths are available throughout New Zealand.

» Phone cards come in NZ$5, NZ$10, NZ$20 and NZ$50 denominations and can be bought from many retail outlets, post and visitor information offices, fuel stations and hostels. Do not use these cards for anything other than domestic calls within New Zealand.

» Coin phones take 10c, 20c, 50c, NZ$1 and NZ$2 coins.

| AREA CODES WITHIN NEW ZEALAND | |
|---|---|
| Auckland | 09 |
| Northland | 09 |
| Bay of Plenty | 07 |
| Coromandel | 07 |
| Taupo | 07 |
| Ruapehu | 07 |
| Waikato | 07 |
| Eastland | 06 |
| Hawkes Bay | 06 |
| Wanganui | 06 |
| Taranaki | 06 |
| Wellington | 04 |
| South Island | 03 |

| COUNTRY CODES FROM NEW ZEALAND | |
|---|---|
| Australia | 00 61 |
| Belgium | 00 32 |
| Canada | 00 1 |
| France | 00 33 |
| Germany | 00 49 |
| Greece | 00 30 |
| Ireland | 00 353 |
| Italy | 00 39 |
| Netherlands | 00 31 |
| Spain | 00 34 |
| Sweden | 00 46 |
| UK | 00 44 |
| USA | 00 1 |
| New Zealand international code | 00 64 |

» If you dial 013 (instead of 0) before the number the operator will call back after you have finished to let you know the cost of your call, but this service adds NZ$2.80 to the overall cost.

» Local non-business calls cost 50c from public telephones, but are free from residential telephones in New Zealand, so it should not cause offence if you ask to use a host's or a friend's domestic (non-business) telephone for that purpose.

» Toll-free numbers start with 0508 or 0800. 0900 numbers are usually very expensive.

» Cell phone numbers usually start with 027 (Telecom) or 021 (Vodafone).

### INTERNATIONAL CALLS

There are now numerous inexpensive international calling cards and call centres, one of the best being E Phone, www.telstraclear.co.nz, a calling card that accesses the net through an 0800 number. The cards, which vary from NZ$10 to NZ$50, can be bought from shops displaying the E Phone flag sign. Cards come with simple instructions and can be used from any landline telephone. Voice instructions guide you through the

| POST SHOPS WITH POST RESTANTE PICK-UP POINTS | | |
|---|---|---|
| **CITY** | **ADDRESS AND TELEPHONE** | **OPEN** |
| Auckland | 24 Wellesley Street, Bledisloe Street, tel 09-379 6710 | Mon–Fri 7.30–5.30 |
| Christchurch | 3 Cathedral Square, tel 03-377 5411 | Mon–Fri 8–6, Sat 10–4 |
| Dunedin | 243 Princes Street, tel 03-477 3518 | Mon–Fri 8.30–5.30 |
| Nelson | Corner of Trafalgar and Halifax streets, tel 03-546 7818 | Mon–Fri 7.45–5, Sat 9.30–12.30 |
| Queenstown | 15–19 Camp Street, tel 03-422 7670 | Mon–Fri 8.30am–10pm, Sat 9–4 |
| Wellington | 43 Manners Street, tel 04-473 5922 | Mon–Fri 8–5.30, Sat 10–1.30 |

process and tell you how much credit you have available before you make each call.

» Credit cards can be used directly in many public phones.

## INTERNET AND EMAIL

Internet cafés and terminals are everywhere in New Zealand and it is fairly easy to get email access. The major cities are well served with internet outlets and most towns have cafés or terminals, often in visitor information offices or libraries. These charge the standard rates of NZ$2–NZ$5 per hour.

» Speed of access varies considerably around the country.

## POSTAL SERVICES

Post offices, called Post Shops, typically open Monday to Friday 9–5, Saturday 9–12.30.

» Mail can also be sent to Post Restante, CPO (Chief Post Office) in the main cities, where it will be held for up to 30 days.

» If you are being sent mail make sure the sender marks your surname in capitals and underlines it.

» Within New Zealand standard post costs 50c for medium letters and postcards (two to three days); NZ$1 for Fastpost (airmail) to domestic centres (one to two days); NZ$1.50 for airmail letters to Australia and NZ$2 for standard overseas airmail letters to Europe, North America and East Asia.

» When sending cards and letters overseas be sure to use the free blue 'air economy' stickers. Books of stamps are available in Post Shops, as are pre-paid envelopes and a range of purpose-made cardboard boxes. Stamps can also be bought in bookstores, fuel stations and supermarkets.

» Average international delivery times depend on the day of the week the item is posted, and can take anywhere from four to twelve days to the UK or North America.

**INTERNET ACCESS POINTS**

| CITY | ADDRESS | TELEPHONE |
|---|---|---|
| **NORTH ISLAND** | | |
| **Auckland** | City Library, 44–46 Lorne Street | 09-377 0209 |
| | Cyberdate2, 320 Queen Street | 09-377 0320 |
| | Login 1, 1/12 Rialto Centre, 163 Broadway, Newmarket | 09-522 9303 |
| | Net Central Cybercafé, 5 Lorne Street | 09-373 5186 |
| | Net Zone, 4 Fort Street | 09-377 3906 |
| | Email access: Travellers Contact Point, 87 Queen Street | 09-300 7197 |
| **Napier** | Cybers, 98 Dickens Street | 06-835 0125 |
| **Palmerston North** | icafé, corner of the Square and Fitzherbert Avenue | 06-353 7899 |
| **Rotorua** | E-Funz, 1174 Huapapa Street | 07-349 3789 |
| | Cybershed, 1176 Pukuatua Street | 07-349 4965 |
| | Heavenley's Internet Bar and Café, 1195 Fenton Street | 07-348 3288 |
| **Wellington** | Cyber City, 99 Courtenay Place | 04-384 3717 |
| | Cyber Spot, Lambton Square, 180 Lambton Quay | 04-473 0098 |
| | Library, Victoria Street, Civic Square | 04-801 4040 |
| | | |
| **SOUTH ISLAND** | | |
| **Christchurch** | E Blah Blah, 53–57 Cathedral Square | 03-377 2381 |
| | High Net, 230 High Street | 03-366 6100 |
| | Tea Net, 603 Colombo Street | 03-379 6545 |
| **Dunedin** | Dunedin Cue Club and Cyber Café, 65 St. Andrew Street | 03-477 3064 |
| | Webrunner, 237 Moray Place | 03-471 8182 |
| **Greymouth** | Grey District Library, Mackay Street | 03-768 5597 |
| **Nelson** | Aurora Tech, 161 Trafalgar Street | 03-546 6867 |
| | Café Affair, 295 Trafalgar Street | 03-548 8295 |
| **Queenstown** | E Café, 50 Shotover Street | 03-442 9888 |
| | Internet Depot, 26 Shotover Street | 03-442 8581 |

# MEDIA

## MAGAZINES

Several national New Zealand magazines are particularly worth a look for visitors: *The Listener*, covering national issues, politics and the arts; *North and South*, a magazine covering a wide range of traditional and contemporary issues; *New Zealand Geographic*, the quality New Zealand equivalent of the American icon; and two glossy outdoor activity publications, *New Zealand Wilderness* and *New Zealand Outside*. All these magazines are widely available at bookshops or Post Shops.

Most mainstream international magazines and newspapers can be found at specialist outlets such as Magazzino in Auckland.

## MAJOR MAGAZINE RETAILERS:

**Auckland**

Magascene
33 Hurstmere Road, Takapuna
tel 09-489 5953

Magazzino
123 Ponsonby Road
tel 09-376 6933

Magazzino
Extreme on Broadway Newmarket
tel 09-524 0604

Magazine City
Westfield Shoppingtown
West City, Henderson
tel 09-978 6752,
www.nzmagazineshop.co.nz

**Christchurch**

Canterbury Magazines
152 Hereford Street
tel 03-377 0991

**Hamilton**

Accent on Magazines
113 Alexandra Street
tel 07-838 0269

**Nelson**

Page & Blackmore Booksellers
254 Trafalgar Street
tel 03-548 9992
www.pageandblackmore.co.nz

**New Plymouth**

Wadsworth's Bookcentre Ltd
Shop 9, Centre City, Gill Street
tel 06-759 4350

**Wellington**

City Cards and Mags
112 Lambton Quay
tel 04-472 7448

Magnetix, Midland Park
Lambton Quay
tel 04-472 2820

Village Newsagent
6/142 Willis Street
tel 04-385 1230

## NEWSPAPERS

The principal daily newspapers (except Sundays) are the *New Zealand Herald* (Auckland and upper North Island), the *Dominion Post* (Wellington and lower North Island), *The Press* (Christchurch and central South Island) and the *Otago Daily Times* (South Island).

Smaller local newspapers can be accessed online from www.stuff.co.nz and include the *Waikato Times, The Manawatu Standard, The Daily News, The Nelson Mail, The Marlborough Express, The Timaru Herald and The Southland Times.*

## TELEVISION

The four terrestrial TV channels have very little to offer except news and current affairs programmes. The rest of the output chiefly consists of UK or US soaps, reality and quiz shows. All four channels carry advertising, which is heavily repetitive, sometimes featuring the same commercial every 10 minutes for several days. TV One shows news, sports and current affairs; Channel Two mainly drama and light entertainment; both are state-owned. TV3 and TV4 combine news and entertainment and are privately owned. Maori Television broadcasts bilingually in Maori and English, with 90 per cent New Zealand content.

Many New Zealanders (and most hotels and bed-and-breakfasts) subscribe to Sky TV.

There are local TV stations in some cities and towns.

## RADIO

State-owned radio stations include Radio New Zealand Concert (classical music) and Radio New Zealand National (news, drama, light entertainment, talk shows). These broadcast on medium wave and VHF nationwide. There are also several stations broadcasting to Maori audiences. Some areas outside the large centres of population receive only medium wave.

» Tourist Information FM broadcasts 24 hours a day and features items on New Zealand's history and culture, news for visitors and commercials for places to stay and eat. It transmits in English (88.2MHz), Japanese (100.8MHz) and German (100.4MHz).

## BOOKS, MAPS AND FILMS

### BACKGROUND READING

Despite its forbidding extent (some 570 pages) *The Penguin History of New Zealand*, by Michael King (2003), is a readable account of New Zealand's history. King has written other history books, including *Nga Iwi O Te Motu: 1,000 Years of Maori History. The Oxford Illustrated History of New Zealand*, by Keith Sinclair (1997), does it with pictures.

There are anthologies of Maori mythology—the *Reed Book of Maori Mythology*, by AW Reed (2004) is an update of an old favourite.

*Old New Zealand Houses 1800–1940*, by Jeremy Salmond (1986) is a beautifully illustrated account of the country's vernacular architecture, from early Maori dwellings to gingerbread villas, which also acts as a fascinating record of social history.

Two natural history guides are particularly recommended: Geoff Moon's *Reed Field Guide to New Zealand Birds* (2000), and the Collins *Field Guide to New Zealand Wildlife*, by Rod Morris and Terence Linsey.

### GUIDES AND MAPS

If you're planning a tramping (trekking) holiday, the Moirs Guides, published by the New Zealand Alpine Club, are recommended, as is *New Zealand's Great Walks*, by Pearl Hewson. Bruce Ringer's *New Zealand by Bike* is a useful guide for cyclists, while skiers will want to obtain a copy of the annual *Ski and Snowboard* guide, which is available free from Brown Bear Publications, PO Box 31–207, Christchurch, tel 03-388 5331, www.brownbear.co.nz.

The NZ AA produces a road atlas, and a guide to accommodation, updated annually. Wises and Minimaps are the major city and provincial town map companies, producing a range of handbooks and foldout city maps. Visitor information centres also stock free leaflet maps.

### NEW ZEALAND IN FICTION

New Zealand literature is flourishing, with a wealth of new talent writing across all genres. A selective cross-section is suggested in the panel here, and you can find out more about the authors and their works on www.bookcouncil.org.nz.

Katherine Mansfield started the short-story genre in 1906, writing in London but drawing on her Wellington childhood (▷ 35)—and her short stories are widely available. Other names to look for are Frank Sargeson, Maurice Shadbolt and Owen Marshall. Witi Ihimaera's short stories, *Pounamu, Pounamu* (1972), was the first fiction published by a Maori—he came to wider world attention when his novel *The Whale Rider* (1987) was filmed.

English artist and writer Samuel Butler, who farmed in Canterbury around 1860, was one of the first to describe the landscape of the high country in his satire *Erewhon* (1872). A better picture of New Zealand appears in his letters to his father, published as *A First Year in Canterbury Settlement* (1863).

Novelists flourished in the second half of the 20th century—look for authors such as Janet Frame, Maurice Gee, Maurice Shadbolt, C.K. Stead, Alan Duff and Dame Ngaio Marsh—the country's best known writer of detective fiction.

James K. Baxter is New Zealand's most celebrated poet, but a wealth of other names includes Fleur Adcock and Alan Curnow.

### FILMS

The movie scene has been dominated in recent years by the success of Peter Jackson's filming of the *Lord of the Rings* trilogy against a New Zealand backdrop. Check out the locations with Ian Brodie's *The Lord of the Rings Location Guide* (2000), complete with GPS references. The 13-year-old actress at the heart of *Whale Rider*, Keisha Castle-Hughes, was a New Zealand star in the 2004 Oscars firmament.

Jackson's earlier film *Heavenly Creatures*, based on the story of two schoolgirl murderers in Christchurch in the 1950s, was a popular success. Jane Campion's *The Piano* (1993) was the award-winning tale of a mute immigrant. Lee Tamahori's *Once Were Warriors* (1995) is the shockingly violent and highly praised film of Alan Duff's novel about a poor Maori family in inner-city Auckland.

### 10 TOP NZ READS

*The New Zealanders*, by Maurice Shadbolt (1959): The author's first short stories, rarely out of print, reveal an emerging New Zealand identity.

*A Good Keen Man*, by Barry Crump (1960): The first in a series of tales of a rugged outdoor bloke by a Kiwi icon, who went on to sell more than 1 million books in New Zealand alone.

*A River Rules My Life*, by Mona Anderson (1963): A classic account of life on an isolated high-country sheep station, Mount Algidus, in the mid-20th century.

*To the Is-land*, by Janet Frame (1982): The first volume of her autobiography tells of a remarkable childhood of poverty, tragedy and rich imagination.

*The Bone People*, by Keri Hulme (1984): Reality and dreams, past and present meld together in a Booker-winning novel about bi-culturality, identity, love and hurt.

*All Visitors Ashore*, by C.K. Stead (1984): A time-shot of a youthful bohemian community and its relationship with the outside world in the 1950s.

*Potiki*, by Patricia Grace (1986): A remarkable novel about life on a *marae* in a changing world, which reveals much about Maori ways and thoughts.

*The Man Who Never Lived*, by Kevin Ireland (1997): A hilarious novel of selfishness, self deception and families.

*The Denniston Rose*, by Jenny Pattrick (2003): A well-told historic tale of life, love and survival in a tough West Coast mining community.

*Barking*, by Joe Bennett (2003): Sharp, humorous articles composed originally for *The Press*, with a wry eye for the follies of daily life.

## SHOPPING

Wits used to quip that they had visited New Zealand, but it was closed. Not any more. Liberalized trading hours mean you can shop every day in the cities and major towns. Although in the tourist resorts you might be forgiven for thinking there is little to buy except fluffy sheep or kiwis dressed in rugby jerseys, shopping in New Zealand can be a rewarding experience, and the quality of locally made goods is generally high. In the cities, you'll find everything from chic boutiques and old-fashioned department stores to lively markets, factory outlets, craft co-operatives and supermarkets. In many places, undercover suburban shopping malls are replacing traditional central-city shops.

### ARTS AND CRAFTS

New Zealand culture has a strong basis in craft. Wherever you go, you'll probably find a gallery, craft co-operative or community market selling paintings, pottery, wood or stone carving, hand-knits, weaving or the produce of country kitchens. Places such as the Christchurch Arts Centre (▷ 197) enable you to meet the artist and buy direct. Much of the art reflects the vibrant blues and greens of the environment. Native woods, such as kauri and rimu, are fashioned into bowls, ornaments and furniture.

### MAORI ART

The Maori carvings on canoes and meeting houses depict ancestors and tell traditional stories. Greenstone (New Zealand jade, or pounamu)—traditionally used for weapons and symbolic gifts—is now made into jewellery. Pendants, associated with status and fertility, are carved from bone and greenstone and often depict sacred animals or spirits. If you buy such an object, it is customary to offer it as a gift. Paua (abalone) is harvested naturally under strict controls and the shells are a by-product. You can buy the shells polished and varnished, or as iridescent jewellery.

### SHEEP PRODUCTS

In a country with an estimated ten sheep to every person, sheepskin and woollen goods are ubiquitous. Choose from jumpers, hats, coats, gloves, full sheepskins and slippers.

**Opposite** *Queens Shopping Arcade in Auckland has many specialist outlets*

The knits are usually homespun, hand-knitted and high quality. Wool is also made into rugged Swanndri bush jackets and luxuriously soft merino underwear. Lanolin is used in popular skincare products.

## CLOTHING

You will see the All Black rugby jerseys, made by Adidas, wherever you go, and the original Canterbury Clothing Company (CCC) jerseys worn by other international sides are excellent quality cotton. The company also makes leisurewear, and has stores up and down the country and a factory shop in Christchurch. Christchurch is a good place for all types of outdoor adventure clothing and high-tech sports gear.

New Zealand fashion designers are making a name for themselves and their designs are often available here at a much better price than overseas. Look out for labels such as Zambesi, Karen Walker and Kate Sylvester. Some designers have their own boutiques, but larger cities also have fashion quarters that are worth exploring—try Newmarket in Auckland, Cuba Street in Wellington and High Street in Christchurch.

## WINE AND FOOD

New Zealand is best known for Marlborough Sauvignon blanc, but the country also produces other excellent and distinctive wines, including Pinot noir, Chardonnay, Riesling, red blends and sparkling wines. You can buy wine in supermarkets, but you'll get a better range at specialist stores such as the Glengarry chain in Auckland and Wellington and Vino Fino in Christchurch. Many wines are made in such small quantities that they may be available only at restaurants or from the winery itself.

Most New Zealanders shop for food at the supermarket, but the quality is often better and the produce fresher at specialist stores such as the Auckland Seafood Market and Moore Wilson Fresh in Wellington. In the country, buy from roadside stalls and farms selling local produce. Native flower honeys, such as rata and manuka, make attractive gifts. Kiwifruit (zespri) and other fruits are made into chocolates and preserves.

## OPENING HOURS

» Most shops open Monday to Saturday 9 to 5 or 5.30pm and have one late shopping night (usually Friday). In larger places and tourist areas, many open on Sunday.
» Large mall multi-complexes are open daily.
» Larger supermarket chains open daily 8am to 9pm at least, some 24 hours, and the small convenience stores known as 'dairies' often open until 10 or 11pm.

## PAYMENT

Most city shops accept credit cards and take EFTPOS transactions. You may have to pay cash in rural areas and at markets.

## TAX REFUNDS

Goods posted direct to overseas destinations are free of the 12.5 per cent GST tax. Many stores offer mailing and shipping services for visitors' purchases.

**Below** *You'll find local crafts on display and for sale in galleries, co-operatives and markets as well as shops throughout the country*

## ENTERTAINMENT AND NIGHTLIFE

New Zealand has a strong musical culture, both from its Maori roots and from its Pacific Island and European immigrants. Maori history is told through song and story, with games and dances originally devised to train and support warriors. The culture of Kapa Haka is taught in schools and contested in competitions. You can experience a version of it in concert parties in Rotorua and most large cities. Auckland's Pacific Island cultures are expressed in the Pasifika festival (⊳ 93). Choral singing is particularly strong in Christchurch, while Dunedin celebrates its Scottish roots in Burns' Night festivities.

Many New Zealand cities have attractive Victorian theatres and modern venues hosting concerts and shows. Drama, orchestral concerts, ballet, dance, comedy, rock and jazz are all well represented, including tours by international performers. In rural New Zealand, people are used to making their own entertainment through amateur theatrical societies, choirs and local DJs.

By world standards, New Zealand nightlife may be nothing remarkable, but there's still plenty to keep you entertained, especially in the cities. Auckland has a humming club life focusing on Karangahape Road, Wellington's Courtenay Place buzzes with night-time activity, Christchurch has the cafés along the restaurant strip and Dunedin has hangouts popular with students. Queenstown is the place most dedicated to fun, with bars and clubs regularly open until 5am. There are casinos in Auckland, Christchurch, Hamilton, Queenstown and Dunedin, which are open most of the night. By law you need to be 20 to enter a casino, and dress codes are applied.

### DRAMA

The Auckland Theatre Company lacks a home venue and performs in various places. Wellington has a lively drama scene, with professional companies performing at Downstage, Circa and the alternative Bats, as well as touring shows. Christchurch's Court Theatre and Dunedin's Fortune Theatre are both professional companies presenting repertory seasons.

### BALLET AND CONTEMPORARY DANCE

The Royal New Zealand Ballet Company (www.nzballet.org.nz) is based at the Westpac St. James Theatre in Wellington. It presents classical and modern works, and tours the country. Contemporary dance tends to be presented by troupes created for specific events. A wide range of dance styles is incorporated in festivals such as Wellington's Dance Your Socks Off (www.feelinggreat.co.nz) in September, Auckland's Tempo (www.tempo.co.nz) and Christchurch's The Body (www.thebody.co.nz), both in September or October.

### OPERA

The NBR New Zealand Opera (www.nzopera.com) combines companies in Auckland and Wellington. They present several seasons of classic opera a year, to a high standard.

### CLASSICAL MUSIC

The New Zealand Symphony Orchestra (www.nzso.co.nz) is based in Wellington at the Michael Fowler Centre. It presents classical and modern works and tours widely. The main cities also support excellent semi-professional orchestras—the Auckland Philharmonia (www.akl-phil.co.nz), Wellington Symphonia, Christchurch Symphony (www.christchurchsymphony.co.nz) and Dunedin Symphonia, which give regular performances. Christchurch also has a fine choir, the Christchurch City Choir (www.christchurchcitychoir.co.nz), which gives several performances a year. Chamber music concerts by local and visiting groups are arranged by Chamber Music New Zealand (www.chambermusic.co.nz), with nationwide tours.

### MAORI PERFORMANCES

Maori groups in the main cities organize performances for tourists. Check with the visitor information office for details.

**Below** *Dunedin's Scottish heritage is celebrated with bagpipe music and traditional cultural performances*

## CINEMA

Cinemas range from country halls to multi-venue city complexes where the popcorn is pushed as hard as the movie. Most big cities also have art-house cinemas, and most cinemas show first-release films.

Many city complexes have daytime showings for parents accompanied by children, with prices to match, and specials early in the week. Typical ticket prices range from NZ$8 to NZ$14, with children around NZ$7.

## BOOKING TICKETS AND INFORMATION

Ticketek are the main national administrators for information and ticketing; their website (www.ticketek.co.nz) lists up-and-coming shows and events.

Other good sources of information are local newspapers—the *New Zealand Herald* in Auckland, the *Dominion Post* in Wellington, *The Press* in Christchurch and the *Otago Daily Times* in Dunedin.

## PUBS AND BARS

Traditionally, pubs in New Zealand were the preserve of hard-drinking men. Such places still exist, typically in rural areas, but in most places you can now enjoy a beer in mixed company by a fire in winter or outside in the summer. Some boutique breweries also have their own bars. Irish pubs have become common, and although some are gimmicky, others try to be authentic and have a good selection of beers to match. Many restaurants and cafés have bars with outdoor seating, popular in summer.

Pubs and bars are generally open from 11am to 10.30pm. They serve a standard range of food, and many have an extended licence to midnight or 3am on weekends. Many also host gigs, some of which don't start until nearly midnight. You need to be 18 and have proof of age.

## GAY AND LESBIAN SCENE

Gay sex was decriminalized in New Zealand only in 1986. Although some homophobia still exists, the larger cities are generally gay- and lesbian-friendly.

Gaytravel New Zealand (www.gaytravel.net.nz) and Go Gay New Zealand (www.gaynewzealand.co.nz) give information on gay and lesbian holidays, accommodation, venues, bars and activities, including events such as the Hero Parade (www.gaynz.com) in Auckland and Gay Ski Week (www.gayskiweeknz.com) in Queenstown.

**Above** *Classical music concerts are performed regularly by professional and semi-professional orchestras*

## SPORTS AND ACTIVITIES

New Zealanders are avid followers of spectator sports. Sport takes up a sizeable chunk of daily news coverage on television, radio and in newspapers, and armchair enthusiasts can spend all Saturday afternoon tuned into coverage of their chosen sports. As for activities—New Zealanders love the great outdoors. The vast range of outdoor pursuits available is a big attraction to visitors. The major cities are at or near the sea, and the countryside is never far away. Many Kiwis spend their leisure time at the family bach (holiday home) by the sea or in the mountains, tramping (hiking) in the bush (native rainforest), fishing from the family boat or gathering shellfish.

### SPECTATOR SPORTS

Rugby is the national game, followed obsessively by young and old alike, who don team jerseys and travel to watch their heroes in action. Soccer, by contrast, has never really taken off. In summer, cricket is the major sport, and horse racing, motor sport and netball are all popular, New Zealand having won international events in these disciplines.

The country also gets solidly behind the national sailing team during the America's Cup, particularly when the event was held in Auckland. New Zealand also prides itself on mounting some of the world's toughest multi-sport and endurance events.

#### CRICKET

Cricket is popular at both local and national levels. During the summer, city parks and rural domains (parks) are filled with white-clad players and the thwack of bat on ball. New Zealand Cricket (www.blackcaps.co.nz) operates the New Zealand cricket team, known as the Black Caps, organizing test tours and one-day internationals with other nations. It also organizes domestic cricket matches, including the State Championship first-class competition and the State Shield one-day competition. On sunny summer days, crowds of New Zealanders equipped with rugs, food and drinks settle on grassy embankments to watch the game, or tune in to the radio to keep score wherever they are on holiday.

#### ENDURANCE EVENTS

Held in February, the Coast to Coast (www.coasttocoast.co.nz, ▷ 17) across the Southern Alps is one of the most gruelling and well-known multi-sport events in the world.

In March, the Ironman New Zealand Triathlon (www.ironman.co.nz) draws crowds in Taupo to cheer on the more than 1,450 competitors from 39 countries who swim 3.8km (2.4 miles) in the lake, cycle 180km (112 miles) and run 42km (26 miles) through the town. Travel in the vicinity is likely to be

**Opposite** *Netball is a very popular sport in New Zealand and the national team has been world champion several times*

slow on competition days, as roads may be partly closed.

### GOLF

With 400 golf courses—more per person than anywhere else in the world—New Zealand has a full calendar of events at both amateur and professional levels. New Zealand Golf (www.pga.org.nz) organizes a number of competitions, including the New Zealand Open, held at a different links each year in February. Also held in February, the NZPGA championship (www.pgachampionship.co.nz), hosted by the Clearwater Golf Club in Christchurch, attracts some of the world's top golfers and an estimated 25,000 spectators.

### HORSE RACING

Horse racing, in both thoroughbred (the gallops) and harness (the trots) forms, is so popular that even the smallest towns are likely to have a racecourse, and races are held throughout the year. The main events are a great excuse to dress up and drink up: Cup Week in Christchurch in November, which includes the New Zealand Trotting Cup at Addington Raceway and the New Zealand Cup at Riccarton Park; Derby Day at Ellerslie—Auckland Racing Club on 26 December; and the Auckland Cup in March. Details of events are available through Harness Racing New Zealand (www.hrnz.co.nz) and New Zealand Racing (www.nzracing.co.nz). Bookmaking is banned; wagers are totalizator-based and the minimum bet is NZ$1.

### MOTOR SPORTS

Motor sports in all their forms have a keen following, with New Zealand having produced world champions in Formula One Grand Prix and motor-cycle racing. Although most spectators watch the races on television, you can catch the sound and smell of live action at raceways such as Manfeild (Manawatu) and Ruapuna (Christchurch), the Rally of New Zealand based in Manukau in April or the Asia Pacific World Rally Championships in Whangarei in May. For details of events, see www.nzmotorsport.co.nz and www.motorcyclesport.co.nz (V8 Supercars, 2L touring cars and karting).

### NETBALL

After rugby, the winter sport with the second-highest player numbers is netball (a game similar to basketball). It is the number one sport for women and is played extensively in schools. The Southern Sting, based in Invercargill, has been a frequent national champion and the national team, the Silver Ferns, has won the world championship several times. Go to www.netballnz.co.nz for details of matches.

### RUGBY

Rugby Union is the most popular spectator sport in New Zealand, and the fortunes of New Zealand's national rugby team, the All Blacks—the world's best, according to international ranking—are followed with much enthusiasm. When they win, it's a national celebration; when they lose, it's a time of national soul-searching.

Rugby has three levels of competition. The international Tri-Nations is played between New Zealand, South Africa and Australia. Super 14 Rugby, played in late summer and autumn, has teams from regions in the three countries. The domestic teams—the Highlanders based in Dunedin, Crusaders based in Christchurch, Hurricanes based in Wellington, Chiefs in Hamilton and Blues in Auckland—all command passionate regional followings.

At the next level down is the Air New Zealand Cup, which is played in winter and is divided into two pools. The most coveted provincial trophy is the Ranfurly Shield. In addition, there are occasional test matches between Australia and New Zealand. All the main cities have large stadia that host national matches and international tests. It's worth attending a live game, if you can, to catch the atmosphere; otherwise, try to find a pub with a big screen, where passions among the crowd run equally high. The New Zealand Rugby Union's dedicated website (www.allblacks.com) gives full details of matches.

Rugby League (www.rugby-league.co.nz) has a single professional team, the New Zealand Warriors, who are based in Auckland and play in the Australian National Rugby League.

New Zealand is also a participant in the IRB Sevens World Series (www.sevens.co.nz), the New Zealand leg of which is usually held in Wellington.

### SAILING

New Zealand sailors have won more than 60 world titles, and sailing is the country's most successful Olympic sport. Youngsters start early, and you will see them sailing their P-class yachts in regattas all over the country. The Royal New Zealand Yacht Squadron (www.rnzys.co.nz) in Auckland is home to Team New Zealand, the only non-US syndicate to have successfully defended the America's Cup. The Club organizes events such as the New Zealand Match Racing Championships, held in November. Yachting New Zealand (www.yachtingnz.org.nz), the national body for competitive and recreational sailing, has details of events.

### SKIING

Competitors in the New Zealand Speed Ski Championships (www.speed ski.co.nz), held at Turoa in October, hurtle down the mountain at speeds of up to 173kph (107mph). Other events include the Australia New Zealand Cup final at Whakapapa in September, the ANZ FIS (International Ski Federation) series held at Mount Hutt in August, and the New Zealand nationals held at Turoa in September. The Ski

**Above** *Jet-boating is a thrilling way to experience New Zealand's rivers; trips range from the full adrenalin rush to the scenic*

Racing New Zealand website (www.skiracing.org.nz) lists upcoming events.

### SURF LIFE-SAVING

Throughout the summer, the main New Zealand beaches are patrolled by surf life-savers. Surf Life Saving New Zealand (www.slsnz.org.nz) trains children in water safety and also holds contests including swimming, running, paddling a surf ski, board or canoe, rowing a surfboat or racing an inflatable rescue boat. The national championships are held every two years, and a tri-nations series between Australia, South Africa and New Zealand is hosted by one of these nations in alternate years.

### TENNIS

One of New Zealand's richest sporting events for women, the ASB Classic international women's tennis tournament is part of the WTA Tour and attracts players among the top 25 in the world. It is played in the first week of January each year at the ASB Bank Tennis Centre in Auckland and is followed by the Heineken Open for men. Tickets start from NZ$32. The website of Auckland Tennis (www.aucklandtennis.co.nz) carries details.

The ITF International Women's tournament, held at the Renouf Tennis Centre in Wellington, is the largest international tournament in New Zealand for juniors. The Wellington Tennis website (www.wellingtontennis.org.nz) has details.

## ACTIVITIES

For visitors, New Zealand has become synonymous with outdoor activities, along with adventure sports such as jet-boating, bungy jumping, kayaking, whitewater rafting, sky-diving and ever more daring variations on the theme. Queenstown calls itself the Adventure Capital of New Zealand, but most of these activities are available in other tourist spots as well. Ensure that your insurance covers you to participate in such extreme sports.

### BUNGY JUMPING

Diving off a very high bridge with a rubber band attached to your ankles is the best known of New Zealand's thrill-seeking activities (▷ 17).

### CAVING

Virtually every part of New Zealand has caves, formed in limestone, marble or volcanic rocks. The most important caving areas are at Waitomo, northwest Nelson and north Westland. The region around Waitomo contains most of the North Island's best-known caves. The New Zealand Speleological Society (www.caves.org.nz) and many guided tours operate from there.

In Nelson, the marble mountains at Takaka Hill, Mount Arthur and Mount Owen contain New Zealand's deepest and longest caves: the Bulmer Cavern (39km/ 24 miles), Ellis Basin system (28km/17 miles) and Nettlebed Cave (24km/15 miles). Harwoods Hole, one of the world's largest sinkholes, is just off the main Motueka–Takaka road.

On the west coast, Karamea has the 13km (8-mile) Honeycomb Hill Cave, with 70 entrances and New Zealand's largest limestone arches. The Nile River caves also have glow-worm and stalactite displays. Guided caving trips are listed on www.newzealand.com.

### FISHING

As well as being one of the best trout-fishing areas in the world, New Zealand provides superb sea- and big-game fishing. The prime trout-fishing spots in the North Island are the lakes around Taupo and Rotorua; in the South Island, around Gore in Southland. Both experienced and novice anglers are well catered for, with numerous boat charters and guides. The warm Pacific waters around the North Island attract dozens of salt-water species from snapper to marlin. Areas particularly well geared up for game- and sea-fishing include the Bay of Islands, Tutukaka (Northland), Whitianga (Coromandel) and Tauranga/Whakatane (Bay of Plenty). Options range from the three-hour novice trip to the highly organized three-day 'Hemingway' trips to catch that prize marlin. Check www.fishing.net.nz for information.

### FLIGHTSEEING

Almost every provincial airport, airstrip or local flying club in New Zealand offers flights in a small, fixed-wing aircraft or a helicopter. There are several operators on the West Coast and the Southern Lakes district. If you take only one flight, make it the helicopter flight around the glaciers and summit of Mount Cook/Aoraki. For a more sedate ride consider a hot-air balloon trip, available in a number of locations (see the local visitor information office). Alternatively, you can don goggles and scarf and get strapped into a biplane. The flightseeing section of www.newzealand.com lists many of the operators.

**FLY-BY-WIRE**
This is claimed to be the world's fastest adventure ride, reaching speeds of 171kph (106mph). Brave souls are strapped to what resembles a metal hospital stretcher with a microlight engine on the back and suspended from a wire. Rides are available only in Queenstown.

**GOLF**
New Zealand has hundreds of golf courses, from those that require a cute wedge shot to avoid sheep to others with well-manicured greens fit for an open championship. They are frequently set in stunning surroundings, overlooking snowy mountains, lakes, seascapes or forests. World-class courses in New Zealand include Formosa in Auckland, Wairakei in Taupo and Millbrook in Arrowtown. The main season is March to October, both because the winters are relatively mild and because in summer many New Zealanders concentrate on water sports. Most courses have clubs for hire. Green fees start at around NZ$15, and attitudes to golfing etiquette tend to be relaxed. The New Zealand Golf website is www.nzga.co.nz.

**HIKING**
See Tramping, ⊳ 284–285.

**HORSE-TREKKING**
The New Zealand landscape is ideal for horse-trekking, and it can be enjoyed around almost every provincial town. Both the experienced and the novice are well catered for in treks lasting from an hour to several days. The approach tends to be informal, and specialized riding gear is not usually necessary. Helmets are provided. For additional information countrywide contact the International League for the Protection of Horses (ILHNZ), www.horsetalk.co.nz, or the national tour organization via www.ridenz.com.

**JET-BOATING**
This usually involves whizzing down a river at high speed in remarkably shallow water, and turning 180 degrees. Although it looks scary, it is actually great fun. A New Zealand invention, the jet-boat was developed by a Canterbury farmer, Bill Hamilton, to navigate the shallow local rivers. Jet-boating is now one of New Zealand's best-known adventure activities. Some of the most exhilarating trips are available near Queenstown, the Buller Gorge, and the Waiau, Whanganui and Waikato rivers, but jet-boating is available on most New Zealand rivers. Not all are adrenalin-pumping trips; some (especially in the North Island) are more scenic affairs. The website www.newzealand.com lists many of the operators.

**KAYAKING**
New Zealand is a renowned playground for kayaking and canoeing, whether on river, lake, sea or fiord. It is also popular as an eco-sensitive way of interacting with wildlife, such as seals, dolphins and birds. Guided trips are particularly popular in the Abel Tasman National Park, but they are also available throughout New Zealand, and kayak operators can be found in just about every major town. Multi-day trips are available in all the main tourist spots, ranging from family-oriented paddles on calm rivers to the adrenalin rush of whitewater and rapids. The website www.newzealand.com lists many of the operators.

**MOUNTAIN BIKING**
New Zealand is a paradise for mountain bikers, with a choice of on- and off-road trails in spectacular locations. Cycling is also a great way to see the country, and many operators offer tours in which your gear is carried from one destination to the next. Some even drive you uphill so you only have to ride the downhill sections. Bicycle hire is available in most towns, and you can choose from gentle family expeditions to the multi-day Otago Central Rail Trail or heli-biking from mountain peaks. The New Zealand Mountain Bike website www.mountainbike.co.nz is a comprehensive resource.

**MOUNTAINEERING**
New Zealand's major peaks, although not especially high, are spectacular, challenging and potentially dangerous. The majority are in the South Island. The Mount Cook Range, Mount Aspiring (Wanaka) and the peaks of the Nelson Lakes National Park are the most accessible. Mountain guides are available and are definitely recommended.

Mount Taranaki/Egmont in the North Island is the country's most-climbed mountain. Other grand peaks in the North Island include Mount Ruapehu and the little-climbed (but superb) Hikurangi in Eastland. If you are a novice, seek advice and above all go well prepared: Check the weather forecast and tell someone of your intentions. Many lives have been lost through a lack of common sense and over-confidence. Numerous guided trips are available, especially around Taranaki and Mount Cook/Aoraki (Franz Josef and Fox Glaciers).

For specialist enquiries contact the NZ Alpine Club, based in Christchurch, www.alpineclub.org.nz. The NZ Mountain Guides Association, www.nzmga.org.nz, is also good for further information and contacts.

**PARAFLYING AND PARAPENTING**
Paraflying (or parasailing) involves sitting on a seat under a parachute being pulled by a boat. Suitable for all ages, it requires no skill and is available at coastal and lake resorts.

Parapenting (or paragliding) is great fun but is difficult to master. As with skydiving, the novice is taken in tandem with an expert. There are a limited number of tourist venues: Te Mata Peak in Hawke's Bay is the North Island's top site, while Wanaka is the capital for the South Island.

## RAFTING

This is another premier New Zealand activity. The principal locations are the rivers of central and east North Island and throughout the South Island. Rivers and the rapids are graded from I to VI. Although the 45-minute trips are great fun and packed with adrenalin-pumping moments, the real rafting experience only comes with a multi-day expedition. Trips are generally well organized and safe; most will even do the campfire cooking for you. The New Zealand Rafting Association's website is www.nz-rafting.co.nz.

## RIVER SLEDDING

River sledding involves rafting down a river on a body-board with little except a wet suit, flippers and a crash helmet. The prime location is the Waingongoro River in Hawera.

## ROCK CLIMBING

Many locations offer great rock climbing—but remember, you need tuition and a guide. Many places also have climbing walls for practice. Visitor information offices can give you contacts.

## SAILING

For the experienced sailor New Zealand—and in particular the Hauraki Gulf, off Auckland, and the Bay of Islands—provides one of the best sailing playgrounds in the world, and novices are well catered for. Try at least a few hours out on the water and, if you can, go on a multi-day trip. Bare boating gives you a choice of any vessel that matches your expertise. Skippered yacht charter/rental companies are based in Auckland and the Bay of Islands. Picot's (www.charterguide.co.nz) has a comprehensive list of yacht charter operators.

## SCUBA DIVING

New Zealand has some world-class dive sites, including the Poor Knights Islands off Tutukaka (www.diving.co.nz) in Northland, famed for their geology, marine life and water clarity. In many locations local operators will take you for a full- or half-day basic first dive experience. The main diving locations in the North Island are the Hauraki Gulf (Auckland), Whitianga (Coromandel) and New Plymouth (Taranaki). In the South Island they are the Marlborough Sounds, Fiordland and Stewart Island/Rakiura. There are also many accessible wrecks on the coast. The prime months are February to June. The website www.newzealand.com lists many operators.

## SKIING AND SNOWBOARDING

New Zealand is the principal skiing and snowboarding venue in the southern hemisphere. Most of the major commercial ski fields are in the South Island. They include Coronet Peak and the Remarkables near Queenstown (▷ 240), Treble Cone and Cardrona near Wanaka, Mount Hutt, Mount Potts and Porter Heights west of Christchurch, and the Craigieburn ranges, Arthur's Pass, Hanmer Springs and Nelson regions. The choice is vast. For an authentic Kiwi experience, try skiing the club fields, where the facilities are basic and the skiing is challenging, but the welcome is friendly and the cost is comparatively modest. The Canterbury Snowsports Association (www.skisouth.org.nz) has 13 affiliated clubs, from Tukino in the North Island to Fox Peak in the South. In the North Island the commercial fields are on the slopes of Ruapehu (Whakapapa and Turoa) in the Tongariro National Park.

There are packages that include lift pass, equipment hire and one or more lessons. For contacts, see www.nzski.com, www.snow.co.nz, and www.brownbear.co.nz.

**Opposite** *The cliffs at Wilyabrup provide excellent rock climbing opportunities*

## SKYDIVING

Tandem skydiving is available in many locations throughout both islands. Jumps range in height from 2,744m (9,000ft) to 4,573m (15,000ft). The latter will give you about 40 seconds free-fall. Prices increase the higher you go, although commercial operators will generally not take first-timers higher than 4,570m (15,000ft).

## SURFING

The North Island's west coast locations of Raglan and Piha are perhaps the most famous for surfing, but other great surf spots include Whangamata (Coromandel), the Eastland beaches, and the beaches on Surf Highway 45 around Mount Taranaki/Egmont. To get a taste of surfing, try boogie-boarding or bodysurfing. Boogie-boards, about half the size of a surfboard and made of compressed foam, are readily available and inexpensive to buy or rent. The website www.surf.co.nz gives an overview of surfing across New Zealand.

## SWIMMING

Rotorua and Taupo are the natural hot-pool capitals but there are many other hot springs throughout the country, including Waiwera north of Auckland, Te Aroha in the Waikato, and Hanmer Springs in Canterbury. You can swim in all the lakes in the Rotorua region, except the Green Lake, which is sacred to Maori.

Coastal swimming can be very dangerous, with notorious riptides, so take care and swim only between the flags on beaches patrolled by surf lifeguards. If in difficulties raise your arm and keep it aloft; lifeguards will come to your rescue.

## TRAMPING (HIKING)

Not only is tramping one of the principal pastimes for many New Zealanders, it is also the reason many visitors come to the country. There is a vast network of routes

and literally thousands of kilometres of track the length and breadth of the country, from the famous and well-trodden Milford Track to the sporadic trail and markers of the lesser-known Dusky Track (▷ 234).

Under the administration and advocacy of the Department of Conservation (DoC), all advertised tracks are clearly marked, well maintained and have designated campsites and huts offering clean water, basic accommodation, cooking facilities and toilets. Detailed tramping information is available, including route descriptions, with the tracks classified by type and fitness required, and up-to-date weather forecasts. Guided trips are also offered for those who would like to be accompanied by an expert.

A word of warning: Many of the tracks are very busy, so accommodation must be reserved weeks in advance. Always make sure you are well prepared, properly equipped and at the required level of fitness. Unless you are experienced, tramping alone on the more remote tracks is not advisable.

For detailed information about tramping tracks and Great Walks contact the DoC Field Centre, www.doc.govt.nz. For accommodation reservations and information, visit the office or send an email to: greatwalksbooking@doc.govt.nz.

**WALKING**

The opportunities are endless and most visitor information offices or regional DoC offices compile lists of the most notable walks in each region. For New Zealand walk suggestions, see the region chapters of this book, or try www.doc.govt.nz; another useful site is www.sparc.org.nz.

**WHALE- AND DOLPHIN-WATCHING**

The Bay of Islands and Whakatane are the dolphin-watching and swimming capitals of the North Island, while Kaikoura in the South Island is world-famous for both dolphins and whales. The tiny, endangered Hector's dolphin can also be viewed from Curio Bay in the Catlins, Southland, and around Banks Peninsula in Canterbury. Encounter success rates are generally very high in New Zealand, to the extent that many operators offer a refund or another trip if the whales and dolphins do not turn up.

**WINDSURFING**

New Zealand is very well suited to the experienced windsurfer, with endless locations. The Estuary in Christchurch is particularly popular with novices, as you can travel considerable distances without getting deeper than chest height in water. Windsurfing schools and board hire are available at most of the principal beach resorts. Contact www.windsurfingnz.co.nz.

**ZORBING**

Invented in Rotorua, zorbing (www.zorb.co.nz) involves climbing into a clear plastic bubble and rolling down a hill (▷ 130). The hair-raising ride lasts about 10 seconds.

## HEALTH AND BEAUTY

New Zealand is located on the active volcanic geothermal belt known as the Pacific Rim of Fire, and is dotted with hot spring mineral water sites, the most famous of which are around Rotorua. Local Maori had long known of the geothermal region's therapeutic powers, and in 1840 gave the new town an area of thermal springs 'for the benefit of the people of the world'. The Government lavished money on making Rotorua 'the spa city of the South Pacific', with a sanitarium, bath houses and landscaped gardens to draw people to 'take the cure'. The famous Blue Baths were one of the first public swimming pools in the world to allow mixed bathing for recreation. Thermal springs in other parts of New Zealand have been developed on a less grand scale.

### PUBLIC POOLS

Most of New Zealand's major hot springs have been developed commercially for recreation, with hot pools of varying temperatures, swimming pools, toddlers' pools, waterslides, picnic areas and cafés. Towels and swimsuits are often available for hire. The main complexes are located at Waiwera, Rotorua, Taupo, Te Aroha and Hanmer Springs.

Swimming complexes in the major towns and cities offer a wide variety of pools and recreational facilities. The most modern complexes also offer fitness classes and are equipped with saunas, steam rooms and a gym. Pool entrance charges start at NZ$6 adult, NZ$4 child.

### SPA TREATMENTS

Spa treatments involving a combination of thermal pools, mud baths, steam rooms, wet and dry massage and beauty therapies are available at the major thermal resorts, including Waiwera, Polynesian Spa and Hell's Gate Wai Ora at Rotorua, Taupo Hot Springs Spa at Lake Taupo, and Hanmer Springs. Spa packages are often available, involving a choice of pampering experiences for both men and women, such as aromatic massage, body wraps, facials, manicures and pedicures. Expect to pay from NZ$40 for a half-hour treatment. Similar massage and beauty therapies are available at day spas attached to luxury hotels and lodges, and in the major cities.

Beauty salons tend to offer a more limited range of services, such as facials, make-up and manicures.

### GYMS

City-dwelling New Zealanders are keen users of gyms and fitness facilities, which provide a range of workout options, including men's, women's and mixed gyms, aerobics classes, weight training, yoga and personal trainers. Some have child day-care facilities and a café.

Casual rates are usually available, starting at around NZ$15. Health and fitness venues should be listed in the Yellow Pages of the telephone directory.

**Above** *Adults and children enjoy the Hot Salt Water Pools at Mount Maunganui*

## FOR CHILDREN

New Zealand is a generally child-friendly destination. Families can happily spend the day at a beach patrolled by lifeguards, take well-marked bush walks, or visit parks and playgrounds for free. During the summer holidays, from mid-December to the end of January, many local councils organize free concerts and family activities. Shopping malls in the big cities have children's play areas, and most public gardens have well-equipped playgrounds for young children. There are swimming pool complexes with waterslides in most large towns, cinemas have special rates for children, and many attractions such as zoos and theme parks have reasonable family combo prices.

### ACTIVITIES AND ATTRACTIONS

In New Zealand, children can do things which may be more expensive in other countries, such as horse-riding, skiing, farm experiences and water sports. Tame versions of jet-boating and rafting are available for families in many places, and although age restrictions apply to activities such as bungy jumping and paragliding, they may be open to children as young as 10.

Many cities and holiday areas have themed attractions that are popular with children. In Wellington, the national museum, Te Papa, has a range of activities, including Story-Place, a haven for small children.

Visitor information offices are a good source of information about facilities and activities. There are also useful websites:

» Kidz Go! (www.kidzgo.co.nz) website and free magazine focuses on Christchurch and Queenstown, Wanaka and Fiordland, with sections on accommodation, activities, free things to do, age limits for adventure activities, and child-minding services.

» Kidsport (www.kidspot.com) is an online magazine.

» KidsNewzealand.com (www.KidsNewzealand.com) is a shopping and information site for families with children.

## FESTIVALS AND EVENTS

From wild foods in Hokitika to art deco in Napier, Kiwis enjoy any excuse for a festival. Whether the official reason is fruit trees in blossom in Hastings, autumn foliage in Arrowtown, or the pohutukawas in the Coromandel, communities celebrate with everything from parades and concerts to art exhibitions, races, shop window competitions, flea markets and balls. In summer many councils sponsor free or low-cost entertainment, with buskers in the street, lunchtime concerts, family picnics and children's activities. Highlights are the free evening concerts in local parks, which draw huge crowds to join in Christmas carols or listen to opera, classical music or popular singers. For many, the most significant national event is Waitangi Day (6 February), when the founding treaty of the nation is celebrated at Waitangi and in *marae* (sacred meeting places) all over the country.

### WINE AND FOOD

Almost every city holds a wine and food festival. One of the oldest and best known is Wine Marlborough (February). Held under marquees in a vineyard, it has tastings from local wineries, food stalls, entertainment and seminars on wine-related subjects. At Toast Martinborough (November), you go from vineyard to vineyard, where tastings are matched with food prepared by local chefs, and the music ranges from jazz to string quartets. The focus is on local bounty of a different sort in Kaikoura's Seafest (October) and the Bluff Oyster and Southland Seafood Festival (April).

### ARTS

The largest cities hold biennial arts festivals, those in Auckland and Christchurch alternating with the month-long International Festival of the Arts, held in February and March in even years in Wellington. Literary, dance and jazz festivals are held annually in the main cities.

### AGRICULTURAL SHOWS

Agricultural and pastoral shows are important events in each region of New Zealand—even in the cities, when the country comes to town. Competitions for prize cattle, sheep-shearing and wood-chopping are held alongside food stalls and funfairs. The most popular are Auckland's Royal Easter Show and Showtime Canterbury, held in Christchurch in November.

» Tourism New Zealand's website has more details (www.newzealand.com).

**You can eat almost any kind of food in New Zealand. The country's European heritage is largely British, with a tradition of roast meat, 'three veg' and hearty breakfasts, which can still be widely found. Good home baking still characterizes many cafés. A typical family meal is likely to be a barbecue of sausages, chops or seafood that folk have caught or gathered themselves, usually washed down with beer or wine.**

Eating out in New Zealand is getting more sophisticated, as Kiwis embrace the café society and bring back a taste for international cuisines from their overseas travels. Modern New Zealand chefs draw inspiration from Asia, the Mediterranean and the Pacific, developing a style of cooking that reflects New Zealand's position in the world. Often called Pacific Rim cuisine, it aims to enhance the tastes of fresh local produce. Indigenous ingredients, traditionally used by Maori, are increasingly being incorporated, with exciting results. With a climate ranging from subtropical to temperate, New Zealand can grow anything from oranges to avocados, saffron to swede, and sheep and cattle are fed year round on pasture. The quality of ingredients is superb.

Immigrants from many countries have opened restaurants, too, so it's easy to find Indian, Chinese, Malaysian, Thai, Japanese, Korean, Italian, Greek and Mexican food. Sometimes they modify their cooking to what they perceive as New Zealand tastes—so in a Chinese restaurant, for example, you may need to ask for the Chinese menu to get authentic dishes. Although New Zealand is still largely a nation of meat eaters, most restaurants offer vegetarian options.

## WHAT TO EAT

New Zealand lamb is arguably the best in the world. Farm-raised venison, known as cervena, is also a speciality (▷ 21). Farmed green-lip mussels, oysters and salmon are also of high quality, thanks to the pristine waters in which they are grown. Despite New Zealand's reputation as perhaps the best trout-fishing country in the world, buying and selling trout is illegal. However, if you catch your own, many restaurants will be happy to cook it for you.

**Above** *Seafood is one of the main ingredients of Pacific Rim cuisine*

When you can get wild seafood, seize the chance. As an island nation, New Zealand's seafood resources are vast, but more than 80 per cent is exported, so chefs in New York, Tokyo or Sydney have a better chance of getting a regular supply than the locals. Look for snapper, monkfish, blue cod, hapuka, turbot, flounder (cooked on the bone is best) and swordfish. For an authentic experience, catch the fish yourself and barbecue it. Other seafood treats include crayfish (spiny lobster), Bluff oysters, paua (abalone), pipi, tuatua, cockles, scampi, koura (freshwater crayfish) and scallops.

Below ground, the kumara (sweet potato) is prized by Maori and used in many ways. Kiwifruit or 'zespri' are deservedly celebrated and most often appear sliced on top of New

Zealand's most famous dessert, the pavlova—a concoction of meringue, whipped cream and fresh fruit. Other locally grown fruits worth trying are the feijoa and tamarillo.

**WHERE TO EAT**

Throughout New Zealand there are eateries to suit every taste and budget, from international fast-food joints to world-class restaurants. The main cities are rich in choice (reputedly, Wellington has more cafés and restaurants per capita than New York) with cafés, café-bars, brasseries, traditional and specialist restaurants flying the flags of many countries. Generally, there is little to distinguish between cafés and restaurants, although cafés tend to be more informal during the day and serve more substantial dishes at night. They also almost always serve coffee, breakfast or brunch, are often licensed (or at least welcome BYO) and often provide outdoor seating.

Kiwis are a casual lot and few restaurants expect formal attire. The restaurants of many of the top hotels, motels and lodges are open to non-residents and can be a good option. If what you want is a hearty feed, you can generally find good pub grub in the cities and most major towns, particularly in popular Irish- and English-style pubs. Fish and chips is New Zealanders' most popular takeaway—with a menu so you can choose what fish you want.

**OPENING HOURS**

Hours vary and are often seasonal. Most cafés open for breakfast between 7 and 9am, often remaining open until 5pm. Some also stay open late into the evening or the early hours. This usually applies seven days a week, with special Sunday brunch hours. Most mid-range restaurants open daily for lunch (often 11–2) and dinner (from 6). The more exclusive establishments usually open for dinner from about 6, with some (especially in winter) opening selected weekday evenings only and at weekends.

**BRING YOUR OWN (BYO)**

BYO restaurants or cafés are licensed for the consumption of (but not the sale of) alcohol and allow you to bring your own wine or bottled beers, sometimes charging a corkage fee (typically NZ$2–NZ$10). Some restaurants are both licensed and BYO wine.

**FOODSTORES**

The main supermarket chains are Foodtown, Woolworths and New World, with Pak 'n Save and Countdown being marginally less expensive. Try to buy fresh vegetables and fruit from roadside stalls or wholesale fruit markets, where the prices are lower and the quality fresher than supermarkets.

**BEER**

Steinlager may be internationally famous, but the most interesting New Zealand beers are the boutique brews. Try Galbraith's in Auckland (Mount Eden Road), Dux de Lux in Christchurch and Emerson's in Dunedin. More beers worth trying are Speight's (the tipple of the Southern Man), Monteith's (especially lauded on the West Coast of the South Island) and Mac's, originally brewed in Nelson. Main international brands and some specialist ones are available, also New Zealand-brewed Guinness.

Beer and lager is usually sold by the 'handle' (pint) or the 'jug' (up to three pints). Half-pints come in a 12fl oz (350ml) glass. Rarely is a pint a full imperial pint; it's usually just under. Drinks generally cost from NZ$6 to NZ$7 for a pint, about NZ$4 to NZ$5 for a jug of Lion Red and up to NZ$7 for a double shot. Drinks cost much less in rural pubs and RSAs (Returned Services Association clubs), where you can usually get yourself signed in. The minimum drinking age is 18. Liquor shops are everywhere and in most places you can buy alcohol seven days a week. For further information on Kiwi beer visit the websites www.Realbeer.co.nz or www.brewing.co.nz.

**WINE**

New Zealand's diversity of climates and soil types has produced a distinctive array of wines. Wine is made all over the country, but the Hawke's Bay and Nelson/Marlborough areas are the principal wine-producing regions. Sauvignon blanc from Marlborough is New Zealand's most acclaimed wine, but there is growing recognition for its Chardonnay, Pinot noir, *méthode traditionelle* sparkling wine, Riesling, Cabernet Sauvignon and Merlot. Striking contemporary architecture and Pacific Rim cuisine combine at vineyard restaurants. Fruit wines, including kiwifruit, are also produced. Many vineyards offer tastings and cellar-door sales.

**NON-ALCOHLIC DRINKS**

All the major soft-drink brands are available. New Zealand has its own soft drink, a brand called L&P, which stands for Lemon and Paeroa. The 'Lemon' speaks for itself and Paeroa relates to a town in the Waikato where the drink was originally made using local mineral-rich spring water. The traditional recipe is still used. Bright green spirulea drinks contain a mineral-rich seaweed.

Given New Zealand's colonial roots, tea is popular and widely available. Increasingly, the standard Bell teabag is being joined by green and herbal teas, often served in specialist shops. New Zealanders expect a high standard from their coffee, and support a number of local roasteries. Expect to ask for a flat white, latte, cappuccino, ristretto, long or short black, or any number of permutations.

**TIPPING**

Tipping is not normal in New Zealand, and most New Zealanders don't tip, but a service charge of 10 to 15 per cent may be included at some smarter restaurants.

**SMOKING**

New Zealand has banned smoking in the workplace—which includes restaurants, bars, pubs and clubs.

**aubergine:** eggplant
**BBQ:** barbecue
**cervena:** New Zealand venison
**BYO:** restaurants or cafés that allow you to bring your own wine or beer
**capsicum:** bell pepper
**entrée:** appetizer or hors d'oeuvre
**feijoa:** an aromatic fruit, also known as the pineapple guava
**fritter:** as in whitebait or crab fritters (also known as patties)—seafood or fish cakes
**hokey pokey:** aerated toffee, usually in vanilla ice cream
**jug:** as in jug of beer (about 4 pints)
***hangi*:** traditional Maori feast cooked on hot stones underground
***kai*:** Maori word for food *(kai moana*—seafood)
**kumara:** sweet potato. Originally from Peru, the kumara came to New Zealand via Samoa and was a staple food of Maori. Very popular because of its sweet taste and versatility, it may be steamed, boiled, baked or eaten raw
**kina:** sea eggs with a prickly shell and edible roe, usually eaten raw and an acquired taste
**lollies:** sweets or confectionery
**manuka honey:** honey with a distinctive taste from the flowers of the manuka (tea tree, known for its medicinal properties)
**muttonbird:** the young of the sooty petrel, with a strong, fishy taste
**paua:** abalone (a mollusc)
**Pavlova:** also known as 'Pav'. A pudding of cream and meringue. Though claimed on both sides of the Tasman Sea, it was thought to have originated in the 1930s to celebrate a visit to New Zealand by Russian ballerina Anna Pavlova
**schooner:** large glass of beer, usually 0.4L (0.75 pint)
**stubby:** a small bottle of beer
**tamarillo:** egg-shaped, deep-red or gold-skinned fruit with tart flesh and edible seeds

## HANGI

Pronounced 'hungi', this is the traditional Maori and Pacific Island method of cooking. It's a great social occasion as much as anything else.

Traditionally, the men would light a large fire and place river stones in the embers. While the stones were heating, a pit was dug in the earth (in active thermal areas, such as around Rotorua, the stones and pit might be naturally heated).

The stones were then placed in the pit with sacking or plant material onto which the meat was laid. Nowadays this includes chicken, wild pig and lamb, but formerly it would have been moa, pigeon, seafood and vegetables, including kumara and watercress. Smaller items were wrapped in leaves or in cooking foil and placed in a basket, which was then covered with earth. The steam slowly cooked the food, sealing in the wonderful flavours.

Although—due to modern health and safety requirements—it is not possible to sample an authentic *hangi*, the feasts produced for visitors are a good second-best.

**Above** *A sweet omelette topped with berry fruits and ice cream*

# STAYING

New Zealand offers a wide choice of accommodation, from backpackers' hostels to luxury lodges in stunning locations. Whichever part of the country you are in, you will rarely end up without a bed for the night, but book ahead in the high season (November to end February). To encounter real Kiwi hospitality, try to stay in a home or farmhouse. Visitor information offices can reserve all kinds of accommodation.

## HOTELS

The hotels in New Zealand usually fall into one of the following four categories:

**Large luxury hotels:** There are a number of large, modern, luxury (four- or five-star) hotels in the main cities. Most are part of major international or trans-Tasman chains and prices range from about NZ$250 to NZ$500 per night. All rooms are equipped with the latest technology, including laptop plug-in ports and satellite TV. Restaurants and leisure facilities such as swimming pools, spas and gyms are standard.

**Standard chain hotels:** Available in all the major cities and most of the larger provincial towns, they charge rates between about NZ$175 to NZ$300, but they have regular weekend or off-season deals. Like the luxury hotels, most standard chain hotels have in-house restaurants and additional facilities such as a heated pool.

**Boutique hotels:** Often used to enhance marketing, the 'boutique' label should still ensure that the hotel is small, luxurious and offers something a little different, be it in décor, location or service. The owners may live on site and extend a personal welcome. Very often the rooms or suites are themed. Although most boutique hotels are urban, you will find the boutique label applied to anything from a modern country home to a heritage building in a city suburb. Dinner is often available by arrangement. On average, double rooms cost from NZ$175 to NZ$400.

**Traditional pubs and budget hotels:** Many rural towns have retained their traditional old wooden hotels. Some of these may look grand from the outside, but invariably the interior doesn't match up. A basic, comfortable room can often be found, but there may be late-night noise from the bar. Prices are usually pitched somewhere between a standard backpackers' hostel and a basic motel unit (from NZ$20 to NZ$60).

## LODGES

From heritage buildings furnished with antiques to purpose-built sporting retreats with fishing, hunting or golf, lodges are usually highly luxurious and often in outstanding rural locations. They may have up to 20 suites, often in self-contained units in secluded, park-like grounds, with opulent reception rooms in the main building. The price usually includes dinner, bed and breakfast, and extras such as pre-dinner drinks. Personal guiding, individuality and good food are assured. Prices range from NZ$200 to NZ$2,600 per night.

» www.lodgesofnz.co.nz.

## BED-AND-BREAKFAST (B&B)

This covers a wide variety of hosted accommodation, from guesthouses to rooms in private homes, and can consist of anything from a basic double room with shared bathroom and cereal for breakfast to a luxurious room with private bathroom and full breakfast. Again prices vary, with the standard cost being around NZ$100 to NZ$150 for a double room. When looking at prices bear in mind a full breakfast costs at least NZ$12 in a café or restaurant. Many B&Bs also offer evening meals at extra cost, but advance notice is usually required.

## HOMESTAYS AND FARMSTAYS

These give you the chance to stay in a family home and mix with your hosts. Breakfast is usually included, and an optional evening meal may be available on request. Farmstays offer the additional attraction of a taste of rural life. You are welcome to help around the farm, and children are particularly welcome. Rates for both homestays and farmstays are comparable with B&B prices.

» New Zealand Farm Holidays, based near Auckland, produce a free catalogue listing about 300 establishments, tel 09-412 9649, www.nzfarmholidays.co.nz.

» For farmstay options in Southland contact Western Southland Farm Hosting Group, tel 03-225 8608, www.farmhost.co.nz.

» Visitor information offices can help you find homestays or farmstays, and the Tourism New Zealand website (www.newzealand.com) also has a detailed listing of nationwide farmstays.

## HOSTELS AND BACKPACKER ORGANIZATIONS

As a popular destination for the independent traveller or backpacker, New Zealand is well served with hostels and budget accommodation.

The Youth Hostels Association NZ (part of the international YHA network) runs 64 hostels, from modern, purpose-built establishments in the cities to ex-churches. Many have double rooms, some with private bathroom.

**Left** *Larger holiday parks may have a café in addition to sports facilities and a store*

You can expect free linen, bedding and pillows, adequately equipped kitchens, laundry facilities, games room or TV room, secure storage facilities, phones and the internet. Prices vary from NZ$12 to NZ$20 for a dormitory bed, depending on season, and NZ$22 to NZ$30 per adult for doubles. Membership is available from www.yha.org.nz. The annual fee is NZ$40 (NZ$30 for renewals). YHA membership cards also entitle you to a number of discounts, including up to 30 per cent off air and bus travel.
Other organizations include:

» VIP group, PO Box 60177, Titirangi, Auckland, tel 09-816 8903, www.vip.co.nz.

» Budget Backpacker Hostels Ltd (BBH), Foley Towers, 208 Kilmore Street, Christchurch, tel 03-379 3014, www.bbh.co.nz.

» Nomads, Travellers' Contact Point, 87 Queen Street, Auckland, tel 09-300 7197, www.travellersnz.com.

## MOTORCAMPS AND CABINS

New Zealand is very well served with motorcamps (also known as holiday parks), where there are both powered sites for motor vehicles and tent pitches for campers. Camps are usually equipped with laundry facilities, hot showers and kitchens. Larger parks may also have a pool, games and sports facilities, a general store and café.

Motorcamps often also have a range of cabins, units or tourist apartments for rent. Cabins are the most basic, with little except a bed, sink and electric supply, but some also have a small kitchen. They cost between NZ$35 and NZ$60 for two. Units and apartments are similar to motels, being fully self-contained, some with multiple rooms. They vary in price but rarely exceed NZ$100 per night (for two people), with an additional charge of NZ$12 to NZ$15 per extra person.

» The Top Ten chain of motorcamps has a good reputation and a 'Club Card' scheme offering a 10 per cent discount, tel 03-377 9900, www.topparks.co.nz.

## CAMPSITES

The Department of Conservation (DoC; www.doc.govt.nz) manages more than 200 vehicle-accessible campsites all over the country, many in prime locations.

Campsites are typically basic, provide clean running water, toilet facilities and barbecue areas, but rarely allow open fires. Sites in the national parks have well-equipped huts. The camping fee is NZ$2 to NZ$10 a night. Fees for huts are anything from NZ$5 to NZ$40 per night, depending on category and location. If you plan to use DoC campsites and huts, it is advisable to book well in advance.

## SELF-CATERING

Holiday homes of all kinds, including tiny country cottages known as baches, are available for rent. Bach is pronounced 'batch', and is a shortened version of 'bachelor pad'. Most self-catering accommodation operates on a minimum weekend or week-long stay basis. Look in the travel or house-rental sections of national newspapers. Regional visitor offices may also be able to help you find accommodation.

Motels are the choice of most New Zealanders. They range from the utilitarian to luxurious condos with a spa pool, but have at least a shower, kitchen facilities and a TV, and are usually clean and comfortable. Studio units cost about NZ$80 to NZ$100, one-bedroom units NZ$90 to NZ$120 and suites are available for an additional charge for each adult. Many of the larger motel complexes have a restaurant and a swimming pool, plus spas. Most motels offer breakfast, delivered to the door at extra charge.

## RESERVATIONS AND PAYING

It is advisable to reserve at least three days in advance during the high season (November to March) and further ahead during New Zealand's summer holidays (from Christmas to the end of January). Payment is generally straightforward, with most establishments taking all major credit cards through EFTPOS (Electronic Funds Transfer at Point of Sale). Cash is also readily accepted, and recommended at B&Bs and homestays.

### QUALMARK

Qualmark is New Zealand tourism's official symbol of quality, instigated to encourage high standards of hospitality and service. Lists of Qualmark-rated places to stay, graded from two to five stars, are available from visitor information offices and AA Travel Centres.

## SPEAKING 'KIWI'

English is the common language of New Zealand, and in its written form generally follows British rather than US spelling conventions. There is little difference in pronunciation from one part of the country to another, although you may detect a burr in the southern half of the South Island and other locations where localized settlement was particularly strong. New Zealand has developed its own slang words and phrases, a selection of which are listed below.

**bach** holiday cottage (pronounced 'batch', originates from a shortened form of 'bachelor', referring to a dwelling fit for a single man)
**Beehive** the main government building in Wellington
**bludge** scrounge, borrow
**bush** forest, native woodland
**BYO** a café or restaurant that allows you to take your own beer or wine

**chook** chicken
**cocky** farmer (usually 'cow cocky')
**chilly-bin** portable cooler box for a picnic
**crib** holiday cottage (South Island)
**crook** sick, ill
**cuppa** cup of tea

**dag** a character, or entertaining person
**dairy** general grocery store

**good as gold** fine, OK

**handle** beer glass with a handle

**jandals** flip-flops, thongs
**judder bars** speed bumps in the road

**morning tea** mid-morning tea or coffee break
**mozzie** mosquito

**Pakeha** person of European descent

**smoko** tea or coffee break

**she'll be right** that's OK
**shout a round** pay for a round of drinks

**togs** swimwear

**wopwops** the back of beyond
**wowser** killjoy

## MAORI WORDS AND PHRASES

Maori words and phrases are used throughout New Zealand and the Maori language is generally encouraged and spoken with pride within the *whanau* and *iwi* (Maori family and tribes). It is wise to be aware of a few basic rules before arriving in the country. The easiest way to say Maori words is to pronounce each syllable phonetically. Perhaps the most important feature is the pronunciation of 'wh' as the English 'f'. For example, *whanau* is pronounced 'fha-now' and Whangarei 'Fhongarei'. Vowels are pronounced openly, as in Italian, and all words end in a vowel.

**ana** cave
**Aotearoa** New Zealand
**ara** path, road
**ariki** tribal leader
**atua** spiritual being
**au** rain
**awa** river, valley

**haere mai** welcome
**haera ra** farewell
**hangi** Maori feast
**hau** wind
**harakeke** flax plant, leaves
**Hawaiiki** ancestral Polynesian homeland
**hapu** sub-tribe/to be pregnant
**he ao** a land or a world
**he tangata** the people
**hei tiki** carved figure worn round the neck, usually shortened to tiki
**hoe** paddle
**hongi** traditional greeting (pressing noses)
**huka** spray, snow

**iti** small
**iwi** tribe, bone

**kahu** blue
**kai** eat
**Kaikaiawaro** a dolphin (also known as Pelorus Jack) who cruised the Marlborough Sounds and became a guardian to *iwi*
**kaitiaki** protector, caretaker
**kainga** village
**kapa haka** group of Maori performers
**kia ora** welcome
**kaumatua** elders
**kawa** protocols
**kete** basket
**kohu** mist, fog
**kowhaiwhai** rafter patterns

**ma** stream, white
**mana** integrity, prestige, control
**manawhenua** people with tribal affiliations with the area
**manu** bird
**Maori** ordinary people
**Maoritanga** Maoriness
**marae** sacred courtyard or plaza
**maunga** mountain
**mauri** life essence
**moana** lake, sea
**moko** tattoo
**motu** island, or anything isolated
**muka** flax fibre

**namu** sandfly
**Ngati** people of
**nui** big, plenty

**o** of, the place of
**one** sand, beach, mud

**pa** fortified village
**Pakeha** foreigner, white person, European
**papa** broad, flat
**poi** ball attached to flax string
**pounamu** sacred greenstone
**puke** hill
**puna** spring of water

**rangatira** tribal leader

**rangi** sky
**roa** long
**roto** lake

**taiaha** a fighting staff
**tangata** people/person
**tangihanga** death ritual
**taonga** treasure, prized object (often passed down by ancestors)
**tapu** sacred, out of bounds
**te** the
**Te Ika-a-Maui** North Island
**tiki** see **hei tiki**
**tipuna** ancestor
**tukutuku** wall panels

**utu** cost, retribution

**wahakatauki** proverb or saying
**wai** water
**waiata** song, flute music
**wairua** soul
**waka** canoe
**whakairo** carvings
**whakapapa** origins or genealogy
**whanau** extended family/to give birth
**whanga** bay, inlet
**whare** house
**whare runanga** meeting house
**whenua** land
**whero** red

## GLOSSARY FOR US VISITORS

| | |
|---|---|
| **A&E** | emergency room (hospital department) |
| **anticlockwise** | counterclockwise |
| **aubergine** | eggplant |
| **bill** | check (at restaurant) |
| **biscuit** | cookie |
| **bonnet** | hood (car) |
| **boot** | trunk (car) |
| **busker** | street musician |
| **caravan** | house trailer or RV |
| **car park** | parking lot |
| **carriage** | car (on a train) |
| **chemist** | pharmacy |
| **chips** | french fries |
| **coach** | long-distance bus |
| **corridor** | hall |
| **courgette** | zucchini |
| **crèche** | day care |
| **dual carriageway** | two-lane highway |
| **en suite** | a bedroom with its own private bathroom; may also just refer to the bathroom |
| **football** | Rugby (sometimes soccer) |
| **full board** | a hotel tariff that includes all meals |
| **garden** | yard (residential) |
| **GP** | doctor |
| **half board** | hotel tariff that includes breakfast and either lunch or dinner |
| **handbag** | purse |
| **high street** | main street |
| **hire** | rent |
| **jelly** | Jello™ |
| **junction** | intersection |
| **layby** | rest stop; also payment of a deposit to secure an article |
| **level crossing** | grade crossing |
| **loo** | rest room |
| **lorry** | truck |
| **licensed** | a café or restaurant that has a license to serve alcohol |
| **lift** | elevator |
| **nappy** | diaper |
| **note** | bill (when referring to money) |
| **pants** | underpants (men's) |
| **pavement** | sidewalk |
| **petrol** | gas |
| **plaster** | Band-Aid or bandage |
| **post** | mail |
| **pudding** | dessert |
| **purse** | change purse |
| **pushchair** | stroller |
| **return ticket** | roundtrip ticket |
| **rocket** | arugula |
| **roundabout** | traffic circle or rotary |
| **self-catering** | accommodation including a kitchen |
| **single ticket** | one-way ticket |
| **stalls** | (in theatre) orchestra seats |
| **subway** | underpass |
| **surgery** | doctor's office |
| **tailback** | stalled line of traffic |
| **takeaway** | takeout |
| **taxi rank** | taxi stand |
| **ten-pin bowling** | bowling |
| **T-junction** | an intersection where one road meets another at right angles (making a T shape) |
| **toilets** | restrooms |
| **torch** | flashlight |
| **trolley** | cart |
| **trousers** | pants |
| **way out** | exit |

## TIMELINE

**AD 800** Polynesian navigator Kupe lands at Hokianga, in Northland.

**1000** Polynesians move southeast to Pacific Islands from Asia.

**1300** Polynesian colonies established on North Island and some tribes are clearing bush and hunting in the South Island.

**1642** Dutch explorer Abel Tasman, commissioned by East India Company, sights the land he calls Staten Landt, later renamed Nieuw Zeeland.

**1769** British explorer Captain James Cook makes the first of three voyages to New Zealand on the *Endeavour*, claiming the country for King George III.

**1773** Cook lands at Dusky Cove on the *Resolution* and returns to Ship Cove via the west coast.

**1776** Cook returns to Ship Cove and the Sounds before sailing to Hawaii, where he is killed.

**1791** *The William and Ann*, the first whaling vessel, anchors at Doubtless Bay, heralding a period of intensive whaling, sealing and timber- and flax-trading.

**1814** British missionary Samuel Marsden establishes an Anglican mission station in the Bay of Islands.

**1820–35** Maori Musket Wars: fierce inter-tribal warfare.

**1833** Official British Resident James Busby arrives in Waitangi and encourages adoption of United Tribes flag.

**1835** Declaration of Independence by United Tribes of New Zealand signed by 34 northern chiefs.

**1839** Captain William Hobson appointed Lieutenant Governor with remit to transfer sovereignty of land from Maori Chiefs to British Crown.

**1840** Treaty of Waitangi signed, proclaiming British sovereignty. French settlers land at Akaroa.

**1844** Chief Hone Heke cuts down British flagpole and instigates two-year War of the North.

**1848** Dunedin founded as a Scottish Presbyterian colony.

**1850** Christchurch founded as an Anglican colony.

**1852** Constitution Act creates General Assembly and provinces. Discovery of gold in Coromandel.

**1855** Earthquake changes the face of Wellington.

**1858** Te Wherowhero installed as first Maori king, taking the name Potatau I.

**1860s** Gold boom attracts thousands of prospectors.

**1865** Wellington becomes capital of New Zealand. Native Lands Act investigates Maori land ownership and distributes land titles.

**1867** First Maori Members of Parliament elected.

**1882** First refrigerator ship sails to London with a cargo of frozen lamb, heralding a new economic era.

**1893** New Zealand is the first country to give women the vote.

**1907** New Zealand constituted as a British Dominion.

**1914–18** New Zealand suffers the most casualties per head of population of any World War I nation.

**1931** Earthquake destroys Napier.

**1938** Government lays basis of welfare state.

**1939–45** New Zealand fights on the Allied side in World War II.

**1945** New Zealand is one of the founding member states of the United Nations.

**1947** New Zealand is declared an independent nation.

**1952** Population tops 2 million.

**1953** New Zealander Edmund Hillary conquers Mount Everest.

**1966** International airport opens at Auckland.

**1973** Preferential trade with Britain ends when the UK joins the Common Market.

**1980s** Anti-nuclear policy is adopted. Deregulation of economy.

**1985** Greenpeace vessel *Rainbow Warrior* is bombed by French Secret Service in Auckland harbour.

**1987** Maori Language Act gives Maori language official status. All Blacks win first Rugby World Cup.

**1988** Unemployment exceeds 100,000.

**1990** Dame Catherine Tizard becomes the first woman Governor-General.

**1993** Referendum votes in favour of mixed-member proportional representation.

**1995** Peter Blake's *Black Magic* crew wins the America's Cup.

**1997** Jenny Shipley of the National Party becomes New Zealand's first woman prime minister.

**2004** *The Return of the King*, last in the *Lord of the Rings* trilogy, scoops 11 Oscars at the Academy Awards.

**2008** New Zealand voters elect the government for the next three years.

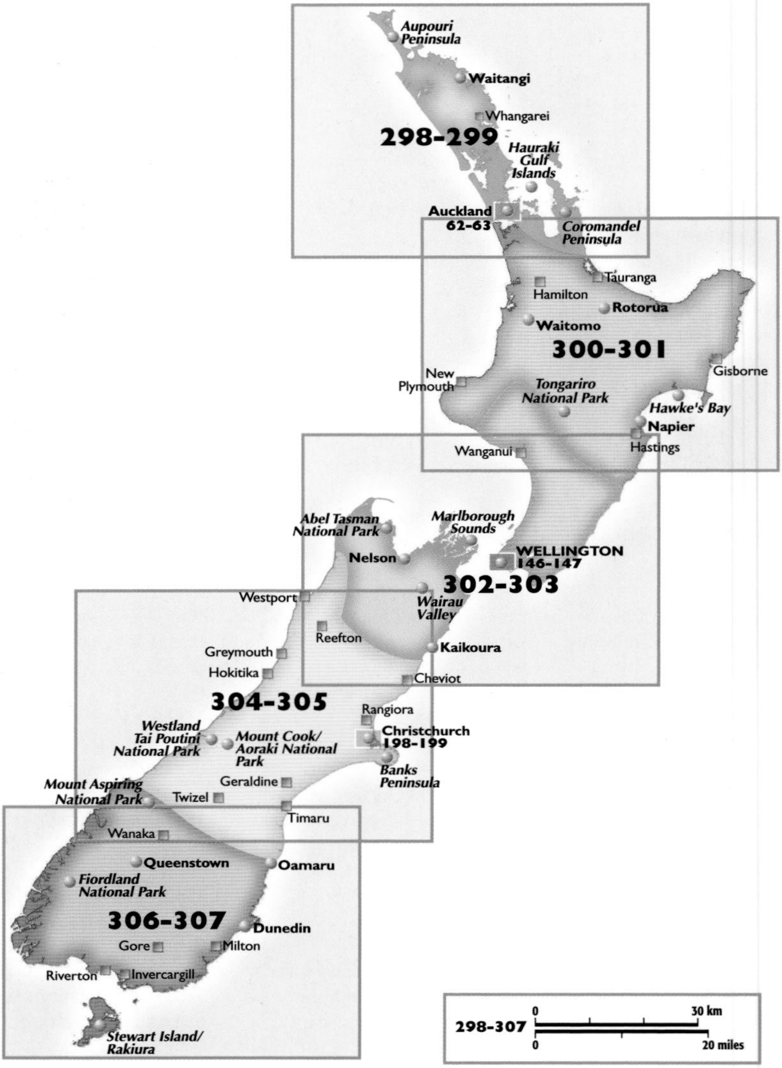

Aupouri Peninsula
Waitangi
Whangarei
298-299
Hauraki Gulf Islands
Auckland 62-63
Coromandel Peninsula
Tauranga
Hamilton
Rotorua
Waitomo
300-301
Gisborne
New Plymouth
Tongariro National Park
Hawke's Bay
Napier
Hastings
Wanganui
Abel Tasman National Park
Marlborough Sounds
Nelson
WELLINGTON 146-147
302-303
Westport
Wairau Valley
Reefton
Kaikoura
Greymouth
Hokitika
Cheviot
304-305
Rangiora
Westland Tai Poutini National Park
Mount Cook/ Aoraki National Park
Christchurch 198-199
Banks Peninsula
Geraldine
Mount Aspiring National Park
Twizel
Timaru
Wanaka
Queenstown
Oamaru
Fiordland National Park
306-307
Dunedin
Gore
Milton
Riverton
Invercargill
Stewart Island/ Rakiura
298-307
0
30 km
0
20 miles

- Motorway (Expressway)
- National road
- Regional road
- Local road
- Minor road
- Built-up area
- City / Town
- National park / Reserve
- Forest
- Marine reserve
- Glacier
- Featured place of interest
- Airport
- 621 Height in metres

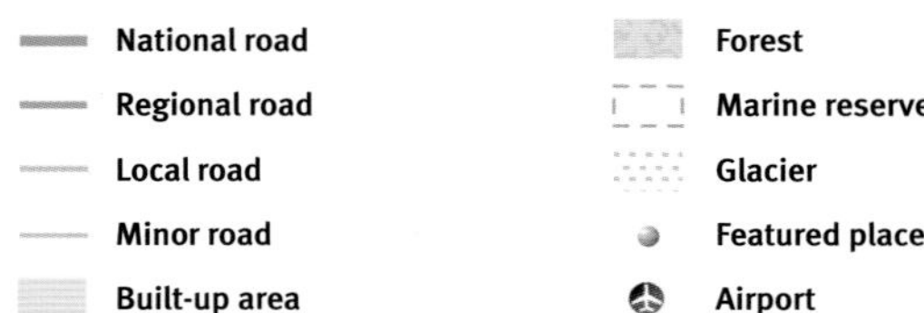

# MAPS

Map references for the sights refer to the atlas pages within this section or to the individual town plans within the regions. For example, Auckland has the reference 299 J4, indicating the page on which the map is found (299) and the grid square in which Auckland sits (J4).

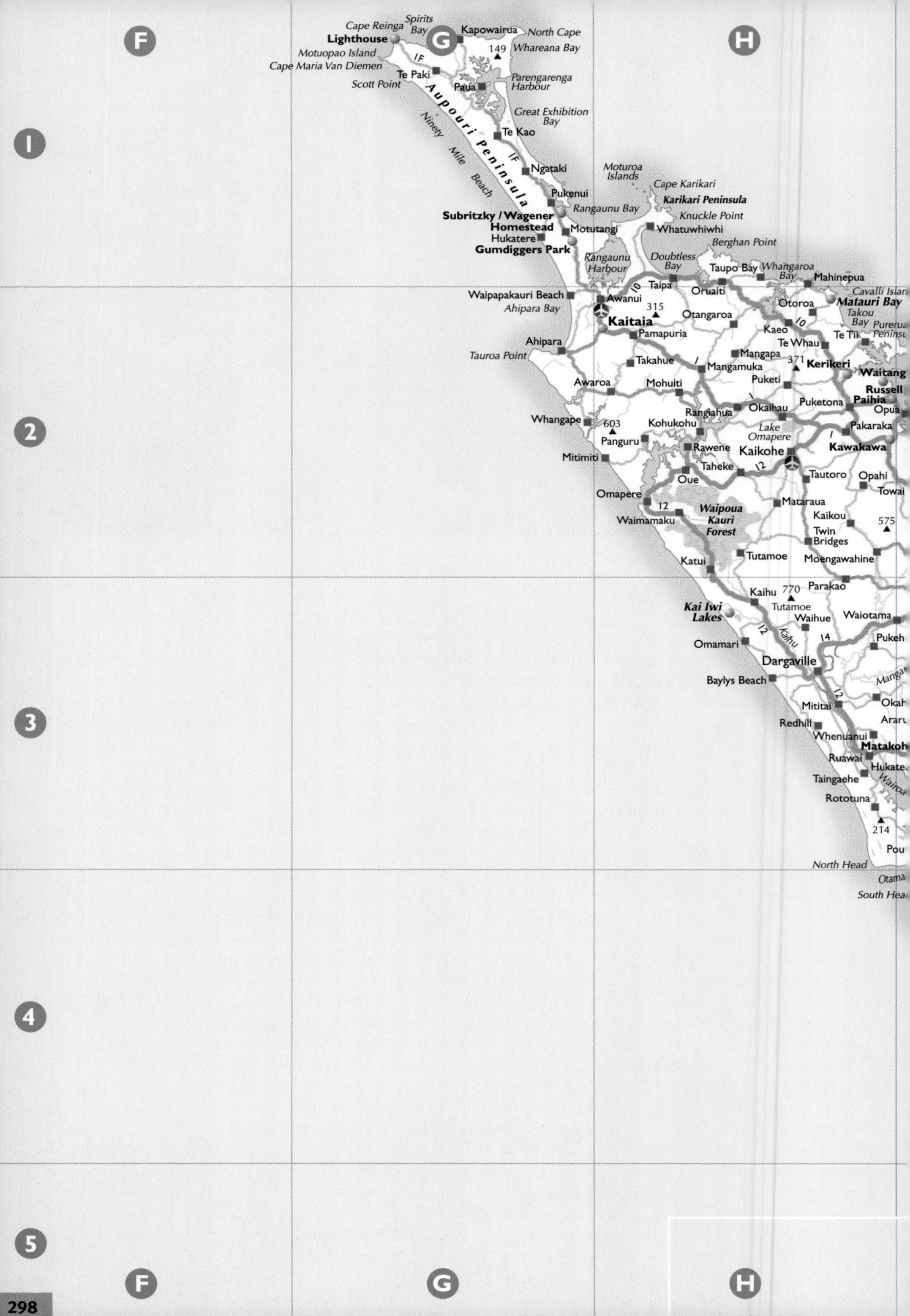

F
G
H
I
2
3
4
5
Cape Reinga
Lighthouse
Spirits Bay
Kapowairua
North Cape
Whareana Bay
149
Motuopao Island
Cape Maria Van Diemen
Te Paki
Scott Point
Paua
Parengarenga Harbour
Great Exhibition Bay
Aupouri Peninsula
Ninety Mile Beach
Te Kao
Ngataki
Moturoa Islands
Cape Karikari
Karikari Peninsula
Pukenui
Rangaunu Bay
Knuckle Point
Subritzky / Wagener Homestead
Motutangi
Whatuwhiwhi
Hukatere
Gumdiggers Park
Berghan Point
Rangaunu Harbour
Doubtless Bay
Taupo Bay
Whangaroa Bay
Mahinepua
Taipa
Oruaiti
Waipapakauri Beach
Awanui
Otoroa
Matauri Bay
Ahipara Bay
315
Kaitaia
Otangaroa
Takou Bay
Kaeo
Te Tii
Pamapuria
Te Whau
Ahipara
Mangapa
Tauroa Point
Takahue
Mangamuka
371
Kerikeri
Waitang
Puketi
Awaroa
Mohuiti
Russell
Paihia
Puketona
Opua
Okaihau
Rangiahua
Whangape
603
Kohukohu
Lake Omapere
Pakaraka
Panguru
Rawene
Kaikohe
Kawakawa
Mitimiti
Taheke
Tautoro
Opahi
Oue
Towai
Omapere
Mataraua
Waipoua Kauri Forest
Waimamaku
Kaikou
575
Twin Bridges
Tutamoe
Moengawahine
Katui
Kaihu
770
Parakao
Tutamoe
Kai Iwi Lakes
Waihue
Waiotama
Omamari
Kaihu
Pukeh
Dargaville
Baylys Beach
Mititai
Okah
Araru
Redhill
Whenuanui
Matakoh
Ruawai
Hukate
Taingaehe
Wairoa
Rototuna
214
Pou
North Head
Otama
South Hea
10
1F
1
12
14

J
K
L
1
2
3
4
5
Bay of Islands Maritime and Historic Park
Bay of Islands
Cape Brett
Rawhiti
Taupiri Bay
Waihaha
Whangaruru Harbour
Poor Knights Islands Marine Reserve
Poor Knights Islands
Whananaki
Motutara Point
Whakapara
Matapouri
Ngunguru
Tutukaka Coast
Kamo
Ngunguru Bay
Whangarei
Parua Bay
Pataua North
Awarua Rock
Whangarei Harbour
Ocean Beach
Marsden Bay
Bream Head
Ruakaka
Ruarangi
Hen and Chickens Islands
Bream Bay
Waipu
Bream Tail
Brynderwyn
Paparoa
Mangawhai
Jellicoe Channel
Little Barrier Island
Cradock Channel
Aiguilles Island
Motairehe
Rakitu Island
Port Fitzroy
Whakatautuna Point
Awana Bay
Whangaparapara
Claris
Great Barrier Island
Tryphena
Cape Barrier
Kaiwaka
Te Arai
Port Albert
Wellsford
Pakiri
Goat Island
Goat Island Marine Reserve
Leigh
Cape Rodney
Omaha Bay
Takatu Point
Matakana
Warkworth
Tauhoa
Colville Channel
Kaipara Harbour
South Head
Woodcocks
Kawau Island
Hauraki Gulf Islands
Cape Colville
Port Jackson
Port Charles
Araparera
Puhoi
Hauraki Gulf Marine Park
Coromandel Forest Park
Tahekeroa
Whangaparaoa Bay
Orewa
Waiaro
Waikawau Bay
Great Mercury Island
Kaukapakapa
Tiritiri Matangi Island
Colville
Waikawau
Dairy Flat
Whangaparaoa
Hauraki Gulf
New Chums Beach
Red Mercury Island
Rakino Island
Tokarahu Point
Albany
Motutapu Island
Papaaroha
Kuaotunu
Wharepapa
Waiheke Island
Coromandel
Te Rerenga
Waimauku
Kumeu
Rangitoto Island
Oneroa
Rotoroa Island
Coromandel Harbour
Coromandel Peninsula
Mercury Bay
Muriwai Beach
Whitianga
Swanson
AUCKLAND
Ponui Island
Cooks Beach
Te Henga
Maraetai
Kereta
Hot Water Beach
Waiatarua
Coroglen
Piha
Whitford
Te Ororoa Point
Waitakere Ranges Regional Park
Clevedon
Kawakawa Bay
Orere Point
Cornwallis
The Aldermen Islands
Tapu
Coromandel Forest Park
Whatipu
Papakura
Pauanui
Awhitu
Manukau Harbour
Hunua
Firth of Thames
Hikuai
Slipper Island
Coromandel Range
Clarks Beach
Te Hihi
Runciman
Kaiaua
Thames
Wharekawa Harbour
Opoutere
Pukekohe
Bombay
Miranda
Kopu
Mangatawhiri
Whangamata Harbour
Whangamata
Waiuku
Tuakau
Pokeno
Waitakaruru
Waihou
Maramarua
Ngatea
Otaua
Tauranganui
Meremere
Omahu
Whiritoa
Mayor Island
Mataora Bay
Port Waikato
Pukekawa
Okaeria
Netherton
Coromandel Forest Park
Waikato
Te Kauwhata
Kaihere
Paeroa
Piako
Waihi
Wairamarama
Waihi Beach
Glen Murray
Lake
300
301

Waitakere Ranges Regional Park
428
Whatipu
Cornwallis
Manukau Harbour
Papakura
Hunua
477
Tapu
Coromandel Forest Park
The Aldermen Islands
Pauanui
Slipper Isl
H
298
J
Awhitu
Te Hihi
22
Runciman
Kaiaua
K
Firth of Thames
Hikuai
Thames
Coromandel Range
Wharekawa Harbour
Opoutere
Clarks Beach
Bombay
Miranda
Kopu
664
Whangamata Harbour
Pukekohe
Mangatawhiri
Waitakaruru
Waihou
Waiuku
Tuakau
Pokeno
Maramarua
2
25
Omahu
Whangamata
Whiritoa
Otaua
Tauranganui
Meremere
Ngatea
Coromandel Forest Park
Mataora Bay
Port Waikato
Pukekawa
Waikato
Okaeria
Kaihere
Netherton
Piako
Paeroa
Waihi
Wairamarama
Te Kauwhata
390
Waihi Beach
5
Glen Murray
Lake Whangape
Lake Waikare
Tirohia
Pios Beach
Limestone Downs
Ohinewai
Matahuru
Tahuna
Ruawaro
Orini
Otway
Woodlands
Matakana Island
Waikorea
Lake Waahi
Huntly
Te Aroha
Tauranga Harbour
Mangateparu
Dunmore
Te Akatea
Tatuarui
Shaftesbury
Te Akau
Morrinsville
848
Omokoroa
Ngaruawahia
Gordonton
Ngarua
Gordon
Tauranga
Waingaro Landing
Eureka
Kaimai Mamaku Forest Park
Kaimai Range
HAMILTON
Kiwitahi
Raglan
Whatawhata
Matamata
Te Uku
756
Mount Karioi
Te Mata
Karamu
Cambridge
Rahanui
Ohaupo
Piarere
Te Poi
Makomako
959
Mount Pirongia
Pirongia
Te Awamutu
797
Tirau
Tapapa
Ngaware
Mangapapa
Kawhia
Kawhia Harbour
Albatross Point
Parawera
Arapuni
Putaruru
Agrodor
Tihiroa
Te Rauamoa
Puniu
Lichfield
6
Tasman Sea
Taharoa
Kinohaku
Rotongata
Mamaku
Otorohanga
Waikato
Te Anga
Waitomo
Wharepuhunga
Tokoroa
Tauraroa
771
Kiritehere
Ngapaenga
Te Kuiti
Ngaroma
Waipapa
Wairek
Waipa
806
Tirua Point
Maungamangero
Mangakino
Wawa
Atiamuri
Waikawau
Piopio
Whakamaru
Mokau
Waipapa
Orakei Korako Geothermal Reserve
Aria
Aratoro
Benneydale
Barryville
1165
Mokai
Mapara Wildlife Reserve
Pureora
Te Pouwhakatutu
Awakino
Mahoenui
Tangitu
Piropiro
Tihoi
Wairakei Park
Huka Falls
Mokau
Pureora Forest Park
Hauhungaroa Range
Kinloch
Maungatupoto
Taupo
Mohakatino
Matiere
Te Koura
Lake Taupo (Taupomoana)
7
Ahititi
Ohura
Ngakonui
Kotare
533
Mount Damper
Taumarunui
Aukopae
Manunui
1078
Hauhungaroa
Pukearuhe
Kuratau Junction
Motutere
Waitara
Wanganui
Tokaanu
New Plymouth
Sugar Loaf Island
Onaero
Okoki
Waitara
Tahora
632
Owhango
Kirikau
Turangi
391
Papakai
Lake Rotoaira
Taurewa
Rangipo
1517
Tarata
Retaruke
Kaitieke
1967
Mount Tongariro
Ngapuketurua
Okato
Matau
Inglewood
Pohokura
Whanganui National Park
2294
Mount Ngauruhoe
Kaimanawa Forest Park
Tongariro
Newall
North Egmont
Tariki
Retaruke
National Park
Whakapapa Village
Cape Egmont
2518
Mount Taranaki/Mount Egmont
Strathmore
Ruatiti
Tongariro National Park
Rangitikei
Mount Egmont National Park
Toko
Matemateaonga Range
Whanganui
Pokaka
2797
Mount Ruapehu
Rahotu
Stratford
Puniwhakau
Tohunga Junction
Rangipo Desert
Mangamingi
Ohakune
Opunake
Awatuna
Eltham
Moeroa
Raetihi
Lake Moawhango
Lake Rotorangi
Karioi
Waitotara
Waiouru
45
Whenuakura
49
8
Manaia
Ararata
Pipiriki
Rangiwaea Junction
1116
Hihitahi
Erewhon
1372
Oeo
Hawera
Ohangai
Makakaho Junction
Ranana
669
Hihitahi
Moawhango
356
Whanganui National Park
Pukeokahu
Hurleyville
Kakatahi
Rongoiti Junction
Manutahi
Patea
Mangawhio
Orangimea
Paparangi
Mangawhero
Papanui Junction
Taihape
Rangitikei
Waverley
Turakina
Utiku
Taoroa Junction
Ruahine Range
Patea
Whakaihuwhaka
Tiriraukawa
Waitotara
Maxwell
Mangamahu
Wakara
Otairi
Ruahine
Brunswick
Upokongaro
Ohingaiti
Wanganui
302
Kuangaroa
Pemberton
Ruahine Forest Park
Makare
Rewa
Umutoi
H
Tasman Sea
J
Porewa
K
Turakina
Marton
Kimbolton
Ngamoko
Koitiata
Komako

L
M
N
P
299
303
5
6
7
8
Mayor Island
White Island
Motiti Island
Mount Maunganui
Bay of Plenty
Cape Runaway
Lottin Point
Whangaparaoa
Potaka
Matakaoa Point
Hicks Bay
Te Araroa
Papatea Bay
Waikawa Point
Papatea
East Island
East Cape
Maketu
Okurei Point
Te Puke
Pukehina
Otamarakau
Matata
Moutohora Island
Te Kaha
Otehirinaki
Tikitiki
Whakawhitira
Whakatane
Paroa
Ohiwa Harbour
Hawai
Raukumara Forest Park
Hikurangi
Raukumara Range
Hiruharama
Whareponga
Opotiki
Omarumutu
Puketoetoe
Rotorua
Hell's Gate
Rotoiti
Te Ngae
Lake Okataina
Kawerau
Te Teko
Awakeri
Taneatua
Kererutahi
Takaputahi
Ihungia
Waipiro Bay
Te Puia Springs
Tamarara
Huiarua
Tokomaru Bay
Mawhai Point
Anaura Bay
Arero
Tutamoa
Tauwhareparae
Kaiaua Bay
Tolaga Bay
Pourewa Island
Takapau
Whatatutu
Kanakanaia
Matahanea
Toatoa
Nukuhou North
Ruatoki North
Matahi
Waiohau
Oponae
Te Waiti Hill
Motu
Matawai
Whakarau
Otoko
Te Karaka
Waimata
Waihau Bay
Gable End Foreland
Whangara
Ormond
Gisborne
Matawhero
Ngatapa
Tahunga
Rere
Maungatopoto
Koranga
Te Urewera National Park
Tawharemanuka
Kopuriki
Ikawhenua Range
Waimangu
Lake Rerewhakaaitu
Rerewhakaaitu
Wai-O-Tapu
Kaingaroa Forest
Parekarangi
Murupara
Broadlands
Wairapukao
Te Whaiti
Te Waiti
Papueru
Huiarau Range
Manuoha
Papuni
Matea
Whirinaki Forest Park
Waikaremoana
Lake Waikaremoana
Ruakituri
Waerengaokuri
Poverty Bay
Tuaheni Point
Young Nicks Head
Waingake
Bartletts
Te Reinga
Whakapunake
Tarapatiki
Ardkeen
Tukemokihi
Rangitaiki
Tarawera
Willow Flat
Frasertown
Wairoa
Nuhaka
Whakaki
Opoutama
Mahia
Table Cape
Mahia Peninsula
Long Point
Ahuriri Point
Portland Island
Te Haroto
Raupunga
Waihua
Putorino
Waikoau
Tutira
Te Pohue
Puketitiri
Patoka
Waipatiki Beach
Tangoio
Kuripapango
Rissington
Bay View
Hawke's Bay
Puketapu
Napier
Crownthorpe
Fernhill
Hastings
Clive
Clifton
Cape Kidnappers
Maraekakaho
Pakipaki
Havelock North
Ocean Beach
Opapa
Waimarama
Otane
Ongaonga
Patangata
Kairakau Beach
Waipukurau
Omakere

F
G
H
300
9
10
11
12
Cape Farewell
Puponga
Farewell Spit
Puponga Farm Park
Whanganui Inlet
Farewell Spit Nature Reserve
Pakawau
Paturau River
Golden Bay
Collingwood
Rockville
916
Bainham
Aorere
Kahurangi Point
Puramahoi
60
Separation Point
Totaranui
Awaroa Bay
Takaka
Motupipi
Te Waikoropupu Springs
Rawhiti Cave
Big Bay
Mackay Downs
Heaphy
East Takaka
Abel Tasman National Park
1784
Devil River Peak
Adele Island
Marahau
Kaiteriteri
Gunner Downs
Tasman Mountains
Cobb
Upper Takaka
Riwaka
Kahurangi
National
Park
Cobb Reservoir
Motueka
Karamea
Ngatimoti
Tasman
Mapua
Woodstock
Upper Moutere
Kongahu
Nelson
Richmond
1762
Mount Kendall
Little Wanganui
Tapawera
Wakefield
Karamea Bight
Corbyvale
Belgrove
Summerlea
1876
Mount Owen
Korere
Kaka
Golden Downs
Granity
67
Owen River
Kawatiri
Kikiwa
Fairdown
Denniston
Westport
Newton Flat
Lyell
Buller
Te Kuha
Murchison
Rotoroa
St Arnaud
Lake Rotoiti
Berlins
Inangahua
Lake Rotoroa
Nelson Lakes National Park
1460
Mount Euclid
Rotokohu
Paenga
Matakitaki
2338
Mount Travers
1640
Mount Victoria
Burnbrae
Reefton
Victoria Range
Victoria Forest Park
Maimai
Maruia
2156
Mount Burn
Spenser Mountains
Lake Tennyson
2013
Mount Sebastopol
Ikamatua
Waiuta
Grey
305
Springs Junction
Ahaura
Maruia Springs
Lewis Pass
Lewis Pass National Reserve
Clarence
Waiau
Lake Hochstetter
1379
Mount Elliot
Upper Grey
Hanmer Springs
Haupiri
Hanmer
Rotomanu
Lake Sumner Forest Park
Hope
1612
Mount Tekoa
Lake Sumner
Taramakau
Crawford Range
1839
Balmoral
Culverden
Stephens Island
Cape Stephens
Patuki
D'Urville Island
Rangitoto Islands
Tasman Bay
Haukawakawa
Admiralty Bay
French Pass
Sauvage Point
Forsyth Island
Cape Jackson
Marlborough Sounds
Cape Soucis
Okiwi Bay
Tennyson Inlet
Endeavour Inlet
1203
Mount Stokes
Cape Koamaru
Delaware Bay
Pepin Island
Wakapuaka
Pelorus Sound
Manaroa
Arapawa Island
Kenepuru Head
Queen Charlotte Sound
Rai Valley
Havelock
Picton
Pelorus Bridge
1330
Robertson Point
Okaramio
Tuamarina
Cloudy Bay
Richmond Range
Mount Richmond Forest Park
Te Rou
Renwick
Blenheim
Wairau
Hillersden
Wairau Valley
63
Waihopai
Seddon
Lake Grassmere
Clifford Bay
1579
Mount Horrible
Altimarloch
Cape Campbell
2009
Ward
Peggioh
Gladstone
Wharanui
Langridge
Awatere
2621
Mitre Peak
Kekerengu
Molesworth
Inland Kaikoura Range
Clarence
Acheron
Seaward Kaikoura Range
2610
Manakau
Rakautara
Hawk Hills
Kowhai
Kaikoura
Kaikoura Peninsula
70
Oaro
Claverley
Ferniehurst
Waiau
594
Parnassus
Leamington
Cheviot

J
K
L
M
Mangawhio
Orangimea
Whanganui National Park
Papanui Junction
Rongoiti Junction
Taihape
Kereru
Hastings
Clifton
Cape Kidnapper
Waverley
Paparangi
Whakaihuwhaka
Utiku
Taoroa Junction
1015
Wakarara
Pakipaki
Havelock North
Ruahine Range
Waitotara
Maxwell
Tiriraukawa
Opapa
Ocean Beach
Mangamahu
Otairi
Tikokino
301
Brunswick
Upokongaro
Ohingaiti
Ruahine
Waimarama
Kuangaroa
Wanganui
Pemberton
Ruahine Forest Park
Makaretu
Ongaonga
Otane
Waipawa
Patangata
Rewa
Porewa
Turakina
Kairakau Beach
Umutoi
Ngamoko
Waipukurau
444
Rangitikei
Kimbolton
Takapau
Omakere
Koitiata
Marton
Oroua
Komako
Oueroa
Paoanui Point
Santoft
Halcombe
Cheltenham
Umutaoroa
Whetukura
Wanstead
Pourerere
Bulls
1035
734
Raumai
Sanson
Feilding
Dannevirke
Ahiweka
Wallingford
Blackhead
Blackhead Point
9
Tangimoana
Awahuri
Waiaruhe
Mangahei
Ashhurst
Glen Oroua
Woodville
Motea
Porangahau
Himatangi Beach
Kairanga
Palmerston North
Manawatu
Waitahora
Bainesse
Kohinui
Coonoor
Weber
Foxton
Linton
Pahiatua
Nikau
Wimbledon
Makuri
Puketoi Range
Cape Turnagain
Shannon
Tararua Range
Hamua
Pongaroa
415
Herbertville
578
Hokio Beach
Tane
Panui
Kakariki
Mount Marchant
Owahanga
Levin
Eketahuna
Rakaunui
Akitio
Tiraumea
Mount Bruce Pukaha Wildlife Centre
Alfredton
Manakau
Owahanga
Kapiti Island Nature Reserve and Marine Reserve
Castlehill
Mount Bruce
Ihuraua
Te Horo
Otaki
1571
Mitre
Mauriceville
Mataikona
Tararua Forest Park
364
Tauweru
Kapiti Island
Waikanae
409
Kaituna
Bideford
Whakataki
Otaki Forks
Opaki
Tinui
Paraparaumu
Masterton
Awatoitoi
Castlepoint
10
924
Carrington
Paekakariki
Tauweru
Whareama
Cloustonville
Carterton
Te Rewarewa Point
Mana Island
Plimmerton
Pakuratahi
Wairarapa
Wainuioru
Greytown
Porirua
Upper Hutt
Gladstone
Riversdale Beach
Tawa
Featherston
Ohariu Bay
Lower Hutt
Longbush
Te Wharau
Lake Wairarapa
Makara
Wainuiomata
Tablelands
Martinborough
Cape Terawhiti
Flat Point
Somes/Matiu Island
Tuhitarata
Hinakura
WELLINGTON
Rimutaka Range
Ruakokoputuna
Haurangi Forest Park
Glendhu
Cook Strait
Orongorongo
Lake Ferry
Aorangi Range
Tuturumuri
Palliser Bay
Turakirae Head
404
Putangirua Pinnacles
Te Humenga Pt
Tora
Haurangi Forest Park
Ngawi
Te Kaukau Pt
Cape Palliser
11
12
J
K
L

B
C
D
11
12
13
14
15
Pukekura
Lake Ianthe
Abut Head
Harihari
Okarito Lagoon
Rotokino
Okarito
Whataroa
Westland Tai Poutini National Park
Lake Mapourika
Newton Pe
Gillespies Beach
Franz Josef Glacier
Fox Glacier
Franz Josef Glacier
Karangarua
Fox Glacier
Mount Cook/ Aoraki NP
Bruce Bay
Jacobs River
Westland Tai Poutini National Park
3754
Mount Cook / Aoraki
Godley
Mahitahi
3157
Mount Sefton
Lilybank
Munroe Beach
Ship Creek
Knights Point
Mount Cook Village
Lake Moeraki
Lake Paringa
2652
Mount Hooker
Lake Tekapo
Mataketake Range
Haast
Okuru
Haast
Southern Alps
Lake Alexandrina
Haast
Jackson Head
Jackson Bay
Jackson Bay
Waiatoto
Okuru
Ben Ohau Range
2200
Lake Tekapo
Lake Pukaki
Cascade Point
Arawhata
Haast Pass
2499
Mount Huxley
Mackenzies Peak
Tekapo
Lake Ellery
Arawata
Haast Range
Siberia
1134
Mount Theta
Olivine Range
2149
Mount Turner
Makarora
Young Range
Hunter
Lake Ohau Lodge
Lake Ohau
Twizel
Makarora
Ohau
Awarua Point
Big Bay
Pyke
Cascade
Mount Aspiring National Park
1877
Birch Hill
Ahuriri
Clearburn
Haldon
Hakatarame Dow
Martins Bay
Lake Wilmot
3033
Mount Aspiring
Lake Wanaka
Lake Benmore
Omarama
Kirkliston Range
2446
Climax Peak
Mount Aspiring
Lake Hawea
Yates Point
Lake McKerrow
Waitangi
Milford Sound
2723
Mount Tutoko
Lake Alabaster
Dart
Lochnager
306
Glendhu Bay
Lake Hawea
1779
Otematata
Lake Aviemore
Maungatiro
1692
Mitre Peak
Maungawera
St Bathans Range
Lake Waitaki
Hakataramea
Wanaka
Lindis Valley

E
F
G
H
Cape Foulwind
Tauranga Bay
Fairdown
Westport
Denniston
Newton Flat
Owen River
Kawatiri
Bull
Wairau
Waihopai
Lyell
Murchison
Rotoroa
St Arnaud
Lake Rotoiti
2009
Nine Mile Beach
Te Kuha
Charleston
Berlins
Inangahua
Lake Rotoroa
Nelson Lakes National Park
Gladstone
1460
Mount Euclid
Rotokohu
Paenga
Matakitaki
Langridge
Awatere
2621
Mitre Peak
Tiromoana
1640
Mount Victoria
2338
Mount Travers
Molesworth
Perpendicular Point
Punakaiki
Paparoa National Park
Paparoa Range
Reefton
Victoria Range
Burnbrae
Inland Kaikoura Range
Victoria Forest Park
Maimai
Maruia
302
2156
Mount Burn
Spenser Mountains
Barrytown
Lake Tennyson
2013
Mount Sebastopol
Clarence
Seaward Kaikoura Range
2610
Manakau
Ikamatua
Waiuta
Grey
Springs Junction
Acheron
12
Blackball
Ahaura
Maruia Springs
Lewis Pass
Hawk Hills
Kowhai
Runanga
Ngahere
Lewis Pass National Reserve
Waiau
Greymouth
Stillwater
Lake Hochstetter
1379
Mount Elliot
Upper Grey
Hanmer Springs
Oaro
Paroa
Ahaura
Shantytown
Aratika
Haupiri
Hanmer
Kumara Junction
Lake Brunner
Lake Sumner Forest Park
Hope
Claverley
Ferniehurst
Kumara
Waiau
Awatuna
Mitchells
Rotomanu
1612
Mount Tekoa
594
Hokitika
Humphreys
Inchbonnie
Taramakau
Crawford Range
Lake Sumner
Parnassus
Kaniere
1839
Culverden
Leamington
Wainihinihi
Otira
Balmoral
Cheviot
Lake Kaniere
Hurunui
Ethelton
Kokatahi
Otira Viaduct
Arthur's Pass National Park
Horsley Downs
Hurunui Mouth
Hokitika
Arthur's Pass
Scargill
Puketeraki Range
Pyramid Valley
Waikari
2294
Mount Greenlaw
Bealey
Cass
Omihi
13
Craigieburn Forest Park
Waipara
2141
Mount Beaumont
Waipara
Motunau Beach
934
Lees Valley
White Rock
Mount Gray
Rolleston Range
Avoca
Leithfield
Castle Hill
Loburn
Ashley Gorge
Rakaia
Lake Coleridge
Oxford
Rangiora
Pegasus Bay
1657
Ben More
Springfield
Springbank
Woodend
Horrellville
Kaiapoi
Sheffield
Eyre
Eyreton
Lake Coleridge
Whitecliffs
McLeans Island
Belfast
Lake Heron
Homebush
Darfield
Erewhon
2215
Old Man Peak
Windwhistle
Hororata
West Melton
CHRISTCHURCH
Ashburton
Aylesbury
Templeton
Godley Head
Lake Clearwater
Alford Forest
Hakatere
Greendale
Lyttelton
Pigeon Bay
Mesopotamia
Methven
Te Pirita
Rolleston
Diamond Harbour
Barrhill
Lincoln
Little Akaloa
Taitapu
769
Ashburton Forks
Selwyn
Selwyn
Duvauchelle
14
Mount Somers
Lauriston
Doyleston
Motukarara
Little River
Banks Peninsula
Rangitata
Rakaia
Lake Ellesmere
Le Bons Bay
Mount Peel
Mayfield
Westerfield
Winchmore
Chertsey
Southbridge
Great Island
Wainui
Akaroa
Taumutu
Kaitorete Spit
Birdlings Flat
Orari
Ashburton
Akaroa Harbour
Clayton
Maronan
Pendarves
Tinwald
Ashwick Flat
Four Peaks Range
Arundel
Wakanui
Hinds
Willowby
Woodbury
Canterbury Bight
Rangitata
Hakatere
Geraldine
Longbeach
Beautiful Valley
Orton
Opuha
Winchester
Coldstream
Waitohi
Tengawai
Temuka
Pleasant Point
Cave
Claremont
Timaru
15
Motukaika
Pareora
Otaio Gorge
Otaio
Hunter
307
Waimate
Wainono Lagoon
Waihao Downs
Willowbridge
Morven

A
B
C
15
16
17
18
19
304
Martins Bay
Lake Wilmot
3033
Mount Aspiring
Lake Wanaka
Lake Hawea
2446
Climax Peak
Lake McKerrow
Yates Point
Lake Alabaster
Dart
Mount Aspiring
Lochnager
Milford Sound
2723
Mount Tutoko
1692
Mitre Peak
Maungawera
Glendhu Bay
Wanaka
Luggate
Poison Bay
Milford Sound
Humboldt Mountains
Paradise
Rees
Shotover
Harris Mountains
2245
Mount Aurum
1840
Middle Peak
Sutherland Sound
Lake Ada
Hollyford
Queensberry
Bligh Sound
Bounty Haven
Kinloch
Glenorchy
Skippers Canyon
Richardson Mountains
Cardrona
Pisa Range
George Sound
1966
Barrier Peak
Lake Gunn
Cascade Creek
Pigeon Island
Arrowtown
Lowburn
Pig Island
Eglinton
Knobs Flat
Franklin Mountains
Mt Creighton
Frankton
Gibbston
Cromwell
1314
Expedition Peak
2036
Mount McDougall
Queenstown
Caswell Sound
Charles Sound
1990
Mount Mavora
Mt Nicholas
Lake Wakatipu
The Remarkables
Bannockburn
North Fjord
Nancy Sound
Middle Fjord
Nevis Crossing
Thompson Sound
Clyde
1484
Double Peak
Te Anau Downs
Secretary Island
Lake Te Anau
North Mavora Lake
Nevis
Fruitlands
Murchison Mountains
Doubtful Sound
2022
Jane Peak
Mountains
Kingston
Lake Roxburgh
South Fjord
1889
Rocky Mount
Shingle Creek
1305
Mount Forbes
Fiordland
Te Anau
1453
Eyre
Fairlight
Dagg Sound
National
Lake Manapouri
Garvie Mountains
Eyre
Athol
1474
Roxburgh
Mararoa
Lake Beattie
Hall Arm
Oreti
Breaksea Island
Park
Manapouri
The Key
Mataura
Five Rivers
1612
Mount Cusack
1569
Gladstone Peak
Cattle Flat
Waikaia
Waiau
Mossburn
Wet Jacket Arm
1615
Waikaia
Resolution Island
Lumsden
Hauroko
Aparima
Josephville
Waiparu
845
Mount Wendon
Park Hill
Monowai
Blackmount
Balfour
Wendon
Green Lake
Glenure
Dusky Sound
Lake Monowai
Kelso
Dipton
Riversdale
Waikaka
Cook Channel
Otama
981
Mount Bradshaw
Hokonui Hills
671
Waimea Hill
Mandeville
Pomahaka
Birchwood
Nightcaps
Waikoikoi
West Cape
1722
Pukemutu
Cameron Mountains
Woodlaw
Otapiri
Mary Island
Lake Hauroko
Clifden
Gore
Pukerau
Cape Providence
Merrivale
Waimumu
Winton
Hokonui
Lake Poteriteri
Tuatapere
Happy Valley
Otautau
Drummond
Te Tipua
Chalky Island
Mataura
Otaraia
Coal Island
Lochiel
Hedgehope
Te Waewae
Tussock Creek
Puysegur Point
Te Waewae Bay
Fairfax
Waiarikiki
Dacre
Edendale
Thornbury
Sand Hill Point
Orepuki
Lorneville
Redan
Pahia Point
Riverton
Kennington
Mokoreta
Wakapatu
Howells Point
Waituna
Glenham
Mokoreta
Colac Bay
Wakaputa Point
Invercargill
Oreti Beach
Waimahaka
Quarry Hills
Centre Island
Gorge Road
Awarua
Fortrose
Greenhills
Chaslands
Otara
Waikawa
Foveaux Strait
Bluff
Tiwai Point
Toetoes Bay
Waipapa Point
Porpoise Bay
Curio Bay
Haldane Bay
Black Rock Point
Ruapuke Island
980
Mount Anglem
Christmas Village Bay
Codfish Island
Edwards Island
Halfmoon Bay
Masons Head
Bench Island
Mason Bay
Paterson Inlet
Ulva Island
Ernest Islands
Stewart Island / Rakiura National Park
East Cape
Doughboy Bay
750
Mount Allen
Shelter Point
South Red Head Point
Stewart Island/ Rakiura
Muttonbird Islands
Pearl Island
470
Broad Head
Big South Cape Island
South Cape

Omarama
Lake Benmore
Hakataramea Downs
Motukaika
Pareora
Otaio Gorge
Otaio
305
Waitangi
Otematata
Lake Aviemore
Kirkliston Range
Hakataramea
The Hunters Hills
Waihao
Maungatiro
Hunter
Lake Waitaki
Hakataramea
Waihaorunga
Waimate
Wainono Lagoon
Willowbridge
Morven
Lindis Valley
St Bathans Range
Dunstan
Hawkdun Range
Clear
Strachans
Waihao Downs
Takiroa
Ikawai
Tawai
Duntroon
Waitaki Valley
Waitaki
St Bathans
Falls Dam
1692
Mount Ida
Kyeburn Diggings
Maerewhenua
Awamoko
Ngapara
Becks
Idaburn
Naseby
Danseys Pass
Tapui
Enfield
Pukeuri
Matakanui
Five Forks
Oamaru
Cape Wanbrow
North Rough Ridge
Poolburn
Ranfurly
Kyeburn
Kakanui
1304
Mount Dasher
Maheno
Kakanui
Gimmerburn
Herbert
Galloway
Taieri
Patearoa
Morrisons
Poolburn Reservoir
Rough Ridge
Hyde
Rock And Pillar Range
Macraes Flat
Dunback
Moeraki Boulders
Manorburn Reservoir
Katiki
Paerau
Stoneburn
Greenland Reservoir
Nenthorn
Shag Point
Middlemarch
Palmerston
710
Mount Royal
Mount Stoker
Lake Onslow
Waikouaiti
Taieri
Merton
1132
Puketeraki
Shannon
Lammerlaw Range
Clarks Junction
Hindon
Mount Allan
Waitati
Clutha
Taiaroa Head
Raes Junction
Lake Mahinerangi
Whare Flat
Port Chalmers
Portobello
Beaumont
Outram
Otago Peninsula
Mosgiel
Waipori Falls
Lawrence
Allanton
DUNEDIN
Berwick
Rongahere
Round Hill
Waihola
Tuapeka Mouth
Taieri Mouth
Awamangu
Milton
Pukeawa
Crichton
Glenledi
Toko Mouth
Balclutha
Kaitangata
Waitepeka
Romahapa
Molyneux Bay
Purekireki
Kaka Point
Owaka
Nugget Point
Cannibal Bay
Surat Bay
Papatowai
Tautuku Bay
D
E
F
15
16
17
18
19

## A



## B



## C



## D

**O**



**P**



**Q**



**R**

## PICTURES

The Automobile Association wishes to thank the following photographers and organisations for their assistance in the preparation of this book.

Abbreviations for the picture credits are as follows – (t) top; (b) bottom; (l) left; (r) right; (c) centre; (AA) AA World Travel Library

2 Destination Northland;
3i Photolibrary Group;
3ii AA/A Belcher;
3iii AA/P Kenward;
3iv AA/A Belcher;
4 AA/P Kenward;
5 Destination Lake Taupo (Marcel Tromp);
6 AA/M Langford;
7 AA/P Kenward;
8 AA/M Langford;
10 AA/P Kenward;
11 AA/A Belcher;
12 AA/M Langford;
13 AA/M Langford;
14 © Ross Land/Getty Images;
15t AA/M Langford;
15b © Wire Image/Getty Images;
16 AA/P Kenward;
17l AA/P Kenward;
17r AA/A Resinger & V Meduna;
18 AA/A Belcher;
19l © Wire Images/Getty Images;
19r AA/M Langford;
20 AA/M Langford;
21l AA/M Langford;
21r AA/M Langford;
22 AA/M Langford;
23l New Zealand Tourist Board;
23r AA/M Langford;
24 © Ross Land/Getty Images;
25 © Hulton Archive/Getty Images;
26 AA/P Kenward;
27l Private Collection/The Bridgeman Art Library;
27r The Art Archive;
28 Mary Evans Picture Library;
29t © National Library of Australia, Canberra, Australia/The Bridgeman Art Library;
29r © Hulton Archive/Getty Images;
30 AA/A Belcher;
31t © Corbis;
31b Mary Evans Picture Library;
32 AA/M Langford;
33l AA/M Langford;
33r © National Library of Australia, Canberra, Australia/The Bridgeman Art Library;
34 AA/P Kenward;
35l © Topical Press Agency/Getty Images;
35r AA/M Langford;
36 © Kevin Fleming/Corbis;
37l © Barry Durrant/Getty Images;
37r Photodisc;
38 © Peter Macdiarmid/Getty Images;
39 AA/A Belcher;
40 Air New Zealand;
41 AA/A Belcher;
42 Britz;
43 AA/M Langford;
44 AA/M Langford;
45 AA/M Langford;
46 AA/A Belcher;
48 AA/M Langford;
49 AA/M Langford;
50 AA/M Langford;
51 AA/A Belcher;
52 AA/M Cawood;
53 AA/M Langford;
54 AA/N Sumner;
55 © Trevor Geise/Alamy;
56 AA/A Belcher;
58 Robert Harding Picture Library/Richard Cummins;
59 SkyCity Auckland;
60 AA/A Belcher;
61t SkyCity Auckland;
61b AA/A Belcher;
64 AA/A Belcher;
65 AA/M Langford;
66t SkyCity Auckland;
66b AA/M Langford;
67 AA/M Langford;
68 Photolibrary Group;
69 Destination Northland (courtesy of Fullers BOI);
70 AA/M Langford;
71 AA/M Langford;
72 AA/A Belcher;
73 AA/M Langford;
74 AA/M Langford;
75 AA/A Belcher;
76 Destination Northland;
77 AA/P Kenward;
78 AA/A Belcher;
79 AA/M Langford;
80 AA/M Langford;
81 AA/M Langford;
82 Photolibrary Group;
83 AA/M Langford;
84 AA/M Langford;
85 AA/M Langford;
86 AA/M Langford;
88 AA/A Belcher;
91 Matana Confections;
92 Pakiri Beach Horse Riding;
93 Stockbyte;
94 AA/M Langford;
96 AA/M Langford;
98 AA/M Langford;
100 AA/M Langford;
101 AA/M Langford;
102 Hawkes Bay Tourism;
103 AA/M Langford;
104 AA/P Kenward;
105 AA/M Langford;
106 AA/M Langford;
107 AA/M Langford;
108 AA/A Belcher;
109 AA/A Belcher;
110t AA/M Langford;
110b AA/M Langford;
111 AA/M Langford;
112 AA/M Langford;
114 AA/A Belcher;
115 AA/A Belcher;
116 Black Water Rafting;
117 AA/M Langford;
118 AA/M Langford;
120 AA/P Kenward;
121t AA/M Langford;
121b AA/M Langford;
122 Lake Taupo Tourism;
124 Black Water Rafting;
125t Waitomo Caves;
125b AA/M Langford;
126 AA/P Kenward;
129 AA/P Kenward;
130 AA/A Belcher;
132 AA/M Langford;
134 Mangatautari Lodge;
136 AA/M Langford;
138 © Angelo Cavalli/Image Bank/Getty Images;
139 Martinborough Wine Centre;
140 AA/M Langford;
141 Wairarapa Tourism;
142 Te Papa, Wellington;
143 Te Papa, Wellington;
144 AA/P Kenward;
145 AA/A Belcher;
148t AA/M Langford;
148b AA/A Belcher;
149 AA/A Belcher;
150 AA/A Belcher;
152 Gaynor James/Highfield Estate;

154 Efil Doog Garden of Art;
157 AA/P Kenward;
158 AA/M Langford;
160 Wharekauhau Country Estate;
162 AA/M Langford;
164 © Dave Walsh/Alamy;
165 Nelson Tourism;
166 AA/P Kenward;
168 AA/M Langford;
169 AA/P Kenward;
170 AA/M Langford;
171 AA/M Langford;
172 AA/M Langford;
173l AA/M Langford;
173r AA/M Langford;
174 AA/M Langford;
175 Photolibrary Group;
176 © Ull Wiesmeier/Zefa/Corbis;
177 AA/M Langford;
178 AA/M Langford;
179 AA/M Langford;
180t D. Parer & E. Parer-Cook/ AUSCAPE;
180b Kaikoura Information and Tourism Inc;
181t AA/P Kenward;
181b Kaikoura Information and Tourism Inc;
182 Happy Valley Adventures;
184 AA/A Belcher;
186 AA/M Langford;
188 Fyffe Country Lodge;
190 AA/A Belcher;
192 AA/A Belcher;
193 AA/A Belcher;
194 AA/A Belcher;
195 AA/P Kenward;
196 AA/M Langford;
197l AA/M Langford;
197r AA/M Langford;
200 AA/P Kenward;
201t AA/M Langford;
201b AA/M Langford;
202 Jochen Schlenker/Robert Harding;
203 AA/M Langford;
204 AA/M Langford;
205 AA/M Langford;
206 AA/A Belcher;
208 AA/P Kenward;
209 AA/M Langford;
210 AA/M Langford;
211 AA/A Belcher;
212 AA/M Langford;
213t AA/M Langford;
213b AA/M Langford;
214 Addington Raceway;
216 AA/M Langford;
219 Barker's Berry Barn;
220 AA/M Langford;
222 AA/M Langford;
224 AA/M Langford;
226 AA/A Belcher;
228 AA/M Langford;
229 AA/P Kenward;
230 AA/A Belcher;
232 AA/P Kenward;
233 AA;
234 AA/A Belcher;
235t AA/P Kenward;
235b AA/P Kenward;
237 AA/P Kenward;
238 Robin Bush/Nature Photographers;
239 AA/M Langford;
240 AA/P Kenward;
241l AA/A Belcher;
241r AJ Hackett;
242 AA/M Langford;
243 AA/M Langford;
244 AA/P Kenward;
245l AA/M Langford;
245r AA/M Langford;
246 AA/P Kenward;
247 AA/M Langford;
248 AA/M Langford;
251 Kingston Flyer;
252 AA/A Resinger & V Meduna;
253 AA/C Sawyer;
254 AA/M Langford;
256 Corstorphine House Private Hotel;
258 AA/M Langford;
259 AA/P Kenward;
260 Lake Taupo Tourism (Credit: Craig Wilson);
262 AA/P Kenward;
263 AA/M Langford;
265 AA/J Tims;
266 AA/M Langford;
267 AA/P Kenward;
268 AA/A Belcher;
269 AA/A Belcher;
272 AA/A Belcher;
273 AA/M Langford;
274 AA/M Langford;
276 AA/M Langford;
277 AA/M Langford;
278 AA/C Coe;
279 Digitalvision;
280 AA/M Langford;
282 Destination Lake Taupo;
285 AA/S Watkins;
286 AA/M Langford;
288 Lake Taupo Tourism;
290 AA/M Langford;
292 AA/M Langford;
297 AA/A Belcher

Every effort has been made to trace the copyright holders, and we apologise in advance for any accidental errors. We would be happy to apply any corrections in the following edition of this publication.

## CREDITS

**Managing editor**
Sheila Hawkins

**Project editor**
Lodestone Publishing Ltd

**Design**
Drew Jones, pentacorbig, Nick Otway

**Cover design**
Chie Ushio

**Picture research**
Vivien Little

**Image retouching and repro**
Sarah Montgomery

**Main contributors**
Mavis Airey, Jane Bellerby, Darroch Donald, Kathryn Fitzpatrick, Michael Mellor

**Updater**
Michael Gebicki

**Indexer**
Marie Lorimer

**Production**
Karen Gibson





**See It New Zealand**
**ISBN 978-1-4000-0361-7**
**Third Edition**

Published in the United States by Fodor's Travel and simultaneously in Canada by Random House of Canada Limited, Toronto.
Published in the United Kingdom by AA Publishing.
Fodor's is a registered trademark of Random House, Inc., and Fodor's See It is a trademark of Random House, Inc.
Fodor's Travel is a division of Random House, Inc.



Color separation by Keenes, Andover, UK
Printed and bound by Leo Paper Products, China
10 9 8 7 6 5 4 3 2 1

Special Sales: This book is available for special discounts for bulk purchases for sales promotions or premiums. Special editions, including personalized covers, excerpts of existing books, and corporate imprints, can be created in large quantities for special needs.
For more information, write to Special Markets/Premium Sales, 1745 Broadway, MD 6-2, New York, NY 10019
or e-mail specialmarkets@randomhouse.com
Important Note: Time inevitably brings changes, so always confirm prices, travel facts, and other perishable information when it matters. Although Fodor's cannot accept responsibility for errors, you can use this guide in the confidence that we have taken every care to ensure its accuracy.

**Dear Traveler,**

From buying a plane ticket to booking a room and seeing the sights, a trip goes much more smoothly when you have a good travel guide. Dozens of writers, editors, designers, and cartographers have worked hard to make the book you hold in your hands a good one. Was it everything you expected? Were our descriptions accurate? Were our recommendations on target? And did you find our tips and practical advice helpful? Your ideas and experiences matter to us. If we have missed or misstated something, we'd love to hear about it. Fill out our survey at www.fodors.com/books/feedback/, or e-mail us at seeit@fodors.com. Or you can snail mail to the See It Editor at Fodor's, 1745 Broadway, New York, New York 10019. We'll look forward to hearing from you.

**Tim Jarrell**
Publisher